STREE

CW00324501

Warwickshire
and Coventry

First published in 1995 by

Philip's, a division of
Octopus Publishing Group Ltd
2-4 Heron Quays, London E14 4JP

Third colour edition 2006
First impression 2006
WARCA

ISBN-10   0-540-08759-9 (pocket)
ISBN-13   978-0-540-08759-4 (pocket)

© Philip's 2006

Ordnance Survey®

This product includes mapping data licensed from
Ordnance Survey® with the permission of the
Controller of Her Majesty's Stationery Office.
© Crown copyright 2006. All rights reserved.
Licence number 100011710.

Printed by Toppan, China

Contents

III   **Key to map symbols**

IV   **Key to map pages**

VI   **Route planning**

X   **Administrative and Postcode boundaries**

1   **Street maps** at 2⅔ inches to 1 mile

112   **Street maps** at 1⅓ inches to 1 mile

143   **Street maps** at 2⅔ inches to 1 mile

151   **Street map of Coventry city centre**
at 5⅓ inches to 1 mile

152   **Index** of towns and villages

154   **Index** of streets, hospitals, industrial estates, railway
stations, schools, shopping centres, universities
and places of interest

Digital Data

The exceptionally high-quality mapping found in this atlas is available as digital data in TIFF
format, which is easily convertible to other bitmapped (raster) image formats.

The index is also available in digital form as a standard database table. It contains all the details
found in the printed index together with the National Grid reference for the map square in which
each entry is named.

For further information and to discuss your requirements, please contact Philip's on
020 7644 6932 or james.mann@philips-maps.co.uk

Key to map symbols

III

Motorway with junction number

Primary route – dual/single carriageway

A road – dual/single carriageway

B road – dual/single carriageway

Minor road – dual/single carriageway

Other minor road – dual/single carriageway

Road under construction

Tunnel, covered road

Rural track, private road or narrow road in urban area

Gate or obstruction to traffic (restrictions may not apply at all times or to all vehicles)

Path, bridleway, byway open to all traffic, road used as a public path

Pedestrianised area

Postcode boundaries

DY7

County and unitary authority boundaries

Railway, tunnel, railway under construction

Tramway, tramway under construction

Miniature railway

Railway station
Walsall

Private railway station

Metro station
South Shields

Tram stop, tram stop under construction

Bus, coach station

Ambulance station

Coastguard station

Fire station

Police station

Accident and Emergency entrance to hospital

H **Hospital**

+ **Place of worship**

i **Information Centre** (open all year)

Shopping Centre

P P&R **Parking, Park and Ride**

PO **Post Office**

X **Camping site, caravan site**

▶ ✕ **Golf course, picnic site**

Important buildings, schools, colleges, universities and hospitals
Prim Sch

Built up area

Woods

River Medway **Water name**

River, weir, stream

Canal, lock, tunnel

Water

Tidal water

Church **Non-Roman antiquity**

ROMAN FORT **Roman antiquity**

87 **Adjoining page indicators and overlap bands**
237 The colour of the arrow and the band indicates the scale of the adjoining or overlapping page (see scales below)

Acad	**Academy**	Inst	**Institute**
Allot Gdns	**Allotments**	Ct	**Law Court**
Cemy	**Cemetery**	L Ctr	**Leisure Centre**
C Ctr	**Civic Centre**	LC	**Level Crossing**
CH	**Club House**	Liby	**Library**
Coll	**College**	Mkt	**Market**
Crem	**Crematorium**	Meml	**Memorial**
Ent	**Enterprise**	Mon	**Monument**
Ex H	**Exhibition Hall**	Mus	**Museum**
Ind Est	**Industrial Estate**	Obsy	**Observatory**
IRB Sta	**Inshore Rescue**	Pal	**Royal Palace**
	Boat Station	PH	**Public House**
Recn Gd	**Recreation Ground**		
Resr	**Reservoir**		
Ret Pk	**Retail Park**		
Sch	**School**		
Sh Ctr	**Shopping Centre**		
TH	**Town Hall/House**		
Trad Est	**Trading Estate**		
Univ	**University**		
W Twr	**Water Tower**		
Wks	**Works**		
YH	**Youth Hostel**		

■ The small numbers around the edges of the maps identify the 1 kilometre National Grid lines
■ The dark grey border on the inside edge of some pages indicates that the mapping does not continue onto the adjacent page

Enlarged mapping only

Railway or bus station building

Place of interest

Parkland

The scale of the maps on the pages numbered in blue is 4.2 cm to 1 km • 2⅔ inches to 1 mile • 1: 23810	0 ¼ ½ ¾ 1 mile
	0 250m 500m 750m 1 kilometre

The scale of the maps on pages numbered in green is 2.1 cm to 1 km • 1⅓ inches to 1 mile • 1: 47620	0 ¼ ½ ¾ 1 mile
	0 250m 500m 750m 1 kilometre

The scale of the maps on pages numbered in red is 8.4 cm to 1 km • 5⅓ inches to 1 mile • 1: 11900	0 220 yards 440 yards 660 yards ½ mile
	0 125m 250m 375m ½ kilometre

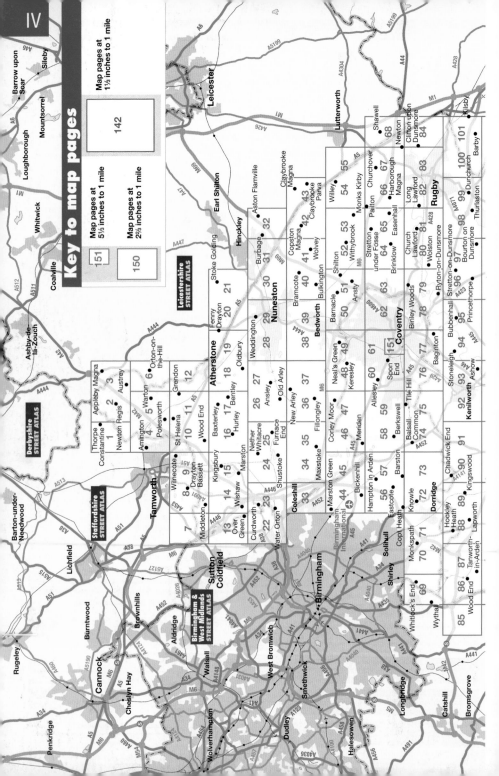

IV

Key to map pages

Map pages at 1⅓ inches to 1 mile

142

Map pages at 5⅓ inches to 1 mile
151

Map pages at 2⅔ inches to 1 mile
150

Leicestershire STREET ATLAS

Derbyshire STREET ATLAS

Staffordshire STREET ATLAS

Birmingham & West Midlands STREET ATLAS

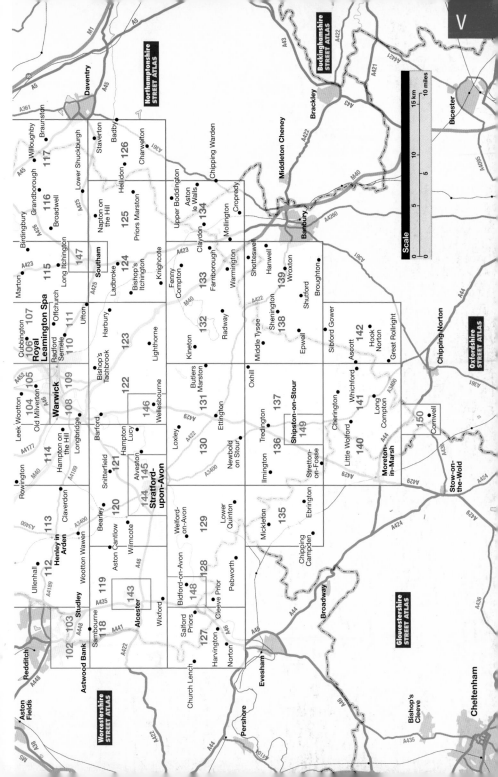

V

Scale

15 km
10 miles

Redditch
Aston Fields
M5
A38

Astwood Bank
102 103
118 Studley
119
143 Alcester
144 Stratford-upon-Avon
145
146
Wellesbourne
147 Southam
Warwick
108 109
104 105
106 107 Royal Leamington Spa
Cubbington
Old Milverton
Leek Wootton
110 111
112 Henley in Arden
113 Claverdon
114 Hampton on the Hill
Rowington
M40
Ullenhall
Wootton Wawen
Bearley
Aston Cantlow
Wilmcote
120
121 Snitterfield
Barford
Longbridge
Hampton Lucy
Lighthorne
Harbury
Bishop's Tachbrook
122 123
Loxley
130
Welford-on-Avon
129 Lower Quinton
Mickleton
135
Ebrington
Chipping Campden
Broadway
Bidford-on-Avon
128
Cleeve Prior
Pebworth
Salford Priors
127 Harvington
Norton
Church Lench
Evesham
Pershore
Bishop's Cleeve
Cheltenham

Daventry
M1
A5
A45
A361
A5

Braunston
Willoughby
117
Grandborough
116 Broadwell
Birdingbury
115
Marton
Long Itchington
Ladbroke
124
Bishop's Itchington
125 Napton on the Hill
Priors Marston
Knightcote
Staverton
Badby
126 Hellidon
Charwelton
Lower Shuckburgh
Upper Boddington
Aston le Walls
134 Mollington
Claydon
Cropredy
Chipping Warden
133 Farnborough
132 Radway
Fenny Compton
Kineton
131 Butlers Marston
Ettington
Newbold on Stour
Tredington
136 Ilmington
137 Shipston-on-Stour
149 Stretton-on-Fosse
138 Middle Tysoe
Shenington
Epwell
Oxhill
Warmington
Shotteswell
Hanwell
139 Wroxton
Shutford
Broughton
142 Hook Norton
Great Rollright
Sibford Gower
Ascott
141 Whichford
Cherington
140 Long Compton
Little Wolford
150 Cornwell
Moreton-in-Marsh
Stow-on-the-Wold
Chipping Norton

Northamptonshire STREET ATLAS
Buckinghamshire STREET ATLAS
Brackley
Middleton Cheney
Banbury
Bicester
Oxfordshire STREET ATLAS
Gloucestershire STREET ATLAS
Worcestershire STREET ATLAS

M40
A43
A422
A422
A421
A4095
A43
A4260
A361
A44
A3400
A429
A424
A436
A46
A44
A435
A410
A422
A441
A4189
A4177
A452
A46
A425
A423
A426
A45
A45
A361

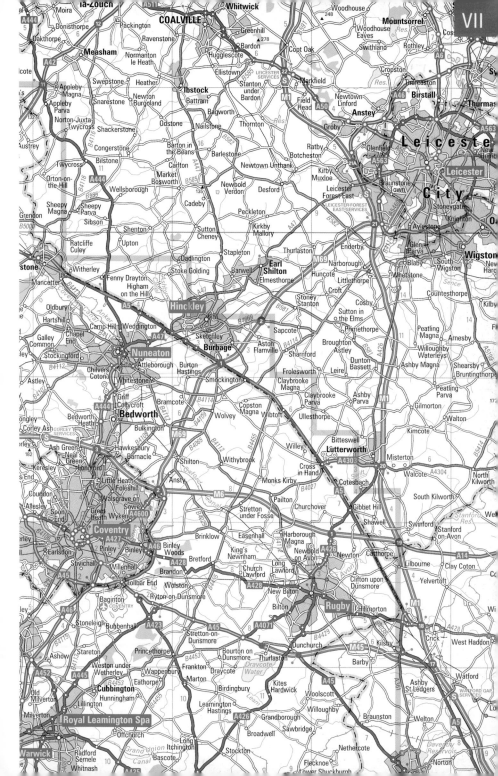

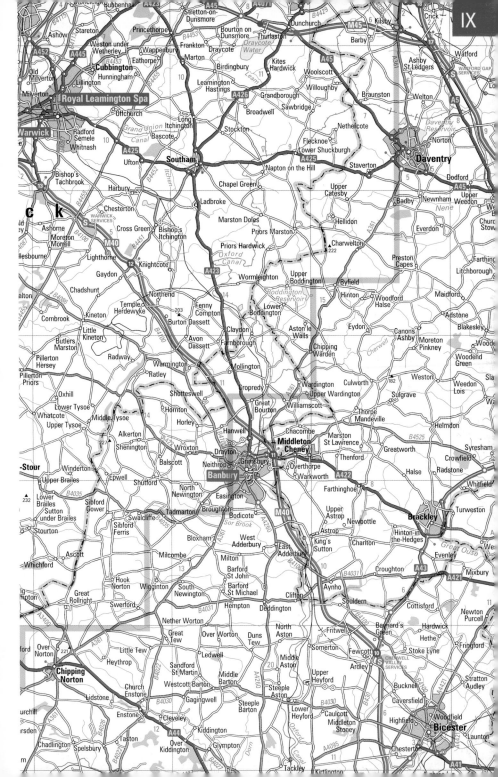

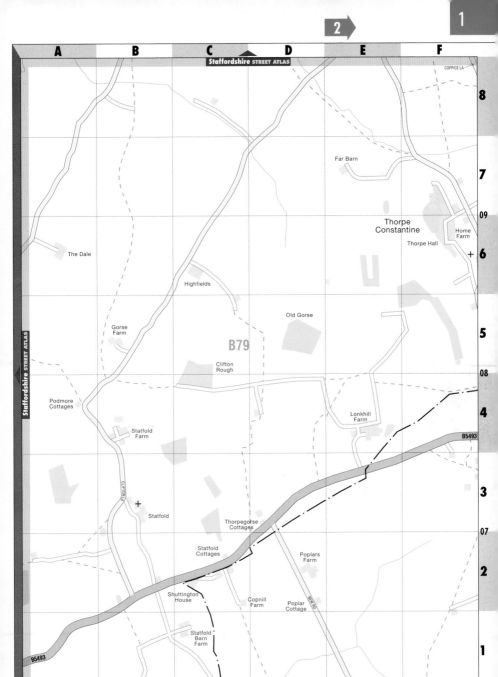

2

Staffordshire STREET ATLAS

COPPICE LA

8

Far Barn

7

09

Thorpe
Constantine

Home
Farm

6

Thorpe Hall

The Dale

Highfields

Old Gorse

Gorse
Farm

B79

5

Clifton
Rough

08

Podmore
Cottages

Lonkhill
Farm

4

Statfold
Farm

B5493

CLIFTON LA

3

Statfold

Thorpegorse
Cottages

07

Statfold
Cottages

Poplars
Farm

2

Shuttington
House

Copnill
Farm

Poplar
Cottage

Statfold
Barn
Farm

1

B5493

06

4

2

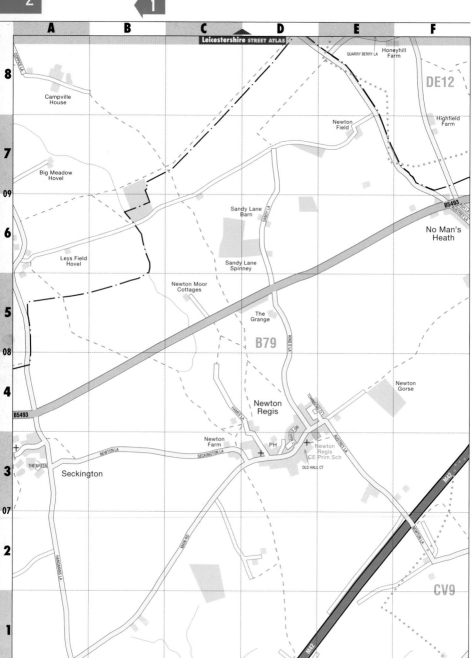

Leicestershire STREET ATLAS

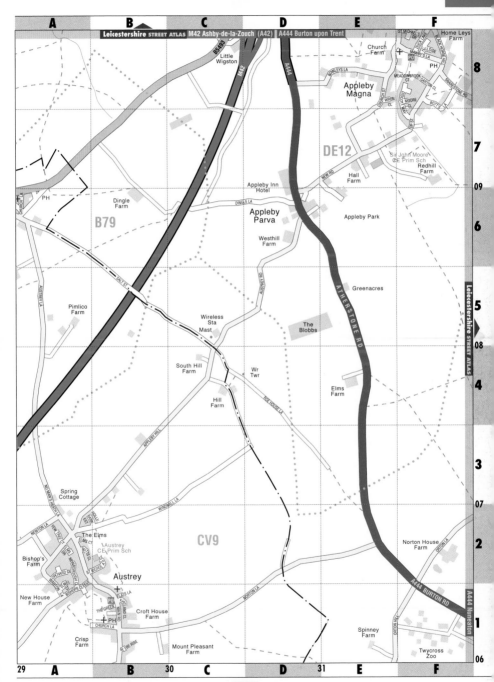

A

B

C

D

E

F

Little
Wigston

M42

A444

St Michael
ROCK BANK
Home Leys
Farm

HILLSIDE
Church
Farm

MANBY'S LA
PO
PH

BONILEYS LA

BLACK HORSE HILL
SAXTON CL
MEADOWBROOK

8

Appleby
Magna

WREN
CL

MOORE
CL

DUCCOT WAY

SWANBESTONE RD

BOTT ST

7

DE12

Sir John Moore
CE Prim Sch

Redhill
Farm

09

PH

CHURCH LA

Dingle
Farm

NEW RD

Hall
Farm

Appleby Inn
Hotel

DINGLE LA

B79

Appleby
Parva

Appleby Park

6

Westhill
Farm

DE LA ZOUCH RD

Pimlico
Farm

Greenacres

ATHERSTONE RD

5

Wireless
Sta
Mast

The
Blobbs

08

AUSTREY LA

SALT ST

South Hill
Farm

Wr
Twr

Elms
Farm

4

Hill
Farm

RIDE HOUSE LA

APPLEBY HILL

Leicestershire STREET ATLAS

3

Spring
Cottage

WINDMILL LA

07

CV9

The Elms

Austrey
CE Prim Sch

Norton House
Farm

ORTON LA

2

Bishop's
Farm

ELMS CT

NEWTON LA

ORCHARD CT
ST BICHOL'S

NORTON LA

A444 BURTON RD

New House
Farm

Austrey

A444 Nuneaton

Croft House
Farm

BLAIS LA

PH
CHURCH LA

Spinney
Farm

ORTON LA

1

Crisp
Farm

GLEBE RISE

Mount Pleasant
Farm

Twycross
Zoo

06

29

A

B

30

C

D

31

E

F

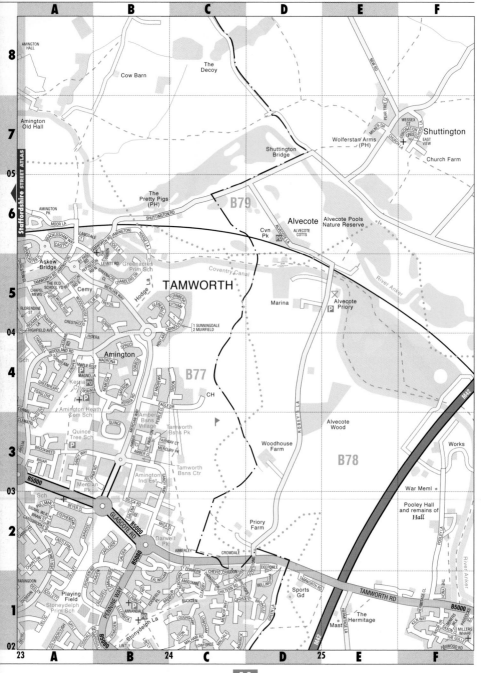

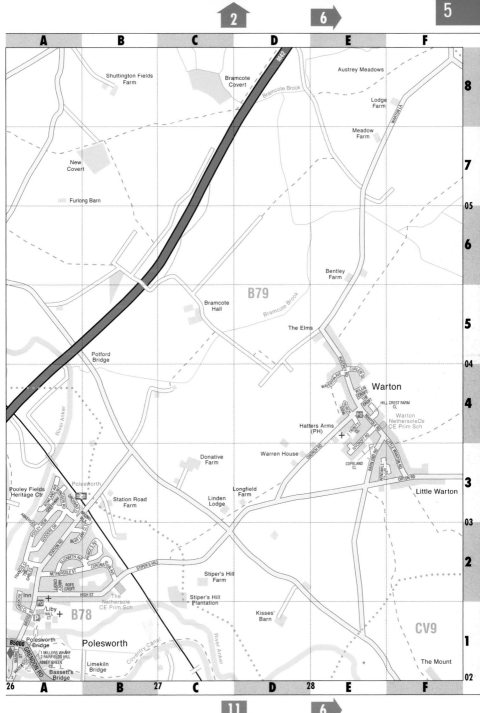

8

7

05

6

5

04

4

03

3

2

1

02

Shuttington Fields Farm

Bramcote Covert

Austrey Meadows

Lodge Farm

M42

Bramcote Brook

Meadow Farm

WARTON LA

New Covert

Furlong Barn

Bentley Farm

B79

Bramcote Brook

Bramcote Hall

The Elms

Potford Bridge

WATERLANE RD

AUSTREY RD

CURLEW CL

WILLIS CROFT

Warton

HILL CREST FARM CL

CHURCH

River Anker

Hatters Arms (PH)

TRINITY CL

SHEEPY RD

Warton Nethersole's CE Prim Sch

RICKYARD CL

LITTLE WARTON RD

Pooley Fields Heritage Ctr

Polesworth

Donative Farm

Warren House

CHURCH RD

COPELAND CL

BARN LANE CL

WINDMILL LA

Little Warton

ANKER CL

POOLEY VIEW
GROSVENOR RD

ORCHARD CL

BRICK KILN CL

Station Road Farm

BEAR LANE

Linden Lodge

Longfield Farm

ORTON RD

PRINCE'S RD
ELIZABETH AVE

STATION RD

CORONATION AVE

THE GABLES

FRANCIS CL

NETHERSOLE ST

Stiper's Hill

Stiper's Hill Farm

ABBEY CROFT
ROFS CROFT

HIGH ST

The Nethersole CE Prim Sch

Stiper's Hill Plantation

Kisses' Barn

CV9

Inn

Liby HALL CT

B78

Polesworth

Coventry Canal

River Anker

B5000

GRENDON RD

Polesworth Bridge

1 MILLERS WHARF
2 FAIRFIELDS HILL

ABBEY GREEN CL

Limekiln Bridge

Bassett's Bridge

MARKET ST
WHARF TCE

The Mount

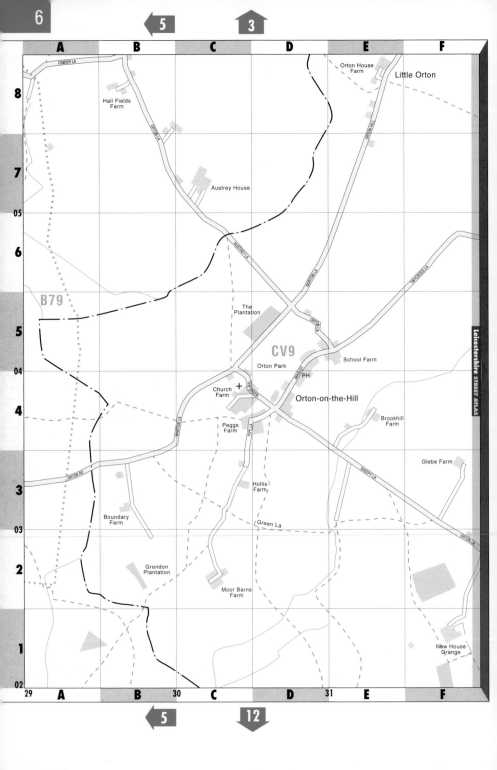

A B C D E F

CINDER LA

8

Hall Fields
Farm

Orton House
Farm

Little Orton

7

Austrey House

05

6

B79

The
Plantation

Orton La

CV9

School Farm

TWYCROSS LA

Leicestershire STREET ATLAS

5

04

Orton Park

PH

4

Church
Farm

Orton-on-the-Hill

Brookhill
Farm

Peggs
Farm

Glebe Farm

ORTON RD

3

Hollis
Farm

Boundary
Farm

Green La

SHEEPY LA

ORTON LA

03

2

Grendon
Plantation

Moor Barns
Farm

1

New House
Grange

02

29 A B 30 C D 31 E F

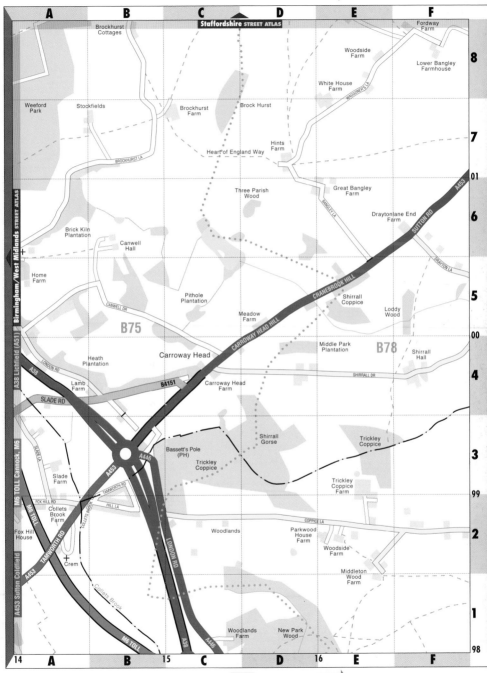

Staffordshire STREET ATLAS

Birmingham/West Midlands STREET ATLAS

| | A | B | C | D | E | F | |

8
Brockhurst Cottages
Fordway Farm
Woodside Farm
Lower Bangley Farmhouse
White House Farm
WAGGONER'S LA

Weeford Park
Stockfields
Brockhurst Farm
Brock Hurst

7
BROCKHURST LA
Heart of England Way
Hints Farm

A453

01

Three Parish Wood
Great Bangley Farm
Draytonlane End Farm
SUTTON RD

6
Brick Kiln Plantation
Canwell Hall
BANGLEY LA
DRAYTON LA

Home Farm
CANWELL DR
Pithole Plantation
Shirrall Coppice
Loddy Wood

5
CRANEBROOK HILL
Meadow Farm

B75

CARROWAY HEAD HILL

Middle Park Plantation

B78
Shirrall Hall

00

Heath Plantation
Carroway Head
SHIRRALL DR

4
LONDON RD
A38 Lichfield (A51)
A38
Lamb Farm
B4151
Carroway Head Farm

SLADE RD

Slade Farm
A453
A446
Bassett's Pole (PH)
Shirrall Gorse
Trickley Coppice

3
M6 TOLL Cannock, M6
SLADE LA
Trickley Coppice
Trickley Coppice Farm

TAMWORTH RD
FOX HILL RD
HILL LA
Collets Brook Farm
COPPICE LA

99

Fox Hill House
FOX HILL RD
COLLETS BROOK
Woodlands
Parkwood House Farm
Woodside Farm

2
A453 Sutton Coldfield
TAMWORTH RD
A453
Crem
Collets Brook
LONDON RD
Middleton Wood Farm

1
M6 TOLL
A38
A446
Woodlands Farm
New Park Wood

98

| 14 | A | B | 15 | C | D | 16 | E | F | |

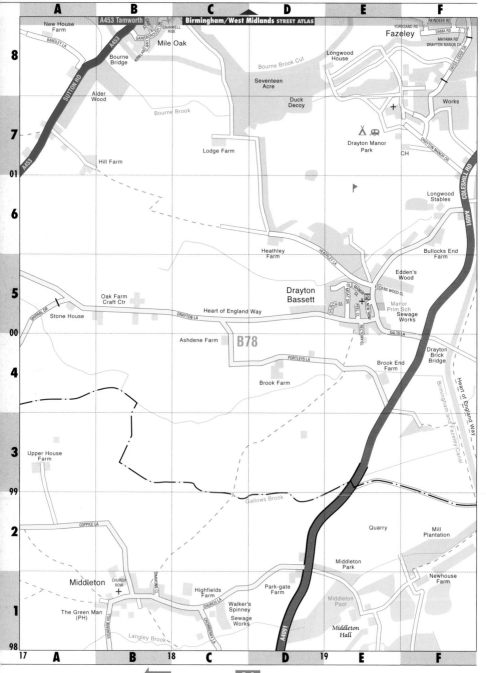

Birmingham/West Midlands STREET ATLAS

A B C D E F

New House
Farm

A453 Tamworth

Mile Oak

Fazeley

YORKSAND RD

REINDEER RD

DAMA RD

MAYAMA RD

DRAYTON MANOR DR

IRIS LODGE DR

BANGLEY LA

CRANWELL
RISE

GAINSBOROUGH

KIRKLAND WAY

CARLTON

CASTLE

Bourne
Bridge

A453

SUTTON RD

Longwood
House

Works

Alder
Wood

Bourne Brook Cut

Seventeen
Acre

Duck
Decoy

Bourne Brook

Drayton Manor
Park

CH

DRAYTON MANOR DR

COLESHILL RD

A4091

Hill Farm

Lodge Farm

Longwood
Stables

Heathley
Farm

HEATHLEY LA

Edden's
Wood

Bullocks End
Farm

Oak Farm
Craft Ctr

Drayton
Bassett

EDDENS WOOD DL

Manor
Prim Sch

Stone House

SHIRRAL DR

DRAYTON LA

Heart of England Way

OLD BANDITT CL

VICAR DR

PEEL CL

CHURCH CL

NEW ROW

Sewage
Works

Drayton
Brick
Bridge

Ashdene Farm

B78

RECTORY CL

SALTS LA

PORTLEYS LA

Brook End
Farm

Brook Farm

Birmingham and Fazeley Canal

Heart of England Way

Upper House
Farm

Gallows Brook

COPPICE LA

Quarry

Mill
Plantation

Middleton
Park

Newhouse
Farm

Middleton

CHURCH
ROW

SMALLING CL

Highfields
Farm

Park-gate
Farm

Middleton
Pool

The Green Man
(PH)

VICARAGE HILL

CHURCH LA

Walker's
Spinney

CROSS HEATH LA

Sewage
Works

A4091

Middleton
Hall

Langley Brook

17 A B 18 C D 19 E F

7

14

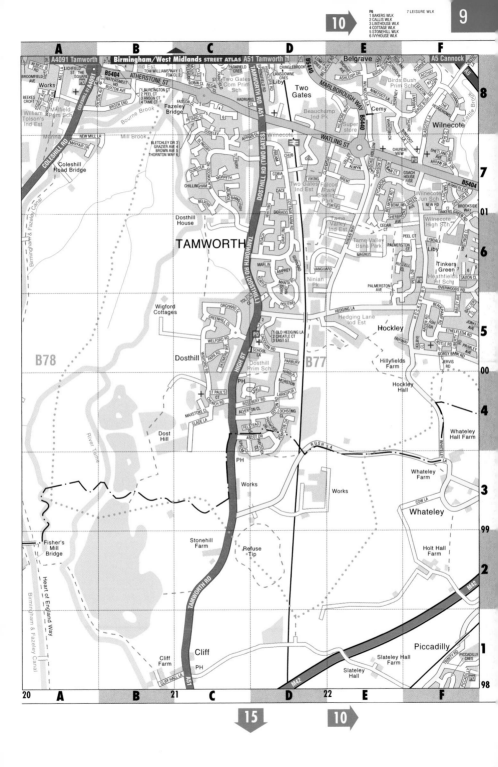

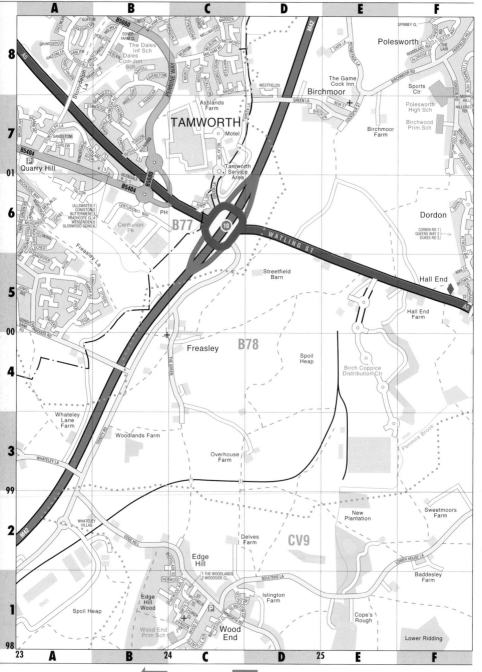

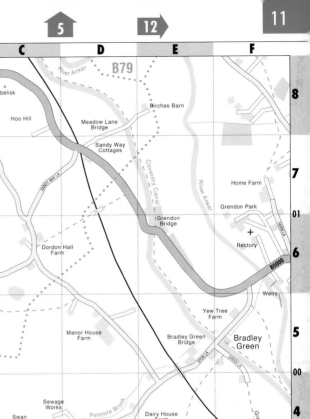

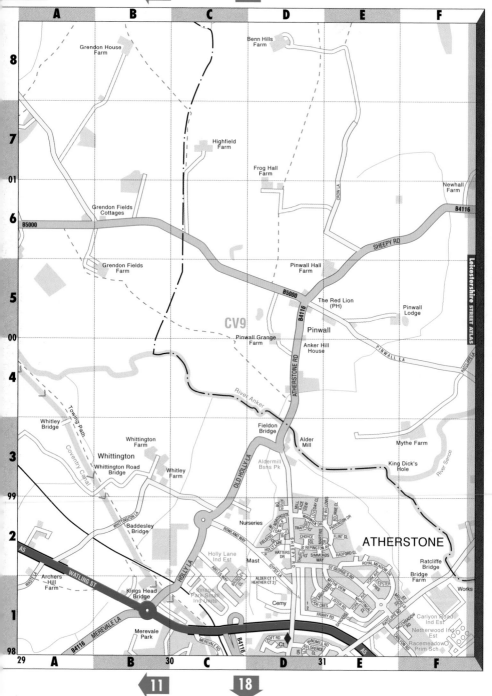

8
7
97
6
5
96
4
3
95
2
1
94

A   B   C   D   E   F

Langley Brook
Riding Stables
Roger's Coppice
Stables
Ash End House Farm
Ash End Farm
Hunts Green
Park Farm
Coneybury Farm
Gravel Pit
CROMWELL LA
A4091
Coneybury Wood
Hunts-green Farm
Cross Green Farm
B78
Pool House Farm
BRICK KILN LA
Sports Gd
Lower Farm
GREEN LA
BISHOPS LA
Stoke End Farm
Primrose Cottage
BODYMOOR HEATH RD
A446
Tidy Cottage
Maple Leaf
Middleton House Farm
Cheatle's Farm Bridge
PH
Boundary Plantation
Lea Farm
Noel Grange
North Wood
Birmingham and Fazeley Canal
Wishaw Hall Farm
Fox Wood
Marston Farm Hotel
M42
Moxhull Pool
The Belfry Golf Ctr
CUTTLE MILL LA
LICHFIELD RD
THE GRANGE
The Belfry (Hotel)
B76
Cuttle Mill Farm
Mill Pools
Cocksparrow House Farm
T2
A4091
Grange Farm Cottages
White Bridge
Church Farm
THE GRANGE
RYEFIELD LA
Wishaw
School Farm
A4097
CHURCH LA
Rye Farm
DUNTON LA
Marston Lane Bridge
MARSTON LA
KINGSBURY RD
Church Pit
BLUNTS LA
M6 TOLL
A446
Willday's Farm Bridge
Fox's Bridge
Marston Lane Bridge
M42
Mullensgrove Farm
BLACKGREAVES LA
Blackgreaves Farm

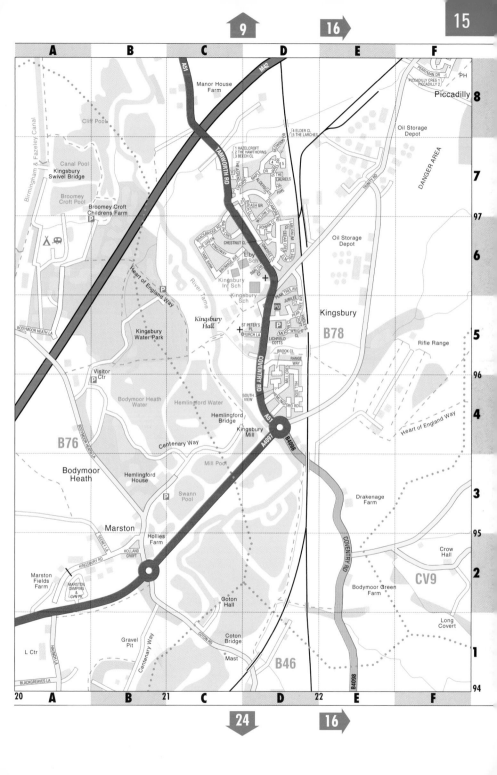

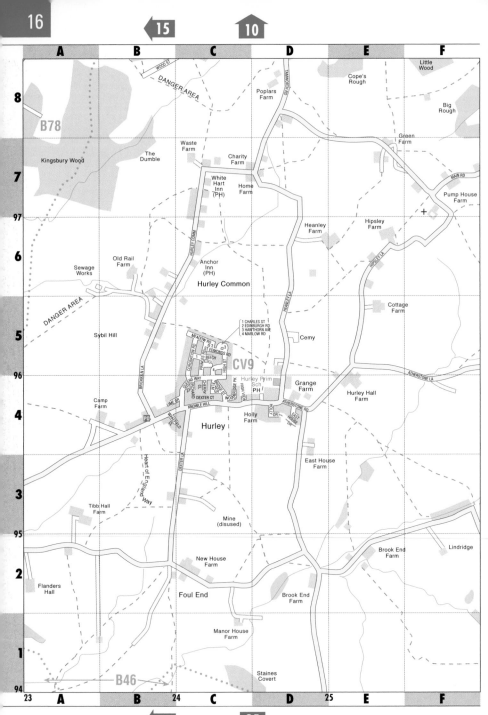

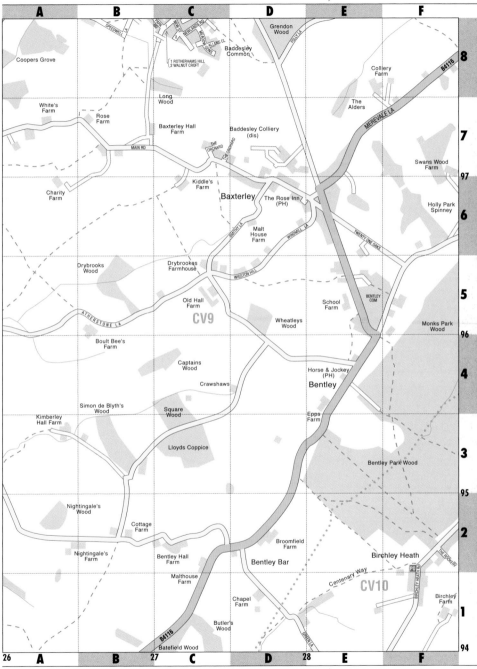

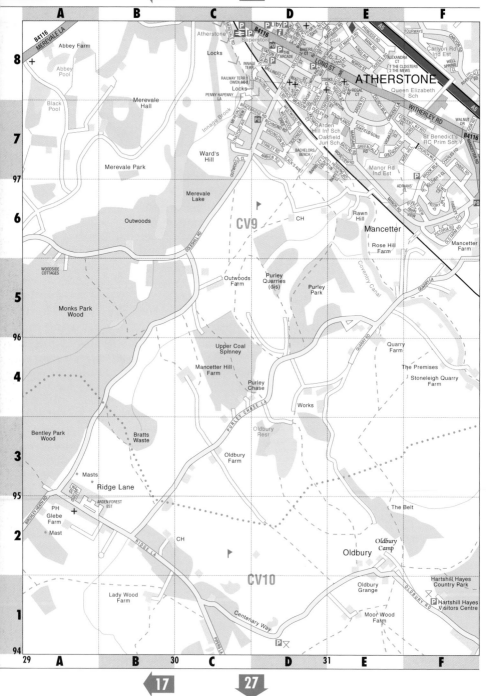

A   B   C   D   E   F

B4116
MEREVALE LA

Abbey Farm

Atherstone

Locks

8

Abbey
Pool

Black
Pool

Merevale
Hall

Innage Brook

Superstore

Liby

B4116

THE
ARCADE

LONG ST

BAKERS
CT

PRINCESS RD

KINGS AVE

ATHERSTONE

Queen Elizabeth
Sch

FOURWAYS

Carlyon Rd
Ind Est

A5

WELL
SPRING

WITHERLEY RD

B4116

WALNUT
DR

RIVERSDALE RD

7

Merevale Park

Ward's
Hill

97

Merevale
Lake

6

Outwoods

CV9

CH

Rawn
Hill

Mancetter

Arden
Hill Inf Sch
Oakfield
Jun Sch

St Benedict's
RC Prim Sch

Rose Hill
Farm

Manor Rd
Ind Est

ADRIANS'

Mancetter
Farm

WOODSIDE
COTTAGES

Monks Park
Wood

5

Outwoods
Farm

Purley
Quarries
(dis)

Purley
Park

Coventry Canal

QUARRY LA

Quarry
Farm

96

4

Upper Coal
Spinney

Mancetter Hill
Farm

Purley
Chase

Works

QUARRY RD

The Premises

Stoneleigh Quarry
Farm

Bentley Park
Wood

Bratts
Waste

PURLEY CHASE LA

Oldbury
Resr

3

Masts

Ridge Lane

ARDEN FOREST
EST

PH
Glebe
Farm

Mast

Oldbury
Farm

The Belt

95

BIRCHLEY HEATH RD

RIDGE LA

CH

CV10

Oldbury
Camp

Oldbury

Oldbury
Grange

OLDBURY RD

Hartshill Hayes
Country Park

Hartshill Hayes
Visitors Centre

2

1

Lady Wood
Farm

Centenary Way

Moor Wood
Farm

94

29   A   B   30   C   D   31   E   F

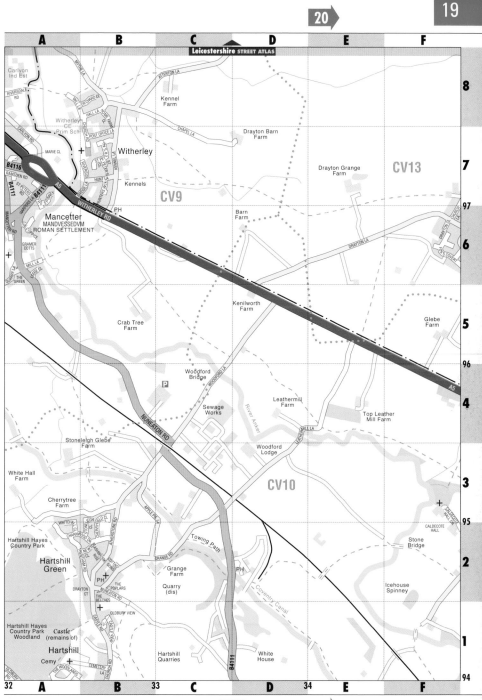

Leicestershire STREET ATLAS

Carlyon Ind Est

RIVERSDALE RD

Kennel Farm

Witherley CE Prim Sch

MARIE CL

Witherley

ATTERTON LA

CHAPEL LA

Drayton Barn Farm

Drayton Grange Farm

CV13

B4116

B4111

WARFORD LA

WITHERLEY RD

Kennels

CV9

Mancetter
MANDVESSEDVM
ROMAN SETTLEMENT

GRAMER COTTS

MILL LA

THE GREEN

Barn Farm

Drayton La

97

6

Crab Tree Farm

Kenilworth Farm

Glebe Farm

5

Woodford Bridge

WOODFORD LA

96

Sewage Works

River Anker

Leathermill Farm

Top Leather Mill Farm

4

NUNEATON RD

MILL LA

LEATHERMILL

Woodford Lodge

Stoneleigh Glebe Farm

White Hall Farm

CV10

3

Cherrytree Farm

Caldecote Hall

95

Hartshill Hayes Country Park

Hartshill Green

APPLE PIE LA

ORANGE RD

Towing Path

Stone Bridge

2

PH

DRAYTON CT

THE POPLARS

THE BEECHES

Grange Farm

Quarry (dis)

PH

Coventry Canal

Icehouse Spinney

Hartshill Hayes Country Park Woodland

Castle (remains of)

Hartshill

Cemy

OLDBURY VIEW

CASTLE RD

CEMETERY LA

B4111

Hartshill Quarries

White House

94

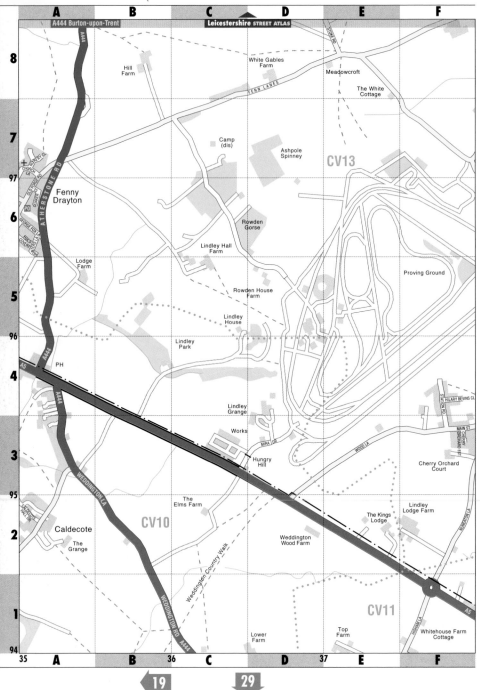

19

A444 Burton-upon-Trent

Leicestershire STREET ATLAS

8

Hill Farm

White Gables Farm

Meadowcroft

The White Cottage

FENN LANES

STONE RD

7

Camp (dis)

Ashpole Spinney

CV13

97

Fenny Drayton

ATHERSTONE RD

6

Rowden Gorse

Lindley Hall Farm

Lodge Farm

Rowden House Farm

5

Lindley House

96

Lindley Park

Proving Ground

A444

A5

PH

4

Lindley Grange

Works

HILARY BEVINS CL

ST KILIAN RD

MAIN ST

3

MIRA DR

Hungry Hill

WOOD LA

Cherry Orchard Court

WEDDINGTON LA

95

The Elms Farm

Lindley Lodge Farm

The Kings Lodge

2

Caldecote

CV10

The Grange

Weddington Wood Farm

Weddington Country Walk

1

WEDDINGTON RD

A444

CV11

A5

Lower Farm

Top Farm

Whitehouse Farm Cottage

94

19

29

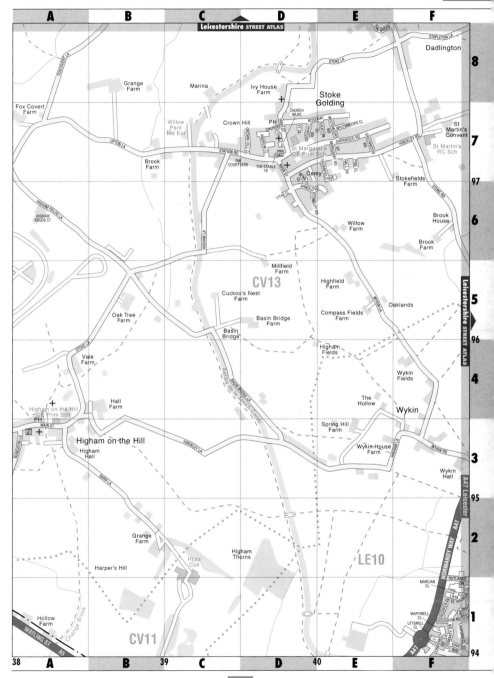

A   B   C   D   E   F

Dadlington

8

Grange
Farm

Marina

Ivy House
Farm

Stoke
Golding

Fox Covert
Farm

CHURCH
WLKS

St
Martin's
Convent

Crown Hill

PH

ROSEWAY

WHITEMOORS CL

St Martin's
RC Sch

7

Willow
Park
Ind Est

CHURCH ST

SHELTON

SHERWOOD RD

GREENWOOD

HINCKLEY RD

UPTON LA

ANDREW CL

IVY CL

STATION RD

PO

St Margaret's
CE Prim Sch

Brook
Farm

THE
COURTYARD

THE STABLE
YD

PINE CL

HALL DR

Stokefields
Farm

97

Cemy

TITHE CL

ARNOLD RD

STOKELEY RD

THORNEYCROFT

CAVE

Brook
House

HIGHAM FIELDS LA

Willow
Farm

Brook
Farm

6

HIGHAM
FIELDS CT

Millfield
Farm

CV13

Highfield
Farm

LA HIGHAM

Cuckoo's Nest
Farm

Compass Fields
Farm

Oaklands

WYKIN LA

5

Oak Tree
Farm

Basin Bridge
Farm

Basin
Bridge

Higham
Fields

96

Vale
Farm

STOKE LA

Ashby Zouch Canal

BASIN BRIDGE LA

Wykin
Fields

4

Hall
Farm

The
Hollow

Wykin

Higham on the Hill
CE Prim Sch

PH

MAIN ST

Spring Hill
Farm

HINCKLEY LA

Wykin-House
Farm

HIGHAM LA

WYKIN RD

3

KINGTON LA

PO

Higham on the Hill

Higham
Hall

Wykin
Hall

95

BARN LA

A47 Leicester

Grange
Farm

Higham
Thorns

LE10

NORMANDY WAY

2

Harper's Hill

Hijaz
Coll

MARCIAN
CL

OUTLANDS

A47

CV11

Hollow
Farm

Change Brook

WATLING ST

A5

MARYWELL
CL

LEYSMILL
CL

CROSSKIRK RD

A47

1

94

38   A   B   39   C   D   40   E   F

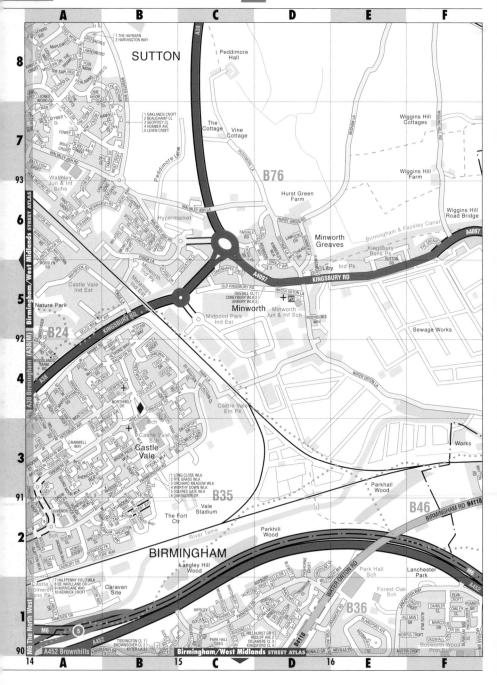

SUTTON

1 THE HAYBARN
2 HARVINGTON WAY

Peddimore
Hall

The
Cottage

Vine
Cottage

1 OAKLANDS CROFT
2 BEAUCHAMP CL
3 GEOFFREY CL
4 HUMBER AVE
5 LEVEN CROFT

Wiggins Hill
Cottages

B76

Hurst Green
Farm

Wiggins Hill
Farm

Walmley
Jun & Inf
Schs

Wiggins Hill
Road Bridge

Hypermarket

WALMLEY ASH LA

HURST GREEN RD

Birmingham & Fazeley Canal

A4097

Minworth
Greaves

Kingsbury
Bsns Pk

THE GREAVES

FARVALE
RD

Liby Ind Pk

SUTTON
RD

KINGSBURY RD

Castle Vale
Ind Est

Nature Park

B24

OLD KINGSBURY RD

A4097

WATER ORTON LA

PO

Minworth

Midpoint Park
Ind Est

Minworth
Jun & Inf Sch

ROBINSON'S
WAY

Sewage Works

OXSTALL CL 1
CONEYBURY WLK 2
ARBURY WLK 3

Castle Vale
Ent Pk

WATER ORTON LA

Castle Vale
Sch

NORTHOLT
DR

CRANWELL
WAY

Castle Vale
Sch

Works

MYTTON
RD

Castle
Vale

1 LONG CLOSE WLK
2 RYE GRASS WLK
3 ORCHARD MEADOW WLK
4 WORTHY DOWN WLK
5 SQUIRES GATE WLK
6 OAKINGTON DR

B35

Parkhall
Wood

B46

BIRMINGHAM RD B4118

Vale
Stadium

The Fort
Ctr

River Tame

Parkhill
Wood

WATER ORTON RD

A452

BIRMINGHAM

Langley Hill
Wood

Park Hall
Sch

Lanchester
Park

1 HALFPENNY FIELD WLK
8 DE HAVILLAND DR
9 HURRICANE WAY
10 KENRICK CROFT

Caravan
Site

Forest Oak
Sch

B36

Castle
Bromwich
Bsns Pk

M6 The North West

HILLHURST GR 1
REDLIFF AVE 2
DELAMERE CL 3
KINGSFORD CL 4

PARK HALL
CRES

B4118

Bosworth Wood
Prim Sch

M6

5

A452 Brownhills

TIDDINGTON CL 1
BROWNSOVER CL 2
KYTER LA 3

A452

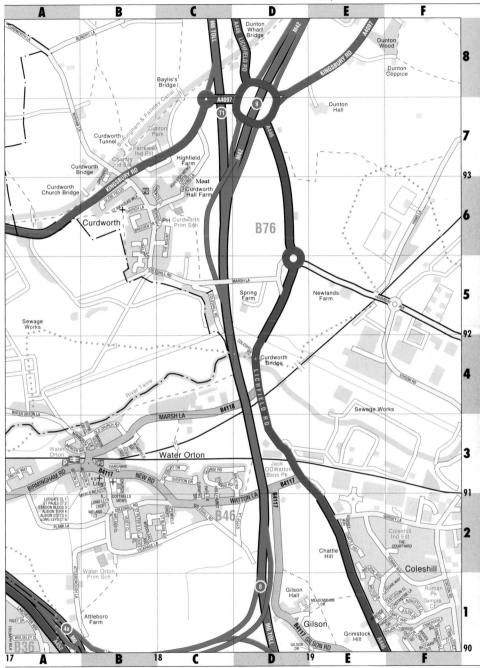

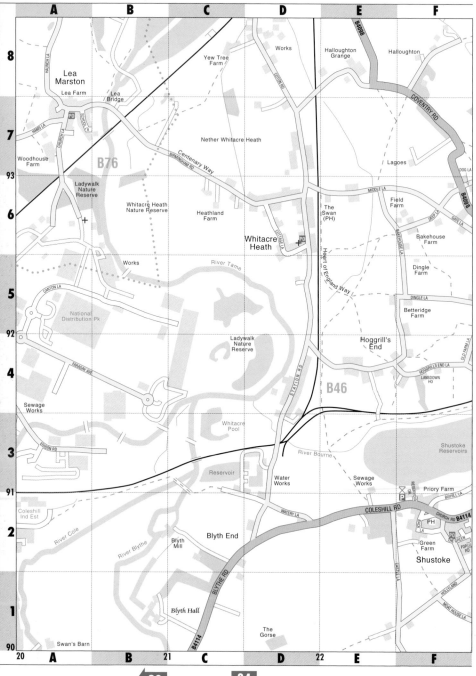

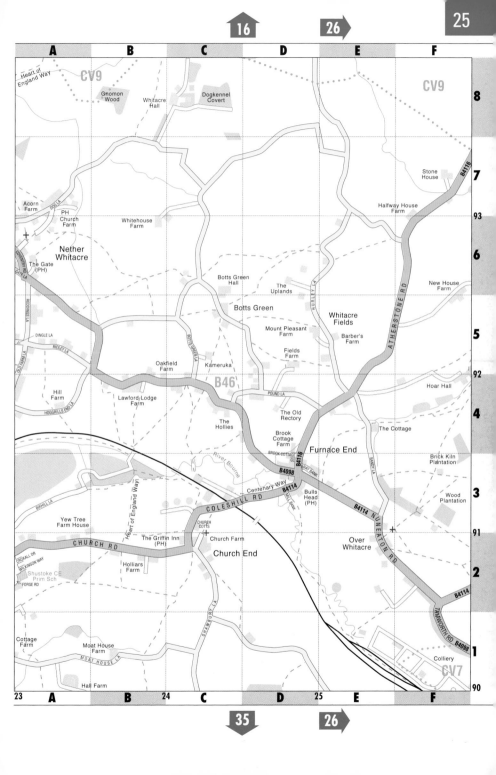

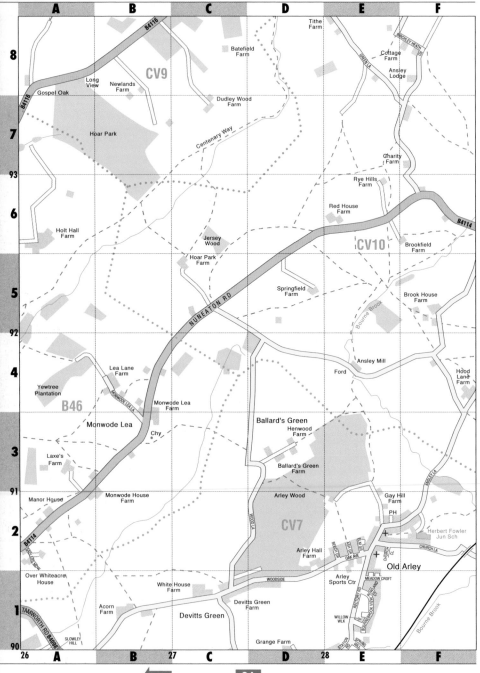

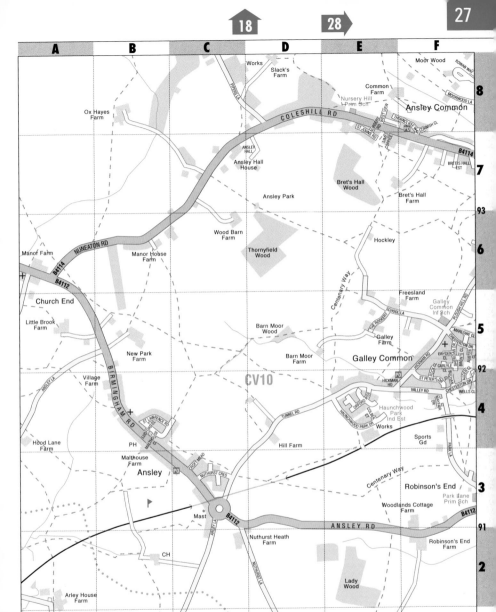

18
28

Moor Wood

ROWAN WAY

MOORWOOD LA

Common Farm

Nursery Hill Prim Sch

Ansley Common

Works

Slack's Farm

8

COLESHILL RD

FIELDS LA

ST JOHNS RD

WEST VIEW

LANGSBY

TYBURN CL

FACK

CORNISH CL

B4114

BRETTS HALL EST

ANSLEY HALL

Ansley Hall House

7

Ansley Park

Bret's Hall Wood

Bret's Hall Farm

93

Ox Hayes Farm

Wood Barn Farm

Thornyfield Wood

Hockley

6

Manor Farm

NUNEATON RD

Manor House Farm

Centenary Way

Freesland Farm

Galley Common Inf Sch

B4114

B4112

Church End

Little Brook Farm

Barn Moor Wood

SCHOOL LA

THE ROOKERY

Galley Farm

MARLOWE CL

CHESTERTON DR

DRYDEN CL

RUSKIN CL

CARLYLE

HICKMAN RD

5

New Park Farm

Barn Moor Farm

Galley Common

P0

HICKMAN RD

ST PETER'S DR

CHESTERTON DR

WELLS CL

92

CV10

BIRMINGHAM RD

Village Farm

ANSLEY LA

HICKMAN HO

VALLEY RD

MAYFAIR

HAUNCHWOOD PARK DR

OXFORD

COLLEGE

4

Hood Lane Farm

ST LAWRENCE RD

MALTHOUSE

PH

Malthouse Farm

Ansley

CROFT MEAD

TUNNEL RD

Hill Farm

Works

Sports Gd

PARK LA

NUTHURST CRES

Centenary Way

Robinson's End

Park Lane Prim Sch

3

Mast

ARLEY LA

B4112

Woodlands Cottage Farm

B4112

91

ANSLEY RD

Nuthurst Heath Farm

Robinson's End Farm

CH

NUTHURST LA

2

Arley House Farm

Lady Wood

CV7

HILL TOP

CHURCH LA

Church Farm

Lodge Farm

1

90

37
28

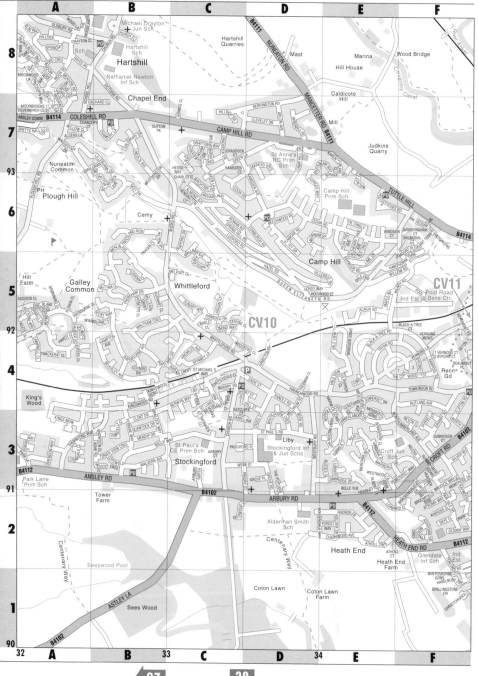

A B C D E F

8

Michael Drayton
+ Jun Sch
Hartshill
Quarries
B4111
Mast
Marina
Wood Bridge

Hartshill
Sch
Hill House
Caldicote
Hill

OLDBURY RD
HILLSIDE
SPRING
Sch
Nathaniel Newton
Inf Sch

MOORWOOD
LA
HAYES RD
PO

Hartshill

MANCETTER RD B4111
NUNEATON RD
Coventry
Canal

7

MOORBROOKE
SILVERBIRCH CL 2
ANSLEY COMM
B4114
COLESHILL RD
CHANCERY
PO
SUTTON
PK
Mill
Judkins
Quarry

CHAPEL END
ORCHARD CL
GRANGE CL
HILLSID
BERRINGTON RD
CLEVELEY RD
ARLIN RD
WINDMILL
BRETTS HALL EST
WILLOW CL
ALDERS LA
CAMP HILL RD

93

Nuneaton
Common
DRAYTONS WAY
CRADDOCK
CT
RAMSDEN
CT
St Anne's
RC Prim
Sch
CARROYD DR
CUL
SEAM
TUTTLE HILL

PH
Plough Hill
HEDGE
WAY
CHARLOTTE
ORCHARD WAY
CYPRESS WAY
SPRUCE
Camp Hill
Prim Sch
THE HEDGES
B4114

6

Cemy
MID RISE
FRASER CL
BINLEY RD
EDINBURGH RD
LUDFORD RD
BEECHWOOD RD
CEDAR RD
PO
SYCAMORE RD
ELM GR
THE DINGLE
WINDSOR
CT
BALMORAL
CT

Hill
Farm
Galley
Common
Whittleford
CV10
CV11
Pool Road
Ind Est
Bsns Ctr.

5

ADDISON CL
CL
DR
SEV BY WAY
WIMBOURNE DR
RANNOCH DR
KATRINE CL
WHITTLEFORD RD
WOODROW
QUEEN ELIZABETH
HOLYROOD CT
ACACIA RD
BLACK-A-TREE RD
VERNONS
MEWS

92

THACKERAY CL
COOMBE
DR
BEVERLEY AVE
ST MICHAEL'S
WAY
WINDSOR GDNS
BLACK-A-TREE
J VERNONS CT
BYFORD ST
BEAUMONT
PL
Recn
Gd

4

King's
Wood
KINGS MDW
CLENT DR
QUANTOCK DR
BENYON WAY
KINGSWOOD
MENDIP DR
QUARRY YD
SHORT ST
LEADE ST
RANDLE RD
HAUNCHWOOD RD
TOMKINSON RD
RUTLAND AVE
B4102

3

B4112
Park Lane
Prim Sch
ANSLEY RD
St Paul's
CE Prim Sch
Stockingford
PADDIFORD PL
RATCLIFFE
RD
ST LUKE'S
DANIEL AVE
ST PAUL'S RD
Liby
Stockingford Inf
& Jun Schs
CROFT RD
WESTWOOD
BELLE VUE
SUNNYSIDE
SKYE CL
PO

91

Tower
Farm
B4102
ARBURY RD
Alderman Smith
Sch
PO
RADNOR
CT
B4112
HEATH END RD
Glendale
Inf Sch
Ind
Est
B4112

2

Centenary
Way
Centenary
Way
FOREST
WAY
CHARNWOOD AVE
ROSEDALE
Heath End
ATHOLL
CT
Heath End
Farm
WINTERBORNE
GDNS
HASELBURY
SHILLINGSTONE
DR

1

ASTLEY LA
Seeswood Pool
Sees Wood
Coton Lawn
Coton Lawn
Farm

90

32
A
B
33
C
D
34
E
F

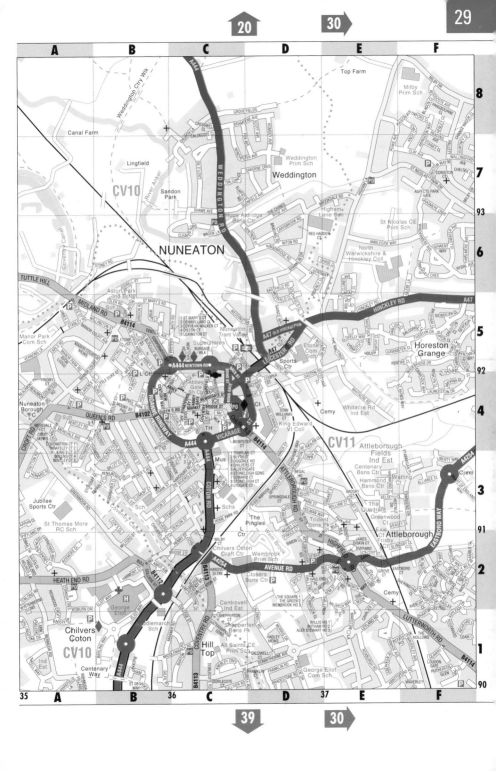

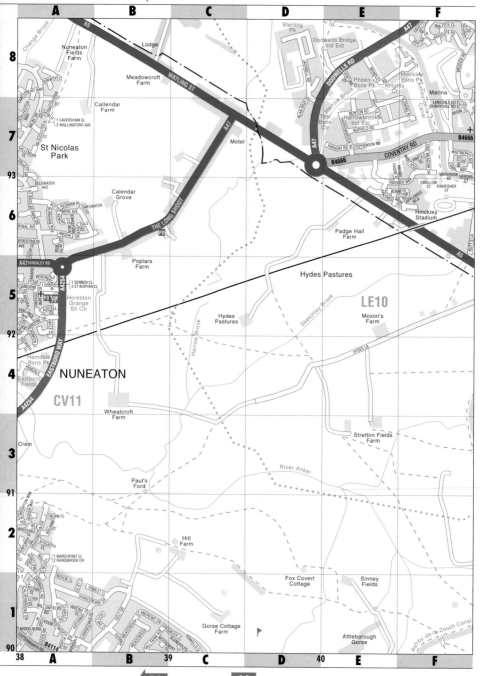

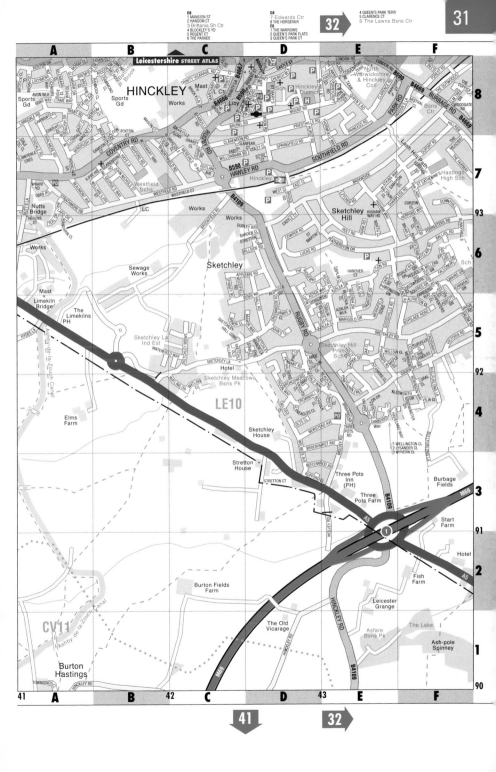

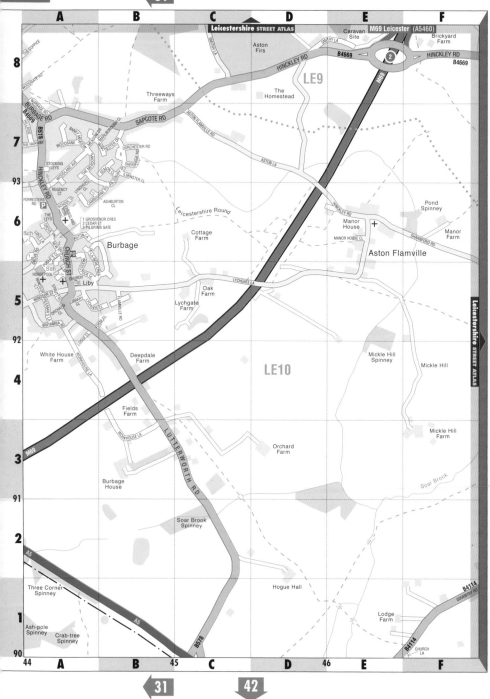

31

Leicestershire STREET ATLAS

Leicestershire STREET ATLAS

A **B** **C** **D** **E** **F**

8

7

93

6

5

92

4

3

91

2

1

90

44 45 46

A **B** **C** **D** **E** **F**

31

42

Caravan Site
Brickyard Farm
M69 Leicester (A5460)
HINCKLEY RD
B4669
B4669
Aston Firs
HINCKLEY RD
SMITHY LA
SOUTH LA
ASTON FLAMVILLE RD
LE9
The Homestead
Threeways Farm
SAPCOTE RD
BURBAGE RD
B578
HINCKLEY RD
BANKS'
WOODBANK
THE MEADOWS
MANOR BOURNE CL
CHESTER DR
DORCHESTER RD
SHERIDAN
ASTON LA
STOCKING LEYS
WOODLAND AVE
MINSTER CL
ASHBURTON CL
CAMBRIDGE
LYNDHURST
REGENCY CT
THE LEYS
FORRESTERS RD
Sch
CHURCH ST
Burbage
1 GROSVENOR CRES
2 CEDAR CT
3 PILGRIMS GATE
Leicestershire Round
Cottage Farm
ASTON LA
HINCKLEY RD
Manor House
MANOR HOUSE CL
Pond Spinney
Manor Farm
SHARNFORD RD
Aston Flamville
Sch
HORSEPOOL
Liby
Oak Farm
LYCHGATE LA
Lychgate Farm
FLAMVILLE RD
LIBRARY
GATE CL
WINDSOR ST
BRITANNIA
ORCHID
LODGE CL
BONHOUSE LA
White House Farm
Deepdale Farm
LE10
Mickle Hill Spinney
Mickle Hill
M69
Fields Farm
LUTTERWORTH RD
Orchard Farm
Mickle Hill Farm
Soar Brook
Burbage House
91
Soar Brook Spinney
A5
Three Corner Spinney
Hogue Hall
B4114
COVENTRY RD
Ash-pole Spinney
A5
Crab-tree Spinney
B578
Lodge Farm
CHURCH LA
B4114

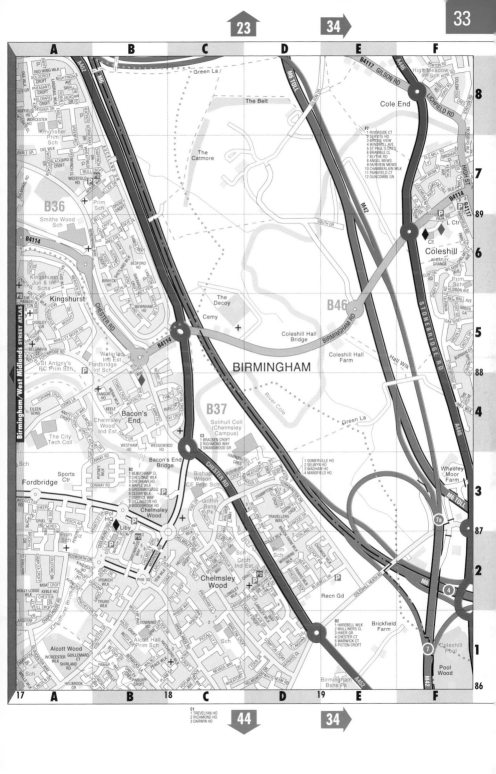

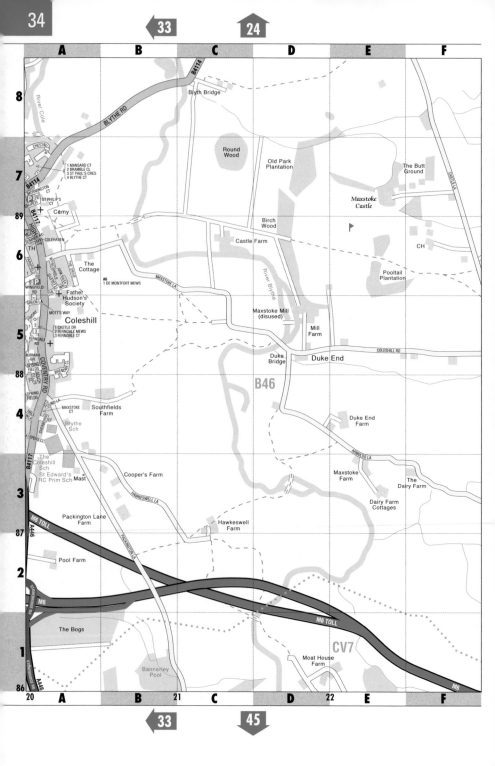

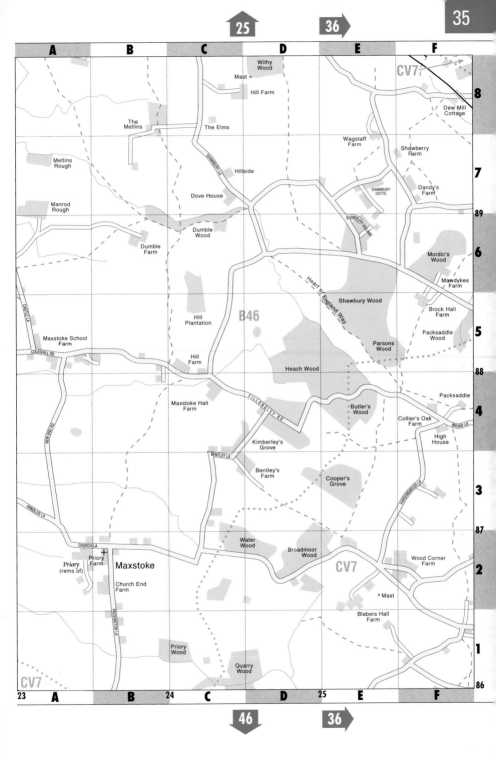

CV7

8

A
B
C
D
E
F

Mast
Withy Wood
Hill Farm
The Elms
The Metlins
Hillside
Metlins Rough
Dove House
Manrod Rough
Dumble Wood
Dumble Farm

Dew Mill Cottage
Wagstaff Farm
Shawberry Farm
Shawbury Cotts
Dandy's Farm

SHAWBURY LA

7

89

SHAWBURY VILLAGE

Mordic's Wood
Mawdykes Farm

6

Shawbury Wood
Heart of England Way
B46
Hill Plantation
Brock Hall Farm
Packsaddle Wood

5

Maxstoke School Farm
COLESHILL RD
CASTLE LA
Hill Farm
Parsons Wood
Heach Wood

88

Maxstoke Hall Farm
FILLONGLEY RD
Butler's Wood
Packsaddle
Collier's Oak Farm
High House
BROAD LA

4

NEW END RD
Kimberley's Grove
BENTLEY LA
Bentley's Farm
Cooper's Grove
HARDINGWOOD LA

3

ARNOLDS LA
CHURCH LA
Water Wood
Broadmoor Wood

87

Priory (rems of)
Priory Farm
Maxstoke
Church End Farm
CV7
Wood Corner Farm

2

Mast
Blabers Hall Farm

PACKINGTON LA
Priory Wood
Quarry Wood

1

CV7

86

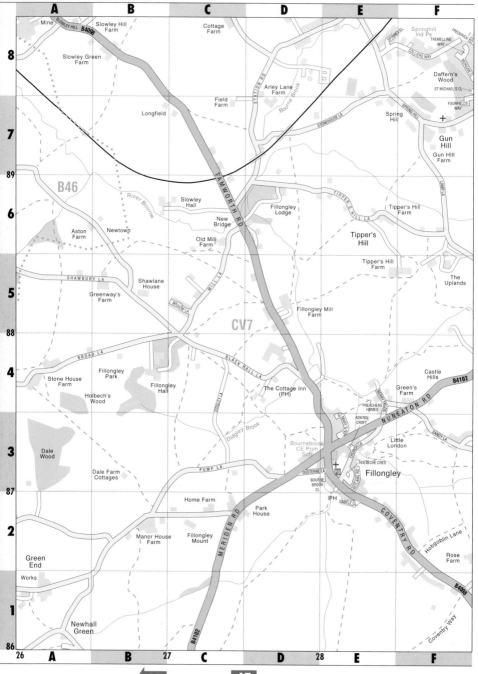

35 26

A **B** **C** **D** **E** **F**

Mine
SLOWLEY HILL
B4098
Slowley Hill
Farm
Cottage
Farm
Springhill
Ind Pk
SPRINGEY CL
TREMELLING
WAY
FREDERICK RD
MOSELEY CL

8

Slowley Green
Farm
COLLIERS WAY
Daffern's
Wood
ST MICHAEL'S CL
FOURFIELDS
WAY

Arley Lane
Farm
STONEHOUSE LA
SPRING HILL
Spring
Hill
Gun
Hill
Longfield
Field
Farm

7

STATION RD
Bourne Brook
Gun HIll
Farm
CAMP LA

89

B46
River Bourne
Slowley
Hall
Fillongley
Lodge
TIPPER'S HILL LA
Tipper's Hill
Farm

6

New
Bridge
Fillongley
Lodge
Tipper's Hill
Farm
Aston
Farm
Newtown
Old Mill
Farm
Tipper's
Hill
The
Uplands
Tipper's Hill
Farm

SHAWBURY LA
Shawlane
House
Greenway's
Farm
WILLOW LA
MILL LA
Fillongley Mill
Farm

5

CV7

88

BROAD LA
BLACK HALL LA
Stone House
Farm
Fillongley
Park
Fillongley
Hall
The Cottage Inn
(PH)
Castle
Hills
B4102
Green's
Farm

4

Holbech's
Wood
DUGDALE LA
PREACHERS
HOMES
NUNEATON RD
Didgley Brook
ADKINS
CROFT
Little
London
SANDY LA

3

Dale
Wood
Bournebrook
CE Prim
Sch
HOLBECHE CRES
PUMP LA
Dale Farm
Cottages
Home Farm
OUSTERNE LA
Fillongley
BOURNE
BROOK
CL

87

Park
House
IPH
CASTLE CL
Manor House
Farm
Fillongley
Mount
MERIDEN RD
COVENTRY RD
Hobgoblin Lane

2

Green
End
Rose
Farm

Works
B4098

1

Newhall
Green
B4102
Coventry Way

86

35 47

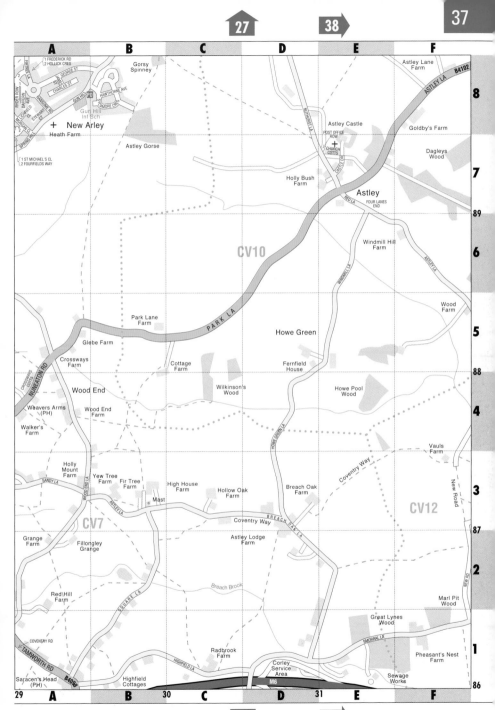

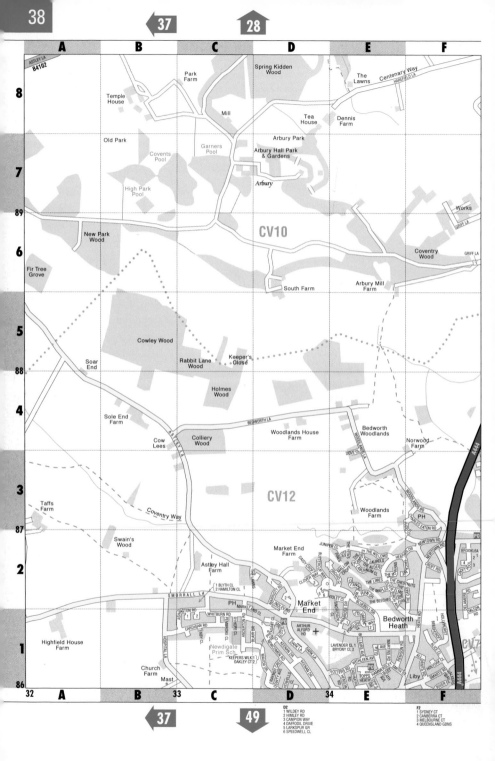

B4102
ASTLEY LA

Temple
House

Park
Farm

Spring Kidden
Wood

The
Lawns

Centenary Way

HAREFIELD LA

Mill

Tea
House

Dennis
Farm

Old Park

Covents
Pool

Garners
Pool

Arbury Park

Arbury Hall Park
& Gardens

High Park
Pool

Arbury

CV10

Works

GRIFF LA

89

New Park
Wood

Coventry
Wood

GRIFF LA

Fir Tree
Grove

South Farm

Arbury Mill
Farm

Cowley Wood

Keeper's
Close

Soar
End

Rabbit Lane
Wood

88

Holmes
Wood

Sole End
Farm

BEDWORTH LA

Bedworth
Woodlands

Norwood
Farm

Cow
Lees

Colliery
Wood

Woodlands House
Farm

WOODLANDS LA

DOVE LA

A444

ASHLEY LA

CV12

Woodlands
Farm

PH

CHARLES EATON RD

Taffs
Farm

Coventry Way

NEWTOWN RD

BROOKLEA

Swain's
Wood

Astley Hall
Farm

Market End
Farm

JUNIPER CL

NEWTOWN RD

CROFT RD

SMORRALL LA

THE LAWNS

1 BLYTH CL
2 HAMILTON CL

PH

MARKET END CL

Market
End

Bedworth
Heath

CV7

DALTON RD

WHITBURN RD

CARDIGAN RD

HOSPITAL LA

PEMBROKE CL

NEWDIGATE RD

ARTHUR
ALFORD
HO

HOLLYHURST

DALTON RD

Highfield House
Farm

Newdigate
Prim Sch

KEEPERS WLK 1
OAKLEY CT 2

LAVENDER CL 1
BRYONY CL 2

KATHLEEN AVE

Liby

Church
Farm

Mast

TOPPS
HEATH

D2
1 WILDEY RD
2 HIMLEY RD
3 CAMPION WAY
4 DAFFODIL DRIVE
5 LARKSPUR GR
6 SPEEDWELL CL

F2
1 SYDNEY CT
2 CANBERRA CT
3 MELBOURNE CT
4 QUEENSLAND GDNS

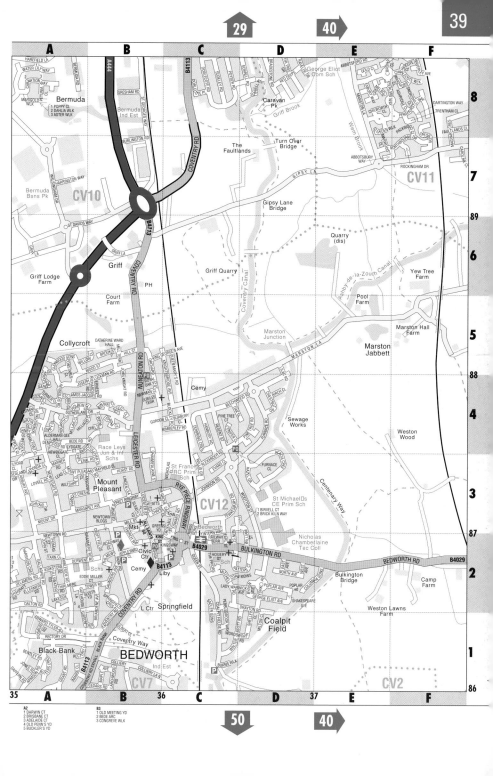

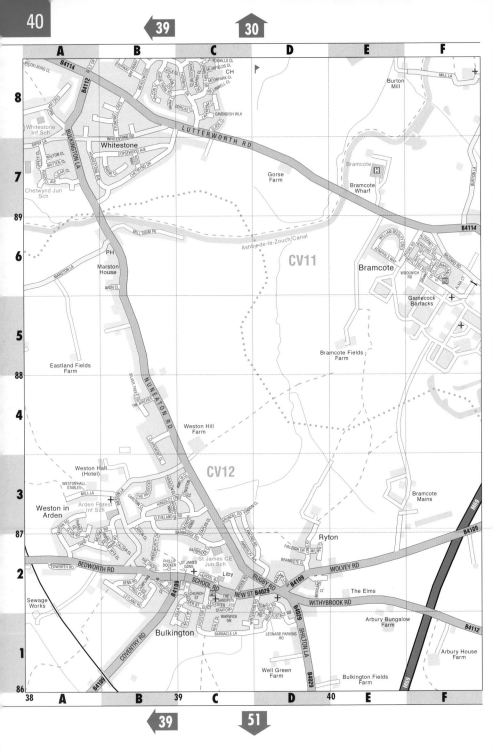

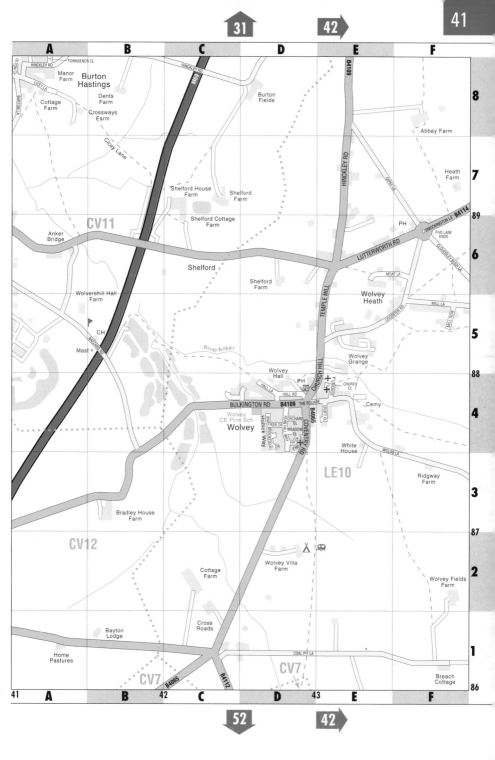

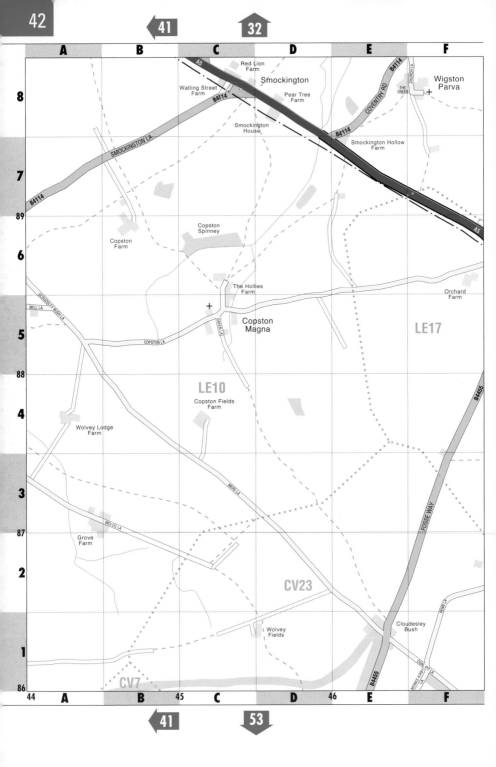

41
32

A B C D E F

8

Red Lion
Farm

A5

Smockington

Watling Street
Farm

B4114

Pear Tree
Farm

COVENTRY RD

B4114

THE
GREEN

CHURCH LA

Wigston
Parva

Smockington
House

7

SMOCKINGTON LA

Smockington Hollow
Farm

B4114

89

B4114

A5

Copston
Spinney

Orchard
Farm

6

Copston
Farm

The Hollies
Farm

LE17

5

MILL LA

FOUSELEY BRIGG LA

COPSTON LA

GREEN LA

Copston
Magna

88

LE10

Copston Fields
Farm

B4455

4

Wolvey Lodge
Farm

3

WOLDS LA

MERE LA

87

Grove
Farm

FOSSE WAY

2

CV23

PEN LA

1

Wolvey
Fields

Cloudesley
Bush

B4455

COAL PIT LA

MONKS KIRBY LA

86

CV7

44 A B 45 C D 46 E F

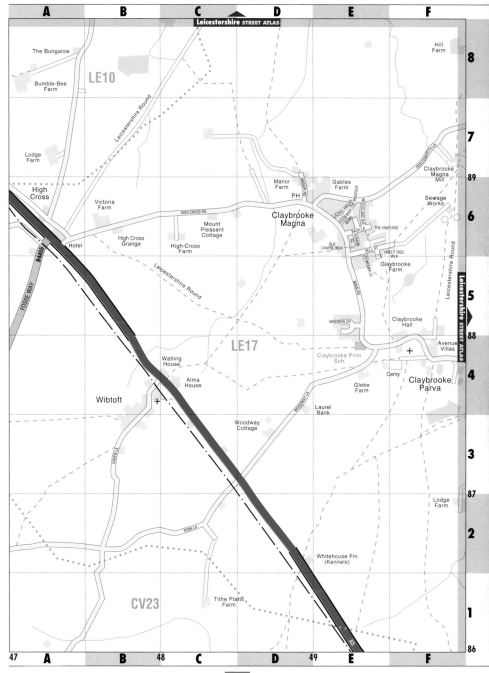

The Bungalow

LE10

Bumble-Bee Farm

Lodge Farm

Leicestershire Round

High Cross

Victoria Farm

Hotel

High Cross Grange

HIGH CROSS RD

Mount Pleasant Cottage

High-Cross Farm

Manor Farm

PH

MANOR RD

Claybrooke Magna

Gables Farm

LAUREL FIELDS
ROSEWAY TER
BACK LA
GUNHAM
OLD CHAPEL WLK
BELL ST
HOLLY TREE WLK

WOODLAND AVE

PADDOCK

THE VINEYARD

Claybrooke Farm

Hill Farm

Claybrooke Magna Mill

Sewage Works

Leicestershire Round

B4455

FOSSE WAY

Leicestershire Round

LE17

Watling House

Alma House

Wibtoft

Woodway Cottage

Laurel Bank

WESTERN DR

Claybrooke Prim Sch

Cemy

Glebe Farm

WOODWAY LA

Claybrooke Hall

Avenue Villas

Claybrooke Parva

GREEN LA

PENN LA

Whitehouse Fm (Kennels)

CV23

Tithe Platts Farm

A5

Lodge Farm

8
7
89
6
5
88
4
3
87
2
1
86

47   A   B   48   C   D   49   E   F

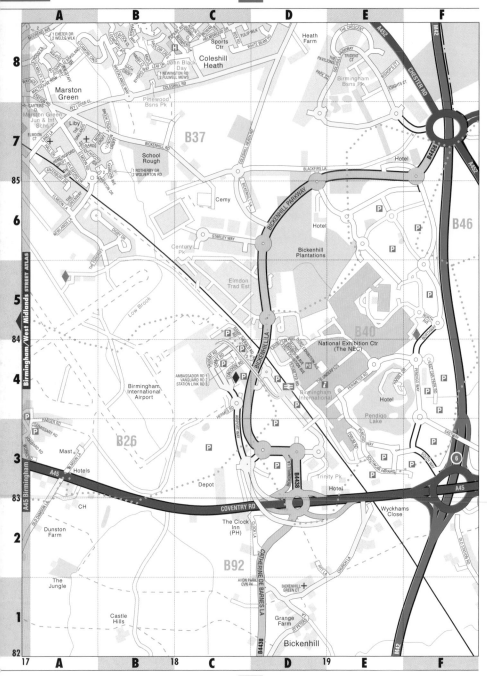

Birmingham/West Midlands STREET ATLAS

A45 Birmingham

8

85

7

6

5

84

4

83

3

2

1

82

A   B   C   D   E   F

Marston Green

Marston Green Jun & Inf School

Liby

Coleshill Heath

Sports Ctr

John Black Day

Heath Farm

Birmingham Bsns Pk

The Pavilions

CHESTER RD

B37

Pinewood Bsns Pk

School Rough

1 ROTHERBY GR
2 WOLVERTON RD

Cemy

BLACKFIRS LA

Hotel

BICKENHILL PARKWAY

B46

Century Pk

STARLEY WAY

Hotel

Bickenhill Plantations

Elmdon Trad Est

Low Brook

B40

BICKENHILL LA

National Exhibition Ctr (The NEC)

AMBASSADOR RD 1
VANGUARD RD 2
STATION LINK RD 3

Birmingham International Airport

B26

Mast

HANGER RD

COMMISSARY RD

Hotels

CH

Dunston Farm

The Jungle

Castle Hills

Depot

COVENTRY RD

Birmingham International

Pendigo Lake

Hotel

Trinity Pk

B4438

Hotel

6

A45

Wyckhams Close

The Clock Inn (PH)

CLOCK LA

B92

CATHERINE DE BARNES LA

AVON PARK CVN PK

BICKENHILL GREEN CT

Grange Farm

Bickenhill

B4438

M42

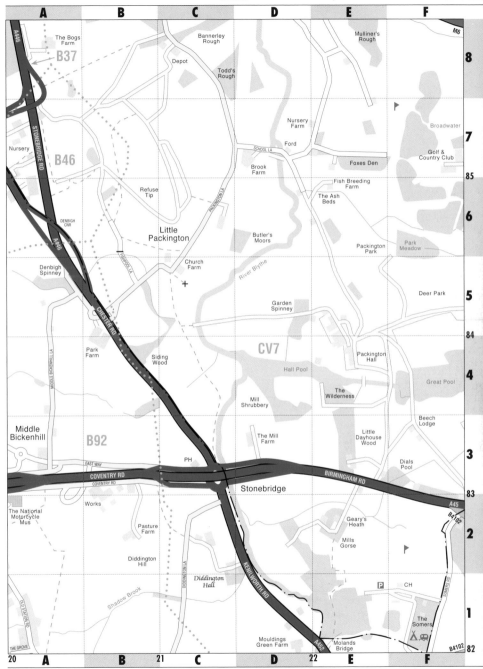

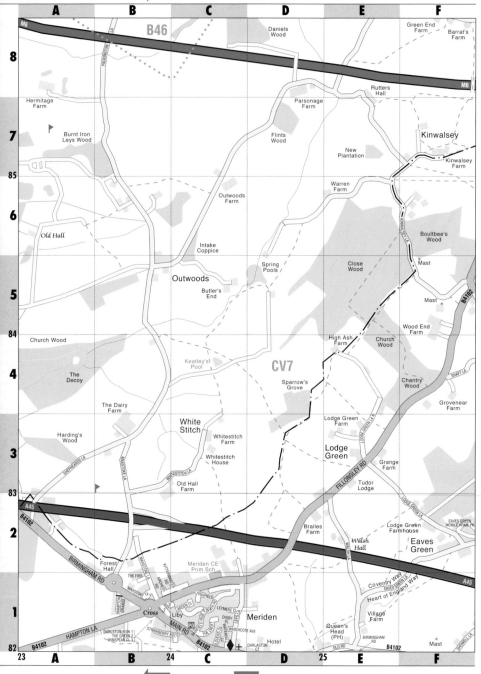

A B C D E F

M6

B46

Daniels
Wood

Green End
Farm

Barrat's
Farm

8

M6

Rutters
Hall

Hermitage
Farm

Parsonage
Farm

Kinwalsey

7

Burnt Iron
Leys Wood

Flints
Wood

New
Plantation

Kinwalsey
Farm

85

Warren
Farm

Old Hall

6

Boultbee's
Wood

Intake
Coppice

Close
Wood

Mast

Spring
Pools

5

Outwoods

Butler's
End

B4102

Wood End
Farm

84

Church Wood

High Ash
Farm

Church
Wood

Mast

CV7

4

Keatley's
Pool

The
Decoy

Sparrow's
Grove

Chantry
Wood

SHAFT LA

Grovenear
Farm

The Dairy
Farm

White
Stitch

Lodge Green
Farm

Harding's
Wood

Whitestitch
Farm

LODGE GREEN LA

Lodge
Green

3

Whitestitch
House

Grange
Farm

SHEPHERDS LA

MAXSTOKE LA

WHITESTITCH LA

FILLONGLEY RD

Old Hall
Farm

Tudor
Lodge

83

A45

LODGE GREEN LA

B4102

Eaves Green
MOBILE HOME PK

2

BIRMINGHAM RD

Brailes
Farm

Walsh
Hall

Lodge Green
Farmhouse

Eaves
Green

Forest
Hall

Meriden CE
Prim Sch

A45

THE FIRS

KITTERMASTER RD

ARDERS RD

MAXSTOKE LA

Coventry Way

EAVES GREEN LA

Heart of England Way

MAIN RD

HIGHFIELD

Village
Farm

Cross

Liby

LEYMERE CL

ARDEN CL

1

PO

DIGBY

Meriden

Queen's
Head
(PH)

HAMPTON LA

DARLSTON ROW
THE GREEN
WINSPEAR CL

STRAWBERRY FIELDS

WHICHCOTE AVE

Hotel

BIRMINGHAM
RD

OLD RD

B4102

Mast

82

B4102

B4102

DARLASTON
CT

SHIONELL LA

23 A B 24 C D 25 E F

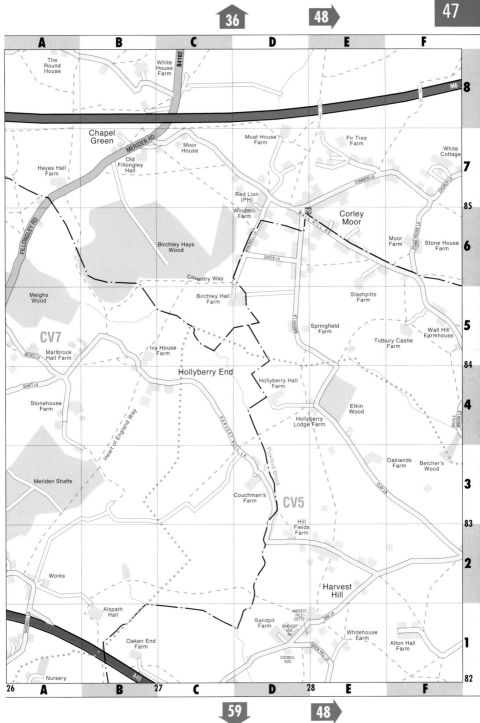

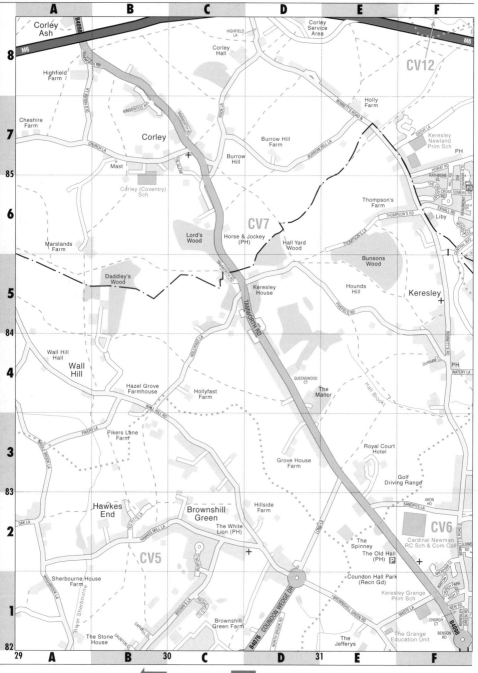

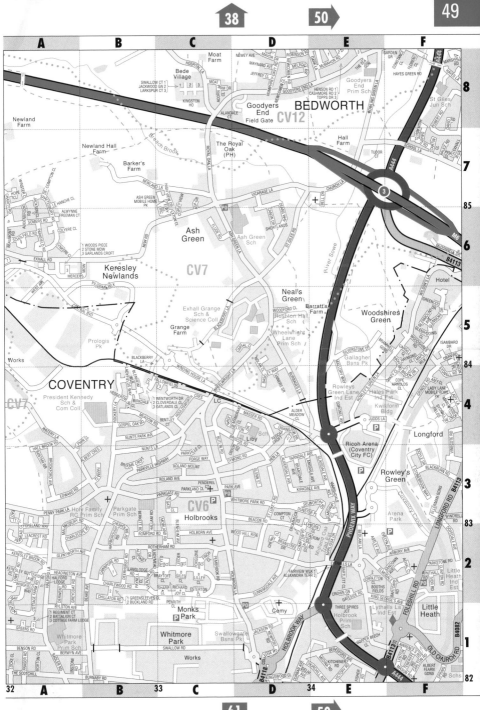

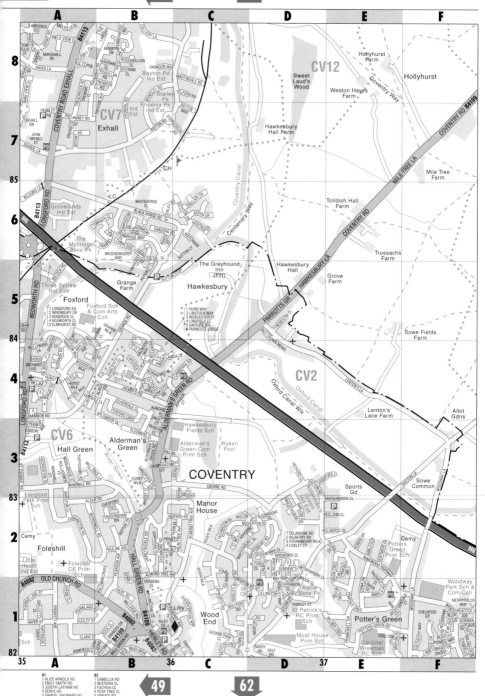

49
39

CV12

Hollyhurst Farm

Hollyhurst

Weston Hayes Farm

Coventry Way

Sweet Laud's Wood

Hawkesbury Hall Farm

Coventry Canal

Mile Tree Farm

Mile Tree La

Coventry Rd B4109

8

7

85

Sch

Lawrence Cl

Melville Cl

Field View Cl

B4113

Coolley La

Paragon Way

Martindale Rd

Telford Rd

Bayton Rd Ind Est

Phoenix Pk Ind Est

Starley Ct

Marshall Rd

Kennym La

Mawmans Cl

De Devoran Cl

Rosemullion Cl

CV7

Exhall

Coventry Road Exhall

Longford Rd

CH

Tolldish Hall Farm

Coventry Rd

Trossachs Farm

6

Grovelands Ind Est

B4113

M6

LC

Whitehorse Cl

Black Horse Rd

Aspen Dr

Sinclair Dr

The Moorings Bsns Pk

Canal Side

Lythalls La

Sanders Rd

Brockenhurst Way

Watermede

Sutton Cl

Centenary Way

The Greyhound Inn (PH)

Hawkesbury

Hawkesbury Hall

Grove Farm

Parrotts Gr

Sowe Fields Farm

5

84

Three Spires Ind Est

Bedworth Rd

Grange Farm

Foxford

1 Longford Sq
2 Wrenbury Dr
3 Hendrick Cl
4 Kegworth Cl
5 Elmhurst Rd

Foxford Sch & Com Arts Coll

1 Hurn Way
2 Linstock Way
3 Worcester Ct
4 Lingfield Ct
5 Sapcote Gr
6 Farmcote Lodge

Old Crown News

Lenton's La

CV2

Oxford Canal Wlk

Oxford Canal

Lenton's Lane Farm

Allot Gdns

4

Longford Rd

Oakmoor Rd

Hollybush La

Orchard Ho

Woodcliffe

Hurst Wlk

Silverdale Cl

Wildmoor Cl

Foxford Cl

Prior's Sch

Newmarket Rd

Seaford Cl

Jacker's Rd

Cheadle Cl

Kanzan Rd

Camborne Cl

Hawkesbury Fields Sch

Wyken Pool

Shelton La

3

83

B4113

CV6

Hall Green

River Sowe

Alderman's Green

Alderman's Green Com Prim Sch

Coop Rive

Mill Rd

Eburne Rd

COVENTRY

Alderman's Green Rd

Sports Gd

Marshbrook Cl

Sowe Common

M6

82

Longford Park Prim Sch

Cemy

Foleshill

Little Heath Ind Est

Foleshill CE Prim Sch

Old Church Rd

B4082

Hall Green Rd

Manor House

Heather Rd

River Sowe

Milverton Rd

Almond Tree Ave

Binswood Cl

1 Celandine Rd
2 Bilberry Rd
3 Strawberry Wlk
4 Loxley Ct

Alpha Bsns Pk

Cemy

Potters Green Prim Sch

Woodway Park Sch & Com Coll

Merryfields Way

Peacock Ave

2

Pauline Ave

Lillington

St Patrick's RC Prim Sch

Potter's Green

Potters Green Rd

Chelwood Gr

Powell Rd

Dorothy Rd

1

Thomas Lane St

Gayer St

Clark St

B4082

B4109

Liby

Riley

Penley Gr

B4082

Wood End

George Park Cl

Gatehouse Cl

Barry Rd

Delf Ho

Moat House Prim Sch

Cardinal Wiseman RC Sch

Doulton Cl

Deanston Croft

Wiley Ct

82

49
62

35
36
37

A B C D E F

B1
1 ALICE ARNOLD HO
2 EMILY SMITH HO
3 JOSEPH LATHAM HO
4 DEWIS HO
5 SAMUEL HAYWARD HO

B2
1 CAMELLIA RD
2 WISTARIA CL
3 FUCHSIA CL
4 PEAR TREE CL
5 SPRUCE RD

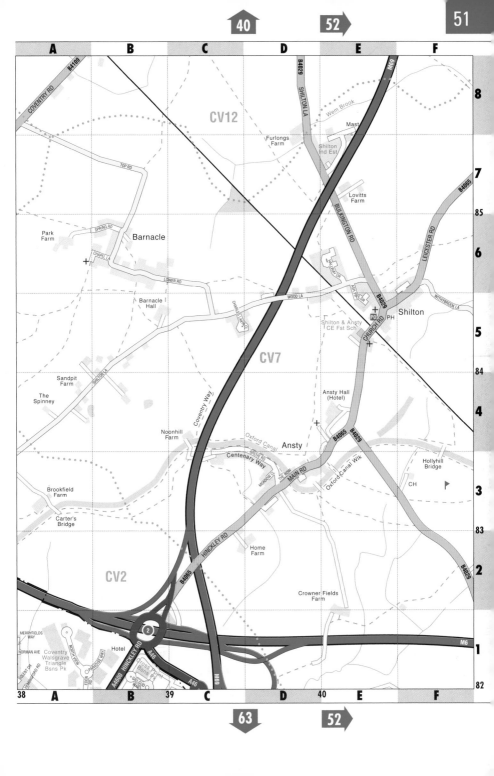

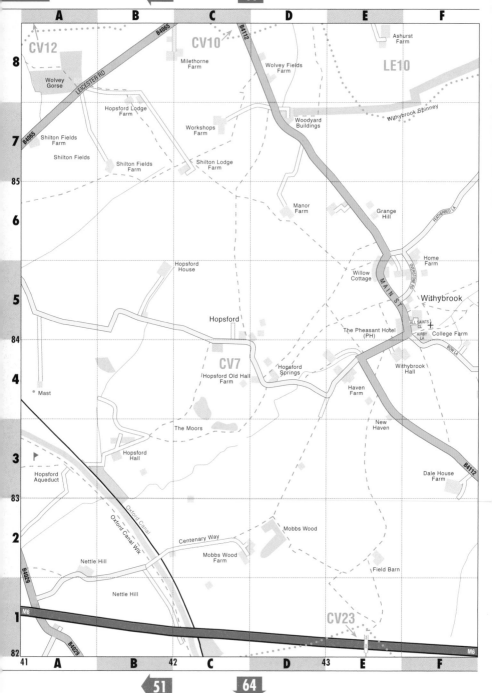

CV12

Wolvey Gorse

LEICESTER RD

B4065

B4112

CV10

Milethorne Farm

Ashurst Farm

Wolvey Fields Farm

LE10

Hopsford Lodge Farm

Workshops Farm

Woodyard Buildings

Withybrook Spinney

B4065

Shilton Fields Farm

Shilton Fields

Shilton Fields Farm

Shilton Lodge Farm

Manor Farm

Grange Hill

FEATHERBED LA

Home Farm

Hopsford House

Willow Cottage

STREET

Withybrook

MAIN ST

CHESTNUT RD

Hopsford

CV7

Hopsford Old Hall Farm

Hopsford Springs

The Pheasant Hotel (PH)

ALL SAINTS CL

KIRBY LA

College Farm

BOW LA

Mast

Haven Farm

Withybrook Hall

The Moors

Hopsford Hall

New Haven

Dale House Farm

B4112

Hopsford Aqueduct

Oxford Canal

Oxford Canal Wlk

Centenary Way

Mobbs Wood

Nettle Hill

Mobbs Wood Farm

Field Barn

B4029

Nettle Hill

M6

CV23

B4029

M6

8 7 85 6 5 84 4 3 83 2 1 82

A B C D E F

41 42 43

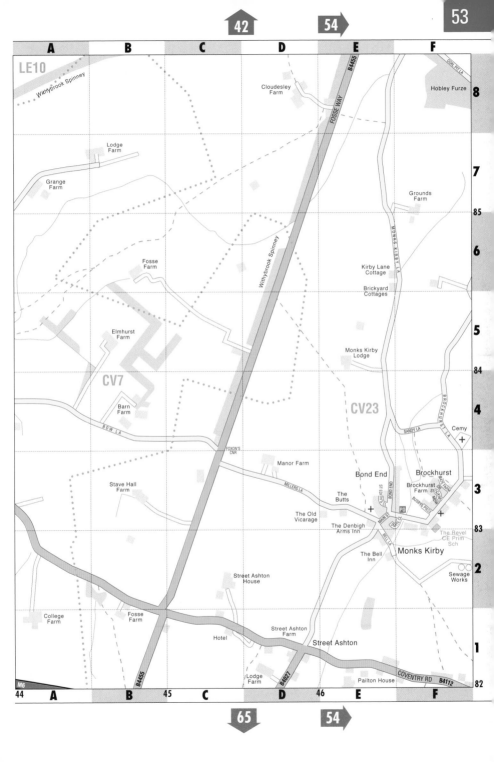

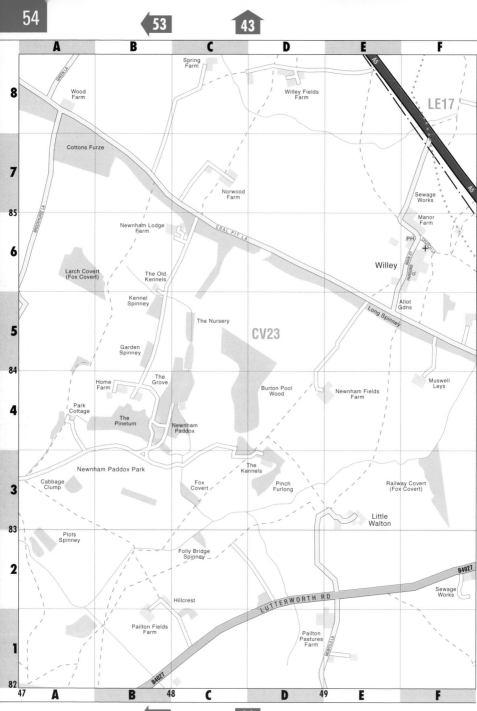

LE17

8

Spring Farm

Wood Farm

Willey Fields Farm

Cottons Furze

7

Norwood Farm

85

Newnham Lodge Farm

COAL PIT LA

Sewage Works

Manor Farm

6

Larch Covert (Fox Covert)

The Old Kennels

Willey

PH

Kennel Spinney

The Nursery

CV23

Allot Gdns

5

Garden Spinney

Long Spinney

84

The Grove

Home Farm

Burton Pool Wood

Newnham Fields Farm

Muswell Leys

4

Park Cottage

The Pinetum

Newnham Paddox

3

Cabbage Clump

Newnham Paddox Park

Fox Covert

The Kennels

Pinch Furlong

Railway Covert (Fox Covert)

Little Walton

83

Plots Spinney

Folly Bridge Spinney

B4027

2

Hillcrest

Sewage Works

LUTTERWORTH RD

1

Pailton Fields Farm

Pailton Pastures Farm

B4027

82

47 48 49

A B C D E F

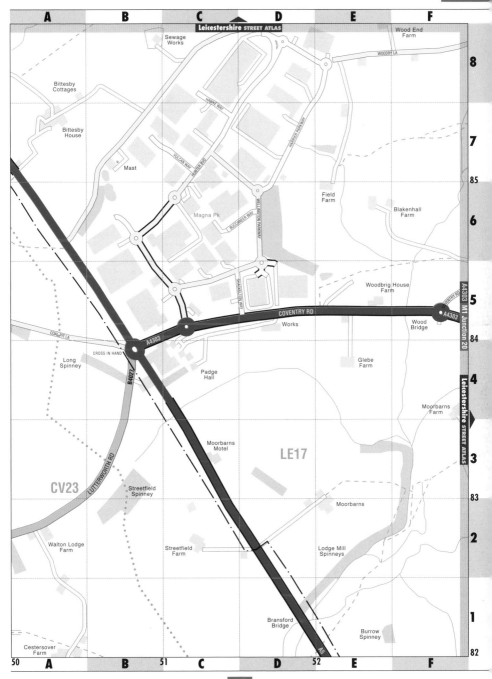

Wood End Farm

WOODBY LA

Sewage Works

Bittesby Cottages

HAWKE WAY

Bittesby House

Mast

VULCAN WAY

HUNTER RD

85

Field Farm

Blakenhall Farm

6

Magna Pk

BUCCANEER WAY

WELLINGTON PARKWAY

HARRIER PARKWAY

Woodbrig House Farm

SHACKLETON WAY

COVENTRY RD

A4303 M1 Junction 20

Leicestershire STREET ATLAS

5

COALPIT LA

A4303

Works

Wood Bridge

A4303

84

Long Spinney

CROSS IN HAND

B4027

Glebe Farm

Moorbarns Farm

4

Padge Hall

LUTTERWORTH RD

Moorbarns Motel

LE17

3

CV23

Streetfield Spinney

83

Moorbarns

Walton Lodge Farm

Streetfield Farm

Lodge Mill Spinneys

2

Bransford Bridge

Burrow Spinney

1

A5

82

Cestersover Farm

50   A   B   51   C   D   52   E   F

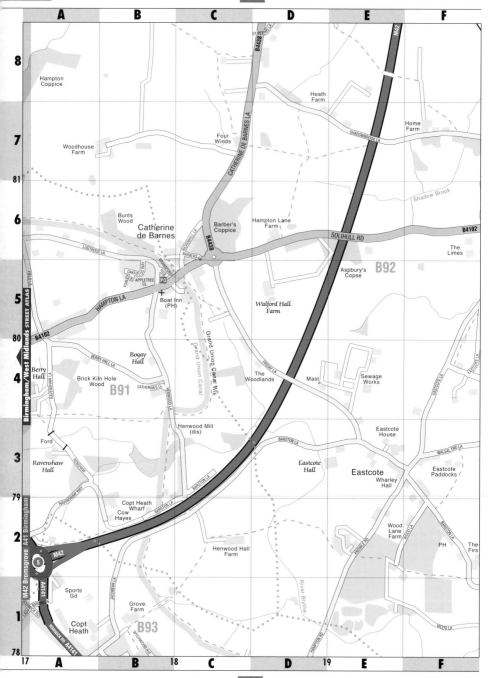

8

7

81

6

5

80

4

3

79

2

1

78

A   B   C   D   E   F

Hampton
Coppice

Woodhouse
Farm

Four
Winds

Heath
Farm

Home
Farm

SHADOWBROOK LA

Shadow Brook

Bunts
Wood

Catherine
de Barnes

Barber's
Coppice

Hampton Lane
Farm

SOLIHULL RD

B4102

The
Limes

B92

Aspbury's
Copse

LUGTROUT LA

BICKENHILL LA

BARBERS

B4438

OAKLEY WAY

FOXLEY DR

APPLETREE
CL

PO

HAMPTON LA

Boat Inn
(PH)

Walford Hall
Farm

B4102

Bogay
Hall

BERRY HALL LA

Grand Union Canal Wlk

Grand Union Canal

The
Woodlands

FRIDAY LA

Mast

Sewage
Works

Berry
Hall

Brick Kiln Hole
Wood

B91

RAVENSHAW LA

CATHERINE'S CL

HENWOOD LA

Henwood Mill
(dis)

BARSTON LA

Eastcote
House

WALSAL END LA

EASTCOTE LA

Ford

Ravenshaw
Hall

PENSHAW

Eastcote
Hall

Eastcote

Eastcote
Paddocks

Wharley
Hall

RAVENSHAW WAY

Copt Heath
Wharf

BARSTON LA

BARSTON LA

Henwood Hall
Farm

Wood
Lane
Farm

MOOR LA

WOOD LA

BARSTON LA

PH

The
Firs

Cow
Hayes

M42

5

A4141

M42 Bromsgrove A41 Birmingham

WARWICK RD A4141

Sports
Gd

JACOBEAN LA

Grove
Farm

B93

WYCHWOOD AVE

Copt
Heath

River Blythe

HAMPTON RD

WOOD LA

A   B   18   C   D   19   E   F

17

72

CATHERINE DE BARNES LA

ST PETER'S LA

Birmingham/West Midlands STREET ATLAS

A41 Birmingham

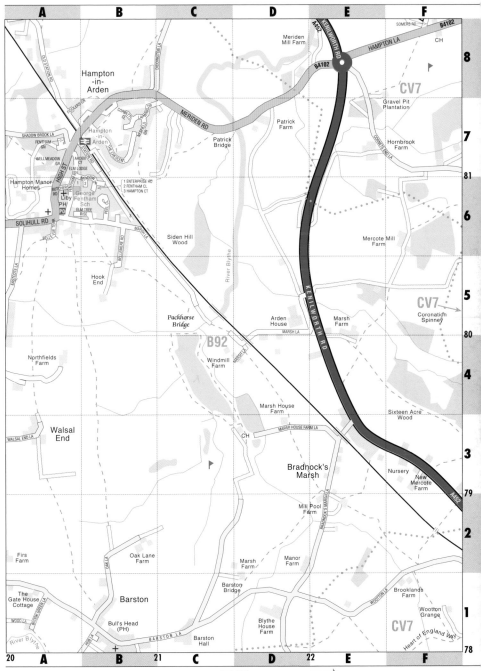

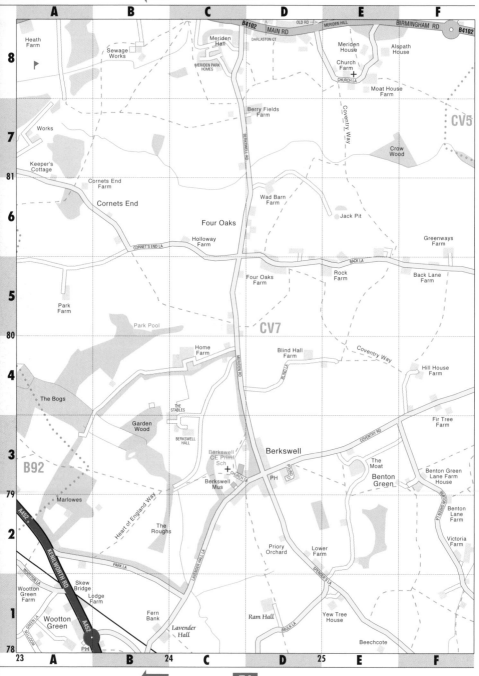

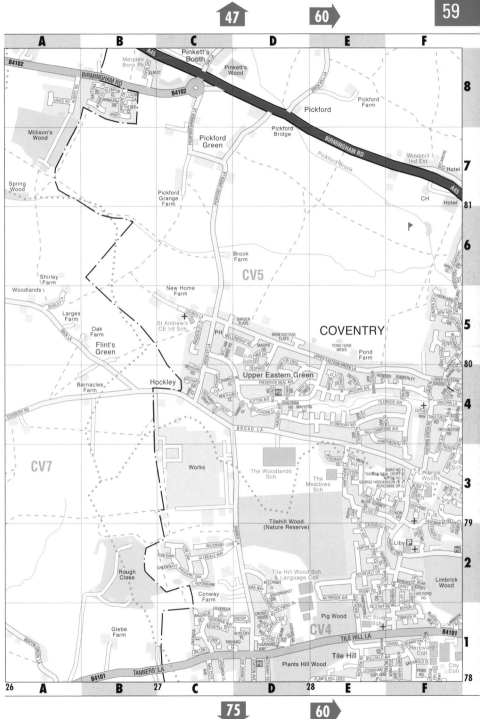

A B C D E F

8

7

81

6

5

80

4

3

79

2

1

78

B4102

BIRMINGHAM RD

Pinkett's Booth

Pinkett's Wood

Meriden Bsns Pk

A45

B4102

Pickford Green

Pickford Wood

Pickford Bridge

Pickford

Pickford Farm

Pickford Brook

BIRMINGHAM RD

A45

Windmill Ind Est

Hotel

CH

Hotel

Millison's Wood

GRACE RD

ALBERT RD

Spring Wood

Pickford Grange Farm

Brook Farm

CV5

Shirley Farm

Woodlands

SHIRLEY LA

Larges Farm

New Home Farm

Oak Farm

Flint's Green

BACK LA

St Andrew's CE Inf Sch

CHURCH LA

PH

MELLOWSHIP RD

GARDEN FLATS

ROSE COTTAGE FLATS

Jun Sch

DESPARD

COVENTRY

Pond Farm Mews

Pond Farm

Barnacles Farm

Hockley

ORCHARD DR

MORGANS

Upper Eastern Green

Upper Eastern Green La

COVENTRY RD

Works

CV7

The Woodlands Sch

BROAD LA

CHILTERN HO

MALVERN

Stonebury Ave

Faulconbridge Ave

HANDSWORTH

Limbrick Wood Sch

The Meadows Sch

Tilehill Wood (Nature Reserve)

Rough Close

WICKMANS DR

GLENDALE WAY

FERN BANK

GREENWAYS

PLEASANT OAK

HERONBANK

Conway Farm

Tile Hill Wood Sch & Language Coll

BEECHNUT

OAK WAY

BROOKHURST

NUTBROOK AVE

Pig Wood

Limbrick Wood

RC Prim Sch

Liby

Glebe Farm

BENTON GREEN LA

DEVEREUX

MAURSON

GOODMAN WAY

EDGEHILL RD

PATRICIA

DRAYTON CL

WINCEBY

TANYARD

SAMMONS' WAY

CROMES WOOD

HOLLYWELL

CV4

Plants Hill Wood

Tile Hill

TILE HILL LA

Hereward Coll

City Coll

B4101

B4101

TANNERS LA

PLANTS HILL CRES

26 A B 27 C D 28 E F

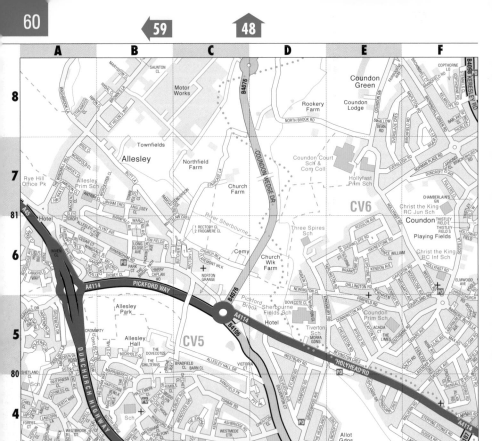

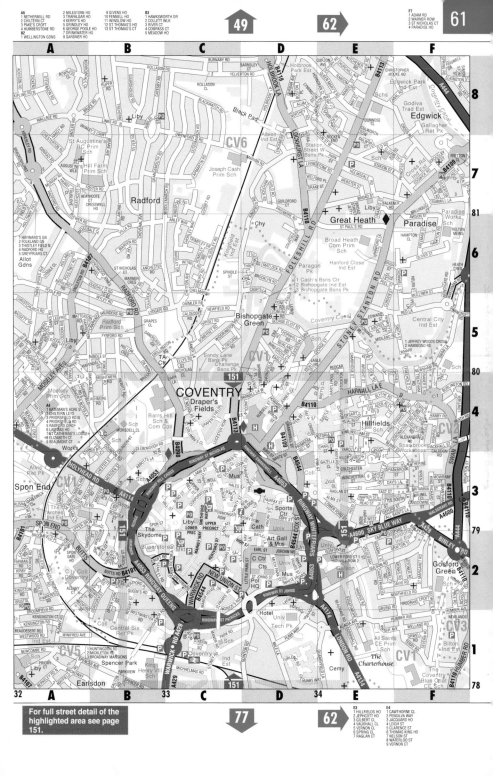

A5
1 NETHERMILL RD
2 CHILTERN CT
3 PAKE'S CROFT
4 HUMBERSTONE RD
B2
1 WELLINGTON GDNS

2 MILESTONE HO
3 TRAFALGAR HO
4 KERRY'S HO
5 GRINDLEY HO
6 GEORGE POOLE HO
7 DRINKWATER HO
8 GARDNER HO

9 GIVENS HO
10 FENNELL HO
11 WINSLOW HO
12 ST THOMAS'S HO
13 ST THOMAS'S CT

B3
1 HAWKSWORTH DR

F7
1 ADAM RD
2 WARNER ROW
3 ST NICHOLAS CT
4 PARADISE CT

1 HAYWARD'S GN
2 FOLKLAND ST
3 THISTLEY FIELD N
4 RADFORD HO
5 GREYFRIARS CT
Allot
Gdns

A4
1 BATEMAN'S ACRE C
2 CHILTERN LEYS
3 PRIORSFIELD HO
4 PRIORS ELM RD
5 RADFORD DRIVE
6 LAMMAS HO
7 ST CATHERINE'S LODGE
8 ELIZABETH CT
9 BEAUMONT CT

For full street detail of the
highlighted area see page
151.

E3
1 HILLFIELDS HO
2 JEPHCOTT HO
3 GILBERT CL
4 VAUXHALL CL
5 VERNON CL
6 SPRING CL
7 RAGLAN CT

E4
1 CAWTHORNE CL
2 PENSILVA WAY
3 JACQUARD HO
4 LEIGH ST
5 CLARENCE ST
6 THOMAS KING HO
7 NELSON ST
8 WATERLOO ST
9 VERNON CT

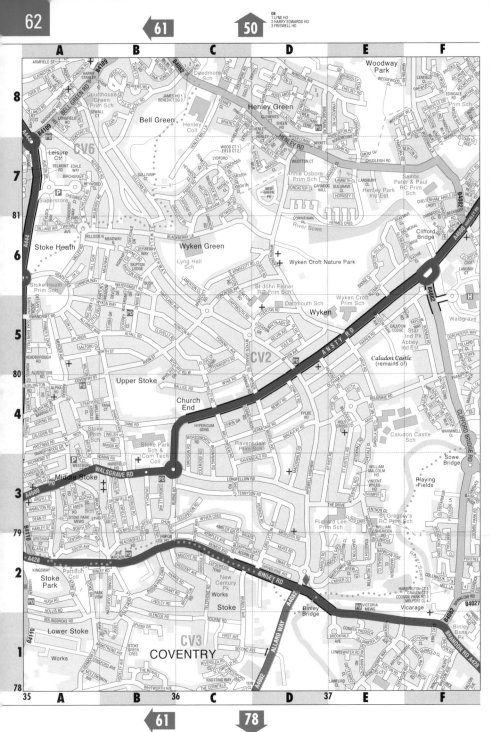

D8
1 LYNE HO
2 HARRY EDWARDS HO
3 FRISWELL HO

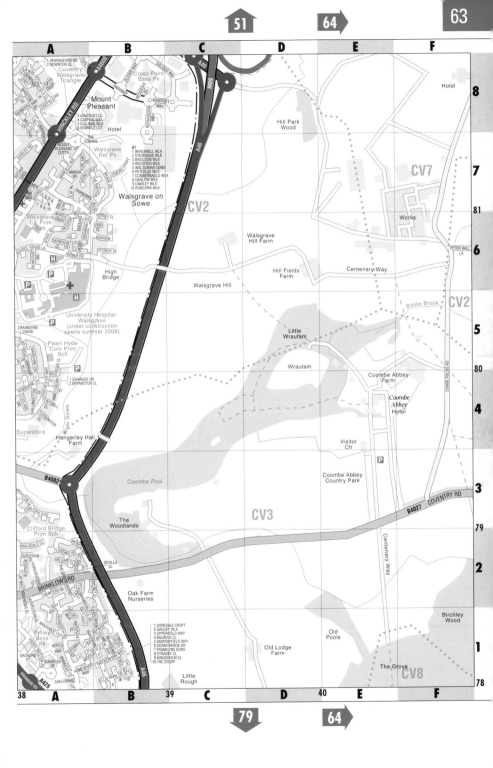

A B C D E F

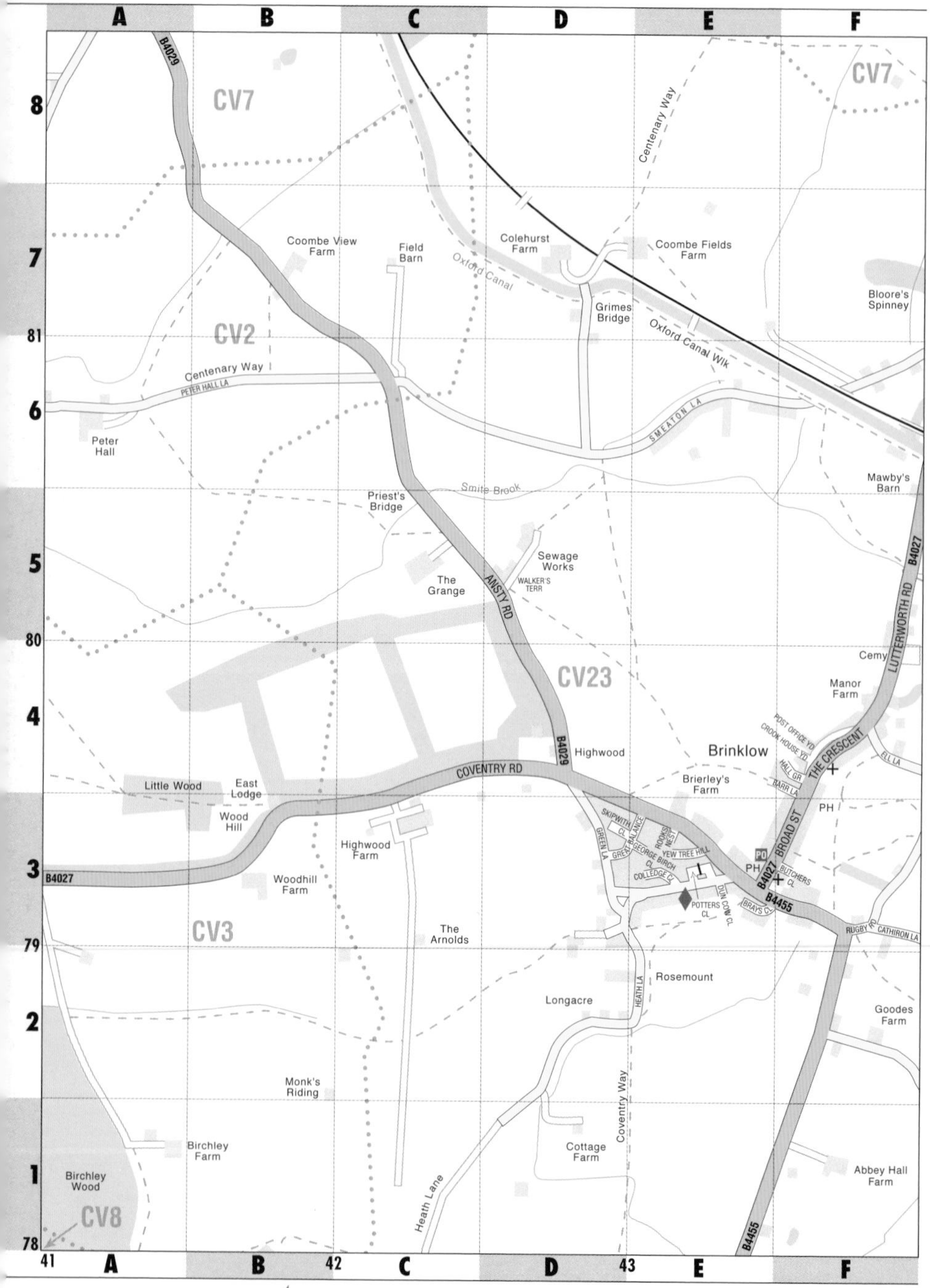

8
81
6
5
80
4
3
79
2
1
78

CV7
CV7
CV2
CV23
CV3
CV8

B4029
B4027
B4455

Coombe View Farm
Field Barn
Colehurst Farm
Coombe Fields Farm
Centenary Way
Bloore's Spinney

Oxford Canal
Grimes Bridge
Oxford Canal Wlk

Peter Hall La
Centenary Way
Peter Hall
Smite Brook
Mawby's Barn
Sneaton La

Priest's Bridge
The Grange
Walker's Terr
Sewage Works
Ansty Rd
Cemy
Manor Farm
Lutterworth Rd

Highwood
Brinklow
The Crescent
Coventry Rd
Brierley's Farm
PH
Ell La

Little Wood
East Lodge
Wood Hill
Highwood Farm
Woodhill Farm
Skipwith La
Green La
George Birch
Yew Tree Hill
College
Broad St
Butchers Cl
Post Office Yd
Crook House Yd
Hill La
Barr La
PH

The Arnolds
Potters Cl
Low Cl
Rugby
Cathiron La
Rosemount
Goodes Farm

Longacre
Heath La
Coventry Way

Monk's Riding
Birchley Farm
Birchley Wood
Cottage Farm
Abbey Hall Farm

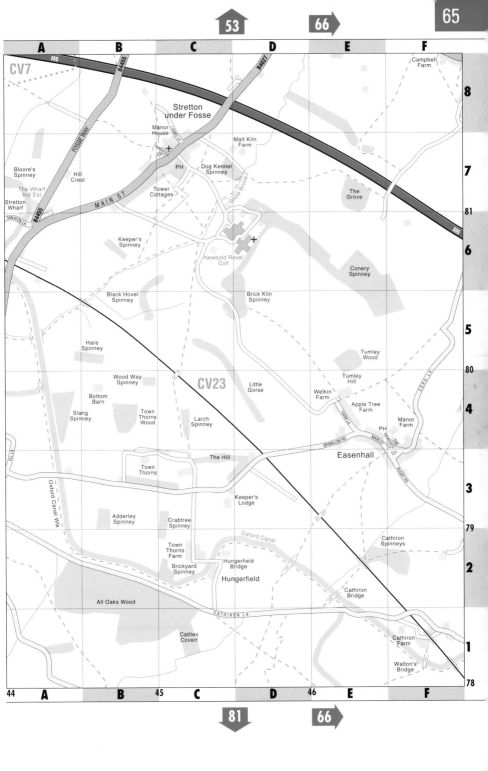

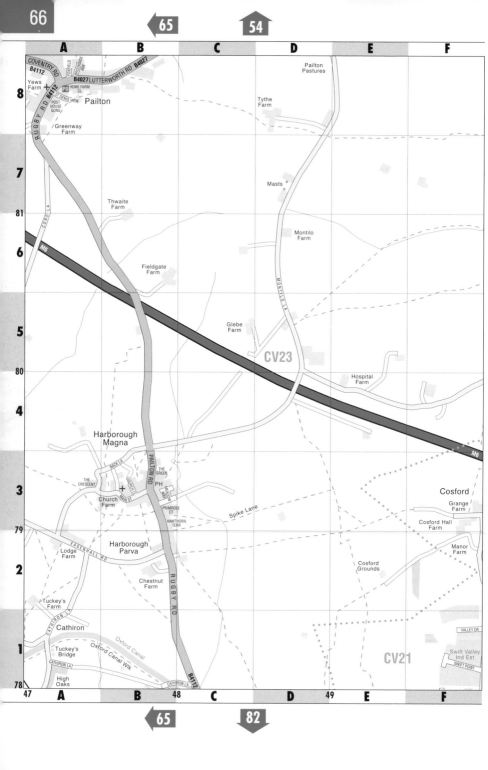

A B C D E F

8

COVENTRY RD
B4112
Yews
Farm
FOXFIELD
FOXFORD AVE
B4027 LUTTERWORTH RD B4027
ST DENIS VIEW
HOME FARM CL
POST
HOUSE
GDNS
RUGBY RD B4112
Pailton
Greenway
Farm

Pailton
Pastures

Tythe
Farm

7

Thwaite
Farm

Masts

81

CORD LA

M6

6

Fieldgate
Farm

Montilo
Farm

MONTILO LA

5

Glebe
Farm

CV23

80

Hospital
Farm

4

M6

Harborough
Magna

BACK LA
THE
CRESCENT
CHURCH
MAIN ST
PAILTON RD
THE
GREEN
PH
MEADOW
WAY

Cosford

Grange
Farm

3

Church
Farm
PRIMROSE
CT
HAWTHORN
TERR

Spike Lane

Cosford Hall
Farm

Manor
Farm

79

EASENHALL RD
Lodge
Farm

Harborough
Parva

Chestnut
Farm

Cosford
Grounds

2

RUGBY RD

CATHIRON LA
Tuckey's
Farm

Cathiron

Oxford Canal

VALLEY DR

Swift Valley
Ind Est
SWIFT POINT

CV21

1

Tuckey's
Bridge
CATHIRON LA

Oxford Canal Wlk

High
Oaks

78

CATHIRON LA B4112

47 A B 48 C D 49 E F

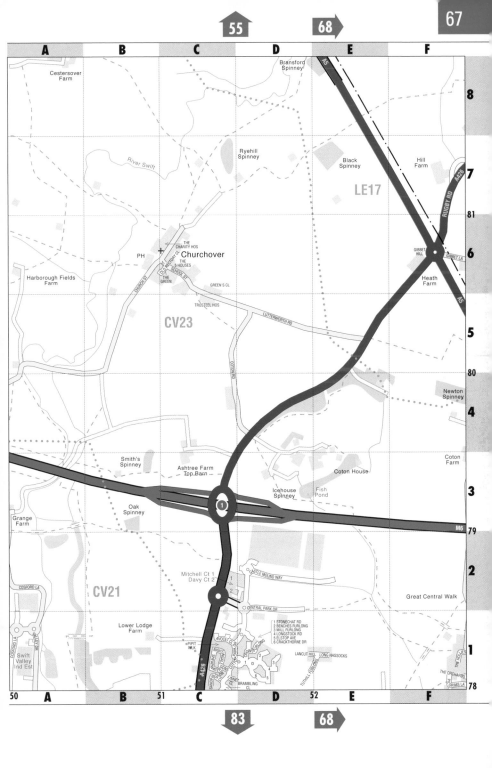

A   B   C   D   E   F

Cestersover
Farm

Bransford
Spinney

A5

8

Ryehill
Spinney

River Swift

Black
Spinney

Hill
Farm

LE17

7

RUGBY RD

A426

81

THE CHARITY HOS
THE 5 HOUSES
Churchover

GIBBET
HILL

GIBBET LA

6

PH

CHURCH ST
OLD RECTORY CL
SCHOOL ST
THE
GREEN

Heath
Farm

A5

Harborough Fields
Farm

GREEN'S CL

TRUSTEEL HOS

CV23

LUTTERWORTH RD

5

COTON RD

80

Newton
Spinney

4

Smith's
Spinney

Ashtree Farm
Top Barn

Coton House

Coton
Farm

Icehouse
Spinney

Fish
Pond

3

Oak
Spinney

1

M6

79

Grange
Farm

Mitchell Ct 1
Davy Ct 2

CASTLE MOUND WAY

2

COSFORD LA

CV21

CENTRAL PARK DR

Great Central Walk

Lower Lodge
Farm

1 STONECHAT RD
2 BENCHES FURLONG
3 MILL FURLONG
4 LONGSTOCK RD
5 ELSTOP AVE
6 CRACKTHORNE DR

PIPIT
WLK

AVOCET CL

Swift
Valley
Ind Est

A426

BRAMBLING
CL

LANCUT HILL   LONG HASSOCKS

TUTHILL FURLONG

THE ORCHARDS

GRIMS LA

THE RYE

1

78

50   A   B 51 C   D 52 E   F

8

81

7

6

LE17

5

80

4

3

79

2

CV23

1

78

53   A   B   54   C   D   55   E   F

Town End
Farm

Lodge
Plantations

Home
Farm

Spinney
Farm

Shawell
Wood

West
Cottages

Cotesbach Fields
Farm

Hill
Farm

Shawell Lodge
Farm

South
Lodge

RUGBY RD

A426

M1

LUTTERWORTH RD

SHAWELL RD

Barn Farm

GIBBET LA

Holme Close
Farm

Middle Barn
Farm

Shawell

Works

PH

MAIN ST

SWINFORD RD

Hill Top
Farm

Shawell
Manor

Mast

Tripontium
Bsns Ctr

BULLACES LA

CHURCH LA

CATTHORPE RD

Shawell
Hall

Grange
Farm

Tomley Hall
Farm

SHAWELL RD

M1

Works

WATLING ST

M6

M1 Northampton (A45)

M6 M1 Junction 19

414

A14

Europark
Ind Est

Old Barn
Farm

THE LEYS

P

Newton

Depot

Catthorpe

ELM LA

Manor
Farm

HERMITAGE
CL

CATTHORPE
MANOR

PH

PH

LEYS LONDON LA

1 NEWTON RD
2 THE PADDOCK

A5

PH

67

84

B14

Hollywood

Major's
Green

Truemans Heath
Farm

Trueman's
Heath

Blounts Hole
Farm

Whitlocks End

B90

Little
Trueman's Heath
Farm

Tyburn
Farm

Little Tyburn
Coppice

Cvn
Site

Ford

Whitlock's
End

Betteridges
Farm

Birchy
Farm

Liby

The Coppice
Prim Sch

The Woodrush
Com High Sch

Drakes
Cross

Barn
Hill

B47

HOUNDSFIELD
FARM

Yewtree
Farm

Big
Dickens'
Wood

Little
Dickens'
Wood

Grimes
Hill

Wythall

Norton Dr

Lowbrook
Farm

Tidbury
Green
Sch

Tidbury
Green
Farm

Tidbury
Green

Big
Cleobury
Farm

Lowbrook
Bridge

Bleakhouse
Farm

Manor
Farm

River Cole

Rumbush

Nursery

Meadow Green
Prim Sch

Wythall

Fulford
Hall

Fulford
Heath

Rumbush
Farm

B94

Little
Tanners Green
Farm

Mast

Little
Fulford
Farm

Kidpile
Farm

Willow Tree
Farm

Manor Farm
Craft Centre

CH

Tanner's
Green

Earlswood

Wood La

New Fallings
Coppice

C8
1 HARWOOD GR
2 SHIRLEYDALE
3 SHELTONDALE
4 HENLEYDALE
5 QUINTONDALE
6 ARDENDALE
7 YARNINGDALE

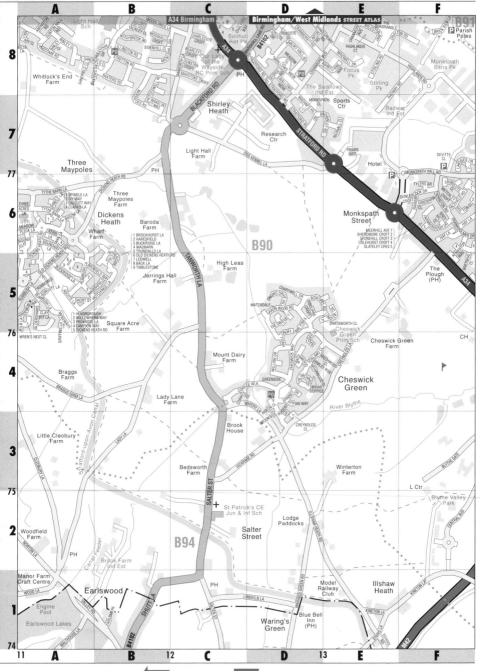

A6
1 HIMBLETON CROFT
2 SLIMBRIDGE CL
3 HIGHDOWN CRES
4 OLDBERROW CL
5 BELLINGTON CROFT
6 WESTGROVE AVE

B8
1 CHADBURY CROFT
2 LITTLEWOOD CL
3 HILLFIELD MEWS
4 MAYTHORN GR
5 GREYHURST CROFT
6 HUNNINGHAM GR

C9
1 CHIPSTONE CL
2 GLENFIELD CL
3 CHERRYWOOD CRES
4 LIBBARDS GATE
5 MERRINGTON CL
6 LITTLETON CROFT

7 THORNGROVE AVE

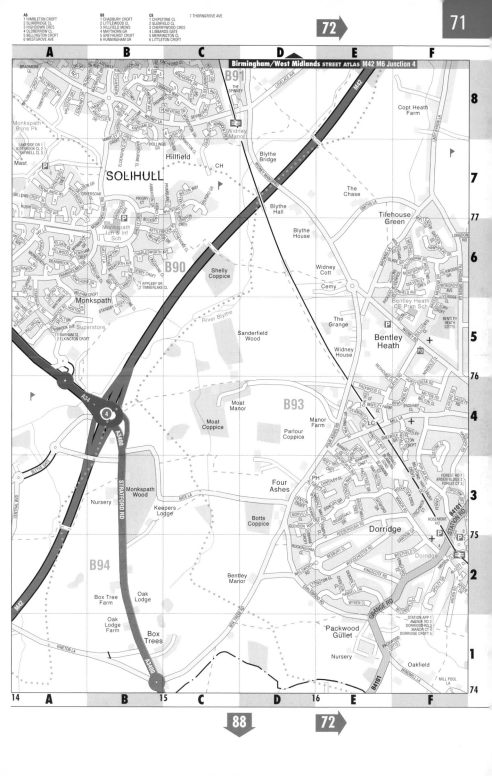

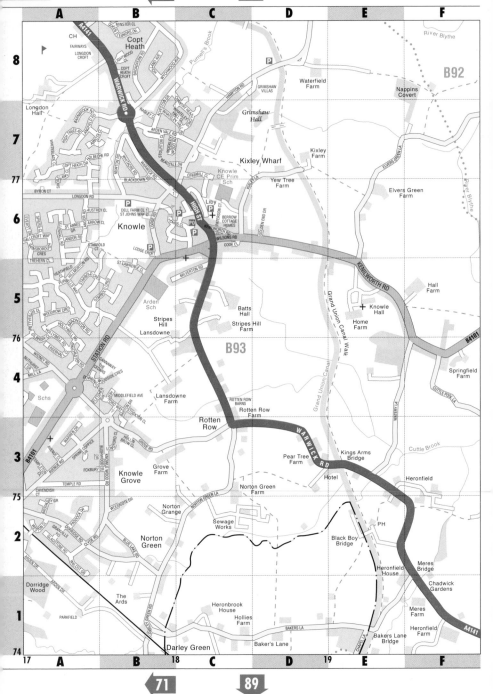

River Blythe

B92

Nappins
Covert

CH
FAIRWAYS
LONGDON
CROFT

Copt
Heath

Purnell's Brook

Waterfield
Farm

GRIMSHAW
VILLAS

Longdon
Hall

WARWICK RD

RADLEY LA

ARDEN VALE RD

Grimshaw
Hall

Elvers Green
Farm

Kixley
Farm

Kixley Wharf

River Blythe

ELVERS GREEN LA

Knowle
CE Prim
Sch

Yew Tree
Farm

BYRON CT

LONGDON RD

BLACKDOWN

DELL FARM CL
ST JOHNS WAY

HIGH ST

Liby

BERROW
COTTAGE
HOMES

GOLDEN END DR

Knowle

KENILWORTH RD

WILSONS RD

COOK CL

Hall
Farm

STARBOLD
CT

LODGE CROFT

ST LAWRENCE CL

MILVERTON RD

Knowle
Hall

Home
Farm

KENILWORTH RD

B101

Arden
Sch

Batts
Hall

Stripes
Hill
Lansdowne

Stripes Hill
Farm

Grand Union Canal Walk

STATION RD

B93

Springfield
Farm

CUTTLE ROW LA

B4101

Schs

Middlefield Ave

Lansdowne
Farm

Grand Union Canal

ROTTEN ROW
BARNS

Rotten Row
Farm

WATERY LA

Cuttle Brook

Rotten
Row

WARWICK RD

Kings Arms
Bridge

Heronfield

B4101

Knowle
Grove

Grove
Farm

Pear Tree
Farm

Hotel

TEMPLE RD

CAVENDISH
CT

Norton Green
Farm

Norton
Grange

NORTON GREEN LA

Sewage
Works

Black Boy
Bridge

PH

Norton
Green

BLUE LAKE RD

Meres
Bridge

Heronfield
House

Chadwick
Gardens

Dorridge
Wood

ARDEN DR

PARKFIELD

The
Ards

Heronbrook
House

Hollies
Farm

BAKERS LA

Meres
Farm

Heronfield
Farm

A4141

Darley Green

Baker's Lane

Bakers Lane
Bridge

COPT LA

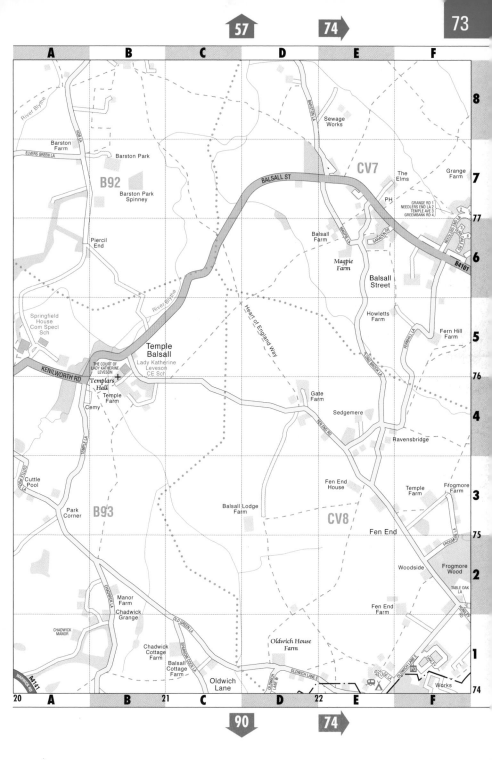

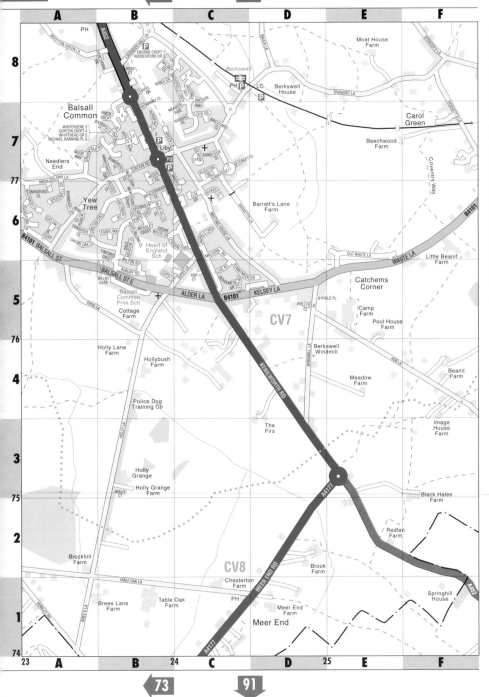

A   B   C   D   E   F

8

PH

WOOTTON GREEN LA

EBORNE CROFT 1
HUDDESFORD DR 2

ROSE CT

Moat House
Farm

SPENCER'S LA

BALK LA

Berkswell

PH

LC

Berkswell
House

TRUGGIST LA

CHAPEL DR

BIRCH DR

RIPPLE DR

HATHAWAY CL

WATSON
WAY

Carol
Green

HOLLY LA

7

Balsall
Common

WINTERDENE 3
GORTON CROFT 4
WHITEHEAD GR 5
MICHAEL BANNING PL 6.

FINCH
CROFT

MEGS BANK
MORFE RIDE

BRICK KILN

LLOYD GR

Liby

Beechwood
Farm

Coventry Way

77

Needlers
End

GLEBE
WAY

GREENLAND CT

STATION RD

ARDEN
CL

SUNNYSIDE
(248)

DEVEMERE CL

Yew
Tree

WINSFORD
CL

NEEDLERS END LA

SPEEDWELL CL

HAMPTON RD

BROOKS

CROFT

BRADLEY
CROFT

CEDAR
WOOD DR

CROXTON CHASE

RUSHTON
CL

Barratt's Lane
Farm

6

B4101 BALSALL ST

COX LA

THOMAS

WAY

CHILDS OAK CL

FOXES WAY

Heart of
England
Sch

MALVERN

CLIVE RD

OLD WASTE LA

WASTE LA

Little Beanit
Farm

B4101

FINFORD
CROFT

DALTON RD

GIPSY CT

ASH
CT

DEVEMERE
DR

Catchems
Corner

Beanit
Farm

5

WELBY
GATE

Balsall
Common
Prim Sch

ALDER LA

B4101

KELSEY LA

WELLFIELD
CL

BYFIELD PL

Camp
Farm

Pool House
Farm

FROG LA

Cottage
Farm

CV7

76

Holly Lane
Farm

Hollybush
Farm

WINDMILL LA

Berkswell
Windmill

HOB LA

4

Police Dog
Training Ctr

Meadow
Farm

Image
House
Farm

3

Holly
Grange

KENILWORTH RD

The
Firs

75

HOLLY
CT

Holly Grange
Farm

Black Hales
Farm

A4177

2

Brockhill
Farm

TABLE OAK LA

CV8

MEER END RD

Redfen
Farm

Chesterton
Farm

Brook
Farm

Springhill
House

A452

1

BREES LA

HOME FM RD

Brees Lane
Farm

Table Oak
Farm

PH

Meer End
Farm

Meer End

A4177

74

23   A   24   B   C   25   D   E   F

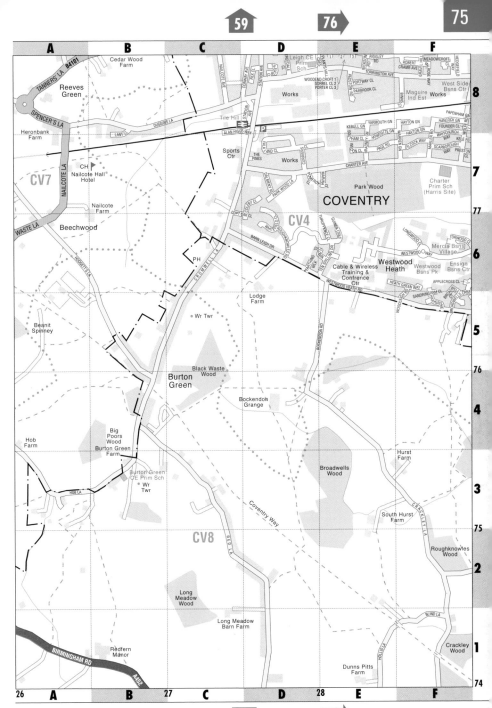

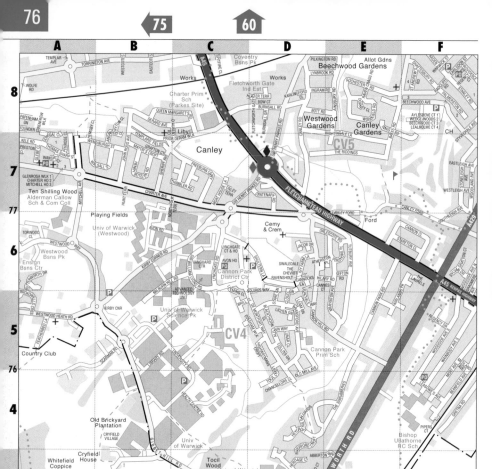

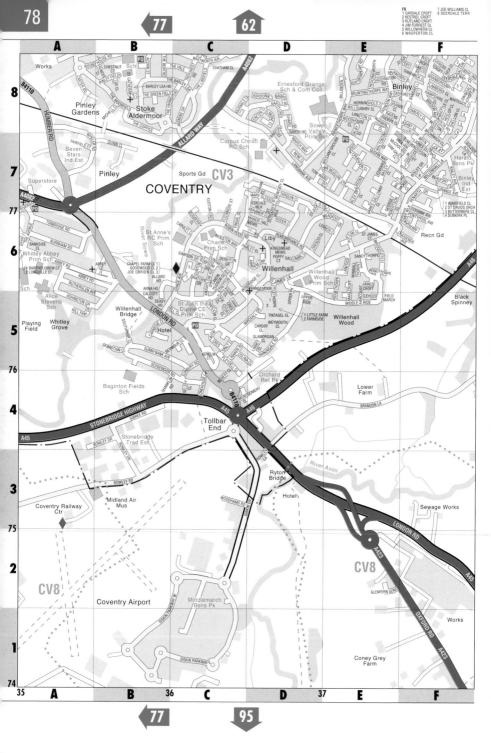

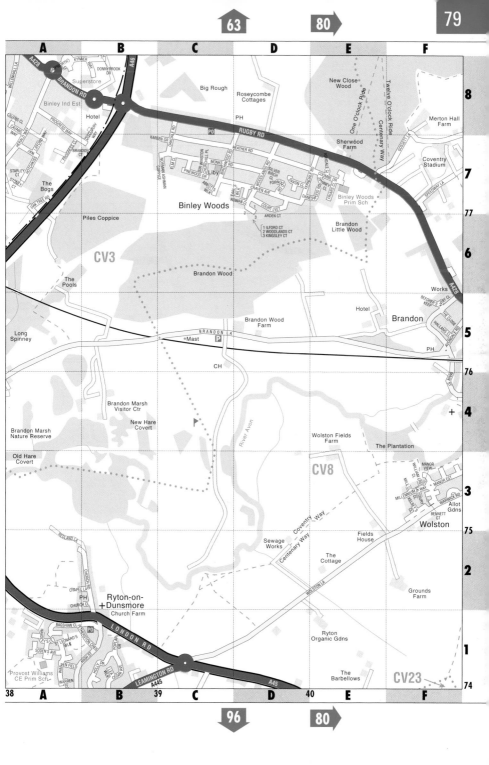

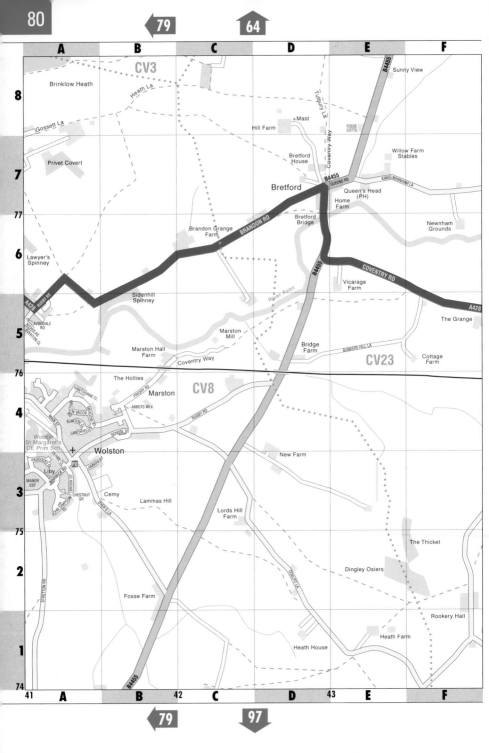

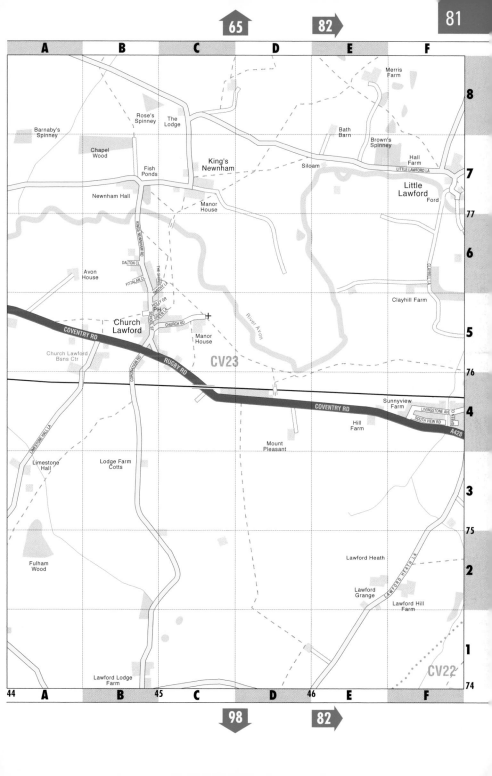

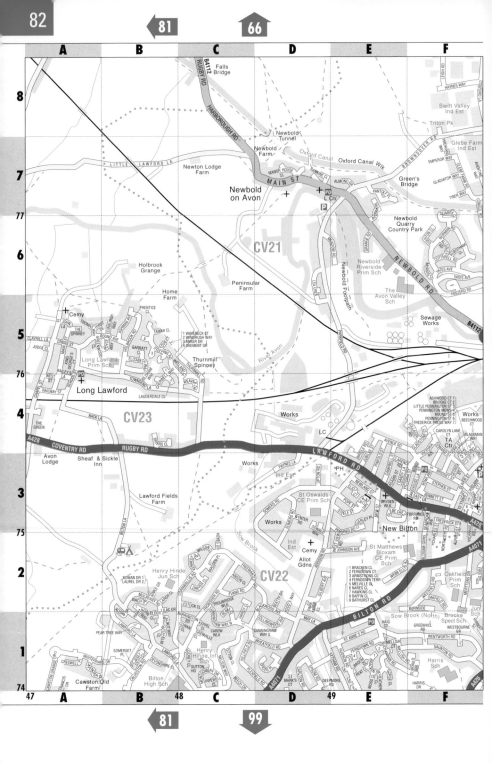

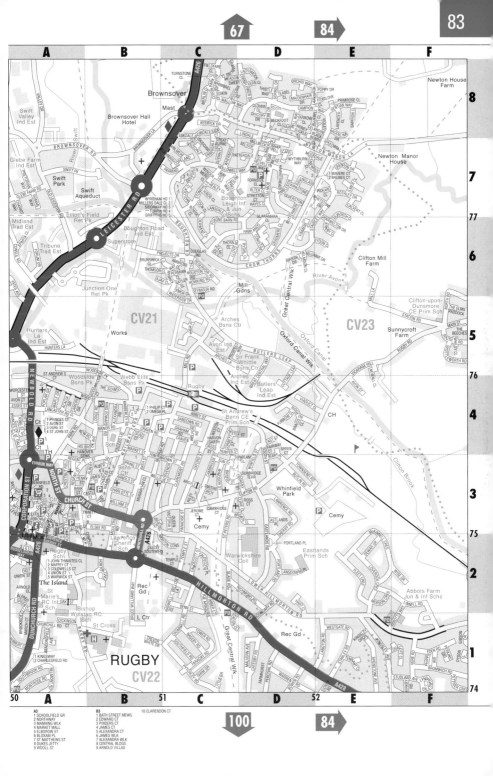

A3
1 SCHOOLFIELD GR
2 NORTHWAY
3 MANNING WLK
4 MARKET MALL
5 ELBOROW ST
6 BLOXAM PL
7 ST MATTHEWS ST
8 DUKES JETTY
9 WOOLL ST

B3
1 BATH STREET MEWS
2 EDWARD CT
3 PINDERS CT
4 JAMES CT
5 ALEXANDRA CT
6 JAMES WLK
7 ALEXANDRA WLK
8 CENTRAL BLDGS
9 ARNOLD VILLAS

10 CLARENDON CT

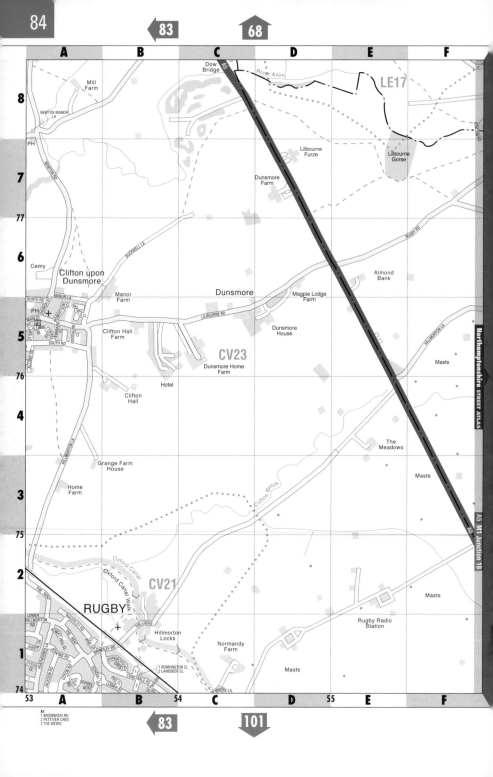

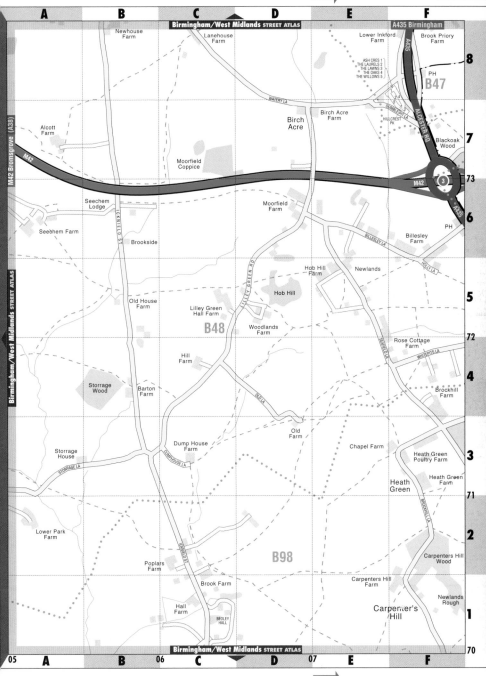

A   B   C   D   E   F

8
7
73
6
5
72
4
3
71
2
1
70

Newhouse Farm
Lanehouse Farm
Lower Inkford Farm
Brook Priory Farm
ASH CRES 1
THE LAURELS 2
THE LAWNS 3
THE OAKS 4
THE WILLOWS 5
B47
WATERY LA
Birch Acre Farm
Birch Acre
HILLCREST PK
PH
Alcott Farm
Blackoak Wood
M42 Bromsgrove (A38)
Moorfield Coppice
Birmingham/West Midlands STREET ATLAS
M42
Seechem Lodge
Moorfield Farm
PH
Billesley Farm
Seechem Farm
ICKNIELD ST
Brookside
BILLESLEY LA
HOLLY LA
Old House Farm
Hob Hill Farm
Newlands
LILLEY GREEN RD
Hob Hill
Lilley Green Hall Farm
B48
Woodlands Farm
Rose Cottage Farm
BEOLEY LA
WHITEPITS LA
Hill Farm
Storrage Wood
Barton Farm
OLD LA
Brockhill Farm
Storrage House
Dump House Farm
PUMPHOUSE LA
Old Farm
Chapel Farm
Heath Green Poultry Farm
STORRAGE LA
Heath Green
Heath Green Farm
BROCKHILL LA
Lower Park Farm
B98
Carpenters Hill Wood
Poplars Farm
Carpenters Hill Farm
Newlands Rough
ICKNIELD ST
Brook Farm
Hall Farm
BEOLEY HALL
Carpenter's Hill

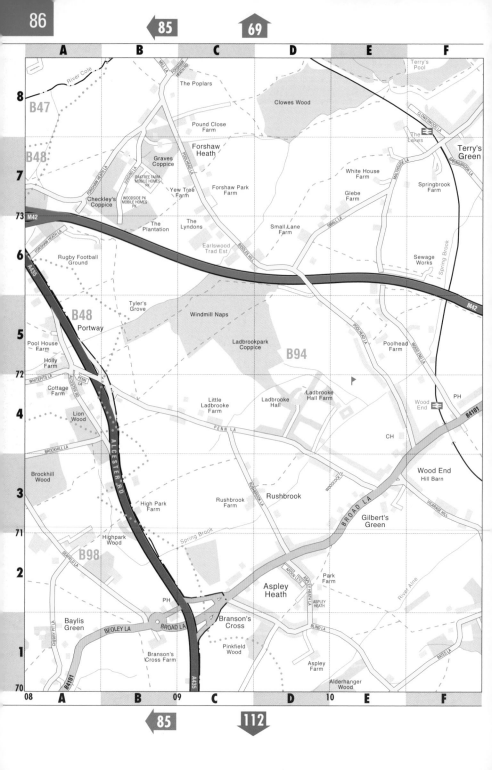

85
69

A **B** **C** **D** **E** **F**

River Cole

8

B47

The Poplars

Clowes Wood

Terry's Pool

The Lakes

7

B48

Pound Close Farm

Forshaw Heath

Graves Coppice

Terry's Green

White House Farm

Springbrook Farm

Springbrook

OAKTREE FARM MOBILE HOMES PK

Checkley's Coppice

WOODSIDE PK MOBILE HOMES PK

Yew Tree Farm

Forshaw Park Farm

Glebe Farm

73 M42

The Plantation

The Lyndons

Small Lane Farm

6

Rugby Football Ground

Earlswood Trad Est

Sewage Works

M42

Spring Brook

Tyler's Grove

Windmill Naps

5

B48

Portway

Ladbrookpark Coppice

B94

Poolhead Farm

Pool House Farm

Holly Farm

72

Cottage Farm

Little Ladbrooke Farm

Ladbrooke Hall

Ladbrooke Hall Farm

PH

Wood End

4

Lion Wood

PENN LA

CH

B4101

BROCKHILL LA

Brockhill Wood

Wood End

Hill Barn

3

High Park Farm

Rushbrook Farm

Rushbrook

Gilbert's Green

BROAD LA

71

Highpark Wood

Spring Brook

Park Farm

2

B98

Aspley Heath

ASPLEY HEATH

River Alne

PH

BEOLEY LA

BROAD LA

Branson's Cross

Baylis Green

Branson's Cross Farm

Pinkfield Wood

BLIND LA

Aspley Farm

1

B4101

A435

Alderhanger Wood

BATES LA

70

08 **A** **B** **09** **C** **D** **10** **E** **F**

85
112

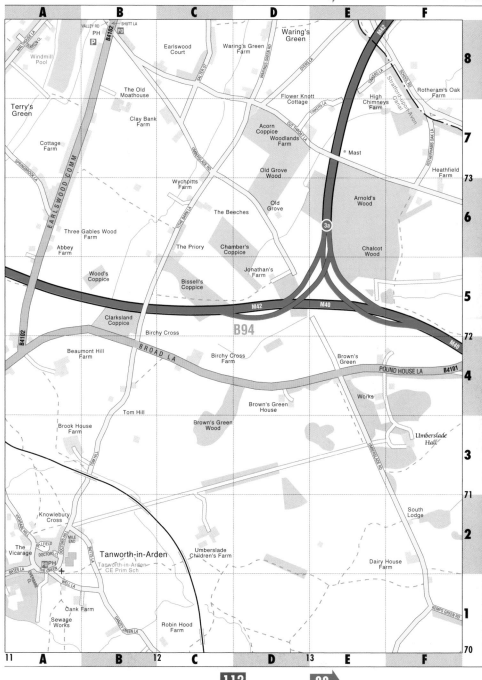

A	B	C	D	E	F

70

88

8

7

73

6

5

72

4

3

71

2

1

70

Windmill Pool

MALTHOUSE LA

MASON CL

Terry's Green

VALLEY RD
PH
SHUTT LA
PO
P
B4102

Earlswood Court

Waring's Green Farm

Waring's Green

WARINGS GREEN RD

DYERS LA

M42

The Old Moathouse

SALTER ST

Flower Knott Cottage

High Chimneys Farm

TIMBERS LA

SCHOOL RD

Rotheram's Oak Farm

Cottage Farm

Clay Bank Farm

Acorn Coppice

Woodlands Farm

CUT THROAT LA

TIMBERS LA

Stratford-upon-Avon Canal

ROTHERAMS OAK LA

Heathfield Farm

SPRINGBROOK LA

EARLSWOOD COMM

Wychpitts Farm

UMBERSLADE RD

Old Grove Wood

Mast

Three Gables Wood Farm

The Beeches

THE BARN LA

Old Grove

Arnold's Wood

Abbey Farm

The Priory

Chamber's Coppice

3a

Wood's Coppice

Bissell's Coppice

Jonathan's Farm

Chalcot Wood

B4102

Clarksland Coppice

M42

M40

B94

Birchy Cross

BROAD LA

Birchy Cross Farm

Brown's Green

M40

72

Beaumont Hill Farm

POUND HOUSE LA

B4101

Tom Hill

Brown's Green House

Works

Brook House Farm

Brown's Green Wood

UMBERSLADE RD

Umberslade Hall

TOM HILL

Knowlebury Cross

South Lodge

VICARAGE HILL

BELLFIELD

DOCTORS HILL

MILE END

BUTTS LA

The Vicarage

Tanworth-in-Arden

Umberslade Children's Farm

Dairy House Farm

BATES LA

THE GREEN

PO PH

Tanworth-in-Arden CE Prim Sch

WELL LA

RAVENSHAW CL

Cank Farm

DANZEY GREEN LA

Sewage Works

Robin Hood Farm

KEMPS GREEN RD

11 A B 12 C D 13 E F 70

112

88

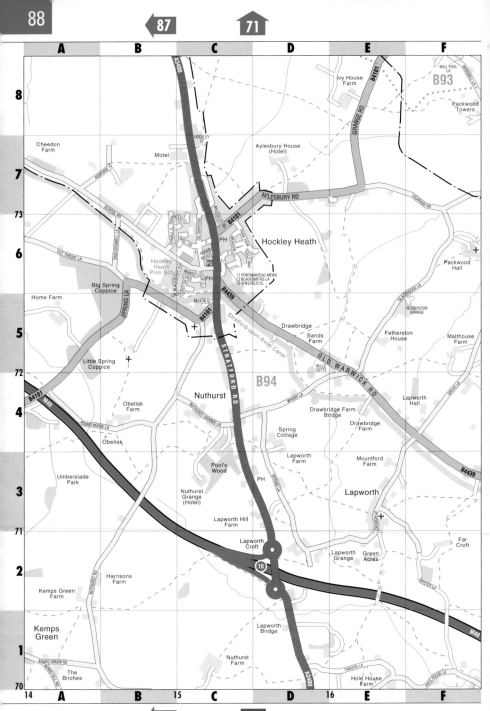

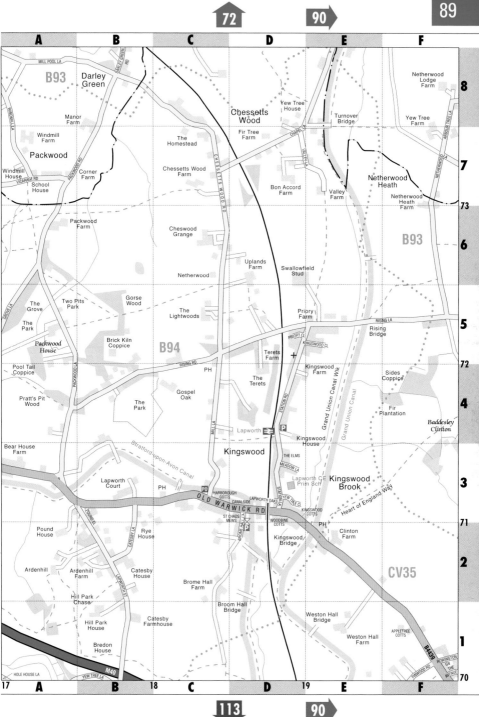

A   B   C   D   E   F

B93   Darley Green

8

Netherwood Lodge Farm

Manor Farm

Chessetts Wood

Yew Tree House

Turnover Bridge

Yew Tree Farm

Windmill Farm

The Homestead

Fir Tree Farm

CHAPEL LA

7

Packwood

Chessetts Wood Farm

Bon Accord Farm

Netherwood Heath

Windmill House

Corner Farm

Valley Farm

73

School House

Packwood Farm

Cheswood Grange

Netherwood Heath Farm

B93

6

Netherwood

Uplands Farm

Swallowfield Stud

Two Pits Park

Gorse Wood

The Grove

The Lightwoods

Priory Farm

RISING LA

5

Rising Bridge

The Park

Brick Kiln Coppice

B94

Packwood House

RISING RD

PH

PRIORY CL   KINGSWOOD CL

Terets Farm

Kingswood Farm

72

Sides Coppice

Pool Tail Coppice

The Terets

The Park

Gospel Oak

Grand Union Canal Wlk

Grand Union Canal

Fir Plantation

4

Baddesley Clinton

Pratt's Pit Wood

MILL LA

Lapworth

Kingswood House

Bear House Farm

Stratford-upon-Avon Canal

Kingswood

THE ELMS

MEADOW LA

Kingswood Brook

Heart of England Way

3

Lapworth Court

PH

OLD WARWICK RD

HARBOROUGH COTTS

CANALSIDE

LAPWORTH OAKS

Lapworth CE Prim Sch

STATION LA   YEW TREE CL

KINGSWOOD COTTS

PH

71

Pound House

PONND EL

CATESBY LA

Rye House

ST CHADS MEWS

WOODBINE COTTS

Kingswood Bridge

Clinton Farm

2

Ardenhill

Ardenhill Farm

LAPWORTH ST

Catesby House

Brome Hall Farm

Weston Hall Bridge

CV35

Hill Park Chase

Hill Park House

Catesby Farmhouse

Broom Hall Bridge

Weston Hall Farm

APPLETREE COTTS

B4439

1

Bredon House

HOWINGTON GN

THE AVENUE

HOLE HOUSE LA

M40   YEW TREE LA

FARWOOD RD

70

17   A   B   18   C   D   19   E   F

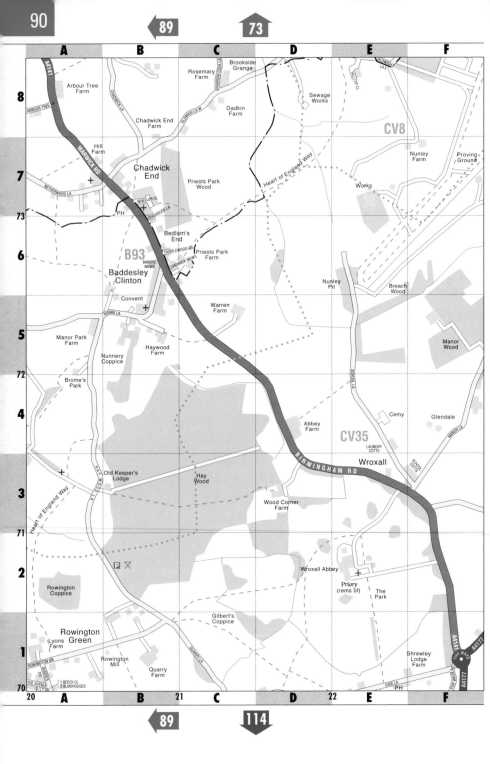

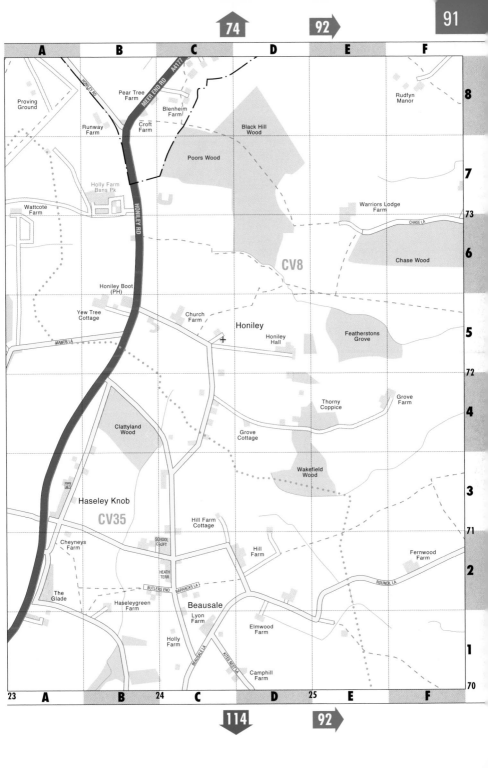

A   B   C   D   E   F

8

Proving
Ground

HONLEY RD

Pear Tree
Farm

MEER END RD   A4177

Blenheim
Farm

Runway
Farm

Croft
Farm

Black Hill
Wood

Rudfyn
Manor

7

Holly Farm
Bsns Pk

Poors Wood

73

Wattcote
Farm

HONLEY RD

Warriors Lodge
Farm

CHASE LA

6

CV8

Chase Wood

Honiley Boot
(PH)

Yew Tree
Cottage

Church
Farm

Honiley

Honiley
Hall

Featherstons
Grove

5

MANOR LA

+

72

Clattyland
Wood

Grove
Cottage

Thorny
Coppice

Grove
Farm

4

Wakefield
Wood

3

PO

Haseley Knob

CV35

Hill Farm
Cottage

71

Cheyneys
Farm

SCHOOL
CROFT

Hill
Farm

Fernwood
Farm

2

HEATH
TERR

BUTLERS END   BARRACKS LA

ROUNDL LA

The Glade

Haseleygreen
Farm

Beausale

Lyon
Farm

Elmwood
Farm

1

Holly
Farm

BEAUSALE LA

RITES WELL LA

Camphill
Farm

70

23   A   B   24   C   D   25   E   F

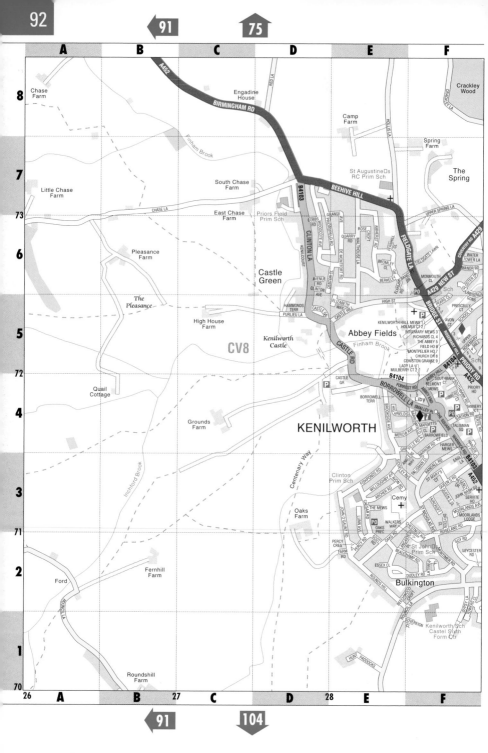

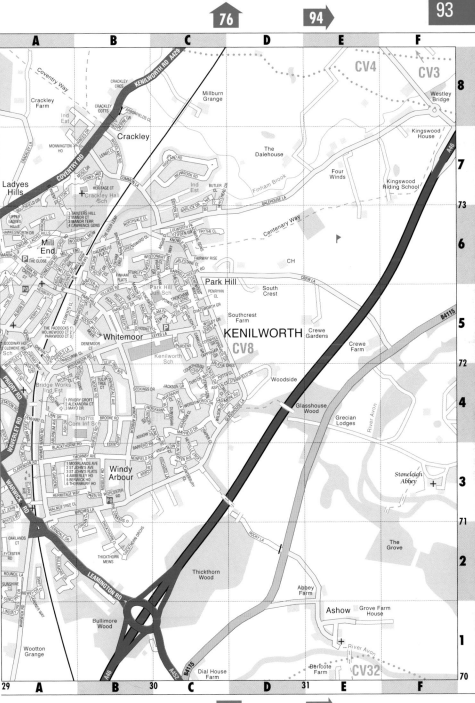

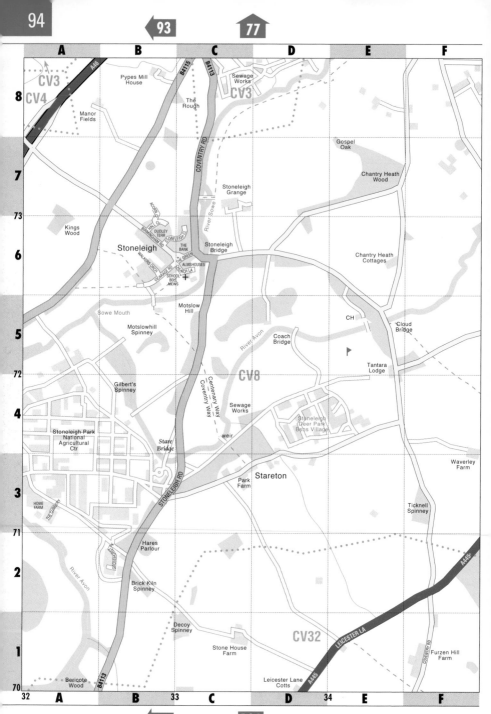

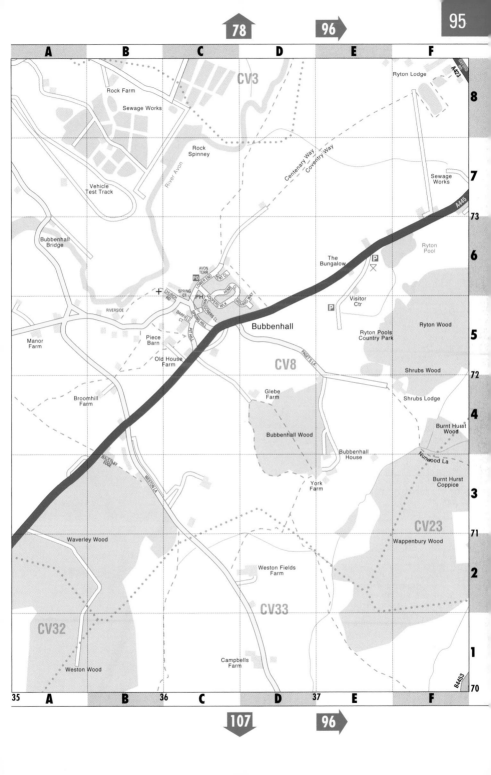

A B C D E F

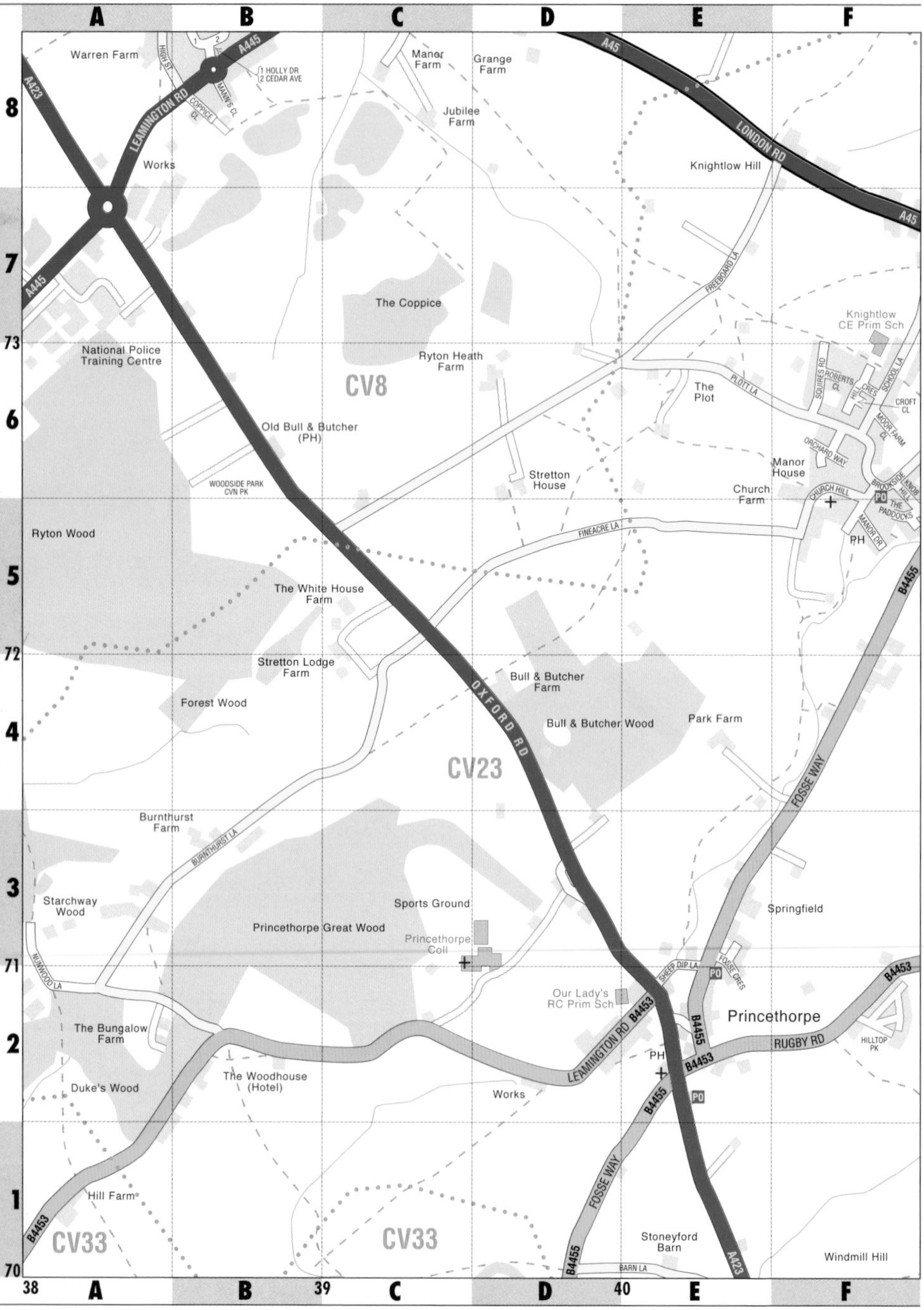

8
Warren Farm
LEAMINGTON RD
A445
HIGH ST
MIERS CL
1 HOLLY DR
2 CEDAR AVE
COPPICE
Works
A23
A445
Manor Farm
Grange Farm
Jubilee Farm
A45
LONDON RD
Knightlow Hill

7
National Police Training Centre
A445
The Coppice
Ryton Heath Farm
CV8
Knightlow CE Prim Sch
FREEBOARD LA
PLOTT LA

73
SOUTHS RD
ROBERTS CL
SCHOOL LA
CROFT CL

6
Old Bull & Butcher (PH)
The Plot
Manor House
ORCHARD WAY
CHURCH HILL
BIRCHEN BANK
THE PADDOCKS
MANOR DR

WOODSIDE PARK CVN PK
Stretton House
Church Farm
PH

Ryton Wood
FINEACRE LA
B4455

5
The White House Farm

72
Stretton Lodge Farm
Bull & Butcher Farm

4
Forest Wood
OXFORD RD
Bull & Butcher Wood
Park Farm
FOSSE WAY
CV23

3
Burnthurst Farm
BURNTHURST LA
Springfield

Starchway Wood
Sports Ground
Princethorpe Great Wood
Princethorpe Coll
FOSSE CRES
SHEEP DIP LA
B4453
PO
B4453
HILLTOP PK

71
Our Lady's RC Prim Sch
B4453
Princethorpe
B4455
RUGBY RD

2
The Bungalow Farm
LEAMINGTON RD
PH
B4453
PO

The Woodhouse (Hotel)
Works
B4455

Duke's Wood
FOSSE WAY

1
Hill Farm
B4453
CV33
Stoneyford Barn
A423
Windmill Hill
B4455
BARN LA

70
CV33

38 A B 39 C D 40 E F

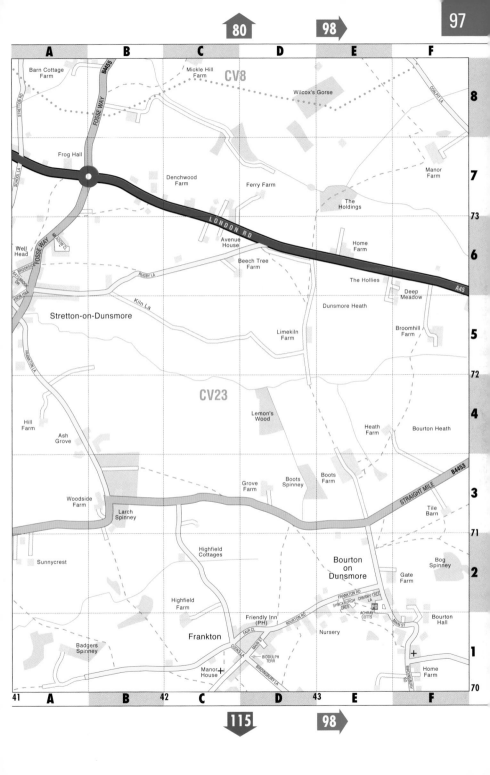

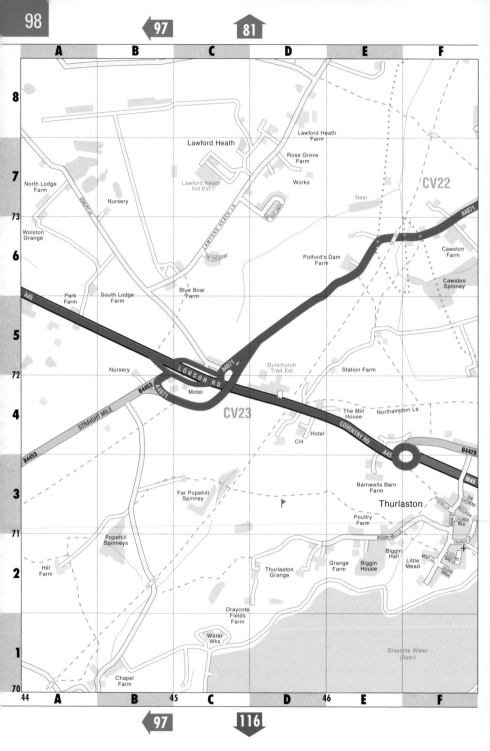

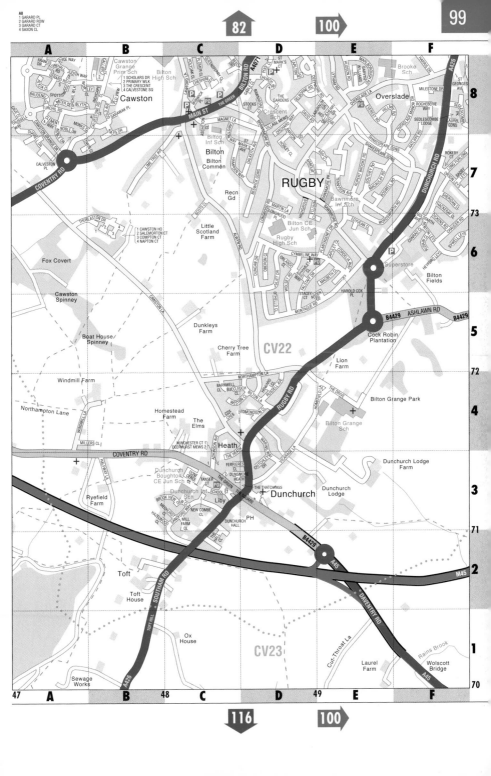

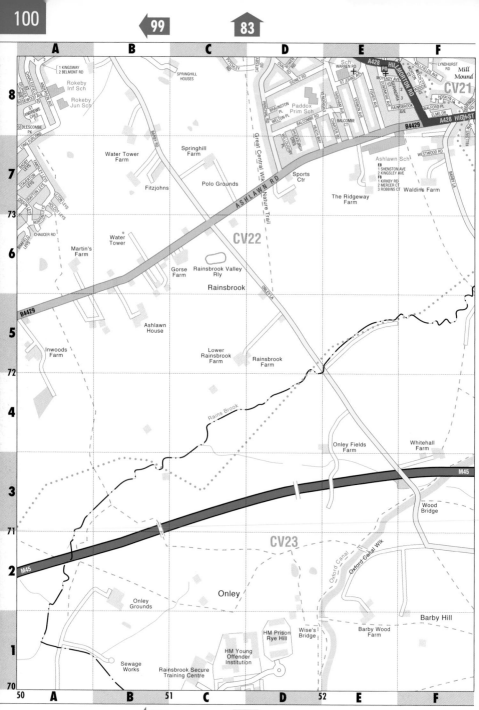

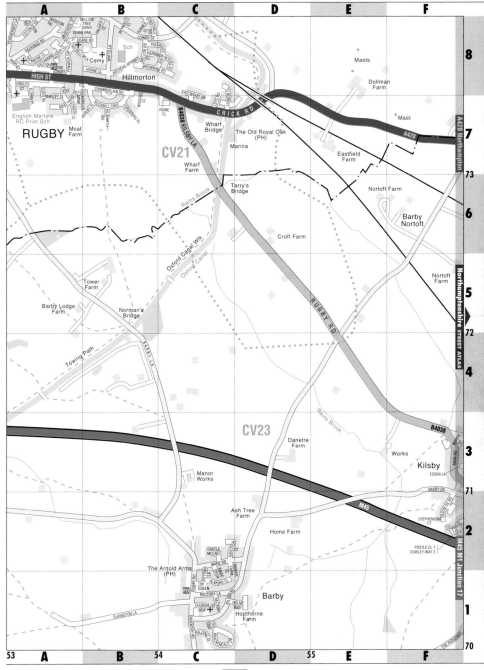

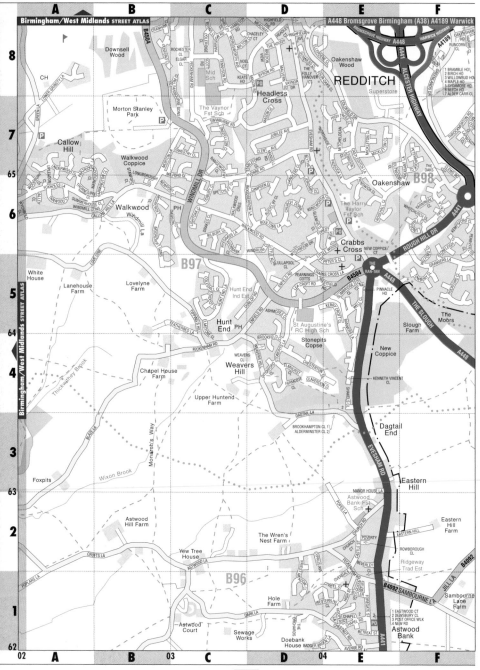

A448 Bromsgrove Birmingham (A38) A4189 Warwick

REDDITCH
Superstore

1 BRAMBLE HO
2 BIRCH HO
3 WILLOWBUD HO
4 MAPLE HO
5 SYCAMORE HO
6 BEECH HO
7 ALDER CARR HO

Downsell
Wood

Oakenshaw
Wood

Headless
Cross

Oakenshaw

B98

CH

Morton Stanley
Park

The Vaynor
Fst Sch

The Harry
Taylor
Fst Sch

The Oaks

Callow
Hill

Walkwood
Coppice

Crabbs
Cross

NEW COPPICE

THE
PAN-TAN

ROUGH HILL DR

A441

Walkwood

Windmill La

B97

PINNACLE
HO

Slough
Farm

The
Moors

White
House

Lanehouse
Farm

Lovelyne
Farm

Hunt End
Ind Est

Fearnings
Cotts

St Augustine's
RC High Sch

New
Coppice

THE SLOUGH

A448

Hunt
End

Brookfield

Stonepits
Copse

Chapel House
Farm

Weavers
Hill

Kenneth Vincent
Cl

EVESHAM RD

Upper Huntend
Farm

BROOKHAMPTON CL 1
ALDERMINSTER CL 2

Dagtail
End

Thickwhiney Brook

Foxpits

Wixon Brook

MANOR HOUSE LA

Eastern
Hill

Astwood
Hill Farm

Yew Tree
House

The Wren's
Nest Farm

Astwood
Bank Fst
Sch

POVERTY
CL

ROWBOROUGH
CL

Eastern
Hill
Farm

Monarch's Way

B96

Ridgeway
Trad Est

B4092

Hole
Farm

Sambourne
Lane
Farm

B4092 SAMBOURNE LA

Astwood
Court

Sewage
Works

Doebank
House

1 EASTWOOD CT
2 DEWSBURY CL
3 POST OFFICE WLK
4 NEW RD

Astwood
Bank

A441

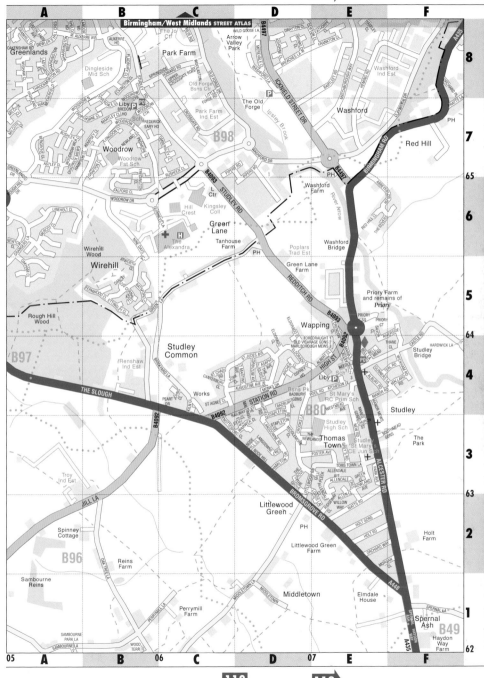

Birmingham/West Midlands STREET ATLAS

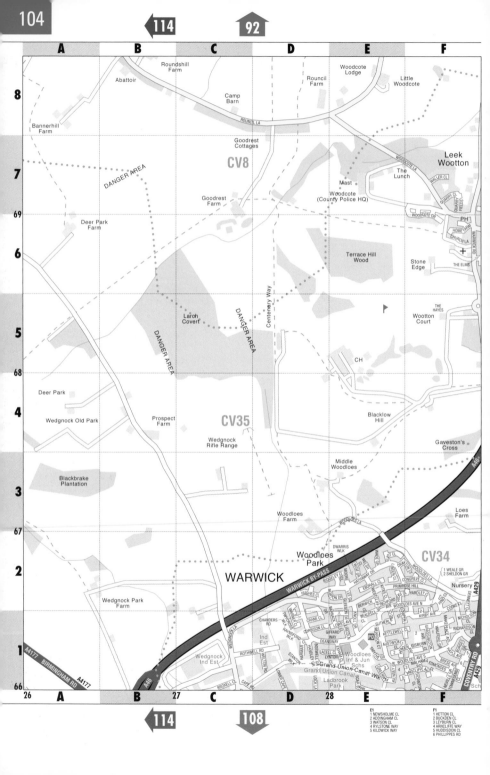

	A	B	C	D	E	F

8

Abattoir

Roundshill Farm

Camp Barn

Rouncil Farm

Woodcote Lodge

Little Woodcote

Bannerhill Farm

ROUNCIL LA

Goodrest Cottages

CV8

Leek Wootton

WOODCOTE LA

7

DANGER AREA

Goodrest Farm

Mast

Woodcote (County Police HQ)

The Lunch

WALLER CL

QUARRY CL

OLD MILL AV

WOODCOTE DR

PH

69

Deer Park Farm

HOME FARM

CHURCH LA

THE ELMS

+

6

Terrace Hill Wood

Stone Edge

5

Larch Covert

DANGER AREA

Centenery Way

THE HAYES

Wootton Court

68

DANGER AREA

CH

4

Deer Park

Wedgnock Old Park

Prospect Farm

CV35

Wedgnock Rifle Range

Blacklow Hill

Gaveston's Cross

A46

3

Blackbrake Plantation

Middle Woodloes

Loes Farm

67

Woodloes Farm

WOODLOES LA

DWARRIS WLK

CV34

2

Woodloes Park

WARWICK

WARWICK BY-PASS

1 WEALE GR
2 SHELDON GR

Nursery

A429

1

Wedgnock Park Farm

A4177 BIRMINGHAM RD

Wedgnock Ind Est

Ind Est

ROTHWELL RD

Grand Union Canal Wlk

Grand Union Canal

Woodloes Inf & Jun Schs

Ladbrook Park

COVENTRY RD

A46

66

26	A	B	27	C	D	28	E	F

E1
1 NEWSHOLME CL
2 ADDINGHAM CL
3 WATSON CL
4 RYLSTONE WAY
5 KILDWICK WAY

F1
1 HETTON CL
2 BUCKDEN CL
3 LEYBURN CL
4 ARNCLIFFE WAY
5 HUDDISDON CL
6 PHILLIPPES RD

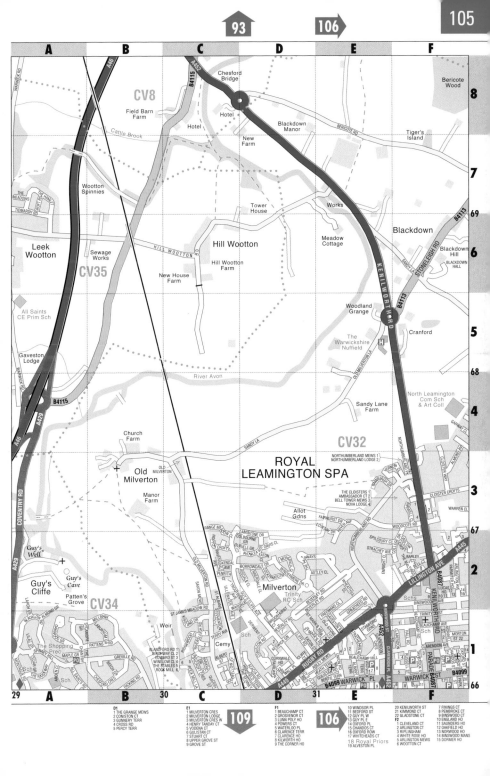

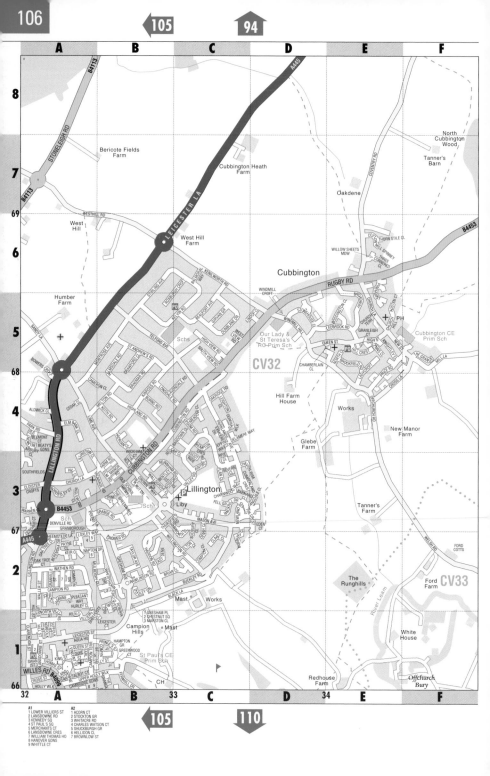

A1
1 LOWER VILLIERS ST
2 LANSDOWNE RD
3 KENNEDY SQ
4 ST PAUL'S SQ
5 MERCHANTS CT
6 LANSDOWNE CRES
7 WILLIAM THOMAS HO
8 HANOVER GDNS
9 WHITTLE CT

A2
1 ACORN CT
2 STOCKTON GR
3 WHITACRE RD
4 CHARLES WATSON CT
5 SHUCKBURGH GR
6 HELLIDON CL
7 BROWNLOW ST

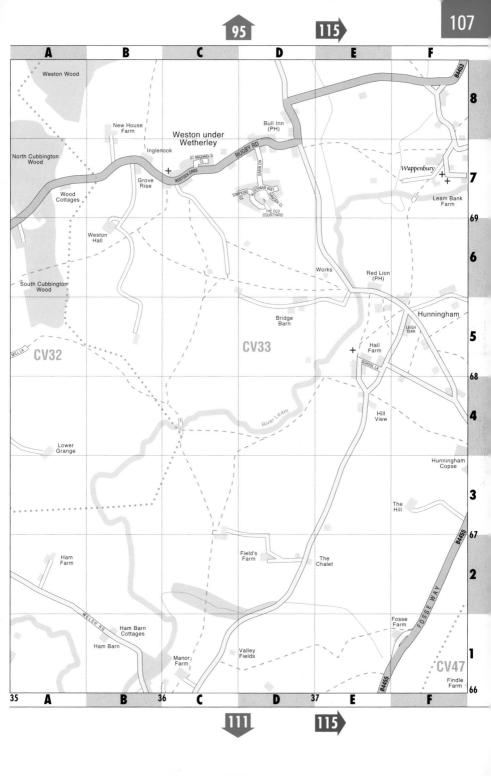

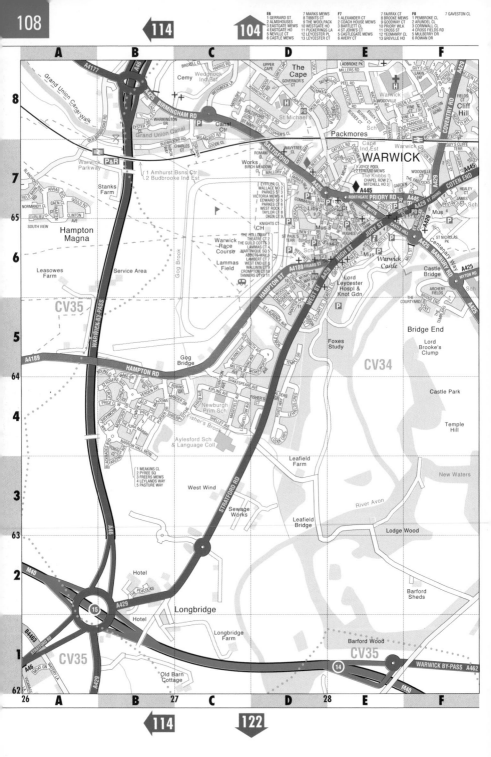

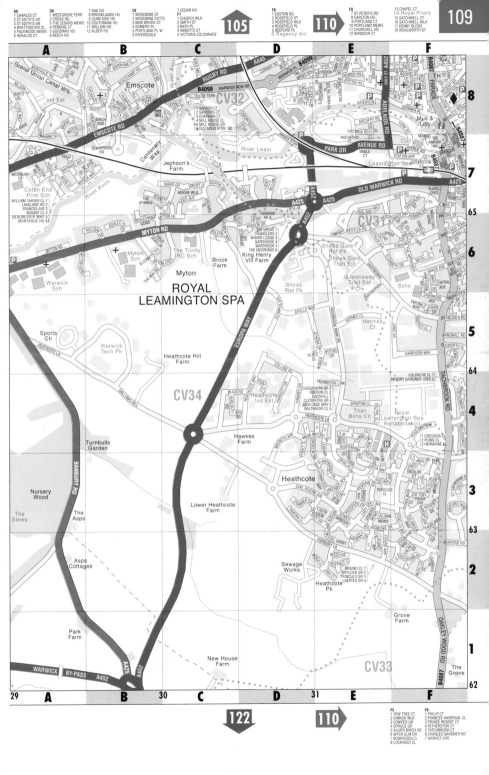

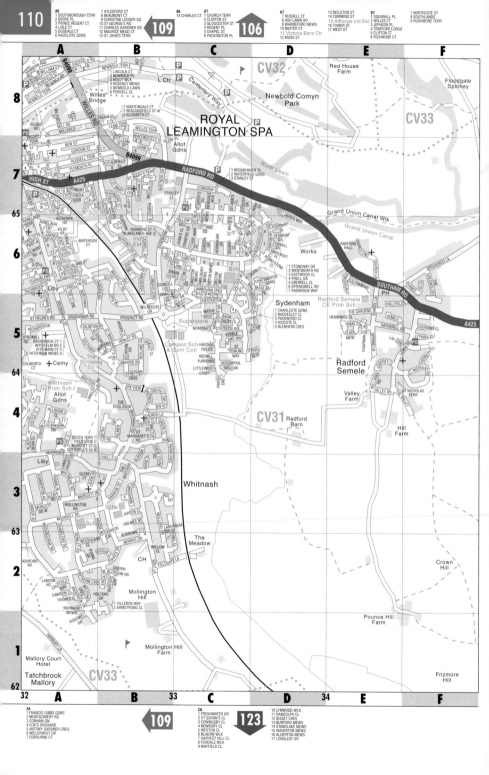

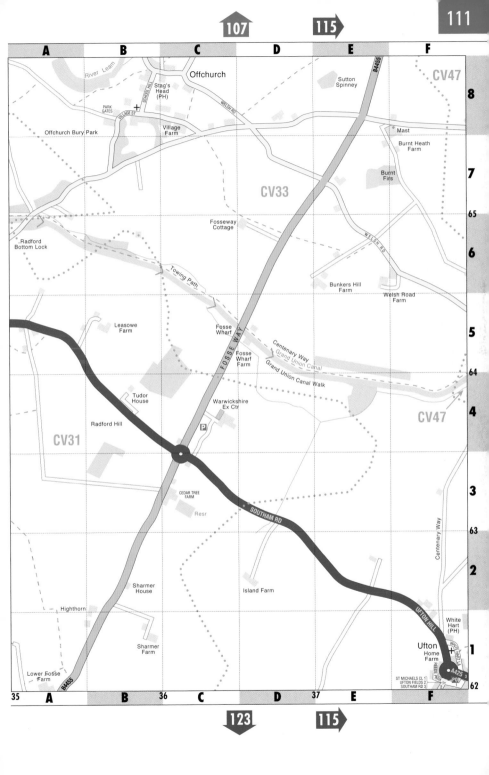

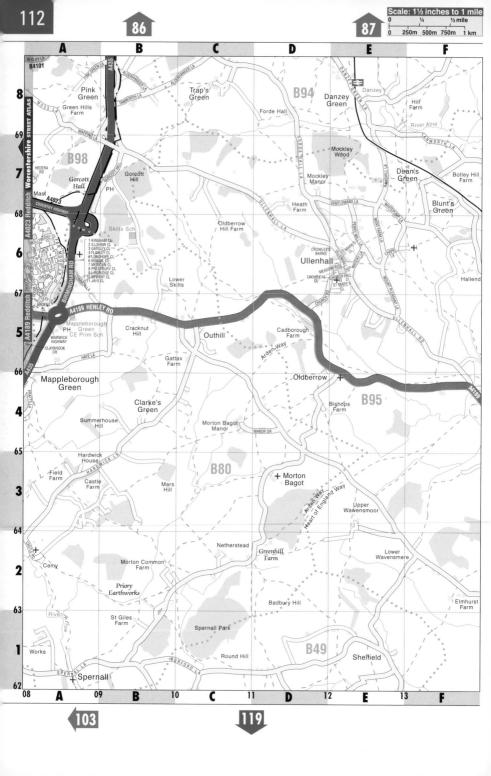

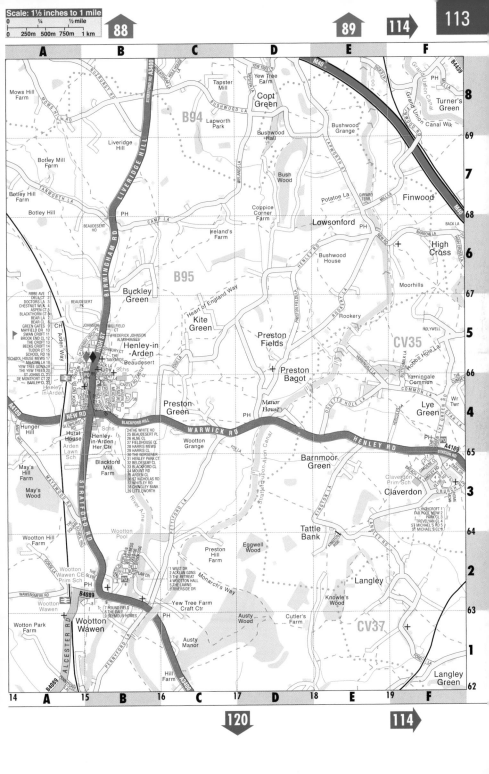

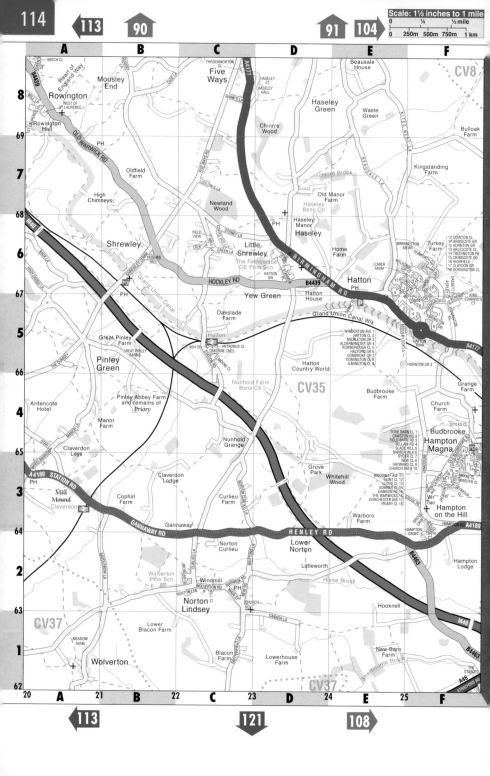

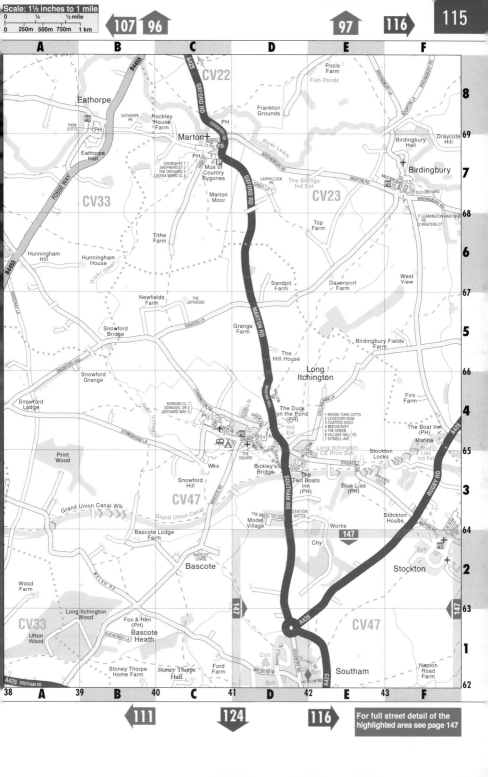

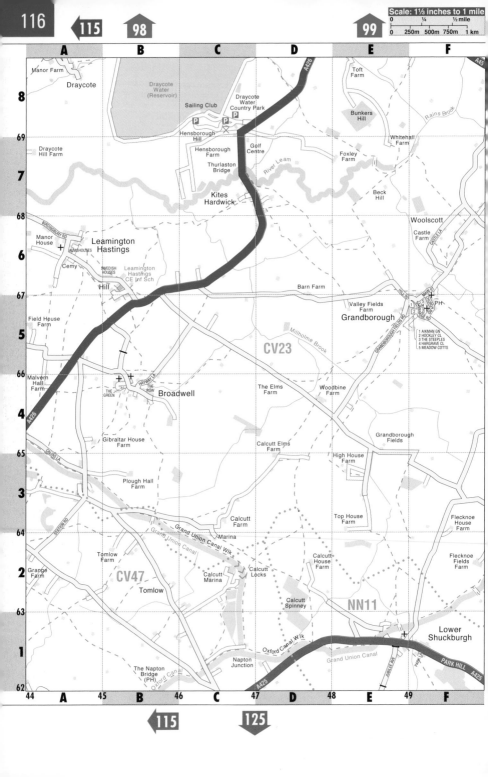

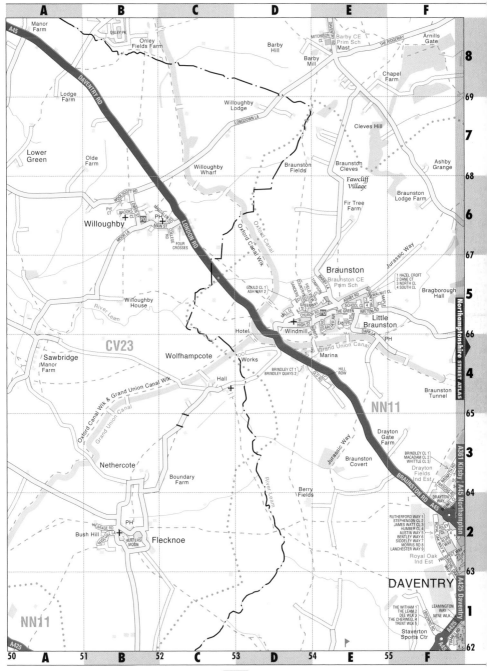

Scale: 1½ inches to 1 mile

Northamptonshire STREET ATLAS

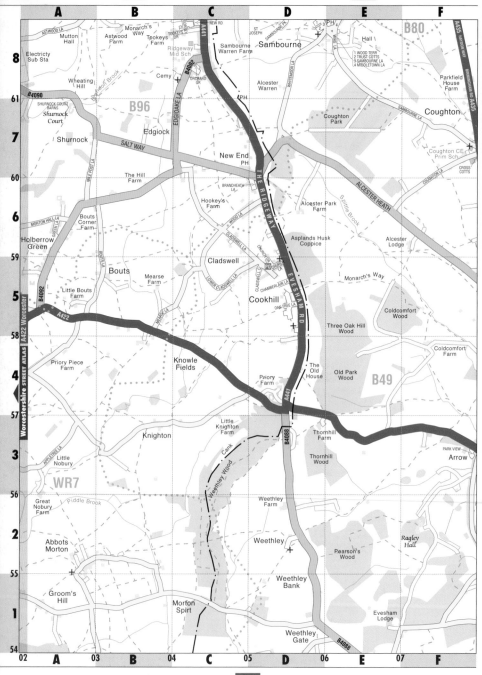

Scale: 1⅓ inches to 1 mile

0   ¼   ½ mile

0   250m   500m   750m   1 km

B80

A435 EVESHAM WAY

A435

A   **B**   **C**   **D**   **E**   **F**

ASTWOOD LA

Electricty
Sub Sta

Mutton
Hall

Monarch's
Way

Astwood
Farm

Tpokeys
Farm

TOOKEYS
DR

NEW RD

A441

St
JOSEPH

Sambourne
Warren Farm

Sambourne

WIKE LA

PH

Hall

1 WOOD TERR
2 TRUST COTTS
3 SAMBOURNE LA
4 MIDDLETOWN LA

Parkfield
House
Farm

8

Wheating
Hill

Cemy

ORCHARD
GR

Alcester
Warren

WHITTMOOR LA

Coughton

Ridgeway
Mid Sch

B4092

EDGIOAKE LA

PH

61

B4090

SHURNOCK COURT
BARNS

Shurnock
Court

B96

Edgiock

Coughton
Park

SAMBOURNE LA

Coughton CE
Prim Sch

COUGHTON LA

CROSS
COTTS

7

Shurnock

SALT WAY

New End
PH

THE RIDGEWAY

ALCESTER HEATH

60

The Hill
Farm

MILE POSTA

BRANDHEATH
LA

Alcester Park
Farm

Spittle Brook

6

MORTON HALL LA

GREEN LA

Bouts
Corner
Farm

Hookey's
Farm

WOOD LA

Asplands Husk
Coppice

Monarch's Way

Alcester
Lodge

Holberrow
Green

CLADSWELL LA

Cladswell

OAK CROFT
LA

EVESHAM RD

59

ARREW LA

Bouts

Mearse
Farm

LOWER CLADSWELL LA

ST EDMOND'S
CL

Coldcomfort
Wood

5

B4092

A422 Worcester

Little Bouts
Farm

MEARSE LA

Cookhill

CHAMBERLAIN LA

OAK TREE LA

Three Oak Hill
Wood

Coldcomfort
Farm

Worcestershire STREET ATLAS

A422

58

Priory Piece
Farm

Knowle
Fields

Priory
Farm

The
Old
House

A441

Old Park
Wood

B49

4

57

ASPLEBREA LA

Little
Nobury

Knighton

Little
Knighton
Farm

Cank

B4088

Thornhill
Farm

Thornhill
Wood

PARK VIEW

Arrow

3

WR7

Piddle Brook

Weethley Wood

Weethley
Farm

56

Great
Nobury
Farm

Weethley

Pearson's
Wood

Ragley
Hall

2

Abbots
Morton

Weethley
Bank

Evesham
Lodge

55

Groom's
Hill

Morton
Spirt

Weethley
Gate

B4088

1

54

02   **A**   **03**   **B**   **04**   **C**   **05**   **D**   **06**   **E**   **07**   **F**

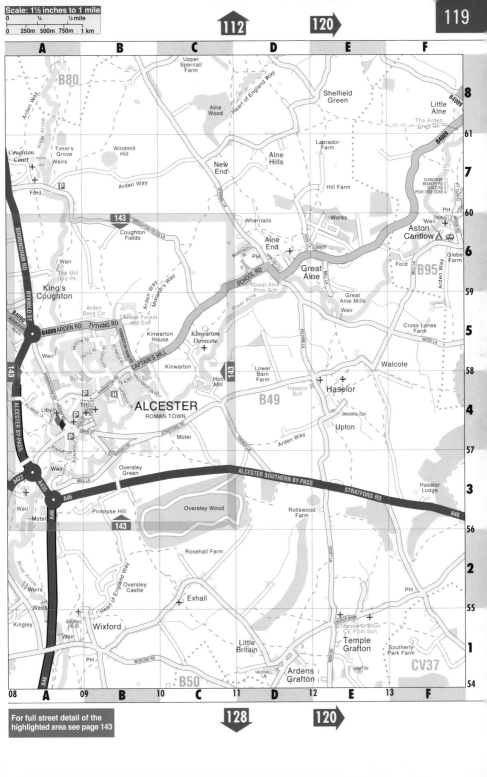

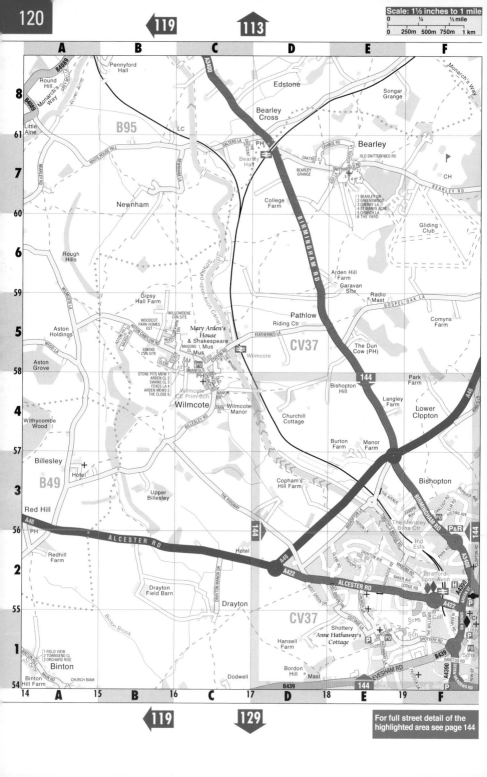

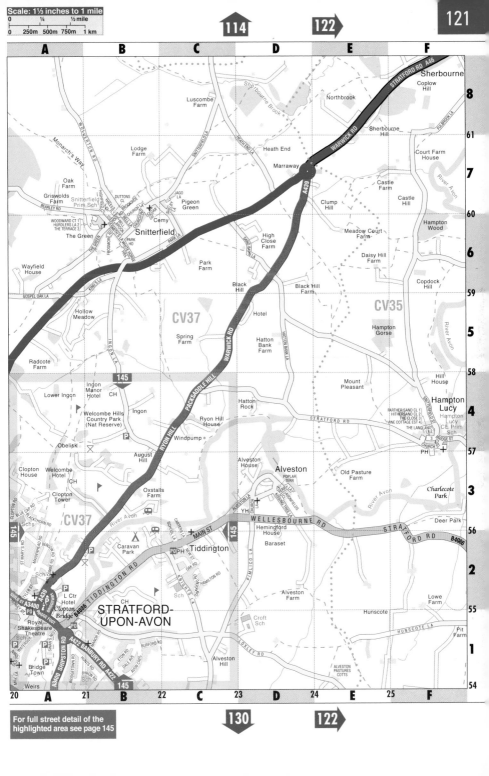

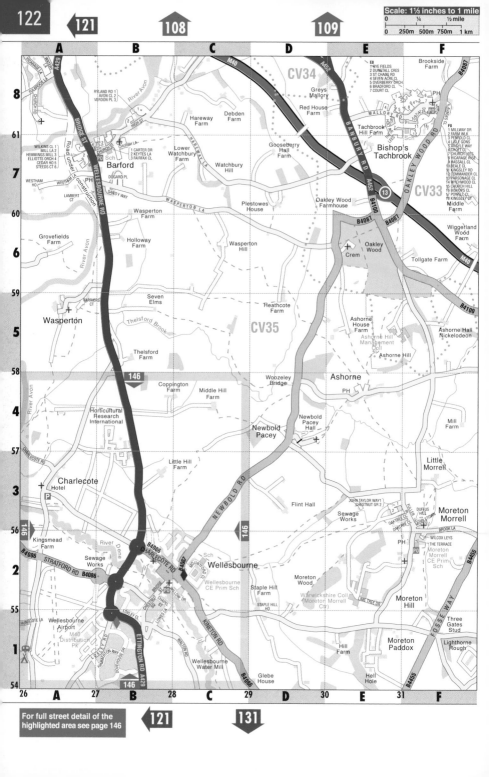

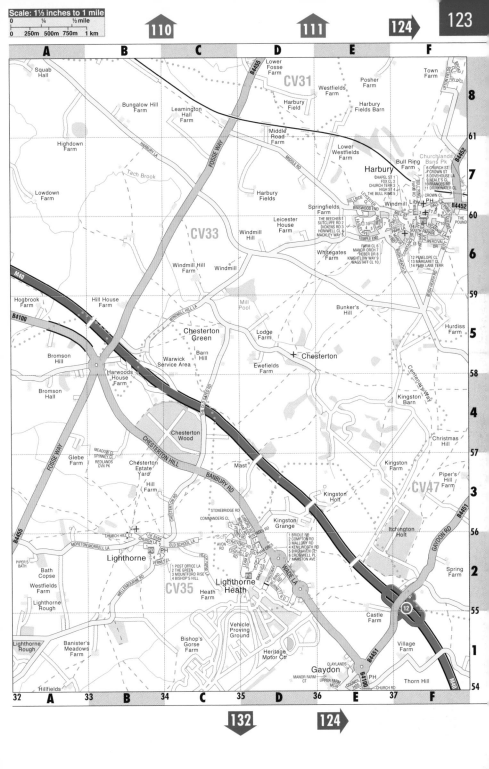

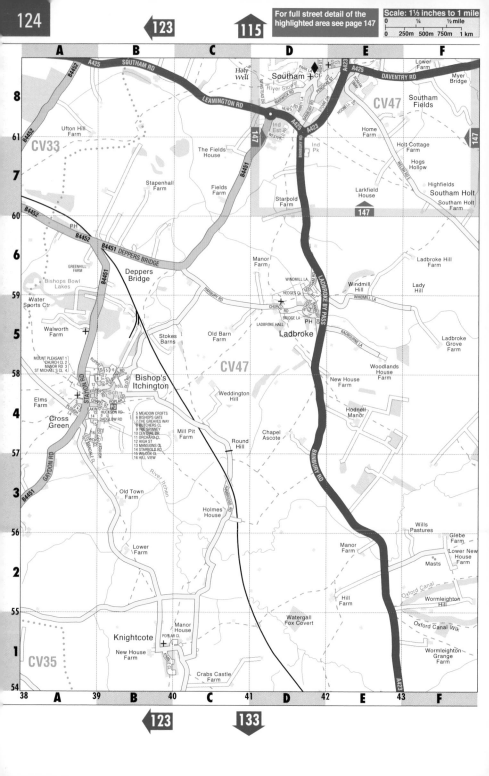

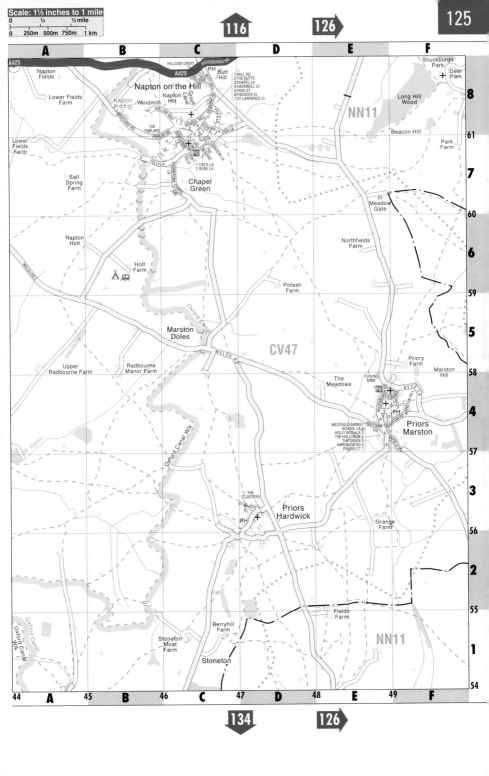

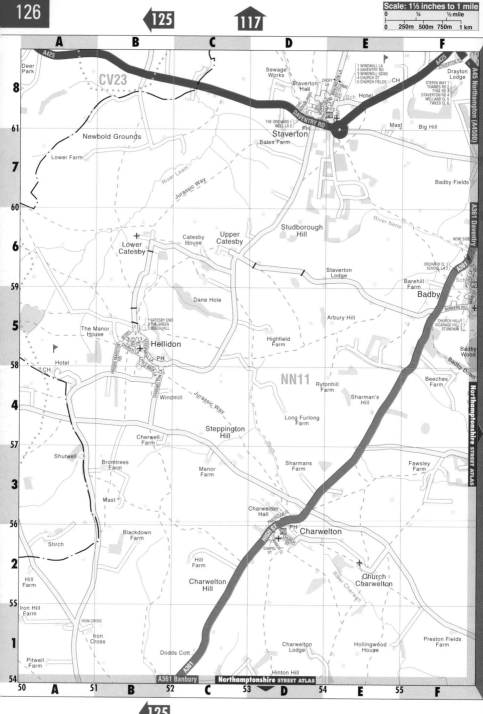

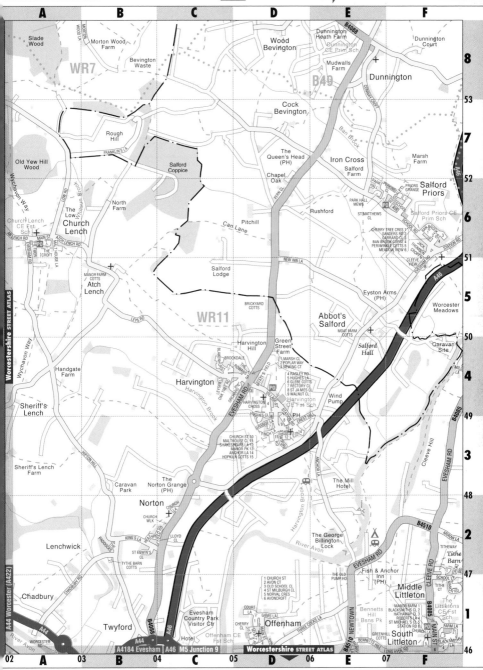

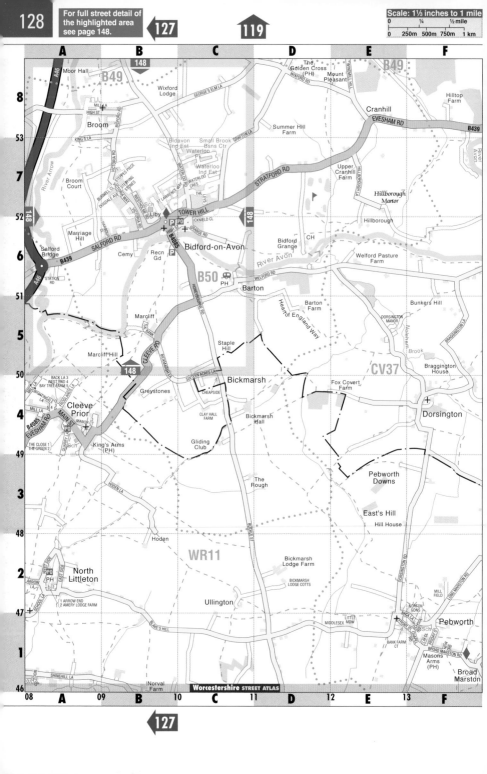

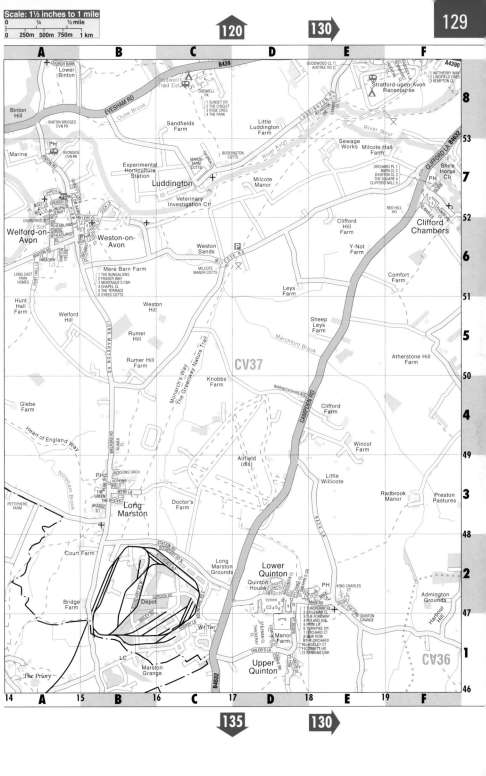

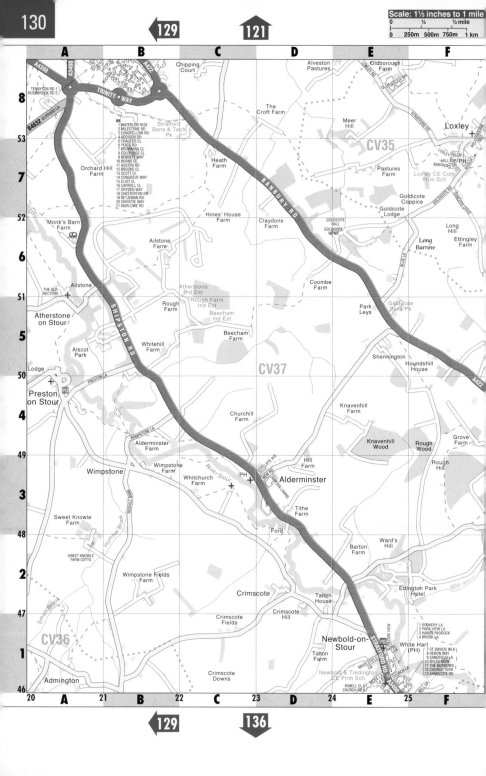

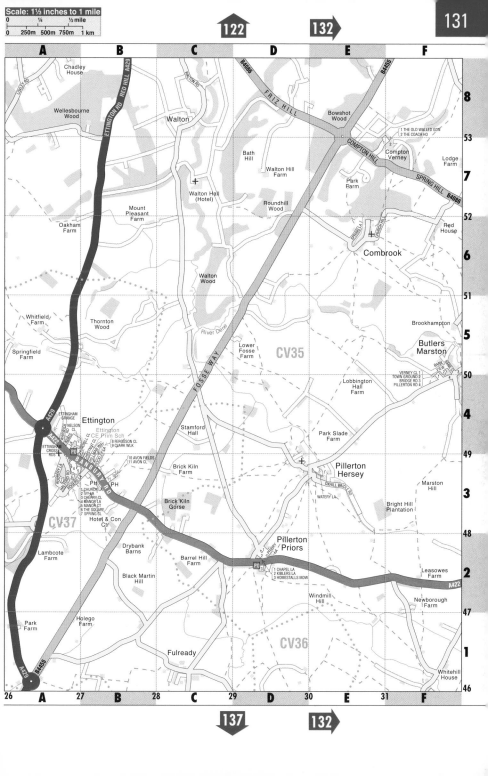

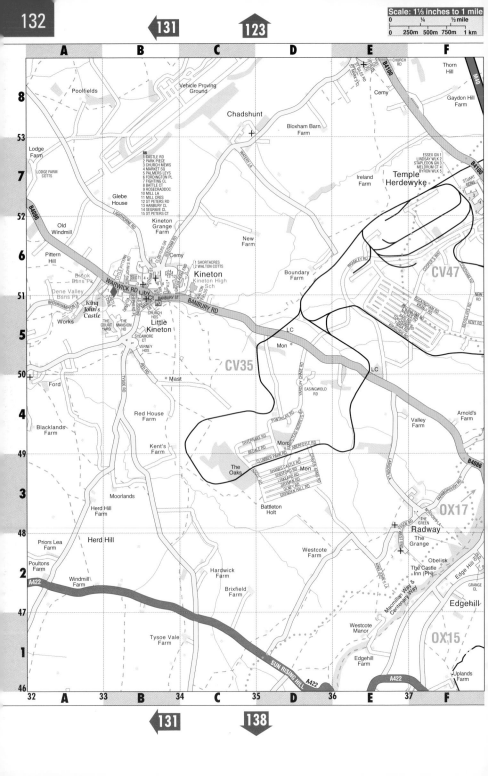

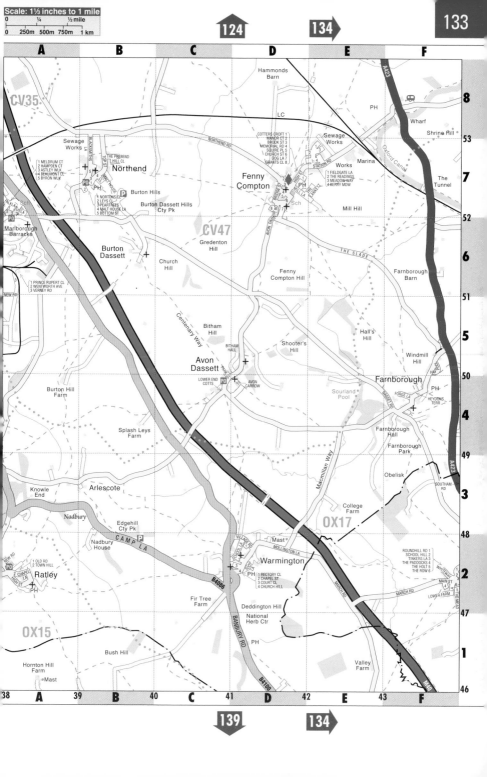

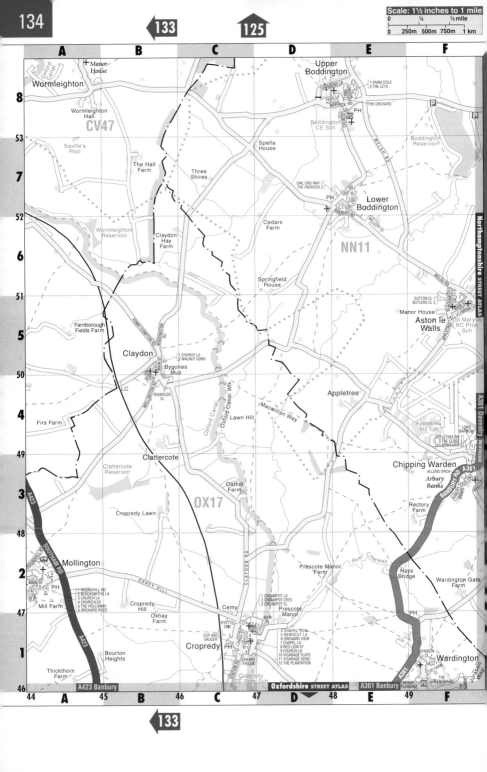

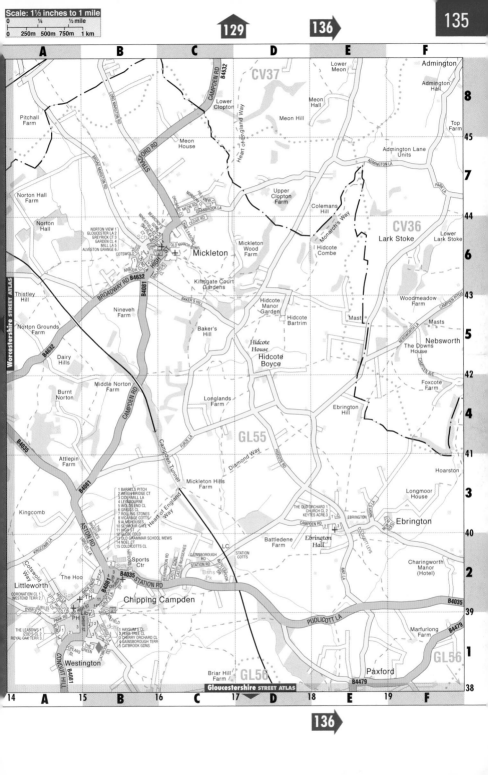

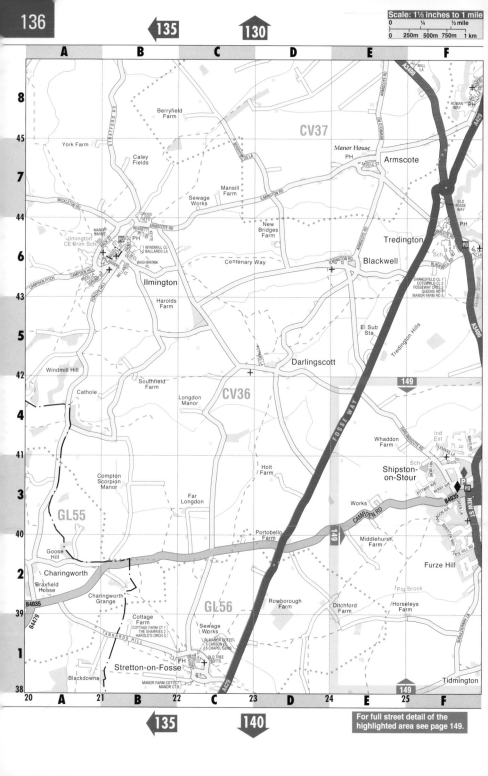

135 130

Scale: 1⅓ inches to 1 mile

0   ¼   ½ mile
0   250m 500m 750m 1 km

A **B** **C** **D** **E** **F**

8

MILL LA

ROMAN WAY PH

A3400

45

CV37

York Farm

Berryfield Farm

Manor House PH

Armscote

MIDDLE ST

7

STRATFORD RD

Caley Fields

Mansill Farm

Sewage Works

OLD FOSSE WAY

PH

44

MICKLETON RD

CROSS LEYS

ARMSCOTE RD

New Bridges Farm

Tredington

ARMSCOTE RD

Sch PO

Ilmington CE Prim Sch

MANOR BARNS

BENNETT KEYTE

1 WINDMILL CL
2 BALLARDS LA

WASHBROOK PL

Blackwell

ILMINGTON RD

BLACKWELL RD

6

CAMPDEN HILL

PH

WELL LA

MILL LA

Centenary Way

SHANESFIELD CL 1
COTSWOLD CL 2
FOSSEWAY CRES 3
QUEENS RD 4
MANOR FARM RD 5

43

GROVE ST

HACCY HILL

Ilmington

Harolds Farm

El Sub Sta

River Stour

CAMPDEN PITCH

5

Tredington Hills

42

Windmill Hill

Southfield Farm

Darlingscott

A3400

Cathole

Longdon Manor

CV36

FOSSE WAY

149

4

Whaddon Farm

DARLINGSCOTE RD

Ind Est

41

Compton Scorpion Manor

Holt Farm

Shipston-on-Stour

Sch
Sch
TILEMANS LA

MAYO RD

3

GL55

Far Longdon

Works

CAMPDEN RD

PO P

NEW ST

BERRY AVE
FITTWAY AVE

B4035

40

149

Portobello Farm

Middlehurst Farm

Furze Hill

Goose Hill

2

Charingworth

Braxfield Hobse

Charingworth Grange

Rowborough Farm

Pig Brook

Ditchford Farm

Horseleys Farm

B4035

39

B4479

GL56

Cottage Farm

COTTAGE FARM CT 1
THE SHARRIES 2
HAROLD'S ORCH 3

Sewage Works

4 MANOR COTTS
5 CARSON CL
6 CHAPEL GDNS

SHOULDERWAY LA

1

TANKARDS HILL

PH

OLD TREE COTTS

A429

149

38

Blackdowns

Stretton-on-Fosse

MANOR FARM COTTS 7
MANOR CT 8

Tidmington

20 **A** 21 **B** 22 **C** 23 **D** 24 **E** 25 **F**

135 140

For full street detail of the highlighted area see page 149.

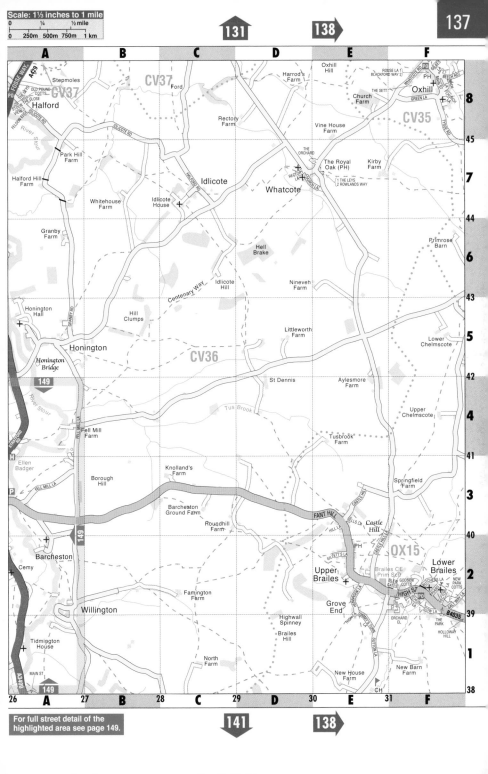

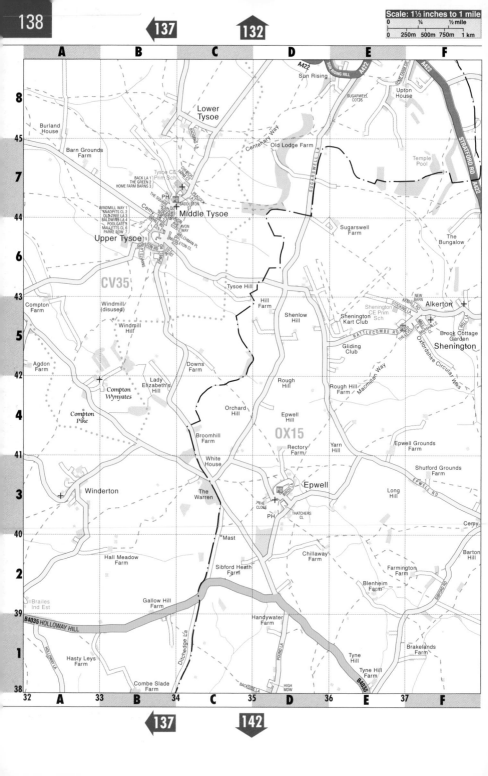

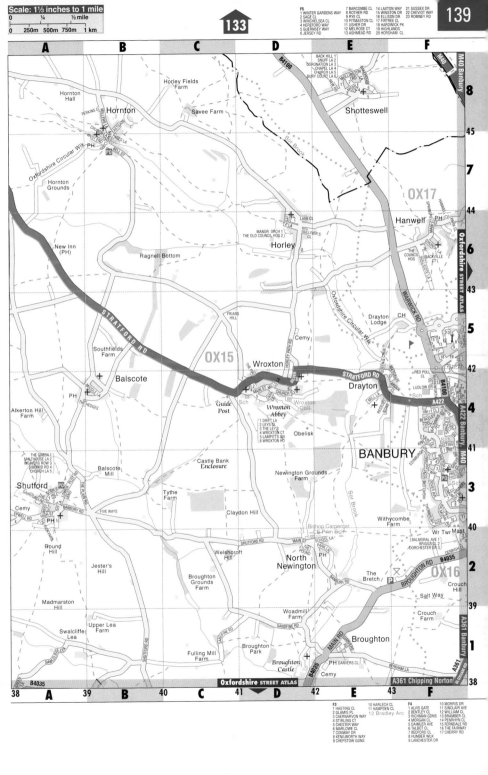

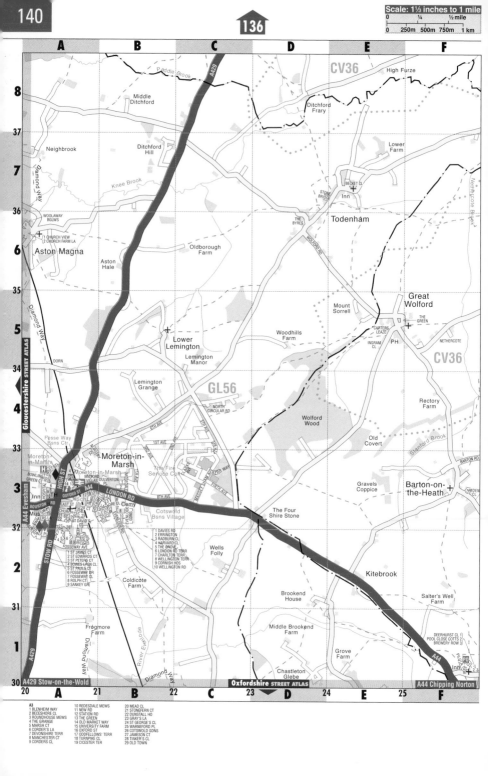

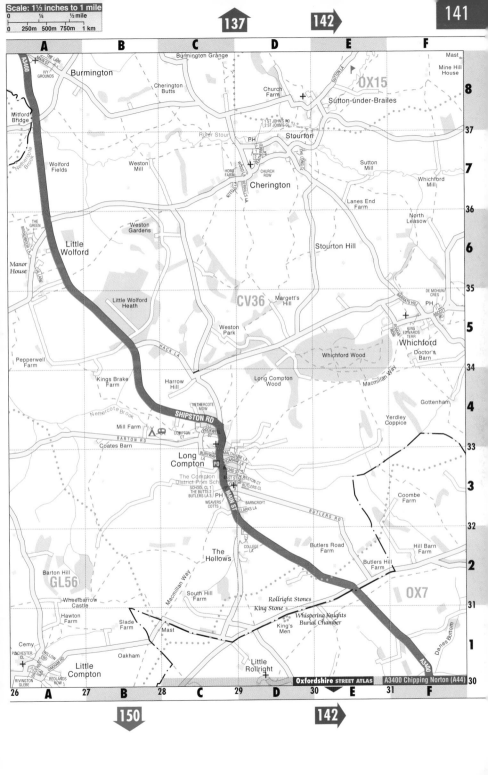

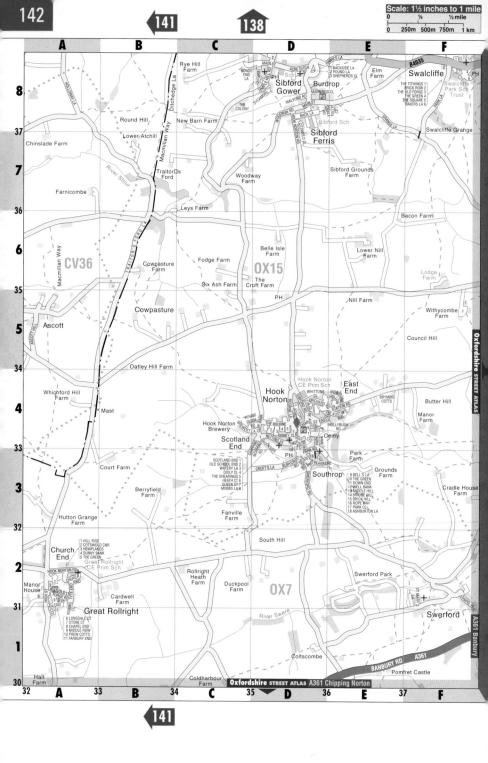

Scale: 1⅓ inches to 1 mile

0 ¼ ½ mile
0 250m 500m 750m 1 km

8

37

7

36

6

35

5

34

4

33

3

32

2

31

1

30

A B C D E F

Rye Hill Farm

BONKS LA

Swalcliffe

B4035

BONDS END LA

MAIN ST

ACRE DITCH

1 BACKSIDE LA
2 POUND LA
3 SHEPHERDS CL

Elm Farm

Mus

PH

Sibford Gower

Burdrop

THE COLONY

SYCAMORE

MANNINGS CL

WALFORD RD

WOODWAY RD

BACK LA

MAIN ST

Sibford Sch

THE TITHINGS
BRICK ROW 2
THE OLD FORGE 3
THE GREEN 4
THE SQUARE 5
BAKERS LA 6

Swalcliffe Park Sch Trust

New Barn Farm

Sibford Ferris

GRANGE LA

Swalcliffe Grange

Round Hill

Lower Atchill

Chinslade Farm

River Stour

Traitor's Ford

Leys Farm

Woodway Farm

Sibford Grounds Farm

Bacon Farm

Farnicombe

CV36

Macmillan Way

TRAITOR'S FORD LA

Cowpasture Farm

Fodge Farm

Belle Isle Farm

Six Ash Farm

The Croft Farm

OX15

PH

Lower Nill Farm

Nill Farm

Lodge Farm

Withycombe Farm

Ascott

ASCOTT RD

Cowpasture

Oatley Hill Farm

Council Hill

Whichford Hill Farm

Mast

Court Farm

Hook Norton CE Prim Sch

WHITTONS

East End

Butter Hill

BRYMBO COTTS

Manor Hill

Hook Norton

ORCHARD

CHAPEL ST

STATION RD

Hook Norton Brewery

BREWERY

ROUND CLOSE RD

Scotland End

1
2
3 4 5

THE BOURNE

NETTING CLOSE

HOLLYBUSH RD

Cemy

SCOTLAND END 1
OLD SCHOOL END 2
WATERY LA 3
DOILY CL 4
THE SHEARINGS 5
HEATH CT 6
QUEEN ST 7
MOBBS LA 8

CROFT'S LA

BURYCROFT

SIBFORD RD

PH

PARK RD

BELL

SEANACRE

Southrop

Park Farm

Berryfield Farm

Fanville Farm

Grounds Farm

Cradle House Farm

9 BELL'S LA
10 THE GREEN
11 DOWN END
12 WELL BANK
13 MIDDLE HILL
14 BIRDIE HILL
15 BRICK HILL
16 ROPE WAY
17 PARK CL
18 ASHBURTON LA

Hutton Grange Farm

Church End

1 HILL RISE
2 COTSWOLD CNR
3 HEMPLANDS
4 SUNNY BANK
5 THE GREEN

Great Rollright CE Prim Sch

South Hill

Rollright Heath Farm

Duckpool Farm

OX7

Swerford Park

Manor House

HOOK NORTON RD

HIGH ST

CHURCH

Cardwell Farm

Great Rollright

6 LONSDALE CT
7 STONE CT
8 CHAPEL END
9 MIDDLE ROW
10 PREW COTTS
11 FARBURY END

River Swere

Swerford

ST MARY'S RD

Coltscombe

BANBURY RD

A361

Pomfret Castle

Half Farm

Coldharbour Farm

A361 Banbury

Oxfordshire STREET ATLAS

32 33 34 35 36 37

A B C D E F

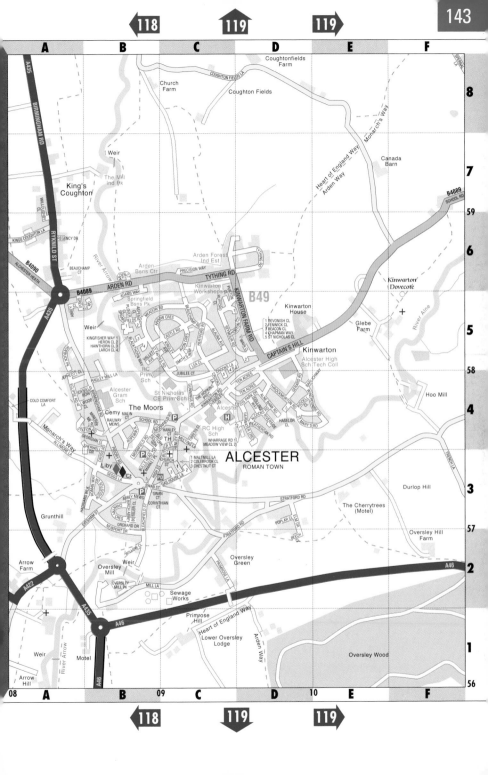

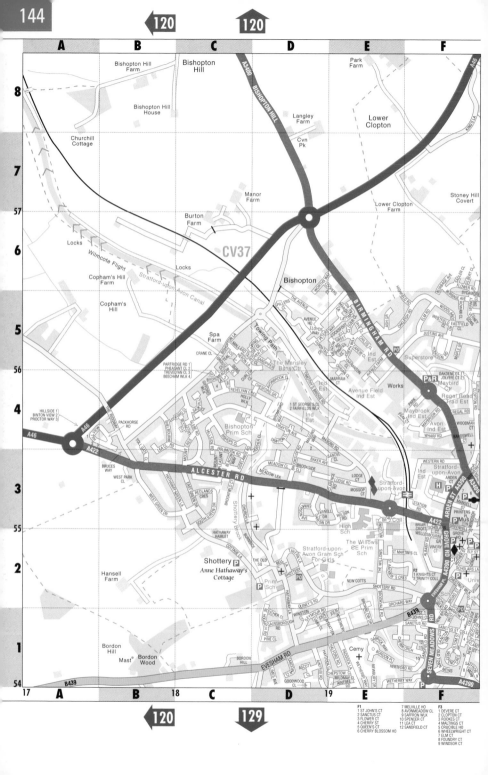

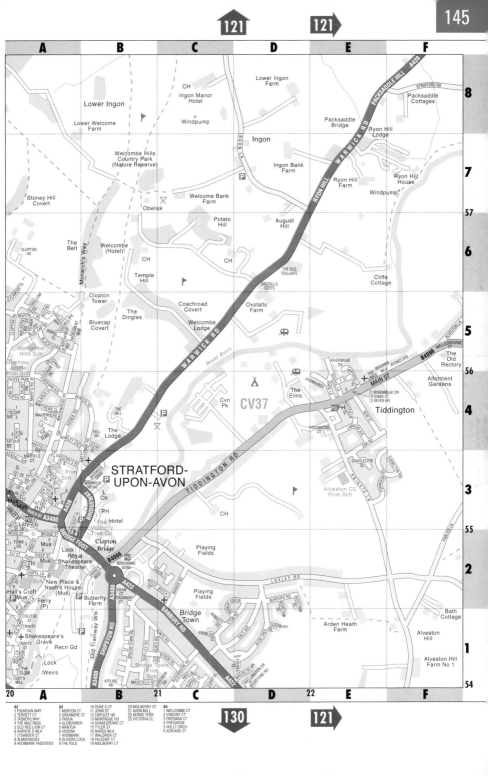

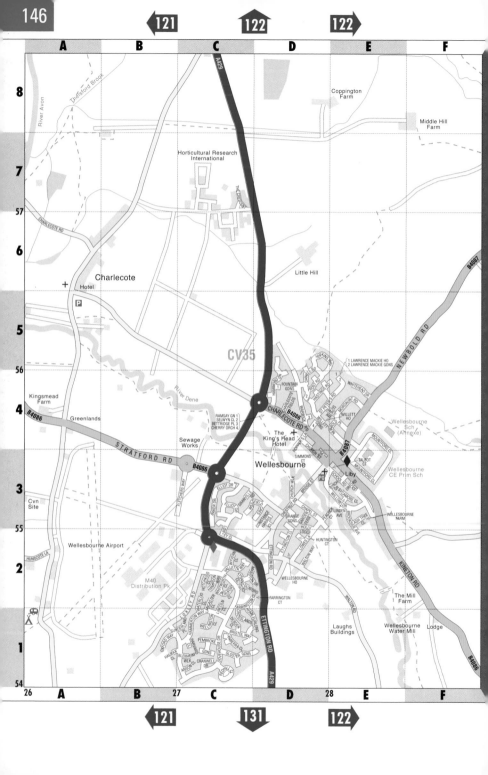

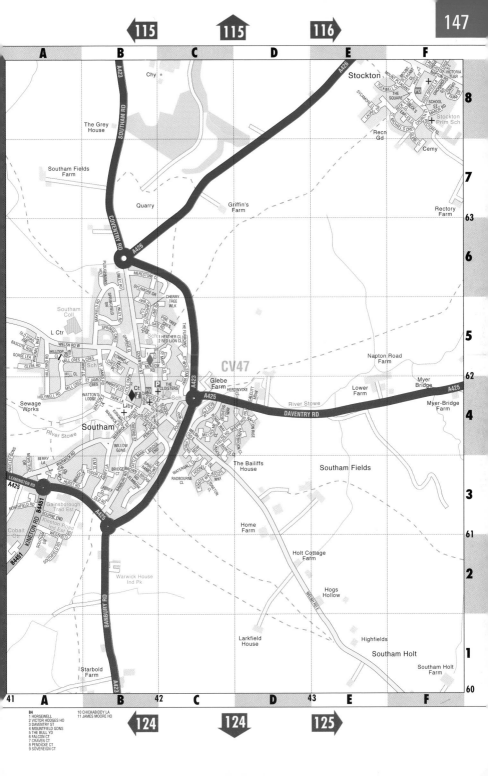

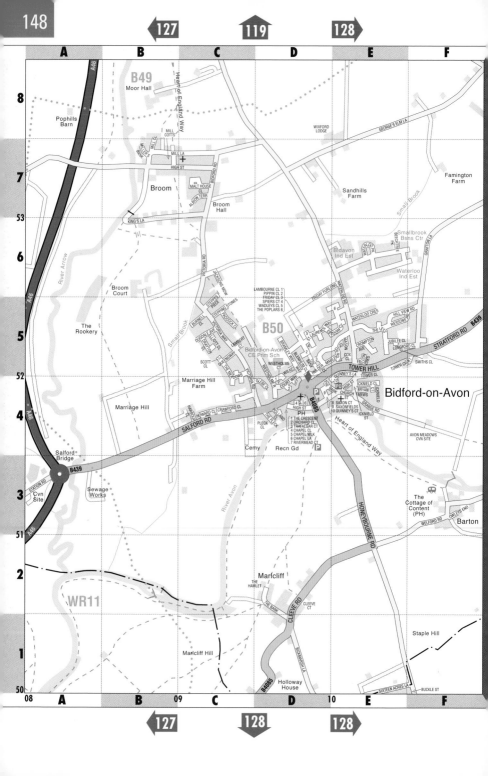

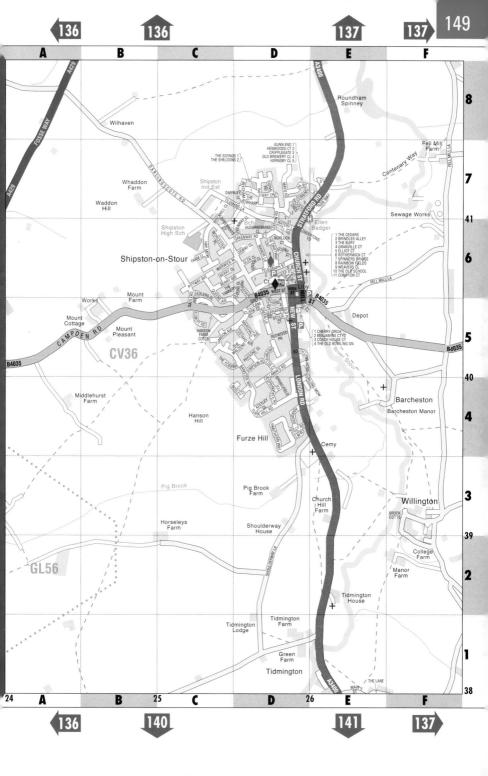

A B C D E F

FOSSE WAY
A429

Wilhaven

Roundham
Spinney

A3400

Fell Mill
Farm

FELL MILL LA

Centenary Way

Whaddon
Farm

DARLINGSCOTE RD

Waddon
Hill

GUNN END 1
HENWOODS CT 2
CRIPPLEGATE 3
OLD BREWERY CL 4
HORNSBY CL 5.

THE SIDINGS 1
THE SHELDONS 2.

Shipston
Ind.Est

Sewage Works

STRATFORD RD

Shipston
High Sch

Sch
HUSBANDMANS

Ellen
Badger

1 THE CEDARS
2 BRINDLES ALLEY
3 THE BURY
4 GRANVILLE CT
5 ELLIOT CT
6 ROTHERWICK CT
7 SPINNERS BRIDGE
8 RAINBOW FIELDS
9 WEAVERS CL
10 THE OLD SCHOOL
11 COMPTON CT

GREENWAY RD

Shipston-on-Stour

CHURCH ST

Fell Mill La

B4035

Depot

Works

Mount
Farm

HAY MDW

Mount
Cottage

CAMPDEN RD

Mount
Pleasant

WEST ST

HIGH ST

MILL ST

P

B4035

B4035

River Stour

B4035

CV36

NEW ST

P

1 CHERRY ORCH
2 BENJAMINS CTYD
3 COACH HOUSE CT
4 THE OLD BOWLING GN

REDWOOD

PK

Middlehurst
Farm

Hanson
Hill

LONDON RD

Barcheston

Barcheston Manor

Furze Hill

Cemy

Willington

BROOK
COTTS

Pig Brook

Pig Brook
Farm

Church
Hill
Farm

College
Farm

GL56

Horseleys
Farm

SHOLDERWAY LA

Shoulderway
House

Manor
Farm

Tidmington
House

Tidmington
Lodge

Tidmington
Farm

Green
Farm

Tidmington

A3400

MAIN ST

THE LANE

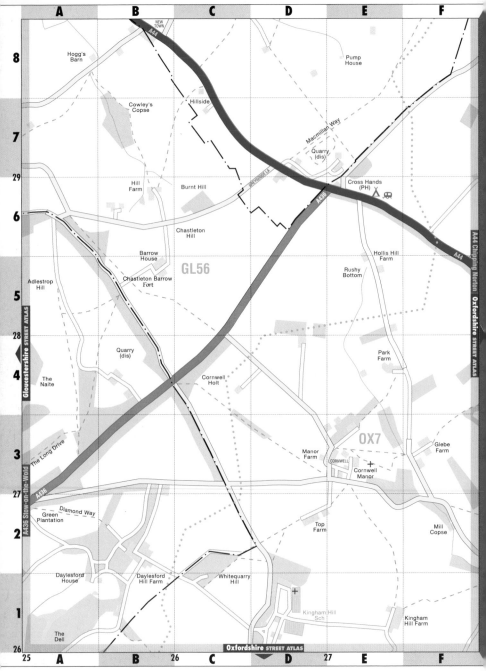

A B C D E F

8

NEW TOWN

Hogg's
Barn

Cowley's
Copse

Hillside

Pump
House

7

Macmillan Way

Quarry
(dis)

29

Hill
Farm

Burnt Hill

Cross Hands
(PH)

6

Chastleton
Hill

Hollis Hill
Farm

Barrow
House

GL56

Rushy
Bottom

Adlestrop
Hill

Chastleton Barrow
Fort

5

28

Quarry
(dis)

Park
Farm

4

The
Naite

Cornwell
Holt

OX7

Glebe
Farm

3

The Long Drive

Manor
Farm

CORNWELL

Cornwell
Manor

27

A436 Stow-on-the-Wold

Diamond Way

Green
Plantation

Top
Farm

Mill
Copse

2

Daylesford
House

Daylesford
Hill Farm

Whitequarry
Hill

1

Kingham Hill
Sch

Kingham
Hill Farm

26

The Dell

25 A 26 B C 26 D 27 E F

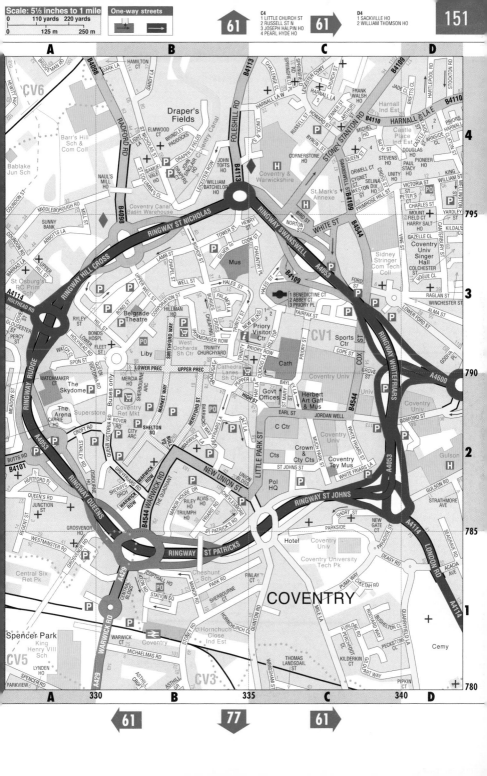

Index

Place name May be abbreviated on the map	**Church Rd** **6** Beckenham BR2..........**53** C6
Location number Present when a number indicates the place's position in a crowded area of mapping	
Locality, town or village Shown when more than one place has the same name	
Postcode district District for the indexed place	
Page and grid square Page number and grid reference for the standard mapping	

Public and commercial buildings are highlighted in magenta   Places of interest are highlighted in blue with a star*

Abbreviations used in the index

Acad	**Academy**	Comm	**Common**	Gd	**Ground**	L	**Leisure**	Prom	**Promenade**
App	**Approach**	Cott	**Cottage**	Gdn	**Garden**	La	**Lane**	Rd	**Road**
Arc	**Arcade**	Cres	**Crescent**	Gn	**Green**	Liby	**Library**	Recn	**Recreation**
Ave	**Avenue**	Cswy	**Causeway**	Gr	**Grove**	Mdw	**Meadow**	Ret	**Retail**
Bglw	**Bungalow**	Ct	**Court**	H	**Hall**	Meml	**Memorial**	Sh	**Shopping**
Bldg	**Building**	Ctr	**Centre**	Ho	**House**	Mkt	**Market**	Sq	**Square**
Bsns, Bus	**Business**	Ctry	**Country**	Hospl	**Hospital**	Mus	**Museum**	St	**Street**
Bvd	**Boulevard**	Cty	**County**	HQ	**Headquarters**	Orch	**Orchard**	Sta	**Station**
Cath	**Cathedral**	Dr	**Drive**	Hts	**Heights**	Pal	**Palace**	Terr	**Terrace**
Cir	**Circus**	Dro	**Drove**	Ind	**Industrial**	Par	**Parade**	TH	**Town Hall**
Cl	**Close**	Ed	**Education**	Inst	**Institute**	Pas	**Passage**	Univ	**University**
Cnr	**Corner**	Emb	**Embankment**	Int	**International**	Pk	**Park**	Wk, Wlk	**Walk**
Coll	**College**	Est	**Estate**	Intc	**Interchange**	Pl	**Place**	Wr	**Water**
Com	**Community**	Ex	**Exhibition**	Junc	**Junction**	Prec	**Precinct**	Yd	**Yard**

Index of localities, towns and villages

A

Abbey Fields..........92 E5
Abbots Morton..........118 A2
Abbot's Salford..........127 E5
Admington..........130 A1
Alcester..........143 D3
Alderman's Green..........50 B3
Alderminster..........130 D3
Alkerton..........138 F5
Allen End..........13 F6
Allesley..........60 B7
Alne End..........119 D6
Alne Hills..........119 D7
Alvecote..........4 D6
Alveston..........121 D3
Amington..........4 B4
Ansley..........27 B3
Ansley Common..........27 F8
Ansty..........51 D4
Appleby Magna..........3 E8
Appleby Parva..........3 D6
Appletree..........134 E4
Ardens Grafton..........119 D1
Arlescote..........133 B3
Armscote..........136 E7
Arrow..........118 F3
Ascott..........142 A5
Ash Green..........49 C6
Ashorne..........122 E4
Ashow..........93 E1
Aspley Heath..........86 D2
Astley..........37 E7
Aston Cantlow..........119 F6
Aston Flamville..........32 E6
Aston le Walls..........134 F5
Aston Magna..........140 A6
Astwood Bank..........102 F1
Atch Lench..........127 B5
Atherstone..........18 E8
Atherstone on Stour..........130 A5
Attleborough..........29 F2
Austrey..........3 B2
Avon Dassett..........133 C5

B

Bacon's End..........33 B4
Badby..........126 F5
Baddesley Clinton..........90 B6
Baddesley Ensor..........11 D1
Baginton..........77 F2
Ballard's Green..........26 D3
Balsall Common..........74 A7
Balsall Street..........73 E6
Balscote..........139 B4

Banbury..........139 E3
Barby..........101 D1
Barby Nortoft..........101 F6
Barcheston..........149 F4
Barford..........122 B7
Barnacle..........51 B6
Barnmoor Green..........113 E3
Barston..........57 B1
Barton-on-the-Heath..........140 F3
Bascote..........115 C2
Bascote Heath..........115 B1
Baxterley..........17 D6
Bedworth..........39 B1
Bedworth Heath..........38 C1
Beechwood..........75 A6
Beechwood Gardens..........76 E8
Belgrave..........9 E8
Bell Green..........62 B8
Bentley..........17 E4
Bentley Bar..........17 D2
Bentley Heath..........71 E5
Benton Green..........58 E3
Berkswell..........58 E3
Bermuda..........39 A8
Bickenhill..........44 D1
Bickmarsh..........128 C4
Bidford-on-Avon..........148 F4
Billesley..........120 A3
Bilton..........99 C7
Binley..........79 E8
Binley Woods..........79 C7
Binton..........120 A1
Birch Acre..........85 D7
Birchley Heath..........17 F2
Birchmoor..........10 E8
Birdingbury..........115 F7
Birmingham..........33 D5
Bishopgate Green..........61 D5
Bishops Itchington..........123 B4
Bishops Tachbrook..........122 E7
Bishopton..........144 D6
Black Bank..........39 A1
Blackdown..........105 F6
Blackwell..........136 E6
Blunt's Green..........112 F7
Blyth End..........24 C2
Bodymoor Heath..........15 A3
Bond End..........53 E3
Botts Green..........25 D5
Bourton on Dunsmore..........97 E2
Bouts..........118 B5
Box Trees..........71 B1
Bradley Green..........11 F5
Bradnock's Marsh..........57 D3

Bramcote..........40 E6
Brandon..........79 F5
Branson's Cross..........86 C2
Braunston..........117 E5
Bretford..........80 D7
Bridge End..........108 F5
Bridge Town..........145 C1
Brinklow..........64 E4
Broad Marston..........128 F1
Broadwell..........116 B4
Brockhurst..........53 F3
Broom..........148 B7
Broughton..........139 E1
Brownshill Green..........48 C2
Brownsover..........83 C8
Bubbenhall..........95 D5
Buckley Green..........113 B6
Budbrooke..........114 F4
Bulkington..........40 B1
Burbage..........32 B6
Burdrop..........142 D8
Burmington..........141 B8
Burton Dassett..........133 B6
Burton Green..........75 C4
Burton Hastings..........41 B8
Butlers Marston..........131 F5

C

Caldecote..........20 A2
Callow Hill..........120 A7
Camp Hill..........28 E5
Canley..........76 C7
Canley Gardens..........76 E8
Carol Green..........74 F7
Carpenter's Hill..........85 F1
Carraway Head..........7 C4
Castle Green..........92 D6
Castle Vale..........22 B3
Catchems Corner..........74 E5
Catherine de Barnes..........56 B6
Cathiron..........66 A1
Cathorpe..........68 E1
Cawston..........99 B8
Chadbury..........127 A1
Chadshunt..........132 C8
Chadwick End..........90 B7
Chapel End..........28 B7
Chapel Fields..........60 E3
Chapel Green..........125 C7
Charingworth..........136 A2
Charlecote..........146 B6
Charwelton..........126 D2
Chelmsley Wood..........33 C2
Cherington..........141 D7
Chessetts Wood..........89 D8
Chesterton..........123 D5

Chesterton Green..........123 C5
Cheswick Green..........70 E4
Cheylesmore..........77 E7
Chilvers Coton..........29 A1
Chipping Campden..........135 B2
Chipping Warden..........134 F3
Church Charwelton..........126 E2
Church End Coleshill..........25 C2
 Coventry..........62 C4
 Hook Norton..........142 A2
 Nuneaton..........27 A5
Church Lawford..........81 B5
Church Lench..........127 A6
Churchover..........67 C6
Cladswell..........118 C5
Clarke's Green..........112 B4
Clattercote..........134 B3
Claverdon..........113 F3
Claybrooke Magna..........43 D6
Claybrooke Parva..........43 F4
Claydon..........134 B5
Cleeve Prior..........128 A4
Cliff..........9 C1
Cliff Hill..........108 F8
Clifford Chambers..........129 F6
Clifton upon Dunsmore..........84 A6
 Coalpit Field..........28 D1
Cock Bevington..........127 D7
Cole End..........33 E8
Coleshill..........23 F2
Coleshill Heath..........44 C8
Collycroft..........39 A5
Combrook..........131 E6
Cookhill..........118 D5
Copston Magna..........42 C5
Copt Green..........113 D8
Copt Heath..........72 B8
Corley..........48 B7
Corley Ash..........48 A8
Corley Moor..........47 E6
Cornets End..........58 B6
Cornwell..........150 E3
Cosford..........66 F3
Coughton..........118 F7
Coundon..........60 F6
Coundon Green..........60 E8
Coventry..........151 C1
Cowpasture..........142 B5
Crabbs Cross..........102 E6
Crackley..........93 B7
Cranhill..........128 E8
Crimscote..........130 D2
Cropredy..........134 C1
Cross Green..........124 A4
Cubbington..........106 D6
Curdworth..........23 B6

D

Dadlington..........21 F8
Dagtail End..........102 E3
Danzey Green..........112 E8
Darley Green..........89 B8
Darlingscott..........136 D5
Daventry..........117 F1
Dean's Green..........112 F7
Deppers Bridge..........124 B6
Devitts Green..........26 C1
Dickens Heath..........70 B6
Dordon..........10 F6
Dorridge..........71 E3
Dorsington..........128 F4
Dosthill..........9 C5
Drakes Cross..........69 A6
Draper's Fields..........151 B4
Draycote..........116 A8
Drayton Banbury..........139 E4
 Stratford-upon-Avon..........120 C2
Drayton Bassett..........8 D5
Duke End..........34 D5
Dunchurch..........99 D3
Dunnington..........127 E8
Dunsmore..........84 C6

E

Earlsdon..........61 A1
Earlswood..........70 B1
Easenhall..........65 E3
Eastcote..........58 C3
East End..........142 E4
Eastern Hill..........102 F3
Eathorpe..........115 B8
Eaves Green..........46 F2
Ebrington..........135 F3
Edgehill..........132 F2
Edge Hill..........10 C2
Edgiock..........118 B7
Edingale..........61 F8
Edstone..........120 D8
Emscote..........109 B8
Epwell..........138 D3
Ettington..........131 B4
Exhall Alcester..........119 C2
 Bedworth..........50 B7

F

Falcon Lodge..........13 A6
Farnborough..........133 F4
Fazeley..........8 F8
Fen End..........73 E3

Fenny Compton 133 D7
Fenny Drayton 20 A6
Fillongley 36 E3
Finham 77 C3
Finwood 113 F7
Five Ways 114 C8
Flecknoe 117 C2
Flint's Green 59 B5
Foleshill 50 A2
Fordbridge 33 A3
Forshaw Heath 86 C7
Foul End 16 C2
Four Ashes 71 D3
Four Oaks 58 C6
Foxford 50 A5
Frankton 97 C1
Freasley 10 C4
Fulford Heath 69 D2
Fulready 131 C1
Furnace End 25 E4
Furze Hill 149 D4

G
Galley Common 27 E5
Gaydon 123 E1
Gibbet Hill 76 E2
Gilbert's Green 86 E3
Gilson 23 E1
Goodyers End 49 D8
Gosford Green 61 F2
Grandborough 116 E5
Great Alne 119 E6
Great Heath 61 E6
Great Rollright 142 B1
Great Wolford 140 F5
Green End 36 A2
Greenlands 103 A8
Green Lane Coventry 77 B5
  Redditch 103 C6
Grendon 11 D3
Grendon Common 11 C2
Griff 39 B6
Grimes Hill 69 B4
Groom's Hill 118 A1
Grove End
  Shipston-on-Stour 137 E2
  Sutton Coldfield 13 F3
Gun Hill 36 F7
Guy's Cliffe 105 A2

H
Halford 137 A8
Hall End 10 F5
Hall Green 50 A3
Hampton-in-Arden 57 B8
Hampton Lucy 121 F4
Hampton Magna 114 F4
Hampton on the Hill 114 F3
Hanwell 139 F6
Harborough Magna 66 B4
Harborough Parva 66 B2
Harbury 123 E7
Hartshill 19 A1
Hartshill Green 19 A2
Harvest Hill 47 E2
Harvington 127 C4
Haseley 114 D6
Haseley Green 114 D8
Haseley Knob 91 B3
Haselor 119 E4
Hatton 114 E6
Hawkesbury 50 C5
Hawkes End 48 B2
Headless Cross 102 D8
Heath 99 C4
Heathcote 109 D3
Heath End 28 E2
Heath Green 85 F3
Hellidon 126 B5
Henley Green 62 D8
Henley-in-Arden 105 C5
Hidcote Boyce 135 D5
Higham on the Hill 21 B3
High Cross Claverdon 113 F6
  Claybrooke Magna 43 A6
Hill 116 B6
Hillfield 71 C7
Hillfields 61 E4
Hillmorton 101 B8
Hill Top New Arley 27 B1
  Nuneaton 29 C1
Hill Wootton 105 C6
Hinckley 31 B8
Hockley Coventry 59 C4
  Tamworth 9 E5
Hockley Heath 88 D6
Hoggrill's End 24 E4
Holberrow Green 118 A6
Holbrooks 49 C3
Hollyberry End 47 C4
Hollyhurst 50 F8
Hollywood 69 B8
Holywell 113 F5
Honiley 91 D5
Honington 137 A5
Hook Norton 142 D4
Hopsford 52 C5
Horeston Grange 29 F5
Horley 139 D6
Hornton 139 B8
Hungerfield 65 D2
Hunningham 107 F5
Hunt End 102 C5
Hunts Green 14 C7

Hurley 16 C4

I
Idlicote 137 C7
Illshaw Heath 70 E1
Ilmington 136 B6
Ingon 145 D7
Iron Cross 127 E7

K
Kemps Green 88 A1
Kenilworth 93 D5
Keresley 48 F5
Keresley Newlands 49 B6
Kineton 132 C6
Kingsbury 15 E5
King's Coughton 143 A7
Kingshurst 33 A5
King's Newnham 81 C7
Kingswood 89 D3
Kingswood Brook 89 E3
Kinwalsey 46 F7
Kinwarton 143 E5
Kitebrook 140 E2
Kite Green 113 C5
Kites Hardwick 116 C7
Kixley Wharf 72 D7
Knightcote 123 B6
Knighton 118 B3
Knowle 72 B6
Knowle Fields 118 C4
Knowle Grove 72 B3

L
Ladbroke 124 D5
Ladyes Hills 93 A7
Langley 113 E2
Langley Green 113 F1
Lapworth 88 E3
Lark Stoke 135 F6
Lawford Heath 98 C7
Lea Marston 24 A8
Leamington Hastings 116 B6
Leek Wootton 104 F7
Lenchwick 127 A2
Lighthorne 123 B2
Lighthorne Heath 123 C2
Lillington 106 C3
Lime Tree Park 60 C8
Little Alne 119 F8
Little Braunston 117 E5
Little Britain 119 D1
Little Compton 141 A1
Little Heath 49 F1
Little Kineton 132 B5
Little Lawford 81 F7
Little Morrell 122 F3
Little Orton 6 F8
Little Packington 45 C6
Little Rollright 141 D1
Little Shrewley 114 C6
Little Walton 54 E3
Little Warton 5 F3
Little Wolford 141 A6
Littlewood Green 103 D2
Littleworth 135 A2
Lodge Green 46 E3
Longbridge 108 C2
Long Compton 141 C3
Longford 49 F4
Long Itchington 115 E4
Long Lawford 82 A4
Long Marston 129 B3
Lower Boddington 134 E7
Lower Brailes 137 F2
Lower Catesby 126 B6
Lower Eastern Green 60 A3
Lower Green 117 A7
Lower Lemington 136 D8
Lower Norton 114 D2
Lower Quinton 129 D2
Lower Shuckburgh 116 F1
Lower Stoke 62 A1
Lower Tysoe 138 C8
Lowsonford 113 E6
Loxley 130 F8
Luddington 129 C7
Lye Green 113 F4

Major's Green 69 D8
Mancetter 19 A6
Manor House 50 C2
Mappleborough Green 112 A4
Market End 38 D2
Marlcliff 148 D2
Marston Kingsbury 15 B3
  Wolston 80 B4
Marston Doles 125 C5
Marston Green 44 A8
Marston Jabbett 39 E5
Marton 119 C1
Maxstoke 35 B2
Meer End 74 D1
Meriden 46 D1
Mickleton 135 C6
Middle Bickenhill 45 A3
Middle Littleton 127 F1
Middle Stoke 62 A3

Middleton 8 A1
Middletown 103 D1
Middle Tysoe 138 C7
Mile Oak 8 B8
Mill End 93 A6
Milverton 105 D2
Minworth 22 C5
Minworth Greaves 22 D6
Mollington 134 A2
Monks Kirby 53 F2
Monks Park 49 C1
Monkspath 71 B5
Monkspath Street 70 E6
Monwode Lea 26 B3
Moreton Hill 122 F2
Moreton-in-Marsh 140 B3
Moreton Morrell 122 F3
Moreton Paddox 122 F1
Morton Bagot 112 D3
Morton Spirt 118 C1
Mount Pleasant Bedworth 39 B3
  Coventry 63 B8
Mousley End 114 B8

N
Napton on the Hill 125 C8
Neal's Green 49 D5
Nebsworth 135 F5
Nethercote 117 B3
Nether Whitacre 25 A6
New Arley 37 A8
New Bilton 82 E3
Newbold on Avon 82 C7
Newbold-on-Stour 130 E1
Newbold Pacey 122 D4
New End Alcester 119 C7
  Redditch 118 C7
Newhall Green 36 A1
Newnham 120 B7
Newton 68 A1
Newton Regis 2 D4
No Man's Heath 2 F6
Northend 133 B7
North Littleton 128 A2
North Newington 139 D2
Norton 127 B2
Norton Green 72 B2
Norton Lindsey 114 C2
Nuneaton 29 C6
Nuthurst 88 C4

O
Oakenshaw 102 E6
Offchurch 111 C8
Offenham 127 D1
Old Arley 26 E2
Oldberrow 112 D4
Oldbury 18 E2
Old Milverton 105 B3
Oldwich Lane 73 C1
Onley 100 C2
Orton-on-the-Hill 6 D4
Over Green 33 C8
Overslade 99 E8
Over Whitacre 25 E2
Oxhill 137 F8

P
Packmores 108 E8
Packwood 89 A7
Packwood Gullet 71 E1
Pailton 66 A8
Paradise 61 F6
Park Farm 103 C8
Park Hill 93 C6
Pathlow 120 D5
Paxford 135 E1
Pebworth 128 F1
Piccadilly 15 F8
Pickford 59 E8
Pickford Green 59 C7
Pillerton Hersey 131 E3
Pillerton Priors 131 D2
Pinket's Booth 59 C8
Pinley 78 B7
Pinley Gdns 78 A8
Pinley Green 114 B5
Pinwall 12 D5
Plough Hill 28 A6
Polesworth 5 B1
Portway 86 A5
Potter's Green 50 E1
Preston Bagot 113 D5
Preston Fields 113 D5
Preston Green 113 C4
Preston on Stour 130 A4
Princethorpe 96 E2
Priors Hardwick 125 D3
Priors Marston 125 F4

Q
Quarry Hill 10 A7

R
Radford 61 B7
Radford Hill 111 B4
Radford Semele 110 E5
Radway 132 F3

Rainsbrook 100 C6
Ratley 133 A2
Redditch 102 E8
Red Hill 120 A3
Reeves Green 75 A8
Ridge Lane 18 B3
Robinson's End 27 F3
Rotten Row 72 A2
Rowington 114 A8
Rowington Green 90 A1
Rowley's Green 49 F3
Royal Leamington Spa 109 C5
Rugby 83 B1
Rumbush 69 E3
Rushbrook 86 D3
Ryton 40 D2
Ryton-on-Dunsmore 79 B2

S
St Helena 11 A8
St Nicolas Park 30 A7
Salford Priors 127 F6
Salter Street 70 D2
Sambourne 118 D8
Sawbridge 117 A4
Scotland End 142 C4
Seckington 2 A3
Shawell 68 D5
Shelfield 112 E1
Shelfield Green 119 E8
Shelford 41 C6
Shenington 138 F5
Sherbourne 121 F8
Sheriff's Lench 127 A4
Shilton 51 F5
Shipston-on-Stour 149 B6
Shirley Heath 70 C7
Shottery 144 C2
Shotteswell 139 E8
Shrewley 114 B6
Shurnock 118 A7
Shustoke 24 F2
Shutford 139 A3
Shuttington 4 F7
Sibford Ferris 142 D7
Sibford Gower 142 D8
Sketchley 31 C6
Sketchley Hill 31 E7
Smockington 42 D8
Snitterfield 121 B6
Solihull 71 B7
Southam 147 B4
South Littleton 127 F1
Southrop 142 D3
Spencer Park 151 A1
Spernal 112 A1
Spernal Ash 103 F1
Spon End 61 A3
Springfield 39 C2
Stareton 94 D3
Staverton 126 D7
Stivichall 77 D5
Stockingford 28 C3
Stockton 147 E8
Stoke 62 C2
Stoke Aldermoor 78 B8
Stoke End 13 F7
Stoke Golding 21 E8
Stoke Heath 62 A6
Stoke Park 62 A2
Stonebridge 45 D3
Stoneleigh 94 B6
Stoneton 125 C1
Stourton 141 D7
Stourton Hill 141 E6
Stratford-upon-Avon 145 B3
Street Ashton 53 E1
Stretton-on-Dunsmore 97 A5
Stretton on Fosse 136 B1
Stretton under Fosse 65 C8
Studley 103 F4
Studley Common 103 C4
Sutton Coldfield 13 B3
Sutton-under-Brailes 141 E8
Swalcliffe 142 F8
Swerford 142 F1
Sydenham 110 D5

Tollbar End 78 C4
Tomlow 116 B2
Tredington 136 E6
Trueman's Heath 69 C7
Turner's Green 113 F8
Two Gates 9 D8
Twyford 127 B1

U
Ufton 111 F1
Ullenhall 112 D6
Upper Boddington 134 D8
Upper Brailes 137 E2
Upper Catesby 126 C6
Upper Eastern Green 59 D4
Upper Quinton 129 D1
Upper Stoke 62 B4
Upper Tysoe 138 B6
Upton 119 E4

W
Walcote 119 F5
Walkwood 102 B6
Wall Hill 48 A4
Walsal End 57 A3
Walsgrave on Sowe 63 B7
Walton 131 C8
Wapping 103 E5
Wardington 134 F1
Waring's Green 70 D1
Warmington 133 D2
Warton 5 E4
Warwick 108 E7
Washford 103 E7
Wasperton 122 A5
Water Orton 23 C3
Weavers Hill 102 C4
Weddington 29 D7
Weethley 118 D2
Weethley Bank 118 D1
Weethley Gate 118 D1
Welford-on-Avon 129 B6
Wellesbourne 146 D3
Westington 135 A1
Weston in Arden 40 A3
Weston-on-Avon 129 B6
Weston under Wetherley 107 C8
Westwood Gardens 76 D8
Westwood Heath 75 E6
Whatcote 137 D7
Whateley 9 F3
Whichford 141 F5
Whitacre Fields 25 E5
Whitacre Heath 24 D6
Whitemoor 93 B5
Whitemore Park 49 C1
White Stitch 46 C3
Whitestone 40 B7
Whitlock's End 69 E6
Whitnash 110 C3
Whittington 12 B3
Whittleford 28 C5
Whoberley 60 D2
Wibtoft 43 B4
Wigston Parva 42 F8
Willenhall 78 D6
Willey 54 E6
Willington 149 F3
Willoughby 117 B6
Wilmcote 120 C4
Wilnecote 9 F8
Wimpstone 130 B3
Winderton 138 A3
Windy Arbour 93 B3
Wirehill 103 B5
Wishaw 14 B2
Witherley 19 B7
Withybrook 52 F5
Wixford 119 B1
Wolfhamcote 117 E4
Wolston 80 B4
Wolverton 114 B1
Wolvey 41 D4
Wolvey Heath 41 E5
Wood Bevington 127 D8
Wood End Coventry 50 C1
  Fillongley 37 A4
  Nuneaton 10 C1
  Tanworth-in-Arden 86 F7
Woodloes Park 104 D2
Woodrow 103 B7
Woodshires Green 49 E5
Woodway Park 62 E8
Woolscott 116 F6
Wootton Green 58 A1
Wootton Wawen 113 B1
Wormleighton 134 A8
Wroxall 90 E3
Wroxton 139 D5
Wyken 62 D5
Wyken Green 62 C6
Wykin 21 F4
Wythall 69 B3

Y
Yew Green 114 D5
Yew Tree 74 A6

154 1st – Ard

1st Ave GL56 ....140 B4
2nd Ave GL56 ....140 B4
3rd Ave GL56 ....140 B3
5 Houses The CV23 ....67 C6
5th Ave GL56 ....140 C4
6th Ave GL56 ....140 B4
7th Ave GL56 ....140 B3
8th Ave GL56 ....140 B3

A

Abberley B77 ....4 C2
Abberton Gr B90 ....71 B7
Abberton Way CV4........76 E3
Abbey CE Sch CV11.......29 B5
Abbey Cl
  Alcester B49 ....143 A5
  Southam CV47 ....147 B3
Abbey Ct
  Coventry CV1..........151 C3
  Coventry,Pinley CV3....78 B6
Abbeydale Cl CV3 ....62 F2
Abbey End CV8 ....92 F4
Abbeyfields Dr B80 ....103 E6
Abbey Gate CV1..........29 C4
Abbey Gate Sh Ctr CV11..29 C4
Abbey Gn CV8 ....29 B5
Abbey Green Ct B78 ....5 A1
Abbey Hill CV8 ....92 F5
Abbey Ind Est CV2 ....62 F5
Abbey La CV47...........147 B3
Abbey Mews B49 ....143 B3
Abbey Rd CV3 ....78 A6
Abbey St
  Nuneaton CV11 ....29 B5
  Rugby CV21 ....83 C4
Abbey The CV8 ....92 F5
Abbey View B78 ....11 B8
Abbey Way CV3 ....77 F6
Abbotsbury Cl CV2......63 A4
Abbotsbury Way CV11...39 F7
Abbots Cl B93 ....72 A7
Abbots Farm Jun & Inf Schs
  CV21 ....83 F1
Abbotsford Rd CV11 ....29 E1
Abbotsford Rd CV8 .....92 F6
Abbots Way CV34 ......108 D6
Abbots Wlk CV8 ....80 B4
Abbots Wood Cl B98...112 A6
Abbots Gn LE10..........31 F5
Abbotts La CV1 ....151 A3
Abbotts St 4 CV31 ....109 F7
Abbotts Way CV21 ......83 F2
Abbotts Wlk CV3 ....79 C7
Abeles Way CV9 ....12 C2
Abelia B77 ....4 A3
Abercorn Rd CV5 ....60 E2
Aberdeen Cl CV5 ....60 A5
Aberdeen Rd CV11........29 E1
Aberfoyle Rd CV35 .....132 D4
Abergavenny Wlk CV3...78 F6
Abingdon Way
  Birmingham B35 ....22 A3
  Nuneaton CV11 ....29 F7
Ab Lench Rd WR11......127 A6
Abu Sultan Rd CV47 ...132 F5
Acacia Ave CV1..........61 E3
Acacia Ct CV6 ....60 E5
Acacia Gr CV21 ....83 A4
Acacia Rd
  Nuneaton CV10 ....28 E5
  Royal Leamington Spa
    CV32 ....105 D1
Achal Cl CV6 ....49 F2
Achilles Cl CV34 ....109 E4
Achilles Rd CV6 ....62 A7
Achray Cotts CV9 ....97 E1
Acklam Gdns B95 ......113 B2
Acorn Cl
  Bedworth CV12 ....49 C8
  Stoneleigh CV8 ....94 B7
Acorn Ct
  1 Royal Leamington Spa
    CV32 ....106 A2
  Coventry CV2 ....62 C2
Acorn Dr CV22............82 B1
Acorn St CV3 ....78 B8
Acre Cl CV31 ....110 A4
Acre Ditch OX15 ....142 D8
Acton Ho CV4 ....59 F3
Adam Rd 1 CV6 ....61 F7
Adams St CV21 ....82 C2
Adams Way B49 ....143 B5
Adare Dr CV3.............77 C8
Adcock Dr CV8 ....93 B5
Addenbrooke Rd CV7...49 A6
Adderley St CV1..........61 E4
Addingham Cl 2 CV34..104 E1
Addison Cl CV10..........28 A5
Addison Dr 4 CV37....130 B8
Addison Rd B46 ....23 B3
Addison Rd
  Coventry CV6...........61 A8
  Rugby CV22 ....82 D2
Adelaide Ct 3 CV12 ....39 A2
Adelaide Rd CV31,CV32..109 E8
Adelaide St CV1 ....151 D4

Adkins Croft CV7 ....36 E3
Adkinson Ave CV22 .....99 C4
Admington Dr CV35....114 F5
Admington La CV36....135 E7
Admiral Gdns CV8 ......93 C6
Admirals Way CV11......40 E6
Adrians' Cl CV9 ....18 F6
Adrians Ct 6 CV37 ....144 C1
Advanced Tech Unit CV4..76 C6
Agincourt Rd CV3.......77 E7
Aikman Gn CV23........116 F5
Ainsbury Rd CV5.........76 E8
Ainsdale Cl CV6 ....50 B4
Aintree Cl
  Bedworth CV12 ....39 B4
  Coventry CV6 ....61 E5
Aintree Dr CV32 ....106 C3
Aintree Rd CV37 ....144 D1
Airport Way B26 ....44 C3
Ajax Cl CV21.............83 C6
Akon Ho CV6 ....48 F2
Alan Bray Cl LE10......30 D7
Alandale Ave CV5.......59 E4
Alandale Ct CV12 ....40 C4
Alan Higgs Way CV4 ...75 C8
Alauna Ave B49.........143 C5
Albany Ct CV1 ....61 A2
Albany Rd
  Coventry CV5...........61 A1
  Stratford-u-A CV37 ...144 F2
Albany Terr CV32 .....105 E1
Albert Bean Cl CV31 ..110 A4
Albert Cl B80 ....103 E4
Albert Cres CV6 ....49 B3
Albert Fearn Gdns CV6...49 F1
Albert Rd
  Allesley CV5.............59 A8
  Fazeley B78 ....9 A8
Albert Sq CV21 ....83 B3
Albert St
  Coventry CV1...........61 E4
  Nuneaton CV10 ....28 E3
  Royal Leamington Spa
    CV32 ....105 C1
  Rugby CV21 ....83 B3
  Warwick CV34 ....108 D7
Albion Cotts B46 ....23 B3
Albion Ct CV11 ....29 D3
Albion Ind Est CV6.......61 B5
Albion St CV8 ....93 A5
Albion Terr
  Broom B50..............148 C7
  Water Orton B46.......23 B3
Albrighton Wlk CV10 ...30 A2
Albury Rd B80 ....103 E4
Alcester Gram Sch B49..143 B4
Alcester Heath B49....118 E6
Alcester High Sch Tech Coll
  B49. ....143 D5
Alcester Highway B98..102 F8
Alcester Hospl B49 ....143 C4
Alcester Rd
  Hollywood B47..........69 A8
  Portway B47,B48........86 B3
  Stratford-u-A CV37 ...144 C3
  Studley B80 ....103 E3
  Wootton Wawen B95...113 A1
Alcocks Rd B49 ....143 D4
Alcott Cl B93 ....71 F2
Alcuin Ct CV8 ....93 A6
Aldbourne Rd CV1.......61 C5
Aldbury Rise CV5........60 C4
Alderbrooke Dr CV11...30 A1
Alder Carr Cl B98......102 F8
Alder Cl B47.............69 B6
Alder Ct CV9 ....12 D1
Alder Dr B37 ....33 B1
Alderhanger La B94,B98..112 A8
Alder Ho 12 CV34 .....109 D8
Alder La CV7 ....74 C5
Alderman Callow Sch & Com
  Coll CV4 ....76 A6
Alderman Gee Hall CV12..50 C3
Alderman's Green Com Prim
  Sch CV2 ....50 C3
Alderman's Green Ind Est
  CV2 ....50 D2
Alderman's Green Rd CV2..50 B3
Alderman Smith Sch
  CV10 ....28 D2
Alderman Way CV33...107 D7
Alder Meadow Cl CV6...49 D4
Aldermill Bsns Pk CV9..12 D3
Alderminster Gr CV35..114 F5
Alderminster Rd
  Coventry CV5...........60 A4
  Solihull B91 ....71 C8
Aldermoor Farm Prim Sch
  CV3 ....78 B8
Aldermoor La CV3 ......62 A1
Alderney Cl
  Bramcote CV11.........40 F6
  Coventry CV6 ....49 B2
Alder Rd CV6 ....50 A2
Alders Dr B98 ....112 A6
Aldersgate
  Kingsbury B78 ....15 D7
  Nuneaton CV11 ....29 C3
Alders La CV10 ....28 A7

Alders The CV12 ....38 E2
Alderton Mews 10 CV31..110 C6
Aldrich Ave CV4 ....75 C7
Aldridge Cl B78 ....10 F8
Aldridge Rd LE10 ....31 D6
Aldrin Way CV4..........76 D5
Aldwick Cl CV32 ....106 A4
Alesworth Dr LE10......31 F4
Alexander Ct 1 CV34..108 F7
Alexander Rd CV12 .....39 C3
Alexandra Ct
  5 Rugby CV21 ....83 B3
  Atherstone CV9 ....18 E8
  Kenilworth CV8..........93 A4
Alexandra Rd
  Coventry CV1...........61 F4
  Royal Leamington Spa
    CV31..................110 B6
  Rugby CV21 ....83 B4
Alexandra St CV11 .....29 A4
Alexandra Terr CV6 ....49 E2
Alexandra Wlk 7 CV21..83 B3
Algate Cl CV6 ....49 C3
Alice Arnold Ho 1 CV2..50 B7
Alice Cl CV12 ....38 F1
Alice Stevens Sch CV3..78 A6
Alison Sq CV10 ....50 B4
Alan Rd CV6 ....60 F4
Allans Cl CV23...........84 A5
Allans Dr CV23 ....84 A5
Allans La CV23...........84 A5
Allard Ho CV3 ....78 B6
Allard Way CV3 ....78 C7
Allen Cl B80 ....103 E3
Allendale Ave B80 ....103 E3
Allendale Cres B80 ...103 E3
Allendale Ct B80 .....103 E3
Allens Orch OX17 .....134 F3
Allens Cl CV2 ....62 E2
Allesley Croft CV5 ......60 A6
Allesley Ct CV5...........60 A6
Allesley Hall Dr CV5....60 C5
Allesley Hall Prim Sch
  CV5......................60 B5
Allesley Old Rd CV5....60 D3
Allesley Prim Sch CV5..60 A7
Allesley Rd CV21........82 F6
Alliance Cl CV11 ....29 F3
Alliance Way CV2........62 A5
Allibone Cl CV31 ....110 C6
Allied Cl CV6 ....49 D2
Allimore La B49 ....143 A4
Allitt Gr CV8.............93 B5
All Saints CE Inf Sch
  CV12 ....39 C2
All Saints' CE Jun Sch
  CV34 ....105 A1
All Saints CE Prim Sch
  Bedworth CV12 ....38 C1
  Coventry CV6...........50 B4
Andertons Yd CV36 ....149 D6
Andrew Cl CV31 ....21 D7
Andrews Cl CV8 ....77 F2
Angela Ave CV2..........50 E1
Angel Mews 8 B49.....143 A7
Anglesey Ave B36......33 B6
Anglesey Cl CV5 ....60 B7
Angless Way CV8 ....92 F3
Angus Cl
  Coventry CV5...........60 A4
  Kenilworth CV8.........93 C6
Anker Dr CV23...........82 B5
Ankerside B78 ....5 A3
Anker St CV11 ....29 D3
Anker View B78..........11 A8
Anley Way CV6 ....61 C6
Annandale B77...........4 B1
Annes Cres CV3 ....77 E8
Anne Hathaway's Cott*
  CV37 ....144 C2
Ann Rd B47..............69 A3
Anns La CV23............65 C2
Ansell Dr CV6 ....50 A4
Ansell Way CV34.......108 D7
Ansley Comm CV10 ....28 A7
Ansley Hall CV10.......27 D7
Ansley La CV7 ....26 F3
Ansley Rd CV10 ....27 F8
Anson Cl
  Rugby CV22 ....82 C2
  Wellesbourne CV35....146 C1
Anson Ct B78 ....9 B8
Anson Way CV2 ....62 F8
Anstey Croft B37 ....33 A4
Ansty Rd
  Brinklow CV23 ....64 D5
  Coventry CV2 ....62 F7
Antelope Gdns CV34 ..108 C8
Anthony Way CV2........62 C2

Anton Dr B76............22 A6
Antony Gardner Cres 5
  CV31 ....110 A7
Antrim Cl CV5 ....60 B7
Antrobus Cl CV35 .....114 C5
Apollo Way CV34 ......109 D5
Appian Cl B77 ....9 D7
Appian Way B90 ....70 D4
Applebee Rd LE10 ......31 D6
Applebees Mdw LE10 ..30 D6
Applebees Wlk LE10 ...30 F6
Appleby Cl
  Banbury OX16 ....139 F4
  Great Alne B49 ....119 D6
Appleby Dr B90 ....71 B6
Appleby Hill CV9.........3 B3
Applecross Cl CV4 .....75 F6
Appledore Dr CV5 ......59 F5
Apple Gr CV22...........82 B2
Apple Pie La CV10 .....19 B3
Appletree Cl B91 ....56 A5
Appletree Cotts CV5 ....4 B3
Appletree Ind Est OX17..134 F4
Appletree La
  Aston le W NN11.......134 F5
  Cookhill WR7 ....118 A3
Appletree Rd OX17.....134 F3
Appleyard Cl CV12 .....39 B2
Approach The CV31 ...109 F6
Apsley Gr B93 ....71 F2
Aqua Ho CV32 ....106 A1
Aqua Pl CV21............83 C5
Aragon Dr CV34 ....109 D6
Aragon Ho CV3 ....77 C8
Arboretum The CV4 ....76 D3
Arborfields Cl CV8 ......93 B8
Arbor Way B37 ....33 C1
Arbour Cl
  Kenilworth CV8 ....93 B3
  Mickleton GL55 ....135 B6
  Rugby CV22 ....99 D7
Arbours The CV22 ......89 A7
Arbour Tree La B93 ....89 F7
Arbury Ave
  Bedworth CV12 ....39 A3
  Coventry CV6 ....49 F2
Arbury Banks OX17 ...134 F3
Arbury Cl CV32 ....106 A4
Arbury Ct CV10 ....28 C3
Arbury Garth CV10 .....28 C3
Arbury Hall Park & Gdns*
  CV10 ....78 E8
Arbury Hall Rd B90 ....70 D8
Arbury Rd CV10 ....28 C3
Arbury Wlk B76..........22 D5
Arcade The
  Atherstone CV9 ....18 C4
  Coventry CV3...........78 B5
Archer Ave NN11 ......117 C5
Archer Cl B80 ....103 D4
Archer Rd CV8...........92 E3
Archers Spinney CV21..100 C8
Archery Fields CV34 ..108 F6
Archery Rd
  Meriden CV7 ....46 B1
  Royal Leamington Spa
    CV31 ....109 E8
Arches Bsns Ctr CV21..83 C5
Arches Ind Est CV21....83 C5
Arches Ind Est The CV5..61 A1
Arches La CV21..........83 C5
Arden Ave CV9 ....18 E8
Arden Bldgs B93........71 F5
Arden Bsns Ctr B49...143 B6
Arden Cl
  Balsall Common CV7....74 B7
  Drayton OX15 ....139 E4
  Henley-in-A B95.......113 B4
  Meriden CV7 ....46 C1
  Rugby CV22 ....99 E6
  Warwick CV34 ....105 A1
  Whitnash CV31 ....110 B5
  Wilmcote CV37 ....120 C5
Arden Craft Ctr The B95..119 F8
Arden Croft B46.........23 F1
Arden Ct
  Alcester B49 ....143 B6
  Bishops Wood CV3 .....79 D6
  Hampton-in-A B92......57 A7
  Stratford-u-A CV37 ...144 F3
Ardendale 6 B90........70 D4
Arden Dr
  Dorridge B93...........72 A1
  Sutton Coldfield,Falcon Lodge
    B75...................13 B5
Arden Forest Est CV10..18 B3
Arden Forest Ind Est
  B49. ....143 C6
Arden Forest Inf Sch
  CV12 ....40 B3
Arden Hill Inf Sch CV9..18 E7
Arden Lawn Sch B95...113 A4
Arden Leys B94..........86 D2
Arden Meads B95 ....87 A6
Arden Mews CV37 .....120 C5
Arden Rd
  Alcester B49 ....143 B6
  Bulkington CV12 ....40 C2
  Dorridge B93...........71 F1
  Henley-in-A B95.......113 B4
  Hollywood B47.........69 A7

Arden Rd *continued*
Kenilworth CV8 . . . . .93 B3
Nuneaton CV11 . . . . .30 A1
Tamworth B77 . . . . .9 F5
Arden Sch B93 . . . . .72 B5
Ardens Cl B98 . . . . .112 A5
Arden St
Atherstone CV9 . . . . .18 E7
Coventry CV5 . . . . .76 F8
Stratford-u-A CV37 . . . . . . .144 C3
Arden Vale Rd B93 . . . . . . .72 B7
Arderne Dr B37 . . . . .33 A1
Arena Pk CV6 . . . . .49 F3
Argyle St CV21 . . . . .83 C3
Argyle Way 5 CV31 . . . . . .122 F8
Argyll St CV2 . . . . .62 A3
Ariel Way CV22 . . . . .99 D6
Arkle Dr CV2 . . . . .62 F7
Arkle B77 . . . . .9 D4
Arklet Cl CV10 . . . . .28 C5
Arlescote Cl CV35 . . . . . . .114 F6
Arleston Way B90 . . . . .70 E8
Arley La CV10 . . . . .27 C3
Arley Mews CV32 . . . . . . .105 E1
Arlidge Cres CV8 . . . . .93 C5
Arlington Ave CV32 . . . . . .105 F1
Arlington Ct 2 CV32 . . . . .105 F2
Arlington Mews 5 CV32 . .105 F2
Arlington Way CV11 . . . . . .29 F2
Arlon Ave CV10 . . . . .28 D7
Armarna Dr CV5 . . . . .59 B8
Armfield St CV6 . . . . .62 A8
Armorial Rd CV3 . . . . .77 B7
Armour Cl CV11 . . . . .31 D5
Armscote Dr CV35 . . . . . . .114 E6
Armscote Rd
Blackwell CV36 . . . . .136 E6
Ilmington CV36 . . . . .136 B6
Newbold-on-S CV37 . . . . . .136 E8
Armscott Rd CV2 . . . . .62 C6
Armson Rd CV7 . . . . .39 A1
Armstrong Ave CV3 . . . . . .62 B1
Armstrong Cl
Rugby CV22 . . . . .82 E1
Whitnash CV31 . . . . .110 A2
Armstrong Dr B36 . . . . . . .22 F1
Arno Ho CV3 . . . . .78 B6
Arncliffe Cl CV11 . . . . .30 A1
Arncliffe Way 4 CV34 . . . .104 F1
Arne Rd CV2 . . . . .63 A6
Arnhem Cnr CV3 . . . . .78 D6
Arnold Ave CV3 . . . . .77 C5
Arnold Cl CV22 . . . . .82 A1
Arnold Lodge Sch CV32 . .105 F2
Arnold Rd CV13 . . . . .21 D6
Arnolds La B46 . . . . .34 E3
Arnold St CV21 . . . . .83 B3
Arnold Villas 9 CV21 . . . . .83 B3
Arnside Cl CV1 . . . . .151 D4
Arran Cl CV10 . . . . .29 A3
Arran Dr B77 . . . . .9 F7
Arran Way B36 . . . . .33 B7
Arras Bvd CV35 . . . . .108 A7
Arrow Cl B93 . . . . .72 A6
Arrow Cres B49 . . . . .143 C5
Arrow End WR11 . . . . .128 A2
Arrow La WR11 . . . . .127 F2
Artemis Dr CV34 . . . . .109 E5
Arthingworth Cl CV23 . . . . .62 E1
Arthur Alford Ho CV12 . . . .38 D1
Arthur Rd CV37 . . . . .145 A4
Arthur St
Coventry CV1 . . . . .151 C4
Kenilworth CV8 . . . . .93 A5
Artillery Rd CV11 . . . . .40 F6
Arundel Cl 2 CV34 . . . . . .108 F8
Arundel Pl OX16 . . . . .139 F3
Arundel Rd
Bulkington CV12 . . . . .40 C3
Coventry CV3 . . . . .77 D6
Arundel B77 . . . . .9 C7
Arun Way B76 . . . . .13 A1
Asbury Rd CV7 . . . . .74 B5
Ascot Cl
Bedworth CV12 . . . . .39 B4
Coventry CV3 . . . . .78 C6
Stratford-u-A CV37 . . . . . .144 D1
Ascot Dr B77 . . . . .9 C4
Ascote La B90 . . . . .70 A5
Ascote Way CV47 . . . . . . .147 C3
Ascot Rd CV35 . . . . .132 D3
Ascot Ride CV32 . . . . .106 C3
Ascott Hill CV36 . . . . .142 A5
Ascott Rd CV36 . . . . .141 F5
Asfare Bsns Pk B49 . . . . .143 C5
Ashborough Dr B91 . . . . . .71 C8
Ashbourne Way B90 . . . . . .70 E8
Ashbridge Rd CV5 . . . . . . .60 C4
Ashbrook Cres B91 . . . . . .71 C8
Ashbrook Rise CV10 . . . . . .19 B2
Ashburton Cl LE10 . . . . . . .31 B6
Ashburton La OX15 . . . . . .142 D3
Ashburton Rd CV2 . . . . . . .62 E8
Ashbury Ct B95 . . . . .113 B5
Ashby Cl CV3 . . . . .78 F8
Ashby Ct CV11 . . . . .29 D3
Ashby Rd NN11 . . . . .117 E5
Ash Cl CV35 . . . . .114 C5
Ashcombe Dr CV4 . . . . . . .59 F3
Ash Cres B47 . . . . .85 F8
Ashcroft Cl CV2 . . . . .63 A8
Ashcroft Way CV2 . . . . . . .63 B8
Ash Ct
Balsall Common CV7 . . . . . .74 C5
Rugby CV22 . . . . .99 E2
Ashdale Cl CV3 . . . . .79 E7
Ashdene Gdns CV8 . . . . . .93 B4
Ashdown Cl CV3 . . . . .78 D8

Ashdown Dr CV10 . . . . . . .28 F2
Ash Dr
Hartshill CV10 . . . . .28 A8
Kenilworth CV8 . . . . .93 A4
Ash End House Farm*
B78 . . . . .14 B8
Ash Rd CV10 . . . . .28 B3
Ashfield Ave CV4 . . . . .59 D1
Ashfield Rd CV8 . . . . .93 B4
Ashford Dr CV12 . . . . .39 A3
Ashford Gdns CV31 . . . . .109 F3
Ashford La B94 . . . . .88 B7
Ashford Rd
Hinckley LE10 . . . . .31 B7
Whitnash CV31 . . . . .109 F2
Ashfurlong Cl CV7 . . . . . . .74 B6
Ash Gr CV7 . . . . .49 C7
Ash Green La CV7 . . . . . . .49 C8
Ash Green Mobile Home Pk
CV7 . . . . .49 C7
Ash Green Sch CV7 . . . . . .49 D6
Ash Gr
Bearley CV37 . . . . .120 E7
Newton Regis B79 . . . . .2 F6
Ash Lawn Ho 8 CV31 . . . .110 A7
Ashlawn Rd CV22 . . . . . . .100 C7
Ashlawn's Sch CV22 . . . . .100 D7
Ashlea B78 . . . . .10 F5
Ashleigh Ct CV23 . . . . . . .101 C2
Ashleigh Dr
Nuneaton CV11 . . . . .29 F1
Tamworth B77 . . . . .9 F8
Ashleigh Mews Cotts B76 .23 C6
Ashley Cres CV34 . . . . . . .109 A8
Ashley Way CV7 . . . . .74 B7
Ashman Ave CV23 . . . . . . .82 B5
Ashmead Rd 13 OX16 . . . .139 F5
Ashmore Rd CV6 . . . . .61 B4
Ashmores Cl B97 . . . . . . .102 D5
Ashorne Cl
Coventry CV2 . . . . .50 C2
Redditch B98 . . . . .103 A4
Ashorne Hall Nickelodeon*
CV33 . . . . .122 F5
Ashorne Hill Management
Coll CV33 . . . . .122 E5
Ashow Cl CV8 . . . . .93 B4
Ash Priors Cl CV4 . . . . . . .60 B1
Ashridge Cl CV11 . . . . .39 F8
Ashstead Cl B76 . . . . .22 B6
Ash Tree Ave CV4 . . . . . . .60 A1
Ash Tree Cl CV35 . . . . . . .146 E3
Ash Tree Gr CV7 . . . . .51 E5
Ashurst Cl CV6 . . . . .50 B5
Ash Way NN11 . . . . .117 D5
Ashwood Ave CV6 . . . . . . .60 F5
Ashwood Ct CV21 . . . . . . .82 F3
Ashwood Dr B37 . . . . .33 D3
Ashwood Rd CV10 . . . . . . .28 E5
Aspbury Croft B36 . . . . . . .22 D1
Aspects Park Gate CV37 . . .29 F7
Aspen Cl
Alcester B49 . . . . .143 B5
Coventry CV4 . . . . .59 D1
Aspen Ct B95 . . . . .113 B5
Aspen Dr
Bedworth CV6 . . . . .50 C6
Birmingham B37 . . . . .44 C8
Aspen Gr B47 . . . . .69 B5
Aspens The B78 . . . . .15 C7
Asplen Ct CV8 . . . . .93 C4
Aspley Ct CV35 . . . . .114 F6
Aspley Heath La B94 . . . . .86 D2
Aspley Heath B94 . . . . .86 D2
Assheton Cl CV22 . . . . . . .99 C8
Aster Cl
Hinckley LE10 . . . . .31 E6
Nuneaton CV11 . . . . .30 A1
Aster Way LE10 . . . . .31 D6
Aster Wlk CV10 . . . . .39 A8
Asthill Croft CV3 . . . . .77 C8
Asthill Gr CV3 . . . . .77 C8
Astley Cl
Redditch B98 . . . . .103 A4
Royal Leamington Spa
CV32 . . . . .105 D2
Astley La
Astley CV10 . . . . .37 F6
Bedworth CV12 . . . . .38 C4
Fillongley CV7 . . . . .37 B3
Nuneaton CV10 . . . . .28 B1
Aston Cantlow Rd CV37,
B95 . . . . .120 B5
Aston Flamville Rd LE10 . .32 D7
Aston Hill CV37 . . . . .120 B5
Aston La
Aston Flamville LE10 . . . . .32 D7
Aston Pk Ind Est CV11 . . . .29 B5
Astley Rd
Chipping Campden GL55 . .135 B3
Coventry CV5 . . . . .60 F1
Nuneaton CV11 . . . . .29 B5
Astwood Bank Fst Sch
B96 . . . . .102 E2

Astwood La B96 . . . . .102 C2
Atcheson Cl B80 . . . . .103 E4
Atch Lench Rd WR11 . . . . .127 A6
Athena Dr CV34 . . . . .109 E5
Athena Gdns CV6 . . . . .50 A1
Atherstone La CV9 . . . . . . .17 B5
Atherstone Rd
Appleby Magna DE12 . . . . . .3 E5
Atherstone CV9 . . . . .12 D4
Fenny Drayton CV10,CV13 . .20 A6
Furnace End B46 . . . . .25 F5
Hartshill Green CV10 . . . . . .19 B2
Hurley CV9 . . . . .16 D4
Atherstone St B77,B78 . . . . .9 B8
Atherston Pl CV4 . . . . .76 C6
Atherstone Sta CV9 . . . . . .18 C8
Atherton Rd CV35 . . . . . . .114 C5
Athol Cl CV2 . . . . .63 B4
Atholl Ct CV10 . . . . .28 E2
Atkins Cl CV2 . . . . .63 A6
Atkins Rd CV10 . . . . .31 E7
Atkins Wlk B78 . . . . .11 A8
Atterton La CV9 . . . . .17 A6
Attleborough Fields Ind Est
CV11 . . . . .29 E3
Attleborough La B46 . . . . . .23 A1
Attleborough Rd CV11 . . . . .29 D3
Attoxhall Rd CV2 . . . . .62 E4
Attwood Cres CV2 . . . . . . .62 C7
Atworth Cl B98 . . . . .103 B5
Auckland Dr B36 . . . . .33 B7
Auden Cl CV10 . . . . .27 F4
Augusta Pl CV32 . . . . .109 F8
Augustine Ave B80 . . . . . .103 B2
Augustus Dr B49 . . . . .143 B3
Augustus Ct B49 . . . . .143 B3
Augustus Rd CV1 . . . . .61 F4
Austcliff Cl CV11 . . . . .30 A1
Austcliff Dr B91 . . . . .71 C8
Austen Cl CV10 . . . . .27 F5
Austen Ct CV32 . . . . .106 C5
Austin Croft B36 . . . . .22 E1
Austin Dr
Banbury OX16 . . . . .139 F4
Coventry CV6 . . . . .62 A7
Austin Edwards Dr CV34 . .109 B8
Austin's Way OX15 . . . . . .142 E4
Austin Way NN11 . . . . . . .117 F2
Austrey CE Prim Sch CV9 . .3 B2
Austrey Cl B93 . . . . .72 A6
Austrey La
Newton Regis B79 . . . . .2 E3
No Man's Heath B79 . . . . . .3 A5
No Man's Heath B79 . . . . . .3 A5
Orton-on-t-H CV9 . . . . .6 C6
Austrey Rd
Appleby Magna DE12 . . . . . .3 D5
Warton B79 . . . . .5 E5
Austwick Cl CV34 . . . . . . .104 E1
Auxerre Ave B98 . . . . .103 B8
Auxerre B98 . . . . .103 B8
Avebury Cl CV11 . . . . .29 F2
Aventine Way CV21 . . . . . .82 F7
Avenue Cl B93 . . . . .72 A3
Avenue Farm Ind Est
CV37 . . . . .144 E5
Avenue Farm CV37 . . . . . .144 E5
Avenue Field Ind Est
CV37 . . . . .144 E4
Avenue Ho CV37 . . . . .144 D5
Avenue Rd
Astwood Bank B96 . . . . . .102 E1
Dorridge B93 . . . . .72 A3
Kenilworth CV8 . . . . .92 D6
Nuneaton CV11 . . . . .29 D2
Royal Leamington Spa
CV31 . . . . .109 F7
Rugby CV21 . . . . .82 E4
Stratford-u-A CV37 . . . . . .145 A4
Avenue The
Coventry CV3 . . . . .78 A6
Rowington Green CV35 . . . .90 A1
Stratford-u-A CV37 . . . . . .144 D5
Avery Ct 6 CV34 . . . . . . .108 F7
Aviemore Cl CV10 . . . . .29 A2
Avill B77 . . . . .10 A5
Avocet Cl
Coventry CV2 . . . . .50 B3
Rugby CV23 . . . . .67 C1
Avon Ave CV35 . . . . .138 B6
Avonbank 7 B37 . . . . .145 A3
Avonbank Cl B97 . . . . . . .102 C6
Avonbank Dr CV37 . . . . . .145 A2
Avonbank Paddocks 9
CV37 . . . . .145 A2
Avonbrook Cl CV37 . . . . . .144 D4
Avon Carrow CV47 . . . . . .133 D4
Avon Cl
Barford CV35 . . . . .122 B8
Bulkington CV12 . . . . .40 B6
Ettington CV37 . . . . .131 B3
Avon Cres
Alcester B49 . . . . .143 C5
Stratford-u-A CV37 . . . . . .145 D1
Avon Ct
Kenilworth CV8 . . . . .92 F5
Offenham WR11 . . . . .127 D1
Rugby CV21 . . . . .83 A4
Avondale Rd
Brandon CV8 . . . . .79 F5
Coventry CV5 . . . . .77 A8
Royal Leamington Spa
CV32 . . . . .106 C4

Avon Dassett Rd CV47 . . .133 D6
Avonfields Cl CV37 . . . . . .121 D3
Avon Fields CV37 . . . . . . .131 B3
Avon Ho CV4 . . . . .76 C6
Avonhurst CV37 . . . . .145 E4
Avon Ind Est
Rugby CV21 . . . . .83 C5
Stratford-u-A CV37 . . . . . .144 F4
Avonlea Rise CV32 . . . . . .105 D2
Avon Lodge CV11 . . . . .41 A4
Avonmeadow Cl 8 CV37 .144 F1
Avonmere CV21 . . . . .82 E7
Avon Mill 21 CV37 . . . . . .145 A3
Avon Park Cvn Pk B92 . . . .44 D1
Avon Rd
Coventry CV4 . . . . .76 B6
Kenilworth CV8 . . . . .93 B4
Lighthorne Heath CV33 . . .123 D2
Whitnash CV31 . . . . .110 A5
Avonside CV37 . . . . .129 A7
Avonside CV37 . . . . .145 A1
Avon St
Clifton u D CV23 . . . . .83 E4
Coventry CV2 . . . . .62 A5
Rugby CV21 . . . . .83 A4
Warwick CV34 . . . . .109 A7
Avon B77 . . . . .10 A5
Avon Terr CV8 . . . . .95 C6
Avon Valley Sch CV21 . . . .82 E6
Avon Way CV35 . . . . .138 B6
Avon Wlk CV10 . . . . .31 A8
Avro Way B35 . . . . .22 B2
Awson St CV6 . . . . .61 F6
Axholme Rd CV2 . . . . .62 E4
Axminster Cl CV11 . . . . . . .29 F5
Aylesbury Cl B94 . . . . .88 C6
Aylesbury Rd B94 . . . . .88 D7
Aylesdene Ct CV5 . . . . . . .76 F8
Aylesford Ct 7 CV31 . . . .110 A6
Aylesford Dr B37 . . . . .44 A7
Aylesford Sch & Language
Coll CV34 . . . . .108 C4
Aylesford St
Coventry CV1 . . . . .61 E4
Royal Leamington Spa
CV31 . . . . .110 A6
Aylstone Cl CV37 . . . . . . .129 D2
Aynho Cl CV5 . . . . .60 A3
Aysgarth Cl CV11 . . . . .30 A2
Azalea Cl LE10 . . . . .31 E5
Azalea Dr LE10 . . . . .31 E5
Azalea Wlk LE10 . . . . .31 E5

B

Babbacombe Rd CV3 . . . . .77 D5
Bablake Cl CV6 . . . . .60 F8
Bablake Jun Sch CV1 . . . .151 A4
Bablake Sch CV1 . . . . . . .151 A4
Bachelors Bench CV9 . . . . .18 D7
Back Ends GL55 . . . . .135 B2
Back Hill CV7 . . . . .139 E8
Back La
Birdingbury CV23 . . . . . . .115 F7
Claverdon CV35 . . . . .113 A3
Claybrooke Magna LE17 . . .43 E6
Cleeve Prior WR11 . . . . . .128 A4
Harborough Magna CV23 . . .66 B3
Henley-in-A B95 . . . . .113 B5
Long Compton CV36 . . . . .141 D3
Long Lawford CV23 . . . . . .82 A4
Lower Quinton CV37 . . . . .129 E2
Meriden CV7 . . . . .58 E5
Mickleton GL55 . . . . .135 B6
Middle Tysoe CV35 . . . . . .138 B7
Oxhill CV35 . . . . .137 F8
Pebworth CV37 . . . . .128 F2
Shustoke B46 . . . . .24 F2
Sibford Ferris OX15 . . . . . .142 D8
Solihull B90 . . . . .70 A5
Warwick CV34 . . . . .108 C6
Wolvey LE10 . . . . .42 A3
Backside La OX15 . . . . . . .142 D8
Badbury Cl B80 . . . . .103 D4
Badbury Gdns B80 . . . . . .103 D4
Badby Leys CV22 . . . . .99 F7
Badby Sch NN11 . . . . . . .126 F6
Baddesley Clinton* B93 . .89 F4
Baddesley Cl CV31 . . . . . .110 D6
Badger Brook La B96 . . . .102 D1
Badger Cl B90 . . . . .70 D4
Badger Dr CV6 . . . . .50 A3
Badgers Cres CV4 . . . . . . .59 F1
Badgers Field GL55 . . . . .135 B2
Badgers La CV35 . . . . . . .138 C8
Baffin Cl CV22 . . . . .82 E1
Baginton Fields Sch CV3 .78 C4
Baginton Rd
Birmingham B35 . . . . .22 B4
Coventry CV3 . . . . .77 C5
Bagot Way CV34 . . . . .109 E3
Bagshaw Cl CV8 . . . . .79 A1
Bailey Ave B77 . . . . .9 F5
Bailey Rd CV37 . . . . .129 B1
Bailey's La CV23 . . . . .82 A4
Bakehouse La
Chadwick End B93 . . . . . . .90 B6
Nether Whitacre B46 . . . . .24 F6
Rugby CV21 . . . . .83 A4
Shotteswell OX17 . . . . . . .139 E8
Baker Ave
Royal Leamington Spa
CV31 . . . . .109 F6

Baker Ave *continued*
Stratford-u-A CV37 . . . . . .144 D3
Baker Dr CV35 . . . . .146 C3
Bakers Croft CV9 . . . . .11 C1
Bakers Ct CV9 . . . . .18 D8
Baker's Hill GL55 . . . . . . .135 C5
Baker's La
Coventry CV5 . . . . .60 E2
Dorridge B93 . . . . .72 D1
Swalcliffe OX15 . . . . .142 F8
Bakers Mews B93 . . . . . . .90 B6
Baker St CV6 . . . . .50 B6
Bakers Wlk 1 B77 . . . . .9 F6
Bakewell Cl CV3 . . . . .78 F8
Balcombe Ct CV22 . . . . . .100 E8
Balcombe Rd CV22 . . . . . .100 D8
Balding Cl CV23 . . . . .101 C1
Baldwin Croft CV6 . . . . . . .50 B1
Baldwins La CV35 . . . . . . .138 B6
Balfour Cl LE10 . . . . .31 E7
Ballantine Rd CV6 . . . . . . .61 B6
Ballards Cl CV35 . . . . . . .135 B6
Ballards La CV36 . . . . . . .136 B6
Ballard Wlk B37 . . . . .33 A6
Ballingham Cl CV4 . . . . . . .60 A2
Balliol Rd
Coventry CV2 . . . . .62 C4
Hinckley LE10 . . . . .31 F6
Balmoral Ave
Banbury OX16 . . . . .139 F2
Banbury OX16 . . . . .139 F3
Balmoral Cl CV2 . . . . .62 E6
Balmoral Ct CV10 . . . . . . .28 E5
Balmoral Rd B36 . . . . .33 A7
Balmoral Way CV32 . . . . .106 C3
Balsall Common Prim Sch
CV7 . . . . .74 B5
Balsall St E CV7 . . . . .74 B5
Balsall St B93,CV7 . . . . . . .73 D7
Balthazar Cl CV34 . . . . . .109 E4
Bamburgh Gr CV32 . . . . . .105 E3
Bamburgh B77 . . . . .9 C7
Ban Brook Copse WR11 . .127 E4
Ban Brook Rd WR11 . . . . .127 E6
Banbury Rd
Chipping Warden OX17 . . .134 F3
Ettington CV37 . . . . .131 B3
Kineton CV35 . . . . .132 C5
Ladbroke CV47 . . . . .124 D3
Lighthorne Heath CV35 . . .123 C2
Lower Boddington NN11 . .134 C3
North Newington OX15 . . .139 E2
Shutford OX15 . . . . .139 A3
Southam CV47 . . . . .147 B1
Stratford-u-A CV37 . . . . . .130 D7
Bancroft Pl CV37 . . . . . . .145 A3
Bangley La
Drayton Bassett B78 . . . . . . .7 E6
Drayton Bassett B78 . . . . . . .8 A8
Bangor Ho B37 . . . . .33 B4
Banister Way CV36 . . . . . .149 D4
Bank Cl CV35 . . . . .131 F5
Bank Croft CV31 . . . . .110 C5
Bank Farm Ct CV37 . . . . .128 E1
Bankfield Dr CV32 . . . . . .105 C1
Bank Rd CV9 . . . . .18 E8
Bankside Cl CV3 . . . . .78 A6
Banks Rd CV6 . . . . .61 A5
Bank St CV21 . . . . .83 A3
Bank The
Bidford-on-A B50 . . . . . . .148 D4
Bidford-on-A B50 . . . . . . .148 D5
Lighthorne CV35 . . . . .123 B2
Marlcliff B50 . . . . .148 D2
Stoneleigh CV8 . . . . .94 C6
Bank View CV35 . . . . .131 F5
Banky Mdw LE10 . . . . .32 A7
Banner La CV4 . . . . .59 D2
Banners Ct B97 . . . . .102 C3
Banning Cnr CV37 . . . . . . .129 D2
Banquo App CV34 . . . . . . .109 F3
Bantam Gr CV6 . . . . .49 A3
Bantock Rd CV4 . . . . .59 E2
Barbers La B91 . . . . .56 C6
Barber Wlk CV35 . . . . . . .114 F4
Barbican Rise CV2 . . . . . . .62 E2
Barbourne CV3 B91 . . . . .71 B7
Barbridge Cl CV12 . . . . . . .40 C2
Barbridge Rd CV12 . . . . . . .40 C3
Barby CE Prim Sch CV23 .117 E8
Barby La
Braunston NN11 . . . . .117 E5
Rugby CV22,CV23 . . . . . .101 B4
Barby Rd
Kilsby CV23 . . . . .101 F3
Rugby CV22 . . . . .100 B7
Barcheston Dr CV35 . . . . .114 F6
Barcheston Mews CV37 . . .72 A4
Barcheston Rd B93 . . . . . . .72 A4
Bardeley Cr B77 . . . . .61 C6
Bardon View Rd B78 . . . . . .11 A7
Bardswell Ct
Stratford-u-A CV37 . . . . . .144 F4
Stratford-u-A CV37 . . . . . .145 A3
Bards Wlk 16 CV37 . . . . . .145 A3
Barford App CV31 . . . . . . .110 D6
Barford Cl CV3 . . . . .78 D8
Barford Rd CV8 . . . . .93 B4
Barford St Peter's CE Prim
Sch CV35 . . . . .122 B7

Barham Cl B90 .... 71 A5
Bari Rd CV35 .... 132 E5
Barker's Butts La CV6 .... 61 A4
Barkers' Butts La CV6 .... 61 A5
Barkers La B47 .... 69 A1
Barkus Cl CV47 .... 147 C4
Barle Gr B36 .... 33 A7
Barley Cl
 Henley-in-A B95 .... 113 B4
 Rugby CV21 .... 101 A8
 Sibford Gower OX15 .... 142 D8
Barley Cl CV32 .... 105 F2
Barley Lea Ho CV3 .... 78 B8
Barley Lea The CV3 .... 78 C8
Barlichway B49 .... 143 D4
Barling Way CV10 .... 29 B1
Barlow Cl B78 .... 15 D6
Barlow Rd CV2 .... 50 D2
Barnack Ave CV3 .... 77 B5
Barnack Dr CV34 .... 104 E1
Barnacle La CV12 .... 40 C1
Barnard Cl
 Birmingham B37 .... 33 D1
 Royal Leamington Spa CV32 ... 106 C3
Barnbrook Rd B93 .... 72 A7
Barn Cl
 Clifford Chambers CV37 ..129 F7
 Coventry CV5 .... 60 C5
 Dordon B78 .... 10 F6
 Whitnash CV31 .... 110 B3
Bancroft CV36 .... 141 C3
Barne Cl CV11 .... 40 B7
Barn End Rd B79 .... 5 E3
Barnfield Ave CV5 .... 60 B6
Barn La CV23 .... 96 E1
Barn Leigh Dr CV4 .... 75 D6
Barnsley Cl CV9 .... 18 D7
Barnsley Ct CV6 .... 61 D8
Barnstaple Cl CV5 .... 59 F5
Barnwell Cl CV22 .... 99 C4
Baron's Croft CV3 .... 77 E7
Barons Croft CV10 .... 28 C4
Baron's Field Rd CV3 .... 77 E8
Barpool Rd CV10 .... 28 F4
Barrack Cl B75 .... 13 A6
Barracks Gn CV35 .... 130 F7
Barracks La CV35 .... 91 C2
Barrack St CV34 .... 108 E7
Barracks Way CV1 .... 151 B2
Barra Croft B35 .... 22 B4
Barras Ct CV2 .... 62 A4
Barras Gn CV2 .... 62 A4
Barras La CV1 .... 61 B2
Barrats Hill CV36 .... 141 F5
Bar Rd CV3 .... 77 E8
Barrels Pitch GL55 ..... 135 B2
Barretts La CV7 .... 74 C6
Barrie Cl CV32 .... 145 C1
Barrington Rd CV22 ...... 82 C1
Barr La
 Brinklow CV23 .... 64 F4
 Higham on t H CV13 .... 21 B3
Barrow Cl CV2 .... 63 B6
Barrowfield Ct CV8 ...... 92 F4
Barrowfield La CV8 ...... 92 F4
Barrow Rd CV8 .... 92 F3
Barr's Hill Sch & Com Coll CV1 ... 151 A4
Barry Ho CV2 .... 50 D1
Barsby Cl CV9 .... 18 D7
Barston Cl CV6 .... 50 A2
Barston La
 Balsall Common CV7 ..... 73 D8
 Barston B92 .... 57 C1
 Catherine de B B92 .... 56 B2
 Eastcote B92 .... 56 D3
Bartholomew Ct CV3 ..... 78 A6
Bartleet Rd B98 .... 103 E8
Bartlett Cl
 [3] Warwick CV34 .... 108 F7
 Coventry CV6 .... 49 C2
Barton Cres CV31 ...... 110 C6
Barton Dr B93 .... 72 B4
Barton Fields CV37 ..... 129 A6
Barton Rd
 Bedworth CV12 .... 39 A4
 Coventry CV6 .... 49 F2
 Long Compton CV36 ....141 B4
 Nuneaton CV10 .... 29 C2
 Rugby CV22 .... 99 D8
 Welford-on-A CV37 .... 129 A6
Barton's Mdw CV2 .... 62 B6
Barwell Cl
 Dorridge B93 .... 71 E4
 Royal Leamington Spa CV32 ... 105 F3
Basant Cl CV34 .... 109 A7
Bascote Chase CV47 .... 115 C2
Bascote Rd CV47 ...... 115 C3
Bascote Rise CV47 .... 147 A5
Baseley Way CV6 .... 49 D4
Basford Brook Dr CV6 ... 49 F4
Basildon Wlk [3] CV2 .... 63 A7
Basin Bridge La CV13 ... 21 C4
Bassett Rd CV6 .... 61 A5
Bateman Rd B46 .... 23 F1
Bateman's Acre S [1] CV6 .. 61 A4
Bates Cl B75 .... 22 B8
Bates La B94 .... 86 F1
Bates Rd CV5 .... 76 E8
Bath Pl [3] CV31 .... 109 F7
Bath Rd
 Atherstone CV9 .... 18 E7
 Nuneaton CV11 .... 29 C5

Bath Cl CV1 .... 151 C4
Bath Street Mews [1]
 CV21 .... 83 B3
Bath St
 Royal Leamington Spa CV31 ... 109 F7
 Rugby CV21 .... 83 B3
Bathurst Cl CV22 .... 82 E1
Bathurst Rd CV6 .... 61 A6
Bathway Rd CV3 .... 77 A4
Batsford Cl B98 .... 103 B5
Batsford Rd CV6 .... 60 F4
Battalion Ct CV6 .... 49 A1
Battledown Cl B49 .... 143 E3
Baulk La CV7 .... 58 D1
Bawnmore Ct CV22 ...... 99 D8
Bawnmore Inf Sch CV22 ..99 E2
Bawnmore Pk CV22 ..... 99 E2
Bawnmore Rd CV22 ..... 99 D7
Baxter Cl
 Atherstone CV9 .... 18 E7
 Coventry CV4 .... 60 A2
 Royal Leamington Spa CV32 ... 109 F8
Bayley La CV1 .... 151 C2
Bayliss Ave CV31 ...... 50 A4
Bayton Rd CV7 .... 50 B7
Bayton Road Ind Est CV7 .50 B8
Bayton Way CV7 .... 50 C7
Bay Tree Cl CV2 .... 50 F3
Bay Tree Farm WR11 ... 128 A4
Baywell Cl [7] B90 ..... 71 A7
Bazzard Rd CV11 .... 41 B5
Beacon Cl B49 .... 143 C5
Beacon Rd CV6 .... 49 D3
Beaconsfield Ave CV22 .. 83 A1
Beaconsfield Ct CV11 ... 29 D5
Beaconsfield Rd CV6 .... 62 B2
Beaconsfield St W CV31 . 110 B8
Beaconsfield St CV31 ... 110 B8
Beake Ave CV6 .... 61 B7
Beale Cl
 [10] Bishops Tachbrook CV33 .. 122 F8
 Birmingham B35 .... 22 A2
Beamish Cl CV2 .... 63 A6
Beanacre OX15 .... 142 D3
Beanfield Ave CV3 ...... 76 F4
Bear Cl B95 .... 113 B6
Bearcroft Gdns GL55 ... 135 C6
Bear La B95 .... 113 A5
Bear Lane Cl B78 .... 5 A2
Bearley Croft B90 ...... 70 C8
Bearley Grange CV37 ... 120 E7
Bearley Hall B95 .... 120 D7
Bearley Rd
 Aston Cantlow B95 ..... 120 A7
 Snitterfield CV37 ...... 121 A7
Beaty Dr CV22 .... 82 D2
Beaty's Gdns CV32 .... 106 A4
Beauchamp Ave CV32 ... 105 F1
Beauchamp Cl
 [1] Birmingham B37 .... 33 B2
 Sutton Coldfield B76 ... 22 B7
Beauchamp Ct
 [1] Royal Leamington Spa CV32 ... 105 F1
 Alcester B49 .... 143 A6
Beauchamp Gdns CV34 . 109 B6
Beauchamp Hill CV32 .. 105 E1
Beauchamp Ind Pk B77 ...9 D8
Beauchamp Rd
 Alcester B49 .... 143 C5
 Kenilworth CV8 .... 92 F2
 Royal Leamington Spa CV32 ... 105 F1
 Tamworth B77 .... 9 F5
 Warwick CV34 .... 109 B8
Beaudesert Cl
 Henley-in-A B95 .... 113 B4
 Hollywood B47 .... 69 A6
Beaudesert Ho B95 .... 113 B6
Beaudesert La B95 .... 113 B5
Beaudesert Rd
 Coventry CV5 .... 61 A1
 Hollywood B47 .... 69 A6
Beaufell Cl CV34 ..... 104 E1
Beaufort Ave CV32 .... 106 C5
Beaufort Cl
 Hinckley LE10 .... 31 E4
 Wellesbourne CV35 ... 146 C2
Beaufort Dr CV3 .... 78 F7
Beaulieu Pk CV31 ..... 110 D6
Beaumaris Cl
 Banbury OX16 .... 139 F4
 Coventry CV5 .... 59 F5
Beaumont Ave LE10 .... 31 A7
Beaumont Cl CV47 .... 133 A7
Beaumont Cres CV6 .... 61 A4
Beaumont Ct
 [8] Royal Leamington Spa CV31 ... 110 A6
 [9] Coventry CV6 ..... 61 A4
Beaumont Pl CV11 ..... 29 A4
Beaumont Rd
 Keresley CV7 .... 49 A6
 Nuneaton CV11 .... 29 A4
Beauvevoir Way CV34 .. 109 A8
Beausale Dr B93 .... 72 C7
Beausale La CV35 ..... 114 E7
Beceshore Cl [2] GL56 . 140 E4
Beche Way CV5 .... 60 B5
Beckbury Rd CV2 .... 62 F6

Becket Cl GL56 .... 140 E7
Beckfoot Cl CV21 ...... 83 D8
Beckfoot Dr CV2 .... 50 F1
Beckford Croft B93 ..... 71 F3
Beck's Cl CV47 .... 147 F8
Becks Croft B95 ..... 113 B4
Becks La CV7 .... 47 A5
Beck's La CV47 .... 147 F8
Beconsfield Cl B93 ..... 71 F2
Bedale Rd CV35 ..... 132 D4
Bede Arc [2] CV12 ..... 39 B3
Bede Rd
 Bedworth CV12 .... 39 A4
 Coventry CV6 .... 61 B6
 Nuneaton CV10 .... 28 D3
Bedford Cl [7] OX16 ... 139 F4
Bedford Ho B36 .... 33 B6
Bedford Pl [8] CV32 ... 109 F8
Bedford St
 Coventry CV1 .... 61 A2
 Royal Leamington Spa CV32 ... 109 F8
Bedlam La CV6 .... 49 E2
Bedworth Cl CV12 ...... 40 B2
Bedworth La CV12 ...... 38 D4
Bedworth Rd
 Bedworth CV12 .... 39 F2
 Bulkington CV12 ...... 40 A2
 Coventry CV6,CV7 ..... 50 A5
Bedworth Sta CV12 ...... 39 C2
Beecham Ind Est CV37 . 130 C5
Beecham Rd CV36 ..... 149 D7
Beecham Wlk CV37 .... 144 C4
Beech Ave B37 .... 33 B1
Beech Cl
 Kingsbury B78 .... 15 C7
 Rowington CV35 ..... 114 A8
 Southam CV47 .... 147 A3
 Stratford-u-A CV37 ... 145 C2
Beechcroft
 Bedworth CV12 .... 38 F1
 Long Itchington CV47 . 115 D4
Beechcroft Rd B36 ..... 22 C1
Beech Ct
 Royal Leamington Spa CV34 ... 109 C2
 Rugby CV22 .... 100 F8
 Stratford-u-A CV37 ... 145 B2
Beech Dr
 Kenilworth CV8 .... 93 B5
 Rugby CV22 .... 99 C8
 Thurlaston CV23 ...... 98 F3
Beecher's Keep CV8 ..... 79 F5
Beeches The
 Bedworth CV12 .... 38 E2
 Clifton u D CV23 ...... 83 F5
 Harbury CV33 .... 123 F7
 Hartshill Green CV10 .. 19 B2
 Polesworth B78 .... 11 A8
Beeches Wlk CV37 ..... 145 E4
Beech Gr
 Old Arley CV7 .... 26 E2
 Warwick CV34 .... 105 B1
Beech Hill NN11 ..... 126 B5
Beech Rd
 Coventry CV6 .... 61 B5
 Hollywood B47 .... 69 B6
 Oxhill CV35 .... 137 F8
Beech Tree Ave CV4 ..... 60 B2
Beechtree Pk B50 ..... 148 E6
Beechwood Ave
 Coventry CV5 .... 76 F8
 Hinckley LE10 .... 31 D3
Beechwood Cl B90 ...... 70 D4
Beechwood Croft CV8 ... 92 F2
Beechwood Ct
 Coventry CV5 .... 76 F8
 Rugby CV21 .... 82 F4
Beechwood Rd
 Bedworth CV12 .... 39 D4
 Nuneaton CV10 .... 28 D6
Beehive Hill CV8 .... 92 E7
Beehive La B76 .... 23 C6
Beekes Croft B78 .... 9 A8
Beeston Cl CV3 .... 78 F8
Begonia Cl LE10 .... 31 E5
Begonia Dr LE10 .... 31 E5
Belcony GL56 .... 136 C1
Beldesert Cl B95 ..... 113 B4
Belfry Cl LE10 .... 31 D4
Belgrade Theatre CV1 .. 151 B3
Belgrave Dr CV21 ...... 83 D6
Belgrave Rd
 Coventry CV2 .... 62 E4
 Tamworth B77 .... 9 E8
Belgrave Sq CV2 .... 62 E4
Belgravia Ct B37 .... 33 A5
Bellairs Ave CV12 ...... 38 E1
Bellam Rd CV35 ...... 114 F4
Bellbrooke Cl CV6 ...... 50 B1
Bell Brook CV37 ..... 121 B6
Bell Cl B36 .... 33 B6
Bell Ct CV32 .... 105 F2
Bell Dr CV7 .... 49 E7
Belle Cotts B94 .... 86 B5
Bellemere Rd B92 ...... 57 B6
Belle Vue CV10 .... 28 E3
Belle Vue Terr B92 .... 57 A6
Bellfield B94 .... 87 A2

Bell Green Rd CV6 ...... 62 A8
Bell Hill OX15 .... 142 D4
Bellingham B77 .... 4 D1
Bellington Croft [5] B90 .. 71 A6
Bell La
 Monks Kirby CV23 ..... 53 E2
 Snitterfield CV37 ...... 121 B6
 Stratford-u-A CV37 ... 144 D2
 Studley B80 .... 103 E4
Bell Mead B80 .... 103 E4
Bell's La OX15 .... 142 D3
Bells La OX15 .... 137 E3
Bell St
 Claybrooke Magna LE17 43 E6
 Hornton OX15 .... 139 B7
Bell Tower Mews CV32 . 105 F3
Bellview Way CV6 ...... 50 B1
Bell Wlk CV21 .... 101 A8
Belmont Ct CV32 ..... 106 A4
Belmont Dr CV32 ..... 106 A4
Belmont Mews CV8 ..... 92 F4
Belmont Rd
 Coventry CV6 .... 62 A7
 Rugby CV22 .... 83 A1
 Tamworth B77 .... 9 E7
Belton Cl B94 .... 88 C5
Belvedere Rd CV5 ...... 77 A8
Belvoir B77 .... 9 C7
Benches Furlong CV23 .. 67 D1
Benedictine Ct CV1 ... 151 C3
Benedictine Rd CV3 ..... 77 C8
Benedict Sq CV2 .... 62 C8
Bengrove Cl B98 ..... 103 A7
Benjamins Ctyd CV36 .. 149 D5
Bennet Cl CV13 .... 21 D7
Bennett Ct CV7 .... 74 C8
Bennett Dr CV34 ..... 109 C7
Bennett Pl CV36 ..... 136 B6
Bennetts Hill Bsns Pk WR11 ... 127 E1
Bennetts Hill WR11 .. 127 E1
Bennett's Rd CV7 ..... 48 F4
Bennett's Road N CV7 .. 48 E7
Bennett's Road S CV6 .. 48 F2
Bennett St CV1 .... 61 D5
Bennett Way [9] 130 B8
Bennfield Rd CV21 ..... 83 A3
Benn Rd CV12 .... 40 B2
Benn St CV22 .... 83 C2
Benson Rd
 Coventry CV6 .... 49 A1
 Stratford-u-A CV37 ... 145 A4
Benthall Rd CV6 ...... 49 F2
Bentley Cl
 [2] Banbury OX16 .... 139 F4
 Royal Leamington Spa CV32 ... 106 B3
Bentley Comm CV9 ..... 17 E5
Bentley Ct
 Coventry CV6 .... 49 C4
 Nuneaton CV11 .... 29 A4
Bentley Farm Cl B93 .. 71 E4
Bentley Heath CE Prim Sch B93 ... 71 F5
Bentley La B46 .... 35 C3
Bentley Rd
 Nuneaton CV11 .... 29 A4
Bentree The CV3 ...... 78 B8
Beoley Hall B98 .... 85 C1
Beoley La B98 .... 86 B1
Berenska Dr CV32 .... 106 A2
Beresford Ave CV6 .... 49 E1
Bericote Rd CV32 .... 105 E8
Berkeley Cl
 Banbury OX16 .... 139 F4
 Nuneaton CV11 .... 29 B3
 Redditch B98 .... 112 A6
Berkeley Rd CV8 .... 92 E6
Berkeley Rd N CV5 .... 61 A1
Berkeley Rd S CV5 .... 77 A8
Berkett Rd CV6 .... 49 B2
Berkshire Cl CV10 .... 28 E3
Berkswell CE Prim Sch CV7 ... 58 C3
Berkswell Hall* CV7 .. 58 C3
Berkswell Mus* CV7 ... 58 C3
Berkswell Rd
 Coventry CV6 .... 50 B2
 Meriden CV7 .... 58 C7
Berkswell Sta CV7 .... 74 C8
Berkswell Windmill* CV7 74 D4
Bermuda Bsns Pk CV10 . 39 A7
Bermuda Ind Est CV10 .. 39 B8
Bermuda Rd CV10 ..... 29 A1
Berners Cl CV4 .... 59 E2
Berrills La CV36 ..... 141 D7
Berrington Rd
 Chipping Campden GL55 135 C2
 Nuneaton CV10 .... 28 D7
 Royal Leamington Spa CV31 ... 110 B6
Berrow Cottage Homes B93 ... 72 C6
Berry Ave CV36 .... 149 C6
Berry Cl CV36 .... 149 C6
Berryfields CV7 .... 36 E4
Berryfields CV36,CV37 . 136 C7
Berry Hall La B91 ..... 56 B4
Berry La
 Hollidon NN11 .... 126 B5
 Southam CV47 .... 147 A3
Berry Mdw CV47 ..... 133 E7
Berrymound View B47 .. 69 C7
Berry St CV1 .... 61 E4

Bertie Rd CV6 .... 93 A4
Bertie Terr CV32 ..... 105 E1
Berwick Cl
 Coventry CV5 .... 60 B4
 Warwick CV34 .... 104 E2
Berwick Ho CV8 .... 93 A3
Berwicks La B37 .... 33 B1
Berwood Pk B35 .... 22 A2
Berwyn Ave CV6 .... 49 A1
Berwyn Way CV10 ..... 28 C4
Besbury Cl B93 .... 71 E2
Besford Gr B90 .... 71 B6
Best Ave CV8 .... 93 C7
Beswick Gdns CV22 .... 99 D7
Betjeman Rd [19] CV37 . 130 B8
Bettina Cl CV10 ...... 28 B5
Bettman Cl CV3 .... 77 E6
Bettridge Pl CV35 .... 146 D4
Bevan Ct CV31 .... 77 D7
Beverley Ave CV10 .... 28 B4
Beverley Cl
 Astwood Bank B96 .... 102 C3
 Balsall Common CV7 ... 74 C7
Beverley Rd CV32 .... 105 D1
Beverly Dr CV4 .... 76 D2
Bevington Cres CV6 ... 60 E5
Bexfield Cl CV5 .... 60 A6
Beyer Cl B77 .... 4 B2
Biart Pl CV21 .... 83 D4
Bicester Sq B35 .... 22 B4
Bickenhill Green Ct B92 . 44 C1
Bickenhill La
 Birmingham B37 .... 44 C6
 Birmingham B40 .... 44 D4
 Catherine de B B92 ... 56 C6
Bickenhill Parkway B37 . 44 D6
Bickenhill Rd B92 .... 44 B7
Bickmarsh La B50 .... 148 D1
Bickmarsh Lodge Cotts WR11 ... 128 D2
Bidavon Ind Est B50 .. 148 E6
Biddles Hill B94 ...... 86 C6
Biddulph Terr CV23 .. 97 D1
Bideford Rd CV2 ...... 62 C7
Bidford-on-Avon CE Prim Sch B50 ... 148 D5
Bidford Rd B50 .... 148 C1
Bigbury Cl CV3 .... 77 E5
Biggin Cl B35 .... 22 A3
Biggin Hall Cres CV3 .. 62 B2
Biggin Hall La CV23 .. 98 E2
Bignolds Cl CV47 .... 134 B4
Bigwood Dr B75 .... 13 A5
Bilberry Rd CV2 ...... 50 D2
Bilbury Cl B97 .... 102 C6
Billesden Cl CV3 ..... 78 E8
Billesley La B48 ...... 85 E6
Billesley Rd CV37 .... 120 C4
Billing Rd CV5 .... 60 D3
Billinton Cl CV2 ..... 62 E2
Bills La B90 .... 70 C8
Bilton CE Jun Sch CV22 . 99 D6
Bilton Grange Sch CV22 . 99 E4
Bilton High Sch CV22 .. 99 C4
Bilton Inf Sch CV22 .. 99 F1
Bilton Ind Est CV3 ... 61 F1
Bilton La
 Dunchurch CV22 ...... 99 D4
 Long Lawford CV22,CV23 82 B3
Bilton Rd CV22 .... 82 E2
Binley Ave CV3 .... 78 F7
Binley Bsns Pk CV3 ... 63 A1
Binley Gr CV3 .... 78 F7
Binley Ind Est CV3 ... 79 A8
Binley Rd CV2,CV3 .... 62 D1
Binley Woods Prim Sch CV3 ... 79 E7
Binns Cl CV4 .... 75 F8
Binswood Ave CV32 ... 105 F2
Binswood Cl CV2 ..... 50 D2
Binswood Ct [9] CV32 . 105 F2
Binswood End CV33 ... 123 F7
Binswood Mans [14] CV32 105 F2
Binswood St CV32 .... 105 E1
Binton Bridges Cvn Pk CV37 ... 129 A8
Binton Cl CV37 .... 120 A1
Binton Rd
 Coventry CV2 .... 50 D2
 Welford-on-A CV37 ... 129 A7
Binton View CV37 .... 144 A4
Birbeck Ho B36 .... 33 B6
Birch Abbey B49 ..... 143 B3
Birch Cl
 Bedworth CV12 .... 39 D4
 Coventry CV5 .... 59 E2
 Kingsbury B78 .... 15 D7
Birch Coppice Distribution Ctr B78 ... 10 C1
Birch Croft B37 ...... 33 C1
Birch Cl CV34 .... 109 E2
Birch Dr CV22 .... 82 B2
Birch End B49 .... 143 A2
Birches La CV8 .... 93 B3
Birches The CV12 .... 40 B4
Birchfield Cl CV9 .... 10 C1
Birchfield Rd
 Coventry CV6 .... 60 F8
 Stratford-u-A CV37 ... 145 A5
Birchgrave Cl CV6 .... 62 A7
Birch Gr
 Balsall Common CV7 ... 74 B8
 Birchmoor B78 .... 10 C7
 Wellesbourne CV35 ... 146 C3
Birch Ho B98 .... 102 F8
Birchley Heath Rd CV10 . 17 F1

Birch Meadow Cl CV34...108 D7
Birchmoor Rd B78.......10 F8
Birchtree Rd CV10......28 C6
Birchway Cl CV32......105 C1
Birchwood Ave B78......1 A7
Birchwood Prim Sch B78 .10 F7
Birchwood Rd CV3......79 C7
Birchy Cl B90..........69 F6
Birchy Leasowes La B90 .64 E5
Bird Grove Ct CV1......61 D5
Birdhaven Cl CV33.....123 D2
Birdhope B77...........4 C1
Birdingbury La CV23...115 E8
Birdingbury Rd
 Birdingbury CV23.....115 F8
 Marton CV23.........115 D7
Bird Rd
 Lighthorne Heath CV33 .123 D2
 Royal Leamington Spa
 CV34...............109 D4
Birds Bush Prim Sch B77 ..9 E8
Birds Bush Rd B77......9 F8
Birds La OX15.........138 D3
Bird St CV1...........151 C3

Birkdale Cl
 Coventry CV6..........49 B4
 Nuneaton CV11.........30 A1
Birmingham Bsns Pk B37 .44 E8
Birmingham Int Airport
 B40................44 D4
Birmingham Int Sta B40..44 D4
Birmingham Rd
 Alcester B49.........143 B4
 Alcester,King's Coughton
 B49...............143 A8
 Allesley CV5..........59 E7
 Ansley CV10..........27 B4
 Burton Green CV8......75 A1
 Coleshill B46.........33 E5
 Henley-in-A B95......113 B6
 Kenilworth CV8........92 C8
 Little Packington CV7...45 E3
 Shrewley CV35.......114 D6
 Stoneleigh CV8........94 B6
 Stratford-u-A CV37...144 E5
 Studley B80,B98......103 E7
 Water Orton B46.......23 A3
 Whitacre Heath B46,B76 ..24 C7
 Wilmcote CV37,B95....120 D6
 Wroxall B93,CV35......90 D3
Birstall Dr CV21........83 D6
Birvell Ct CV12........39 D3
Bishop Carpenter CE Prim
 Sch OX15............139 D2
Bishopgate Bsns Pk CV1 ..61 D5
Bishopgate Ind Est CV1 ..61 D5
Bishops Bowl Lakes Water
 Sports Ctr* CV47.....124 A5
Bishops Cl [16] CV33...122 F8
Bishops Cl CV37.........3 A1
Bishops Cl CV37......144 C4
Bishop's Ct B37.......44 E8
Bishop's Gate CV47...124 B5
Bishop's Hill CV35....123 B2
Bishop St CV1.........151 B3
Bishops Itchington Prim Sch
 CV47...............124 B5
Bishop's Tachbrook CE Prim
 Sch CV33............122 F8
Bishop St CV1.........151 B3
Bishopton Cl CV5.......60 B3
Bishopton Hill CV37...144 D8
Bishopton La CV37....144 C5
Bishopton Prim Sch
 CV37...............144 C4
Bishop Ullathorne RC Sch
 CV3.................76 F4
Bishop Wilson CE Prim Sch
 B37.................33 C3
Bishop Wulstan RC Sch
 CV22.................83 A1
Bisset Cres [12] CV31...110 C6
Bitham Hall CV47.....133 D5
Bitham Rd CV33........23 A3
Bixhill La B46..........25 F3
Black-a-Tree Ct CV10...28 F5
Black-A-Tree Rd CV10...28 E4
Blackbades Bvd CV34...108 B4
Black Bank CV7........39 B1
Blackberry Ave B94.....86 C6
Blackberry Cl CV23.....83 D8
Blackberry La
 Coventry,Neal's Green
 CV7...............49 C5
 Coventry,Wyken Green CV2 ..62 A8
Blackbird Croft B36.....33 A7
Blackburn Rd CV6......49 F3
Blackcat Cl B37........33 A3
Blackdown Hall CV32...105 F6
Blackdown Rd B93......72 B6
Blackdown B77.........4 C1
Blackford Cl B95......113 B4
Blackford Hill B95....113 B4
Blackford Rd B90......70 C8
Blackford Way CV35...137 F8
Blackgreaves La B76....14 F1
Black Hall La CV7......36 C4
Black Horse Hill DE12 ..3 F8
Black Horse Rd CV6,CV7 .50 B6
Blackman Way CV21....82 F4
Black Prince Ave CV3...77 E6
Blackshaw Dr CV2......62 F6
Blacksmiths Cl WR11...127 F1
Blacksmith's La NN11...134 F5

Blacksmiths La
 Hockley Heath B94.....88 C6
 Mollington OX17......134 A2
 Northend CV47.......133 B7
 South Littleton WR11...127 F1
Blackthorn Cl CV4......76 D5
Blackthorn Ct B95.....113 B5
Blackthorn Rd CV8.....93 A3
Blackthorn La CV31.....29 F2
Blackthorn Rd CV37...145 A5
Blackthorn Way B49...143 B5
Blackwatch Rd CV6.....61 C8
Blackwell La CV35....114 F5
Blackwell Rd
 Coventry CV6..........61 E8
 Tredington CV36......136 F6
Blackwood Ave CV32...82 D2
Blackwood Rd B77......9 C7
Blackwood Way CV37..144 C3
Bladon Cl CV11........29 F8
Bladon Wlk [6] CV31...110 C6
Blair Dr CV10.........38 D1
Blair Gr B37..........33 D1
Blake Cl
 Nuneaton CV10.........28 A5
 Rugby CV22..........82 C2
Blakelands Ave CV31...110 B6
Blakenhurst WR11.....127 C4
Blake's Hill WR11.....128 B1
Blandford Ave B36.....22 E1
Blandford Dr CV2......62 F5
Blandford Rd CV32....105 C1
Blandford Way CV35...108 A7
Blanning Ct B93.......71 E3
Blaze La B96,B97......102 A3
Bleaberry CV21........83 C7
Bleachfield St B49....143 B3
Blenheim Ave CV6......49 C2
Blenheim Cl
 Bidford-on-A B50.....148 D5
 Nuneaton CV11........29 F2
Blenheim Cres CV31...110 C5
Blenheim Way
 [1] Moreton-in-M GL56 ..140 A3
 Birmingham,Castle Vale B35 22 B2
Blenheim Wlk
 Coventry CV6..........49 B4
 Wellesbourne CV35....146 C1
Bletchley Dr
 Coventry CV5..........60 B4
 Tanworth B77..........9 C8
Blindpit La B76........23 B8
Bliss Cl CV4...........59 E3
Blockley Rd CV12......40 A3
Blockley's Yd [4] LE10...31 B8
Blondvil St CV3........77 D7
Bloxam Gdns CV22......82 F2
Bloxam Pl [6] CV21.....83 A3
Bloxham Rd OX16......139 F1
Bluebell Cl CV23.......83 D8
Bluebell Dr
 Bedworth CV12........38 E2
 Birmingham B37.......33 E2
Bluebell Wlk CV4.......59 F1
Bluebellwood Rd B76...13 A3
Blue Cap Rd CV37.....145 A5
Blue Lake Rd CV37.....72 B2
Blue La CV35,CV37....130 A6
Blue Lias Ind Est CV47 .115 F4
Bluebells Croft CV37..124 A7
Blundells The CV8......93 A5
Blundell Ave CV7......74 C5
Blyth Cl
 Bedworth CV12........38 C5
 Cawston CV22.........99 A8
Blyth Ct CV11.........29 C3
Blythe Cl B97.........28 C3
Blythe Ct B46.........34 A7
Blythe Gate B90.......70 F3
Blythe Rd
 Coleshill B46.........34 B8
 Coventry CV1.........61 E4
Blythe Valley Pk B90...70 F2
Boar Croft CV4........59 F2
Boat La CV37.........129 A7
Bockendon Rd CV4.....75 E5
Boddington CE Sch
 OX17................134 E8
Boddington Cl CV32...106 E5
Boddington Cotts CV37 .129 D7
Boddington Rd OX17...134 B5
Bodmin Rd CV2........62 F5
Bodnant Way CV8......93 C4
Bodymoor Heath La B76 ..15 A4
Bohun St CV4.........59 F1
Boleyn Cl CV4........109 C6
Bolingbroke Dr CV34...109 E3
Bolingbroke Rd CV3....62 A1
Bolton Cl CV3.........77 E5
Bolyfant Cres CV31...110 A2
Bond Dr B35..........22 E2
Bond End CV23........53 E3
Bond Gate CV11.......29 C4
Bonds End La OX15...142 D8
Bonds Hospl CV1......151 A3
Bond St
 Coventry CV1........151 B3
 Nuneaton CV11........29 C5
 Rugby CV21..........82 F3

Boningale Way B93.....71 E3
Bonington Dr CV12.....39 A4
Bonneville Cl CV5......59 B8
Bonniksen Cl [7] CV31..109 F5
Bonnington Cl CV21....84 B1
Boot Hill CV9.........11 E2
Booths Fields CV6......49 E2
Bordesley Ct CV32....106 A3
Bordon Hill CV37.....144 C1
Bordon Pl CV37.......144 E1
Borough The LE10......31 D8
Borrowdale Cl CV6......61 A8
Borrowdale Dr CV32...105 D2
Borrowell La CV8.......92 E4
Borrowell Terr CV8.....92 E4
Boscobel Rd CV7.......70 D5
Bosley Cl CV36.......149 D4
Bostock Cres CV33....107 C7
Boston Pl CV6.........61 D8
Boswell Dr CV2........62 F8
Boswell Gr CV34......104 D1
Boswell Rd CV22......99 E2
Bosworth Cl CV8.......77 E2
Bosworth Dr B37.......33 A2
Bosworth Wood Prim Sch
 B36.................22 F1
Boteler Cl B49........143 B3
Botham Ho CV11........29 E1
Botoner Rd CV1........61 E3
Bottom St CV47.......133 B7
Bott Rd CV5...........76 D8
Bottrill St CV11.......29 B5
Botts Green La B46.....25 C5
Bott's La DE12.........3 F7
Boucher Cl CV37......144 D1
Boughton Leigh Inf Sch
 CV21.................83 C7
Boughton Leigh Jun Sch
 CV21.................83 C7
Boughton Rd CV21......83 D6
Boughton Road Ind Est
 CV21.................83 B6
Boulters La CV9........10 D1
Boultons La B97......102 D6
Boundary La B90.......70 A6
Boundary Rd E CV37...129 C2
Boundary Rd N CV37...129 C2
Boundary Rd CV1,CV22 ..83 D2
Boundary Rd CV37....110 A8
Bourne CV7............36 E3
Bourne Brook Cl CV7...36 E3
Bournebrook View CV7..26 E1
Bourne Cl CV9.........12 E2
Bourne End CV47.....147 A3
Bourne La CV5........142 D4
Bourne Rd CV3........62 C2
Bourne The OX15.....142 D4
Bourton La CV23.....115 F8
Bourton Rd
 Frankton CV23........97 D1
 Moreton-in-M GL56...140 A3
Bouts La WR7,B96.....118 B5
Bovey Croft B76.......22 A7
Bovingdon Rd B35.....22 A2
Bowbrook Ave B90.....71 A5
Bow Ct CV5...........76 D8
Bowden Way CV3.......62 F1
Bowen Rd CV22........83 D1
Bowers Croft CV32....106 A5
Bowes Lyon Cl GL56...140 A2
Bowfell Cl CV4........60 B4
Bow Fell CV21.........83 D7
Bow La CV7,CV23......53 B4
Bowleys La DE12.......1 F4
Bowling Green Ave B77 ..9 F7
Bowling Green Ct GL56 .140 A3
Bowling Green La CV7,
 CV12................49 E8
Bowling Green St CV34 .108 D6
Bowls Cl CV5..........60 F3
Bowman Gn LE10......31 F6
Bowness Cl CV6.......61 A8
Bowshot Cl B36.......22 D1
Box Cl CV31..........110 B3
Boxhill The CV3.......62 B1
Box Rd B37...........44 C8
Box Trees Rd B93,B94..71 C1
Boyce Way CV23.......82 B5
Boyd Cl CV2..........62 F8
Boyslade Rd LE10......31 F6
Boyslade Road E LE10..31 F5
Bracadale Cl CV3......63 A2
Bracebridge Cl CV7....74 B6
Bracebridge Rd
 Atherstone CV9........18 D7
 Kingsbury B78........15 C6
Bracebridge St CV11...29 B3
Bracken Cl CV22.......82 E1
Bracken Croft [8] B37..33 C3
Brackendale Dr
 Barby CV23..........101 C1
 Nuneaton CV10........28 F3
Bracken Dr
 Rugby CV22..........82 E1
 Sutton Coldfield B75...13 A5
 Wolvey LE10..........41 D4
Brackenhurst Rd CV6...61 A7
Bracklesham Way CV31..69 F7
Brackley Cl CV6.......60 F7
Bracknell Wlk [1] CV2..63 A7
Braddock Cl CV3.......63 A1
Brade Dr CV2..........63 B7
Bradestone Rd CV11....29 D1
Bradewell Rd B36......22 D1
Bradfield Cl CV5......60 C5

Bradford Cl [6] CV33...122 E8
Brading Rd CV10.......29 D6
Bradley Arc [12] OX16...139 F3
Bradley Croft CV7.....74 B6
Bradmore Cl B91......71 A8
Bradney Gn CV4.......75 E7
Bradnock's Marsh La B92 57 E2
Braemar Cl CV2........62 E6
Braemar Rd CV32.....106 B4
Braemar Way CV10.....29 A2
Braeside Croft B37.....33 D2
Brafield Leys CV22....100 A6
Braggington La CV37..128 F5
Braggs Farm La B90....70 A4
Braids Cl CV21........83 D4
Brailes CE Prim Sch
 OX15................137 E2
Brailes Ind Est OX15...138 A2
Brain St B77...........4 A2
Brakesmead CV31......109 F5
Bramber Cl [8] OX16...139 F4
Bramble Cl
 [6] Coleshill B46......33 F7
 Nuneaton CV11........29 F2
Bramble Ho B98......102 F8
Bramble St CV1........61 E2
Brambles The B76......22 A8
Brambling Cl CV23.....83 C8
Brambling B77.........10 A7
Bramcote Cl CV12.....40 E2
Bramcote Hospl CV11...40 E3
Bramdene Ave CV10....29 D8
Bramley Dr B47........69 B6
Bramley Rd CV35.....132 E6
Bramley Way B50.....148 D5
Brampton Way CV12...40 B3
Bramshall Dr B93......71 E3
Bramston Cres CV4.....59 F1
Bramwell Gdns CV6....49 F5
Brancaster Cl B77......4 B4
Brandfield Rd CV6.....60 F8
Brandheath La B96....118 D6
Brandon Cl CV3.......79 C5
Brandon La CV3,CV8....79 C5
Brandon Marsh Nature
 Reserve* CV3........79 A4
Brandon Marsh Visitor Ctr*
 CV3.................79 B4
Brandon Rd
 Bretford CV23........80 D6
 Coventry CV3.........78 D6
 Hinckley LE10........31 B7
Brandon Wood Farm*
 CV8.................79 D5
Branksome Rd CV6.....60 E6
Bransdale Ave CV6.....49 D3
Bransford Ave CV4.....76 A5
Bransford Rise B91....56 B5
Branstree Dr CV6......49 D2
Brascote Rd LE10......31 A8
Bratches The GL55....135 B3
Brathay Cl CV3........77 D8
Braunston CE Prim Sch
 NN11...............117 E5
Braunston La B76......13 A2
Braunston La NN11...126 E8
Braunston Pl CV22....100 D8
Braunston Rd NN11...117 F3
Bray Bank B46........25 D3
Brayford Ave CV3......77 A3
Brays Cl CV37.........64 E3
Bray's La CV2.........62 A3
Brazil St CV4.........59 E2
Breaches La B98......103 D8
Breach La CV35.......113 F3
Breach Oak La CV7.....37 D3
Bream Cl B37.........33 C2
Bream B77............9 D7
Brechin Cl LE10.......31 A8
Bredon Ave CV3.......78 F8
Bredon Ho B98.......103 B7
Bredon View B97.....102 D8
Bree Cl CV5..........60 A7
Breeden Dr B76.......23 B6
Bree's La CV8.........74 A1
Brendan Cl B46.......34 A5
Brendon B77..........4 B1
Brendon Way CV10.....28 A3
Brenfield Dr LE10.....31 A8
Brent B77............9 D7
Brentwood Ave CV3....77 C3
Brentwood Gdns CV3...77 C3
Brese Ave CV34......104 F1
Bretch Hill OX16.....139 F3
Bretford Rd CV7......50 C1
Bretshall Cl B90......70 D3
Bretts Cl CV1........151 D4
Bretts Hall Est CV10...28 A7
Brewer Rd CV12.......40 D2
Brewers Cl CV3.......78 F8
Brewery La OX15.....142 C4
Brewery Row GL56....140 F3
Brewery St CV37.....144 F3
Brewster Cl CV2......62 F4
Briansway CV6.......49 E3
Briar Cl
 Hinckley LE10........31 F6
 Royal Leamington Spa
 CV32...............106 B2
Briar Coppice B90.....70 D4
Briar Croft CV37.....144 B3
Briardene Ave CV12....39 B2
Briar Hill Inf Sch CV31 .110 B3
Briarmead LE10.......31 E4

Briars Cl
 Coventry CV6..........62 C2
 Long Lawford CV23....82 B4
 Nuneaton CV11.........29 E5
Briar B77.............4 A3
Briarwood Cl B90......70 D4
Brickall The CV37.....129 B3
Brickhill Cl CV36.....149 C6
Brickhill Dr B37.......33 A2
Brick Hill OX15......142 D3
Brick Kiln La CV5......59 E8
Brick Kiln La
 Middleton B78........14 D6
 Solihull B91.........70 F8
Brick Kiln Way CV32...39 D3
Brick Row OX15......142 F8
Brickyard Cl CV47.....74 C7
Brickyard Cotts WR11..122 B7
Brickyard La B80.....103 C4
Brickyard Rd CV47...125 B8
Bridal Path The CV5...60 B6
Bridgeacre Gdns CV3...62 F2
Bridgecote CV3........78 E6
Bridge Cl CV47......147 B3
Bridge End
 Southam CV47.......147 B4
 Warwick CV34.......108 F5
Bridge Foot CV37.....145 A2
Bridge Hill OX15.....142 D4
Bridge Ho CV10......110 A8
Bridge La
 Ladbroke CV47........124 D5
 Witherley CV9........19 B7
Bridgeman Rd CV6.....60 E4
Bridge Meadow Dr B93 ..71 F6
Bridge Rd
 Butlers Marston CV35 .131 F5
 Hinckley LE10........31 D7
Bridge St
 Barford CV35.........122 A7
 Coventry CV6.........62 A7
 Fenny Compton CV47 .133 D7
 Hampton Lucy CV35...121 F4
 Hurley CV9...........16 C4
 Nuneaton CV11........29 C2
 Nuneaton CV11........29 C4
 Polesworth B78........5 A1
 Rugby CV21..........83 C3
 Stratford-u-A CV37...145 A2
 Warwick CV34.......109 C8
 Wellesbourne CV35....146 D3
Bridge Town Prim Sch
 CV37................145 B1
Bridgetown Rd CV37...145 B1
Bridget St CV22.......82 F3
Bridge View
 [3] Coleshill B46......33 F7
 Baginton CV8.........77 F2
Bridgeway CV37......145 B3
Bridle Rd
 Lighthorne Heath CV33 .123 D2
 Rugby CV21..........82 E3
Bridport Cl CV2.......63 A4
Brierley Rd CV2.......62 E8
Briggs Cl OX16......139 F2
Bright Rd CV6........61 B4
Brighton St CV2.......61 F3
Bright St CV6........61 B6
Brightwalton Rd CV3...77 D7
Brightwell Cres B93...71 E3
Brill Cl CV4..........76 C5
Brindle Ave CV3......62 C2
Brindles Alley CV36..149 D6
Brindley Cl
 Atherstone CV9.......12 C1
 Daventry NN11......117 F3
Brindley Ct NN11.....117 D4
Brindley Paddocks CV1 .151 B4
Brindley Quays NN11..117 D4
Brindley Rd
 Bedworth CV12.......50 B8
 Hinckley LE10........30 E8
 Rugby CV21..........84 B1
Brinklow Cl B98.....103 D8
Brinklow Rd
 Coventry CV3.........63 A2
 Easenhall CV23.......65 E4
Brisbane Cl CV3......77 E6
Brisbane Ct [2] CV12..39 A2
Briscoe Rd CV6.......49 D4
Bristol Way CV35....146 C1
Britannia B1 GL56....32 A5
Britannia St CV2......61 F3
Briton Rd CV2........62 A4
Brittania Sh Ctr [3] LE10 .31 D8
Britten Cl CV11......40 A7
Brittons La CV35....114 C2
Brixfield Way B90....70 B5
Brixham Cl CV11......29 F5
Brixham Dr CV2.......62 E2
Brixworth Cl CV3.....78 E8
Broad Cl CV33.......123 F6
Broadfern Rd B93....72 B8
Broadgate CV1.......151 B2
Broadhaven Cl CV31..110 C7
Broad Heath Com Prim Sch
 CV6.................61 B6

Broad La
Coventry CV5 59 D4
Fillongley CV7 36 A4
Broadlands Cl CV5 60 C2
Broad La B98 86 E3
Broadlee B77 4 C1
Broad Marston Rd
Mickleton CV37,GL55 135 B7
Pebworth CV37 128 F1
Broadmead Ct CV5 60 C2
Broadmeadow La CV37 144 C4
Broadmere Rise CV5 60 A2
Broadmoor La CV36 141 A6
Broad Oaks B76 13 A1
Broad Park Rd CV2 62 D8
Broad St
Brinklow CV23 64 F3
Coventry CV6 61 E7
Long Compton CV36 141 C3
Broad Street Jetty CV6 61 E7
Broad St
Stratford-u-A CV37 144 F2
Warwick CV34 108 F7
Broadsword Way LE10 31 D4
Broadwater CV5 77 A8
Broadway
Coventry CV5 61 A1
Cubbington CV32 106 E5
Broadway Mans CV5 61 A1
Broadway Rd GL55 135 B6
Broadwell Ct CV4 75 F6
Broadwells Cres CV4 76 A5
Broad Wlk CV37 144 F2
Brockenhurst Way CV6 50 B6
Brockhill La B98 85 F2
Brockhurst Ave LE10 31 D4
Brockhurst Dr CV4 59 D2
Brockhurst La
Carroway Head B75 7 B7
Monks Kirby CV23 53 F4
Solihull B90 70 B5
Brodick Cl LE10 31 A8
Brodick Rd LE10 30 F8
Brodick Way CV10 28 F3
Bromage Ave B78 15 C6
Brome Hall La B94 89 D2
Bromford Way CV37 144 D4
Bromhurst Way CV34 108 B4
Bromleigh Dr CV2 62 C2
Bromleigh Villas CV8 77 F2
Bromley Cl CV8 92 E6
Bromsgrove Highway
B98 102 E8
Bromsgrove Rd B80 103 D2
Bromwich Cl CV3 78 F8
Bromwich Rd CV21 83 F1
Bromyard Ave B76 22 A8
Bronte Cl
Galley Common CV10 27 F5
Rugby CV21 83 D3
Bronze Cl CV11 39 E8
Brook Ave B77 10 A7
Brook Bsns Pk CV35 132 A6
Brook Cl
Coventry CV1 61 E4
Kingsbury B78 15 D5
Shipston-on-S CV36 149 D6
Brook Cottage Cl B46 25 D3
Brook Cottage Gdn*
OX15 138 F5
Brook Cotts CV36 149 F3
Brook Croft B37 44 B7
Brookdale
Harvington WR11 127 C4
Hinckley LE10 31 B7
Brookdale Rd CV10 29 E7
Brooke Cl
12 Stratford-u-A CV37 130 B8
Warwick CV34 108 F5
Brooke Ct CV21 82 F3
Brooke Mews 8 CV34 108 F7
Brook End Cl B95 113 A4
Brook End Dr B95 113 A4
Brook End B78 9 B8
Brooke Rd CV8 93 B4
Brooke Sch CV22 99 E7
Brooke Specl Sch CV22 82 F1
Brook Farm Ind Est B94 70 B2
Brook Farm Wlk B37 33 D2
Brookfield Cl B97 102 D4
Brookfield Ct CV37 144 C3
Brookfield Dr LE10 41 D4
Brookfield Rd
Cubbington CV32 106 E5
Hinckley LE10 31 C6
Brookford Ave CV6 49 A3
Brook Green La B92 57 A1
Brookhampton Cl B97 102 E4
Brookhampton La CV35 132 A5
Brookhurst Ct CV32 105 D1
Brookhurst Prim Sch
CV32 105 C1
Brookhus Farm Rd B76 22 A8
Brook La CV35 122 F3
Brooklands Ho 8 CV34 109 D8
Brooklands Way B37 44 A8
Brook La
Newbold-on-S CV37 130 E1
Nuneaton CV10 29 C6
Brooklea CV12 38 F2
Brooklime Dr CV23 83 E8
Brooklyn Rd CV1 61 D6
Brook Piece Wlk B35 22 B3
Brook Rd B95 119 F6
Brooksby Gr B93 72 A2
Brooks Cl CV23 117 B6
Brooks Croft B35 22 A2
Brookshaw Way CV2 62 F8
Brookside Ave
Coventry CV5 60 C3
Kenilworth CV8 92 E4
Pailton CV23 66 A8
Wellesbourne CV35 146 E3
Brookside B90 70 D3
Brookside Cl
Rugby CV22 83 A2
Stratford-u-A CV37 144 D3
Brookside
Hinckley LE10 31 E7
Hook Norton OX15 142 D4
Brookside Rd CV37 144 D3
Brookside
Snitterfield CV37 121 B7
Stretton-on-D CV23 96 F6
Brookside Way B77 10 A6
Brookside B95 113 B2
Brook St
Bedworth CV12 39 B5
Fenny Compton CV47 133 D7
Brookstray Flats CV5 60 B3
Brook St
Warwick CV34 108 E6
Wolston CV8 80 A3
Brook Turn Cotts CV47 115 D4
Brookvale Ave CV3 62 E1
Brookvale Rd CV37 144 E2
Brook View CV22 99 C3
Brookweed B77 4 A3
Brook Wlk CV9 18 F7
Broom Cl CV22 82 E1
Broome Croft CV6 49 B3
Broomey Croft Childrens
Farm* B76 15 B7
Broomfield Ave B78 9 A8
Broomfield Pl CV5 61 A2
Broomfield Rd CV5 61 A1
Broomfield Rise CV10 28 F2
Broom La B90 70 A6
Broomybank CV8 93 B6
Broughton Castle*
OX15 139 D1
Broughton Rd OX15,OX16 139 F2
Browett Rd CV6 61 A5
Brown Ave B77 9 C8
Browning Ave CV34 108 C5
Browning Cl
7 Stratford-u-A CV37 130 B8
Nuneaton CV10 28 A5
Browning Rd
Coventry CV2 62 C3
Rugby CV21 101 B8
Brownley Rd B90 70 E7
Brownlow Dr CV37 144 E1
Brownlow St 7 CV32 106 A2
Brown's Bridge Rd CV47 147 B3
Brownshill Ct CV6 60 F8
Brownshill Green Rd CV6 48 E1
Brown's La
Brownshill Green CV5 48 C1
Dordon CV9 11 A5
Browns La B93 71 E6
Brownsover Cl B36 22 B1
Brownsover Com Inf Sch
CV23 83 D8
Brownsover La CV21 83 B8
Brownsover Rd
Rugby CV21 82 F7
Rugby CV21 83 A7
Browns Rd NN11 117 F1
Broxell Cl CV34 104 C1
Bruce Rd
Bedworth CV7 49 F7
Coventry CV6 61 B8
Bruces Way CV37 144 B3
Bruce Williams Way CV22 83 B2
Brudenell Cl CV22 99 A8
Brunel Cl
Coventry CV2 61 F3
Daventry NN11 117 F2
Whitnash CV31 110 B2
Brunel Rd LE10 31 C8
Brunel Wlk B78 5 A3
Brunes Ct CV21 83 D7
Brunswick Cl CV21 83 C6
Brunswick Ct CV31 110 A5
Brunswick Rd CV1 61 B2
Brunswick St CV31 110 A5
Bruntingthorpe Way CV3 78 E8
Brunton Cl CV3 63 B1
Brutus Dr B46 23 E1
Bryan Mews B50 148 E4
Bryanston Cl CV2 63 A4
Bryant Rd CV7 50 A7
Brymbo Cotts OX15 142 E4
Brympton Rd CV3 62 C2
Bryn Jones Cl CV3 78 F7
Bryn Rd CV6 61 F7
Bryony Cl CV12 38 E1
Bubbenhall Rd CV8 77 F1
Buccaneer Way LE17 55 D6
Buccleuch Cl CV22 99 C4
Buchanan Rd CV22 82 E1
Buchan Cl
Galley Common CV10 27 F4
Stratford-u-A CV37 130 B8
Buckbury Croft B90 71 B6
Buckden Cl 2 CV34 104 F1
Buckden B77 4 C1
Buckfast Cl CV3 77 E5
Buckhold Dr CV5 60 B5
Buckingham Cl CV10 29 B1
Buckingham Rd CV47 132 F5
Buckingham Rise CV5 60 B4
Buckland Rd CV6 49 B2
Buckler's Yd 5 CV12 39 A2
Buckle St WR11,B50 128 C3
Buckley Ho CV5 60 F1
Buckley Rd CV32 106 C2
Buckminster Dr B93 71 E4
Bucknill Cres CV21 101 B7
Buckridge La B90 70 A5
Bucks Hill CV10 28 C6
Buckwell La CV23 84 B6
Budbrooke Cl CV2 50 D2
Budbrooke Ind Est CV34 108 B7
Budbrooke Prim Sch
CV35 114 F4
Budbrooke Rd CV34 108 B7
Bufferys Cl B91 71 B8
Bulkington La CV11 40 A7
Bulkington Rd
Bedworth CV12 39 D2
Shilton CV7 51 E6
Wolvey LE10 41 D4
Bullaces La LE17 68 C4
Bullfield Ave CV4 59 E1
Bullfurlong La LE10 31 F4
Bullimore Gr CV8 93 A2
Bullivents Cl B93 71 F5
Bull Ring Farm Rd CV33 123 F7
Bull Ring CV10 29 B2
Bull Ring The CV33 123 F6
Bull's Head La CV3 62 B2
Bulls Head Yd B49 143 B3
Bull's La B76 13 E1
Bull St
Nuneaton CV11 29 D2
Southam CV47 147 B4
Stratford-u-A CV37 144 F1
Bull Yd CV1 151 B2
Bull Yd The 5 CV47 147 B4
Bulwer Rd CV6 61 A6
Bulwick Cl CV3 63 B1
Bungalows The CV37 129 B7
Bunkers Hill NN11 126 F5
Bunkers Hill La CV23 80 E5
Bunneys Mdw LE10 30 E6
Burbage Ave CV37 144 F5
Burbage CE Inf Sch LE10 32 A5
Burbage Jun Sch LE10 31 F6
Burbage Rd LE10 32 A7
Burbages La CV6 49 D4
Burberry Gr CV7 74 A6
Burbury Cl
Bedworth CV12 39 C4
Royal Leamington Spa
CV32 106 C2
Burbury Ct CV34 109 B8
Burford La B49,B80 112 C1
Burford Mews 13 CV31 110 C6
Burford Rd
Hollywood B47 69 A6
Stratford-u-A CV37 145 D2
Burgage Pl CV11 29 C4
Burgage Wlk CV11 29 C4
Burges CV1 151 B3
Burges Gr CV34 104 F1
Burghley Cl CV11 29 F2
Burhill Way B37 33 B5
Burleigh Cl CV7 74 B7
Burlington Ct B78 9 B8
Burlington Rd
Coventry CV2 61 F4
Nuneaton CV10 39 B7
Burman Dr B46 34 A5
Burnaby Cl CV10 28 B5
Burnaby Rd CV6 49 B1
Burnaston Cres B90 71 C6
Burnell Cl B50 148 C5
Burnett Rd CV33 123 D2
Burnham Rd CV3 78 A6
Burnham Rise CV11 30 A6
Burnsall Gr CV5 76 D8
Burnsall Rd CV5 76 D8
Burns Ave CV34 108 C5
Burns Cl
10 Stratford-u-A CV37 130 B8
Redditch B97 102 C8
Burnside
Coventry CV3 63 A2
Rugby CV22 82 F2
Stratford-u-A CV37 144 C2
Burns Rd
Coventry CV2 62 B3
Royal Leamington Spa
CV32 106 B4
Burns Wlk CV12 39 C1
Burnthurst Cres B90 71 A7
Burnthurst La CV23 96 B3
Burrow Hill La CV7 48 D7
Burrows Cl CV31 110 B3
Burrows The CV37 130 E1
Burton Cl CV5 48 C2
Burton Dassett Hills Ctry Pk*
CV47 133 B7
Burton Green CE Prim Sch
CV8 75 B3
Burton La CV11 40 F7
Burton Rd CV9 3 F1
Bury Court La OX17 139 E8
Burycroft Rd OX15 142 D3
Bury Ho CV4 59 F3
Bury Rd CV31 109 F7
Bury The CV36 149 D6
Buryway La CV36 141 C3
Busby Cl CV3 78 F7
Busbys Piece CV23 53 F3
Bushbery Ave CV4 59 F2
Bushbury Croft B37 33 C3
Bush Cl CV4 59 F3
Bush Ct CV2 62 B6
Bushelton Cl CV1 151 C1
Bush Heath La CV33 123 F6
Bush Heath Rd CV33 123 F6
Bush Hill La CV23 117 B2
Bushley Cl B98 103 A7
Bushley Croft B91 71 B8
Bushwood Dr B93 72 B3
Bushwood La B94,B95 113 C8
Bushy End CV34 109 E4
Butchers Cl
Bishops Itchington CV47 124 A4
Brinklow CV23 64 F3
Butcher's La CV5 60 C6
Butchers La OX15 137 F2
Butchers Rd B92 57 A6
Butler Cl CV8 93 C7
Butlers Cl
Aston le W NN11 134 F5
Long Compton CV36 141 D3
Butlers Cres CV7 39 A1
Butlers End CV35 91 C2
Butlers La
Baddesley Ensor CV9 11 C2
Long Compton CV36 141 C3
Butlers Leap Ind Est CV21 83 D4
Butlers Leap CV21 83 D5
Butlers Rd CV36,OX7 141 E3
Butler St B96 102 E1
Butlin Rd
Coventry CV6 49 C4
Rugby CV21 83 D3
Buttercup Way CV12 38 D2
Buttermere Ave CV11 30 A6
Buttermere Cl CV3 78 F7
Buttermere
Rugby CV21 83 D7
Tamworth B77 10 B7
Buttermilk La CV35 113 F5
Butter St B49 143 C3
Butterworth Dr CV4 76 A6
Butt Hill CV47 125 C8
Butt La
Allesley CV5 60 B7
Harbury CV33 123 F6
Butts Cl CV9 3 A2
Butts CV1 61 A2
Butts La B94 87 B2
Butts Rd CV1 61 B2
Butts The
Long Compton CV36 141 C3
Napton on t H CV47 125 C8
Warwick CV34 108 E7
Buxton Ave B78 9 B8
Byefield Rd OX17 134 F4
Byfield Pl CV7 74 D5
Byfield Rd
Coventry CV6 60 E5
Priors Marston CV47 125 F4
Byford Ct CV10 28 F4
Byford St CV10 28 F4
Byford Way B37 44 B8
Bygones Mus* OX17 134 B4
By Pass Rd B77 4 A5
Byres The GL56 140 D6
Byron Ave
Bedworth CV12 39 D2
Warwick CV34 108 C4
Byron Ct B93 72 A6
Byron Rd
Redditch B97 102 D8
Stratford-u-A CV37 145 C1
Byron St CV1 151 C4
Byron Wlk CV47 132 F7
Bywater Cl CV3 77 B5

C

Cadbury Dr B35 22 A2
Cadden Dr CV4 60 B2
Cadman Cl CV12 39 C3
Cadogan Rd B77 9 D5
Caen Cl CV35 108 A7
Caernarfon Dr CV11 29 D3
Caernarvon Way 3
OX16 139 F3
Caesar Rd CV8 92 E3
Caesar Way B46 23 E1
Caister B77 4 A6
Caistor Cl B78 8 B8
Caithness Cl CV5 60 A4
Calcott Ho CV3 78 B5
Calcutt Mdw CV47 147 D4
Calcutt Way B90 70 A6
Caldecote Cl CV10 29 C8
Caldecote Hall CV10 19 F2
Caldecote Hall Dr CV10 19 F3
Caldecote Rd CV6 61 C5
Caldecott Pl CV21 83 C2
Caldecott St CV21,CV22 83 C2
Caldeford Ave B90 71 A7
Calder Cl
Bulkington CV12 40 B2
Coventry CV3 77 E7
Calder Dr B76 22 A7
Calder B77 4 B2
Calder Wlk CV31 110 C6
Caldon Cl LE10 31 B8
Caldwell Ct CV11 29 D1
Caldwell Rd CV11 29 D1
Calf's La GL55 135 B2
Calgary Cl CV3 63 A2
Calias La CV23 116 A3
Caliban Mews CV34 109 E3
Callaways Rd CV36 149 D5
Callendar Cl CV11 30 A7
Callier Cl CV22 99 B8
Callis Wlk 2 B77 9 F6
Callow Hill La B97 102 B6
Calmere Cl CV2 62 F8
Calpurnia Ave CV34 109 E2
Caludon Castle Sch CV2 62 E4
Caludon Lodge CV2 62 E5
Caludon Park Ave CV2 62 E5
Caludon Rd CV2 62 A4
Calvert Cl
Coventry CV3 77 D6
Rugby CV21 83 E7
Calvestone Pl CV22 99 A7
Calvestone Rd CV22 99 B8
Calvestone Sq CV22 99 B8
Camberwell Terr CV31 110 A7
Camborne Dr CV11 29 F5
Cambourne Rd LE10 32 A6
Cambria Cl B90 69 E7
Cambrian B77 4 A2
Cambridge Ct CV21 83 C3
Cambridge Dr
Birmingham B37 33 A1
Nuneaton CV10 28 E3
Cambridge Gdns CV32 106 A1
Cambridge St
Coventry CV1 61 E5
Rugby CV21 83 C3
Camden Cl GL56 140 F3
Camden St CV2 62 A4
Camellia Rd 1 CV2 50 B2
Camelot Gr CV8 93 C5
Cameron Cl
Allesley CV5 60 A7
Royal Leamington Spa
CV32 106 A4
Camhouses B77 4 B1
Campbell Cl CV10 28 A4
Campbell St CV21 82 E3
Campden Ave CV36 135 F5
Campden Cl B97 102 D6
Campden Gr CV35 114 F6
Campden Hill CV36 136 A6
Campden Lawns CV37 130 D3
Campden Pitch CV36 136 A6
Campden Rd
Ebrington GL55 135 D3
Lower Quinton CV37 129 D4
Mickleton GL55 135 B4
Shipston-on-S CV36 149 A5
Camp Hill Dr CV10 28 D7
Camp Hill Prim Sch CV10 28 E6
Camp Hill Rd CV10 28 C7
Campion Cl CV3 77 D6
Campion Gn CV32 106 A2
Campion Rd CV32 106 A2
Campion Sch & Com Coll
CV31 110 C5
Campion Terr CV32 106 A1
Campion Way
3 Bedworth CV12 38 D2
Rugby CV23 83 D8
Solihull B90 70 A5
Camp La
Henley-in-A B95 113 B6
Warmington OX17 133 B2
Camplea Croft B37 33 A2
Campling Cl CV12 40 B2
Campriano Dr CV34 109 A8
Campton Cl LE10 31 E7
Camville CV3 63 A2
Canada La CV35 114 D1
Canal Rd
Coventry CV6 61 F8
Hatton CV35 114 E5
Canalside
Bedworth CV6 50 B6
Kingswood B94 89 D3
Canal Way LE10 30 F7
Canberra Cl CV35 146 C1
Canberra Ct 2 CV12 38 F2
Canberra Rd CV2 50 C4
Canberra Way LE10 31 E4
Canford Cl CV3 77 C3
Canley Ford CV4,CV5 76 E7
Canley Rd CV5 76 D8
Canley Sta CV5 60 D1
Cannes Ct CV4 76 D6
Cannocks La CV4 76 D6
Cannon Cl CV4 76 F6
Cannon Hill Rd CV4 76 D5
Cannon Park District Ctr
CV4 76 C6
Cannon Park Prim Sch
CV4 76 D5
Cannon Park Rd CV4 76 E5
Canon Dr CV7 49 D6
Canon Evans CE Inf Sch
CV12 39 A2
Canon Hudson Cl CV3 78 C6
Canon Maggs CE Jun Sch
CV12 39 B2
Canon Young Rd CV31 110 B3
Canterbury Cl
Kenilworth CV8 93 C3
Studley B80 103 C4
Canterbury Dr B37 44 A7
Canterbury St CV1 151 D3
Canterbury Way CV11 30 A8
Cantlow Cl CV5 60 A3
Canton La B46 24 A5
Canwell Dr B75 7 B5
Cape Ind Est CV34 108 E7
Cape Rd CV34 108 D8
Capmartin Rd CV6 61 C7
Captain's Hill B49 143 D5
Capulet Cl
Coventry CV3 78 C6
Rugby CV22 99 E6
Capulet Dr CV34 109 E3

Capulet Ho 12 CV37 . . . . . 145 A3
Caradoc Cl CV2 . . . . . 62 D7
Caradoc Hall CV2 . . . . . 62 D7
Caradoc B77 . . . . . 4 A2
Cardale Croft 1 CV3 . . . . . 78 F8
Cardiff Cl CV3 . . . . . 78 D5
Cardigan Rd CV12 . . . . . 38 C1
Cardinal Newman RC Sch & Com Coll CV6 . . . . . 48 F2
Cardinal Wiseman RC Sch CV2 . . . . . 50 E1
Carding Cl CV5 . . . . . 59 F4
Carew Cl CV37 . . . . . 144 E5
Carew Wlk CV22 . . . . . 82 C1
Carey St CV6 . . . . . 62 B8
Carey B77 . . . . . 10 A5
Cargill Cl CV6 . . . . . 49 F5
Carhampton Rd B75 . . . . . 13 A5
Carisbrooke Ave B37 . . . . . 33 C2
Carisbrooke B77 . . . . . 4 A2
Carisbrook Rd CV10 . . . . . 29 D6
Carlcroft B77 . . . . . 4 B2
Carlton Cl CV12 . . . . . 40 B3
Carlton Ct CV5 . . . . . 60 F2
Carlton Gdns CV5 . . . . . 77 A8
Carlton Ho 8 CV32 . . . . . 109 F8
Carlton Rd
Coventry CV6 . . . . . 49 F1
Rugby CV22 . . . . . 82 D1
Carlyle Cl CV10 . . . . . 27 F5
Carlyon Rd CV9 . . . . . 18 F8
Carlyon Road Ind Est CV9 12 F1
Carmelite Rd CV1 . . . . . 61 E2
Carnation Way CV10 . . . . . 39 A8
Carnbroe Ave CV3 . . . . . 78 F7
Carnegie Cl CV3 . . . . . 78 B5
Carnoustie Cl CV11 . . . . . 40 C8
Carnoustie B77 . . . . . 4 C5
Caroline Cl CV11 . . . . . 39 F7
Carolyn Lane Ct CV21 . . . . . 82 F4
Carpenters Cl LE10 . . . . . 31 F5
Carrie Ho CV1 . . . . . 151 A2
Carroll Cl 16 CV37 . . . . . 130 B8
Carroway Head Hill B78 . . . . . 7 D4
Carsal Cl CV7 . . . . . 49 D5
Carson Cl GL56 . . . . . 136 C1
Carter Dr CV35 . . . . . 122 A7
Carter Rd CV3 . . . . . 78 A8
Carters Cl B37 . . . . . 44 A7
Carters La CV37 . . . . . 145 E4
Carters Leaze CV36 . . . . . 140 E5
Carthusian Rd CV3 . . . . . 77 C7
Cartmel Cl CV5 . . . . . 60 A4
Cart's La CV9 . . . . . 11 C2
Carvell Cl CV5 . . . . . 48 B1
Carver Cl CV2 . . . . . 62 E2
Cascade Cl CV3 . . . . . 77 E6
Case La CV35 . . . . . 114 B8
Casern View B75 . . . . . 13 A6
Cashmore Ave CV31 . . . . . 109 F5
Cashmore Rd
Bedworth CV12 . . . . . 38 E1
Kenilworth CV8 . . . . . 93 C4
Cash's Bsns Ctr CV1 . . . . . 61 D5
Cash's La CV1 . . . . . 61 D6
Casita Gr CV8 . . . . . 93 C4
Caspian Way CV2 . . . . . 63 A8
Cassandra Cl CV4 . . . . . 76 D3
Cassandra Gr CV34 . . . . . 109 D4
Castello Dr B36 . . . . . 22 D1
Castle Bromwich Bsns Pk B35 . . . . . 22 A1
Castle Cl
Coventry CV3 . . . . . 77 D6
Fillongley CV7 . . . . . 36 E2
Henley-in-A B95 . . . . . 113 B4
Warwick CV34 . . . . . 108 E6
Castle Cres CV35 . . . . . 132 B5
Castle Ct
Hinckley LE10 . . . . . 31 D6
Kenilworth CV8 . . . . . 93 A6
Castleditch La B98 . . . . . 102 E7
Castle Dr
Astley CV10 . . . . . 37 E7
Coleshill B46 . . . . . 33 F5
Castlegate Mews 5 CV34 . . . . . 108 F7
Castle Gdns GL55 . . . . . 135 C2
Castle Gn CV8 . . . . . 92 D5
Castle Gr CV8 . . . . . 92 E4
Castlehall B77 . . . . . 4 A2
Castle Hill CV8 . . . . . 92 E5
Castle Hill La OX15 . . . . . 137 E2
Castle Hill
Upper Brailes OX15 . . . . . 137 E3
Warwick CV34 . . . . . 108 E6
Castle La
Grandborough CV23 . . . . . 116 F6
Maxstoke B46 . . . . . 34 F7
Warwick CV34 . . . . . 108 E6
Castle Mews 6 CV34 . . . . . 108 E6
Castle Mound CV23 . . . . . 101 C2
Castle Mound Way CV23 . . . . . 67 D2
Castle Nurseries GL55 . . . . . 135 C2
Castle Place Ind Est CV1 151 D4
Castle Rd
1 Kineton CV35 . . . . . 132 B6
Alcester B49 . . . . . 143 C5
Hartshill CV10 . . . . . 19 B1
Henley-in-A B95 . . . . . 113 B4
Kenilworth CV8 . . . . . 92 E5
Nuneaton CV10 . . . . . 29 C7
Studley B80 . . . . . 103 F4
Tamworth B77 . . . . . 9 F5
Castle St
Astwood Bank B96 . . . . . 102 E2
Coventry CV1 . . . . . 151 D4
Hinckley LE10 . . . . . 31 D8
Castle St *continued*
Rugby CV21 . . . . . 83 B3
Warwick CV34 . . . . . 108 E6
Castle Vale Ent Pk B76 . . . . . 22 C4
Castle Vale Ind Est B76 . . . . . 22 A5
Castle Vale Sch B35 . . . . . 22 B3
Castle View CV10 . . . . . 19 B1
Caswell Rd CV31 . . . . . 110 B6
Catbrook Cl GL55 . . . . . 135 B1
Catbrook Gdns GL55 . . . . . 135 A1
Catesby End NN11 . . . . . 126 B5
Catesby La B94 . . . . . 89 B2
Catesby Rd
Coventry CV6 . . . . . 61 B8
Rugby CV22 . . . . . 83 D1
Cathedral Lanes Sh Ctr CV1 . . . . . 151 B3
Catherine de Barnes La
Bickenhill B92 . . . . . 44 D1
Catherine de B B92 . . . . . 56 C7
Catherines Cl B91 . . . . . 56 B4
Catherine St CV2 . . . . . 61 F3
Catherine Ward Hall CV12 39 B5
Cathiron La
Cathiron CV23 . . . . . 66 A1
Easenhall CV23 . . . . . 65 C1
Harborough Magna CV23 . . . . . 66 B1
Cattell Dr B75 . . . . . 13 B5
Cattell Rd CV34 . . . . . 108 E7
Catthorpe Manor LE17 . . . . . 68 F1
Catthorpe Rd LE17 . . . . . 68 C4
Cavalier Cl CV11 . . . . . 29 E2
Cavans Cl CV3 . . . . . 79 A8
Cavans Way CV3 . . . . . 79 A8
Cave Cl CV22 . . . . . 99 A8
Cavendish Cl CV22 . . . . . 82 A1
Cavendish Ct B93 . . . . . 72 A3
Cavendish Rd CV4 . . . . . 59 E2
Cavendish Wlk CV11 . . . . . 40 C8
Caversham Cl CV11 . . . . . 30 A7
Cawdon Gr B93 . . . . . 71 F3
Cawnpore Rd CV6 . . . . . 49 B2
Cawston Grange Dr CV22 . 99 A8
Cawston Grange Prim Sch CV22 . . . . . 99 B8
Cawston Ho
Hampton Magna CV35 . . . . . 114 F4
Rugby CV22 . . . . . 99 B6
Cawston La CV22 . . . . . 99 B5
Cawston Way CV22 . . . . . 99 C8
Cawthorne Cl 1 CV1 . . . . . 61 E4
Cecil Ct CV31 . . . . . 110 A8
Cecil Leonard Knox Cres CV11 . . . . . 40 F6
Cecily Rd CV3 . . . . . 77 E7
Cedar Ave CV8 . . . . . 79 B1
Cedar Cl
Royal Leamington Spa CV32 . . . . . 106 A4
Stratford-u-A CV37 . . . . . 145 B4
Cedar Cres B78 . . . . . 15 D6
Cedar Ct
Allesley CV5 . . . . . 60 A6
Hinckley LE10 . . . . . 32 A6
Tamworth B77 . . . . . 9 E6
Cedar Dr CV37 . . . . . 121 B7
Cedar Gr CV34 . . . . . 105 A1
Cedar Ho
7 Royal Leamington Spa CV32 . . . . . 109 E8
Barford CV35 . . . . . 122 A7
Cedar Rd
Mickleton GL55 . . . . . 135 C6
Nuneaton CV10 . . . . . 28 D6
Cedars Ave CV6 . . . . . 60 F5
Cedars Mews The 3 CV32 . . . . . 109 D8
Cedars Rd CV7 . . . . . 39 B1
Cedars The
Dorridge B93 . . . . . 72 A4
Shipston-on-S CV36 . . . . . 149 D6
Cedar Tree Farm CV31 . . . . . 111 C3
Cedar Wlk 6 B37 . . . . . 33 B2
Cedar Wood Dr CV7 . . . . . 74 B6
Cedric Cl CV3 . . . . . 78 C5
Celandine Rd CV2 . . . . . 50 D2
Celandine CV23 . . . . . 83 E8
Celandine Way CV12 . . . . . 38 E2
Cemetery La CV10 . . . . . 19 B1
Centaur Rd CV5 . . . . . 60 F2
Centenary Bsns Ctr CV11 . . 29 E3
Centenary Rd CV4 . . . . . 76 D7
Central Ave
Coventry CV2 . . . . . 62 A2
Nuneaton CV11 . . . . . 29 B5
Royal Leamington Spa CV31 . . . . . 109 F6
Central Bldgs
8 Rugby CV21 . . . . . 83 B3
Coventry CV3 . . . . . 151 B1
Central Bvd
Cheswick Green B90 . . . . . 71 A3
Coventry CV6,CV7 . . . . . 49 A5
Central City Ind Est CV6 . . . 61 F5
Central Dr CV47 . . . . . 124 B4
Central Park Dr CV23 . . . . . 67 D2
Central Six Ret Pk CV1 . . . 151 A1
Centrovell Ind Est CV11 . . . 29 C2
Centurion Cl B46 . . . . . 23 F1
Centurion Pk B77 . . . . . 10 B6
Centurion Way B77 . . . . . 10 B6
Century Pk B26 . . . . . 44 C6
Ceolmund Cres B37 . . . . . 33 B2
Chace Ave CV3 . . . . . 78 C6
Chaceley Cl CV2 . . . . . 63 A8
Chaceley Ct B97 . . . . . 102 D8
Chace Prim Sch CV3 . . . . . 78 C6
Chadbury Croft 1 B91 . . . 71 B8
Chadbury Rd WR11 . . . . . 127 A1
Chadshunt Cl B36 . . . . . 22 D2
Chadstone Cl B90 . . . . . 71 B6
Chadwick Cl CV5 . . . . . 60 B3
Chadwick La
Chadwick End B93 . . . . . 90 B8
Temple Balsall B93 . . . . . 73 B2
Chadwick Manor B93 . . . . . 73 A1
Chadwick Mews
Chadwick End B93 . . . . . 90 B6
Redditch B98 . . . . . 103 A7
Chadworth Ave B93 . . . . . 71 E3
Chaffinch Dr B36 . . . . . 33 B7
Chalfont Cl
Bedworth CV12 . . . . . 39 A4
Coventry CV5 . . . . . 60 B4
Chalford way 7 B90 . . . . . 70 C8
Challenge Bsns Pk CV1 . . . 61 D5
Challenge Cl CV1 . . . . . 151 C4
Chamberlain Cl CV32 . . . . . 106 E5
Chamberlaine St CV12 . . . . . 39 B3
Chamberlain La B49 . . . . . 118 D5
Chamberlain Rd CV21 . . . . . 101 B8
Chamberlain's Gn CV6 . . . . . 60 F7
Chamberlain Wlk 10 B46 . . 33 F7
Chance Fields CV31 . . . . . 110 F6
Chancellors Cl CV4 . . . . . 76 D4
Chancery Ct CV10 . . . . . 28 A7
Chancery La CV10 . . . . . 28 B7
Chanders Rd CV34 . . . . . 104 D1
Chandlers Cl B97 . . . . . 102 D7
Chandlers Dr B77 . . . . . 4 B5
Chandlers Rd CV31 . . . . . 110 A2
Chandlers CV31 . . . . . 109 D7
Chandos Ct 15 CV32 . . . . . 105 F1
Chandos St
Coventry CV2 . . . . . 62 A3
Nuneaton CV11 . . . . . 29 A4
Royal Leamington Spa CV32 . . . . . 105 F1
Change Brook Cl CV11 . . . . . 29 F8
Channel Way CV6 . . . . . 50 B6
Chantries The CV1 . . . . . 61 E5
Chantry Cl B47 . . . . . 69 A7
Chantry Cres B49 . . . . . 143 B3
Chantry Heath Cres B93 . . 72 C7
Chantry Ind Est B76 . . . . . 23 B7
Chantry The CV34 . . . . . 105 A1
Chapel Cl
Bidford-on-A B50 . . . . . 148 D4
Welford-on-A CV37 . . . . . 129 B6
Chapel Ct
13 Royal Leamington Spa CV32 . . . . . 109 F8
Astwood Bank B96 . . . . . 102 E1
Chapel Dr
Balsall Common CV7 . . . . . 74 B8
Wythall B47 . . . . . 69 A3
Chapel End OX7 . . . . . 142 A2
Chapel Farm Cl CV3 . . . . . 78 C6
Chapel Gdns GL56 . . . . . 136 C1
Chapel Gn CV47 . . . . . 125 C7
Chapel Hill OX7 . . . . . 142 F2
Chapelhouse Rd B37 . . . . . 33 A1
Chapel La
Aston Cantlow B95 . . . . . 119 F7
Barnacle CV7 . . . . . 51 B6
Bidford-on-A B50 . . . . . 148 D4
Cropredy OX17 . . . . . 134 C1
Kingswood B94 . . . . . 89 D7
Mickleton GL55 . . . . . 135 B6
Napton on t H CV47 . . . . . 125 C8
Newbold-on-S CV37 . . . . . 130 E1
Pillerton Priors CV35 . . . . . 131 D2
Ratley OX15 . . . . . 133 A2
Ryton-on-D CV8 . . . . . 79 B2
Shotteswell OX17 . . . . . 139 E8
Stratford-u-A CV37 . . . . . 145 A2
Ullenhall B95 . . . . . 112 E6
Witherley CV9 . . . . . 19 C7
Chapel Mews B77 . . . . . 4 A5
Chapelon B77 . . . . . 4 A2
Chapel Rd
Astwood Bank B96 . . . . . 102 E1
Pebworth CV37 . . . . . 128 F1
Chapel Row
Cropredy OX17 . . . . . 134 C1
Warwick CV34 . . . . . 108 E7
Chapel St
5 Royal Leamington Spa CV31 . . . . . 110 A7
Astwood Bank B96 . . . . . 102 E1
Bedworth CV12 . . . . . 39 C3
Bishops Itchington CV47 . . 124 A4
Charwelton NN11 . . . . . 126 D2
Coventry CV1 . . . . . 151 B3
Harbury CV33 . . . . . 123 F6
Hook Norton OX15 . . . . . 142 D4
Long Lawford CV23 . . . . . 82 A4
Nuneaton CV11 . . . . . 29 C4
Rugby CV21 . . . . . 83 A3
Stratford-u-A CV37 . . . . . 145 A2
Warmington OX17 . . . . . 133 D2
Warwick CV34 . . . . . 108 E7
Welford-on-A CV37 . . . . . 129 B6
Wellesbourne CV35 . . . . . 146 D3
Chapel Wlk B50 . . . . . 148 D4
Chapman Cl CV31 . . . . . 110 E5
Chapman Ct CV34 . . . . . 109 C8
Chapman Way B49 . . . . . 143 C5
Chard Rd CV3 . . . . . 78 D8
Charingworth Dr CV35 . . . 114 F5
Chariot Way CV21 . . . . . 83 A7
Charity Hos The CV23 . . . . . 67 C6
Charity Rd CV7 . . . . . 49 A7
Charlbury Mews CV31 . . . . . 110 C6
Charlecote Cl CV37 . . . . . 145 E3
Charlecote Croft B90 . . . . . 70 C8
Charlecote Fields CV35 . 146 D4
Charlecote Gdns CV31 . . 110 D5
Charlecote Pk* CV35 . . . . . 121 F3
Charlecote Rd
Charlecote CV35 . . . . . 146 A6
Coventry CV6 . . . . . 49 A2
Wellesbourne CV35 . . . . . 146 D4
Charlecote Wlk CV11 . . . . . 39 F8
Charles Ct
14 Royal Leamington Spa CV31 . . . . . 110 A6
1 Warwick,Emscote CV34 . . . . . 109 B8
Warwick CV34 . . . . . 108 C7
Charles Eaton Rd CV12 . . . 38 F3
Charlesfield Rd CV22 . . . 100 A8
Charles Gardner Rd 6 CV31 . . . . . 109 F6
Charles Lakin Cl CV7 . . . . . 51 C5
Charles Rd CV9 . . . . . 18 F7
Charles St
Coventry CV1 . . . . . 151 D4
Hurley CV9 . . . . . 16 C5
New Arley CV7 . . . . . 37 A8
Nuneaton CV11 . . . . . 29 A5
Rugby CV21 . . . . . 82 F3
Warwick CV34 . . . . . 109 A8
Charles Warren Cl CV21 . . . 83 B3
Charles Watson Ct 4 CV32 . . . . . 106 A2
Charlesworth Ave B90 . . . . . 71 B6
Charlewood Rd CV6 . . . . . 49 B2
Charlotte Cl CV10 . . . . . 28 C6
Charlotte St
Royal Leamington Spa CV31 . . . . . 109 F6
Rugby CV21 . . . . . 83 B3
Charlton Terr GL56 . . . . . 140 B3
Charminster Dr CV3 . . . . . 77 D4
Charnwood Ave CV10 . . . . . 28 E2
Charnwood Dr CV10 . . . . . 19 B2
Charnwood Way CV32 . . . 106 C3
Charter App CV34 . . . . . 108 D5
Charter Ave CV4 . . . . . 76 B7
Charter Ho CV4 . . . . . 76 A7
Charterhouse Rd CV1 . . . . . 61 E2
Charter Prim Sch (Harris Site) CV4 . . . . . 75 F7
Charter Prim Sch (Parkes Site) CV4 . . . . . 76 C8
Charter Rd CV22 . . . . . 100 E8
Chartley Cl B93 . . . . . 71 E3
Chartwell Cl CV11 . . . . . 29 F1
Chartwell Dr B90 . . . . . 70 D5
Charwelton Dr CV21 . . . . . 83 E6
Charwelton La NN11 . . . . . 126 B4
Chase Cl CV11 . . . . . 29 E6
Chase La CV8 . . . . . 92 B7
Chater Dr B76 . . . . . 13 A1
Chaters Orch CV47 . . . . . 115 D4
Chatham Cl CV3 . . . . . 78 C8
Chatillon Cl CV34 . . . . . 109 E3
Chatsworth Cl
Cheswick Green B90 . . . . . 70 E5
Hinckley LE10 . . . . . 31 F6
Chatsworth Dr CV11 . . . . . 29 F2
Chatsworth Gdns CV31 . . 110 D6
Chatsworth Gr CV8 . . . . . 93 C5
Chatsworth Rise CV3 . . . . . 77 E6
Chattaway Dr CV7 . . . . . 74 B6
Chattle Hill B46 . . . . . 23 E2
Chaucer Cl 5 CV37 . . . . . 130 B8
Chaucer Dr CV10 . . . . . 28 A4
Chaucer Rd CV22 . . . . . 99 F6
Chauntry Pl CV1 . . . . . 151 C3
Chauson Gr B91 . . . . . 71 A8
Chaytor Dr CV10 . . . . . 28 B6
Chaytor Rd B78 . . . . . 11 A8
Cheadle Cl CV2 . . . . . 50 A4
Cheam Cl CV6 . . . . . 50 A1
Cheapside B50 . . . . . 128 C4
Cheatle Ct B77 . . . . . 9 D5
Cheedon Cl B93 . . . . . 71 E2
Cheetah Rd CV1 . . . . . 151 C1
Chelmarsh CV6 . . . . . 61 C6
Chelmsley Ave B46 . . . . . 33 F6
Chelmsley Circ B37 . . . . . 33 B2
Chelmsley La B37 . . . . . 44 A8
Chelmsley Rd B37 . . . . . 33 C2
Chelmsley Wood Ind Est B37 . . . . . 33 B4
Chelney Wlk CV3 . . . . . 63 A1
Chelsea Cl CV11 . . . . . 29 F7
Chelsey Rd CV2 . . . . . 62 E8
Cheltenham Cl CV12 . . . . . 39 B4
Cheltenham Croft CV2 . . . 62 F7
Cheltondale 3 B90 . . . . . 70 C8
Chelveston Rd CV6 . . . . . 60 E5
Chelwood Gr CV2 . . . . . 50 F1
Chenies Cl CV5 . . . . . 60 B3
Chepstow Cl
Coventry CV3 . . . . . 78 C5
Stratford-u-A CV37 . . . . . 144 E1
Chepstow Gdns 9 OX16 . 139 F3
Chequer St CV12 . . . . . 40 C2
Cheriton Cl CV5 . . . . . 60 D4
Cherry Blossom Gr CV31 . 110 B2
Cherry Blossom Ho 6 CV37 . . . . . 144 F1
Cherrybrook Way CV2 . . . . . 50 C1
Cherry Cl
Coventry CV6 . . . . . 49 D2
Ettington CV37 . . . . . 131 A3
Hurley CV9 . . . . . 16 C4
Offenham WR11 . . . . . 127 D1
Cherryfield Cl CV10 . . . . . 19 B2
Cherry Fields OX17 . . . . . 134 C1
Cherry Gr CV22 . . . . . 99 E8
Cherry La
Bearley CV37 . . . . . 120 E7
Hampton Magna CV35 . . . . . 114 F4
Cherry Orchard Cl GL55 . 135 B1
Cherry Orchard Est CV13 . . 20 F3
Cherry Orch
Henley-in-A B95 . . . . . 113 B5
Kenilworth CV8 . . . . . 93 A5
Shipston-on-S CV36 . . . . . 149 D5
Stratford-u-A CV37 . . . . . 144 E1
Wellesbourne CV35 . . . . . 146 D4
Cherry Pit La B98 . . . . . 86 A1
Cherry Rd 17 OX16 . . . . . 139 F4
Cherry St
4 Stratford-u-A CV37 . . . . . 144 F1
Warwick CV34 . . . . . 108 F7
Cherry Tree Ave CV10 . . . . . 28 E6
Cherry Tree Cres WR11 . . . 127 F6
Cherry Tree La CV23 . . . . . 97 E2
Cherry Tree Wlk CV47 . . . . . 147 B5
Cherry Way CV8 . . . . . 93 A5
Cherry Wlk B47 . . . . . 69 B5
Cherrywood Cres 3 B91 . . 71 C8
Cherrywood Gr CV5 . . . . . 59 F5
Cherwell Cl LE10 . . . . . 31 A8
Cherwell The NN11 . . . . . 117 F1
Cherwell Way CV23 . . . . . 82 B4
Chesford Cres
Coventry CV6 . . . . . 50 B2
Warwick CV34 . . . . . 105 B1
Chesford Gr CV37 . . . . . 144 D4
Chesham St CV31 . . . . . 110 B7
Cheshire Cl CV22 . . . . . 99 C8
Chesholme Rd CV6 . . . . . 49 B2
Cheshunt Ho 3 B37 . . . . . 33 B2
Cheshunt Sch CV1 . . . . . 151 B1
Chesils The CV3 . . . . . 77 D6
Chessetts Wood Rd B94 . . 89 C7
Chester Cl B37 . . . . . 33 A2
Chester Ct 4 B37 . . . . . 33 D2
Chester Rd
3 Birmingham B36,B37 . . . . . 33 C3
Birmingham,Chelmsley Wood B37 . . . . . 44 F8
Hampton-in-A B46,B92,CV7 . . 45 B5
Chester St
Coventry CV1 . . . . . 61 B3
Rugby CV21 . . . . . 83 C4
Chesterton Cl B97 . . . . . 102 D4
Chesterton Dr
18 Stratford-u-A CV37 . . . . . 130 B8
Nuneaton CV10 . . . . . 28 A5
Royal Leamington Spa CV31 . . . . . 110 C5
Chesterton Hill CV35 . . . . . 123 B4
Chesterton Rd
Coventry CV6 . . . . . 61 A7
Lighthorne CV35 . . . . . 123 C3
Chester Way 5 OX16 . . . . . 139 F3
Chesterwood B47 . . . . . 69 A6
Chestnut Ave CV8 . . . . . 92 F3
Chestnut Cl
Ettington CV37 . . . . . 131 B3
Kingsbury B78 . . . . . 15 D6
Chestnut Cres CV10 . . . . . 28 E6
Chestnut Ct
Alcester B49 . . . . . 143 C3
Coventry CV3 . . . . . 78 B8
Royal Leamington Spa CV34 . . . . . 109 E2
Chestnut Dr CV11 . . . . . 29 E3
Chestnut Field CV21 . . . . . 83 A3
Chestnut Gr
Coleshill B46 . . . . . 34 A7
Coventry CV4 . . . . . 60 A2
Moreton Morrell CV35 . . . . . 122 E3
Wolston CV8 . . . . . 80 A3
Chestnut Pl CV47 . . . . . 147 B5
Chestnut Rd
Astwood Bank B96 . . . . . 102 E1
Bedworth CV12 . . . . . 39 D4
Mollington OX17 . . . . . 134 A2
Chestnut Sq
Royal Leamington Spa CV32 . . . . . 106 B2
Wellesbourne CV35 . . . . . 146 D3
Chestnuts The CV12 . . . . . 38 E2
Chestnut Tree Ave CV4 . . . 60 A2
Chestnut Wlk
2 Birmingham B37 . . . . . 33 B2
Henley-in-A B95 . . . . . 113 A5
Stratford-u-A CV37 . . . . . 144 F2
Cheswick Cl
Coventry CV6 . . . . . 62 A7
Redditch B98 . . . . . 112 A6
Cheswick Green Prim Sch B90 . . . . . 70 E4
Cheswick Way B90 . . . . . 70 D4
Cheswood Dr B76 . . . . . 22 B6
Chetton Ave CV6 . . . . . 61 C6
Chetwode Cl CV5 . . . . . 60 B4
Chetwynd Ave B78 . . . . . 11 A8
Chetwynd Dr CV11 . . . . . 40 B7
Chetwynd Jun Sch CV11 . . 40 A7
Cheveral Ave CV6 . . . . . 61 B6
Cheveral Rd CV12 . . . . . 39 A3
Cheverel Pl CV11 . . . . . 29 B2
Cheverel St CV11 . . . . . 29 B3
Cheviot Cl CV10 . . . . . 28 B3
Cheviot Rise CV32 . . . . . 106 C3
Cheviot B77 . . . . . 4 C1
Cheviot The CV4 . . . . . 76 D6
Cheviot Way 22 OX16 . . . 139 F5
Cheylesmore CV1 . . . . . 151 B2
Chichester Cl CV11 . . . . . 30 A7

Chichester Gr B37 . . . . .33 B1
Chichester La CV35 . . . . .114 F3
Chickabiddy La **10** CV47. .147 B4
Chicory Dr CV23 . . . . .83 D8
Chideock Hill CV3 . . . . .77 A6
Chiel Cl CV5 . . . . .59 F4
Chigwell Cl B35 . . . . .22 A3
Childs Cl CV37 . . . . .144 E5
Childs Oak Cl CV7 . . . . .74 A6
Chilham Dr B37 . . . . .33 C2
Chillaton Rd CV6 . . . . .49 B2
Chillingham B77 . . . . .9 C7
Chiltern Cl **2** CV6 . . . . .61 A5
Chiltern Ho CV5 . . . . .59 D4
Chiltern Leys **2** CV6 . . . . .61 A5
Chiltern Rd B77 . . . . .4 C1
Chilterns The CV5 . . . . .60 B4
Chilvers Coton Com Inf Sch
  CV11 . . . . .29 B3
Chilvers Coton Craft Ctr
  CV11 . . . . .29 C2
Chilvers Cl CV11 . . . . .29 C3
Chilworth Cl CV11 . . . . .39 E8
Chines The CV10 . . . . .29 D7
Chingford Rd CV6 . . . . .50 A4
Chingley Bank B95 . . . . .113 B4
Chipping Campden Bsns Pk
  GL55 .135 C2
Chipping Campden Sch
  GL55 .135 B2
Chipping Norton Rd
  OX15 .142 D4
Chipstone Cl B91 . . . . .71 C8
Chiswick Wlk B37 . . . . .33 E2
Chivenor Ho B35 . . . . .22 A2
Chivenor Jun & Inf Sch
  B35 . . . . .22 A2
Chivington Cl B90 . . . . .71 B6
Chorley Way CV6 . . . . .61 C6
Choyce Cl CV9 . . . . .12 D2
Christchurch Cl CV10 . . . . .28 F1
Christchurch Rd CV6 . . . . .61 A5
Christie Way CV37 . . . . .130 B8
Christine Ledger Sq **9**
  CV31 .110 A6
Christopher Hooke Ho
  CV6 . . . . .61 E8
Christ the King RC Inf Sch
  CV6 . . . . .60 F6
Christ the King Jun Sch
  CV6 . . . . .60 F7
Chub B77 .9 D7
Chudleigh Rd CV2 . . . . .62 E7
Church Ave B46 . . . . .23 B3
Church Bank
  Binton CV37 . . . . .129 A8
  Temple Grafton B49. . . . . .119 E1
Church Cl
  Birmingham B37 . . . . .33 A6
  Bishops Itchington CV47. . . . .124 A4
  Drayton Bassett B78. . . . . .8 E5
  Ebrington GL55 . . . . .135 E3
  Harborough Magna CV23 . . . . .66 B3
  Hartshill CV10 . . . . .28 B8
  Hinckley LE10 . . . . .32 A6
  Luddington CV37 . . . . .129 C7
  Old Arley CV7 . . . . .26 E2
  Ryton-on-D CV8 . . . . .79 B2
  Stoke Golding CV13. . . . . .21 D7
  Wardington OX17 . . . . .134 F1
  Whitnash CV31 . . . . .110 B4
  Wolvey LE10 . . . . .41 E4
  Wood End CV9 . . . . .10 C1
Church Cotts
  Astley CV10 . . . . .37 E7
  Church End B46 . . . . .25 C3
Church Ct
  Astwood Bank B96 . . . . .102 E2
  Coventry CV6 . . . . .48 F1
Churchdale Cl CV10 . . . . .28 C4
Church Down Cl B97 . . . . .102 D6
Church Dr
  Cookhill B49. . . . . .118 D5
  Kenilworth CV8 . . . . .92 F5
Church End
  Great Rollright OX7 . . . . .142 A2
  Radford Semele CV31 . . . . . . .110 E6
Church Farm Ct CV35 . . . . . . .138 C7
Church Farm La GL56 . . . . . . .140 A6
Church Fields
  Staverton NN11 . . . . .126 E8
  Wixford B49 . . . . .119 A1
Churchfield CV37 . . . . .129 A7
Church Hill
  15 Bishops Tachbrook
    CV33 . . . . .122 F8
  Badby NN11. . . . . .126 F5
  Coleshill B46 . . . . .34 A7
  Combrook CV35 . . . . .131 E6
Church Hill Ct CV35. . . . . .123 B2
Church Hill
  Cubbington CV32 . . . . .106 E5
  Royal Leamington Spa
    CV32 . . . . .109 E8
  Stretton-on-D CV23 . . . . .96 F6
  Ullenhall B95 . . . . .112 E6
  Warmington OX17 . . . . .133 D2
  Wilmcote CV37 . . . . .120 C5
Church Hos CV35 . . . . .132 B5
Churchill Ave
  Coventry CV6 . . . . .61 E8
  Kenilworth CV8 . . . . .93 A6
Churchill Cl CV37 . . . . .131 A4
Churchill Ho **11** CV32 . . . . .109 F8
Churchill Par B75. . . . . .13 A5

Churchill Rd
  Rugby CV22 . . . . .83 A1
  Sutton Coldfield,Falcon Lodge
    B75. . . . . .13 A5
Church La
  Alveston CV37 . . . . .121 D3
  Ash Green CV7 . . . . .49 E7
  Aston Cantlow B95 . . . . .119 F6
  Austrey CV9 . . . . .3 B1
  Barford CV35. . . . . .122 B7
  Bearley CV37. . . . . .120 E7
  Berkswell CV7 . . . . .58 C3
  Bickenhill B92 . . . . .44 E2
  Claydon OX17 . . . . .134 B5
  Cookhill B49. . . . . .118 D5
  Corley CV7 . . . . .48 B7
  Coventry,Middle Stoke CV2 . .62 B3
  Coventry,Upper Eastern Green
    CV5 . . . . .59 C5
  Cropredy OX17 . . . . .134 C1
  Cubbington CV32 . . . . .106 E5
  Curdworth B76 . . . . .23 B6
  Ettington CV37 . . . . .131 A3
  Fenny Drayton CV13 . . . . .19 F6
  Fillongley CV7 . . . . .36 E3
  Gaydon CV35. . . . . .132 E8
  Hanwell OX17 . . . . .139 F6
  Hellidon NN11 . . . . .126 B5
  Hornton OX15 . . . . .139 B7
  Kingsbury B78 . . . . .15 D5
  Lapworth B94 . . . . .88 E3
  Lea Marston B76 . . . . .24 A7
  Leek Wootton CV35. . . . . .104 F6
  Lighthorne CV35 . . . . .123 B2
  Maxstoke B46 . . . . .35 A2
  Meriden CV7 . . . . .58 E8
  Middleton B78 . . . . .8 C1
  Mollington OX17 . . . . .134 A2
  Newbold-on-S CV37 . . . . .130 E1
  No Man's Heath B79 . . . . .3 A6
  Norton WR11 . . . . .127 C2
  Nuneaton CV10 . . . . .29 C7
  Old Arley CV7 . . . . .26 F2
  Oxhill CV35 . . . . .137 F8
  Radford Semele CV31. . . . . . .110 E6
  Royal Leamington Spa
    CV32. . . . . .106 A3
  Shawell LE17 . . . . .68 C4
  Shotteswell OX17 . . . . .139 E8
  Shutford OX15. . . . . .139 A3
  Shuttington B79. . . . . .4 E7
  Snitterfield CV37 . . . . .121 B7
  South Littleton WR11. . . . . . .127 F1
  Stoneleigh CV8 . . . . .94 C6
  Stratford-u-A CV37 . . . . .144 C3
  Thurlaston CV23 . . . . .98 F2
  Welford-on-A CV37 . . . . .129 A7
Church Lawford Bsns Ctr
  CV23 . . . . .81 A5
Church La
  Whatcote CV36 . . . . .137 D7
  Whitnash CV31 . . . . .110 B4
  Wigston Parva LE10 . . . . .42 F8
  Willey CV23 . . . . .54 F6
  Wishaw B76 . . . . .14 A2
Churchlea OX17 . . . . .134 A2
Church Lees **7** CV33 . . . . . .122 F8
Church Lench CE Fst Sch
  WR11 .127 A6
Church Mews **3** CV35 . . . .132 B6
Church Park CV6 . . . . .48 F1
Church Path CV35 . . . . .114 F3
Church Rd
  Astwood Bank B96 . . . . .102 E2
  Baginton CV8. . . . . .77 F2
  Barford CV35. . . . . .122 A8
  Braunston NN11 . . . . .117 D5
  Bubbenhall CV8 . . . . .95 C6
  Church Lawford CV23 . . . . . . .81 C5
  Claverdon CV35. . . . . .113 F3
  Dordon B78 . . . . .11 A5
  Gaydon CV35. . . . . .132 E8
  Grandborough CV23 . . . . .116 F5
  Hartshill CV10 . . . . .28 B8
  Ladbroke CV47 . . . . .124 D5
  Long Itchington CV47. . . . . . .115 D4
  Newbold-on-S CV37 . . . . .130 E1
  Norton Lindsey CV35 . . . . . . .114 A8
  Nuneaton,Stockingford
    CV10. .28 C3
  Ryton-on-D CV8 . . . . .79 B2
  Shilton CV7 . . . . .51 E5
  Shustoke B46 . . . . .25 B2
  Snitterfield CV37 . . . . .121 B6
  Tamworth B77 . . . . .9 C4
  Ullenhall B95 . . . . .112 D5
  Upper Boddington NN11. . . .134 E8
  Warton B79 . . . . .5 E3
  Wilmcote CV37 . . . . .120 C4
  Wythersey CV9 . . . . .19 B7
Church Row
  Cherington CV36 . . . . .141 D7
  Middleton B78 . . . . .8 B1
Church St
  Alcester B49 . . . . .143 C3
  Appleby Magna DE12. . . . . .3 E8
  Atherstone CV9 . . . . .18 D8
  Barford CV35. . . . . .122 B7
  Bidford-on-A B50. . . . . .148 E4
  Bulkington CV12 . . . . .40 C2
  Charwelton NN11 . . . . .126 C7
  Chipping Campden GL55. . . .135 B2
  Churchover CV23. . . . . .67 B6
  Clifton u D CV23 . . . . .84 A5
  Coventry CV1. . . . . .151 C4

Church St continued
  Fenny Compton CV47. . . . . . .133 D7
  Hampton Lucy CV35. . . . . . . .121 F4
  Harbury CV33 . . . . .123 F6
  Harvington WR11 . . . . .127 D3
  Hinckley LE10 . . . . .32 A5
  Marton CV23 . . . . .115 C7
  Moreton-in-M GL56 . . . . .140 A3
  Nuneaton CV11 . . . . .29 C4
  Offenham WR11. . . . . .127 D1
  Royal Leamington Spa
    CV31. . . . . .110 A7
  Rugby CV21. . . . . .83 A3
  Shipston-on-S CV36. . . . . .149 D6
  Staverton NN11. . . . . .126 D8
  Stockton CV47 . . . . .147 F8
  Stratford-u-A CV37 . . . . .145 A2
  Studley B80 . . . . .103 E3
  Warwick CV34 . . . . .108 E6
  Welford-on-A CV37 . . . . .129 A7
  Wellesbourne CV35 . . . . .146 D3
  Wroxton OX15 . . . . .139 D4
Church Terr
  1 Royal Leamington Spa
    CV31. . . . . .110 A7
  Cubbington CV32 . . . . .106 E5
  Harbury CV33 . . . . .123 F7
  Newbold-on-S CV37 . . . . .130 E1
Church View
  Aston Magna GL56 . . . . .140 A6
  Tamworth B77 . . . . .9 F7
  Warton B79 . . . . .5 E4
Church Way CV12. . . . . .39 B2
Church Wlk
  1 Royal Leamington Spa
    CV31. . . . . .109 F7
  Allesley CV5 . . . . .60 C6
  Atherstone CV9 . . . . .18 F7
  Barby CV23 . . . . .101 C1
  Hinckley LE10 . . . . .31 D8
  Norton WR11. . . . . .127 C2
  Rugby,Bilton CV22 . . . . .99 D8
  Rugby CV21,CV22 . . . . .83 A2
  Cleopatra Gr CV34 . . . . .109 E4
  Church Wlkes CV13 . . . . .21 D7
  Wellesbourne CV35 . . . . .146 D3
Chylds Ct CV5 . . . . .60 A5
Cicero App CV34. . . . . .109 E2
Cicester Terr **10** GL56 . . . .140 A3
Cidermill La CV35 . . . . .41 A8
Cinder La CV9 . . . . .3 A4
Circle The CV10 . . . . .28 F4
Circuit The CV47 . . . . .129 C8
Circus Ave B37 . . . . .33 C2
City Arc CV1 . . . . .151 C2
City Coll Coventry (Butts Ctr)
  CV1 . . . . .61 A2
City Coll Coventry (Maxwell
  Ctr) CV1 . . . . .61 B1
City College Coventry (Tile
  Hill Ctr) CV4 . . . . .59 F1
City Tech Coll The B37 . . . . . . .33 A4
Cladswell La B49. . . . . .118 D5
Cladswell La B49,B96. . . . . . . .118 C6
Clapham Sq CV31 . . . . .110 B7
Clapham St CV31 . . . . .110 B6
Clapham Terrace Com Prim
  Sch CV31 . . . . .110 B7
Clapham Terr CV31. . . . . .110 B7
Clara St CV2 . . . . .62 A2
Clare Cl CV32 . . . . .106 C2
Clare St CV21. . . . . .82 F3
Claremont Cl CV12. . . . . .40 B4
Claremont Rd
  Royal Leamington Spa
    CV31. . . . . .109 F6
  Rugby CV21 . . . . .83 C3
Claremont Wlk CV5 . . . . .60 C6
Clarence Ct **5** LE10. . . . . . . .31 E8
Clarence Ho **7** CV32. . . . . .105 F1
Clarence Rd
  Hinckley LE10 . . . . .31 E8
  Rugby CV21 . . . . .82 E3
  Stratford-u-A CV37 . . . . .144 D3
Clarence St
  5 Coventry CV1 . . . . .61 E4
  Nuneaton CV11 . . . . .29 A4
  Royal Leamington Spa
    CV31. . . . . .110 A6
Clarence Terr **6** CV32 . . . .105 F1
Clarendon Ave CV32 . . . . .105 F1
Clarendon Cres CV32 . . . . . . .105 E1
Clarendon Ct **8** CV21 . . . . . .83 B3
Clarendon Ho LE10 . . . . .31 B7
Clarendon Pl CV32 . . . . .105 F2
Clarendon Rd
  Hinckley LE10 . . . . .31 C7
  Kenilworth CV8 . . . . .93 A3
Clarendon Sq CV32 . . . . .105 F1
Clarendon St
  Coventry CV5 . . . . .60 F1
  Royal Leamington Spa
    CV32. . . . . .106 A1
Clarewell Ave B91 . . . . .71 B8
Clark Cl CV36 . . . . .149 D5
Clarke Ave GL56 . . . . .140 C3
Clarke's Ave CV8 . . . . .93 A3
Clarks La CV36 . . . . .141 D3
Clarkland Gr B37 . . . . .44 A8
Clarks La B90. . . . . .70 A6
Clarkson Dr CV31 . . . . .110 A4
Clark St CV6 . . . . .50 A1
Claverdon Cl B97 . . . . .102 D4
Claverdon Ho CV34 . . . . .109 B8

Claverdon Prim Sch
  CV35 . . . . .113 F3
Claverdon Rd CV5 . . . . .60 B3
Claverdon Sta CV35. . . . . .114 A3
Clay Ave CV11 . . . . .29 F7
Clay Bank OX15. . . . . .142 D4
Clayborook Dr B98. . . . . .103 F7
Claybrooke Prim Sch
  LE17 . . . . .43 E4
Claydon Gr CV35. . . . . .114 F6
Claydon Rd OX17 . . . . .134 C2
Clay Hall Farm B50 . . . . .128 C4
Clayhill La CV23 . . . . .81 F6
Clay La
  Coventry CV2. . . . . .62 A4
  Harvest Hill CV5 . . . . .47 E3
Claylands CV35 . . . . .123 E1
Claymore B77 . . . . .9 E7
Clay Pit La B90 . . . . .70 A5
Clayton Rd CV6 . . . . .60 E5
Clayton Wlk B35 . . . . .22 A2
Cleasby B77 . . . . .4 C1
Cleaver Gdns CV10 . . . . .29 C6
Clebe Rd CV35 . . . . .113 F3
Cleeve Ct B50 . . . . .148 D2
Cleeve Prior CE Fst Sch
  WR11 .128 A4
Cleeve Rd
  Marlcliff B50 . . . . .148 D2
  Middle Littleton WR11. . . . . .127 F2
Cleeves Ave CV34 . . . . .109 D6
Cleeve View WR11 . . . . .127 F5
Clematis B77 . . . . .4 A3
Clemens St CV31 . . . . .110 A7
Clement Ho CV8 . . . . .93 A5
Clements Cl CV8 . . . . .93 A5
Clements St CV2 . . . . .62 A3
Clement St CV11 . . . . .29 B3
Clement Way CV22 . . . . .99 A8
Clennon Rise CV2 . . . . .62 D8
Clent Ave B97 . . . . .102 D7
Clent Dr CV10 . . . . .28 B3
Cleopatra Gr CV34 . . . . .109 E4
Clevedon Gn WR11 . . . . .128 C4
Cleveland Ct **1** CV32 . . . . .105 F2
Cleveland Rd
  Bulkington CV12 . . . . .40 B3
  Coventry CV2. . . . . .62 A4
  Hinckley LE10 . . . . .31 C8
Cleveley Dr CV10 . . . . .28 D7
Clews Rd B98 . . . . .103 C2
Clifden Gr CV8. . . . . .93 C6
Cliffe Ct CV32 . . . . .105 D1
Cliffe Rd CV32 . . . . .105 D1
Cliffe Way CV34 . . . . .109 A8
Cliff Hall La B79. . . . . .9 C1
Clifford Bridge Prim Sch
  CV3 . . . . .63 A3
Clifford Bridge Rd CV3. . . . . . .62 F4
Clifford La CV37 . . . . .130 A8
Clifford Mill CV37 . . . . .129 F7
Clifford Rd B93 . . . . .71 F4
Clifton Cl B98 . . . . .103 E8
Clifton Ct **5** CV31 . . . . .110 B7
Clifton La B79 . . . . .1 B3
Clifton Rd
  Nuneaton CV10 . . . . .28 F4
  Rugby CV21. . . . . .83 D3
Clifton St CV1 . . . . .151 D4
Clifton-upon-Dunsmore CE
  Prim Sch CV23 . . . . .83 F5
Clinic Dr CV11. . . . . .29 C3
Clinton Ave
  Hampton Magna CV35. . . . . .108 A7
  Kenilworth CV8 . . . . .92 D6
Clinton La CV8 . . . . .92 D6
Clinton Prim Sch CV8. . . . . . . .92 E3
Clinton Rd
  Coleshill B46 . . . . .33 F6
  Coventry CV6. . . . . .49 F2
  Solihull B90 . . . . .70 D8
Clinton St **2** CV31 . . . . .110 A7
Clipstone Rd CV6 . . . . .60 E6
Cliveden Wlk CV11. . . . . .39 E8
Clive Rd CV7 . . . . .74 C5
Clock La B92 . . . . .44 D2
Clock Towers Sh Ctr The
  CV21 . . . . .83 A3
Cloister Croft CV2 . . . . .62 F6
Cloister Crofts CV32 . . . . .105 F3
Cloisters The
  Atherstone CV9 . . . . .18 E8
  Priors Hardwick CV47 . . . . . .125 D3
  Royal Leamington Spa
    CV32. . . . . .105 F3
  Southam CV47 . . . . .147 C4
  Studley B80 . . . . .103 D4
Cloister Way CV34 . . . . .105 F3
Clopton Cres B37 . . . . .33 C4
Clopton Ct **2** CV37 . . . . . . .144 F3
Clopton Ho CV37 . . . . .144 F3
Clopton Rd CV37. . . . . .145 A6
Closers Bsns Ctr CV11 . . . . . . .29 D2
Close The
  Brandon CV8 . . . . .79 F5
  Chipping Warden OX17 . . . . .134 F3
  Cleeve Prior WR11 . . . . .128 A4
  Clifford Chambers CV37. . . . .129 F7
  Epwell OX15 . . . . .138 D3
  Halford CV36 . . . . .137 A8
  Hampton Lucy CV35. . . . . . . .121 F4
  Hollywood B47. . . . . .69 A5
  Kenilworth CV8 . . . . .93 A6
  Lower Quinton CV37 . . . . . . .129 E2
  Stratford-u-A CV37 . . . . .145 A1
  Whitnash CV31 . . . . .110 A5
  Wilmcote CV37 . . . . .120 C5

Closters Gn CV35 . . . . .132 B6
Cloud Gn CV4 . . . . .76 D5
Cloudsley Bush La LE10. . . . . .42 A5
Clovelly Gdns CV2 . . . . .62 C5
Clovelly Rd CV2 . . . . .62 B5
Clovelly Way CV11 . . . . .29 E5
Clover Ave B37 . . . . .33 D2
Clover Cl
  Rugby CV23 . . . . .83 D8
  Stratford-u-A CV37 . . . . .144 E5
Cloverdale Cl CV6 . . . . .49 B4
Clover Way CV12. . . . . .38 D2
Clowes Rd CV37. . . . . .86 F8
Clumber Park Rd CV35. .132 D3
Clunes Ave CV11 . . . . .29 E6
Clyde Rd
  Bulkington CV12 . . . . .40 A2
  Dorridge B93. . . . . .72 A6
Coach Ho The CV3 . . . . .62 E6
Coach House Ct CV36. . . . . .149 D5
Coach House Mews **2**
  CV34 . . . . .108 F7
Coach House Rise B77. . . . . .9 F7
Coalpit Fields Rd CV12. . .39 C1
Coal Pit La CV23 . . . . .54 C6
Coal Pit La CV8. . . . . .80 D2
Coal Pit Pit La LE10. . . . . .33 B6
Coat Of Arms Bridge Rd
  CV3 . . . . .77 A6
Cobalt Ctr CV47 . . . . .147 A3
Cobbs Rd CV8 . . . . .92 D6
Cobden Ave CV31 . . . . .110 C5
Cobden St
  Coventry CV6 . . . . .61 E5
  Warwick CV34 . . . . .108 D8
Cobham Gn **3** CV31 . . . . . .110 A4
Cobia B77 .9 D7
Coburg Ho CV5 . . . . .60 E3
Cockerills Mdw CV21 . . . . . . .101 A8
Cockermouth Cl CV32. . . . . . .105 D2
Cocksfoot Cl CV37 . . . . .144 E5
Cocksparrow St CV34 . . . . . .108 D7
Cockspur St B78. . . . . .10 E4
Coffee Pot La CV5 . . . . .114 C6
Colbek Ct CV10 . . . . .28 E7
Colbourne Gr CV32 . . . . .105 D2
Cold Comfort La B49. . . . . . . .143 A4
Coldfield Dr B98. . . . . .102 F2
Coldicott Leys GL55. . . . . . . .135 E3
Coldicotts Cl CV35 . . . . .135 B2
Coldwells Ct CV22 . . . . .83 A2
Colebridge Cres B46. . . . . . . .35 F8
Colebrook Cl
  Alcester B49 . . . . .143 C3
  Coventry CV3. . . . . .62 F2
Coleby Cl CV4 . . . . .75 D7
Cole Ct B37 . . . . .33 A2
Coleford Dr B37. . . . . .33 A2
Colehaven Ave B46. . . . . .34 A4
Colehurst Croft B90 . . . . .70 F6
Coleman St CV4 . . . . .59 F3
Colemeadow Rd B46. . . . . . . .33 F7
Coleridge Cl
  3 Stratford-u-A CV37 . . .130 B8
  Redditch B97 . . . . .102 C8
Coleridge Rd CV2 . . . . .62 C3
Coleshill CE Prim Sch
  B46. . . . . .34 A3
Coleshill Cl B97 . . . . .102 C5
Coleshill Heath Rd
  Birmingham B37 . . . . .44 C7
  Coleshill B37,B46. . . . . .33 E2
Coleshill Heath Sch B37 . .33 C1
Coleshill Ind Est B46. . . . . . .23 F2
Coleshill Rd
  Ansley Common CV10 . . . . . . .27 D8
  Atherstone CV9 . . . . .18 C6
  Birmingham,Marston Green
    B37. . . . . .44 B8
  Church End B46. . . . . .25 C3
  Curdworth B76 . . . . .23 C5
  Fazeley B78 . . . . .9 A2
  Hartshill CV10 . . . . .28 A7
  Maxstoke B46 . . . . .34 E5
  Shustoke B46 . . . . .24 E2
  Water Orton B46. . . . . .23 D2
Coleshill Sch The B46. . . . . .34 A4
Coleshill St
  Atherstone CV9 . . . . .18 D8
  Fazeley B78 . . . . .9 A8
Colesleys The B46 . . . . .34 A6
Coleville Rd B76. . . . . .22 B6
Coley Cl LE10. . . . . .31 D7
Colina Cl CV3 . . . . .78 C5
Colledge Cl CV23 . . . . .64 E3
Colledge Rd CV6. . . . . .49 D1
Colledge Dr CV32 . . . . .105 F2
College La
  Balsall Common CV7 . . . . .73 E1
  Long Compton CV36 . . . . . . .141 D2
  Stratford-u-A CV37 . . . . .144 F1
College Mews CV37 . . . . .144 F1
College Rd CV23. . . . . .117 C6
College St
  Nuneaton CV10 . . . . .29 C1
  Stratford-u-A CV37 . . . . .144 F1
Colletts Brook B75 . . . . .7 A2
Collett B77 . . . . .4 D1
Collett Wlk **2** CV1. . . . . . . .61 B3
Colliers Way CV7 . . . . .36 F8
Colliery La CV7 . . . . .39 B1
Colliery La N CV7 . . . . .39 B1
Collingham La CV47 . . . . .115 E4
Colling Wlk B37 . . . . .33 C3
Collingwood Ave CV22. . . . . . .82 D1
Collingwood Rd CV5 . . . . .61 A2
Collins Gr CV4 . . . . .76 D5
Collins Rd CV34 . . . . .109 D5
Collins Way B49 . . . . .143 D4
Colmore Dr B75 . . . . .7 A3

Colony The OX15. . . . . . . 142 C8
Colts Cl LE10 . . . . .31 D4
Columbia Gdns CV12. . . . . .39 B2
Columbine Way CV12 . . . .38 E1
Colyere Cl CV7 . . . . .49 A4
Combe Fields Rd CV3 . . . . .63 F4
Combroke Gr CV35. . . . . . 114 F5
Comet Rd B26. . . . . .44 C4
Commainge Cl CV34 . . . . 108 D7
Commander Cl ⓬ CV33 .122 F8
Commanders Cl CV33 .123 C3
Commissary Rd B26 . . . . . .44 A3
Common La
  Claverdon CV35. . . . . . . .113 F4
  Corley Moor CV7 . . . . .47 E7
  Kenilworth CV8 . . . . .93 B7
  Mappleborough Green B80 112 A6
  Redditch B78. . . . . .11 A8
Common The CV9 . . . . .11 A1
Common Way CV2 . . . . . . .62 A6
Compass Ct ⓭ CV1 . . . . . .61 B3
Compton Cl CV32 . . . . . . 106 C2
Compton Croft B37 . . . . . .33 D1
Compton Ct
  Coventry CV6. . . . . .49 D2
  Long Compton CV36 . . . .141 C4
  Rugby CV22 . . . . .99 B6
  Shipston-on-S CV36. . . . .149 D6
Compton District Prim Sch
  The CV36 . . . . .141 C3
Compton Hill CV35. . . . . .131 E7
Compton Rd
  Coventry CV6. . . . . .49 D2
  Lighthorne Heath CV33 . . .123 D2
  Compton Verney* CV35 .131 F7
Comrie Cl CV2 . . . . .62 F6
Comyn St CV32 . . . . .106 B1
Concorde Rd B26. . . . . . . .44 C4
Conduit Hill GL55. . . . . . .135 A1
Coneybury Wlk B76 . . . . . .22 D5
Congleton Cl CV6 . . . . .49 E2
Congreve Cl CV34 . . . . . . 104 F2
Congreve Wlk ⓫ CV37 .130 B8
Congreve Wlk ⓯ CV3 . . . . .39 B3
Conifer Cl CV32 . . . . .39 C4
Conifer Gr ⓷ CV31 . . . . .109 F5
Conifer Paddock CV3 . . . . .62 E1
Conifers The CV8 . . . . .93 B3
Coningsby Cl ⓷ CV31 . . .110 C6
Coniston Cl
  Bulkington CV12 . . . . .40 C3
  Rugby CV21 . . . . .83 D6
Coniston Ct
  ② Royal Leamington Spa
    CV32. . . . . .105 D1
  Nuneaton CV11 . . . . .29 F7
Coniston Dr CV5 . . . . .59 D4
Coniston Grange CV8 . . . . .92 F5
Coniston Rd
  Coventry CV5. . . . . .60 F1
  Royal Leamington Spa
    CV32. . . . . .105 D1
Coniston B77 . . . . .10 B7
Coniston Way CV11 . . . . . .29 F7
Conrad Cl CV22. . . . . .99 F6
Conrad Rd CV6 . . . . .61 A7
Constable Cl CV12 . . . . . . .39 A5
Constable Rd CV21 . . . . . .84 B1
Constance Cl CV12. . . . . . .49 F8
Constance Harris Cl
  CV35 . . . . .146 D3
Constantine La B46. . . . . . .23 F1
Consul Rd CV21. . . . . .83 A6
Convent Cl
  Atherstone CV9 . . . . .18 F7
  Kenilworth CV8 . . . . .93 A7
Convey Ct CV9 . . . . .18 E7
Conway Ave CV4 . . . . .75 D8
Conway Croft B49 . . . . . .127 E8
Conway Dr ⓷ OX16 . . . . .139 F3
Conway Rd
  Birmingham B37 . . . . .33 B3
  Royal Leamington Spa
    CV32. . . . . .109 D8
Conwy Cl CV11 . . . . .29 D3
Cook Cl
  Knowle B93 . . . . .72 C6
  Rugby CV21 . . . . .83 C7
Cooke Cl
  Coventry CV6. . . . . .50 A4
  Warwick CV34 . . . . .104 F2
Cooks Cl CV9 . . . . .18 D8
Cook's Hill OX15. . . . . . . .139 A3
Cooks La
  Baddesley Ensor CV9. . . . .11 C2
  Birmingham B37 . . . . .33 C1
  Frankton CV23. . . . . .97 C1
Cook St CV1 . . . . .151 B3
Coombe Abbey Ctry Pk*
  CV3 . . . . .63 E3
Coombe Abbey Visitor Ctr*
  CV3 . . . . .63 E4
Coombe Ave CV3 . . . . .78 F7
Coombe Ct CV3. . . . . .63 A2
Coombe Dr
  Binley Woods CV3 . . . . . . .79 A7
  Nuneaton CV10 . . . . .28 B4
Coombe Park Rd CV3 . . . . .62 F2
Coombe St CV3 . . . . .62 B2
Co-Operative St CV2. . . . . .50 B3
Cooper St CV37. . . . . .144 D6
Cooper St CV11 . . . . .29 D4
Cooper's Way CV47 . . . . .132 F6
Coopers Wlk CV8 . . . . .95 C5
Cope Arnolds Cl CV6. . . . . .49 F4
Copeland CV21 B79. . . . . .5 E4
Copeland CV21 . . . . .83 C7

Cope St CV1. . . . . .151 C3
Copland Pl CV4. . . . . .59 E1
Copland Cl CV7 . . . . .74 A6
Copperas St CV2. . . . . .50 B2
Copper Beech Cl CV4 . . . . .49 E1
Copperfield Rd CV2 . . . . . .62 B3
Coppice Cl
  Cheswick Green B90. . . . . .70 C4
  Redditch B98 . . . . .96 B8
  Stratford-u-A CV37 . . . . .145 A5
Coppice Dr B78. . . . . .11 A6
Coppice Gdns B47 . . . . . . .69 A7
Coppice La
  Middleton B78 . . . . .7 D2
  Newton Regis B79 . . . . .2 A8
Coppice Prim Sch The
  B47. . . . . .69 A6
Coppice Rd CV31 . . . . . . .110 B2
Coppice The
  Atherstone CV9 . . . . .19 A6
  Coventry CV3. . . . . .78 B8
  Hinckley LE10 . . . . .31 F8
  Nuneaton CV10 . . . . .29 C7
Coppice Way ⓬ B37 . . . . .33 B2
Coppice Wlk B90 . . . . .70 D4
Copps Rd CV32 . . . . .109 D6
Copse Dr CV5 . . . . .59 B8
Copse The CV5 . . . . .50 A8
Copsewood Ave CV11 . . . . .40 B7
Copsewood Terr CV3 . . . . .62 C2
Copstone Dr B93 . . . . .71 F3
Copston La LE10 . . . . .42 B5
Copthall Ho CV1. . . . . . . .151 B1
Copt Heath Croft B93 . . . .72 B8
Copt Heath Dr B93 . . . . . .72 A7
Copthorne Lo CV6 . . . . . . .60 F8
Copthorne Rd CV6 . . . . . . .60 F8
Copt Oak Cl CV4 . . . . .75 C6
Coral Cl
  Coventry CV5. . . . . .60 C2
  Hinckley LE10 . . . . .31 F4
Coralin Cl B37 . . . . .33 C2
Corbett Rd CV6 . . . . .61 C7
Corbett Ho CV37. . . . . . . .129 D2
Corbett Rd B47. . . . . .69 A7
Corbetts Cl B92. . . . . .57 B7
Corbett St CV21 . . . . .83 C4
Corbin Rd B78. . . . . .11 A6
Corbison Ct CV34 . . . . . . .104 D1
Corbizum Ave B80 . . . . . .103 D4
Cordelia Gn CV2 . . . . .99 E6
Cordelia Way CV22. . . . . . .99 E6
Corders Cl ⓷ GL56 . . . . .140 A3
Corder's La ⓭ GL56 . . . . .140 A3
Cord La CV23 . . . . .65 F4
Corfe Cl CV2 . . . . .62 F5
Corinne Croft B37 . . . . . . .33 A4
Corinthian Ct B49. . . . . . .143 B3
Corinthian Pl CV2. . . . . . . .62 F6
Coriolanus Sq CV34. . . . . .109 F3
Corley (Coventry) Sch
  CV7. . . . . .48 B6
Corley View CV7 . . . . .49 C6
Corncrake Dr B36 . . . . .33 A7
Cornel Cl B37 . . . . .44 C8
Cornelius St CV3 . . . . .77 D8
Cornel B77 . . . . .4 A4
Corner Ho The ⓭ CV32 .105 F1
Cornerstone Ho CV1. . . . .151 C4
Cornet's End La CV7 . . . . . .56 B4
Cornets End La CV7. . . . . .57 E7
Cornfield Croft B37 . . . . . .33 D3
Cornfield The CV13 . . . . . . .62 C1
Cornflower Dr CV23. . . . . .83 D8
Cornhill Gr CV8. . . . . .93 C5
Cornish Cl CV10 . . . . .27 F8
Cornish Cres CV10. . . . . . . .29 A2
Cornish Hos GL56. . . . . . .140 B3
Corn Mdws CV12 . . . . .39 C2
Cornwall Cl CV34 . . . . . . .108 F8
Cornwall Ho CV32 . . . . . .105 D1
Cornwall Pl CV32 . . . . . . .105 D1
Cornwall Rd CV1 . . . . .61 E1
Cornwall Cl B98 . . . . .103 B5
Cornwell Cl CV47. . . . . . .150 E3
Coronation Ave B78. . . . . . .5 B2
Coronation Cl GL55. . . . . .135 A2
Coronation Cres ⑤ 4 F7
Coronation La OX17. . . . . .139 E8
Coronation Rd
  Church Lawford CV23 . . . . .81 B5
  Coventry CV1. . . . . .61 F4
  Hurley CV9. . . . . .16 C5
Coronel Ave CV6. . . . . .49 E4
Corporation St
  Coventry CV1. . . . . .151 B3
  Nuneaton CV11 . . . . .29 B5
  Rugby CV21 . . . . .82 F2
Corpus Christi RC Sch
  CV3 . . . . .78 D7
Correen B77. . . . . .4 C1
Corsham Rd CV47. . . . . . .132 F6
Corston Mews CV31. . . . . .110 C6
Corunna Rd CV34 . . . . . . .108 C7
Cosford Cl CV32 . . . . .106 B3
Cosford Cres B35. . . . . .22 A3
Cosford La
  Rugby CV21 . . . . .67 A2
  Rugby CV21 . . . . .82 F8
Costard Ave
  Royal Leamington Spa
    CV34. . . . . .109 E3
  Shipston-on-S CV36. . . . .149 D5
Costock Cl CV37 . . . . .44 B8
Coten End Prim Sch
  CV34 . . . . .108 C7

Coten End CV34 . . . . .108 F7
Cotes Rd LE10. . . . . .31 F5
Cotheridge Cl B90 . . . . . . .71 A6
Cotman Cl CV12 . . . . .39 A4
Coton Park Dr CV23 . . . . . .67 C8
Coton Rd
  Churchover CV23 . . . . .67 C5
  Nether Whitacre B46. . . . .15 C1
  Nuneaton CV11 . . . . .29 C3
  Rugby CV21 . . . . .84 A1
Cotsmore Cl GL56. . . . . . .140 B3
Cotswold Bsns Village
  GL56. . . . . .140 B3
Cotswold Cl
  Sibford Ferris OX15. . . . . .142 D8
  Tredington CV36. . . . . . . .136 F6
Cotswold Cnr OX7 . . . . . .142 A2
Cotswold Cres CV10 . . . . . .28 B3
Cotswold Dr CV3 . . . . .77 C3
Cotswold Edge GL55 . . . .135 B6
Cotswold Gdns ⓲⓴ GL56 . 140 A3
Cottage Cl
  Nuneaton CV11 . . . . .29 D4
  Royal Leamington Spa
    CV31. . . . . .110 C6
Cottage Farm Ct GL56 . . .136 C1
Cottage Farm Lodge CV5 .49 A1
Cottage Farm Rd
  Coventry CV6. . . . . .49 A2
  Tamworth B77 . . . . .9 C7
Cottage Gdns CV10 . . . . . .19 B2
Cottage La
  Minworth B76 . . . . .22 D6
  Stratford-u-A CV37 . . . . .144 C2
  Whitacre Heath B46 . . . . . .24 D6
Cottage Leap CV21. . . . . . .83 D5
Cottage Sq CV31. . . . . . . .110 C6
Cottage Wlk ⓸ B77. . . . . . .9 F6
Cotterell Rd CV21. . . . . . . .82 F6
Cotterill's Cl CV31 . . . . . .110 B3
Cotters Croft CV47 . . . . . .133 D7
Cottesbrook Cl CV3 . . . . . .62 E1
Cotton Dr CV8 . . . . .93 C6
Cotton Mill Spinney
  CV32. . . . . .106 A6
Cotton Park Dr CV23 . . . . .67 C1
Cottrells Mews B46. . . . . . .23 B2
Coughton CE Prim Sch
  B49. . . . . .118 F7
Coughton Ct* B49. . . . . . .118 F7
Coughton Dr CV31. . . . . . .110 D5
Coughton Fields La B49. 143 C8
Coughton La B49 . . . . . . .118 F7
Council Hos
  Gaydon CV35 . . . . .123 E1
  Harvest Hill CV5 . . . . .47 D1
Council Hos The OX17. . .139 F6
Coundon Court Sch & Com
  Coll CV6 . . . . .60 E7
Coundon Gn CV6 . . . . .60 E8
Coundon Prim Sch CV6 . . .60 E5
Coundon Rd CV1 . . . . .61 B3
Coundon St CV1 . . . . .151 A4
Coundon Wedge Dr CV5,
  CV6 . . . . .60 D7
Countess Rd CV11 . . . . . . .29 A4
Countess's Croft The CV3 .77 D7
Countryside NN11 . . . . . .117 D5
Courtaulds Way CV6 . . . . . .61 D6
Court Cl
  ⓫ Bishops Tachbrook
    CV33 . . . . .122 E8
  Warmington OX17 . . . . . .133 D2
Courthouse Croft CV8. . . . .93 C4
Courthouse Green Prim Sch
  CV6. . . . . .62 A8
Courtland Ave CV6. . . . . . .60 F5
Court La WR11. . . . . .127 D1
Court Leet CV3 . . . . .79 D7
Court Leet Rd CV3 . . . . . . .77 E7
Courtney Cl CV11 . . . . .29 F7
Court of Lady Katherine
  Leveson The B93 . . . . .73 B5
Court St CV31 . . . . .110 A7
Court Way B50 . . . . .148 C4
Court Way B50. . . . . .23 F2
Court Yard The CV35 . . . .132 B5
Courtyard The
  Stoke Golding CV13. . . . . .21 C7
  Warwick CV34 . . . . .108 F5
Coventry Airport CV8 . . . . .78 B2
Coventry Blue Coat CE Sch
  The CV1. . . . . .61 F1
Coventry Bsns Pk CV5 . . . .60 D1
Coventry Canal Basin
  Warehouse CV1. . . . . . . .151 B4
Coventry Cath Church of St
  Michael* CV1 . . . . .151 C3
Coventry Gram Sch CV5. . .60 F1
Coventry Highway B98. . .112 A7
Coventry Muslim Sch CV6 61 E8
Coventry Prep Sch CV3 . . .77 B8
Coventry Railway Ctr CV8 .78 A3
Coventry Rd
  Aston Flamville LE10 . . . . .32 F1
  Baginton CV8. . . . . .77 F2
  Barnacle CV7,CV12. . . . . .51 A8
  Bedworth CV12 . . . . .39 B2
  Bedworth,Hawkesbury CV7 .50 C6
  Berkswell CV7 . . . . .58 E3
  Bickenhill B26,B92. . . . . . .45 A3
  Brinklow CV23. . . . . .64 C4
  Bulkington CV12 . . . . .40 B1
  Cawston CV22 . . . . .99 A7
  Church Lawford CV23 . . . . .80 E6
  Coleshill B46. . . . . .34 A5
  Cubbington CV32 . . . . . . .106 E2
  Dunchurch CV22 . . . . .99 B3

Coventry Rd continued
  Fillongley CV7 . . . . .36 F2
  Hampton-in-A B92 . . . . . . .45 B3
  Hinckley LE10 . . . . .31 B7
  Hinckley,Sketchley Hill LE10 .31 F5
  Kenilworth CV8 . . . . .93 A7
  Kingsbury B78 . . . . .15 D5
  Kingsbury B78. . . . . .9 B8
  Long Lawford CV23 . . . . . .81 E4
  Marton CV23 . . . . .115 C8
  Nether Whitacre B46. . . . .24 F7
  Nuneaton CV10 . . . . .39 C7
  Pailton CV23 . . . . .66 A8
  Southam CV47 . . . . .147 B5
  Stoneleigh CV8,CV3 . . . . .94 C7
  Thurlaston CV23 . . . . .98 A4
  Wibtoft CV23 . . . . .108 F8
  Willey LE17 . . . . .55 D5
  Wolvey LE10 . . . . .41 C3
Coventry Ret Mkt CV1. . .151 B2
Coventry Road Exhall CV7 50 B8
Coventry Sta CV1 . . . . . . .151 B1
Coventry St
  Coventry CV2. . . . . .62 A4
  Nuneaton CV11 . . . . .29 C4
  Southam CV47 . . . . .147 B5
Coventry Toy Mus* CV1 .151 C2
Coventry Univ CV1. . . . . .151 B2
Coventry University Tech Pk
  CV1 . . . . .61 C2
Coventry Walsgrave Triangle
  Bsns Pk CV2. . . . . .51 A1
Coventry & Warwickshire
  Hospl CV1 . . . . .151 C4
Cove Pl CV2 . . . . .62 C7
Cover Croft B76 . . . . .13 A1
Coverley Pl CV22 . . . . .82 E3
Covers The B80. . . . . .103 E6
Cowan Cl CV22 . . . . .82 C1
Cowdray Cl CV31 . . . . . . .110 C7
Cow La
  Lower Brailes OX15. . . . . .137 F2
  Whateley B78 . . . . .9 F3
Cowley Cl B36. . . . . .22 C1
Cowley Rd CV2 . . . . .62 D4
Cowley Way CV23 . . . . . .101 F2
Cowper Cl CV34 . . . . .104 E1
Cowper Rd LE10 . . . . .31 D6
Cox Cl B50 . . . . .148 E5
Cox Cres CV22 . . . . .99 C4
Cox's Cl CV10. . . . . .29 B3
Cox's La
  Hellidon NN11 . . . . .126 B5
  Napton on H CV47 . . . . .125 C7
Cox St CV1 . . . . .151 C3
Cozens Cl CV12 . . . . .38 D2
Crabbs Cross La B97. . . . .102 E5
Crabmill Cl B93 . . . . .72 A3
Crabmill La CV6 . . . . .61 F7
Crabtree Gr CV31 . . . . . . .110 C6
Crackley Cotts CV8 . . . . . .93 B8
Crackley Cres CV8 . . . . . . .93 B8
Crackley Hall Sch CV8 . . . .93 B7
Crackley La
  Coventry CV8. . . . . .75 F3
  Kenilworth CV8 . . . . .76 A3
Crackthorne Dr CV23 . . . . .67 D1
Craddock Ct CV10 . . . . . . .28 C7
Craddock Dr CV10 . . . . . . .28 C7
Craig Cl CV31. . . . . .110 B6
Craig Croft B37. . . . . .33 D2
Craigends Ave CV3 . . . . . . .78 E6
Crakston Cl CV2 . . . . .62 E2
Cramond Cl LE10 . . . . .31 B8
Cramper's Field CV6 . . . . . .61 A5
Cranborne Chase CV2. . . . .63 A5
Cranebrook Hill B78 . . . . . .7 F7
Crane Cl
  Stratford-u-A CV37 . . . . .144 C5
  Warwick CV34 . . . . .104 D1
Cranford Rd CV5. . . . . .60 D4
Cranham Cl B97 . . . . .102 B8
Cranmer Cl CV34 . . . . . . .109 D3
Cranmore Ave B90. . . . . . .70 C8
Cranmore Bvd B90 . . . . . . .70 D8
Cranmore Rd
  Birmingham B36 . . . . .22 E1
  Solihull B90 . . . . .70 D8
Crantock Way CV11 . . . . . .29 F4
Cranwell Dr CV35 . . . . . . .146 C1
Cranwell Rise B78 . . . . .8 B8
Cranwell Way B35 . . . . . . .22 A3
Crathie Cl CV2. . . . . .62 F6
Craven Arms Rd CV35 . . .132 D3
Craven Ave CV3. . . . . .79 D7
Craven Ct
  ⓷ Southam CV47 . . . . .147 B4
  Coventry CV3. . . . . .63 B2
Craven La CV47. . . . . .147 B4
Craven Rd CV21 . . . . .83 C4
Craven St CV5 . . . . .60 F2
Craven B77. . . . . .4 B1
Crawford Cl
  Bidford-on-A B50. . . . . . .148 C4
  Royal Leamington Spa
    CV32. . . . . .106 B5
Crawshaws Rd B36 . . . . . . .22 C1
Creampot Cl OX17 . . . . . .134 D1
Creampot Cres OX17. . . . .134 C1
Creampot La OX17 . . . . . .134 C1
Crecy Rd CV3 . . . . .77 E7
Crediton Cl CV11 . . . . .29 F4
Crendon Cl B80. . . . . .103 E5
Crescent Ave CV3 . . . . .62 D2
Crescent Sch CV22. . . . . . .99 D8

Crescent The
  Baddesley Ensor CV9. . . . .11 C3
  Bidford-on-A B50. . . . . . .148 D4
  Birmingham,Coleshill Heath
    B37. . . . . .44 E8
  Brinklow CV23. . . . . .64 F4
  Cawston CV22 . . . . .99 B8
  Charlecote CV35 . . . . . . .146 C7
  Hampton-in-A B92 . . . . . . .57 B7
  Harborough Magna CV23 . .66 A3
  Keresley CV7 . . . . .48 F6
  Lawford Heath CV23 . . . . .98 C6
  Nether Whitacre B46 . . . .123 C7
  Wootton Wawen B95. . . .120 C7
Cressage Rd CV2 . . . . .63 A6
Cressida Cl CV34 . . . . . . .109 F3
Cresswell Cl CV10 . . . . . . .29 C3
Cresswell Ho CV6 . . . . .61 B7
Crest Hill WR11 . . . . .127 D3
Crest The CV32 . . . . .106 D3
Creswell Pl CV22 . . . . .82 A1
Crew La CV8 . . . . .93 E6
Creynolds Cl B90 . . . . .70 D4
Creynolds La B90. . . . . . . .70 E4
Cricket Cl CV5 . . . . .60 F3
Crick Rd CV23 . . . . .101 D7
Crigdon B77 . . . . .4 C1
Crimscote Cl B90 . . . . .70 F6
Crimscote La CV35 . . . . . .114 C6
Cringlebrook B77 . . . . .9 D8
Cripplegate CV36 . . . . . . .149 D7
Critchley Dr CV22 . . . . . . .99 D3
Crockwell St CV36 . . . . . .141 C4
Croft Cl
  ⓺ Bishops Tachbrook
    CV33. . . . . .122 F8
  Stretton-on-D CV23 . . . . . .96 F6
  Warwick CV34 . . . . .109 C7
  Wolvey LE10 . . . . .41 C4
Croft Field CV47 . . . . .125 C7
Croft Fields CV12 . . . . .39 B2
Croft Holm B36. . . . . .140 B3
Croft Ind Est B37 . . . . .33 D2
Croft Jun Sch CV10 . . . . . .28 F3
Croft La
  Shrewley CV35 . . . . .114 C6
  Staverton NN11 . . . . .126 D8
  Temple Grafton B49. . . . .119 E2
Croft Mead CV10 . . . . .27 C3
Croft Mews CV10 . . . . .29 A4
Croft Pool CV12 . . . . .38 F2
Croft Rd
  Atherstone CV9 . . . . .12 D1
  Bedworth CV12 . . . . .38 F2
  Coventry CV1. . . . . .151 A2
  Leek Wootton CV35 . . . . .105 A7
  Middle Littleton WR11 . . .127 F2
  Nuneaton CV10 . . . . .28 F3
Croft CV37 . . . . .121 D1
Croft's La B96. . . . . .102 B2
Crofts The B76. . . . . .22 A8
Croft Rd
  Bulkington CV12 . . . . .40 B2
  Church Lench WR11 . . . .127 A6
  Coventry CV6. . . . . .49 F4
  Henley-in-A B95. . . . . . . .113 B4
  Meriden CV7 . . . . .46 C1
  Rugby CV21 . . . . .101 A8
  Warton B79 . . . . .5 E4
Cromarty Cl CV5 . . . . .60 A5
Cromarty Dr LE10. . . . . . . .21 F1
Cromdale Cl CV10 . . . . . . .28 A3
Cromdale B77 . . . . .4 C1
Cromer Rd CV32 . . . . .106 B2
Cromes Wood CV4 . . . . . . .59 D1
Crompton Ave B50. . . . . . .148 C5
Crompton Ct CV34 . . . . . .108 D6
Crompton St CV34 . . . . . .108 D6
Cromwell La CV4,CV8. . . . .75 C6
Cromwell Pl CV33 . . . . . . .123 D2
Cromwell Rd CV22 . . . . . . .83 C1
Cromwell St CV6 . . . . .61 F6
Crondal Rd CV7. . . . . .50 B7
Crook House Yd CV23 . . . .64 F4
Crooks La
  Alcester B49 . . . . .143 C5
  Studley B80 . . . . .103 D3
Cropredy CE Prim Sch
  OX17 . . . . .134 C1
Cropthorne Cl B98. . . . . . .103 B7
Cropthorne Dr B47 . . . . . . .69 B7
Crosbie Rd CV5. . . . . .60 E3
Cross Cheaping CV1. . . . .151 B3
Cross Cotts B49 . . . . .118 F7
Crossfell B77 . . . . .4 C1
Cross Fields Rd ⓭ CV34 .108 F8
Crossgate Rd B98 . . . . . . .103 C7
Cross In Hand LE17 . . . . . .55 B4
Crosskirk Rd LE10 . . . . . . .21 F1
Cross La
  Braunston NN11 . . . . . . .117 C5
  Cubbington CV32 . . . . . . .106 E4
Crossland Row LE10 . . . . .32 A6
Crossley Ct CV6 . . . . .151 C4
Crossleys Cl CV36 . . . . . .146 C1
Crossley Ct CV6 . . . . .61 F7
Cross Leys CV36 . . . . .149 C4
Cross Point Bsns Pk CV2. .63 B8
Cross Rd
  ② Royal Leamington Spa
    CV32. . . . . .105 D1
  Alcester B49 . . . . .143 B3
  Coventry CV6. . . . . .61 F8

Cross Rd *continued*
Keresley CV7 . . . . .48 F6
Cross Road Ind Est CV6 . . . . . .61 F7
Cross St
11 Warwick CV34 . . . . .108 F7
Coventry CV1 . . . . .151 C4
Long Lawford CV23 . . . . .82 A5
Nuneaton CV10 . . . . .28 D3
Royal Leamington Spa
  CV32 . . . . .106 A1
Rugby CV21 . . . . .83 C4
Crossway Rd CV3 . . . . .77 B4
Crossways Cotts CV7 . . . . .37 A4
Crossways LE10 . . . . .31 F5
Cross Wlk B78 . . . . .11 A6
Crowberry La B78 . . . . .14 C8
Crowden Rd B77 . . . . .4 A1
Crow Hill CV9 . . . . .11 C1
Crowhill Rd CV11 . . . . .30 A1
Crow La CV9 . . . . .12 E6
Crowley's Barns B95 . . . . .112 D6
Crowleys Cl B95 . . . . .112 E6
Crowmere Rd CV2 . . . . .62 F7
Crown Cl CV33 . . . . .123 F7
Crown Gn CV6 . . . . .49 E2
Crown Hill Cl CV13 . . . . .21 D7
Crownhill Rd LE10 . . . . .31 D4
Crown Ho CV5 . . . . .60 E3
Crown St CV33 . . . . .123 F7
Crown Way CV32 . . . . .106 B3
Crowsfurlong CV23 . . . . .67 D1
Crow Thorns CV21 . . . . .83 D6
Croxall Dr B46 . . . . .25 A2
Croxhall St CV12 . . . . .39 C3
Croydon Cl CV3 . . . . .77 E6
Croy Dr B35 . . . . .22 B4
Crucible Ho **6** CV37 . . . . . . .144 F3
Crutmock Cl CV6 . . . . .49 D3
Crutchley Way CV31 . . . . .110 A2
Cryersoak Cl B90 . . . . .71 A6
Cryfield Grange Rd CV4,
  CV8 . . . . .76 C2
Cryfield Hts CV4 . . . . .76 D2
Cryfield Village CV4 . . . . .76 B4
Cubbington CE Prim Sch
  CV32 . . . . .106 F5
Cubbington Rd
Coventry CV6 . . . . .50 A2
Royal Leamington Spa
  CV32 . . . . .106 B3
Cuckoo La CV1 . . . . .151 C3
Culey Wlk B37 . . . . .33 D2
Culpepper Cl CV10 . . . . .28 E4
Culverley Cres B93 . . . . .71 F6
Culworth Cl
Rugby CV21 . . . . .83 E7
Whitnash CV31 . . . . .109 F5
Culworth Ct
Coventry CV6 . . . . .61 F7
Whitnash CV31 . . . . .110 A5
Culworth Rd CV31 . . . . .134 F3
Culworth Row CV6 . . . . .61 E8
Cumberland Cres CV32 . .106 C3
Cumberland Dr CV10 . . . . .28 E3
Cumberland Wlk B75 . . . . . . .13 B5
Cumbernauld Wlk **7** CV3 .63 A7
Cumbria Cl CV1 . . . . .61 A3
Cumming St CV31 . . . . .110 A7
Cumsey The CV35 . . . . .114 A5
Cundall Cl CV31 . . . . .110 B6
Cunnery The CV8 . . . . .94 A3
Cunningham Way N CV22 .82 C1
Cunningham Way S CV22 .82 C1
Cup & Saucer OX17 . . . . .134 C1
Curdworth La B76 . . . . .23 A8
Curdworth Prim Sch B76 .23 C6
Curie Cl CV21 . . . . .83 D3
Curlew Cl
Stratford-u-A CV37 . . . . .144 C4
Warton B79 . . . . .5 C4
Curlew Ct CV6 . . . . .61 E7
Curlieu Cl CV35 . . . . .108 A7
Curlieu La CV35 . . . . .114 C2
Curran Cl CV31 . . . . .110 B4
Curriers Cl CV4 . . . . .75 D7
Curtis Rd CV2 . . . . .62 D6
Curzon Ave CV6 . . . . .61 E8
Curzon Cl LE10 . . . . .31 F7
Curzon Gr CV31 . . . . .110 C6
Cut Throat La B94 . . . . .87 D7
Cuttle Mill La B76 . . . . .14 D3
Cuttle Pool La B93 . . . . .72 F4
Cutworth Cl B76 . . . . .13 A3
Cygnet Ct CV1 . . . . .151 C4
Cymbeline Way
  CV34 . . . . .109 E4
Cypress Croft CV3 . . . . .78 F8
Cypress La CV31 . . . . .110 B3
Cypress Way CV10 . . . . .28 D6
Cyprus Ave B96 . . . . .102 D2

D

Dace B77 . . . . .9 D7
Dadglow Rd CV47 . . . . .124 B4
Daffern Ave CV7 . . . . .37 A8
Daffern Rd CV7 . . . . .39 A1
Daffodil Dr **4** CV12 . . . . . . .38 D2
Dagtail La B97 . . . . .102 D3
Dahlia Cl LE10 . . . . .31 E6
Dahlia Wlk CV10 . . . . .39 A8

Daimler Ave **6** OX16 . . . . . .139 F4
Daimler Cl B36 . . . . .22 F1
Daimler Rd CV6 . . . . .61 C5
Daintree Croft CV3 . . . . .77 C7
Dairyground The OX15 . .139 A3
Daisy Croft CV12 . . . . .38 D2
Dalby Cl CV3 . . . . .78 E8
Dale Ave CV37 . . . . .145 D1
Dale Cl
Long Itchington CV47 . . . . . . .115 C4
Warwick CV34 . . . . .109 A8
Dale End Cl LE10 . . . . .31 A7
Dale End CV10 . . . . .28 E5
Dalehouse Flats CV8 . . . . .93 B6
Dalehouse La CV8 . . . . .93 D7
Dale Meadow Cl CV7 . . . . .74 B6
Dales Com Jun Sch B77 . .10 B8
Dales Inf Sch The B77 . . . .10 B8
Dale St
Royal Leamington Spa
  CV32 . . . . .109 C8
Rugby CV21 . . . . .83 A4
Dale The B95 . . . . .113 B2
Daleway Rd CV3 . . . . .77 B4
Dalkeith Ave CV22 . . . . .99 D7
Dallington Rd CV6 . . . . .60 E6
Dalmahoy Cl CV11 . . . . .40 C8
Dalmeny Rd CV4 . . . . .75 D7
Dalton Cl CV23 . . . . .81 B6
Dalton Gdns CV2 . . . . .62 F4
Dalton Rd
Bedworth CV12 . . . . .39 A2
Coventry CV5 . . . . .61 B1
Dalwood Way CV6 . . . . .50 B4
Daly Ave CV35 . . . . .114 F3
Dama Rd B78 . . . . .8 F8
Dame Agnes Gr CV6 . . . . .62 B8
Damson Cl CV35 . . . . .102 C6
Damson Ct LE10 . . . . .31 B7
Damson Rd CV35 . . . . .114 F3
Danbury Cl B76 . . . . .13 A2
Dancers Dr CV35 . . . . .130 F7
Dane Ct NN11 . . . . .117 E5
Dane Rd CV2 . . . . .62 B4
Danesbury Cres CV31 . . . . . .110 D6
Daneswood Rd CV3 . . . . .79 E7
Daniel Ave CV10 . . . . .28 C3
Daniell Rd CV35 . . . . .146 D4
Daniel Rd CV9 . . . . .18 F7
Danvers Cl OX15 . . . . .139 E1
Danvers Rd OX15 . . . . .139 E1
Danzey Cl B98 . . . . .103 B5
Danzey Green La B94 . . . . .87 B1
Danzey Green Rd B36 . . . . . . .22 B1
Danzey Sta B94 . . . . .112 E8
Daphne Cl CV2 . . . . .50 C3
Darfield Ct CV8 . . . . .95 C5
Dark La
Astwood Bank B96 . . . . .102 D1
Bedworth CV12 . . . . .38 D1
Birchmoor B78 . . . . .10 E8
Braunston NN11 . . . . .117 E5
Coventry CV1 . . . . .151 B4
Hollywood B47 . . . . .69 A6
Tiddington CV37 . . . . .145 E4
Wroxton OX15 . . . . .139 D4
Darlaston Ct CV7 . . . . .46 D1
Darley Green Rd B93 . . . . .72 B1
Darley Rd LE10 . . . . .31 E6
Darlingscote Rd CV36 . . . . . .149 C7
Darlow Dr CV37 . . . . .144 D3
Darlston Row CV7 . . . . .46 B1
Darnbrook B77 . . . . .4 C1
Darnford Cl CV2 . . . . .62 F7
Darnley Cl CV36 . . . . .149 D7
Darrach Cl CV2 . . . . .50 E1
Dart Cl LE10 . . . . .31 A8
Dartington Way CV11 . . . . .39 F8
Dartmouth Rd CV2 . . . . .62 C5
Dartmouth Sch CV2 . . . . .62 D5
Dart B77 . . . . .10 A5
Darwell Pk B77 . . . . .4 A2
Darwin Cl
Coventry CV2 . . . . .63 A6
Darwin Ct **1** CV12 . . . . .39 A2
Darwin Ho **3** B37 . . . . .33 C1
Dassett CE Prim Sch The
  CV47 . . . . .133 D7
Dassett Cl CV35 . . . . .114 F5
Dassett Rd B93 . . . . .71 F4
Datchet Cl CV5 . . . . .60 C4
D'aubeny Rd CV4 . . . . .76 C3
Davenport Dr B35 . . . . .22 C3
Davenport Lodge Sch
  CV5 . . . . .77 B8
Davenport Rd CV5 . . . . .77 B8
Davenport Terr LE10 . . . . .31 E8
Daventry Rd
Barby CV23 . . . . .101 C1
Coventry CV3 . . . . .77 D7
Rugby CV22 . . . . .99 E2
Southam CV47 . . . . .147 D4
Staverton NN11 . . . . .126 D8
Daventry St **3** CV47 . . . . . .147 B4
David Rd
Bedworth CV7 . . . . .49 F8
Coventry CV1 . . . . .61 F2
Rugby CV22 . . . . .99 D8
Davidson Ave CV31 . . . . .110 A7
Davies Rd
Bedworth CV7 . . . . .49 F7
Moreton-in-M GL56 . . . . .140 B3
Davis Cl CV32 . . . . .105 D2
Davy Ct CV23 . . . . .67 C2
Dawes Cl CV2 . . . . .62 A3
Dawley Cres B37 . . . . .33 B1
Dawley Wlk **9** CV2 . . . . .63 A7
Dawlish Cl CV11 . . . . .29 E5

Dawlish Dr CV3 . . . . .77 D5
Dawson Cl CV31 . . . . .110 A2
Dawson Rd CV3 . . . . .62 A1
Days Cl CV1 . . . . .61 E3
Day's La CV1 . . . . .61 F3
Daytona Dr CV5 . . . . .59 B8
Deacon Cl CV22 . . . . .83 C1
Deacon St CV11 . . . . .29 C3
Deanbrook Cl B90 . . . . .71 A6
Deane Par CV21 . . . . .101 A8
Deane Rd CV21 . . . . .101 B8
Dean St CV2 . . . . .62 A3
Deanston Croft CV2 . . . . .50 F1
Deans Way CV7 . . . . .49 D6
Deansway CV34 . . . . .104 E1
Deasy Ho CV3 . . . . .78 B5
Deasy Rd CV1 . . . . .151 C1
Debden Cl
Dorridge B93 . . . . .71 E2
Wellesbourne CV35 . . . . .146 C1
De-Compton Cl CV7 . . . . .49 A7
Deedmore Rd CV2 . . . . .50 D1
Deedmore Sch CV2 . . . . .62 C8
Deegan Cl CV2 . . . . .62 A5
Deeley **7** CV7 . . . . .4 A1
Deepdale B77 . . . . .4 A2
Deep La B46 . . . . .24 F6
Deepmore Rd CV22 . . . . .99 D8
Deerdale Terr **8** CV3 . . . . . .78 F8
Deerdale Way CV3 . . . . .78 F8
Deerhill B77 . . . . .4 C1
Deerhurst Cl GL56 . . . . .140 F1
Deerhurst Mews CV2 . . . . .99 C3
Deerhurst Rd CV6 . . . . .49 B2
Deer Leap The CV8 . . . . .93 B6
Deerpark Dr CV34 . . . . .108 E8
Dee Wlk
Birmingham B36 . . . . .33 A7
Birmingham B36 . . . . .33 A8
Daventry NN11 . . . . .117 F1
Dehaviland Cl CV11 . . . . .29 B5
De Havilland Dr B35 . . . . .22 A2
De Havilland Way LE10 . .31 E4
Deighton Gr CV3 . . . . .78 C6
De-La-Bere Cres LE10 . . .32 A6
Delage Cl CV6 . . . . .50 B4
Delamere Cl B36 . . . . .22 D1
Delamere Rd CV12 . . . . .38 F2
Delamere Way CV32 . . . . . . .106 C4
Delancey Keep B75 . . . . .13 A5
Delaware Rd CV3 . . . . .77 B5
Delf Ho CV2 . . . . .50 D1
Delhi Ave CV6 . . . . .49 D1
Delius St CV4 . . . . .59 E3
Dell Cl CV3 . . . . .78 C5
Dell Farm Cl B93 . . . . .72 B6
Dell The B95 . . . . .113 B2
Delmore Way B76 . . . . .22 B6
Delves Cl CV23 . . . . .109 E4
Deltic B77 . . . . .4 A1
Delves Cres CV9 . . . . .10 C1
De Mohun Cres CV36 . . . . . .141 F5
De Montfort St B95 . . . . .113 B4
De Montfort Mews 1
  B46 . . . . .34 A6
De Montfort Rd CV8 . . . . .92 E6
De Montfort Way CV4 . . . . . . .76 B6
Dempster Ct CV11 . . . . .29 C4
Dempster Rd CV12 . . . . .39 A4
Denbigh Cl B93 . . . . .139 F2
Denbigh Cnr B46 . . . . .45 A6
Denbigh Rd CV6 . . . . .60 E5
Denby Bldgs **17** CV32 . . . .109 F8
Denby Cl CV32 . . . . .106 C3
Denby Croft B90 . . . . .71 A6
Dencer Dr CV8 . . . . .93 C4
Dene Cl CV35 . . . . .132 B5
Denegate Dr CV7 . . . . .74 B7
Denham Ave CV5 . . . . .60 A2
Denham Ct CV9 . . . . .18 E8
Denis Rd LE10 . . . . .31 D5
Denne Cl CV37 . . . . .145 A5
Dennett Cl CV34 . . . . .104 F2
Dennis Rd CV2 . . . . .62 C4
Denshaw Croft CV2 . . . . .63 A8
Denton Cl CV8 . . . . .92 D6
Denton Croft B93 . . . . .71 D3
Denville Rd CV32 . . . . .106 A3
Deppers Bridge CV33,
  CV47 . . . . .124 B6
Derby Dr B37 . . . . .33 B2
Dereham Ct CV32 . . . . .106 A2
Derek Ave B78 . . . . .11 A6
Dering Cl CV2 . . . . .62 D8
Deronda Cl CV12 . . . . .39 A3
Derry Cl CV8 . . . . .80 A3
Dersingham Dr CV2 . . . . .50 B2
Derwent Cl
Coventry CV5 . . . . .59 E4
Royal Leamington Spa
  CV32 . . . . .105 D1
Rugby CV21 . . . . .83 C6
Derwent Rd
Bedworth CV12 . . . . .39 A2
Coventry CV6 . . . . .49 A2
Derwent Way CV11 . . . . .29 F6
Desdemona Ave CV34 . . . . . .109 E4
Despard Rd CV5 . . . . .59 D4
Devere Ct **1** CV37 . . . . .144 F3

Devereux Cl CV4 . . . . .59 C1
Devitts Cl B90 . . . . .70 F7
Devon Cl CV10 . . . . .28 F3
Devon Gr CV2 . . . . .62 B6
Devonish Cl B49 . . . . .143 C5
Devon Ox Rd CV23 . . . . .101 F2
Devonshire Cl CV22 . . . . .82 B1
Devonshire Terr **7** GL56 .140 A3
Devoran Cl CV7 . . . . .50 A8
Dewar Gr CV21 . . . . .83 E2
Dew Cl CV22 . . . . .99 C3
Dewis Ho **4** CV2 . . . . .50 B1
Dewsbury Ave CV3 . . . . .77 B5
Dewsbury Cl B96 . . . . .102 C1
Dexter Ct CV9 . . . . .16 C4
Dexter La CV9 . . . . .16 C3
Dexter Way B78 . . . . .10 F8
Dey Croft CV34 . . . . .108 B4
Dial House La CV5 . . . . .59 F4
Diana Dr CV2 . . . . .50 E1
Dickens Cl CV10 . . . . .27 F3
Dickens Heath Prim Com Sch
  B90 . . . . .70 A6
Dickens Heath Rd
Solihull B90 . . . . .70 A5
Solihull B90 . . . . .70 A5
Solihull B90 . . . . .70 A5
Dickens Rd
Coventry CV6 . . . . .61 A8
Harbury CV33 . . . . .123 E6
Rugby CV22 . . . . .99 F6
Dickinson Ct CV22 . . . . .83 A1
Dickins Rd CV34 . . . . .105 B1
Dick's La B94 . . . . .113 E8
Didcot Cl B97 . . . . .102 C5
Didcot Way DE12 . . . . .3 F8
Diddington La B92,CV7 . . .45 C1
Didgley Gr B37 . . . . .33 A5
Didgley La CV7 . . . . .36 C4
Didsbury Rd CV7 . . . . .39 A1
Digbey Cl CV5 . . . . .60 B6
Digby Cres CV46 . . . . .23 B3
Digby Dr B37 . . . . .44 B6
Digby Pl CV7 . . . . .46 C2
Digby Rd B46 . . . . .33 F6
Dighton Cl CV37 . . . . .129 F7
Dilcock Way CV4 . . . . .75 F7
Dillam Cl CV6 . . . . .50 A4
Dillington Ho **8** B37 . . . . . . .33 B2
Dillon Ct CV11 . . . . .29 B5
Dillotford Ave CV3 . . . . .77 D6
Dingle Cl CV6 . . . . .61 A6
Dingle La
Appleby Magna B79,DE12 . . . .3 C6
Nether Whitacre B46 . . . . .24 F5
Dingleside Mid Sch B98 . .103 A4
Dingles Way CV37 . . . . .145 A5
Dingle The
Cheswick Green B90 . . . . .70 D5
Nuneaton CV10 . . . . .28 E6
Dingley Rd CV12 . . . . .40 B2
Discovery Way CV3 . . . . .79 B7
Ditchford Cl B97 . . . . .102 D4
Ditton Cl CV22 . . . . .82 C1
Dixon Cl B35 . . . . .22 A2
Dobbie Rd CV47 . . . . .129 D1
Dobson La CV31 . . . . .110 A4
Dockers Cl CV7 . . . . .74 C7
Doctors Cl CV8 . . . . .87 A2
Doctors Hill B94 . . . . .87 A2
Doctors La B95 . . . . .113 B5
Dodd Ave CV34 . . . . .109 C7
Dodgson Cl CV6 . . . . .50 A4
Dodwell Pk CV37 . . . . .129 C8
Dodwells Bridge Ind Est
  LE10 .30 E8
Dodwells Rd LE10 . . . . .30 E8
Dodwell Trad Est CV37 . .129 C8
Doe Bank La CV1 . . . . .61 A3
Dogberry Cl CV3 . . . . .78 C6
Dogberry Way CV34 . . . . .109 F2
Dog Kennel La B90 . . . . .70 D7
Dog La
Fenny Compton CV47 . . . . . .133 D7
Napton on t H CV47 . . . . .125 C8
Doglands The CV31 . . . . .110 B4
Doily Cl OX15 . . . . .142 D4
Dolomite Ave CV4 . . . . .60 D1
Donalbain Cl CV34 . . . . .109 F3
Doncaster Cl CV2 . . . . .62 D7
Done Cerce Cl CV22 . . . . .99 C3
Donegal Cl CV4 . . . . .76 A7
Dongan Rd CV34 . . . . .108 D7
Donibristle Croft B35 . . . . . . .22 A4
Donnington Ave CV6 . . . . .60 E5
Donnington Rd CV36 . . . . . . .149 D7
Donnithorne Ave CV10,
  CV11 .29 D1
Doone Cl CV2 . . . . .62 E6
Dorado B77 . . . . .9 D7
Dorcas Cl CV11 . . . . .40 C8
Dorchester Ave CV35 . . . . . .114 F3
Dorchester Gr OX16 . . . . . . .139 F4
Dorchester Rd LE10 . . . . .32 B7
Dorchester Way
Coventry CV2 . . . . .63 A4
Nuneaton CV11 . . . . .30 A7
Dordon Com Prim Sch
  B78 . . . . .11 A6
Dordon Rd B78 . . . . .11 A6
Doris Rd B46 . . . . .33 F8
Dorlecote Ct CV11 . . . . .29 C1
Dorlecote Pl CV10 . . . . .39 C8
Dorlecote Rd CV10 . . . . .39 C8
Dormer Harris Ave CV4 .59 F1

Dormer Ho **15** CV32 . . . . . .105 F2
Dormer Pl CV32 . . . . .109 F8
Dormston Cl B91 . . . . .71 C8
Dorney Cl CV5 . . . . .76 E8
Dorn Cl GL56 . . . . .140 A4
Dorothy Powell Way CV2 .50 F1
Dorridge Croft B93 . . . . .71 F1
Dorridge Jun & Inf Schs
  B93 . . . . .72 A4
Dorridge Rd B93 . . . . .72 A2
Dorridge Sta B93 . . . . .71 F2
Dorset Cl
Nuneaton CV10 . . . . .28 F3
Rugby CV22 . . . . .82 B1
Dorset Rd CV1 . . . . .61 C5
Dorsington Cl CV35 . . . . .114 F6
Dorsington Manor CV37 .128 E5
Dosthill Prim Sch B77 . . . . .9 C5
Dosthill Rd (Two Gates)
  B77 . . . . .9 B6
Douglas Ho CV1 . . . . .151 D4
Douglas Rd
Hollywood B47 . . . . .69 A7
Rugby CV21 . . . . .83 C6
Doulton Cl CV2 . . . . .50 E1
Dove Cl
Bedworth CV12 . . . . .38 E3
Hinckley LE10 . . . . .31 A8
Dovecote Cl CV6 . . . . .60 D5
Dovecotes The CV5 . . . . .60 B5
Dovedale Ave CV6 . . . . .49 F2
Dovedale Cl CV21 . . . . .83 C7
Dovehouse Dr CV35 . . . . .146 C1
Dovehouse La CV33 . . . . .123 F7
Dover Ave OX16 . . . . .139 F3
Doverdale Cl B98 . . . . .103 B7
Dover Farm Cl B77 . . . . .10 B8
Dover St CV1 . . . . .151 A3
Dovestone B77 . . . . .4 D1
Dovey Dr B76 . . . . .22 A8
Dowler's Hill Cres B98 . . . .103 A8
Dowley Croft CV3 . . . . .63 A6
Downderry Way CV6 . . . . .62 A6
Down End CV3 . . . . .142 D4
Downing Cl B93 . . . . .72 A5
Downing Cres CV12 . . . . .39 C4
Downing Ho B37 . . . . .33 B1
Downton Cl CV2 . . . . .63 A8
Dowty Ave CV12 . . . . .38 D1
Doyle Dr CV6 . . . . .49 F3
Drakes Cl B97 . . . . .102 C4
Drakes Cross Par B47 . . . . . .69 A5
Drake St CV6 . . . . .61 D7
Draper Cl CV8 . . . . .93 C4
Drapers Ct CV1 . . . . .151 B4
Draper's Fields CV1 . . . . . . .151 B4
Drawbridge Rd B90 . . . . .69 E8
Draycote Water Ctry Pk*
  CV23 . . . . .116 E3
Draycote Water* CV23 . .116 B8
Draycott Rd CV2 . . . . .62 C7
Drayton Ave CV37 . . . . .144 D4
Drayton Cl
Bidford-on-A B50 . . . . .148 C5
Fenny Drayton CV13 . . . . .19 F6
Hartshill CV10 . . . . .28 A8
Redditch B98 . . . . .103 D8
Stratford-u-A CV37 . . . . .144 D4
Drayton Ct
Hartshill Green CV10 . . . . .19 B2
Warwick CV34 . . . . .104 E2
Drayton Fields Ind Est
  NN11 . . . . .117 F3
Drayton La
Drayton Bassett B78 . . . . .8 C5
Fenny Drayton CV13 . . . . .19 E6
Drayton Leys CV22 . . . . .100 A7
Drayton Manor Dr
Drayton Bassett B78 . . . . .8 F7
Fazeley B78 . . . . .9 A6
Stratford-u-A CV37 . . . . .120 C2
Drayton Manor Pk* B78 . .8 E7
Drayton Rd
Bedworth CV12 . . . . .39 D2
Solihull B90 . . . . .70 E8
Stratford-u-A OX16 . . . . .139 F4
Drayton Way
Daventry NN11 . . . . .117 F2
Nuneaton CV10 . . . . .28 C7
Drem Croft B35 . . . . .22 A2
Drew Cres CV8 . . . . .93 A4
Dreyer Cl CV22 . . . . .82 C2
Drift La OX15 . . . . .139 D4
Driftway The CV33 . . . . .123 F6
Drinkwater Cl CV33 . . . . .123 F6
Drinkwater Ho **7** CV1 . . . .61 B2
Drivers La GL56 . . . . .141 A1
Drive The
Coleshill B46 . . . . .34 A6
Coventry CV2 . . . . .62 E3
Dunchurch CV22 . . . . .99 E4
Drovers Way CV47 . . . . .147 C4
Droylsdon Park Rd CV3 .77 B3
Dr Phillips Sh Ctr The
  CV2 . . . . .50 D1
Druid Rd CV2 . . . . .62 B3
Drummond Cl CV6 . . . . .60 F7
Drummond Way B37 . . . . .33 C2
Drury La CV21 . . . . .83 A3
Dryborkks Cl CV7 . . . . .74 B6
Dryden Cl
Galley Common CV10 . . . . .27 F5
Kenilworth CV8 . . . . .92 F3
Dryden Pl CV22 . . . . .82 E3
Dryden Way **17** CV37 . . . .130 A3

Dryden Wlk CV22 . . . . .82 E3
Drymen Rd CV35 . . . . . . .132 D3
Duck Lake DE12 . . . . .3 F8
Duck La CV37 . . . . .129 B7
Dudley Gr CV32 . . . . . . .106 B2
Dudley Rd CV8 . . . . .92 F2
Dudley Rise LE10 . . . .31 D6
Dudley St
  Atherstone CV9 . . . . . .18 D7
  Coventry CV5 . . . . .50 A1
Dudley Terr CV8 . . . . .94 B6
Duffus Hill CV35 . . . .122 F3
Duffy Pl CV21 . . . . .101 A8
Dugard Pl CV35 . . . . . .122 B7
Dugdale Ave
  Bidford-on-A B50 . . . .148 C5
  Stratford-u-A CV37 . .145 A5
Dugdale Cl 5 CV31 . .110 A6
Dugdale Ho CV11 . . . . . .29 C3
Dugdale Rd CV6 . . . . . .61 B6
Dugdale St CV11 . . . . .29 C4
Duggins La CV4,CV7 . . .75 B8
Duke Barn Field CV2 . .62 A5
Duke's Cl CV37 . . . . . .145 A3
Duke's Cft 8 CV21 . . . .83 A3
Dukes Rd B78 . . . . .11 A6
Duke St
  2 Rugby CV21 . . . . .83 A4
  Coventry CV5 . . . . .60 F2
  Nuneaton CV11 . . . . . . .29 B4
  Royal Leamington Spa
    CV32 . . . . .106 A1
Dulverton Ave CV5 . . . .60 D4
Dulverton Ct CV5 . . . . .60 D4
Dulverton Pl GL56 . .140 B3
Dumble Pit La B47,B48 .85 F7
Dumphouse La B48 . . . .85 C3
Dunblane Dr CV32 . . .106 C5
Duncan Dr CV22 . . . . . . .99 B6
Dunchurch Boughton CE Jun
  Sch CV22 . . . . .99 C3
Dunchurch Cl CV7 . . . .74 B7
Dunchurch Hall CV22 . .99 C2
Dunchurch Highway CV5 .60 A3
Dunchurch Inf Sch CV22 .99 C3
Dunchurch Rd CV22 . . .99 B3
Dunchurch Trad Est CV23 .98 D5
Duncombe Gn 12 B46 . .33 F7
Dun Cow Cl CV23 . . . . .64 E3
Duncroft Ave CV6 . . . .60 F7
Duncumb Rd B75 . . . . . .13 A5
Dunedin B77 . . . . .4 A1
Dunham Croft B93 . . . .71 D3
Dunhill Ave CV4 . . . . . .59 E3
Dunkirk Pl CV3 . . . . . . .78 F7
Dunley Croft B90 . . . .70 F6
Dunlop Rd CV32 . . . . .102 D5
Dunnerdale CV21 . . . . . .83 D7
Dunnington CE Prim Sch
  B49 . . . . .127 E8
Dunmose Cl CV6 . . . . . .61 E8
Dunn's La B78 . . . . .11 B6
Dunrose Cl CV2 . . . . . .62 E2
Dunsmore Ave
  Coventry CV3 . . . . .78 C6
  Rugby CV22 . . . . .100 C4
Dunsmore Bsns Ctr CV21 .83 B3
Dunsmore Heath CV22 . .99 C3
Dunstall Cres 8 CV33 .122 E8
Dunstall Ho 22 B46 . .140 A3
Dunstan Croft B90 . . .70 C8
Dunster Rd B37 . . . . . .33 D2
Dunster B77 . . . . .9 C7
Dunsville Dr CV3 . . . .70 A4
Dunton Hall Rd B90 . .70 A8
Dunton La B76 . . . . . . .14 C1
Dunton Pk B76 . . . . . . .23 C7
Dunwegan Cl
  Coventry CV3 . . . . .63 A2
  Kenilworth CV8 . . . . . .93 C4
Duport Rd LE10 . . . . . . .31 F7
Durbar Ave CV6 . . . . . .61 D8
Durham Cl CV7 . . . . . . .48 F4
Durham Cres CV5 . . . . .60 B7
Durham Croft B37 . . . .33 B2
Durlston Cl B37 . . . . . . .4 A5
Durrell Dr CV22 . . . . . .99 A7
Dursley La B98 . . . . . .112 A6
Dutton Rd CV2 . . . . . . .50 D3
Duttons Cl CV37 . . . .121 B7
Duxford Cl
  Redditch B97 . . . . . . .102 B8
  Wellesbourne CV35 . .146 C2
Dwarris Wlk CV34 . . .104 E2
Dyas Rd B47 . . . . .69 A7
Dyce Cl B35 . . . . .22 A4
Dyer's La GL55 . . . . . .135 A2
Dyers La B94 . . . . .87 D8
Dyer's La CV37 . . . . . .130 B3
Dyers Rd CV11 . . . . .40 F6
Dymond Rd CV6 . . . . . . .49 D4
Dysart Cl CV1 . . . . .61 E4
Dyson Cl CV21 . . . . .83 F1
Dyson St CV4 . . . . .59 E3

E

Eacott Cl CV6 . . . . .49 A3
Eacott Cl CV10 . . . . . . .28 D4
Eagle Cl CV11 . . . . .40 B8
Eagle Dr B77 . . . . .9 B1
Eagle Ho CV1 . . . . .61 D5
Eagle La CV34 . . . . .92 F3
Eagle St E CV1 . . . . . . .61 D5

Eagle St
  Coventry CV1 . . . . .61 D5
  Royal Leamington Spa
    CV31 . . . . .110 A6
Ealingham B77 . . . . .4 B1
Earles Cl CV47 . . . . . .147 F8
Earl Place Bsns Pk CV4 .60 B1
Earl's Croft The CV3 . .77 E7
Earlsdon Ave CV5 . . . . .77 A8
Earlsdon Ave N CV5 . .60 F1
Earlsdon Ave S CV5 . .77 A8
Earlsdon Ho CV5 . . . . . .77 A8
Earlsdon Prim Sch CV5 .61 A1
Earlsdon St CV5 . . . . . .76 F8
Earlsmere B94 . . . . .70 B1
Earls Rd CV11 . . . . .29 A5
Earls Rivers Ave CV34 .109 D3
Earl St
  Bedworth CV12 . . . . . .39 C2
  Coventry CV1 . . . . . . .151 C2
  Royal Leamington Spa
    CV32 . . . . .106 A1
  Rugby CV21 . . . . .83 B3
Earl's Wlk CV3 . . . . . . .79 D7
Earlsdon Comm CV5 . . .77 A8
Earlswood Rd B93 . . . .71 D2
Earlswood St CV5 . . . .77 A8
Earlswood Sta B94 . . .69 D1
Earlswood Trad Est B94 . .86 C6
Easedale Cl
  Coventry CV3 . . . . .77 B6
  Nuneaton CV11 . . . . . . .30 A6
Easenhall Cl B93 . . . . .72 A4
Easenhall Rd CV23 . . .66 A2
Easingwold Rd CV35 . .132 D4
East Ave
  Bedworth CV12 . . . . . .39 D2
  Coventry CV2 . . . . .62 A2
Eastboro Ct CV11 . . . . .29 E2
Eastboro Fields CV11 . .30 A4
Eastboro Way CV11 . . .29 F2
Eastbourne Cl CV6 . . . .60 E6
East Car Park Rd B40 . .44 F4
East Cl LE10 . . . . .31 D7
Eastcote La B92 . . . . . .56 F4
Eastcotes CV4 . . . . .60 B1
East Dene CV32 . . . . . .106 B2
East End OX15 . . . . . . .142 D4
Eastern Green Jun Sch
  CV5 . . . . .59 D5
Eastern Green Rd CV5 . .59 F4
Eastern Hill B96 . . . . .118 C2
Eastfield Cl CV37 . . .144 F5
Eastfield Pl CV21 . . . .83 A3
Eastfield Rd
  Nuneaton CV10 . . . . . .29 D6
  Royal Leamington Spa
    CV32 . . . . .110 A8
Eastfields NN11 . . . . .117 E5
Eastgate Ho 6 CV34 . .108 E6
Eastgate OX15 . . . . . . .139 B8
Eastgate Mews 3 CV34 . .108 E6
East Green Dr CV37 . .144 C3
East Gr CV31 . . . . .110 A6
East House Dr CV5 . . . .16 D4
Eastlands Gr CV5 . . . . .60 E4
Eastlands Pl CV21 . . . .83 D3
Eastlands Prim Sch CV21 .83 D2
Eastlands Rd CV21 . . .83 D2
Eastleigh Ave CV5 . . . .76 F7
Eastleigh Croft B76 . .22 A7
Eastley Cres CV34 . . .108 B8
Eastnor Gr CV31 . . . . .110 B7
Easton Gr B47 . . . . .69 B7
East Side WR11 . . . . . .128 A2
East St
  Coventry CV1 . . . . .61 E5
  Long Compton CV36 . .141 C3
  Moreton-in-M GL56 . .140 A3
  Rugby CV21 . . . . .83 D4
  Tamworth B77 . . . . .9 C5
East Union St CV22 . . .83 A2
East View B79 . . . . .4 F7
East Way B40 . . . . .45 B3
Eastway CV22 . . . . .99 B2
Eastwood Cl CV31 . . . .110 D6
Eastwood Cl B96 . . . . .102 E1
Eastwood Gr CV21 . . .101 C8
Easy La CV21 . . . . .82 F3
Eathorpe Cl
  Coventry CV2 . . . . .50 C1
  Redditch B98 . . . . . . .103 E8
Eathorpe Pk CV33 . . .115 B8
Eaton Cl CV32 . . . . . . .105 D2
Eaton Ct CV32 . . . . . . .105 D1
Eaton Rd CV1 . . . . .151 B1
Eaves Green La CV7 . . .46 C1
Eaves Green Mobile Home
  Pk CV7 . . . . .46 F2
Ebbw Vale Terr CV3 . . .77 D7
Eborall Cl CV34 . . . . .104 E2
Eborne Croft CV7 . . . . .74 C6
Ebourne Cl CV8 . . . . . . .93 A4
Ebrington Dr CV35 . .114 F5
Ebrington GL55 . . . . . .135 E3
Ebro Cres CV3 . . . . .62 F1
Ebsdorf Cl B50 . . . . .148 E5
Eburne Rd CV2 . . . . .50 C3
Eccles Cl CV2 . . . . .62 C8
Eckington Cl B98 . . . .103 B8
Eclipse Rd B49 . . . . . .143 A4
Ecton Leys CV22 . . . .100 A7
Edale B77 . . . . .9 D3
Edale Way CV6 . . . . . . .62 A7
Eddie Miller Ct CV12 . .39 B2
Eden Cl B80 . . . . .103 D3

Eden Croft CV8 . . . . . . .93 B3
Eden Ct
  Nuneaton CV10 . . . . . .28 C7
  Royal Leamington Spa
    CV32 . . . . .106 D3
Edenfield Pl B77 . . . . . .4 B1
Eden Gr B37 . . . . .33 D1
Eden Rd
  Coventry CV2 . . . . .63 A8
  Rugby CV21 . . . . .83 F1
Eden St CV6 . . . . .61 F7
Edgecote Cl CV21 . . . .83 F1
Edgefield Rd CV2 . . . . .63 A8
Edgehill Cl B98 . . . . . .102 C8
Edgehill Pl CV4 . . . . . .59 C1
Edgehill Rd CV33 . . . .123 C2
Edge Hill CV9 . . . . .10 B2
Edge La B95 . . . . .113 C5
Edgewick Com Prim Sch
  CV6 . . . . .61 E8
Edgioake La B96 . . . . .118 C2
Edgwick Park Ind Est CV6 .61 F8
Edgwick Rd CV6 . . . . . .61 F8
Edinburgh Cl OX16 . .139 F4
Edinburgh Cres CV31 . .109 F5
Edinburgh Rd
  Hurley CV9 . . . . .16 C5
  Nuneaton CV10 . . . . . .28 D6
Edinburgh Villas CV8 . .77 F2
Edinburgh Way
  Banbury OX16 . . . . . .139 F3
  Long Lawford CV23 . .82 B5
Edingale Rd CV2 . . . . . .62 F8
Edison Rd
  Coleshill B46 . . . . . . .24 A3
  Curdworth B46,B76 . .23 F4
Edkins Cvn Site CV37 . .120 B5
Edmondes Cl CV34 . . .104 F1
Edmonds Cl CV37 . . . .129 D1
Edmondscote Rd CV32 . .109 D8
Edmondson Cl CV22 . . .99 D4
Edmund Rd CV1 . . . . . . .61 D5
Edmunds Rd OX16 . . .139 F3
Edstone Cl B93 . . . . . . .71 F4
Edward Bailey Cl CV3 . .78 E7
Edward Ct
  2 Rugby CV21 . . . . . . .83 B3
  Nuneaton CV11 . . . . . .29 C2
Edward Mews CV34 . . .108 E7
Edward Rd
  Bedworth CV12 . . . . . .39 C3
  Coventry CV6 . . . . .49 A3
  Water Orton B46 . . . . .23 C3
Edwards Ctr 7 LE10 . .31 D8
Edwards Gr CV8 . . . . . . .93 C5
Edward St
  Coventry CV6 . . . . .61 E5
  Nuneaton CV11 . . . . . .29 C3
  Royal Leamington Spa
    CV32 . . . . .105 C1
  Rugby CV21 . . . . .82 F3
  Warwick CV34 . . . . . .108 D7
Edward Tyler Rd CV7 . .39 A1
Edwin Cl CV22 . . . . .99 B7
Edyth Rd CV2 . . . . .62 E7
Edyvean Cl CV22 . . . . .99 E6
Edyvean Walker Ct CV11 . .29 B5
Egerton Cl CV21 . . . . . .82 F4
Eglamour Way CV34 . .109 F3
Egret Wlk CV2 . . . . .50 B3
Eileen Gdns B37 . . . . . .33 A4
Elan Cl CV32 . . . . .106 C3
Elborow St 5 CV21 . . .83 A3
Elbury Croft B93 . . . . .71 F5
Elderberry Way CV2 . . .62 A6
Elder Cl
  Kingsbury B78 . . . . . .15 D7
  Rugby CV22 . . . . .82 B1
Eldersfield Gr B91 . . .71 B7
Eldorado Cl B80 . . . . .103 D4
Eld Rd CV6 . . . . .61 F7
Elford Gr B37 . . . . .33 B1
Elgar Cl
  Nuneaton CV10 . . . . . .40 A7
  Redditch B97 . . . . . . .102 C8
Elgar Rd CV6 . . . . .62 C5
Eliot Cl
  15 Stratford-u-A CV37 . .130 B8
  Warwick CV34 . . . . . .104 E2
Eliot Ct CV22 . . . . .82 E3
Eliot Way CV10 . . . . . . .29 B2
Elisabeth Ct CV31 . . .110 B8
Elizabeth Ave B78 . . . . .5 A2
Elizabeth Ct
  8 Coventry CV6 . . . . . .61 A4
  Warwick CV34 . . . . . .109 B6
Elizabeth Rd CV31 . . .109 F6
Elizabeth Way
  Coventry CV2 . . . . .62 F7
  Kenilworth CV8 . . . . . .92 E5
  Long Lawford CV23 . .82 B5
Elkington Croft B90 . .71 A6
Elkington La CV23 . . .101 B1
Elkington St CV6 . . . . .61 F8
Ellacombe Rd CV12 . . .39 C2
Ellen Badger Hospl
  CV36 . . . . .149 E6
Ellerbeck B77 . . . . .4 B1
Ellerdene Cl B98 . . . .102 D8
Ellerman Gdns CV6 . . .49 F3
Ellesmere Rd CV12 . . .39 C2
Ellice Dr B36 . . . . .33 B7
Elliot Cl CV36 . . . . . .149 D6
Elliot Dr CV35 . . . . . .146 C3
Elliott Cl CV21 . . . . . .83 C7
Elliott's Field Ret Pk CV21 .83 A6
Elliotts Orch CV35 . .122 A7

Ellison Dr 16 OX17 . .139 F5
Ellis Park Dr CV3 . . . .63 B1
Ellison Gr CV31 . . . . .110 C6
Ell La CV23 . . . . .64 F4
Ellys Rd CV1 . . . . .61 C5
Elm Bank Cl CV32 . . . .106 A4
Elmbank Rd CV8 . . . . . . .92 E6
Elmbank CV47 . . . . . . .147 B3
Elmbridge Dr B90 . . . .71 B6
Elm Cl
  Binley Woods CV3 . . .79 C7
  Ilmington CV36 . . . . .136 B6
  Pebworth CV37 . . . . . .128 F1
  Southam CV47 . . . . . .147 A2
Elm Ct
  7 Stratford-u-A CV37 . .144 F3
  Allesley CV5 . . . . .59 B8
Elmdene Cl
  Hatton CV35 . . . . . . .114 C5
  Wolston CV8 . . . . .80 A4
Elmdene Rd CV8 . . . . . .93 B4
Elmdon Ct B37 . . . . . . .44 A7
Elmdon La
  Birmingham B37 . . . . .44 A6
  Solihull B26 . . . . .44 A3
Elmdon Rd B37 . . . . . . .44 A6
Elmdon Trad Est B37 . .44 C5
Elm Dr B49 . . . . .143 D3
Elmfield Rd CV10 . . . . .29 C7
Elm Gr
  Balsall Common CV7 . .74 C5
  Birmingham GL55 . . .135 F3
  Hurley CV9 . . . . .16 C4
  Old Arley CV7 . . . . . . .26 E2
Elmhurst Cl B97 . . . . .102 D4
Elmhurst Rd CV6 . . . . . .50 A4
Elm La CV23 . . . . .68 E1
Elm Lodge B92 . . . . . . .57 A7
Elmore Cl
  Birmingham B37 . . . . . .33 A4
  Coventry CV3 . . . . .78 D8
Elmore Rd CV22 . . . . . . .82 F1
Elm Rd
  Royal Leamington Spa
    CV32 . . . . .106 B3
  Shipston-on-S CV36 .149 D4
  Stratford-u-A CV37 . .144 F5
Elm Row CV47 . . . . . . .147 A3
Elm St CV9 . . . . .3 A2
Elmsdale Ave CV6 . . . .49 F2
Elms Paddock The CV23 . .84 A3
Elms The
  Bedworth CV12 . . . . . .38 C2
  Kingswood B94 . . . . . .89 D3
  Leek Wootton CV35 . .104 F6
  Wellesbourne CV35 . .146 D2
Elmstone Cl B91 . . . . .71 A7
Elm Tree Ave CV4 . . . .60 B2
Elm Tree Cl B78 . . . . . .15 D6
Elm Tree Dr LE10 . . . . .31 F8
Elm Tree Rd CV12 . . . .40 D2
Elm Tree Rise B92 . . . .57 B6
Elm Way CV10 . . . . .28 A8
Elmwood Ave CV6 . . . . .60 F5
Elmwood Cl CV7 . . . . . .74 C7
Elmwood Ct CV1 . . . . .151 A4
Elmwood Gr B47 . . . . . .69 A6
Elmwood Rd CV13 . . . . .21 C4
Elphin Cl CV6 . . . . .49 A3
Elsee Rd CV21 . . . . .83 B3
Elstop Ave CV23 . . . . .64 C2
Elter Cl CV21 . . . . .83 D7
Eltham Rd CV3 . . . . .77 E7
Elton Cl CV32 . . . . . . .106 C2
Elton Croft B93 . . . . . .71 F4
Elva Croft B36 . . . . . . .22 F1
Elvers Green La B92,B93 . .72 E7
Ely Circ CV47 . . . . .49 C6
Ely Cl
  Birmingham B37 . . . . . .33 A2
  Coventry CV2 . . . . .63 A4
Ely Gdns CV37 . . . . . .144 F2
Ely St CV37 . . . . .145 A2
Embassy Wlk CV2 . . . . .62 D8
Emerald Way CV31 . . .109 F5
Emerson Rd CV2 . . . . . .62 C3
Emery Cl CV2 . . . . .62 E7
Emily Smith Ho 2 CV2 . .50 B1
Emmerson Ave CV37 . .144 D3
Emmott Dr CV31 . . . . .110 B5
Empire Rd CV4 . . . . .59 E2
Emscote Inf Sch CV34 . .108 E7
Emscote Rd
  Coventry CV2 . . . . .62 C2
  Warwick CV34 . . . . . .109 B8
Ena Rd CV1 . . . . .61 D5
Endemere Rd CV6 . . . . .61 D6
Enderby Cl B93 . . . . . . .71 F4
Endsleigh Gdns CV31 . .110 D6
Enfield Rd
  Coventry CV2 . . . . .62 B3
  Redditch B97 . . . . . . .102 C3
Engine La B77 . . . . .4 A2
England Cres CV31 . . .109 E7
England Ho 10 CV32 . .105 F2
Engleton Rd CV6 . . . . .61 A6
English Martyrs RC Prim Sch
  CV22 . . . . .101 A7
Ennerdale Cl CV32 . .105 D2
Ennerdale Cres CV11 . .29 F6
Ennerdale La CV21 . . .83 C7
Ennerdale CV21 . . . . . .83 C7
Ennersdale Bglws B46 . .23 F1
Ennersdale Cl B46 . . .23 F1
Ennersdale Rd B46 . . .23 F1

Enright Cl CV32 . . . . . .105 E2
Ensign Bsns Ctr CV4 . .75 F6
Ensign Cl CV4 . . . . .59 D5
Ensor Cl CV11 . . . . .30 A6
Ensor Dr B78 . . . . .4 F1
Enterprise Ho B92 . . . .57 A6
Enville Cl B37 . . . . .33 B1
Epperston Ct CV31 . . .109 F7
Epping Way CV32 . . . .106 C4
Epsom Cl
  Bedworth CV12 . . . . . .39 B4
  Redditch B97 . . . . . . .102 C8
  Tamworth B77 . . . . .9 C4
Epsom Dr CV3 . . . . .78 C6
Epsom Rd
  Royal Leamington Spa
    CV32 . . . . .106 C4
  Rugby CV22 . . . . .82 D1
Epwell Rd
  Shutford OX15 . . . . . .138 F3
  Upper Tysoe CV35 . . .138 B6
Erdington Rd CV9 . . . . .18 D7
Erica Ave CV12 . . . . . . .38 F2
Erica Dr CV31 . . . . . . .110 B2
Eric Grey Cl CV2 . . . . .62 A5
Eringden B77 . . . . .4 B1
Erithway Rd CV3 . . . . . .77 A4
Ernesford Grange Prim Sch
  CV3 . . . . .78 E6
Ernesford Grange Sch & Com
  Coll CV3 . . . . .78 D8
Ernest Richards Rd CV12 . .39 B4
Ernsford Ave CV3 . . . . .62 F2
Ernsford Cl B93 . . . . . .71 F2
Errington GL56 . . . . . .140 B3
Esher Dr CV3 . . . . .77 E7
Eskdale Cl CV21 . . . . . .30 A1
Eskdale Cl CV21 . . . . . .83 C8
Eskdale Wlk CV3 . . . . . .78 D7
Essen La CV23 . . . . . . .101 F3
Essex Cl
  Coventry CV5 . . . . .60 B3
  Kenilworth CV8 . . . . . .92 E2
Essex Ct CV34 . . . . . . .108 E8
Essex Gn CV47 . . . . . .132 F7
Essex St CV21 . . . . .83 A4
Essex Way CV10 . . . . . .28 F3
Ethelfield Rd CV2 . . . .62 D3
Ethelfleda Rd B77 . . . . .9 F5
Etone Com Sch CV11 . . .29 D5
Etone Ct CV11 . . . . .29 B5
Eton Rd CV37 . . . . . . .145 C1
Ettingham Cross Rds
  CV37 . . . . .131 A4
Ettingham Grange CV37 .131 A4
Ettingley Cl B98 . . . .103 B5
Ettington Cl
  Dorridge B93 . . . . .71 D2
  Wellesbourne CV35 . .146 D2
Ettington CE Prim Sch
  CV37 . . . . .131 B3
Ettington Rd
  Coventry CV5 . . . . .60 A3
  Wellesbourne CV35 . .146 D2
Eunal Ct B97 . . . . . . .102 E5
Europark Ind Est CV23 . .68 B2
Europa Way CV34 . . . .109 D5
Eustace Rd CV12 . . . . . .40 D1
Euston Cres CV3 . . . . .78 C6
Euston Pl CV32 . . . . . .109 F8
Euston Sq 1 CV32 . . .109 F8
Evans Cl
  Bedworth CV12 . . . . . .39 C3
  Stratford-u-A CV37 . .144 D1
Evans Gr CV31 . . . . . .110 A2
Evans Rd CV22 . . . . .82 C2
Evelyn Ave CV6 . . . . . .49 F2
Evenlode Cl CV31 . . .145 C1
Evenlode Cres CV6 . . .60 F5
Evenlode Gdns GL56 .140 B3
Everard Cl CV33 . . . . . .84 A5
Everard Ct CV11 . . . . . .29 E2
Everdon Cl CV22 . . . .100 E8
Everdon Rd CV6 . . . . . .49 B2
Everest Rd CV22 . . . . . .99 B8
Everglade Rd CV9 . . . .10 C2
Evergreens The CV10 . .28 F6
Everitt Dr B93 . . . . . . .71 F6
Eversleigh Rd CV6 . . . .60 F7
Evesham Country Park
  Visitor Ctr* WR11 . .127 C1
Evesham Ct CV37 . . . .144 F2
Evesham Rd
  Bidford-on-A B50,CV37 . .128 B8
  Church Lench WR11 . .127 A6
  Cookhill B49 . . . . .118 D5
  Harvington WR11 . . . .127 F3
  Middle Littleton WR11 .127 F3
  Redditch B96,B97 . . .102 E3
  Salford Priors WR11 . .127 F5
  Stratford-u-A CV37 . .144 D1
Evesham St B49 . . . . .143 B3
Evesham Wlk CV4 . . . . .76 D3
Evreux Way CV21 . . . . . .83 A3
Exbury Way CV11 . . . . . .39 F8
Exeter Cl CV3 . . . . .78 D8
Exhall Cedars Inf Sch CV7 .50 A8
Exhall Cl CV37 . . . . . .145 A1
Exhall Grange Sch & Science
  Coll CV7 . . . . .49 C5
Exhall Rd CV7 . . . . .49 A6
Exham Cl CV34 . . . . . .104 E1

Exhibition Way B40 . . . . .44 D4
Exis Ct CV11 . . . . .29 E2
Exminster Rd CV3 . . . . .77 E5
Exmoor Dr CV32 . . . . .106 C4
Exmouth Cl CV2 . . . . .62 C7
Exton Cl CV7 . . . . .49 C6
Eydon Cl CV21 . . . . .83 E6
Eyffler Cl CV34 . . . . .108 D7

F

Fabian Cl CV3 . . . . .78 D7
Fabius Cl LE10 . . . . .31 C7
Fairbanks Cl CV2 . . . . .63 A7
Fairbourne Gdns B97 . . . . . .102 C7
Fairbourne Way CV6 . . . . .60 E8
Fair Cl CV23 . . . . .97 D1
Faircroft CV8 . . . . .92 F3
Faircroft Rd B36 . . . . .22 D1
Fairfax Cl CV35 . . . . .122 A7
Fairfax 7 CV34 . . . . .108 F7
Fairfax St CV1 . . . . .151 C3
Fairfield Cl CV3 . . . . .78 A7
Fairfield Rise CV7 . . . . .46 C1
Fairfields Hill B78 . . . . .10 F8
Fairfields Wlk CV37 . . . . .144 D4
Fairhurst Dr CV32 . . . . .105 E3
Fair Isle Dr CV10 . . . . .28 F2
Fairlands Pk CV4 . . . . .76 E5
Fairlawns Cl CV32 . . . . .105 D1
Fairlawns B76 . . . . .22 A8
Fairmile Cl CV3 . . . . .78 C8
Fairview Ind Est B76 . . . . .23 B7
Fairview Mews 9 B46 . . . . . . .33 F7
Fairview Wlk CV6 . . . . .49 E2
Fairwater Cres B49 . . . . .143 D4
Fairway CV1 . . . .
Rugby CV21 . . . . .83 D4
Tamworth B77 . . . . .4 B3
Fairway CV11 . . . . .40 B8
Fairway Rise CV8 . . . . .93 C6
Fairways Cl CV5 . . . . .60 A6
Fairways B93 . . . . .72 A8
Fairways The CV32 . . . . .105 D2
Fairway B77 . . . . .9 F5
Fairway The
5 Banbury OX16 . . . . .139 F4
Hinckley LE10 . . . . .31 F7
Falcon Ave CV3 . . . . .78 F8
Falcon Cl CV11 . . . . .40 B8
Falcon Cres B50 . . . . .148 E5
Falcon Ct 6 CV47 . . . . .147 B4
Falconers Gn LE10 . . . . .31 F6
Falcon Lodge Cres B75 . . . . . .13 A6
Falcon Pk B77 . . . . .9 E7
Falcons The B75 . . . . .13 B5
Falcon B77 . . . . .10 A6
Falkener Ho CV6 . . . . .61 E7
Falkland Cl CV4 . . . . .75 D7
Falkland Pl CV47 . . . . .133 A7
Falkland Way B36 . . . . .33 B5
Falkwood Gr B93 . . . . .71 F6
Fallowfields CV6 . . . . .49 C4
Fallow Hill CV31 . . . . .110 C6
Falmouth Cl CV11 . . . . .30 A5
Falstaff Ave B47 . . . . .69 A6
Falstaff Cl
Nuneaton CV11 . . . . .30 A1
Sutton Coldfield B76 . . . . . .22 B7
Falstaff Ct
18 Stratford-u-A CV37 . . .145 A3
Sutton Coldfield B75 . . . . . .13 C5
Falstaff Dr CV22 . . . . .99 D6
Falstaff Gr CV34 . . . . .109 E3
Falstaff Rd CV4 . . . . .59 E1
Fancott Dr CV8 . . . . .92 F6
Fant Hill OX15 . . . . .137 E3
Faraday Ave
Coleshill B46 . . . . .24 A4
Farnborough B76,B76. . . . .23 F5
Faraday Rd
Hinckley LE10 . . . . .30 E7
Rugby CV22 . . . . .83 C1
Farber Rd CV2 . . . . .63 A6
Farbury End OX7 . . . . .142 A6
Farcroft Ave CV5 . . . . .59 D4
Fareham Ave CV22 . . . . .100 E8
Far Gosford St CV1 . . . . .61 E2
Faringdon B77 . . . . .4 A1
Far Lash LE10 . . . . .31 F7
Farley Ave CV33 . . . . .123 E6
Farley St CV31 . . . . .110 B7
Farlow Cl CV6 . . . . .62 A6
Farman Rd CV5 . . . . .61 A2
Farm Cl
Coventry CV6 . . . . .49 B3
Harbury CV33 . . . . .123 E6
Shipston-on-S CV36 . . . . . .149 C6
Farmcote Cl B97 . . . . .102 D4
Farmcote Lodge CV2 . . . . .50 B4
Farmcote Rd CV2 . . . . .50 B4
Farmer Ward Rd CV8 . . . . . . .93 A3
Farm Gr CV22 . . . . .83 C1
Farmhouse Way B90 . . . . .71 B7
Farmhurst CV22 . . . . .83 C1
Farm La
Easenhall CV23 . . . . .65 E4
Grendon CV9 . . . . .11 F6
South Littleton WR11 . . . . .127 F1
Far Moor La B98 . . . . .112 A6
Farm Rd
Hinckley LE10 . . . . .31 E6
Kenilworth CV8 . . . . .92 E2

Farm Rd continued
Royal Leamington Spa
CV32 . . . . .106 B3
Farmside CV3 . . . . .78 D5
Farmstead The CV3 . . . . .78 B8
Farm St CV33 . . . . .123 E6
Farm Stile NN11 . . . . .134 E8
Farm Wlk 2 CV23 . . . . .122 F8
Farnborough Dr B90 . . . . .70 F6
Farnborough Hall*
OX17 . . . . .133 F4
Farnborough Rd
Birmingham B35 . . . . .22 B3
Radway CV35. . . . . .132 F3
Farndale Ave CV6 . . . . .49 D3
Farndon Ave B37 . . . . .44 B7
Farndon Cl CV12 . . . . .40 B3
Farnell Dr CV37. . . . . .144 D3
Farnworth Gr B36 . . . . .22 E1
Far Pool Mdw CV35 . . . . . . .113 F3
Farr Dr CV4 . . . . .60 B2
Farren Rd CV2 . . . . .62 E5
Farriers Ct
Stretton u F CV23 . . . . .65 C7
Wasperton CV35 . . . . .122 A5
Farriers Way
Hinckley LE10 . . . . .31 F6
Nuneaton CV11 . . . . .29 F2
Farrington Cl CV35 . . . . .146 C2
Farrington Ct CV35 . . . . .146 C2
Farther Sand Cl CV35 . . . . . .121 F4
Farthing La B76 . . . . .23 C6
Farthing Wlk CV4 . . . . .75 D6
Farvale Rd B76 . . . . .22 C6
Farzens Ave CV34 . . . . .108 B3
Faseman Ave CV4 . . . . .59 F3
Fasson Cl B77 . . . . .9 C8
Faulconbridge Ave CV5 . . . . .59 E4
Faulconbridge Way
CV34 . . . . .109 E3
Faultlands Cl CV11 . . . . .39 F8
Fawley Cl CV3 . . . . .78 F6
Fawsley Leys CV22 . . . . .100 A7
Faygate Cl CV3 . . . . .62 F3
Fearnings Cotts B97 . . . . . . .102 D5
Featherbed La
Bascote CV47 . . . . .115 B1
Cherington CV36 . . . . .141 D7
Coventry CV4 . . . . .76 A5
Redditch B97 . . . . .102 C5
Rugby CV21 . . . . .84 A1
Wilmcote CV37 . . . . .120 D5
Withybrook CV7 . . . . .52 D8
Feather Dr LE10 . . . . .31 E6
Featherstone Ct CV10 . . . . . . .29 C2
Feckenham Rd
Astwood Bank B96 . . . . . .102 C2
Redditch,Headless Cross
B97 . . . . .102 C8
Redditch,Hunt End B97 . .102 C4
Feilding Cl CV2 . . . . .63 A6
Feilding Way CV10 . . . . .28 A5
Fen Bank CV4 . . . . .59 C2
Feldon Edge CV36 . . . . .137 A8
Felgate Cl B90 . . . . .71 A6
Fell Gr CV32 . . . . .106 C3
Fell Mill La
Honington CV36. . . . . .149 F7
Shipston-on-S CV36 . . . . .149 E6
Fellmore Gr CV31 . . . . .110 D7
Fellows Way CV21 . . . . .100 F8
Fell's La CV47 . . . . .125 C8
Felspar Rd B77 . . . . .4 B3
Felstead Cl B77 . . . . .9 C4
Felton Cl CV2 . . . . .50 E1
Fencote Ave B37 . . . . .33 A4
Fen End Rd CV8 . . . . .73 E4
Fennell Ho 10 CV1 . . . . .61 B2
Fennis Cl B93 . . . . .71 F3
Fenn Lanes CV13 . . . . .20 D8
Fenny Compton Rd
OX17 . . . . .134 B5
Fennyland La CV8 . . . . .93 B7
Fenside Ave CV3 . . . . .77 D4
Fentham Cl B92 . . . . .57 B6
Fentham Gn B92 . . . . .57 B6
Fentham Rd B92 . . . . .57 A6
Fenton Rd B47 . . . . .69 A7
Fenwick Cl B49 . . . . .143 D5
Fenwick Dr CV21 . . . . .101 A8
Ferguson Cl CV37 . . . . .131 B3
Fern Cl
Coventry CV2 . . . . .50 C2
Rugby CV23 . . . . .83 D8
Salford Priors WR11 . . . . .127 D6
Ferncumbe CE Prim Sch The
CV35 . . . . .114 D6
Ferndale Cl CV11 . . . . .29 E5
Ferndale Ct B46 . . . . .34 A5
Ferndale Dr CV8 . . . . .93 A2
Ferndale Gr LE10 . . . . .31 A7
Ferndale Mews B46 . . . . .34 A5
Ferndale Rd 8 OX16 . . . . . .139 F4
Fern Dale Rd CV7 . . . . .73 F6
Ferndale Rd
Binley Woods CV3 . . . . .79 D7
Coleshill B46 . . . . .34 A5
Ferndown Cl CV4 . . . . .60 A3
Ferndown Ct CV22 . . . . .82 E1
Ferndown Rd CV22 . . . . .82 E1
Ferndown Terr CV22 . . . . . . .82 E1
Fern Gr CV12 . . . . .38 E2
Fernhill Cl CV8 . . . . .92 E6
Fernhill Dr CV32 . . . . .106 B1
Fernhill La CV7,CV8 . . . . .73 F5
Fern Hill Way LE10 . . . . .41 D4
Fernwood Cl B98 . . . . .103 B5
Ferrers Cl CV4. . . . . .59 F2

Ferrieres Cl CV22 . . . . .99 C3
Ferry La CV37 . . . . .121 D3
Fetherston Cres CV37 . . . . . . .94 B6
Fetherston St 4 CV31 . . . .109 F6
Fetherston Grange B94 . . . . .88 F5
Fiddlers Gn B92 . . . . .57 A7
Field Barn Rd CV35 . . . . .108 A7
Field Cl
Harbury CV33 . . . . .123 F8
Kenilworth CV8 . . . . .93 B5
Warwick CV34 . . . . .109 B7
Field Ct CV2 . . . . .62 D7
Fieldfare Cl CV23 . . . . .83 C8
Fieldfare Croft B36 . . . . .33 A8
Fieldgate La
Fenny Compton CV47. . . .133 C7
Kenilworth CV8 . . . . .92 F6
Whitnash CV31 . . . . .110 B2
Fieldgate Lawn CV8 . . . . .92 F6
Field Head La CV34 . . . . .109 B6
Fieldhouse Cl B95 . . . . .113 A4
Fielding Cl CV11 . . . . .12 D2
Field La LE91 . . . . .66 B3
Field March CV3 . . . . .78 E5
Fieldside La CV3 . . . . .62 F3
Fields Park Dr B49 . . . . .143 D4
Field View
Binton CV37 . . . . .120 A1
Braunston NN11 . . . . .117 D5
Cawston CV22 . . . . .99 B8
Field View CV7 . . . . .50 A8
Field View
Shrewley CV35 . . . . .114 C6
Whitnash CV31 . . . . .110 B3
Field Way B94 . . . . .88 C6
Fieldways Cl B47 . . . . .69 A7
Fife Rd CV5 . . . . .60 F2
Fife St CV11 . . . . .29 A4
Fifield Cl CV11 . . . . .29 D2
Fighting Cl 7 CV35 . . . . . . .132 B6
Fillingham Cl B37 . . . . .33 D1
Fillongley Rd
Lodge Green CV7 . . . . .46 E3
Maxstoke B46 . . . . .35 D4
Filton Croft B35 . . . . .22 A4
Fin Cl CV6 . . . . .49 C2
Finch Cl CV5 . . . . .60 D6
Finch Croft CV7 . . . . .74 B7
Finch La WR11 . . . . .127 D3
Findley Cl CV9 . . . . .118 E6
Findon Cl CV12 . . . . .40 C3
Fineacre La CV8,CV23 . . . . . .96 D5
Finford Croft CV7 . . . . .74 B6
Fingal Cl CV3 . . . . .78 C6
Fingest Cl CV5 . . . . .60 B4
Finham Cres CV8 . . . . .93 B6
Finham Flats CV8 . . . . .93 B6
Finham Gr CV3 . . . . .77 C3
Finham Green Rd CV3 . . . . . .77 B3
Finham Park Sch CV3 . . . . . .77 A4
Finham Prim Sch CV3 . . . . . .77 B3
Finham Rd CV8 . . . . .93 B6
Finings Ct 7 CV32 . . . . .105 F2
Finlay Ct CV1 . . . . .151 C1
Finmere CV21 . . . . .83 D6
Finnemore Cl CV3 . . . . .77 B5
Finwood Rd CV35 . . . . .113 F8
Fircroft Ho B37 . . . . .33 A2
Fircroft B78 . . . . .15 D7
Firedrake Croft CV1 . . . . .61 F2
Fire Service Coll The
GL56 . . . . .140 B3
Firethorn Cres CV31 . . . . . . .110 A2
Fir Gr CV4 . . . . .60 A2
Firleigh Dr CV12 . . . . .40 D2
Firs Dr CV22 . . . . .82 F2
First Ave
Birmingham B35 . . . . .22 A5
Coventry CV3 . . . . .62 A1
First Exhibition Ave B40 . . . .44 D4
Firs The
Bedworth CV12 . . . . .38 E2
Kingsbury B78 . . . . .15 D7
Lower Quinton CV37 . . . . .129 E2
Meriden CV7 . . . . .46 B1
Wroxton OX15 . . . . .139 D4
Firth Ave GL56 . . . . .140 C3
Fir Tree Ave CV4 . . . . .60 B2
Firtree Cl CV7 . . . . .37 A8
Fisher Ave CV22 . . . . .100 E8
Fisher Rd
Bishops Itchington CV47. .124 A4
Coventry CV6 . . . . .61 E8
Fishers Cl CV23 . . . . .101 F2
Fisher's Ct CV34 . . . . .108 D4
Fishers Dr B90 . . . . .69 F5
Fishponds Rd CV8 . . . . .92 E3
Fishpool La CV7 . . . . .45 B5
Fitton St CV11 . . . . .29 B3
Fitzalan Cl CV23 . . . . .81 B6
Fitzroy Cl CV2 . . . . .63 B6
Fivefield Rd CV7 . . . . .48 E5
Five Lane Ends LE10 . . . . . . .41 F6
Five Ways Rd CV35 . . . . .114 C7
Five Ways
Shutford OX15 . . . . .139 B3
Wroxall CV35. . . . . .90 F1
Fladbury Cl B98 . . . . .103 B8
Flamboro' Cl CV3 . . . . .78 F8
Flamville Rd LE10 . . . . .32 B5
Flats La CV9 . . . . .3 B1
Flaunden Cl CV5 . . . . .60 B4
Flavel Cres CV31 . . . . .109 F7
Flavel Ct CV9 . . . . .3 A1

Flax Cl B47 . . . . .69 A5
Flaxley Cl B98 . . . . .112 A6
Flecknoe Cl B36 . . . . .22 C1
Flecknose St CV3 . . . . .78 C6
Fleet Cres CV21. . . . . .83 E2
Fleet St CV1 . . . . .151 B3
Fleming Rd LE10 . . . . .30 F7
Fletchamstead Highway
CV5 . . . . .76 D7
Fletcher Gr B93 . . . . .72 B4
Fletcher Rd LE10 . . . . .31 E7
Fletchers Way CV35. . . . . . .146 C3
Fletchworth Gate CV5. . . . . .76 D8
Fletchworth Gate Ind Est
CV4 . . . . .76 D8
Fleur de-lys Ct CV34 . . . . . .109 B8
Flint Cl CV9 . . . . .12 E2
Florence Cl
Atherstone CV9 . . . . .12 D1
Bedworth CV12 . . . . .49 F8
Florence Rd CV3 . . . . .63 A2
Florendine St B77 . . . . .4 A5
Florian Way LE10 . . . . .21 F1
Florin Cl CV4 . . . . .75 E6
Florin Pl CV21 . . . . .83 C5
Flower Cl 8 CV37 . . . . .144 F1
Flowerdale Dr CV2. . . . . .62 B6
Flower Rd CV37 . . . . .144 F6
Floyd Gr CV7 . . . . .74 C7
Flude Rd CV7. . . . . .49 C6
Flying Fields Rd CV47. . . . . .147 C4
Flynt Ave CV5 . . . . .60 B6
Focus Pk B90 . . . . .70 B8
Fold The 8 CV37 . . . . .145 A3
Foldyard Cl B76 . . . . .22 A8
Foleshill CE Prim Sch
CV6 . . . . .50 A2
Foleshill Rd CV1,CV6 . . . . . . .61 D6
Folkland Gn CV6. . . . . .61 A7
Follager Rd CV21 . . . . .82 F4
Folly Ct CV15 . . . . .142 E8
Folly La
Baddesley Ensor CV9. . . . . .17 D8
Napton on t H CV47. . . . . .125 B7
Folly The B97 . . . . .102 D8
Fontmell Cl CV2 . . . . .63 A4
Fordbridge Inf Sch B37 . . . . .33 A5
Fordbridge Rd B37 . . . . .33 A5
Ford Cotts CV33 . . . . .106 F2
Forde Hall La B94,B95. . . . .112 D7
Fordham Ave CV37 . . . . .145 A4
Fordington Pl 6 CV35. . . . .132 B6
Ford La CV37 . . . . .113 F1
Fordrift The B37 . . . . .44 A6
Fordrough The B90 . . . . .69 C7
Fords Rd B90 . . . . .69 E7
Ford St
Coventry CV1. . . . . .151 C3
Nuneaton CV10 . . . . .28 E4
Fordway The CV37 . . . . .129 D2
Fordwell Cl CV5 . . . . .60 F3
Foredraught B80 . . . . .103 E4
Foregate St B96 . . . . .102 E1
Foreland Way CV6 . . . . .49 A3
Forest Ct
Coventry CV5. . . . . .60 A4
Dorridge B93 . . . . .71 F3
Foresters Pl CV21. . . . . . . .101 B7
Forester's Rd CV3. . . . . .77 E6
Forest Oak Sch B36. . . . . . . .22 E1
Forest Rd
Dorridge B93 . . . . .71 F3
Hinckley LE10 . . . . .102 E6
Forest View B97 . . . . .102 E6
Forest Way
Hollywood B47 . . . . .69 B6
Nuneaton CV10 . . . . .28 E2
Forfield Pl CV31 . . . . .110 A7
Forfield Rd CV6 . . . . .60 E5
Forge Croft B76 . . . . .22 B6
Forge La
Farnborough OX17 . . . . . .133 F4
Sutton Coldfield B76 . . . . . .22 B5
Forge Rd
Kenilworth CV8 . . . . .93 A6
Shustoke B46 . . . . .25 A2
Forge Way CV6 . . . . .49 C3
Forknell Ave CV2 . . . . .62 C5
Fornside Cl CV21 . . . . .83 D7
Forresters Cl LE10 . . . . .31 F6
Forresters Rd LE10 . . . . .31 F6
Forrest Rd CV8 . . . . .92 E4
Forryan Rd LE10 . . . . .31 F7
Forshaw Heath La B94. . . . . .86 A7
Forshaw Heath Rd B94. . . . . .69 C1
Forth Dr B37 . . . . .33 B4
Forties B77. . . . . .9 E7
Forum Dr CV21 . . . . .83 A6
Forum Rd B40 . . . . .44 E3
Forward Rd B26 . . . . .44 A3
Fosberry Cl CV34 . . . . .109 B8
Fossdale Rd B77 . . . . .10 A8
Fosse Cl LE10 . . . . .32 A5
Fosse Cotts CV23 . . . . .80 E8
Fosse Cres CV23 . . . . .96 E3
Fosseway Ave GL56 . . . . . . .140 A4
Fosse Way Bsns Ctr
GL56 . . . . .140 A3
Fosseway Cl GL56 . . . . .140 A2
Fosseway Cres CV36 . . . . . .136 F6
Fosse Way GL56 . . . . .140 A2
Fosse Way
Harbury CV33 . . . . .123 C7
Moreton Morrell CV35. . . .123 A3

Fosseway Rd CV3 . . . . .77 B4
Fosse Way
Shipston-on-S CV36 . . . . .149 A8
Stretton-on-D CV23 . . . . . .97 A6
Stretton u F CV23 . . . . .65 B7
Ufton CV31,CV33 . . . . . . .111 C5
Foster Ave B80 . . . . .103 E3
Fosterd Rd CV21. . . . . .82 F6
Foster Rd CV6 . . . . .61 B7
Founder Cl CV4 . . . . .75 F7
Foundry Ct 6 CV37 . . . . . .144 F3
Fountain Gdns CV35 . . . . . .145 A2
Fountain Way 1 CV37 . . . .145 A2
Four Ashes Rd B93 . . . . .71 E4
Four Crosses CV23. . . . . . . .117 C6
Four Foxes CV5 . . . . .60 A6
Four Lanes End CV10 . . . . . . .37 E7
Four Oaks Cl B98 . . . . .102 D8
Four Pounds Ave CV5 . . . . . . .60 F2
Fourways CV9 . . . . .18 F8
Fowey Cl B76 . . . . .22 A7
Fowler Rd
Coventry CV6 . . . . .61 B4
Sutton Coldfield B75 . . . . . .13 B5
Fox Cl CV34 . . . . .59 C2
Fow Oak CV4 . . . .
Fox Ave CV10 . . . . .29 C7
Foxbury Dr B93 . . . . .72 B3
Fox Cl
Harbury CV33 . . . . .123 F6
Rugby CV21 . . . . .84 B1
Tamworth B77 . . . . .9 C8
Foxcote Cl B90 . . . . .70 D8
Foxcote Dr B90 . . . . .70 D8
Foxcote Hill CV36. . . . . .136 A6
Foxcovert La CV21 . . . . .81 A8
Foxdale Wlk 8 CV31. . . . . .110 C6
Foxes La CV37 . . . . .120 C5
Foxes Mdw B76. . . . . .22 A8
Foxes Way
Balsall Common CV7 . . . . . .74 B4
Warwick CV34 . . . . .108 D4
Foxfield CV23 . . . . .66 A8
Foxford Cl B36 . . . . .22 D1
Foxford Cres CV2 . . . . .50 B4
Foxford Sch & Com Arts Coll
CV6 . . . . .50 A5
Foxglove Cl
Bedworth CV12 . . . . .38 E1
Coventry CV6 . . . . .49 C2
Rugby CV23 . . . . .83 E8
Foxglove B77 . . . . .4 A4
Fox Hill Rd B75 . . . . .7 A2
Foxhills Cl CV11 . . . . .30 C1
Foxholes La B97 . . . . .102 A6
Fox Hollies Rd
Sutton Coldfield B76 . . . . . .13 A1
Sutton Coldfield B76 . . . . . .13 B2
Fox la B95. . . . . .113 C4
Foxland Cl
Birmingham B37 . . . . .33 D2
Cheswick Green B90 . . . . . .70 D4
Foxley Dr B91 . . . . .56 A7
Foxons Barn Rd CV21 . . . . . .83 C6
Foxon's Cnr CV23 . . . . .53 C4
Fox's Covert CV13 . . . . .19 F6
Foxtail Cl CV37 . . . . .144 D5
Foxton Ct LE10 . . . . .31 B7
Foxton Rd CV3. . . . . .62 E1
Foxwood Dr CV3 . . . . .79 D7
Foxwood Rd B78. . . . . .10 F8
Framlingham Gr CV8. . . . . . . .93 C6
Frampton Cl B37 . . . . .33 D3
Frampton Wlk CV2 . . . . .62 F4
Frances Ave CV34. . . . . .109 A7
Frances Cres CV12. . . . . .39 A3
Frances Havergal Cl 2
CV31 . . . . .109 F6
Frances Rd
Baginton CV8. . . . . .77 F3
Harbury CV33 . . . . .123 F6
Franciscan Rd CV3 . . . . .77 D8
Francis Cl B78. . . . . .5 A2
Francis Dr CV22 . . . . .99 A8
Francis Gibbs Gdns 3
CV31 . . . . .110 A4
Francis St CV6 . . . . .61 E7
Frankholmes Dr B90 . . . . .71 A6
Frankland Rd CV6 . . . . .50 A1
Franklin Ct CV11. . . . . .29 D1
Franklin Gr CV4 . . . . .59 E1
Franklin Rd
Nuneaton CV11 . . . . .29 D1
Whitnash CV31 . . . . .110 A3
Franklins Gdns CV3 . . . . .63 B1
Franklin's La WR11 . . . . . . .127 B7
Frankpledge Rd CV3 . . . . .77 E7
Frank St CV11 . . . . .29 B3
Frankton Ave CV3 . . . . .77 C5
Frankton Cl B98 . . . . .103 E8
Frankton La CV23 . . . . .97 A5
Frankton Rd CV23 . . . . .97 C2
Frank Walsh Ho CV1 . . . . . .151 C4
Frankwell Dr CV2 . . . . .50 C1
Fraser Cl CV10. . . . . .28 B3
Fraser Rd CV6 . . . . .49 A1
Fraser Way CV37. . . . . .129 B6
Frederick Bird Prim Sch
CV2 . . . . .61 F5
Frederick Eary Ho B98. . . . .103 B7
Frederick Johnson
Almshouses B95. . . . . . . .113 B5
Frederick Neal Ave CV5. . . . .59 D4
Frederick's Rd
CV21 . . . . .82 F3
Frederick Rd CV7 . . . . .37 A8
Frederick St CV21 . . . . .82 F3
Fred Lee Gr CV3 . . . . .77 D4
Freeboard La CV23 . . . . .96 E7

Freeburn Cswy CV4 . . . . .76 C7
Freehold St CV1 . . . . .61 F4
Freeman Cl CV10 . . . . .28 D4
Freeman Ct **3** CV37 . . . 145 A4
Freemans Cl CV32 . . . . . . .105 E2
Freeman's La LE10. . . . . . . .32 A5
Freeman St CV6 . . . . .61 F6
Freemantle Rd CV22 . . . . . .82 C2
Freers Mews CV34 . . . . . .108 B4
Freer St CV11 . . . . .29 E2
Freesland Rise CV10 . . . . . .28 B6
Frensham Cl B37 . . . . .33 C2
Frensham Dr CV10. . . . . . . .28 B5
Freshfield Cl CV5 . . . . .48 C1
Freshwater Gr **1** CV31 . . 110 C6
Freswick Cl LE10 . . . . .21 F1
Fretton Cl CV6 . . . . .61 F7
Frevill Rd CV6 . . . . .62 B8
Friars Cl CV3 . . . . .79 E7
Friar's Gate CV9 . . . . .18 D8
Friars Hill OX15. . . . . .139 C5
Friars' Rd CV1 . . . . .151 B2
Friars St CV34 . . . . .108 D6
Friars Wlk B37 . . . . .33 D2
Friary Ave B90. . . . . .71 A6
Friary Cl CV35 . . . . .114 F3
Friary Rd CV9 . . . . .12 D1
Friary St CV11 . . . . .29 B5
Friary Cl B50. . . . . .148 D5
Friday Furlong B50 . . . . . .148 D6
Friday La B92 . . . . .56 D4
Friday St
  Lower Quinton CV37 . . . . .129 E2
  Pebworth CV37 . . . . .128 F1
Frilsham Way CV5 . . . . .60 B4
Frisby Cl CV11 . . . . .29 E2
Frisby Rd CV4 . . . . .59 E2
Friswell Dr CV6. . . . . .61 F8
Friswell Ho **3** CV2 . . . . .62 D8
Friswell St CV1 . . . . .131 D8
Frobisher Rd
  Coventry CV3. . . . . .77 C5
  Rugby CV22 . . . . .82 C2
Frog La
  Balsall Common CV7 . . . . .74 A5
  Ilmington CV36 . . . . .136 A6
Froglands La WR11 . . . . . .128 A4
Frog La
  Upper Boddington NN11 . .134 E8
  Welford-on-A CV37 . . . . .129 B6
Frogmere Cl CV5 . . . . .60 C6
Frogmore Rd CV8 . . . . .73 F2
Frogmore Rd CV37 . . . . . .121 B6
Frolesworth La LE17 . . . . . .43 F7
Front St
  Ilmington CV36 . . . . .136 B6
  Pebworth CV37 . . . . .128 E1
Frost Rd CV35 . . . . .146 D4
Frosmere Cl CV11 . . . . .71 C8
Fryer Ave CV32 . . . . .105 E3
Frythe Cl CV8. . . . . .93 C6
Fuchsia Cl **3** CV2 . . . . . .50 B2
Fulbrook La CV35. . . . . . . .121 F8
Fulbrook Rd CV2 . . . . .50 C2
Fulford Dr B76 . . . . .22 B5
Fulford Hall Rd B90,B94 . .69 D3
Fullbrook Cl B90 . . . . .71 A5
Fuller Pl CV35 . . . . .122 F3
Fullers Cl CV6 . . . . .49 C1
Fullwood Cl CV2 . . . . .50 E2
Fulwell Mews B37 . . . . .44 B8
Furlong Mdw CV36 . . . . . .149 D4
Furlong Rd CV1 . . . . .151 C1
Furnace Cl CV12 . . . . .39 D4
Furnace Rd CV12 . . . . .39 D4
Furness Cl CV21 . . . . .83 D7
Furr Marsh The CV34 . . . .108 B4
Furrow Cl CV21 . . . . .83 D4
Furrows The CV47 . . . . . . .147 C5
Furze Hill Rd CV36 . . . . . .149 D4
Furze La
  Chipping Campden GL55 . .135 C4
  Redditch B98 . . . . .112 A6
Fylde Ho CV2 . . . . .62 D4
Fynford Rd CV6. . . . . .61 B5

G

Gable Cl CV22 . . . . .99 D8
Gables The B78 . . . . .5 A2
Gabor Cl CV21 . . . . .83 C6
Gadsby Ct CV11 . . . . .29 E3
Gadsby St CV11 . . . . .29 E3
Gadshill CV34. . . . . .109 E4
Gainford Rise CV3 . . . . .63 A3
Gainsborough Cres
  Dorridge B93 . . . . .72 A6
  Rugby CV21 . . . . .84 B1
Gainsborough Dr
  Bedworth CV12 . . . . .39 A4
  Oak Dale B78 . . . . .8 B8
  Royal Leamington Spa
    CV31. . . . . .110 B3
Gainsborough Rd GL55. .135 C5
Gainsborough Rd CV37. .144 D1
Gainsborough Terr GL55. 135 A1
Gainsborough Trad Est
  CV47 . . . . .147 A3
Galena Cl B77 . . . . .4 B2
Galey's Rd CV3 . . . . .77 D8
Gallagher Bsns Pk CV6 . . .49 E5
Gallagher Rd CV12 . . . . . . .39 A2
Gallagher Ret Pk CV6 . . . .61 F8
Galley Common Inf Sch
  CV10 . . . . .27 F5

Galliards The CV4 . . . . .76 D4
Galliers Cl B77 . . . . .9 F5
Gallows Hill CV34 . . . . . . .109 A4
Galmington Dr CV3 . . . . . . .77 B6
Gannaway B93. . . . . .72 A4
Gannaway Rd CV35 . . . . . .114 B3
Garard Ct **3** CV22 . . . . . .99 A8
Garard Pl **1** CV22 . . . . . .99 A8
Garard Row **2** CV22 . . . .99 A8
Garden Cl
  Hinckley LE10 . . . . .31 D6
  Knowle B93 . . . . .71 F6
  Mickleton GL55 . . . . .135 B6
Garden Ct
  Warwick,Emscote CV34. . .109 C8
  Warwick,Packmores CV34. .108 E7
Garden Flats CV15 . . . . . . .59 D5
Garden Gr CV12 . . . . .49 F8
Gardenia Dr CV6 . . . . .60 B6
Gardens The
  Kenilworth CV8 . . . . .93 A3
  Radford Semele CV31 . . . .110 E5
  Rugby CV22 . . . . .99 C7
  Thurlaston CV23 . . . . .98 F3
Garden Terr CV35 . . . . . . .137 E8
Gardner Ho CV1 . . . . .61 B2
Gardner Way CV8 . . . . .93 A2
Garlands Croft CV7 . . . . . . .49 A6
Garlick Dr CV8 . . . . .93 C6
Garnette Cl CV10 . . . . .28 B5
Garrard Cl WR11 . . . . .127 F6
Garratt Cl CV23 . . . . .82 B5
Garrett St CV11 . . . . .29 B4
Garrick Cl CV5 . . . . .59 C4
Garrick Way CV37 . . . . . . .144 E1
Garrigill B77 . . . . .4 B1
Garth Cres CV3 . . . . .78 D8
Garth Ho CV3. . . . . .78 D8
Garton Cl DE12 . . . . .3 F8
Garway Cl CV32. . . . . .105 F4
Garyth Williams Cl CV22 . .99 E8
Gas House La B49 . . . . . . .143 C3
Gas St
  Royal Leamington Spa
    CV31. . . . . .109 F7
  Rugby CV21 . . . . .83 B3
Gate Farm Dr CV23 . . . . . . .53 F3
Gatehouse Cl CV21 . . . . . .101 A8
Gatehouse La CV12 . . . . . . .39 A2
Gatehouse CV31 . . . . .109 D7
Gate La
  Dorridge B93,B94 . . . . . . .71 C3
  Nether Whitacre B46. . . . . .24 F6
Gateley Rd CV8. . . . . .112 A6
Gateside Rd CV6. . . . . .49 E2
Gatwick Rd B35 . . . . .22 B4
Gaulby Wlk CV3. . . . . .63 A1
Gaveston Cl **7** CV34 . . .108 F8
Gaveston Rd
  Coventry CV6. . . . . .60 F6
  Royal Leamington Spa
    CV32. . . . . .105 E1
Gaydon Cl CV6 . . . . .62 A8
Gaydon Rd CV47 . . . . .124 A3
Gayer St CV6 . . . . .50 A1
Gayhurst Cl CV31 . . . . .78 E8
Gayle B77 . . . . .4 A1
Gaza Cl CV4 . . . . .40 A1
Gazelle Cl CV1 . . . . .151 D3
Geeson Cl B35. . . . . .22 B4
Gentian Way CV23 . . . . . . .83 E8
Gentlemans La B94 . . . . . .112 E7
Geoffrey Cl
  Coventry CV2. . . . . .62 B5
  Sutton Coldfield B76 . . . . . .22 B7
George Birch Cl CV23 . . . . .64 E3
George Eliot Ave CV12 . . . .39 E2
George Eliot Com Sch
  CV11 . . . . .29 D1
George Eliot Hospl CV10. .39 D8
George Eliot St CV11. . . . .29 C2
George Fentham Endowed
  Sch B92 . . . . .57 B6
George Fox La CV13 . . . . . .20 A6
George Hodgkinson Cl
  CV4 . . . . .59 F3
George La GL55. . . . . .135 B1
George Marston Rd CV3 . .62 E1
George Park Cl CV2 . . . . . .50 C1
George Poole Ho **6** CV1 .61 B2
George Rd
  Warwick CV34 . . . . .109 A8
  Water Orton B46. . . . . .23 C3
George Robertson Cl CV3 .78 E7
George's Elm La B50. . . . .148 E8
George St
  Coventry CV1. . . . . .61 E5
  Hinckley LE10 . . . . .31 D8
  New Arley CV7 . . . . .37 A8
  Stockton CV23 . . . . .115 F3
George Street Ringway
  CV12 . . . . .39 B3
George St
  Royal Leamington Spa
    CV31. . . . . .110 A7
  Rugby CV21 . . . . .82 F3
  Stockton CV23 . . . . .115 F3
Georgian Cl B49. . . . . .143 B4
Gerard Ave CV4 . . . . .76 B8
Gerard Rd
  Alcester B49 . . . . .143 D4
  Cawston B27 . . . . .99 A8
Gerrards Rd CV36 . . . . . . .149 D5
Gerrard St **1** CV34 . . . .108 E6
Gibbet Hill LE17 . . . . .67 F6

Gibbet Hill Rd CV4. . . . . . .76 B3
Gibbet La LE17 . . . . .68 B6
Gibbons Cl CV4. . . . . .59 F2
Gibbs Cl CV2 . . . . .63 B6
Gibbs St CV37 . . . . .145 E4
Gibson Cres CV12. . . . . . . .39 A1
Gibson Dr CV21 . . . . .84 A1
Gielgud Way CV2 . . . . .63 B8
Giffard Terr B95 . . . . .113 E7
Giffard Way CV34 . . . . . . .104 E1
Gifford Rd CV33 . . . . .123 D3
Gifford Wlk CV37 . . . . . . .144 C4
Gigg La B76 . . . . .14 B3
Gilberry Cl B93 . . . . .72 A4
Gilbert Ave CV22 . . . . .82 D2
Gilbert Cl
  3 Coventry CV1 . . . . .61 E3
  Bedworth CV12 . . . . .39 B2
  Stratford-u-A CV37 . . . . .144 F6
Gilberts Rugby Football
  Mus* CV21 . . . . .83 A3
Giles Cl CV6 . . . . .49 F1
Gilfil Rd CV10. . . . . .29 B1
Gilkes La CV35. . . . . .137 F8
Gillet Cl CV11. . . . . .29 B3
Gillett's La OX15. . . . . . . .137 E2
Gillians Wlk CV2 . . . . .63 A8
Gillows Croft B90. . . . . . . .71 A7
Gilquart Way CV1 . . . . . . .151 C1
Gilson Dr B46 . . . . .33 D8
Gilson Rd B46 . . . . .33 E8
Gilson Way B37. . . . . .33 A5
Gingles Cl CV47 . . . . .101 A8
Ginkgo Wlk **2** CV31 . . . .109 F5
Gipsy Cl CV7 . . . . .74 B5
Gipsy La
  Balsall Common CV7 . . . . .74 C5
  Nuneaton CV10,CV11. . . . .39 D7
  Wolvey LE10 . . . . .41 E7
Girdlers Cl CV3 . . . . .77 A5
Girtin Cl CV12 . . . . .39 A4
Girton Gr CV22 . . . . .106 C5
Gisburn Cl CV34 . . . . .104 F1
Givens Ho **9** CV1. . . . . . .61 B2
Glade The CV5. . . . . .59 F3
Gladiator Way CV1 . . . . . . .61 B2
Gladstone Ct **2** CV32 . .105 F1
Gladstone Rd B93 . . . . . . .72 A2
Gladstone St CV21 . . . . . . .83 F4
Gladstone Terr LE10. . . . . .31 E8
Glaisdale Ave CV6 . . . . . . .49 E3
Glamis Pl **2** OX16 . . . . .139 F3
Glamorgan Cl CV3 . . . . . . .78 D5
Glaramara Cl CV21 . . . . . . .83 D7
Glascote Heath Prim Sch
  B77. . . . . .4 A2
Glascote La B77 . . . . .9 F8
Glasshouse La
  Hockley Heath B94 . . . . . . .88 F6
  Kenilworth CV8 . . . . .93 D4
Gleave Rd CV31 . . . . .110 A3
Glebe Ave CV12 . . . . .38 E1
Glebe Cl
  Bidford-on-A B50. . . . . . . .148 D4
  Coventry CV4 . . . . .76 A7
  Warwick CV34 . . . . .147 F8
Glebe Cotts WR11. . . . . . .127 D3
Glebe Cres
  Kenilworth CV8 . . . . .93 A3
  Rugby CV21 . . . . .82 E3
Glebe Ct CV31 . . . . .110 A3
Glebe Est CV37 . . . . .120 B5
Glebefarm Gr CV3 . . . . . . .62 F3
Glebe Farm Ind Est CV21. .82 F7
Glebe Farm (Mus)*
  CV37 . . . . .120 C5
Glebe Farm Rd CV21. . . . .82 F7
Glebe Fields B76 . . . . .23 B6
Glebe Fold GL55. . . . . .135 B6
Glebe La
  Nuneaton CV11 . . . . .29 F6
  Staverton NN11. . . . . . . .126 E8
Glebe Rd
  Hinckley LE10 . . . . .31 D7
  Nuneaton CV11 . . . . .29 D4
  Southam CV47 . . . . .147 A5
  Stratford-u-A CV37 . . . . .144 C4
Glebe Rise CV9 . . . . .3 B1
Glebe The
  Corley CV7 . . . . .48 C7
  Hook Norton OX15. . . . . . .142 D4
  Wootton Wawen B95. . . . .113 B2
Glebe Way CV7 . . . . .74 A7
Gleeson Dr CV34. . . . . . . .104 E1
Glen Cl CV36 . . . . .149 D6
Glencoe Rd CV3 . . . . .62 B1
Glendale Ave CV8 . . . . .93 A6
Glendale Ct B77 . . . . .10 B6
Glendale Inf Sch CV10 . . . .28 F2
Glendale Way CV4 . . . . . . .59 C2
Glendon Gdns CV12. . . . . .40 C3
Glendower App CV34 . . . .109 E3
Glendower Ave CV5. . . . . .60 D3
Gleneagles Cl
  Hinckley LE10 . . . . .31 D4
  Nuneaton CV11 . . . . .30 C1
Gleneagles Rd CV2 . . . . . . .62 E6
Gleneagles B77 . . . . .4 B5
Glenfern Gdns CV8 . . . . . . .78 E2
Glenfield Ave CV10 . . . . . . .29 D7

Glenfield Cl
  2 Solihull B91 . . . . .71 C8
  Redditch B97 . . . . .102 D6
Glenhurst Rd B95. . . . . . . .113 A4
Glenmore Dr CV6. . . . . . . .49 F5
Glenmount Ave CV6. . . . . .49 F5
Glenn St CV6 . . . . .49 D3
Glenridding Cl CV6 . . . . . . .49 F5
Glenrosa Wlk CV4. . . . . . . .76 A7
Glenroy Cl CV7 . . . . .62 E6
Glentworth Ave CV6 . . . . . .49 A2
Glentworth B76. . . . . .13 A2
Glenville Ave CV10 . . . . . . .10 C1
Glenwood Dr B90. . . . . . . .70 D4
Glenwood Gdns
  Bedworth CV12 . . . . .39 A5
  Tamworth B77 . . . . .10 B6
Gloster Dr CV8 . . . . .92 F6
Gloster Gdns CV35 . . . . . .146 C1
Gloucester Cl CV11 . . . . . . .30 A7
Gloucester La GL55 . . . . . .135 B6
Gloucester St
  3 Royal Leamington Spa
    CV31. . . . . .110 A7
  Coventry CV1. . . . . .61 B3
Gloucester Way B37 . . . . . .33 A1
Glover Cl CV34 . . . . .108 B4
Glover Rd B75 . . . . .13 A5
Glover's Cl CV9 . . . . .18 F7
Glovers Cl CV7 . . . . .46 C1
Glover St CV3 . . . . .77 D8
Godfrey Cl CV31 . . . . .110 E5
Godiva Pl CV1 . . . . .151 C3
Godiva Trad Est CV6 . . . . . .61 F8
Godson Cotts CV5 . . . . . . .137 F2
Godsons La CV47 . . . . .125 C8
Gofton B77 . . . . .10 A8
Goldcare Cl CV31 . . . . . . .109 F4
Gold Ave CV22 . . . . .99 B8
Gold Cl CV11 . . . . .39 E8
Goldcrest Croft B36. . . . . .33 A8
Goldcrest Mews CV37. . . .130 E6
Golden Acres La CV37 . . . .78 F7
Golden End Dr CV8 . . . . . . .72 D6
Goldicote Bsns Pk CV37. .130 E5
Goldicote Rd CV35 . . . . . .130 F7
Goldsmith Ave
  Rugby CV22 . . . . .99 F6
  Warwick CV34 . . . . .108 C5
Goldthorn Cl CV5 . . . . .59 D4
Golf Dr CV11 . . . . .30 B1
Golf La CV31 . . . . .110 A2
Goodacre Cl CV23 . . . . . . .84 A5
Goode Cl CV34 . . . . .108 C7
Goode Croft CV4. . . . . .59 F2
Goodere Ave B78 . . . . .11 A8
Goodere Dr B78 . . . . .5 A2
Goodeve Wlk B75 . . . . .13 B5
Goodfellow St CV32 . . . . .105 C1
Goodman Way CV4 . . . . . .59 C1
Good Shepherd RC Sch
  CV6 . . . . .49 F1
Goodway Ho **9** CV34 . . .108 F7
Goodway Rd
  6 Royal Leamington Spa
    CV31. . . . . .109 D8
  Kenilworth CV8 . . . . .93 A5
Goodwood Cl CV3 . . . . . . .63 B1
Goodyers End La CV12 . . .49 D8
Goodyers End Prim Sch
  CV12 . . . . .49 E8
Goosehills Rd LE10 . . . . . .31 E5
Gorcott Cl B97 . . . . .102 A3
Gorcott La CV7 . . . . .129 D1
Gorcott La B90 . . . . .70 A5
Gordon Cl CV12 . . . . .39 C4
Gordon Rd CV37 . . . . .129 C2
Gordon St
  Coventry CV1. . . . . .61 E5
  Royal Leamington Spa
    CV31. . . . . .110 A7
Gorey Cl CV12 . . . . .82 E1
Goring Rd CV2 . . . . .62 B5
Gorse Farm Rd CV11. . . . .40 A3
Gorse La B95. . . . . .113 A2
Gorse La CV47. . . . . .147 A5
Gorseway CV5 . . . . .60 C3
Gorsey Cl B96 . . . . .118 B6
Gorsey La
  Coleshill B46 . . . . .23 F2
  Wythall B47 . . . . .69 A5
Gorsy Way B46 . . . . .23 F1
Gorsy Way CV10 . . . . .28 D5
Gorton Croft CV7 . . . . .74 A7
Gosford Ind Est CV1 . . . . .61 F2
Gosford Park Prim Sch
  CV1 . . . . .61 F2
Gosford St
  Coventry CV1. . . . . .151 D2
  Royal Leamington Spa
    CV31. . . . . .110 A7
Gospel La CV47 . . . . .120 F5
Gospel Oak Rd CV6 . . . . . .49 B4
Gosport Rd CV6 . . . . .50 A1
Gossett La CV8 . . . . .79 F7
Gould Cl NN11 . . . . .134 E8
Gould Rd CV35 . . . . .108 A7
Governor's Ct CV34 . . . . .108 B5
Grace Rd CV5 . . . . .59 A8
Grafton Cl
  Redditch B98 . . . . .112 A6
  Temple Grafton B49. . . . . .119 F6
Grafton Ct CV23 . . . . .84 A5
Grafton La B49 . . . . .148 F6
Grafton St CV1 . . . . .151 D3
Graham Cl CV6 . . . . .50 B1
Graham Rd CV21. . . . . .83 C4

Graham St CV11 . . . . .29 C5
Gramer Cotts CV9 . . . . . . .19 A6
Granborough Ct
  3 Royal Leamington Spa
    CV32. . . . . .105 A3
Granbrook La GL55 . . . . . .135 C7
Granby Cl LE10 . . . . .31 C7
Granby Rd
  Hinckley LE10 . . . . .31 C7
  Honington CV36. . . . . . . .137 A5
  Nuneaton CV10 . . . . .28 F3
Grandborough Fields Rd
  CV23 . . . . .116 C5
Grand Depot Rd CV11. . . .40 F6
Grange Ave
  Coventry,Binley CV3. . . . . .78 F7
  Coventry,Finham CV3. . . . .77 C3
  Kenilworth CV8 . . . . .92 E7
Grange Cl
  Nuneaton CV10 . . . . .28 C7
  Ratley OX15. . . . . .132 F2
  Southam CV47 . . . . .147 B5
  Tamworth B77 . . . . .9 C8
  Warwick CV34 . . . . .109 C8
Grange Ct CV37. . . . . .129 B3
Grange Dr LE10. . . . . .31 C6
Grange Education Unit The
  CV6 . . . . .48 E1
Grange Farm Dr CV47. . . .147 B9
Grange Farm Prim Sch
  CV3 . . . . .77 B5
Grange Gdns CV35 . . . . . .146 D3
Grangehurst Prim Sch
  CV6 . . . . .50 B4
Grange La
  Harvington WR11 . . . . . .127 D3
  Sibford Ferris OX15. . . . . .142 E8
Grange Mews The **1**
  CV32. . . . . .105 D1
Grangemouth Rd CV6 . . . .61 B7
Grange Pk CV37 . . . . .145 A4
Grange Rd
  Balsall Common CV7 . . . . .73 F7
  Bearley CV37. . . . . .120 E7
  Bidford-on-A B50. . . . . . . .148 E4
  Coventry CV6. . . . . .50 B5
  Dorridge B93 . . . . .71 E2
  Hartshill Green CV10. . . . . .19 C2
  Hockley Heath B94 . . . . . . .88 E8
  Royal Leamington Spa
    CV32. . . . . .106 B3
  Rugby CV21 . . . . .82 E6
Grangers La B98. . . . . . . .102 F5
Grange The
  4 Moreton-in-M GL56 . . .140 A3
  Cubbington CV32. . . . . . .106 F5
  Warwick CV34 . . . . .109 C8
Granhill Cl B98 . . . . .103 A8
Granleigh Ct CV32 . . . . . .106 E3
Granoe Cl CV3 . . . . .78 E8
Grantham St CV2 . . . . .61 F3
Grantley Dr B37 . . . . .33 B3
Grant Rd
  Bedworth CV7 . . . . .39 A1
  Coventry CV3. . . . . .62 B2
Grants Cl CV47 . . . . .133 D7
Granville Ct CV36 . . . . . . .149 D6
Granville Gdns LE10 . . . . .31 C8
Granville Rd
  Dorridge B93 . . . . .72 A2
  Hinckley LE10 . . . . .31 D8
  Wellesbourne CV35 . . . . .146 C3
Granville St CV32 . . . . . . .106 A2
Grapes Cl CV6 . . . . .61 B5
Grasmere Ave CV3 . . . . . . .76 F6
Grasmere Cl CV21 . . . . . . .83 D6
Grasmere Cres CV11 . . . . .29 F7
Grasmere Ct **2** CV37 . .145 A3
Grasmere Rd CV12 . . . . . .39 B2
Grassholme **2** CV21 . . .83 E8
Grassholme B77 . . . . .10 A8
Grassington Ave CV34 . . .104 F1
Grassington Dr CV11. . . . .30 A2
Gratton Ct CV3 . . . . .76 F6
Gravel Hill CV4 . . . . .59 F1
Gravel The CV36 . . . . .14 B2
Graylands The CV3. . . . . . .77 C4
Grayling Wlk B37 . . . . .33 C3
Gray's La CV7 . . . . .35 A5
Grays Orch CV23 . . . . .98 F2
Grayswood Ave CV5. . . . . .60 D4
Grazier Ave B77 . . . . .9 C8
Great Alne Prim Sch
  B49. . . . . .119 D6
Great Balance CV23. . . . . .64 E3
Great Borne CV21 . . . . . . .83 E8
Great Central Walk Nature
  Trail* CV22 . . . . .100 D7
Great Central Way CV21. .83 A3
Great Central Wlk* CV23 .67 F2
Greatheed Rd CV32 . . . . . .105 E1
Great Pinley Barns CV35 .114 B5
Great Rollright CE Prim Sch
  OX7 . . . . .142 A2
Great William St CV37 . . .145 A2
Greaves Cl CV34 . . . . .109 C7
Greaves Cotts CV47 . . . . .115 D3
Greaves The B77 . . . . .10 A7
Greaves Way The CV47 . .124 B4
Greenacres Prim Sch B77. . .4 B5
Greenacres B76 . . . . .22 A8

Greenbank Rd CV7. . . . . .73 F6
Green Cl
Long Lawford CV23 . . . . .81 F4
Studley B80 . . . . .103 E3
Whitnash CV31 . . . . .110 B4
Wythall B47 . . . . .69 A3
Green Ct CV21 . . . . .83 D4
Greendale Cl CV9 . . . . .18 E7
Greendale Rd
Atherstone CV9 . . . . .18 E7
Coventry CV5 . . . . .60 D3
Green End CV47 . . . . .115 D4
Green Farm End CV35 . . . . .132 B6
Greenfield Ave CV7 . . . . .74 A7
Greenfields Cl CV36 . . . . . . .149 D5
Green Field The CV3 . . . . .78 B8
Greenfinch Cl B36 . . . . .33 A7
Greenfinch Rd B36 . . . . .33 A7
Green Gables B47 . . . . .69 A7
Green Gates B95 . . . . .113 B5
Greenheart B77 . . . . .4 A4
Greenhill Cl B77 . . . . .9 C5
Greenhill Cotts WR11 . . . . .127 E1
Greenhill Farm CV47 . . . . . .124 A6
Greenhill Rd
Rugby CV22 . . . . .82 F1
Stoke Golding CV13 . . . . .21 D7
Whitnash CV31 . . . . .110 B4
Greenhill St CV37 . . . . .144 F3
Green La
Balsall Common CV7 . . . . . . .74 B7
Birchmoor B77,B78 . . . . .10 D7
Bouts B96 . . . . .118 A6
Bradley Green CV9 . . . . .11 F5
Brinklow CV23 . . . . .64 D3
Church Lawford CV23 . . . . . .81 C5
Coleshill B46 . . . . .33 F5
Corley Moor CV7 . . . . .47 D6
Coventry CV3 . . . . .77 D4
Grendon CV9 . . . . .11 F3
Middleton B78 . . . . .14 B6
Greenland Ave CV5 . . . . .59 F5
Greenland Ct CV5 . . . . .59 F5
Greenlands Ave B98 . . . . . .103 A8
Greenlands Dr B98 . . . . .102 F8
Greenlands Rd B37 . . . . .33 C1
Green Lane Cl CV36 . . . . . . .149 D5
Green La
Nuneaton CV10 . . . . .28 C7
Old Arley CV10 . . . . .26 E8
Oxhill CV35 . . . . .137 F8
Redditch B97 . . . . .102 A7
Shipston-on-S CV36 . . . . . .149 D5
Shrewley CV35 . . . . .114 C6
Studley B80 . . . . .103 B5
Swalcliffe OX15 . . . . .139 A1
Tamworth B77 . . . . .10 C6
Warwick CV34 . . . . .108 F8
Wibtoft LE17 . . . . .43 B3
Wolvey LE10 . . . . .42 C5
Greenleaf Cl CV5 . . . . .60 A3
Greenlea B77 . . . . .10 A8
Greenmoor Rd
Hinckley LE10 . . . . .31 D5
Nuneaton CV10 . . . . .29 A3
Greenodd Dr CV6 . . . . .49 F5
Greenside B90 . . . . .70 D4
Greenside Cl CV11 . . . . .30 C1
Greensleeves Cl CV6 . . . . . .49 B2
Greens Rd CV6 . . . . .49 A1
Greensward Cl CV8 . . . . .93 B6
Greensward The
Coventry CV3 . . . . .63 A2
Wardington OX17 . . . . .134 F1
Greenswood CV37 . . . . .120 E7
Greens Yd CV12 . . . . .39 C3
Green The
13 Moreton-in-M GL56 . . . .140 A3
Atherstone CV9 . . . . .19 A6
Austrey CV9 . . . . .3 B1
Barby CV23 . . . . .101 C1
Braunston NN11 . . . . .117 E5
Broadwell CV23 . . . . .116 B4
Chipping Campden GL55 . . .135 B1
Churchover CV23 . . . . .67 C6
Claverdon CV35 . . . . .113 F4
Cleeve Prior WR11 . . . . .128 A4
Dadlington CV13 . . . . .21 E8
Dunchurch CV22 . . . . .99 C3
Freasley B78 . . . . .10 C4
Great Rollright OX7 . . . . . . .142 A2
Great Wolford CV36 . . . . . . .140 E5
Harborough Magna CV23 . . .66 B3
Helldon NN11 . . . . .126 B5
Hook Norton OX15 . . . . .142 D4
Hornton OX15 . . . . .139 B7
Kingsbury B78 . . . . .15 C6
Long Itchington CV47 . . . . . .115 D4
Long Lawford CV23 . . . . .82 A4
Long Marston CV37 . . . . . . .129 B3
Meriden CV7 . . . . .46 B1
Middle Tysoe CV35 . . . . . . .138 B7
Nuneaton CV11 . . . . .29 E2
Orton-on-t-H CV9 . . . . .6 C4
Priors Marston CV47 . . . . . .125 E4
Ratley CV35 . . . . .132 F3
Rugby CV22 . . . . .99 C8
Seckington B79 . . . . .2 A3
Shrewley CV35 . . . . .114 D6
Shustoke B46 . . . . .24 F2
Shutford OX15 . . . . .139 A3
Snitterfield CV37 . . . . .121 B6

Green The continued
Stoneleigh CV8 . . . . .94 C6
Swalcliffe OX15 . . . . .142 F8
Tamworth B77 . . . . .4 B5
Tanworth-In-A B94 . . . . .87 A2
Wigston Parva LE10 . . . . .42 E8
Greenway NN11 . . . . .117 D5
Greenway Cl CV36 . . . . .149 D6
Greenway Nature Trail The
CV37 .129 C5
Greenway
Nuneaton CV11 . . . . .40 B8
Polesworth B78 . . . . .5 A3
Greenway Rd CV36 . . . . .149 D6
Greenways CV4 . . . . .59 C2
Greenways Cl CV36 . . . . . . .149 C6
Greenways The CV32 . . . . .106 B3
Greenway The B37 . . . . .44 A6
Greenway CV34 . . . . .104 E1
Greenwood Cl CV23 . . . . . . .82 A5
Greenwood Ct
Nuneaton CV11 . . . . .29 E3
Royal Leamington Spa
CV32 .106 B1
Greenwood Rd CV13 . . . . . . .21 E7
Greenwood Sq 5 B37 . . . . . .33 B2
Greenwood Way B37 . . . . . . .33 B2
Gregory Ave CV3 . . . . .77 A6
Gregory Hood Rd CV3 . . . . . .77 E4
Grenden Hall Rd CV35 . . . .132 D3
Grendon Cl CV4 . . . . .59 C1
Grendon Dr CV21 . . . . .83 E7
Grendon Rd B78 . . . . .11 A8
Grenfell Cl CV31 . . . . .110 D6
Grenville Ave CV2 . . . . .62 B3
Grenville Cl CV22 . . . . .82 C1
Gresham Ave CV32 . . . . .106 B2
Gresham Pl CV32 . . . . .106 B2
Gresham Rd CV10 . . . . .39 B8
Gresham St CV2 . . . . .62 A2
Gresley Rd CV2 . . . . .62 D7
Greswold Cl CV4 . . . . .59 F1
Greswoldes The CV31 . . . . .110 E5
Gretna Rd CV3 . . . . .76 F4
Grevel La GL55 . . . . .135 B2
Greville Ho 15 CV34 . . . . . . .108 F7
Greville Rd
Alcester B49 . . . . .143 A5
Kenilworth CV8 . . . . .92 F4
Warwick CV34 . . . . .105 B1
Greville Smith Ave CV31 . .110 B4
Grewcock Cl LE17 . . . . .43 E6
Greycoat Rd CV6 . . . . .49 A2
Greyfriars Ct CV6 . . . . .61 A7
Greyfriars La CV1 . . . . .151 B2
Greyfriars Rd CV1 . . . . .151 B2
Greygoose La GL56 . . . . . . .150 D6
Greyhurst Croft 5 B91 . . . .71 B8
Grey Mill Cl B90 . . . . .70 F6
Grey Mill La B95 . . . . .120 A8
Greyrick Ct GL55 . . . . .135 B6
Greys Cl OX16 . . . . .139 F3
Grey's Rd B80 . . . . .103 E3
Grey Tree Cres B93 . . . . .71 E3
Griffin Bsns Pk B37 . . . . .33 C3
Griffin Rd CV34 . . . . .109 C7
Griffins La B90 . . . . .70 A5
Griffiths Ho CV21 . . . . .83 C7
Griff La
Nuneaton CV10 . . . . .39 A6
Nuneaton CV10 . . . . .39 A6
Griggs Cl GL55 . . . . .135 B2
Grimshaw Villas B93 . . . . . . .72 D8
Grimston Cl CV3 . . . . .63 A2
Grindle Rd CV6 . . . . .49 F4
Grindley Ho 8 CV1 . . . . .61 B2
Grindsbrook B77 . . . . .10 A8
Grizebeck Dr CV5 . . . . .60 A5
Grizedale CV21 . . . . .83 C7
Grosvenor Cres LE10 . . . . . . .32 A6
Grosvenor Ct 2 CV32 . . . . .105 F1
Grosvenor Ho CV1 . . . . .151 A2
Grosvenor Rd
Coventry CV1 . . . . .151 A1
Rugby CV21 . . . . .83 C3
Whitnash CV31 . . . . .110 A5
Grouse Cl CV37 . . . . .144 C5
Grove Croft CV35 . . . . .114 F3
Grove Ct
Coventry CV5 . . . . .77 B8
Nuneaton CV11 . . . . .29 E2
Grovefield Cres CV7 . . . . . . .74 C8
Grove Fields CV10 . . . . .28 E8
Grove Ho CV37 . . . . .144 F2
Grovehurst Pk CV8 . . . . .94 B2
Grove La
Keresley CV7 . . . . .48 F7
Lapworth B94 . . . . .88 F4
Grovelands Ind Est CV7 . . . .50 A6
Grove La B76 . . . . .13 F2
Grove Pk
Hampton Magna CV35 . . . . .114 F3
Hinckley LE10 . . . . .32 A6
Grove Pl
2 Royal Leamington Spa
CV31 .110 A6
Nuneaton CV10 . . . . .28 D3
Grove Rd
Ansty CV7 . . . . .51 D3
Atherstone CV9 . . . . .18 D8
Dorridge B93 . . . . .72 B3
Hinckley LE10 . . . . .32 A6
Nuneaton CV10 . . . . .28 D3
Stratford-u-A CV37 . . . . . . .144 F2
Grove St
Coventry CV1 . . . . .151 C3
Royal Leamington Spa
CV32 .109 E8

Grove The
Bedworth CV12 . . . . .39 C3
Coleshill B46 . . . . .33 F4
Hampton-in-A B92 . . . . .45 A1
Hinckley LE10 . . . . .31 C8
Moreton-in-M GL56 . . . . . . .140 B3
Studley B80 . . . . .103 D3
Grump St CV36 . . . . .136 A6
Guardhouse Rd CV6 . . . . .61 B8
Guernsey Dr B36 . . . . .33 B6
Guernsey Way 5 OX16. . . . .139 F5
Guild Cotts The CV34 . . . . .108 D6
Guildford Ct CV6 . . . . .61 D7
Guild Rd
Aston Cantlow B95 . . . . .119 F6
Coventry CV6 . . . . .61 D7
Guild St CV37 . . . . .145 A3
Guillemard Ct B37 . . . . .33 B1
Guilsborough Rd CV3 . . . . . .78 E8
Guinea Cres CV4 . . . . .75 E6
Guinness Cl B98 . . . . .102 D8
Gulistan Ct 6 CV32 . . . . . . .105 E1
Gulistan Rd CV32 . . . . .105 E1
Gullet The B78 . . . . .4 A4
Gullicote La CV47 . . . . .139 F6
Gulliman's Way CV31 . . . . .110 D7
Gulliver's Cl OX15 . . . . .139 D6
Gulson Hospl CV1 . . . . .151 D2
Gulson Rd CV1 . . . . .61 E2
Gundry Cl CV31 . . . . .110 A7
Gun Hill Inf Sch CV7 . . . . . . .37 A8
Gun Hill CV7 . . . . .37 A8
Gunn Ct B49 . . . . .119 E6
Gunn End CV36 . . . . .149 D7
Gunner Gr B75 . . . . .13 A6
Gunners La B80 . . . . .103 E4
Gunnery Terr 3 CV32 . . . . .105 D1
Gunnings Rd B49 . . . . .143 C4
Gunton Ave CV3 . . . . .78 C6
Guphill Ave CV5 . . . . .60 D2
Guphill La CV5 . . . . .60 D3
Gurnard B77 . . . . .9 B6
Gurney Cl CV4 . . . . .59 E3
Gutteridge Ave CV6 . . . . .49 A2
Guy Cl 3 CV32 . . . . .105 F1
Guy Pl E CV32 . . . . .105 F1
Guy Pl W 12 CV32 . . . . .105 F1
Guy's Cliffe Ave CV32 . . . . .105 D2
Guy's Cliffe Rd CV32 . . . . . .109 E8
Guy's Cliffe Terr CV34 . . . .108 F7
Guy's Cl CV34 . . . . .109 A8
Guy's Cross Park Rd
CV34 .108 F8
Guy St
Royal Leamington Spa
CV32 .109 F2
Warwick CV34 . . . . .108 F7
Gypsy La
Atherstone CV9 . . . . .12 D2
Dordon CV9 . . . . .11 A4
Kenilworth CV8 . . . . .92 F2
Water Orton B46 . . . . .23 D2

H

Hack La CV36. . . . . .141 C5
Hackwell St CV47 . . . . .125 C8
Haddon End CV3 . . . . .77 E6
Haddon Rd CV32 . . . . .106 B2
Haddon St CV6 . . . . .62 A8
Hadfield Cl CV3 . . . . .84 A5
Hadfield Way B37 . . . . .33 A4
Hadleigh Croft B76 . . . . .22 A6
Hadleigh Rd CV3 . . . . .77 C4
Hadley Cl B47 . . . . .69 A5
Hadley Mews CV11 . . . . .29 D1
Hadleys Croft B78 . . . . .15 D5
Hadrian Cl
Hinckley LE10 . . . . .21 F1
Royal Leamington Spa
CV32 .106 B4
Hadrian Dr B46 . . . . .23 F1
Hadrians Walk CV31 . . . . . . .110 C6
Hadrians Wy CV21 . . . . .82 F7
Hadrians Wlk B49 . . . . .143 B3
Haig Cl CV22 . . . . .82 E1
Halberd Cl LE10 . . . . .31 D5
Hales Cl CV37 . . . . .121 B7
Hales La B47 . . . . .69 C3
Hales Park Ind Est CV6 . . . .49 F4
Hales St CV1 . . . . .151 C3
Halford Gr CV35 . . . . .114 F5
Halford La CV6 . . . . .49 A2
Halford Lodge CV6 . . . . .49 A2
Halford Rd
Ettington CV37 . . . . .131 A3
Idlicote CV36 . . . . .137 C7
Stratford-u-A CV37 . . . . . . .144 E1
Halfpenny Field Wlk B35 . .22 A3
Halfway La CV22 . . . . .99 B3
Halifax Cl
Allesley CV5 . . . . .60 A7
Wellesbourne CV35 . . . . . . .146 B1
Hallam Rd CV6 . . . . .49 B2
Hallams Cl CV3 . . . . .79 F5
Hall Brook Rd CV6 . . . . .49 A4
Hall Cl CV8 . . . . .94 B6
Hall Cl The CV22 . . . . .99 C2
Hallcroft Way B93 . . . . .72 A6
Hall Ct B78 . . . . .5 A3
Hall Dr
Baginton CV8 . . . . .77 E3
Birmingham B37 . . . . .44 A7
Stoke Golding CV13 . . . . .21 E7
Hall End Cl CV11 . . . . .29 D2
Hall End Pl CV11 . . . . .29 D2
Hallfields CV31 . . . . .110 E5

Hall Gr CV23. . . . . .64 F4
Hall Green Rd CV2,CV6 . . . .50 B2
Hall La
Coventry CV2. . . . . .62 F6
Harbury CV33 . . . . .123 F7
Witherley CV9 . . . . .19 B8
Wolvey LE10 . . . . .41 D4
Hall Rd
Hinckley LE10 . . . . .31 D5
Royal Leamington Spa
CV32 .105 F1
Wolvey LE10 . . . . .41 D4
Hall's Cl CV31 . . . . .110 B3
Hall's Croft Mus* CV37 . . .145 A2
Hallway Dr CV7 . . . . .51 E6
Hall Wlk B46 . . . . .33 F4
Halstead Gr B91 . . . . .71 A8
Haltonlea B77 . . . . .10 A8
Hamar Way B37 . . . . .33 B1
Hambridge Rd CV47 . . . . . . .124 C3
Hames La B79 . . . . .2 D3
Hamilton Cl CV12 . . . . .38 C1
Hamilton Ct
Coventry CV1 . . . . .151 B4
Nuneaton CV11 . . . . .30 B1
Rugby CV22 . . . . .99 D6
Hamilton Rd
Coventry CV2 . . . . .62 A3
Radford Semele CV31 . . . . .110 E5
Redditch B97 . . . . .102 C8
Tiddington CV37 . . . . .145 F3
Hamilton Terr CV32 . . . . . . .109 F8
Hamlet Cl
Nuneaton CV11 . . . . .30 B1
Rugby CV22 . . . . .99 D6
Hamlet The
Leek Wootton CV35 . . . . . . .105 A7
Marlcliff B50 . . . . .148 D2
Hammersley St CV12 . . . . . . .38 E1
Hammerton Way CV35 . . . .146 C1
Hammond Bsns Ctr CV11 . .29 E3
Hammond Cl CV11 . . . . .29 E3
Hammond Gn CV35 . . . . .146 D4
Hammond Rd CV2 . . . . .61 F4
Hammonds Terr CV8 . . . . . . .92 D5
Hampden Cl 11 OX16 . . . . .139 F3
Hampden Ct CV47 . . . . .133 A7
Hampden Way CV22 . . . . .99 C7
Hampdon Way CV35 . . . . . . .146 C2
Hampshire Cl CV3 . . . . .78 F8
Hampstead Norreys Rd
CV35 .132 D4
Hampton Ave CV10 . . . . .28 B4
Hampton Cl
Coventry CV6 . . . . .61 F6
Redditch B98 . . . . .103 B7
Hampton Croft CV35 . . . . . .114 F2
Hampton Ct B92 . . . . .57 B6
Hampton Grange CV7 . . . . . .46 B1
Hampton Gr CV32 . . . . .106 B1
Hampton-in-Arden Sta
B92. . . . . .57 A8
Hampton La
Catherine de B B91 . . . . .56 B5
Meriden CV7 . . . . .57 E8
Hampton Lucy CE Prim Sch
CV35 .121 F4
Hampton Rd
Coventry CV6 . . . . .61 F6
Knowle B93 . . . . .72 C8
Warwick CV34 . . . . .108 B5
Hampton St CV6 . . . . .108 D6
Hams La B76 . . . . .23 F6
Hanbury Cl 13 CV35 . . . . . .132 B6
Hanbury Rd
Bedworth CV12 . . . . .39 C4
Dorridge B93 . . . . .71 F4
Hancock Gn CV4 . . . . .75 F8
Hancox Cl CV33 . . . . .107 D7
Handcross Gr CV3 . . . . .77 A5
Handley Gr CV34 . . . . .104 D1
Handley's Cl CV8 . . . . .79 A1
Hands Paddock CV37 . . . . . .130 E1
Handsworth Cres CV5 . . . . . .59 E4
Hanford Close Ind Est
CV6 . . . . .61 E6
Hanger Rd B26 . . . . .44 A3
Hangmans La B79 . . . . .2 A2
Hanley Ct B49 . . . . .143 C4
Hanlith B77 . . . . .10 A8
Hanover Ct
Hinckley LE10 . . . . .31 E6
Redditch B97 . . . . .102 D8
Hanover Gdns
8 Royal Leamington Spa
CV32 .106 A1
Rugby CV21 . . . . .83 B4
Hanover Glebe CV11 . . . . . . .29 C2
Hans Cl CV2 . . . . .61 F4
Hansell Dr B93 . . . . .71 E2
Hanson Ave CV36 . . . . .149 C5
Hanson Farm Cotts
CV35 .149 C5

Harborough Rd continued
Rugby CV23 . . . . .82 C8
Harbour Cl B50 . . . . .148 C4
Harbourne Cl CV34 . . . . .93 A5
Harbury CE Prim Sch
CV33 .123 F6
Harbury Cl B76 . . . . .22 B6
Harbury La
Harbury CV33 . . . . .123 B7
Royal Leamington Spa CV33,
CV34 .109 E2
Harbury Rd CV47 . . . . .124 C6
Harby Cl B37 . . . . .44 B8
Harcourt CV3 . . . . .78 E5
Harcourt Gdns CV11 . . . . . . .29 C3
Hardingwood La CV7 . . . . . . .35 F3
Hardwick Cl CV5 . . . . .60 A4
Hardwick La B80 . . . . .112 B3
Hardwick Pk 18 OX16 . . . .139 F5
Hardwick Rd CV47 . . . . .125 E4
Hardwyn Cl CV3 . . . . .63 A1
Hardy Cl
Nuneaton CV10 . . . . .28 A4
Rugby CV22 . . . . .82 C2
Hardy Rd CV6 . . . . .61 A8
Harebell B77 . . . . .4 A4
Harebell Way CV23 . . . . .83 B4
Harebell Wlk 1 B37 . . . . .33 D2
Harefield Ho CV2 . . . . .62 B3
Harefield La CV12. . . . . .38 F8
Harefield Rd
Coventry CV2 . . . . .62 B3
Nuneaton CV11 . . . . .29 C4
Hare & Hounds La CV10. . . .29 A2
Haresfield B90 . . . . .70 A5
Hareway La CV35 . . . . .122 C7
Harewood Rd CV5 . . . . .60 A3
Harger Ct CV8 . . . . .92 F4
Harger Mews CV8 . . . . .92 F4
Hargrave Cl
Coventry CV3 . . . . .63 A1
Grandborough CV23 . . . . . .116 F5
Water Orton B46 . . . . .23 B3
Harington Rd CV6 . . . . .61 A5
Harlech Cl
10 Banbury OX16 . . . . . . .139 F3
Kenilworth CV8 . . . . .93 C5
Harley St CV2 . . . . .62 A3
Harlow Wlk 8 CV2 . . . . .63 A7
Harmar Cl CV34 . . . . .104 E1
Harmer Cl CV2 . . . . .63 A7
Harmony Ct CV10 . . . . .29 B2
Harnall Cl CV1 . . . . .151 C4
Harnall La E CV1 . . . . .61 C4
Harnall La W CV1 . . . . .151 C4
Harnall Ind Est CV1 . . . . . . .151 C4
Harnall Row
Coventry CV1 . . . . .61 E2
Coventry CV1 . . . . .61 E2
Harold Cox Pl CV22 . . . . .99 E5
Harold Rd CV2 . . . . .62 E2
Harold's Orch CV56 . . . . .136 B1
Harold St CV11 . . . . .29 D2
Harpenden Dr CV5 . . . . .60 A5
Harper Rd CV1 . . . . .61 E2
Harpers La CV9 . . . . .11 F1
Harrier Parkway LE17 . . . . . .55 D7
Harrington Cl CV23 . . . . .62 F2
Harrington Way CV34 . . . . . .39 A7
Harriott Dr CV34. . . . . .109 D4
Harris Cl
Henley-in-A B95 . . . . .113 B4
Redditch B98 . . . . .102 F8
Harris Dr CV22 . . . . .99 F8
Harris Mews B95 . . . . .113 B4
Harrison Cl CV21 . . . . .101 B8
Harrison Cres CV12 . . . . .39 A2
Harrison Rd B97 . . . . .102 C8
Harris Rd
Coventry CV3 . . . . .62 B2
Warwick CV34 . . . . .108 C8
Harris Sch CV22 . . . . .82 C2
Harrowbrook Ind Est
LE10 . . . . .30 E7
Harrowbrook Rd LE10 . . . . . .30 E7
Harrow Cl CV6. . . . . .50 A4
Harrow Rd CV31 . . . . .110 B3
Harry Caplan Ho CV5 . . . . . .60 B6
Harry Edwards Ho 2 CV2 .62 D8
Harry Rose Rd CV2 . . . . .62 E3
Harry Salt Ho CV1 . . . . .151 D3
Harry Stanley Ho CV6 . . . . .61 D3
Harry Taylor Fst Sch The
B97. . . . . .102 C6
Harry Truslove Cl CV6 . . . . .60 F5
Harry Weston Rd CV3 . . . . . .63 A1
Hart Cl CV21 . . . . .83 D2
Hartington Cl B93 . . . . .71 F3
Hartington Cres CV5 . . . . . . .60 F1
Hartington Gn LE10 . . . . .31 E6
Hartland Ave CV2 . . . . .62 B5
Hartlebury Cl B93 . . . . .71 F3
Hartlepool Rd CV1 . . . . .151 D4
Hartley Gdns CV47 . . . . .147 F4
Hartridge Wlk CV5 . . . . .60 B4
Hartshill Hayes Ctry Pk*
CV10 . . . . .19 A5
Hartshill Hayes Visitors Ctr*
CV10 . . . . .19 A4
Hartshill Sch CV10 . . . . .28 B8
Harvard Cl
Moreton-in-M GL56 . . . . . . .140 B3
Wellesbourne CV35 . . . . . . .146 C1

Harvesters Cl CV3 . . . . .63 A2
Harvest Hill Rd 7 CV31. .110 C6
Harvest Hill Cotts CV5 . . . .47 D1
Harvest Hill La CV5,CV7 . . .47 C4
Harvest Hill Pk CV5 . . . . . .47 D1
Harvey Cl CV5 . . . . .60 A7
Harvington Cl Fst Sch
  WR11 . . . . .127 D4
Harvington Cross WR11 .127 D4
Harvington Dr B90 . . . . . . .71 B6
Harvington Way B76 . . . . . .22 A8
Harvon Garth CV21 . . . . . .83 C4
Harwood Dr B77 . . . . .9 D4
Harwood Gr 1 B90 . . . . . . .70 C8
Haselbech Rd CV3 . . . . . . .62 F1
Haselbury Cnr CV10 . . . . . .28 F1
Haseley Bsns Ctr CV35 . .114 D7
Haseley Cl CV31 . . . . .110 B5
Haseley Ct
  Five Ways CV35 . . . . . . .114 D8
  Lower Quinton CV37 . . .129 D2
Haseley Hall CV35 . . . . . .114 D8
Haseley Rd CV2 . . . . .50 C1
Haselor Cl B49 . . . . .143 D4
Haselor Sch B49 . . . . .119 D4
Hasilwood Sq CV3 . . . . . . .62 F3
Haslucks Green Rd B90 . .69 E7
Hassall Cl 9 CV33 . . . . . . .122 F8
Hastang Fields CV31 . . . .110 C5
Hastings Cl
  1 Banbury OX16 . . . . . .139 F3
  Tamworth B77 . . . . .9 F6
Hastings High Sch LE10. .31 F7
Hastings Rd
  Banbury OX16 . . . . .139 F4
  Coventry CV2 . . . . .62 A4
  Wellesbourne CV35. . . .146 D4
Haswell Cl CV22 . . . . .83 C2
Hatchford Wlk B37 . . . . . .33 B1
Hathaway Cl
  Balsall Common CV7 . . .74 B7
  South Littleton WR11. . .127 F1
Hathaway Dr
  Nuneaton CV11 . . . . . . .30 A1
  Warwick CV34 . . . . .104 C2
Hathaway Green La
  CV37 . . . . .144 B3
Hathaway Hamlet CV37 .144 C2
Hathaway La CV37 . . . . . .144 D1
Hathaway Rd CV4. . . . . . . .59 D1
Hatherden Dr B76 . . . . . . .13 A2
Hatherell Rd CV31 . . . . . .110 E5
Hatters Ct CV12. . . . . .39 D2
Hatters Dr CV9 . . . . .12 D2
Hatton Bank La CV37 . . .121 D5
Hatton Cl CV35 . . . . .114 E5
Hatton Ctry World*
  CV35 . . . . .114 D6
Hatton Gn CV35 . . . . .114 D6
Hatton Sta CV35 . . . . .114 F5
Hatton Terr CV35. . . . . . . .114 F5
Haunch La B76 . . . . .24 A8
Haunchwood Park Dr
  CV10 . . . . .27 E4
Haunchwood Park Ind Est
  CV10 . . . . .27 E4
Haunchwood Rd CV10. . . .28 D4
Havendale Cl CV6. . . . . . . .61 B5
Hawbridge Cl B90 . . . . . . .71 B6
Hawfinch B77 . . . . .10 A6
Hawk Cl CV11 . . . . .40 B8
Hawkesbury Fields Sch
  CV2 . . . . .50 C3
Hawkesbury La CV2 . . . . . .50 D5
Hawkes Dr CV34 . . . . .109 D4
Hawkeshead CV21 . . . . . . .83 D7
Hawkes Mill La CV5. . . . . .48 B2
Hawkeswell La B46 . . . . . .34 B3
Hawkesworth Dr CV8 . . . .93 A6
Hawke Way LE17. . . . . .55 C7
Hawkinge Dr B35 . . . . .22 A4
Hawkins Cl CV22 . . . . .82 E1
Hawkins Rd CV5. . . . . .60 A2
Hawkshead Dr B93 . . . . . .71 F6
Hawkside B77 . . . . .10 B8
Hawk's La OX15 . . . . .142 E8
Hawkswood Dr CV7 . . . . . .74 B7
Hawksworth B77 . . . . .74 D3
Hawksworth Dr 1 CV11. .61 B3
Hawlands CV21 . . . . .83 D6
Hawley Rd LE10 . . . . .31 D6
Haworth Gr B76 . . . . .13 A2
Hawthorn Ave CV9 . . . . . . .16 C5
Hawthorn Cl B49 . . . . .143 B5
Hawthorn Cres LE10 . . . . .31 E4
Hawthorn Ct CV4 . . . . .59 E1
Hawthorn Dr CV7 . . . . .74 B8
Hawthorne Ave CV7. . . . . .33 B1
Hawthorne Cl CV8 . . . . . . .80 A4
Hawthorne Terr CV10 . . . .28 E5
Hawthorn La CV4 . . . . .59 E1
Hawthorn Rd CV31. . . . . .109 F6
Hawthorns The B78. . . . . .15 C7
Hawthorn Terr CV23. . . . . .66 B3
Hawthorn Way
  Hartshill CV10 . . . . .28 A8
  Rugby CV22 . . . . .82 B2
  Shipston-On-S CV36. . .149 D4
  Tamworth B76 . . . . .22 A8
Haydock Cl
  Coventry CV6. . . . . .50 B4
  Stratford-u-A CV37 . . . .144 E1
  Tamworth B77 . . . . .9 F7
Haydon Cl B93 . . . . .71 F2
Haydons Cl B55. . . . . .135 B2
Haydon Way B49 . . . . . . .118 F8
Haye La B80 . . . . .112 A5

Hayes Cl CV21 . . . . .83 D7
Hayes Green Rd CV12. . . .49 F8
Hayes La CV7 . . . . .50 A8
Hayes Rd CV10 . . . . .28 A8
Hayes The CV35. . . . . . . .104 F5
Hay La
  Coventry CV1. . . . . .151 C2
  Solihull B90 . . . . .71 A6
Hayle Ave CV34 . . . . .104 F1
Hayle Cl CV11 . . . . .30 A5
Hay Mdw CV36 . . . . .149 C6
Haynestone Rd CV6 . . . . .60 E6
Haynes Way CV21. . . . . . . .82 F3
Hay Pool OX17 . . . . .133 F5
Hays La LE10 . . . . .31 B7
Haysum's Cl GL55. . . . . . .135 B1
Hayton Gn CV4 . . . . .59 E2
Haytor Rise CV2 . . . . .62 C7
Hayward's Gn CV6 . . . . . . .61 A7
Hayway La CV23 . . . . .116 B4
Hay Wood La B93,CV35. . .90 A3
Hazel Cl
  Hartshill CV10 . . . . .28 A8
  Royal Leamington Spa
  CV32. . . . . .106 A2
Hazel Croft
  Birmingham,Chelmsley Wood
  B37. . . . . .33 B1
  Braunston NN11 . . . . . .117 C5
  Hockley Heath B94 . . . . .88 C6
Hazell Way CV10. . . . . .29 A1
Hazel Rd
  Coventry CV6. . . . . .50 B1
  Nuneaton CV10 . . . . . . .28 D4
Hazeltree Gr B93 . . . . .71 E3
Hazelwood Cl CV22 . . . . . .99 C3
Hazlemere Cl CV5 . . . . . . .60 B4
Headborough Rd CV2 . . . .62 A5
Headington Ave CV6 . . . . .49 A2
Headland Cl CV37. . . . . . .129 A6
Headland Rd CV37 . . . . . .129 A6
Headland Rise CV37 . . . .129 A6
Headlands The CV5 . . . . . .60 D4
Headley Cl B97. . . . . .102 D8
Healey Cl CV21 . . . . .83 C7
Healey Ct CV34 . . . . .108 F7
Health Centre Rd CV4. . . .76 C4
Heanley La CV9 . . . . .16 D5
Hearsall Comm CV5 . . . . .60 F2
Hearsall Com Prim Sch
  CV7 . . . . .60 F2
Hearsall Ct CV5. . . . . .60 E2
Hearsall La CV5. . . . . .60 F2
Heart of England Sch
  CV7 . . . . .74 C6
Heart of England Way
  CV11 . . . . .29 E3
Heath Ave CV12. . . . . .38 E1
Heathcote Cl B77 . . . . . . .10 B7
Heathcote Gn CV6 . . . . . . .61 A7
Heathcote Ind Est CV34 .109 D4
Heathcote La
  Royal Leamington Spa
  CV34. . . . . .109 D4
  Warwick CV34 . . . . .109 A5
Heathcote Rd CV31 . . . . .110 A4
Heathcote St CV6. . . . . . . .61 A7
Heathcote Way CV34 . . . .109 D4
Heath Cres CV2 . . . . .62 A6
Heath Ct OX15. . . . . .142 D4
Heath End Rd CV37 . . . . .121 D7
Heath End Rd CV10 . . . . . .28 F2
Heather Cl
  Birmingham B36 . . . . . . .33 A8
  Nuneaton CV10 . . . . . . .28 F3
  Rugby CV22 . . . . .82 B1
  Stratford-u-A CV37 . . . .144 D3
Heather Ct CV9 . . . . .12 D1
Heather Dr CV12. . . . . .38 E2
Heather Rd
  Binley Woods CV3 . . . . .79 D7
  Coventry CV2 . . . . .50 C2
Heath Farm La CV35 . . . .123 C2
Heathfield Cl B93. . . . . . . .72 A5
Heathfield Rd
  Coventry CV5. . . . . .60 C2
  Norton WR11. . . . . .127 B2
Heathgreen Cl B37 . . . . . .33 D3
Heath Green Way CV4 . . . .75 F6
Heath La CV23 . . . . .84 E3
Heathley La B78 . . . . .8 E5
Heath Rd
  Bedworth CV12 . . . . .38 F1
  Coventry CV2. . . . . .62 A4
  Hollywood B47. . . . . .69 A7
Heath Terr
  Beausale CV35 . . . . .91 C2
  Royal Leamington Spa
  CV32. . . . . .105 E1
Heath The CV22 . . . . .99 C4
Heath Way CV10 . . . . .100 D8
Hebden Ave CV34 . . . . . . .105 D1
Hebden B77 . . . . .10 B8
Hebden Way CV11 . . . . . . .30 A2
Heber Dr CV8 . . . . .123 E6
Heckley Rd CV7 . . . . .51 A5
Heddle Gr CV6. . . . . .62 B8
Hedera Rd B98 . . . . .112 A4
Hedgefield Way CV4 . . . . .75 F8

Hedgerows The
  Nuneaton CV10 . . . . . . .28 F6
  Tamworth B77 . . . . .9 F8
Hedgerow Wlk CV6 . . . . . .49 B4
Hedges Cl CV4 . . . . .124 D6
Hedges The OX15 . . . . . .139 A4
Hedgetree Croft B37. . . . .33 C2
Hedge Way CV10 . . . . .28 C7
Hedging Lane Ind Est B77. .9 E5
Hedging La B77 . . . . .9 E5
Hedingham Gr B37 . . . . . .33 D2
Hedley Croft B35 . . . . .22 B4
Heemstede La CV32. . . . .106 A2
Heera Cl CV6. . . . . .61 D8
Helena Cl CV10 . . . . .28 F3
Helen St CV6 . . . . .61 F6
Hele Rd CV3. . . . . .77 D6
Hellidon Cl 6 CV32. . . . .106 A2
Hellidon Rd CV47 . . . . . . .125 F4
Helmdon Cl CV21 . . . . .83 D6
Helmsdale Rd CV22 . . . . . .99 C3
Helmswood Dr B37 . . . . . .44 C8
Helston Cl CV11 . . . . .30 A5
Helvellyn Way CV21. . . . . .83 D7
Hemdale Bsns Pk CV11 . .30 A4
Hemdale CV11. . . . . .30 A4
Hemingford Rd CV3 . . . . . .63 A8
Heming Rd B98. . . . . .103 E8
Hemlingford Croft B37. . . .44 A7
Hemlingford Rd
  Kingsbury B78 . . . . .15 D4
  Sutton Coldfield B76 . . . .22 A6
Hemmings Cl CV31 . . . . . .110 E5
Hemmings Mill CV35. . . . .122 A7
Hemplands OX7 . . . . .142 A2
Hemsby Cl CV4 . . . . .76 A7
Hemsworth Dr CV12 . . . . .40 B2
Henbrook La OX15 . . . . . .137 E2
Henderson Cl CV5 . . . . . . .60 C2
Hendre Cl CV5 . . . . .60 D2
Hen La CV6. . . . . .49 D3
Henley Coll CV2 . . . . .61 E8
Henley Coll CV2 . . . . .62 C8
Henley Ct CV2 . . . . .62 D7
Henleydale 4 B90 . . . . . . .70 C8
Henley-in-Arden Com Prim
  Sch B95. . . . . .113 B4
Henley-in-Arden Her Ctr*
  B95. . . . . .113 B4
Henley-in-Arden High Sch
  B95. . . . . .113 A4
Henley Mill La CV2 . . . . . .62 C7
Henley Park CV35 . . . . . .113 B4
Henley Park Ind Est CV2 .62 E7
Henley Rd
  Claverdon CV35 . . . . . .113 E4
  Coventry CV2. . . . . .62 D7
  Lowsonford B95 . . . . . . .89 D1
  Mappleborough Green B80. 112 A5
  Norton Lindsey CV35. . .114 D3
  Whitnash CV31 . . . . . . .110 B5
Henley St
  Alcester B49 . . . . .143 C4
  Stratford-u-A CV37 . . . .145 A3
Henley Wlk CV2 . . . . .62 D8
Henrietta St CV6 . . . . .61 E5
Henry Boteler Rd CV4. . . .76 B7
Henry Hinde Inf Sch CV22.82 C1
Henry Hinde Jun Sch
  CV22 . . . . .82 B2
Henry Tandy Ct 4
  CV32. . . . . .105 E1
Hensborough B90 . . . . . . .70 A5
Henson Rd CV12. . . . . .38 E1
Henwood La B91 . . . . .56 B4
Henwoods Ct CV10 . . . . . .149 D7
Hepworth Rd CV3. . . . . . . .63 B1
Herald Ave CV5 . . . . .60 D1
Herald Bsns Pk CV3. . . . . .78 F7
Herald Rd B26. . . . . .44 C4
Heralds Ct 6 CV34 . . . . .109 B8
Herald Way
  Coventry CV3. . . . . .79 A7
  Hinckley LE10 . . . . .31 D4
Herbert Art Gall & Mus*
  CV1 . . . . .151 C2
Herbert Fowler Jun Sch
  CV7 . . . . .26 F2
Herbert Gray Coll CV21 . .83 A3
Herbert's La CV8 . . . . .93 A5
Herbert St CV10 . . . . .28 E3
Hercules La CV35 . . . . . . .113 F4
Herdwycke Cl CV47 . . . . .147 D4
Hereford Cl CV10 . . . . .28 E4
Hereford Rd CV11 . . . . . . .40 F6
Hereford Way 4 OX16 . .139 F5
Hereward Coll CV4 . . . . . .59 F1
Hereford Way LE10. . . . . . .31 D4
Heritage Ct
  Coventry CV8 . . . . .93 B7
  Kenilworth CV8 . . . . .93 B7
Heritage Dr CV6 . . . . .50 C6
Heritage Motor Ctr*
  CV35 . . . . .123 D1
Hermes Cl CV34 . . . . .109 E5
Hermes Cres CV2 . . . . . . .62 E6
Hermes Rd CV1. . . . . .109 F3
Hermitage Cl
  Catthorpe CV23 . . . . . . .68 E1

Hermitage Cl continued
  Polesworth B78 . . . . .4 F1
Hermitage Dr B76 . . . . . . .13 A4
Hermitage Rd CV2. . . . . . .62 D7
Hermitage Way CV8. . . . . .93 A3
Hermit's Croft CV3. . . . . . .77 D8
Heronbank CV4 . . . . .59 C2
Heron Cl
  Alcester B49 . . . . .143 B5
  Cheswick Green B90 . . . .70 D4
Heron Ho CV3 . . . . .62 B2
Heron La CV37. . . . . .144 C5
Herons Cl LE10 . . . . .31 A7
Heron Way OX17 . . . . . . .130 E1
Herrick Rd CV2 . . . . .62 D3
Herring Rd CV9. . . . . .18 E7
Hertford Pl CV1 . . . . .151 A2
Hertford Rd
  Alcester B49 . . . . .143 C5
  Stratford-u-A CV37 . . . .144 F1
Hertford St CV1 . . . . .151 B2
Hertford Way B93 . . . . . . .72 B4
Hesleden B77 . . . . .10 B8
Heslop Cl CV3 . . . . .78 F8
Hetton Cl 1 CV34 . . . . . .104 F1
Hewitt Ave CV6 . . . . .61 A8
Hexby Cl CV2 . . . . .63 A6
Hexworthy Ave CV3 . . . . . .77 B5
Heybrook Cl CV2. . . . . .62 C7
Heycroft CV4 . . . . .76 D4
Heydons Terr CV47 . . . . . .133 F4
Heyford Cl CV2 . . . . .50 D3
Heyford Gr B91 . . . . .71 B8
Heyford Leys CV22 . . . . . .99 F6
Heyford Way B35 . . . . .22 B5
Heyville Croft CV8 . . . . . . .93 C3
Heywood Cl CV6. . . . . .62 A7
Hibberd Ct CV8 . . . . .92 F4
Hibbert Cl CV22 . . . . .83 A1
Hickman Ho CV10 . . . . . . .27 E4
Hickman Rd CV10. . . . . . . .27 F5
Hicks Cl CV34 . . . . .104 E2
Hidcote Ave B76. . . . . .22 A8
Hidcote Cl
  Nuneaton CV11 . . . . . . .39 F8
  Royal Leamington Spa
  CV31. . . . . .110 C5
Hidcote Gr B37 . . . . .44 A7
Hidcote Manor Gdn*
  GL55 . . . . .135 D5
Hidcote Rd
  Ebrington GL55. . . . . . .135 D3
  Kenilworth CV8 . . . . .93 C6
Higham Fields Ct CV13. . .21 A6
Higham La CV11 . . . . .21 C6
Higham Lane Sch CV10 . .29 D6
Higham La
  Nuneaton CV11 . . . . . . .29 E7
  Stoke Golding CV13 . . . .21 C6
  Wykin LE10 . . . . .21 C7
Higham on the Hill CE Prim
  Sch CV13 . . . . .21 A6
Higham Way LE10 . . . . . . .31 E7
High Ash Cl CV7 . . . . .49 F7
High Beech CV5 . . . . .60 A6
Highclere Gdns OX16 . . .139 F3
Highcliffe Rd B77 . . . . .9 D8
Highcroft CV35 . . . . .113 F3
Highcroft Cres CV32 . . . .105 C1
High Cross La CV47 . . . . . .76 E6
High Cross Rd LE17 . . . . .43 C6
Highdown Cres 3 B90. . .71 A6
Highdown Rd CV31 . . . . . .110 B6
Highfield Ave
  Redditch B97 . . . . .102 D8
  Tamworth B77 . . . . .4 A5
Highfield Cl
  Kenilworth CV8 . . . . .92 E4
  Sittlerfield CV37 . . . . . .121 B7
Highfield La CV7. . . . . . . .114 F6
Highfield La CV7 . . . . .37 C1
Highfield Rd
  Coventry CV2 . . . . .61 F4
  Nuneaton CV11 . . . . . . .29 E4
  Redditch B97 . . . . .102 D8
  Stratford-u-A CV37 . . . .144 E5
  Studley B80. . . . . .103 D4
Highfield Terr CV32 . . . . .105 D1
Highgrove
  Coventry CV4 . . . . .75 F5
  Rugby CV22 . . . . .99 D7
Highland Rd
  Coventry CV5. . . . . .60 F1
  Royal Leamington Spa
  CV32. . . . . .106 B4
Highlands 10 OX16 . . . . .139 F5
Highlands Cl CV34 . . . . . .109 A8
Highlands Ct B90 . . . . .70 E8
Highlands Rd B90 . . . . . . .70 F8
Highland Way B98 . . . . . .103 A7
High La OX15 . . . . .137 E1
High Mdw Inf Sch B46 . . .33 F8
High Park Cl CV5 . . . . .59 D5
High St
  Alcester B49 . . . . .143 B3
  Astwood Bank B96 . . . .102 E1
  Barford CV35 . . . . .122 B8
  Bedworth CV12 . . . . . . .39 B2
  Bidford-on-A B50. . . . . .148 D4
  Birmingham,Castle Vale B35. 22 B4
  Bishops Itchington CV47. 124 A4

High St continued
  Braunston NN11 . . . . . .117 D5
  Broom B50. . . . . .148 B7
  Charwelton NN11 . . . . .126 D2
  Chipping Campden GL55. .135 B2
  Coleshill B46 . . . . .33 F7
  Coventry CV1 . . . . .151 C2
  Coventry,Keresley CV6 . .48 F1
  Cubbington CV32. . . . . .106 E5
  Fenny Compton CV47. . .133 D7
  Great Rollright OX7 . . . .142 A2
  Hampton-in-A B92 . . . . .57 A7
  Harbury CV33 . . . . .123 F6
  Henley-in-A B95. . . . . . .113 B5
  Hook Norton OX15. . . . .142 D4
  Hurley CV9. . . . . .16 C5
  Keenly CV8 . . . . .92 E5
  Knowle B93 . . . . .72 C6
  Lower Brailes OX15. . . .137 F2
  Marton CV23 . . . . .115 C7
  Mickleton GL55 . . . . . . .135 C6
  Moreton-in-M GL56 . . . .140 A3
  Napton on t H CV47. . . .125 C8
  Nuneaton CV11 . . . . . . .29 B3
  Polesworth B78 . . . . .5 B2
  Royal Leamington Spa
  CV31. . . . . .110 A7
  Rugby CV21 . . . . .83 A3
  Rugby,Hillmorton CV21 . .101 A8
  Ryton-on-D CV8 . . . . . . .79 B1
  Shipston-on-S CV36. . . .149 D6
  Shutford OX15. . . . . . . .139 A3
  Southam CV47. . . . . . . .147 B4
  Stockton CV47. . . . . . . .147 C4
  Stoke Golding CV13 . . . .21 D7
  Stratford-u-A CV37 . . . .145 A2
  Studley B80. . . . . .103 E4
  Tamworth B77 . . . . .9 C5
  Warwick CV34 . . . . .108 E6
  Welford-on-A CV37 . . . .129 A7
High Trees Cl B90. . . . . . .102 E7
High Trees Rd B93 . . . . . .72 A7
High View CV7 . . . . .49 C7
High View Dr CV7 . . . . .49 C7
High View Rd CV32. . . . . .106 C5
Highwaymans Croft CV4 . .76 D5
Hijaz CV11 . . . . .21 C2
Hiker Gr 3 B37 . . . . .33 D1
Hilary Bevins Cl CV13. . . .20 F7
Hilary Dr B76. . . . . .13 A3
Hilary Rd
  Coventry CV4 . . . . .76 E6
  Nuneaton CV11 . . . . . . .28 F5
Hildtch Way CV11 . . . . . . .29 E2
Hillary Rd CV22. . . . . .99 F8
Hillborough La B50 . . . . . .128 E2
Hill Cl
  Northend CV47 . . . . . . .133 B7
  Royal Leamington Spa
  CV32. . . . . .106 A3
Hill Cres CV23 . . . . .96 F6
Hill Crest CV32. . . . . .106 E5
Hill Crest Hosp B98. . . . .103 C6
Hillcrest Pk B47 . . . . .85 F8
Hillcrest Rd
  Nuneaton CV10 . . . . . . .28 B5
  Polesworth B78 . . . . . . .11 A7
Hill Farm Ave CV11 . . . . . .30 B1
Hill Farm Prim Sch CV6. . .61 B7
Hillfield Mews 3 B91. . . .71 B8
Hillfield Rd
  Rugby CV22 . . . . .82 C1
  Solihull B91. . . . . .71 B8
Hillfields Ho 1 CV1 . . . . .61 E3
Hill Fray Dr CV3 . . . . .78 A5
Hill La CV47 . . . . .145 B4
Hillhurst Gr B36 . . . . .22 D1
Hilliard Cl CV12. . . . . .39 B4
Hill La
  Middleton B75. . . . . .7 B2
  Upper Brailes OX15. . . .137 E3
  Upper Quinton CV37 . . .129 D1
Hillman Gr B36 . . . . .22 F1
Hillman Ho CV1 . . . . .151 B3
Hillman Way CV37 . . . . . .144 C5
Hillmorton La
  Clifton u D CV23 . . . . . . .84 A4
  Dunsmore CV23. . . . . . .84 F5
Hillmorton Prim Sch
  CV21 . . . . .101 B8
Hillmorton Rd
  Coventry CV2. . . . . .50 C1
  Dordon B93 . . . . .72 A3
  Rugby CV22 . . . . .83 C2
Hill Rd
  Grandborough CV23 . . .116 E6
  Keresley CV7 . . . . .48 F6
  Lower Boddington NN11. .134 E7
Hill Rise NN11 . . . . .142 A2
Hillrise LE10. . . . . .31 F8
Hill Row CV11 . . . . .117 F4
Hillside DE12 . . . . .3 F8
Hill Side CV2 . . . . .62 A6
Hillside Croft CV47 . . . . .125 C8
Hillside Dr CV10 . . . . .28 C7
Hillside
  Harbury CV33 . . . . .123 E7
  Hartshill CV10 . . . . .19 A3
Hill Side B78 . . . . .15 D4
Hillside CV47 . . . . .125 C8
Hillside N CV2 . . . . .62 A6

Hillside Rd
Hinckley LE10 . . . . .31 D6
Stratford-u-A CV37 . . . . . . .144 C4
Hillside CV37 . . . . .144 A4
Hill St
Bedworth CV12 . . . . .39 B5
Coventry CV1 . . . . .151 B3
Hinckley LE10 . . . . .31 E8
Nuneaton CV10 . . . . .28 D4
Royal Leamington Spa
CV32 . . . . .106 A1
Rugby CV21 . . . . .83 A4
Warwick CV34 . . . . .109 B8
Hill The CV37 . . . . .145 B4
Hill Top CV9 . . . . .11 B2
Hilltop Cl
Honiley CV8 . . . . .90 E8
Southam CV47 . . . . .147 A5
Hill Top
Coventry CV1 . . . . .151 C3
Hill Top CV7 . . . . .27 B1
Loxley CV35 . . . . .130 F7
Hilltop Pk CV23 . . . . .96 F2
Hill View CV47 . . . . .124 A4
Hill View Cl GL55 . . . . .135 C7
Hill View Rd B50 . . . . .148 E5
Hill View CV37 . . . . .144 A4
Hillwood Ave B90 . . . . .71 A6
Hill Wootton Rd CV32,
CV35 . . . . .105 C6
Hillyard Rd CV47 . . . . .147 A5
Hilmore Way B77 . . . . .9 E8
Hilton Ave CV10 . . . . .28 B6
Hilton Ct CV5 . . . . .60 F2
Himbleton Croft ⊞ B90 . . .71 A6
Himley Rd ② CV12 . . . . . . .38 D2
Himley Rise B90 . . . . .70 E4
Hinchwick Ct B93 . . . . .71 F3
Hinckley Bsns Pk LE10 . . . .30 F8
Hinckley & District Hospl
LE10 . . . . .31 D8
Hinckley La CV13 . . . . .21 C3
Hinckley Rd
Ansty CV2,CV7 . . . . .51 C2
Aston Flamville LE10 . . . . . . .32 E6
Burbage LE9 . . . . .32 D8
Burton Hastings CV11,LE10 . .41 C8
Coventry CV2 . . . . .63 A8
Hinckley LE10 . . . . .32 A6
Nuneaton CV11 . . . . .29 E5
Stoke Golding CV13 . . . . .21 F7
Wolvey LE10 . . . . .41 E7
Hinckley Sta LE10 . . . . .31 D7
Hind Cl CV34 . . . . .104 F2
Hinde Cl CV21 . . . . .83 C4
Hindlip Cl B98 . . . . .112 A6
Hintons Coppice B93 . . . . .71 E6
Hipsley Cl B36 . . . . .22 C1
Hipsley La CV9 . . . . .16 E6
Hipswell Highway CV2 . . . .62 D3
Hipton Hill WR11 . . . . .127 B3
Hirdemonsway B90 . . . . . . .70 A5
Hiron Croft CV3 . . . . .77 C8
Hiron The CV3 . . . . .77 C8
Hiron Way CV34 . . . . .108 B7
Hirst Cl CV23 . . . . .82 A5
Hitchman Ct CV31 . . . . . . .110 A5
Hitchman Rd CV31 . . . . . . .110 A5
Hithersand Cl CV35 . . . . . .121 F4
Hitherside B90 . . . . .70 A5
HM Prison Rye Hill CV23 .100 D1
HM Young Offender
Institution CV23 . . . . .100 C1
Hoarestone Ave CV11 . . . . .40 A7
Hobbins The CV36 . . . . . . .149 C5
Hob La
Balsall Common CV7 . . . . . . .74 E4
Burton Green CV8 . . . . .75 A3
Temple Balsall B92 . . . . .73 A8
Hobley Cl CV22 . . . . .99 D7
Hockett St CV3 . . . . .77 D8
Hocking Rd CV2 . . . . .62 E4
Hockley Cl CV23 . . . . .116 F5
Hockley Ct B94 . . . . .88 C7
Hockley Heath Prim Sch
B94 . . . . .88 C6
Hockley La
Coventry CV5 . . . . .59 C5
Ettington CV37 . . . . .131 B3
Hockley Rd
Shrewley CV35 . . . . .114 C6
Tamworth B77 . . . . .9 F5
Hoden La WR11 . . . . .128 B3
Hodge La B77 . . . . .4 B6
Hodgett's La
Balsall Common CV7 . . . . . . .74 F7
Coventry CV7,CV8 . . . . .75 A6
Hodgson Rd CV37 . . . . . . .145 B2
Hodnell Cl B36 . . . . .22 C1
Hodnell Dr CV47 . . . . .147 C3
Hodnet Cl CV8 . . . . .93 B5
Hogarth Cl CV12 . . . . .39 A4
Hogarth Rd CV37 . . . . .144 D1
Hogg End OX17 . . . . .134 F3
Hoggrills End La B46 . . . . .25 A4
Holbeche Cres CV7 . . . . . . .36 E3
Holbeche Rd
Dorridge B93 . . . . .72 A7
Sutton Coldfield B75 . . . . . . .13 B5
Holbein Cl CV12 . . . . .39 A4
Holborn Ave CV6 . . . . .49 C2
Holbrook Ave CV21 . . . . . . .83 B4
Holbrook Gr B37 . . . . .33 A1
Holbrook La CV6 . . . . .49 D2
Holbrook Park Est CV6 . . . .61 D8

Holbrook Prim Sch CV6 . . .49 E1
Holbrook Rd
Long Lawford CV23 . . . . .82 B5
Stratford-u-A CV37 . . . . . . .144 C3
Holbrook Way CV6 . . . . . . .49 D1
Holcot Leys CV22 . . . . .100 A7
Holder Cl B50 . . . . .148 D5
Hole House La B94 . . . . .88 F1
Holioak Dr CV34 . . . . .109 B6
Holland Ave B93 . . . . .72 B8
Holland Cl B50 . . . . .148 D4
Holland Croft B76 . . . . .15 B2
Holland Rd CV6 . . . . .61 A6
Hollick Cres CV7 . . . . .37 A8
Hollicombe Terr CV2 . . . . . .62 D8
Hollies Rd B78 . . . . .11 B8
Hollies The CV23 . . . . .67 F1
Hollin Brow Cl B93 . . . . . . .72 B3
Hollings Gr B91 . . . . .71 B8
Hollington Way B90 . . . . . . .71 C7
Hollinwell Cl CV11 . . . . .40 C8
Hollis La CV8 . . . . .92 E8
Hollis Rd CV3 . . . . .62 A2
Holloway Field CV6 . . . . . . .61 A6
Holloway Hill OX15 . . . . . .138 A1
Holloway La OX15 . . . . .138 A1
Holloway The
Mollington OX17 . . . . .134 A2
Priors Marston CV47 . . . . . .125 E4
Warwick CV34 . . . . .108 D6
Hollow Cres CV6 . . . . .61 B5
Hollowell Way CV21 . . . . . . .83 C7
Hollows The CV11 . . . . .29 F1
Hollow Way CV47 . . . . .125 C8
Holly Bank CV5 . . . . .77 A8
Holly Bank Est CV9 . . . . .3 A2
Hollyberry Ave B91 . . . . . . .71 A8
Hollyberry Cl B98 . . . . .112 A6
Hollybush La CV6 . . . . .50 A4
Holly Bush La CV47 . . . . . .125 E4
Hollybush Rd OX15 . . . . . .142 D4
Holly Cl LE10 . . . . .31 E5
Holly Ct CV7 . . . . .74 B3
Holly Dr
Hollywood B47 . . . . .69 B7
Hurley CV9 . . . . .16 D4
Ryton-on-D CV8 . . . . .79 B1
Holly Farm Bsns Pk CV8 . .91 B7
Hollyfast La CV7 . . . . .48 C4
Hollyfast Prim Sch CV6 . . .60 E7
Hollyfast Rd CV6 . . . . .60 E6
Holly Gr
Church Lawford CV23 . . . . . .81 B5
Coventry CV4 . . . . .60 B2
Hollyhurst CV12 . . . . .38 F1
Hollyhurst Gr B90 . . . . .70 B8
Hollyhurst B46 . . . . .23 C2
Holly La
Atherstone CV9 . . . . .12 C2
Atherstone CV9 . . . . .12 D2
Balsall Common CV7 . . . . . . .74 B3
Hollyland B46 . . . . .24 F1
Holly Lane Ind Est CV9 . . . .12 C2
Holly La
Portway B48 . . . . .85 F5
Wishaw B76 . . . . .13 D4
Holly Lodge CV35 . . . . .146 D3
Holly Lodge Wlk B37 . . . . . .33 A2
Holly Marie Ct CV5 . . . . . . .60 F1
Holly Orch ⑤ CV37 . . . . . .145 A4
Holly Rd CV36 . . . . .149 D4
Hollystitches Rd CV10 . . . . .28 E6
Holly St CV32 . . . . .106 B1
Holly Tree Wlk LE17 . . . . . .43 E6
Hollywell Rd B93 . . . . .72 A5
Holly Wlk
Baginton CV8 . . . . .77 E2
Nuneaton CV11 . . . . .29 F2
Royal Leamington Spa
CV32 . . . . .106 A3
Stratford-u-A CV37 . . . . . . .144 C1
Hollywood Gdns B47 . . . . . .69 A8
Hollywood La B47 . . . . .69 A8
Hollywood Motor Pk B47 . .69 A8
Hollyword Dr B47 . . . . .69 A8
Holman Way CV11 . . . . .29 D3
Holmcroft CV2 . . . . .62 F8
Holme Cl CV21 . . . . .83 C6
Holmes Cl CV8 . . . . .92 F5
Holmes Dr CV5 . . . . .59 D5
Holmes Rd CV31 . . . . .110 B3
Holme Way CV21 . . . . .101 D1
Homewood Cl CV8 . . . . .93 B5
Homewood Ct CV8 . . . . .93 B5
Holmfield Rd CV2 . . . . .62 B3
Holmsdale Rd CV6 . . . . .61 E7
Holroyd Ho CV4 . . . . .59 F2
Holsworthy Cl CV11 . . . . . . .29 E5
Holt Ave CV33 . . . . .122 E8
Holte Rd CV9 . . . . .18 D8
Holt Gdns B80 . . . . .103 E2
Holt Leys CV47 . . . . .147 C4
Holtom St CV37 . . . . .144 F1
Holt Rd
Hinckley LE10 . . . . .31 E6
Studley B80 . . . . .103 E2
Holt The
Mollington OX17 . . . . .133 F2
Royal Leamington Spa
CV32 . . . . .106 B3
Holwick B77 . . . . .10 B8
Holys Cross Ct CV2 . . . . . . .62 E4
Holy Cross RC Prim Sch
B76 . . . . .13 A3
Holy Family RC Prim Sch
CV6 . . . . .61 B6
Holyhead Rd CV5 . . . . .60 E5

Holyoak Cl
Bedworth CV12 . . . . .38 F1
Rugby CV22 . . . . .99 C8
Holyoke Gr CV31 . . . . .110 B2
Holyrood Ct CV10 . . . . .28 D5
Holywell Cl CV4 . . . . .59 D1
Holywell Rd CV35 . . . . .113 F5
Holywell Rd CV47 . . . . .147 A4
Home Cl
Bubbenhall CV8 . . . . .95 C6
Staverton NN11 . . . . .126 E8
Home Farm Barns CV35 . .138 B7
Home Farm CV36 . . . . .141 C7
Home Farm Cl
Pailton CV23 . . . . .66 A8
Witherley CV9 . . . . .19 B8
Home Farm Cres CV31 . . . .110 B4
Home Farm Dr OX15 . . . . .138 E8
Home Farm
Leek Wootton CV35 . . . . . . .104 F6
Stoneleigh CV8 . . . . .94 A3
Homefield La CV22 . . . . .99 E4
Home Furlong CV35 . . . . . .146 C1
Home Mdw CV35 . . . . .113 F3
Home Park Rd CV11 . . . . . . .29 C3
Homer Cl CV34 . . . . .104 F1
Homestalls Mdw CV35 . . . .131 D2
Homeward Way CV3 . . . . . . .63 A1
Honeybourne Cl CV5 . . . . . .60 B3
Honeybourne Rd B50 . . . . .148 E3
Honeyfield Rd CV1 . . . . .61 D5
Honeysuckle Cl CV23 . . . . . .83 D8
Honeysuckle Dr CV2 . . . . . .50 B2
Honiley Ct CV2 . . . . .50 D1
Honiley Rd
Honiley CV8 . . . . .91 B6
Meer End CV8 . . . . .74 A1
Honiley Way CV2 . . . . .50 D1
Honington Cl CV35 . . . . . . .146 C1
Honington Hall* CV36 . . . .137 A5
Honiton Rd CV2 . . . . .62 C5
Honiwell Ct CV33 . . . . .123 E6
Hood St CV1 . . . . .61 E3
Hood's Way CV22 . . . . .82 D2
Hook Norton Brewery*
OX15 . . . . .142 C4
Hook Norton CE Prim Sch
OX15 . . . . .142 D4
Hook Norton Rd
Great Rollright OX7 . . . . . . .142 A2
Sibford Ferris OX15 . . . . . . .142 D8
Hoo La GL55 . . . . .135 A2
Hoopers La B96 . . . . .102 E1
Hope Aldridge Bsns Ctr
CV10 . . . . .29 C6
Hope Cl CV7 . . . . .49 A7
Hopedale Cl CV2 . . . . .62 E3
Hope St CV1 . . . . .61 B2
Hopkin Cotts WR11 . . . . . .127 D3
Hopkins Field CV37 . . . . . . .129 B7
Hopkins Prec The B49 . . . .143 C4
Hopkins Rd CV6 . . . . .61 A4
Hopkins Way CV35 . . . . . . .146 D5
Hopper's La CV35 . . . . .146 D4
Hopton Cl CV5 . . . . .60 A4
Hopton Crofts CV32 . . . . . .105 C2
Horeston Grange Sh Ctr
CV11 . . . . .30 A5
Horley Path Rd OX15 . . . . .139 D5
Hornbeam Dr CV4 . . . . .59 D1
Hornbeam CV31 . . . . .110 C6
Hornbeam B77 . . . . .4 A4
Hornchurch Close Ind Est
CV1 . . . . .151 B1
Hornchurch Cl CV1 . . . . . . .151 B1
Horndean Cl CV6 . . . . .50 A2
Horne Cl CV21 . . . . .101 B8
Horninghold Cl CV3 . . . . . . .78 E8
Hornsby Cl CV36 . . . . .149 E7
Hornsey Cl CV2 . . . . .62 F7
Horton Gr CV35 . . . . .114 E6
Horton Prim Sch OX15 . . .139 B7
Horsefair CV36 . . . . .149 D6
Horsefair The ⑥ LE10 . . . .31 D8
Horse Shoe Rd CV6 . . . . . . .50 A4
Horsepool Hollow CV31 . . .110 C5
Horsewell ⑦ CV47 . . . . . . .147 B4
Horsfall Rd B75 . . . . .13 A5
Horsford Rd CV3 . . . . .77 E6
Horsham Cl 図 OX16 . . . . .139 F5
Horton Cl
Alcester B49 . . . . .143 D5
Bedworth CV7 . . . . .49 F7
Horton Cres CV22 . . . . .83 B2
Horton Gr B90 . . . . .71 A5
Hosiery St CV2 . . . . .39 C2
Hoskyn Cl CV21 . . . . .100 F8
Hospital La CV12 . . . . .38 B1
Hospital of St Cross CV22 .83 B1
Hospital Rd GL56 . . . . .140 A3
Hotchkiss Cl CV35 . . . . . . .146 D2
Hotchkiss Way CV3 . . . . . . .79 A7
Hothorpe Cl CV3 . . . . .62 F1
Houldsworth Cres CV6 . . . .49 C4
Houndsfield Cl B47 . . . . . . .69 C6
Houndsfield Farm B47 . . . . .69 B5
Houndsfield La B47 . . . . . . .69 C6
Houndsfield La B47 . . . . . . .69 C7
Houston Rd CV21 . . . . .83 C6
Hove Ave CV5 . . . . .59 E4
Hovelands Cl CV2 . . . . .62 C8
Howard Cl
Bidford-on-A B50 . . . . .148 C4
Coventry CV5 . . . . .59 E4
Dunchurch CV22 . . . . .99 C4

Howard Rd
Nuneaton CV10 . . . . .29 A3
Redditch B98 . . . . .103 C8
Howard St CV1 . . . . .151 C4
Howard Wlk CV31 . . . . .109 D6
Howat Rd CV7 . . . . .48 F7
Howcombe La CV47 . . . . . .125 C7
Howcotte Gn CV4 . . . . .75 E8
Howe Green La CV7,CV10 . .37 D4
Howells Cl CV12 . . . . .38 D1
Howes Com Prim Sch
CV3 . . . . .77 E5
Howes Croft B35 . . . . .22 A2
Howes La CV3 . . . . .77 D3
Howkins Rd CV21 . . . . .83 E6
Howlette Rd CV4 . . . . .59 E2
Hoylake Cl CV11 . . . . .30 B1
Hoylake B77 . . . . .4 B4
Huckson Rd CV47 . . . . .124 B4
Huddesford Dr CV7 . . . . . . .74 C8
Huddiscon Cl ⑤ CV34 . . . .104 F1
Hudson Ave B46 . . . . .33 F6
Hudson Rd CV22 . . . . .82 E1
Huggins Cl CV7 . . . . .74 C7
Hughes Cl
Harvington WR11 . . . . .127 D4
Warwick CV34 . . . . .104 D2
Whitnash CV31 . . . . .110 A2
Hughes Hill CV35 . . . . .114 B6
Hughes La WR11 . . . . .127 D4
Hughes The CV34 . . . . .108 E6
Hugh Rd CV3 . . . . .62 A2
Hulme Cl CV3 . . . . .63 B1
Humber Ave
Coventry CV1 . . . . .61 F1
Sutton Coldfield B76 . . . . . . .22 A7
Humber Cl NN11 . . . . .117 F2
Humber Gr B36 . . . . .22 F1
Humber Rd CV3 . . . . .78 A8
Humberstone Rd ④ CV6 . . .61 A5
Humber Wlk ⑧ CV34 . . . . .109 B8
Humphrey Burton's Rd
CV3 . . . . .77 C6
Humphrey-Davy Rd CV12 . .49 D8
Humphris St CV34 . . . . .109 B8
Hungerfield Rd B36 . . . . . . .22 C1
Hunningham Gr ⑥ B91 . . .71 B8
Hunscote La CV35 . . . . .121 F1
Hunt Cl CV35 . . . . .114 F3
Hunt End La B97 . . . . .102 C5
Hunt End La B97 . . . . .102 C5
Hunter Bvd LE17 . . . . .55 C7
Hunters Cl CV3 . . . . .63 A2
Hunters La CV13 . . . . .20 A6
Hunters Lane Ind Est
CV21 . . . . .83 A5
Hunters La CV21 . . . . .83 A5
Hunters Moon CV23 . . . . . .117 B2
Hunters Pk CV9 . . . . .11 C1
Hunter St CV21 . . . . .83 C4
Hunters Wlk CV9 . . . . .19 B7
Hunter Terr CV5 . . . . .76 D8
Hunt Hall La CV37 . . . . .129 A6
Huntingdon Rd CV5 . . . . . . .77 A8
Huntingdon Way CV10 . . . . .28 E3
Hunt Paddocks CV8 . . . . . . .92 E1
Hunts Rd CV37 . . . . .145 C1
Hunt Terr CV4 . . . . .76 B7
Hurdlers La CV37 . . . . .121 B6
Hurlbutt Rd CV34 . . . . .109 C4
Hurley Cl CV32 . . . . .106 A2
Hurley Comm CV9 . . . . .16 C6
Hurley La B46 . . . . .25 D6
Hurley Prim Sch CV9 . . . . . .16 D4
Hurn Way CV6 . . . . .50 A4
Hurricane Way B35 . . . . . . .22 A2
Hurst Green Rd
Bentley Heath B93 . . . . .71 F4
Minworth B76 . . . . .22 D6
Hurst Rd
Bedworth CV12 . . . . .39 B3
Coventry CV6 . . . . .50 A4
Hinckley LE10 . . . . .30 D8
Southam CV47 . . . . .147 A3
Hurst The B94 . . . . .69 A6
Hurst Wlk CV6 . . . . .50 A4
Husbandmans Cl CV36 . . . .149 D6
Hutchings La B90 . . . . .70 B5
Hyacinth Way LE10 . . . . .31 D5
Hyde Pl CV32 . . . . .109 E8
Hyde Rd
Coventry CV2 . . . . .62 E4
Kenilworth CV8 . . . . .93 A5
Hydes La LE10 . . . . .30 E4
Hypericum Gdns CV2 . . . . . .62 C4

Ibex Cl CV3 . . . . .62 F1
Ibstock Rd CV6 . . . . .50 A5
Icknield Cl B50 . . . . .148 E4
Icknield St B50 . . . . .148 E4
Icknield Row B49 . . . . .143 B4
Icknield St
Bidford-on-A B50 . . . . .148 E4
Carpenter's Hill B48,B98,B98 .85 C2
Portway B48 . . . . .85 B6
Icknield Street Dr B98 . . . .103 D7
Iden Rd CV1 . . . . .61 E4
Idlicote Rd CV36 . . . . .137 B8
Ilam Pk CV8 . . . . .93 C5
Ilex Ct CV34 . . . . .109 A7
Ilford Cl CV12 . . . . .39 A3
Ilford Ct CV3 . . . . .79 D7
Ilford Dr CV3 . . . . .77 B5

Ilfracombe Gr CV3 . . . . .77 A5
Iliffe Ho LE10 . . . . .31 B7
Illshaw Cl B98 . . . . .112 A6
Illshaw Heath Rd B90,B94 .70 D2
Ilmer Cl CV21 . . . . .83 E7
Ilmington CE Prim Sch
CV36 . . . . .136 A6
Ilmington Cl
Coventry CV3 . . . . .77 B5
Hatton CV35 . . . . .114 C6
Ilmington Rd
Blackwell CV36 . . . . .136 C6
Ilmington CV36,CV37 . . . . .136 D7
Ilminster Cl LE10 . . . . .32 B7
Imogen Gdns CV34 . . . . . . .109 E3
Imperial Rise B46 . . . . .23 E2
Inca Cl CV3 . . . . .78 F8
Inchbrook Rd CV8 . . . . .93 C7
Inchcape Cl CV22 . . . . .99 B8
Inchford Ave CV34 . . . . . . .104 E2
Inchford Cl CV11 . . . . .29 F1
Infantry Pl B75 . . . . .13 A5
Ingle Ct CV21 . . . . .109 E7
Ingleton Cl CV11 . . . . .30 A2
Inglewood Cl CV22 . . . . . . .106 A3
Ingon La CV37 . . . . .121 B5
Ingram Cl CV36 . . . . .140 E5
Ingram Pit La B77 . . . . .4 A5
Ingram Rd CV5 . . . . .76 D8
Innage Cl CV31 . . . . .110 B4
Innage Park Small Ind Units
CV9 . . . . .12 C1
Innage Terr CV9 . . . . .18 D8
Innage The B47 . . . . .69 A5
Innis Rd CV5 . . . . .76 E8
Innsworth Dr B35 . . . . .22 A2
Instone Rd CV6 . . . . .61 A8
Inverary Cl CV8 . . . . .93 C4
Inverlea Ct GL55 . . . . .135 B6
Inverness Cl CV5 . . . . .60 A4
Invicta Rd CV3 . . . . .78 F8
Io Ctr The B98 . . . . .103 C8
Ipswich Wlk B37 . . . . .33 B2
Irelands La B94,B95 . . . . . .113 D7
Ireton Cl CV4 . . . . .59 C1
Iris Cl LE10 . . . . .31 E5
Ironbridge Way CV6 . . . . . . .50 B6
Iron Cross NN11 . . . . .126 A1
Ironmonger Row CV1 . . . . .151 B3
Ironstone Hollow OX15 . . .142 E4
Irving Rd CV1 . . . . .61 E2
Isambard Dr CV6 . . . . .49 F5
Isis Gr B36 . . . . .33 A8
Islington Cres CV9 . . . . .10 C1
Ivanhoe Ave CV11 . . . . .29 E1
Ivor Rd
Atherstone CV9 . . . . .18 C4
Coventry CV6 . . . . .49 F2
Ivybridge Rd CV3 . . . . .77 D6
Ivy Cl CV13 . . . . .21 D7
Ivycroft Rd B79 . . . . .5 E4
Ivy Farm La CV4 . . . . .76 D6
Ivy Gr CV1 . . . . .28 D6
Ivy Grounds CV36 . . . . .141 A8
Ivyhouse Wlk ⑥ B77 . . . . . .9 F6
Ivy La
Ettington CV37 . . . . .131 A3
Harbury CV33 . . . . .123 F6
Mollington OX17 . . . . .134 A2
Shutford OX15 . . . . .139 A3
Ivy Lodge Cl B37 . . . . .44 A7
Ivy Way B90 . . . . .70 A6
Izod's Cl GL55 . . . . .135 A4

J

Jack Cade Way CV34 . . . . . .109 E4
Jackdaw Dr B36 . . . . .33 B8
Jacker's Rd CV2 . . . . .50 B4
Jacklin Dr CV3 . . . . .77 C4
Jacknell Rd LE10 . . . . .30 D8
Jack O'Watton Bsns Pk
B46 . . . . .23 D3
Jackson Cl
Hampton Magna CV35 . . . . .114 F3
Keresley CV7 . . . . .49 A7
Jackson Gr CV8 . . . . .93 A4
Jackson La CV47 . . . . .125 C7
Jackson Rd
Coventry CV6 . . . . .49 D1
Rugby CV21 . . . . .84 A1
Jacksons Mdw B50 . . . . . . .148 C6
Jacksons Orch CV37 . . . . . .129 B3
Jackson Wlk B35 . . . . .22 A2
Jack Thomson Croft
WR11 . . . . .127 F6
Jackwood Gn CV12 . . . . .49 C8
Jacob Dr CV4 . . . . .76 D6
Jacobean La B93 . . . . .56 B2
Jacox Cres CV8 . . . . .93 C5
Jade Cl CV1 . . . . .151 D4
Jago La CV37 . . . . .133 C4
Jamescroft CV3 . . . . .78 E6
James Ct
④ Rugby CV21 . . . . .83 B3
Warwick CV34 . . . . .108 F7
James Dawson Dr CV5 . . . .59 B8
James Diskin Ct CV11 . . . . .29 E2
James Galloway Cl CV3 . . . .78 E7
James Green Rd CV4 . . . . . .59 F2
James Ho CV2 . . . . .62 C8
James Moore Ho ⑪
CV47 . . . . .147 B4
Jameson Ct ㉗ GL56 . . . . .140 A3
James Rd B46 . . . . .33 F8

James St
New Arley CV7 37 A8
Nuneaton CV11 29 A5
Rugby CV21 83 B3
James Watt Cl NN11 117 F2
James Wlk 6 CV21 83 B3
Jaques Cl B46 23 B2
Jardine Cres CV4 59 F2
Jasmine Gr
Coventry CV3 78 C8
Royal Leamington Spa CV32 106 A2
Jasmine Rd B77 4 A4
Javelin Ave B35 22 B2
Jays Cl B98 112 A6
Jean St CV9 11 C1
Jedburgh Gr CV3 77 A4
Jeffrey Cl CV12 49 D8
Jeffrey Woods Cross CV1 61 F4
Jeff's Cl OX15 137 F2
Jeffs Cl CV35 138 B6
Jeliff St CV4 59 F2
Jenkins Ave CV5 59 F4
Jenkins Rd CV21 84 A1
Jenner St CV1 151 C4
Jenton Rd CV31 110 B6
Jephcott Cl B49 143 A4
Jephcott Ho 2 CV1 61 E3
Jephson Ct CV2 50 C4
Jephson Pl 3 CV31 110 B7
Jephsons The CV47 115 C5
Jerome Ct CV21 83 C3
Jersey Croft B36 33 B6
Jersey Dr 6 OX16 139 F5
Jervis Rd B77 9 F5
Jesmond Rd CV1 61 F4
Jesson Rd B75 13 A5
Jetty The OX17 134 F1
Jill La B96 103 B2
Jim Forrest Cl 4 CV3 78 F8
Joanna Dr CV3 77 C3
Joan of Arc Ho CV3 77 E6
Joan's Cl CV31 110 C6
Joan Ward St CV3 77 D8
Job's La CV4 60 A2
Jodrell St CV11 29 B6
Joe OBrien Cl CV3 78 C6
Joe Williams Cl 7 CV3 78 F8
John Black Day Hospl B37 44 C8
Johndory B77 9 D6
John Grace St CV3 77 D8
John Gulson Prim Sch CV1 61 D5
John Haynes Ct CV7 50 A7
John Knight Rd CV12 39 B5
John McGuire Cres CV3 78 E7
John Nash Sq CV8 92 F3
John Nichols St LE10 31 B7
John of Gaunt Ho CV3 77 E6
John O'Gaunt Rd CV8 92 E3
John Rous Ave CV4 76 B7
John's Cl LE10 31 D5
Johns Cl B80 103 C4
John Shelton Com Prim Sch CV6 49 D4
John Shelton Dr CV6 49 D4
John Simpson Cl CV8 80 A3
John Sinclair Ho CV1 151 B4
Johnson Ave CV22 82 E2
Johnson Pl B95 113 B5
Johnson Rd
Bedworth CV12 39 C3
Coventry CV6 62 A8
Johnson St CV9 10 C1
John St
11 Stratford-u-A CV37 145 A3
Bedworth CV12 39 A2
Nuneaton CV11 29 C2
Nuneaton,Stockingford CV10 28 E3
Royal Leamington Spa CV32 109 F8
John Taylor Way CV35 122 E3
John Thwaites Cl CV22 83 A2
John Tofts Ho CV1 151 B4
Jolyffe Ct CV37 144 F4
Jolyffe Park Rd CV37 145 A4
Jonathan Rd CV2 62 F8
Jon Baker Ct LE10 31 E8
Jones Rd CV7 39 A1
Jones Wood Cl B76 22 A7
Jonkel Ave B77 10 A5
Jordan Cl CV8 93 B2
Jordans Cl B97 102 D6
Jordans The CV5 60 C4
Jordan Well CV1 151 C2
Joseph Cash Prim Sch CV6 61 C7
Joseph Creighton Cl CV3 78 E7
Joseph Halpin Ho 3 CV1 151 C4
Joseph Latham Ho 3 CV2 50 B1
Joseph Luckman Rd CV12 39 B4
Joseph Way CV37 144 E5
Jourdain Pk CV34 109 E3
Joyce Pool CV34 108 E7
Joyce Way CV22 99 A8
Jubilee Ave
Lower Shuckburgh NN11 116 E1
Redditch B97 102 D7
Jubilee Cl
Bidford-on-A B50 148 E5
Chipping Campden GL55 135 A2
Jubilee Cres CV6 61 B7
Jubilee Ct
Alcester B49 143 C4
Jubilee Ct *continued*
Kingsbury B78 15 D5
Jubilee St CV21 82 E4
Jubilee Terr CV12 39 B4
Judd Cl CV12 38 F3
Judds La CV6 49 E4
Judge Cl CV23 82 A5
Judith Way CV22 99 A8
Juggins La B94 86 B7
Julian Cl CV2 62 F8
Juliet Cl CV11 30 A1
Juliet Dr
Royal Leamington Spa CV34 109 F3
Rugby CV22 99 D6
Julius Dr B46 23 F1
Junction One Ret Pk CV21 83 B6
Junction St CV1 151 A2
Junewood Cl CV21 83 D7
Juniper Cl CV12 38 E2
Juniper Dr
Coventry CV5 59 F5
Sutton Coldfield B76 22 A7
Juniper B77 4 A4
Juno Dr CV31 109 F5
Jury St CV34 108 E6
Justice Cl CV31 110 A4
Justins Ave CV37 144 F5

K

Kalfs Dr CV22 99 B8
Kanzan Rd CV2 50 B4
Kareen Gr CV3 79 C7
Karen Cl CV10 28 E7
Karlingford Cl CV5 76 D8
Kathleen Ave CV12 38 E1
Katrine Cl CV10 28 C5
Kay Cl CV21 83 C7
Kaysbrook Dr CV23 97 A6
Keats Cl CV10 28 A4
Keats Ho B97 102 C8
Keats Rd
Coventry CV2 62 D2
Stratford-u-A CV37 145 B1
Keble Ho B37 33 A2
Keble Rd GL56 140 A2
Kebull Gn CV4 75 E8
Keele Ho B37 33 B4
Keeling Rd CV8 93 B5
Keenan Dr CV12 38 D1
Keepers Cl B46 34 A4
Keepers Wlk CV12 38 D1
Keetley Cl CV36 149 D4
Kegworth Cl CV6 50 A4
Keir Cl CV32 106 A2
Keith Rd CV32 106 B4
Kele Rd CV4 76 A7
Kelmscote Rd CV6 60 F8
Kelsey Cl CV11 29 E3
Kelsey La CV7 74 D5
Kelsey's Cl CV8 79 F3
Kelsull Croft B37 33 A2
Kelvin Ave CV2 62 D5
Kelvin Rd CV32 106 C5
Kelway CV3 63 A2
Kemble Dr B35 22 A3
Kemerton Way B90 70 F6
Kemp Cl CV34 109 A7
Kempley Ave CV2 62 C2
Kempsey Cl B98 103 B7
Kempsford Cl B98 102 F6
Kemps Green Rd
Balsall Common CV7 74 B6
Kemps Green B94 88 A1
Kempton Cl CV37 129 F8
Kempton Cres CV32 106 C4
Kempton Dr B77 9 D4
Kem St CV11 29 E2
Kendal Ave
Coleshill B46 33 F7
Royal Leamington Spa CV32 105 C2
Kendal Cl
Nuneaton CV11 30 A6
Redditch B98 112 A6
Kendall Ave CV37 145 A3
Kendal Rise CV5 60 C4
Kenderdine Montessori Sch CV5 77 A8
Kendon Ave CV6 60 E6
Kendrick Cl CV6 50 A4
Kenelm Ct CV3 78 C5
Kenhill Rd OX15 138 F5
Kenilcourt CV8 92 D6
Kenilworth Castle* CV8 92 D5
Kenilworth Cl
Balsall Common CV7 74 A6
Redditch B97 102 D6
Kenilworth Ct CV3 77 C8
Kenilworth Dr CV11 29 B3
Kenilworth Hall Mews CV8 92 F5
Kenilworth Rd
Balsall Common CV7,CV8 74 D4
Blackdown CV32 105 E5
Bradnock's Marsh B92 57 E5
Coventry CV4 76 E3
Kenilworth CV8 93 C8
Knowle B93 72 E5
Lighthorne Heath CV33 123 D2
Meriden CV7 45 D1
Royal Leamington Spa CV32 106 C6
Kenilworth Sch Castle Hall Sixth Form CV8 92 F2
Kenilworth Sch CV8 93 C5
Kenilworth St 20 CV32 105 F1
Kenilworth Way 8 OX16 139 F3
Kennan Ave CV31 109 F6
Kennedy Dr CV22 82 C2
Kennedy Sq 3 CV32 106 A1
Kennel La CV9 19 B7
Kennet Cl CV2 62 C8
Kenneth Vincent Cl B97 102 E4
Kenning Cl CV47 115 C4
Kenpas Highway CV3 77 A5
Kenrick Croft B35 22 A2
Kensington Ct
Coventry CV5 61 A1
Nuneaton CV10 28 C6
Kensington Rd CV5 61 A1
Kent Cl CV3 77 E6
Kenthurst Cl CV5 59 C4
Kentmere Cl CV2 50 E2
Kent Rd CV47 132 F5
Kents La CV37 131 A4
Kent The CV21 84 A2
Kenway B47 69 A7
Kenwyn Gn CV7 50 B8
Keppel Cl CV22 82 C1
Keppel St CV1 61 E5
Keresley Brook Rd CV6 49 A2
Keresley Cl CV6 49 A2
Keresley Grange Prim Sch CV6 48 F1
Keresley Green Rd CV6 48 F1
Keresley Newland Prim Sch CV7 48 F7
Keresley Rd CV6 61 A8
Kerns Terr 22 CV37 145 A3
Kerria Ctr B77 4 A4
Kerria Rd B77 4 B4
Kerris Way CV3 63 A1
Kerr La B90 70 A6
Kerr Way GL56 140 C3
Kerry Croft Cl B97 102 E5
Kerry's Ho 4 CV1 61 B2
Kerswell Dr B90 71 A5
Kestrel Cl
Birmingham,Castle Vale B35 22 B3
Hinckley LE10 31 F6
Stratford-u-A CV37 145 A5
Kestrel Croft 2 CV3 78 F8
Kestrel B77 10 A6
Keswick Cl CV11 30 A6
Keswick Dr CV21 83 C8
Keswick Gn CV32 105 D1
Keswick Wlk CV2 62 F4
Kettlebrook Rd B90 71 C6
Kettlewell Cl CV34 104 E1
Keviliok St CV3 77 D6
Kew Cl CV8 93 C5
Kew Ho CV4 59 F3
Kew Rd CV21 83 B4
Keyes Dr CV22 82 C2
Keys Hill CV9 11 C1
Keys La CV47 125 F4
Keyte Rd CV36 136 B6
Keytes Acre GL55 135 E3
Keytes La CV35 122 B7
Kiblers La CV35 131 D2
Kielder Dr CV10 28 E2
Kiftsgate Court Gdns* GL55 135 C6
Kilburn Dr CV5 60 F3
Kilby Ct CV31 110 A6
Kilbye Cl B77 9 F5
Kilby Gn LE10 31 F6
Kilby Gr CV31 110 C5
Kildale Cl CV1 151 D3
Kilderkin Ct CV1 151 C1
Kildwick Way 5 CV34 104 E1
Kiln Cl
Nuneaton CV10 28 E3
Royal Leamington Spa CV32 106 A1
Studley B80 103 C4
Kiln La B90 70 A5
Kilnsey Gr CV34 104 E1
Kiln Way B78 4 F1
Kilsby Gr B91 71 C8
Kilsby La CV21 101 C7
Kilsby Rd CV23 101 C1
Kilworth Ho 8 CV32 105 F1
Kilworth Rd CV21 101 B7
Kimberley Cl CV5 59 F4
Kimberley Rd
Baginton CV8 77 F2
Bedworth CV12 39 C4
Rugby CV21 83 B4
Kimberley B77 9 F7
Kimberley Wlk B76 22 D6
Kimble Cl
Coventry CV5 60 B4
Knightcote CV47 124 B1
Kimmond Ct 21 CV32 105 F1
Kinchford Cl B91 71 B8
Kineton CE Prim Sch CV35 132 B6
Kineton High Sch CV35 132 C6
Kineton La B90,B94 71 A1
Kineton Rd
Coventry CV2 62 C6
Kenilworth CV8 93 C4
Southam CV47 147 A3
Wellesbourne CV35 146 E2
Kineton Road Ind Est CV47 147 A3
King Charles Ct CV37 129 E2
Kingcomb La GL55 135 A2
King Edward Rd
Coventry CV1 61 F4
King Edward Rd *continued*
Nuneaton CV11 29 D4
Rugby CV21 83 B4
King Edward's Ct CV35 114 F5
King Edwards Terr CV36 141 F5
King Edward VI Coll CV11 29 D4
King Edward VI Sch CV37 145 A2
Kingfield Ind Est CV1 61 C6
Kingfield Rd CV1,CV6 61 D7
Kingfisher Ave CV10 28 C5
Kingfisher Ct LE10 30 F6
Kingfisher Dr B36 33 A8
Kingfisher Prim Sch B36 33 A8
Kingfisher B77 10 A6
Kingfisher Way B49 143 B5
King George's Ave
Bedworth CV12 39 B5
Coventry CV6 49 F2
King George's Ct CV23 82 A5
King George's Way LE10 31 B7
Kingham Cl B98 112 A6
Kingham Hill Sch OX7 150 D1
King Henry VIII Sch CV3 151 A1
King John's La CV35 132 E2
King John's Rd CV35 132 B6
Kingland Dr CV32 105 C1
Kingley Ave B49 143 C5
King Richard St CV2 61 F3
Kings Ave CV9 18 E8
Kingsbridge Rd CV10 29 D6
Kingsbrook Dr B91 71 B8
Kingsbury Bsns Pk B76 22 E6
Kingsbury Cl B76 22 D5
Kingsbury Inf Sch B78 15 C6
Kingsbury Jun Sch B78 15 D6
Kingsbury Rd
Birmingham B35,B76 22 B5
Coventry CV6 60 E5
Curdworth B76 23 B6
Marston B76 15 B2
Minworth B76 22 D5
Kingsbury Sch B78 15 D6
Kingsbury Water Park Visitor Ctr* B76 15 B5
Kingsbury Water Pk* B76 15 B6
Kingscote Gr CV3 77 A4
Kingscote Rd B93 71 E2
Kings Coughton La B49 143 A6
King's Ct CV11 29 B4
Kingsford Cl B36 22 D1
Kingsford Rd CV6 61 C7
Kingsgate Ho B37 33 A2
Kings Gdns CV12 39 C2
Kings Gr CV2 62 B3
King's High Sch for Girls The CV34 108 E7
King's Hill La CV3 77 B2
Kingsholm Cl CV3 63 B1
Kingshurst Inf Sch B37 33 A6
Kingshurst Jun Sch B37 33 A6
Kingshurst CV31 110 E6
King's La B50 148 B6
Kingsland Ave CV5 60 F2
Kingsland Dr B93 71 E4
King's La
Newton Regis B79 2 D5
Norton WR11 127 B2
Snitterfield CV37 121 B6
Stratford-u-A CV37 144 F8
Kingsleigh Dr B36 22 B1
Kingsley Ave CV21 83 F1
Kingsley Coll B98 103 C6
Kingsley Cres CV12 40 B3
Kingsley Ct
18 Bishops Tachbrook CV33 122 F8
Binley Woods CV3 79 D6
Kingsley Orch CV21 83 E1
Kingsley Prep Sch B93 72 A4
Kingsley Rd 11 CV33 122 F8
Kingsley Sch The CV32 105 F1
Kingsley Terr CV2 62 E8
Kingsley Wlk CV2 62 F7
Kings Mdw CV10 28 A3
Kingsmead Mews CV3 78 D6
Kings Newnham La CV23 80 E7
Kings Newnham Rd CV23 81 B6
Kings Park Dr CV3 63 B1
King St CV12 39 C2
Kingston Ho CV12 49 C8
Kingston Mews CV31 110 C6
Kingston Rd CV5 60 F2
King St
Royal Leamington Spa CV32 106 A1
Rugby CV21 83 A4
Kingsway Com Prim Sch CV31 109 F6
Kingsway CV2 62 A3
Kingsway Ho CV12 39 C2
Kingsway
Kingsbury B78 15 C6
Lighthorne Heath CV33 123 D2
Nuneaton CV11 29 B4
Royal Leamington Spa CV31 109 F6
Rugby CV22 83 A1
Kingswood Ave CV7 48 B8
Kingswood Cl
Coventry CV6 49 D1
Kingswood B94 89 E5
Kingswood Cotts B94 89 D3
Kingswood Gdns CV10 28 B4
Kingswood Rd CV10 28 B4
Kington La CV35 113 E3
Kington Rise CV35 113 E2
King William St CV1 61 E4
Kinman Way CV21 83 C6
Kinross Cl CV10 28 F2
Kinross Rd CV32 106 B4
Kinross Way LE10 21 F1
Kinsall Gn B77 10 C6
Kinsham Dr B91 71 B8
Kintyre The CV2 63 B7
Kinver Cl CV2 50 E1
Kinver Croft B76 22 A8
Kinwalsey La CV7 46 F6
Kinwarton Dovecote* B49 143 F6
Kinwarton Farm Rd B49 143 D5
Kinwarton Rd B49 143 C4
Kinwarton Workshops B49 143 C6
Kipling Ave CV34 108 C4
Kipling Cl CV10 28 A5
Kipling Rd
Coventry CV6 61 A8
Stratford-u-A CV37 130 A8
Kirby Ave CV34 104 F1
Kirby Cl
Brandon CV8 79 F5
Coventry CV1 61 D6
Kirby Cnr CV4 76 B5
Kirby Corner Rd CV4 76 B6
Kirby La CV7 52 F5
Kirby Rd CV5 60 F2
Kirigushi Rd CV35 132 E5
Kirkby Cl CV21 83 E6
Kirkby Rd CV21 83 F1
Kirkdale Ave CV6 49 D3
Kirkland Way B78 8 B8
Kirkstone Rd CV12 39 A2
Kirkstone CV21 83 D7
Kirkstone Wlk CV11 30 A6
Kirkwall CV47 147 B4
Kirtland Cl CV9 3 B1
Kirton Cl
Coventry CV6 48 F1
Whitnash CV31 110 B3
Kissing Tree La CV37 121 D3
Kitchener Rd
Coventry CV6 61 E8
Long Marston CV37 129 C2
Kitebrook Cl B90 71 A7
Kites Cl CV34 104 E2
Kites Nest La CV35 114 E8
Kittermaster Rd CV7 46 C1
Kitwood Ave B78 10 F6
Kixley La B93 72 C6
Klevedon Cl CV11 30 A1
Knebley Cres CV10 29 C1
Knibbs The CV34 108 E7
Knight Ave CV1 61 E1
Knightcote Dr
Royal Leamington Spa CV32 109 E8
Solihull B91 71 B8
Knight Ct B75 13 C5
Knightley Cl CV32 106 E5
Knightlow Ave CV3 78 C6
Knightlow CE Prim Sch CV23 96 F7
Knightlow Cl CV8 93 C3
Knightlow Way CV33 123 F6
Knightsbridge Ave CV12 39 C4
Knights Cl LE10 31 D4
Knights Ct
1 Stratford-u-A CV37 144 F2
Birmingham B37 44 E8
Hinckley LE10 30 E8
Warwick CV34 108 D6
Knights La CV37 145 E3
Knights Templar Way CV4 60 A1
Knob Hill CV23 96 F6
Knoll Croft
Cheswick Green B90 70 D4
Coventry CV3 77 C6
Knoll Dr
Coventry CV3 77 C6
Warwick CV34 104 E1
Knottesford Cl B80 103 C3
Knotting Way CV3 62 C1
Knowlands Rd B90 71 A7
Knowle CE Prim Sch B93 72 C6
Knowle Hill
Hurley CV9 16 C4
Kenilworth CV8 93 C6
Knowle Rd B92 56 E2
Knowles Ave CV10 28 C4
Knowle Wood Rd B93 72 B3
Knox Cres CV11 29 F8
Kranji Rd CV47 132 F5
Kurtus B77 9 D6
Kwikform Bldg CV6 49 E4
Kyetts Cnr OX17 134 C1
Kynner Way CV3 79 B8
Kyter La B36 22 B1

L

Laburnum Ave
Coventry CV6 60 F5
Kenilworth CV8 93 A4
Laburnum Cl
Bedworth CV12 38 E2
Hollywood B47 69 A5
Kingsbury B78 15 D6
Laburnum Dr
Sutton Coldfield B76 13 A3
Whitnash CV31 110 B3

Laburnum Gr
Nuneaton CV10 . . . . .28 D6
Rugby CV22 . . . . .99 E8
Warwick CV34 . . . . .105 B1
Lacell Cl CV34 . . . . .104 E1
Ladbroke By-Pass CV47 .124 D5
Ladbroke Hall CV47 . . . . .124 D5
Ladbroke Pk CV34 . . . . . . .104 E1
Ladbroke Rd CV47 . . . . . . .124 B4
Ladbroke Cl B98 . . . . .102 E7
Ladbrook Rd CV5 . . . . .60 A4
Lady Byron La
Knowle B93 . . . . .56 A1
Knowle B93 . . . . .71 F8
Ladycroft CV32 . . . . .106 E5
Ladyfields Way CV6 . . . . . . .49 A4
Lady Grey Ave CV34 . . . . .109 E3
Ladygrove Cl B98 . . . . .103 A8
Lady Katherine Leveson CE
Sch B93 . . . . .73 B5
Lady La
Coventry CV6 . . . . .49 F4
Earlswood B90,B94 . . . . .70 B3
Kenilworth CV8 . . . . .92 F4
Lady Lane Mobile Home Pk
CV6 .49 F4
Ladymead Dr CV6 . . . . .49 B2
Ladysmock CV23 . . . . .83 D8
Lady Warwick Ave CV12. .39 D2
Laertes Gr CV34 . . . . .109 F2
Laggan Cl CV10 . . . . .28 C5
Lairhillock Pk CV23 . . . . . .115 D7
Lair The B78 . . . . .9 A4
Lakeland Dr B77 . . . . .10 B7
Lakeland Ho CV34 . . . . . . .109 A4
Lakeside CV12 . . . . .39 A2
Lakeside Dr B90 . . . . .70 F7
Lakeside B95 . . . . .113 B2
Lakes The B94 . . . . .86 F8
Lake View Rd CV5 . . . . .60 F4
Lakin Cl CV34 . . . . .108 F8
Lakin Dr CV47 . . . . .124 A4
Lakin Rd CV34 . . . . .108 F8
Lambert Ct
Barford CV35 . . . . .122 A7
Bidford-on-A B50 . . . . .148 C5
Warwick CV34 . . . . .108 D6
Lambeth Cl
Birmingham B37 . . . . .33 B4
Coventry CV2 . . . . .62 E7
Lambourn Cres CV31. . . . .110 C6
Lambourne Cl
Bidford-on-A B50 . . . . .148 D5
Coventry CV6 . . . . .60 A4
Lamb St CV1 . . . . .151 B3
Lamerton Cl CV2 . . . . .62 C6
Lamintone Dr CV32 . . . . . .105 D2
Lammas Croft CV31 . . . . . .110 A3
Lammas Ct
Warwick CV34 . . . . .108 D6
Wolston CV8 . . . . .80 A3
Lammas Rd CV6 . . . . .61 A4
Lammas Rd CV34 . . . . .60 F4
Lammas Wlk CV34 . . . . . . .108 D7
Lamorna Cl CV11 . . . . .29 F4
Lampitts Gn OX15 . . . . . . .139 D4
Lamp La CV7 . . . . .36 F6
Lamprey B77 . . . . .9 D6
Lancaster Cl
Atherstone CV9 . . . . .12 E1
Wellesbourne CV35 . . . . . . .146 C2
Lancaster Dr B35 . . . . .22 B2
Lancaster Pl CV4 . . . . .92 E2
Lancaster Rd
Hinckley LE10 . . . . .31 D8
Rugby CV21 . . . . .83 A4
Lance Cl LE10 . . . . .31 D5
Lanchester Dr 9 OX16. . .139 F4
Lanchester Rd CV6 . . . . . . .61 B6
Lanchester Way
Birmingham B36 . . . . .22 F1
Daventry NN11 . . . . .117 F2
Lancia Cl CV6 . . . . .50 B4
Lancing Rd CV12 . . . . .40 C2
Lancut Hill CV23 . . . . .67 D1
Land La B37 . . . . .44 A7
Landor Ho CV31 . . . . .110 A2
Landor Rd
Dorridge B93 . . . . .72 A6
Redditch B98 . . . . .103 A8
Warwick CV34 . . . . .108 D8
Whitnash CV31 . . . . .110 A3
Landrail Wlk B36 . . . . .33 A8
Landseer Cl CV21 . . . . .84 B1
Lane Cl OX15 . . . . .139 D6
Lane Croft B76 . . . . .22 A8
Laneside CV3 . . . . .78 E6
Lane The
Burmington CV36 . . . . .149 E6
Little Wolford CV36 . . . . . . .141 A6
Lanfear Ct LE10 . . . . .31 C7
Langbank Ave CV3 . . . . .78 D7
Langbay Ct CV2 . . . . .62 F6
Langcliffe Ave CV34 . . . . . .104 F1
Langcomb Rd B90 . . . . .70 A8
Langdale Ave CV6 . . . . .49 D3
Langdale Cl
Royal Leamington Spa
CV32 . . . . .106 D3
Rugby CV21 . . . . .83 C7
Langdale Ct B77 . . . . .4 A6
Langdale Dr CV11 . . . . .30 A6
Langdale Rd LE10. . . . . .31 A8
Langdon La CV35 . . . . .132 E3

Langfield Rd B93 . . . . .72 A7
Langlands The CV35 . . . . . .121 F4
Langley Croft CV4 . . . . .60 A2
Langley Dr B35 . . . . .22 A1
Langley Hall Dr B75 . . . . . . .13 B5
Langley Hall Rd B75 . . . . . . .13 B5
Langley Heath Dr B76. . . . .13 A3
Langley Rd
Claverdon CV35 . . . . .113 E3
Whitnash CV31 . . . . .110 A3
Langley Specl Sch B75. . . .13 A6
Langley Wlk B37 . . . . .33 D2
Langlodge Rd CV6 . . . . .49 B2
Langnor Rd CV2 . . . . .62 C6
Langton Cl
Birmingham B36 . . . . .33 B6
Coventry CV3 . . . . .78 E8
Langton Rd CV21,CV22 . . . .83 C1
Langwood Cl CV4 . . . . .76 B7
Lankett The CV47 . . . . .133 D7
Lansbury Cl CV2 . . . . .62 E7
Lansdowne Cir CV32 . . . . .106 A1
Lansdowne Cl CV12 . . . . . . .39 A3
Lansdowne Cres
6 Royal Leamington Spa
CV32 . . . . .106 A1
Studley B80 . . . . .103 D3
Tamworth B77 . . . . .9 D8
Lansdowne Pl CV21 . . . . . . .83 D2
Lansdowne Rd
2 Royal Leamington Spa
CV32 . . . . .106 A1
Studley B80 . . . . .103 D3
Lansdowne St
Coventry CV2 . . . . .61 F3
Royal Leamington Spa
CV32 . . . . .106 A1
Lansdown Ho B46 . . . . .24 F4
Lant Cl CV7 . . . . .75 B7
Lapwing Dr B92 . . . . .57 B7
Lapwing B77 . . . . .10 A4
Lapworth CE Prim Sch
B94 . . . . .89 D3
Lapworth Cl B98 . . . . .102 F7
Lapworth Oaks B94 . . . . . . .89 D3
Lapworth Rd CV2 . . . . .50 C1
Lapworth Sta B94 . . . . .89 D4
Lapworth St B94 . . . . .89 B2
Larch Cl
Alcester B49 . . . . .143 B5
Rugby CV22 . . . . .82 B2
Stratford-u-A CV37 . . . . . . .145 A4
Larch Croft B37 . . . . .33 B2
Larches The
Bedworth CV7 . . . . .50 B8
Kingsbury B78 . . . . .15 C7
Larchfields CV8 . . . . .80 A4
Larch Gr CV34 . . . . .105 A1
Larch Tree Ave CV4 . . . . . . .60 A2
Larchwood Rd CV7 . . . . .39 B1
Larchwood Way CV5 . . . . . . .60 A6
Larkin Cl CV12 . . . . .40 A3
Larkin Gr CV2 . . . . .62 F6
Larkspur Cl CV12 . . . . .49 C8
Larkspur Gr 5 CV12 . . . . . .38 D2
Larkspur
Rugby CV23 . . . . .83 B8
Tamworth B77 . . . . .9 F4
Latham Rd CV5 . . . . .61 A2
Latimer Cl CV8 . . . . .92 F2
Lattimore Rd CV37. . . . . . .144 E5
Latymer Cl B76 . . . . .22 A7
Lauderdale Ave CV6 . . . . . . .49 D3
Lauderdale Cl CV23 . . . . . . .82 B4
Launce Gr CV34 . . . . .109 F2
Launceston Dr CV11 . . . . . . .29 F4
Laundry Cotts CV35 . . . . . . .90 E4
Laurel Ave B78 . . . . .11 A8
Laurel Cl CV2 . . . . .50 C2
Laurel Ct CV5 . . . . .60 F1
Laurel Dr
Hartshill CV10 . . . . .28 A7
Rugby CV22 . . . . .82 B1
Stockton CV47 . . . . .147 E8
Laurel Fields LE17 . . . . .43 E6
Laurel Gdns CV22 . . . . .99 F8
Laurels Cres CV7 . . . . .74 C6
Laurels The
Bedworth CV12 . . . . .38 E2
Coventry CV4 . . . . .76 F6
Kingsbury B78 . . . . .15 C7
Portway B47 . . . . .85 F8
Lavender Ave CV6 . . . . .60 F5
Lavender Cl
Bedworth CV12 . . . . .38 E1
Rugby CV23 . . . . .83 E8
Lavender Hall La CV7 . . . . . .58 C2
Lavenham Cl CV11 . . . . .40 C8
Lawford Cl CV3 . . . . .62 E1
Lawford Heath Ind Est
CV23 .98 C2
Lawford Heath La CV23 . . .98 C6
Lawford La CV22 . . . . .82 B1
Lawford Rd
Rugby CV21,CV22 . . . . .82 E3
Whitnash CV31 . . . . .110 B5
Lawley Cl CV4 . . . . .59 E1
Lawns Bsns Ctr The LE10. .31 E8
Lawnsdale Cl B46 . . . . .33 F7
Lawns The
Bedworth CV12 . . . . .38 C2
Hinckley LE10 . . . . .31 E8
Wootton Wawen B95 . . . . . .113 B2
Lawnswood
Hinckley LE10 . . . . .31 A8
Sutton Coldfield B76 . . . . . . .22 A8
Lawrence Dr B76 . . . . .22 D6

Lawrence Gdns CV8. . . . . . .93 A6
Lawrence Mackie Gdns
CV35 . . . . .146 E4
Lawrence Mackie Ho
CV35 . . . . .146 E4
Lawrence Rd
Bedworth CV7 . . . . .50 A8
Rugby CV21 . . . . .83 D3
Lawrence Saunders Rd
CV6 . . . . .61 B5
Lawrence Sheriff Sch
CV21 .82 C2
Lawrence Sheriff St CV22 .83 A2
Lawson Ave CV37 . . . . .145 E4
Lawton Cl LE10 . . . . .30 F8
Laxford Cl LE10 . . . . .21 F1
Laxton Way 14 OX16 . . . . .139 F5
Lay Gdns CV31 . . . . .110 E5
Lea Cl
Alcester B49 . . . . .143 C5
Stratford-u-A CV37 . . . . . . .144 B4
Lea Cres CV21 . . . . .82 D6
Leacrest Rd CV6 . . . . .49 A2
Lea Croft Rd B97 . . . . .102 D5
Lea Ct 11 CV37 . . . . .144 F1
Leacroft Cl CV7 . . . . .77 D4
Leafield Cl CV2 . . . . .63 A5
Leaf La CV3 . . . . .77 E5
Leagh Cl CV8 . . . . .93 B7
Lea Green Dr B47 . . . . .69 C4
Lea Green La B47 . . . . .69 C5
Lealholme Cl CV5 . . . . .76 F8
Leam Cl CV11 . . . . .29 F1
Leam Gn CV4 . . . . .76 D5
Leamington Hastings CE Inf
Sch CV23 . . . . .115 D5
Leamington Hastings Rd
CV23 . . . . .115 F7
Leamington Rd
Coventry CV3 . . . . .77 C6
Kenilworth CV8 . . . . .93 B2
Long Itchington CV47 . . . . .115 C4
Princethorpe CV23 . . . . .96 D2
Ryton-on-D CV8 . . . . .96 B6
Southam CV47 . . . . .124 C8
Leamington Spa Art Gallery
& Mus* CV32 . . . . .109 F8
Leamington Spa Sta
CV31 . . . . .109 F7
Leamington Way NN11. . . .117 F1
Leam Rd
Lighthorne Heath CV33 . . .123 D2
Royal Leamington Spa
CV31 . . . . .109 D7
Leam Side Ho 9 CV34 . . . .109 D8
Leam St CV31 . . . . .110 B7
Leam Terr CV31 . . . . .110 B8
Leam The NN11 . . . . .117 F1
Lear Gr CV34 . . . . .109 E4
Leas Cl CV12 . . . . .39 A3
Leasowe's Ave CV3 . . . . . . .76 F4
Leasows The
Chipping Campden GL55 . . .135 A1
Mickleton GL55 . . . . .135 C6
Leathermill La CV10 . . . . . . .19 D4
Leather St CV47 . . . . .115 D4
Leaward Cl CV10 . . . . .28 E2
Lea Wlk CV8 . . . . .79 B1
Ledbrook Rd CV32 . . . . . . .106 E5
Ledbury Rd CV31 . . . . .110 C5
Ledbury Way B76 . . . . .22 A8
Ledwell B90 . . . . .70 A5
Lee Cl CV34 . . . . .104 E2
Leeder Cl CV6 . . . . .49 C2
Lee Meadow CV34 . . . . . . .108 B4
Leeming Cl CV4 . . . . .76 C6
Lee Rd
Hollywood B47 . . . . .69 A7
Royal Leamington Spa
CV31 . . . . .109 E6
Lees The CV33 . . . . .122 E8
Lee The CV5 . . . . .60 C4
Le Hanche Cl CV7 . . . . .49 A7
Leicester Cres CV9 . . . . .12 E1
Leicester Cswy CV1 . . . . . . .61 D5
Leicester Ct CV12 . . . . .40 C2
Leicester La
Cubbington CV32 . . . . .94 E1
Royal Leamington Spa
CV32 . . . . .106 C6
Leicester Rd
Bedworth CV12 . . . . .39 B4
Nuneaton CV11 . . . . .29 D5
Rugby CV21 . . . . .83 B6
Shilton CV7 . . . . .51 F6
Wolvey LE10 . . . . .41 E5
Leicester Row
Coventry CV1 . . . . .151 B4
Long Itchington CV47 . . . . .115 D4
Leicester St
Bedworth CV12 . . . . .39 B3
Bulkington CV12 . . . . .40 D1
Royal Leamington Spa
CV32 . . . . .106 A1
Leigh Ave CV3 . . . . .77 C3
Leigh CE Prim Sch CV4 . . .75 D8
Leigh Cres CV47 . . . . .115 D3
Leigh Rd
Rugby CV21 . . . . .82 F8
Sutton Coldfield B75 . . . . . . .13 B5
Leigh St 4 CV1 . . . . .61 E4
Leigh Terr CV33 . . . . .107 F5
Leighton Cl
Coventry CV4 . . . . .76 D2
Royal Leamington Spa
CV32 . . . . .106 C4
Leisure Wlk 7 B77 . . . . .9 F6
Lennon Cl CV21 . . . . .101 C7

Lennox Cl CV3 . . . . .78 E6
Lenton's La CV2 . . . . .50 E4
Leofric St CV6 . . . . .61 A5
Leonard Parkins Ho CV12 .40 D2
Leontes Mdws CV34 . . . . .109 E3
Leopold Rd CV1 . . . . .61 F4
Lesingham Dr CV4 . . . . .59 E1
Lesley Souter Ho CV21. . . .83 B2
Lestock Cl CV22 . . . . .82 C2
Letchlade Cl CV2 . . . . .62 C8
Level The OX15 . . . . .138 F5
Leven Cl LE10 . . . . .31 B8
Leven Croft B76 . . . . .22 A7
Leven Way CV2 . . . . .63 A8
Lever Rd CV21 . . . . .84 A1
Leveson Cres CV7 . . . . .74 B6
Levett Rd B77 . . . . .4 B5
Lewis Cl CV21 . . . . .82 F3
Lewis Ct CV9 . . . . .18 F6
Lewis Rd
Coventry CV1 . . . . .61 D5
Radford Semele CV31 . . . . .110 F5
Lexington Ct CV11 . . . . .29 B5
Leyburn Cl
3 Warwick CV34 . . . . .104 F1
Coventry CV6 . . . . .49 E2
Nuneaton CV11 . . . . .30 A2
Leycester Cl CV33 . . . . .123 E7
Leycester Pl 13 CV34 . . . .108 E6
Leycester Pl 12 CV34 . . . .108 E6
Leycester Rd CV8 . . . . .93 A2
Leyes La CV8 . . . . .93 C5
Leyfields Cres CV34 . . . . . .108 D4
Leyland Rd
Bulkington CV12 . . . . .40 B2
Coventry CV5 . . . . .60 D4
Nuneaton CV11 . . . . .29 E1
Leylands Way CV31 . . . . . . .108 B4
Leymere Cl CV7 . . . . .46 C1
Leysbourne GL55 . . . . .135 B2
Leys Cl
Northend CV47 . . . . .133 B7
Wroxton OX15 . . . . .139 D4
Leysfield WR11 . . . . .127 C4
Leyside CV3 . . . . .78 E5
Leys La CV7 . . . . .46 C1
Leysmill Cl LE10 . . . . .21 F1
Leys The
Bidford-on-A B50 . . . . .148 E5
Halford CV36 . . . . .137 A8
Hinckley LE10 . . . . .32 A6
Newton CV23 . . . . .68 A1
Upper Boddington NN11 . . .134 E8
Whatcote CV36 . . . . .137 E7
Ley's The OX15 . . . . .139 D4
Libbards Gate 8 B91 . . . . . .71 C8
Libbards Way B91 . . . . .71 A8
Liberty Rd B77 . . . . .9 F5
Liberty Way CV11 . . . . .29 F3
Library Cl LE10 . . . . .32 A5
Library Rd CV4 . . . . .76 B5
Lichen Gn CV4 . . . . .76 D5
Lichfield Cl
New Arley CV7. . . . . .37 A8
Nuneaton CV11 . . . . .30 A7
Lichfield Cotts B78 . . . . . . .15 D5
Lichfield Rd
Coventry CV3 . . . . .77 D8
Water Orton B46,B76 . . . . . .23 D4
Wishaw B76,B78 . . . . .14 B3
Lichfield St B78 . . . . .9 A8
Lifford Way CV3 . . . . .79 A7
Light Hall Sch B90. . . . . . . .70 B8
Lighthorne Heath Prim Sch
CV33 . . . . .123 C2
Lighthorne Rd CV35. . . . . .132 B6
Light La CV1 . . . . .151 B4
Lightoak Cl B97 . . . . .102 C6
Lightwood Cl B93. . . . . .72 B8
Lilac Ave CV6 . . . . .60 F5
Lilac Cl LE10 . . . . .31 E6
Lilac Dr CV22 . . . . .82 B2
Lilac Gr CV34 . . . . .105 A1
Lilac Rd CV12 . . . . .39 D5
Lilacvale Way CV4 . . . . .76 D5
Lilbourne Rd CV23 . . . . .84 C5
Lilleburne Dr CV10 . . . . .28 B7
Lilley Cl CV6 . . . . .49 C2
Lilley Green Rd B48. . . . . . .85 D5
Lillington Ave CV32 . . . . . .105 F2
Lillington Cl
Royal Leamington Spa
CV32 . . . . .106 A3
Sutton Coldfield B75 . . . . . . .13 A4
Lillington Prim Sch
CV32 . . . . .106 B3
Lillington Rd
Coventry CV2 . . . . .50 D1
Royal Leamington Spa
CV32 . . . . .106 A3
Solihull B90 . . . . .70 B8
Limbrick Ave CV4 . . . . .60 A1
Limbrick Wood Prim Sch
CV4 . . . . .59 F3
Lime Ave CV32 . . . . .106 A4
Lime Cl B47 . . . . .69 A5
Lime Gr
Birmingham,Chemsley Wood
B37 .33 B1
Coventry CV4 . . . . .60 B1
Hurley CV9 . . . . .16 B4
Kenilworth CV8 . . . . .93 A4
Nuneaton CV10 . . . . .28 E5
Limekiln La B94 . . . . .70 D1
Lime Kilns B78 . . . . .11 A8

Lime Rd CV47 . . . . .147 B5
Limes Ave CV37 . . . . .144 D1
Limes Coppice CV10 . . . . . . .27 E7
Limes The
Bedworth CV12 . . . . .38 E2
Coventry CV6 . . . . .60 E5
Tiddington CV37 . . . . .145 E4
Limestone Hall La CV23 . . .81 A4
Lime Tree Ave
Coventry CV4 . . . . .60 A2
Rugby CV22 . . . . .99 B7
Lime Tree Dr CV35 . . . . . . .122 E2
Linaker Rd CV3 . . . . .78 C5
Lincoln Ave CV10 . . . . .28 B7
Lincoln Cl
Warwick CV34 . . . . .104 E1
Wellesbourne CV35 . . . . . . .146 C1
Lincoln Ct CV32 . . . . .110 A8
Lincoln Gr B37 . . . . .33 A1
Lincoln St CV1 . . . . .151 C4
Lincroft Cres CV5 . . . . .60 E4
Lindale CV21 . . . . .83 D8
Linden Ave CV35 . . . . .146 E3
Linden Cl CV34 . . . . .104 E2
Linden Lea CV12 . . . . .39 B3
Lindera B77 . . . . .4 A4
Lindfield The CV3 . . . . .78 C8
Lindhurst Dr B94 . . . . .88 C6
Lindisfarne Dr CV8 . . . . .93 C4
Lindley Rd
Bedworth CV12 . . . . .38 D2
Coventry CV3 . . . . .62 B2
Lindop Cl CV32 . . . . .106 D5
Lindridge Cl B98 . . . . .112 A6
Lindridge Dr B76 . . . . .22 D6
Lindridge Rd B75,B76 . . . . .13 B6
Lindsay Wlk CV47 . . . . .132 F7
Lindsey Cres CV8 . . . . .93 A1
Lineholt Cl B98 . . . . .103 A6
Linen St CV34 . . . . .108 D6
Linford Wlk CV2 . . . . .50 F1
Lingard Rd B75 . . . . .13 A5
Lingfield Cres CV37 . . . . . .129 F8
Lingfield Ct CV6 . . . . .50 B4
Lingwood Dr CV10 . . . . .28 F3
Links Rd CV6 . . . . .61 A8
Linkway CV31 . . . . .109 E6
Linley Rd CV47 . . . . .147 B5
Linnell Rd CV21 . . . . .83 F2
Linnet Cl
Coventry CV3 . . . . .78 D5
Rugby CV23 . . . . .67 C1
Linstock Way CV6 . . . . .50 B4
Linthouse Wlk 3 B77 . . . . . .9 F6
Lintly B77 . . . . .4 B1
Linwood Dr CV2 . . . . .50 F1
Lion Fields Ave CV5 . . . . . . .60 B6
Liskeard Cl CV11 . . . . .30 A5
Liskeard Rd CV35 . . . . .132 D3
Lisle Cl 4 CV31 . . . . .110 A6
Lisle Gdns 7 CV33 . . . . . . .122 F8
Lismore Croft CV2 . . . . .63 A7
Lister Rd CV9 . . . . .12 E1
Lister St CV11 . . . . .29 D3
Little Acre B97 . . . . .102 D6
Little Back La NN11 . . . . . .126 B5
Little Brum CV7 . . . . .11 C2
Little Church St
1 Coventry CV1. . . . . .151 C4
Rugby CV21 . . . . .83 A3
Little Cryfield CV4 . . . . .76 C2
Little Duke St CV11 . . . . . . .29 B4
Little Elborow St CV21 . . . .83 A3
Little Farm CV3 . . . . .78 D5
Little Field CV2 . . . . .62 A5
Little Forge Rd B98 . . . . . .103 C8
Little Gr CV22 . . . . .83 C1
Little Heath Ind Est CV6. . .50 A2
Little Heath Prim Sch CV6 .49 F1
Little La OX15 . . . . .139 D6
Little Lawford La
Little Lawford CV23 . . . . .81 F7
Rugby CV23 . . . . .82 B7
Little London La CV23 . . . . .68 A1
Little Mdw CV37 . . . . .128 E1
Littlemead Rd B90 . . . . .69 F8
Little Park St CV1 . . . . .151 C2
Little Pennington St CV21 .82 E3
Little Pittern CV35 . . . . . . .132 B6
Littleshaw Croft B47 . . . . . .69 C4
Littleshaw La B47 . . . . .69 C4
Little South St CV11 . . . . . . .61 E3
Littlethorpe CV3 . . . . .78 D6
Littleton Cl
Kenilworth CV8 . . . . .93 A7
Sutton Coldfield B76 . . . . . . .13 A2
Littleton Croft 6 B91 . . . . .71 C8
Littletons CE Fst Sch The
WR11 . . . . .127 F1
Little Warton Rd B79 . . . . . . .5 F3
Littlewood Cl 2 B91 . . . . . .71 B8
Littlewood Gn B80. . . . . . . .103 D3
Little Woods B97 . . . . .102 E6
Littleworth GL55 . . . . .135 A2
Littleworth Croft CV11 . . . .110 C5
Littleworth B95 . . . . .113 A3
Litton B77 . . . . .4 C1
Liveridge Cl B93 . . . . .71 F6
Liveridge Hill B95 . . . . .113 B7
Livery St CV32 . . . . .109 F8
Livia Cl LE10 . . . . .31 C8
Livingstone Ave CV23 . . . . .81 F4
Livingstone Rd CV6 . . . . . . .61 F7
Liza Ct CV21 . . . . .83 C8
Llewellyn Rd CV31 . . . . . . .110 A6
Lloyd Cl
Hampton Magna CV35. . . . .114 F3

lloyd Cl *continued*
Norton WR11 . . . . 127 C2
Nuneaton CV11 . . . . 29 D2
lloyd Cres CV2 . . . . 62 E3
lloyd Rd CV21 . . . . 83 C6
lloyds Way CV37 . . . . . . 144 D5
loach Dr CV2 . . . . 62 E7
lobelia Cl CV10 . . . . 31 E5
lochmore Cl LE10 . . . . . 31 A8
lochmore Dr LE10 . . . . . 31 A8
lochmore Way LE10 . . . 31 A8
lochsong Cl B77 . . . . 9 C4
lock St CV3 . . . . 62 C1
lock Cl CV37 . . . . 145 A3
lock La CV34 . . . . 49 A1
lockhart Cl CV8 . . . . 93 A4
lockheed Cl 3 CV31 . . . 109 F5
lockhurst La CV6 . . . . . . 61 D7
locking Croft B35 . . . . . . 22 B3
lock La CV34 . . . . 108 D8
locks The
　Royal Leamington Spa
　CV31 . . . . 109 D7
　Rugby CV21 . . . . 84 B1
loder Cl CV4 . . . . 59 F3
lodge Cl
　Atherstone CV9 . . . . . . 19 A6
　Hinckley LE10 . . . . 32 A5
lodge Cres CV34 . . . . . 108 D4
lodge Croft B93 . . . . 72 B6
lodge Ct CV37 . . . . 144 E3
lodge Farm OX15 . . . . . 142 F6
lodge Green La CV7 . . . 46 F2
lodge Green La N CV7 . . 46 E3
lodge Rd
　Coventry CV3 . . . . 62 B1
　Knowle B93 . . . . 72 B6
　Rugby CV21 . . . . 83 B4
　Stratford-u-A CV37 . . . 144 E3
logan Rd CV2 . . . . 62 E7
lole Cl CV6 . . . . 50 A4
lollard Croft CV3 . . . . . . 77 D8
lomita Cres B77 . . . . 9 D8
lomond Cl LE10 . . . . 31 B8
lomond Way CV10 . . . . . 28 C5
lomsey Cl CV4 . . . . 60 A1
london End NN11 . . . . . 134 E8
london Rd
　Coventry,Cheylesmore
　CV3 . . . . 77 E8
　Coventry,Willenhall CV3 78 B5
　Hinckley LE10 . . . . 31 E8
　Middleton B75,B78 . . . 13 D7
　Moreton-in-M GL56 . . 140 B3
　Ryton-on-D CV8 . . . . . 79 B1
　Shipston-on-S CV36 . . 149 D4
　Stretton-on-D CV23 . . 97 C6
　Sutton Coldfield B75 . . 7 A4
　Thurlaston CV23 . . . . . 98 C5
　Willoughby CV23 . . . . 117 C6
london Road Terr GL56 140 C6
long Barrow NN11 . . . . 134 F4
longborough Cl B97 . . . 102 B6
long Brook La CV7,CV8 . . 73 C5
long Cast Park Homes
　CV37 . . . . 129 A6
long Close Ave CV5 . . . 60 B6
long Close Wlk B35 . . . 22 A3
long Cl The CV36 . . . . . 141 D7
longcroft Cl B35 . . . . . . 22 A3
longdon Cl B98 . . . . . . 103 B7
longdon Croft B93 . . . . 72 A8
longdown La CV3 . . . . . 117 D7
longfellow Ave CV34 . . 108 C4
longfellow Cl B97 . . . . 102 C7
longfellow
　3 Stratford-u-A CV37 . 130 D8
　Coventry CV2 . . . . 62 C3
longfield Ho CV6 . . . . . . 62 A8
longfield Rd CV31 . . . . 110 B6
longford Cl
　Bidford-on-A B50 . . . . 148 E5
　Dorridge B93 . . . . 72 B3
longford Park Prim Sch
　CV6 . . . . 50 A3
longford Rd
　Bedworth CV7 . . . . 50 A6
　Coventry CV7 . . . . 50 A4
longford Sq CV6 . . . . . . 50 A4
long Furlong CV22 . . . . . 99 F7
long Hassocks CV23 . . . 82 C1
longhope Cl B98 . . . . . 112 A6
long Hyde Rd WR11 . . 127 F1
long Itchington CE Prim Sch
　CV47 . . . . 115 C3
long Lawford Prim Sch
　CV23 . . . . 82 B5
longleat Gr B90 . . . . 70 E5
longleat Gr CV31 . . . . . 110 C6
longley Ave B76 . . . . . . 22 C5
long Leys Croft B46 . . . 23 B2
long Leys Rd B46 . . . . . 23 B2
longley Wlk B37 . . . . . . 33 C2
long Marston Rd
　Mickleton CV37,GL55 . 135 B8
　Pebworth CV37 . . . . . 128 F2
　Welford-on-A CV37 . . 129 C4
long Meadow Dr LE10 . . 30 F7
longrood Pl CV22 . . . . . 99 D7
longrood Rd CV22 . . . . . 99 D7
long Shoot The CV11 . . . 30 C6
Long St
　Atherstone CV9 . . . . . . 18 D8
　Bulkington CV12 . . . . . 40 D2
　Dordon B78 . . . . 11 A5

Longstock Rd CV23 . . . . 67 D1
Longstone Cl B90 . . . . . 71 B6
Longville Ct CV3 . . . . . . 78 A6
Longwood Cl CV4 . . . . . 75 F6
Lonscale Dr CV3 . . . . . . 77 B5
Lonsdale Cl CV11 . . . . . 142 A2
Lonsdale Rd CV32 . . . . 106 B4
Lord Leycester Hospl & Knot
　Gdn* CV34 . . . . 108 E6
Lord Lytton Ave CV2 . . . 62 D7
Lords La B80 . . . . 103 E2
Lord St CV5 . . . . 60 F2
Lorenzo Cl CV3 . . . . 78 D6
Lossiemouth Rd LE10 . . 21 F1
Lothersdale B77 . . . . . . 10 C8
Loudon Ave CV6 . . . . . . 61 A5
Loudon Gate CV11 . . . . 29 F1
Loughshaw B77 . . . . 4 C1
Louisa Ward Cl CV3 . . . 115 C7
Loveday Cl CV9 . . . . 12 D2
Loveday Dr CV32 . . . . . 105 E2
Lovelace Ave B91 . . . . . 71 D8
Love La LE10 . . . . 32 A6
Lovell Cl CV7 . . . . 50 A8
Lovell Rd CV12 . . . . 39 A3
Love Lyne B97 . . . . 102 B5
Loverock Cres CV21 . . . 83 E2
Lovetts Cl CV21 . . . . 83 E2
Lowbrook La B90 . . . . . 69 D4
Lowdham B77 . . . . 4 F1
Lower Ave CV31 . . . . . 109 F7
Lower Cape CV34 . . . . 108 D8
Lower Cladswell La B49 118 C5
Lowe Rd CV6 . . . . 49 A2
Lower Eastern Green La
　CV5 . . . . 59 F4
Lower End CV8 . . . . 95 C6
Lower End Cotts CV47 . 133 C4
Lower End OX15 . . . . . 139 A3
Lower Farm CV8 . . . . . 114 E6
Lower Farm La CV47 . . 133 F2
Lower Ford St CV1 . . . . 151 D3
Lower Grinsty La B97 . . 102 A8
Lower High St GL55 . . . 135 A2
Lower Hillmorton Rd
　CV21 . . . . 83 D2
Lower Holyhead Rd CV1 151 A3
Lower House La
　Baddesley Ensor CV9. . . 11 A3
　Wood End CV9 . . . . . . 10 F2
Lower Ladyes Hills CV8 . . 93 A6
Lower Leam St CV31 . . 110 B7
Lower Prec CV1 . . . . . . 151 B3
Lower St CV7 . . . . 51 C6
Lower St
　Rugby CV21 . . . . 101 B8
　Willoughby CV23 . . . . 117 B6
Lower Villiers St 1
　CV32 . . . . 106 A1
Lowes Ave CV34 . . . . . 104 E1
Lowes La CV35 . . . . . . 146 D2
Loweswater Rd CV11 . . . 30 A6
Lowfield Rd CV3 . . . . . . 62 C1
Lowforce B77 . . . . 4 C1
Low Rd WR11 . . . . 127 A6
Lowry Cl CV12 . . . . 39 A4
Lowther St CV1 . . . . . . 151 C4
Loxley CE Com Prim Sch
　CV35 . . . . 130 F7
Loxley Cl
　Coventry CV2. . . . . 50 D2
　Wellesbourne CV35 . . 146 C2
Loxley Ct CV2 . . . . 50 D2
Loxley Fields CV35 . . . 130 F7
Loxley Rd
　Alveston CV37 . . . . . . 121 D1
　Wellesbourne CV35 . . 146 C2
Loxley Way CV32 . . . . . 106 A2
Lucas Ct
　Royal Leamington Spa
　CV32 . . . . 109 D8
　Rugby CV21 . . . . 83 B4
Lucas Ho CV32 . . . . . . 105 F2
Lucas Rd LE10 . . . . 31 D6
Luce Cl B35 . . . . 22 B4
Lucerne Cl CV2 . . . . 50 C3
Lucian Cl CV2 . . . . 63 B7
Lucy's Mill CV37 . . . . . 145 A1
Luddington Rd CV37 . . 129 E8
Ludford Cl
　Ansley CV10. . . . . 27 B4
　Stratford-u-A CV37 . . 144 C4
Ludford Rd CV10 . . . . . . 28 C6
Ludgate Cl B46 . . . . 23 B3
Ludlow Cl B37 . . . . 33 C2
Ludlow Dr OX16 . . . . . 139 F4
Ludlow Rd CV5 . . . . 61 A2
Ludlow's La CV35 . . . . 114 C7
Ludworth Ave B37 . . . . 44 B8
Luff Cl CV3 . . . . 78 B8
Lugtrout La B91 . . . . 56 A6
Lulworth Pk CV8 . . . . . . 93 C6
Lumley Gr B37 . . . . 33 D2
Lumsden Cl CV2 . . . . . . 62 F8
Lunar Cl CV4 . . . . 76 D5
Lundy View B36. . . . . . . 33 B6
Lunn Ave CV8 . . . . 92 E3
Lunn Poly Ho 3 CV32. . 105 F1
Lunt The* CV8 . . . . 77 E3
Lupin Cl LE10 . . . . 31 D5
Lupton Ave CV3 . . . . . . 77 C2
Luscombe Rd CV2 . . . . . 62 E8
Luther Way CV5 . . . . . . 59 F4
Lutterworth Rd
　Brinklow CV23 . . . . . . 64 F5
　Churchover CV23,LE17 67 D5
　Coventry CV2 . . . . 62 C5

Lutterworth Rd *continued*
　Hinckley LE10 . . . . 32 C3
　Nuneaton CV11 . . . . . . 40 C8
　Pailton CV23,LE17 . . . 54 D2
　Shawell LE17 . . . . 68 D6
　Wolvey LE10 . . . . 41 E6
Luxor La CV5 . . . . 59 B8
Lychgate Cl LE10 . . . . . 32 A5
Lychgate La LE10 . . . . . 32 C5
Lydd Croft B35 . . . . 22 B4
Lydford Cl CV2 . . . . 62 C7
Lydgate Ct
　Bedworth CV12 . . . . . . 39 A4
　Nuneaton CV11 . . . . . . 29 C2
Lydgate Rd CV6. . . . . . . 61 B5
Lydstep Gr CV31 . . . . . 110 C7
Lycroft Ave B37 . . . . . . 33 D2
Lye Green Rd CV35 . . . 113 F4
Lymesy St CV3 . . . . 77 D7
Lymington Cl CV6. . . . . . 61 D8
Lymington Dr CV6 . . . . . 50 B6
Lymore Croft CV2 . . . . . 63 A8
Lynbrook Cl B47 . . . . . . 69 A7
Lynbrook Rd CV5 . . . . . 76 D8
Lynchgate Ct CV4 . . . . . 76 C6
Lynchgate Ho CV4 . . . . 76 C6
Lynchgate Rd CV4 . . . . 76 C6
Lynch The
　Nuneaton CV11 . . . . . . 29 D2
　Polesworth B78. . . . . . . 4 F1
Lyndale Cl CV5 . . . . 60 C3
Lyndale Rd CV5. . . . . . . 60 C3
Lyndale B77 . . . . 4 F1
Lynden Ho CV5 . . . . 77 B8
Lyndhurst Cl
　Bedworth CV6 . . . . 50 B6
　Hinckley LE10 . . . . 32 A7
Lyndhurst Croft CV5 . . . 59 C4
Lyndhurst Rd CV21 . . . . 83 F1
Lyndon Croft B37 . . . . . 44 B7
Lyndon Ct CV32 . . . . . 109 E8
Lyndon Rd B37 . . . . 44 A6
Lyneham Gdns B76 . . . 22 A8
Lyng Ho 1 CV2 . . . . 62 D8
Lyng Hall Sch CV2 . . . . 62 C6
Lynmouth Cl CV11 . . . . 29 E5
Lynmouth Rd CV2 . . . . . 62 E8
Lynnon Field CV34 . . . 108 A4
Lynton Cl CV34 . . . . . . 104 E1
Lynton Rd CV6 . . . . 49 F1
Lynwood Wlk 10 CV1 . . 110 C6
Lysander Cl
　Hinckley LE10 . . . . 31 E4
　Wellesbourne CV35 . . 146 C2
Lysander Ct 7 CV37 . . 145 A2
Lysander Way CV35 . . . 22 B2
Lyster Cl CV34 . . . . . . 108 B8
Lytham Cl CV11 . . . . . . 40 E5
Lythalls La CV6 . . . . 49 E2
Lythalls Lane Ind Est CV6 49 F3
Lytham B77 . . . . 22 B6
Lytham Rd CV22 . . . . . . 82 E1
Lytham B77 . . . . 4 C5
Lyttelton Rd CV34 . . . . 108 E8
Lyttleton Cl CV3 . . . . . . 63 A1

M

M40 Distribution Pk
　CV35 . . . . 146 B2
MacAdam Cl NN11 . . . 117 F3
MacAulay Rd
　Coventry CV2. . . . . 62 D4
　Rugby CV22 . . . . 99 E7
Macbeth App CV34 . . . 109 D4
Macbeth Cl CV22 . . . . . 99 E6
MacDonald Rd CV2 . . . . 62 D4
McDonnell Dr CV6,CV7 . 49 F6
Macefield Cl CV2 . . . . . . 50 D2
Mackenzie Cl CV5 . . . . . 60 A7
McKinnell Cres CV21 . . 83 C4
Mackley Way CV33 . . . 123 E6
McMahon Rd CV12 . . . . 49 B8
Madam's Hill Rd B90 . . 70 D7
Madden Pl CV22 . . . . . . 82 C2
Madeira Croft CV5 . . . . 60 E2
Madrona B77 . . . . 4 B4
Maffey Ct CV22 . . . . 83 A2
Magdalen Cl CV37 . . . 129 D2
Magdalen Rd CV23 . . . 117 C6
Magna Pk LE17 . . . . 55 C6
Magnet La CV22 . . . . . . 99 C8
Magnolia Cl CV3 . . . . . . 77 B5
Magnolia B77 . . . . 4 A4
Magnus B77 . . . . 4 A4
Magpie Ho CV5 . . . . 59 D5
Magpie La CV7 . . . . 51 E6
Maguire Ind Est CV4 . . . 75 F8
Magyar Cres CV11 . . . . 40 A5
Maidavale Cres CV3 . . . 77 C4
Maidenhair Dr CV23 . . . 83 D8
Maidenhead Cl CV37 . . 145 A4
Maidenhead Rd CV37 . . 145 A4
Maidwell Dr B90 . . . . . . 70 E8
Main Rd
　Ansty CV7 . . . . 51 D3
　Austrey CV9 . . . . 3 B1
　Baxterley CV9 . . . . 17 F7
　Binton CV37 . . . . 120 A1
　Broughton OX15 . . . . 139 E1
　Claybrooke Magna LE17 43 F3
　Kilsby CV23 . . . . 101 F3
　Lower Quinton CV37 . 129 D2
　Meriden CV7 . . . . 58 D8
　Newton Regis B79. . . . . 2 C2
Main St
　Aston le W NN11 . . . . 134 F5

Main St *continued*
　Badby NN11 . . . . 126 F6
　Birdingbury CV23 . . . 115 F7
　Bourton on D CV23 . . . 97 F1
　Burmington CV36 . . . 141 C2
　Church Lench WR11 . . 127 A6
　Claydon OX17 . . . . . . 134 B5
　Cleeve Prior WR11 . . . 128 A4
　Clifton u D CV23 . . . . . 83 F5
　Easenhall CV23 . . . . . . 65 E4
　Frankton CV23 . . . . . . 97 D1
　Grandborough CV23 . 116 F6
　Hanwell OX17 . . . . . . 139 F6
　Higham on t H CV13 . . 21 A3
　Long Compton CV36 . 141 C3
　Long Lawford CV23 . . . 82 A5
　Middle Tysoe CV35 . . 138 B7
　Mollington OX17 . . . . 134 A2
　Monks Kirby CV23 . . . . 53 E3
　Newton CV23 . . . . 68 A1
　North Newington OX15 139 A6
　Norton Lindsey CV35 . 114 C2
　Offenham WR11 . . . . . 127 D1
　Orton-on-t-H CV9 . . . . . 6 D4
　Oxhill CV35 . . . . 137 F8
　Rugby CV22 . . . . 99 C8
　Rugby,Newbold on A CV21 82 D7
　Shawell LE17 . . . . 68 C5
　Sibford Gower OX15 . 142 D8
　South Littleton WR11 . 127 F1
　Stoke Golding CV13 . . 21 D7
　Stretton u F CV23 . . . . 65 B7
　Thurlaston CV23 . . . . . 98 F3
　Tiddington CV37 . . . . 145 E4
　Willey CV23 . . . . 54 F6
　Willoughby CV23 . . . . 117 C6
　Withybrook CV7 . . . . . . 52 E5
　Wolston CV8 . . . . 80 A4
　Wolvey LE10,CV23 . . . 39 D4
Makepeace Ave CV10 . 104 F1
Malam Cl CV4 . . . . 60 A1
Maldale B77 . . . . 4 C1
Maldens The CV36 . . . 149 D5
Malham Cl CV11 . . . . . . 30 A2
Malham Rd
　Tamworth B77 . . . . 10 C8
　Warwick CV34 . . . . . . 104 F1
Malins The CV34 . . . . . 109 B6
Mallaby Cl B90 . . . . 70 A8
Mallard Ave CV10 . . . . . 28 C6
Mallard Cl CV37 . . . . . 144 C5
Mallard Dr LE10 . . . . . . 31 A7
Mallard Rd B80 . . . . . . 103 F4
Mallender Dr B93 . . . . . 71 F5
Malletts Croft CV10 . . . 28 B8
Malletts Cl CV35 . . . . . 138 B6
Mallory Ct CV34 . . . . . 108 D7
Mallory Rd
　Bishops Tachbrook CV33 122 E8
　Lighthorne Heath CV33 123 D2
Mallory Way CV6 . . . . . . 49 E4
Mallow Croft CV12 . . . . 38 E2
Mallow Way CV23 . . . . . 83 C8
Malmesbury Rd CV6 . . . 49 F5
Malt House Cl
　Fenny Compton CV47 . 133 D7
　Little Compton GL56 . . 140 F3
Malthouse Cl WR11 . . . 127 D1
Malthouse Cl CV47 . . . 133 D4
Malt House La WR11 . . 127 A6
Malthouse La
　Earlswood B94 . . . . 86 E7
　Kenilworth CV8 . . . . . . 92 E4
　Shustoke CV35 . . . . . . 141 C2
Malt House La CV47 . . 133 B7
Malthouse La OX15 . . . 139 A3
Malthouse Row B37 . . . 44 A8
Maltings Cl 4 CV37 . . 144 F3
Maltings The
　3 Stratford-u-A CV37 . 145 A2
　Nuneaton CV11 . . . . . . 28 D8
　Royal Leamington Spa
　CV32 . . . . 105 F2
　Studley B80 . . . . 103 D4
Maltmill La B49 . . . . . . 143 C3
Malvern Ave
　Nuneaton CV10 . . . . . . 28 B3
　Rugby CV22 . . . . 83 D1
Malvern Dr B76. . . . . . . 22 A8
Malvern Rd CV5 . . . . . . 59 D4
Malvern Rd
　Balsall Common CV7 . . 74 C6
　Coventry CV5 . . . . 60 F4
　Redditch B97 . . . . 102 D8
Manby Rd B35 . . . . 22 C5
Mancetter Rd
　Atherstone CV9 . . . . . . 19 A6
　Nuneaton CV10 . . . . . . 28 D7
Manchester Ct 3 GL56 145 A2
Mandale Cl CV47 . . . . . 124 A4
Mandarin Cl LE10 . . . . . 31 A6
Mander Gr CV34 . . . . . 108 C4
Manderley Cl CV5 . . . . . 59 C5
Mandrake Cl CV6 . . . . . 49 D4
Manfield Ave CV3 . . . . . 63 A7
Mannings Cl CV33 . . . . 142 D8
Manning Wlk 3 CV21 . . 83 A3
Mann's Cl CV35 . . . . . 119 C8
Manor Barns CV36 . . . 136 B6
Manor Cl
　Baddesley Ensor CV9. . . 11 B2
　Charwelton NN11 . . . 126 D2
　Hinckley LE10 . . . . 31 C5
Manor Cotts GL56 . . . . 136 C1
Manor Court Ave CV11 . 29 A5
Manor Court Mews CV11 29 A5
Manor Court Rd CV11 . . 29 A5

Manor Ct
　Cleeve Prior WR11 . . . 128 A4
　Dorridge B93 . . . . 71 F2
　Ettington CV37. . . . . . 131 A3
　Fenny Compton CV47. . 133 D7
　Kenilworth CV8 . . . . . . 93 A6
　Royal Leamington Spa
　CV31 . . . . 109 F7
　Stretton on F GL56 . . 136 C1
Manor Dr
　Stretton-on-D CV23 . . . 96 F5
　Ullenhall B80 . . . . 112 D4
　Wilmcote CV37 . . . . . 120 C4
Manor Est CV8 . . . . 79 F3
Manor Farm Cl CV23 . . 101 C2
Manor Farm Cotts
　Church Lench WR11 . . 127 B5
　Luddington CV37 . . . . 129 C7
　Stretton on F GL56 . . 136 C1
Manor Farm Craft Ctr*
　B94 . . . . 69 F2
Manor Farm Cl CV23 . . 123 E1
Manor Farm Rd CV36 . . 136 F6
Manor Farm WR11 . . . 127 F1
Manor Gn CV37 . . . . . 145 C2
Manor Ho CV5 . . . . 78 D6
Manor Ho The CV5 . . . 109 F7
Manor House Cl
　Aston Flamville LE10 . . 32 E6
　Rugby CV21 . . . . 82 D7
Manor House Dr CV1 . . 151 B2
Manor House La
　Astwood Bank B96 . . . 102 E3
　Water Orton B46. . . . . . 23 B3
Manor La
　Claverdon CV35 . . . . . 114 A4
　Clifton u D CV23 . . . . . 84 A6
　Ettington CV37. . . . . . 131 A3
　Honiley CV8,CV35. . . . . 91 A5
　Kineton CV35 . . . . . . 132 B5
　Loxley CV35 . . . . 130 F7
　Shipston-on-S CV36. . 149 D6
　Wroxall CV35 . . . . 90 F4
Manor Mews B80 . . . . 103 E4
Manor Orch
　Harbury CV33 . . . . . . 123 E6
　Horley OX15 . . . . 139 D6
Manor Park Com Sch
　CV11 . . . . 29 A5
Manor Park Prim Sch
　CV3 . . . . 77 D7
Manor Park Rd CV11 . . . 29 A5
Manor Pk
　Claydon OX17 . . . . . . 134 B5
　Harvington WR11 . . . 127 D3
Manor Prim Sch B78 . . . 8 E5
Manor Rd
　Atherstone CV9 . . . . . . 18 F6
　Bishops Itchington CV47 124 A4
　Claybrooke Magna LE17 43 D6
　Coventry CV1 . . . . . . 151 B1
　Dorridge B93 . . . . 71 F3
　Harbury CV33 . . . . . . 123 F6
Manor Rd Ind Est CV7 . 18 E7
Manor Rd
　Kenilworth CV8 . . . . . . 92 F6
　Middle Littleton WR11 127 F1
　Royal Leamington Spa
　CV32 . . . . 106 B3
　Rugby CV21 . . . . 83 B4
　Staverton NN11 . . . . . 126 D8
　Stockton CV47 . . . . . . 147 F8
　Stratford-u-A CV37 . . 145 C2
　Studley B80 . . . . 103 E4
　Wythall B47 . . . . 69 A3
Manor Terr CV8 . . . . . . 93 A6
Manor View CV8 . . . . . . 79 F3
Manor Way LE10 . . . . . . 31 D5
Mansard Ct B46 . . . . . . 34 A4
Manse Cl CV7 . . . . 39 A1
Manse Gdns B80 . . . . . 103 E3
Mansell Rd B97 . . . . . . 102 D7
Mansell St CV37 . . . . . 144 F3
Mansel St CV6 . . . . 61 E8
Mansfield Ho B37 . . . . . 33 D3
Mansion Ho The CV35 . 132 B5
Mansions Cl CV47 . . . . 124 A4
Manston Dr B77 . . . . . . 9 D6
Manta Rd B77 . . . . 9 D6
Mantilla Dr CV3 . . . . . . 77 A5
Manton Croft B93 . . . . . 71 E3
Mantua 5 CV37 . . . . . 145 A3
Maple Ave CV7 . . . . 39 B1
Maple Cl
　Braunston NN11 . . . . 117 C5
　Hinckley LE10 . . . . 31 E5
Maple Dr B78 . . . . 15 D7
Maple Gr
　Rugby CV21 . . . . 83 A4
　Stratford-u-A CV37 . . 144 F5
　Warwick CV34 . . . . . . 105 A1
Maple Ho B98 . . . . 102 F8
Maple Leaf Dr B37 . . . . 44 B8
Maple Rd
　Nuneaton CV10 . . . . . . 28 E5
　Royal Leamington Spa
　CV31 . . . . 109 F6
Maple Rise B77 . . . . 4 A4
Maples The CV12 . . . . . 38 E2
Mapleton Rd CV6 . . . . . 60 F6

Maple Wlk
4 Birmingham B37 . . . .**33** B2
Coventry CV6 . . . .**49** F5
Maplewood B76 . . . .**22** A8
Mapperley Cl CV2 . . . .**63** A8
Mappleborough Green CE
Prim Sch B80 . . . .**112** A5
Marble Alley B80 . . . .**103** E4
Marchant Rd LE10 . . . .**31** C8
March Ct CV22 . . . .**83** A1
Marchfont Cl CV11 . . . .**30** A1
March Rd
Mollington OX17 . . . .**133** F2
Warmington OX17 . . . .**133** E2
March Way CV3 . . . .**78** D7
Marcian Cl LE10 . . . .**21** F1
Marcos Dr B36 . . . .**22** F1
Marcroft Pl CV1 . . . .**110** D6
Mardol Cl CV2 . . . .**62** D7
Mardol Cl B76 . . . .**22** A6
Margaret Ave CV12 . . . .**39** B3
Margaret Cl CV33 . . . .**123** F6
Margaret Rd CV9 . . . .**18** E7
Margeson Cl CV2 . . . .**62** E2
Margetts Cl CV34 . . . .**109** E2
Marie Brock Cl CV4 . . . .**60** B1
Marie Cl CV9 . . . .**19** A7
Marigold Dr LE10 . . . .**31** E5
Marigold Wlk CV10 . . . .**39** A8
Marina Cl CV4 . . . .**75** F7
Marion Rd CV6 . . . .**61** D7
Mark Antony Dr CV34 . . . . .**109** D4
Market Cnr
7 Royal Leamington Spa
CV31 . . . .**109** F6
Baginton CV8 . . . .**77** F2
Market End Cl CV12 . . . .**38** C2
Market Hill CV47 . . . .**147** B4
Market Mall 4 CV21 . . . .**83** A3
Market Pl
Alcester B49 . . . .**143** B3
Hinckley LE10 . . . .**31** D8
Nuneaton CV11 . . . .**29** C4
Rugby CV21 . . . .**83** A2
Shipston-on-S CV36 . . . . . .**149** D6
Warwick CV34 . . . .**108** E6
Market Sq 3 CV32 . . . .**132** B6
Market St
Atherstone CV9 . . . .**18** D8
Polesworth B78 . . . .**5** A1
Rugby CV21 . . . .**83** B4
Warwick CV34 . . . .**108** D6
Market Way CV1 . . . .**151** B2
Markham Dr CV31 . . . .**110** B3
Marks Mews 7 CV34 . . . . .**108** E6
Marlborough Cl LE10 . . . .**32** B7
Marlborough Ct B75 . . . .**13** A6
Marlborough Dr CV31 . . . . .**110** D5
Marlborough Mews B80 . . .**103** E4
Marlborough Rd
Coventry CV2 . . . .**62** A3
Nuneaton CV11 . . . .**29** B3
Rugby CV22 . . . .**99** E8
Marlcroft CV3 . . . .**78** E5
Marleigh Rd B50 . . . .**148** D5
Marlene Croft B37 . . . .**33** C1
Marler Rd CV4 . . . .**75** F7
Marlin B77 . . . .**9** D6
Marlissa Dr CV6 . . . .**49** E2
Marloes Wlk CV31 . . . .**110** C6
Marlow Cl CV5 . . . .**60** B4
Marlowe Cl
8 Banbury OX16 . . . .**139** F3
Galley Common CV10 . . . . . .**27** F5
Marlowe Rd 21 CV37 . . . . .**130** B8
Marlow Rd CV9 . . . .**16** C5
Marlston Wlk CV5 . . . .**60** A6
Marlwood Cl CV6 . . . .**49** F4
Marne Cl CV34 . . . .**109** A8
Marner Cres CV6 . . . .**61** B5
Marner Rd
Bedworth CV12 . . . .**39** A3
Nuneaton CV10 . . . .**29** B1
Marnhull Cl CV2 . . . .**62** F4
Marram Ct CV37 . . . .**144** E4
Marrick B77 . . . .**4** C1
Marriners La CV5 . . . .**60** B5
Marriott Rd
Bedworth CV12 . . . .**38** D2
Coventry CV6 . . . .**61** A4
Marsdale Dr CV10 . . . .**28** E3
Marsett B77 . . . .**10** C8
Marshall Ave CV36 . . . .**149** D5
Marshall Rd CV7 . . . .**49** F8
Marshalls Cl OX15 . . . .**138** F5
Marsham Ct CV34 . . . .**109** B8
Marshbrook Cl CV2 . . . .**50** E3
Marsh Cl CV11 . . . .**127** D4
Marsh St 5 GL56 . . . .**140** A3
Marshdale Ave CV6 . . . .**49** E3
Marshfield Dr CV4 . . . .**76** D2
Marshfield B90 . . . .**70** B5
Marsh Ho CV2 . . . .**63** A7
Marsh House Farm La
B92 . . . .**57** D3
Marsh La
Bradnock's Marsh B92 . . . . .**57** D5
Curdworth B76 . . . .**23** D5
Hampton-in-A B92 . . . .**57** B6
Stratford-u-A CV37 . . . .**144** E5
Water Orton B46 . . . .**23** C3
Marsh Rd CV37 . . . .**120** B5
Marston Ave CV33 . . . .**123** D2
Marston Camping & Cvn Pk
B76 . . . .**15** A2
Marston Cl CV32 . . . .**106** B2
Marston Dr B37 . . . .**33** A5
Marston Green Inf Sch
B37 . . . .**44** A7
Marston Green Jun Sch
B37 . . . .**44** A7
Marston Hill CV47 . . . .**125** F4
Marston La
Bedworth CV12 . . . .**39** D5
Nuneaton CV11 . . . .**39** E8
Wishaw B76 . . . .**14** E1
Marten Cl CV35 . . . .**108** A7
Martin Cl
Coventry CV5 . . . .**59** E4
Stratford-u-A CV37 . . . .**145** A5
Martindale Rd CV7 . . . .**50** C8
Martinique Sq CV34 . . . . . .**108** D6
Martin La CV22 . . . .**99** D7
Martins Dr CV9 . . . .**12** E2
Martins Rd CV12 . . . .**38** E1
Martley Cl B98 . . . .**102** A4
Martley Croft B91 . . . .**71** B8
Marton Hill CV47 . . . .**115** D4
Marton Rd
Birdingbury CV23 . . . .**115** E7
Long Itchington CV47 . . . . .**115** D5
Martyrs' Cl The CV3 . . . .**77** D8
Marwood Cl CV11 . . . .**39** E7
Mary Arden's House &
Shakespeare Mus*
CV37 . . . .**120** C5
Mary Herbert St CV3 . . . .**77** D7
Mary Slessor St CV3 . . . .**78** D7
Marystow Cl CV5 . . . .**60** B8
Marywell Cl LE10 . . . .**21** F1
Masefield Ave CV34 . . . .**108** C4
Masefield Rd CV37 . . . .**145** B1
Maseley Ct CV37 . . . .**129** D2
Mason Ave CV32 . . . .**106** C3
Mason Cl
Bidford-on-A B50 . . . .**148** E5
Redditch B97 . . . .**102** D7
Mason Ct LE10 . . . .**31** B8
Mason Gr CV8 . . . .**93** B5
Mason La B94 . . . .**69** F1
Mason Rd
Coventry CV6 . . . .**49** F1
Redditch B97 . . . .**102** D8
Masons Cl CV37 . . . .**120** C5
Masons Rd CV37 . . . .**144** E4
Masons Way CV37 . . . .**144** D4
Masser Rd CV6 . . . .**49** D4
Massey Sham Ave GL56 . . .**140** C3
Masters Cl CV23 . . . .**115** F7
Masters Rd CV31 . . . .**110** A4
Master's Yd CV23 . . . .**115** F7
Matchborough Way B98 . .**103** E8
Mathe Croft CV31 . . . .**110** C5
Matlock Cl CV21 . . . .**83** C7
Matlock Rd CV1 . . . .**61** D6
Matterson Rd CV6 . . . .**61** A5
Matthews Cl CV37 . . . .**145** A4
Maud Rd B46 . . . .**23** D3
Maudslay Rd CV5 . . . .**60** E2
Maureen Cl CV4 . . . .**59** C1
Maurice Mead Ct 12
CV31 . . . .**110** A6
Mavor Dr CV12 . . . .**38** D1
Mawby's La DE12 . . . .**3** F8
Mawnan Cl CV7 . . . .**50** B8
Max Rd CV6 . . . .**60** F5
Maxstoke Cl
Meriden CV7 . . . .**46** B1
Tamworth B77 . . . .**9** C4
Maxstoke Croft B90 . . . .**70** C8
Maxstoke Ct B46 . . . .**34** A4
Maxstoke Gdns CV31 . . . . .**109** F6
Maxstoke La
Coleshill B46 . . . .**34** B6
Meriden CV7 . . . .**46** A4
White Stitch CV7 . . . .**46** B3
Mayama Rd B78 . . . .**8** F8
Maybird Ctr CV37 . . . .**144** F4
Maybridge Dr B91 . . . .**71** B8
Maybrook Ind Est CV37 . . .**144** F4
Maybrook Rd
Stratford-u-A CV37 . . . .**144** F4
Sutton Coldfield B76 . . . . . .**22** A5
Maycock Rd CV6 . . . .**61** D7
Mayfair Dr
Fazeley B78 . . . .**9** A7
Galley Common CV10 . . . . . .**27** F4
May Farm Cl B47 . . . .**69** A6
Mayfield Ave CV37 . . . .**145** A4
Mayfield Cl
9 Royal Leamington Spa
CV31 . . . .**110** C6
Bedworth CV12 . . . .**39** B3
Mayfield Ct CV37 . . . .**145** A4
Mayfield Dr
Henley-in-A B95 . . . .**113** A5
Kenilworth CV8 . . . .**93** C4
Mayfield Rd
Coventry CV5 . . . .**61** A1
Nuneaton CV11 . . . .**29** E2
Southam CV47 . . . .**147** B5
Mayfield B77 . . . .**10** C8
Mayflower Dr CV2 . . . .**62** E2
Mayhurst Cl B47 . . . .**69** C6
Mayhurst Rd B47 . . . .**69** B6
May La
Ebrington GL55 . . . .**135** G2
Hollywood B47 . . . .**69** A7
Rugby CV22 . . . .**82** D1
Maynard Ave
Bedworth CV12 . . . .**49** D8
Warwick CV34 . . . .**109** A4
Mayne Cl CV35 . . . .**114** F3
Mayo Dr CV8 . . . .**93** A4
Mayo Rd CV36 . . . .**149** D7
Mayor's Croft CV4 . . . .**76** B7
Maypole La CV9 . . . .**11** C1
Maypole Rd B79 . . . .**5** C1
May's Hill CV6 . . . .**113** A4
May St CV6 . . . .**61** E8
Mayswood Rd B95 . . . .**113** A3
Maythorn Ave B76 . . . .**22** A6
Maythorn Gr B91 . . . .**71** B8
Maytree Cl B37 . . . .**33** A2
Mead Cl 2 GL56 . . . .**140** A3
Meadfoot Rd CV3 . . . .**78** E6
Meadowbank Dr B46 . . . .**23** D1
Meadowbrook Ct DE12 . . . . . .**3** F8
Meadow Cl
Ansty CV7 . . . .**51** D3
Hockley Heath B94 . . . .**88** C6
Kingsbury B78 . . . .**15** D5
Lighthorne CV35 . . . .**123** B4
Royal Leamington Spa
CV32 . . . .**106** C4
Solihull B90 . . . .**70** D8
Stratford-u-A CV37 . . . .**144** D3
Stretton-on-D CV23 . . . .**97** A6
Wolvey LE10 . . . .**41** D4
Meadow Cotts CV23 . . . .**116** F5
Meadowcroft Cl CV4 . . . .**75** F8
Meadow Croft CV7 . . . .**26** E1
Meadow Crofts CV47 . . . . . .**124** B5
Meadow Croft B47 . . . .**69** A3
Meadow Ct CV11 . . . .**29** B4
Meadow Dr
Hampton-in-A B92 . . . .**57** B7
Hinckley LE10 . . . .**32** A7
Meadow Farm CV37 . . . .**114** A1
Meadow Gdns CV9 . . . .**17** C8
Meadow Green Prim Sch
B47 . . . .**69** A3
Meadow Ho 5 CV1 . . . .**61** B3
Meadow Lea CV37 . . . .**144** D3
Meadow Pleck La B90 . . . . . .**70** A6
Meadow Rd
Alcester B49 . . . .**143** B5
Coventry CV6 . . . .**49** B4
Hartshill CV10 . . . .**28** A8
Henley-in-A B95 . . . .**113** B4
Hurley CV9 . . . .**16** C5
Rugby CV21 . . . .**82** E6
Southam CV47 . . . .**147** B5
Warwick CV34 . . . .**109** A4
Wolston CV8 . . . .**80** A4
Wythall B47 . . . .**69** A3
Meadow Rise
Balsall Common CV7 . . . . . .**74** C7
Ullenhall B95 . . . .**112** C6
Meadowside Sch The CV4 .**59** E3
Meadow St
Atherstone CV9 . . . .**18** D7
Coventry CV1 . . . .**151** A2
Meadows The
Bidford-on-A B50 . . . .**148** C5
Hinckley LE10 . . . .**32** A7
Leek Wootton CV35 . . . .**105** A7
Meadow St CV11 . . . .**29** B5
Meadow Sweet Rd CV37 . . .**144** E5
Meadowsweet CV23 . . . .**83** C8
Meadow View B49 . . . .**143** D4
Meadow View WR11 . . . .**127** F6
Meadow Way
Fenny Compton CV47 . . . . .**133** E7
Harborough Magna CV23 . . .**66** B3
Meadow CV37 . . . .**129** A6
Mead The OX17 . . . .**133** F2
Meadway CV2 . . . .**62** B6
Meadway N CV2 . . . .**62** B6
Meadway The
Hinckley LE10 . . . .**31** F7
Redditch B97 . . . .**102** D8
Meakins Cl CV34 . . . .**108** B4
Mearse La WR7 . . . .**118** B5
Medhurst Rd CV22 . . . .**99** C3
Medina Rd CV6 . . . .**49** E1
Medland Ave CV3 . . . .**76** F5
Medley Gr CV31 . . . .**109** F3
Meer End Rd CV8 . . . .**91** A6
Meerhill Ave B90 . . . .**71** A6
Meer St CV37 . . . .**145** A3
Meeting House La CV7 . . . . . .**74** C6
Meeting La B49 . . . .**143** C4
Meir Rd B98 . . . .**103** C8
Melbourne Cl CV11 . . . .**39** E8
Melbourne Ct 3 CV12 . . . . . .**38** E2
Melbourne Rd CV5 . . . .**61** A2
Meldon Rd CV47 . . . .**132** F7
Meldrum Rd CV10 . . . .**28** D4
Melfort Cl
Coventry CV3 . . . .**62** F2
Nuneaton CV10 . . . .**28** C5
Melksham Sq B35 . . . .**22** A3
Mellish Ct CV22 . . . .**82** E1
Mellish Rd CV22 . . . .**82** E1
Mellor Rd CV21 . . . .**101** B8
Mellowdew Rd CV2 . . . .**62** E4
Mellowship Rd CV5 . . . .**59** D5
Mellwaters B77 . . . .**10** C8
Melmerby B77 . . . .**10** C8
Melrose Ave CV12 . . . .**49** D8
Melrose Cl LE10 . . . .**31** B8
Melrose Ct 12 OX16 . . . . . .**139** F5
Melton Rd CV32 . . . .**106** B4
Melville Cl
Bedworth CV7 . . . .**50** A8
Rugby CV22 . . . .**82** E1
Melville Ho 7 CV37 . . . . . .**144** F1
Melville Rd CV1 . . . .**61** A3
Memorial Rd CV47 . . . .**133** D7
Menai Wlk B37 . . . .**33** B4
Mendip Dr CV10 . . . .**28** B3
Mendip Way B77 . . . .**4** C1
Meon Cl CV37 . . . .**129** D1
Meon Rd GL55 . . . .**135** C7
Mercer Ave
Coventry CV2 . . . .**62** A5
Water Orton B46 . . . .**23** A3
Mercer Ct 8 CV22 . . . .**100** F8
Mercers Mdw CV7 . . . .**49** A6
Merchants Ct 5 CV32 . . . .**106** A1
Mercia Ave CV8 . . . .**92** F4
Mercia Bsns Village CV4 . . .**75** F6
Mercia Ho CV1 . . . .**151** B3
Mercian Pk B77 . . . .**4** A3
Mercian Way B77 . . . .**4** B3
Mercia Way CV34 . . . .**109** B7
Mercot Cl B98 . . . .**103** A6
Mercury Pk B77 . . . .**4** B3
Mere Ave B35 . . . .**22** B3
Meredith Rd CV2 . . . .**62** D2
Mere La LE10 . . . .**42** C3
Merestone Cl CV47 . . . .**147** B6
Merevale Ave
Hinckley LE10 . . . .**31** C7
Redditch B98 . . . .**103** D8
Merevale Cl
Hinckley LE10 . . . .**31** C7
Redditch B98 . . . .**103** D8
Merevale La CV9 . . . .**17** F7
Merevale Rd CV9 . . . .**12** C1
Merevale View CV9 . . . .**18** C7
Mereways B90 . . . .**70** A5
Meriden Bsns Pk CV5 . . . . . .**59** B8
Meriden CE Prim Sch
CV7 . . . .**46** C1
Meriden Cl B98 . . . .**112** A6
Meriden Cross* CV7 . . . .**46** B1
Meriden Dr B37 . . . .**33** A6
Meriden Hill CV7 . . . .**58** E8
Meriden Park Homes CV7 . . .**58** C8
Meriden Rd
Berkswell CV7 . . . .**58** C4
Fillongley CV7 . . . .**36** C2
Hampton-in-A B92 . . . .**57** C7
Meriden St CV1 . . . .**61** B3
Merlin Ave CV10 . . . .**28** B6
Merlin Cl
Birmingham B35 . . . .**22** A3
Rugby CV23 . . . .**83** C8
Tamworth B77 . . . .**10** A6
Merrick Ct LE10 . . . .**31** F5
Merrifield Gdns LE10 . . . .**31** E5
Merrington Cl 5 B91 . . . .**71** C8
Merrivale Rd CV5 . . . .**60** E3
Merryfields Way CV2 . . . .**50** F1
Merry Hurst Pl LE10 . . . .**30** E7
Merry La WR11 . . . .**127** E1
Mersey Rd CV12 . . . .**39** A3
Merstone Sch B37 . . . .**33** A1
Merttens Dr CV22 . . . .**82** F2
Merynton Ave CV4 . . . .**76** E5
Meschines St CV3 . . . .**77** D6
Metallurg Ind Est B76 . . . . . .**22** B5
Metcalfe Cl OX15 . . . .**139** E4
Metchley Croft B90 . . . .**70** F6
Meteor Ho CV2 . . . .**100** D8
Mews The
3 Rugby CV21 . . . .**84** A1
Atherstone CV9 . . . .**18** E8
Bedworth CV12 . . . .**39** B2
Kenilworth CV8 . . . .**92** E3
Mica Cl B77 . . . .**4** B2
Michael Banning Pl CV7 . . .**74** B7
Michael Blanning Gdns
B93 . . . .**71** E3
Michael Drayton Jun Sch
CV10 . . . .**28** B8
Michaelmas Rd CV3 . . . . . .**151** B1
Michel Ho CV1 . . . .**151** C4
Michell Cl CV3 . . . .**78** B8
Micklehill Dr B90 . . . .**70** B8
Mickle Mdw B46 . . . .**23** B3
Mickleton Cl B98 . . . .**102** E7
Mickleton Dr CV35 . . . .**146** C2
Mickleton Prim Sch
GL55 . . . .**135** B6
Mickleton Rd
Coventry CV5 . . . .**77** A8
Ilmington CV36 . . . .**136** A7
Mickleton B37 . . . .**10** C8
Middelburg Cl CV11 . . . .**30** A1
Middle Bickenhill La B92 . . .**45** A4
Middleborough Rd CV1 . . . .**151** A4
Middlecotes CV4 . . . .**60** B1
Middlefield Ave B93 . . . .**72** B4
Middlefield Cl CV3 . . . .**63** B1
Middlefield La CV37 . . . .**130** C1
Middlefield Rd CV3 . . . .**63** A1
Middle La
Balscote OX15 . . . .**139** B4
Nether Whitacre B46 . . . . . .**24** E6
Shotteswell OX17 . . . .**139** E8
Middle Littleton Tithe Barn*
WR11 . . . .**127** F2
Middle Lock La CV35 . . . . . .**114** F5
Middlemarch Bsns Pk
CV3 . . . .**78** C2
Middlemarch Rd
Coventry CV6 . . . .**61** C7
Nuneaton CV10 . . . .**29** C1
Middlemarch Sch CV10 . . . . .**29** B1
Middlemore Cl B80 . . . .**103** D3
Middle Rd CV33 . . . .**123** D7
Middle Ride CV3 . . . .**78** E5
Middle Row OX7 . . . .**142** A2
Middlesex Cl CV37 . . . .**128** E1
Middlesmoor B77 . . . .**10** C8
Middle St
Armscote CV37 . . . .**136** E7
Ilmington CV36 . . . .**136** B6
Middle Tysoe CV35 . . . .**138** B6
Middleton Hall* B78 . . . .**8** E1
Middleton La B78 . . . .**13** F6
Middletown La B96,B80 . . .**103** D3
Middletown
Moreton Morrell CV35 . . . .**122** F3
Studley B80 . . . .**103** D1
Midland Air Mus* CV8 . . . . .**78** B3
Midland Oak Trad Est
CV6 . . . .**49** E2
Midland Rd
Coventry CV6 . . . .**61** E5
Nuneaton CV11 . . . .**29** C2
Midland Trad Est CV21 . . . . .**83** A4
Midpoint Park Ind Est
B76 . . . .**22** C5
Milburn Hill Rd CV4 . . . .**76** B6
Milburn B77 . . . .**10** C8
Milby Cl CV11 . . . .**29** C2
Milby Dr CV11 . . . .**30** A7
Milby Prim Sch CV11 . . . .**29** F8
Milcote Cl B98 . . . .**103** A4
Milcote Manor Cotts
CV37 . . . .**129** C6
Milcote Rd CV37 . . . .**129** C6
Mildmay Cl CV37 . . . .**144** E1
Mile End B94 . . . .**87** B2
Mile La CV1 . . . .**151** C1
Mile Post La CV6 . . . .**118** A2
Milesbush Ave B36 . . . .**22** D1
Miles Mdw
Coventry CV6 . . . .**50** B1
Newbold-on-S CV37 . . . . . .**130** E1
Milestone Dr CV22 . . . .**99** F8
Milestone Ho 2 CV1 . . . . . .**61** B2
Milestone Rd CV34 . . . .**108** C8
Mile Tree La CV2 . . . .**50** F7
Milfoil Cl LE10 . . . .**30** F7
Milford Cl
Allesley CV5 . . . .**60** A6
Redditch B97 . . . .**102** C6
Milford Ct CV31 . . . .**110** A8
Milford Gr B90 . . . .**71** C7
Milford St CV10 . . . .**29** B2
Milking La B95 . . . .**112** C6
Millais Cl CV12 . . . .**39** A4
Mill Bank CV14 . . . .**25** D3
Mill Bank Mews CV8 . . . .**93** B6
Millbank CV34 . . . .**105** B1
Millbeck CV21 . . . .**83** D7
Mill Cl
Braunston NN11 . . . .**117** D5
Broom B50 . . . .**148** B7
Coventry CV2 . . . .**50** B3
Hollywood B47 . . . .**69** A7
Norton Lindsey CV35 . . . . .**114** C2
Nuneaton CV11 . . . .**29** F1
Southam CV47 . . . .**147** A5
Wolston CV8 . . . .**79** F3
Mill Cotts B50 . . . .**148** B7
Mill Cres
11 Kineton CV35 . . . .**132** B6
Kingsbury B78 . . . .**15** D4
Southam CV47 . . . .**147** A5
Mill Ct CV36 . . . .**149** D5
Mill End CV8 . . . .**93** A6
Millennium Way CV8 . . . .**79** F3
Millers Bank B50 . . . .**148** B7
Millers Cl CV22 . . . .**99** A3
Miller's Cl CV22 . . . .**99** A4
Millers La
Lower Boddington NN11 . .**134** E6
Welford-on-A CV37 . . . . . .**129** B6
Millers Dale Cl CV21 . . . .**83** C7
Millers Gn LE10 . . . .**31** F6
Millers La
Hornton OX15 . . . .**139** B8
Monks Kirby CV23 . . . .**53** D3
Millers Rd CV34 . . . .**108** D8
Millers Wharf B78 . . . .**4** F1
Mill Farm Ct CV22 . . . .**99** C3
Mill Farm Pk CV12 . . . .**40** B6
Millfield Cl CV37 . . . .**129** D2
Millfield CV31 . . . .**113** B5
Mill Field CV37 . . . .**128** F2
Millfield Prim Sch B78 . . . . . .**9** A4
Millfield CV31 . . . .**110** A8
Millfields Ave CV22 . . . .**100** A4
Mill Furlong CV23 . . . .**67** D1
Mill Hill CV8 . . . .**77** D3
Millholme Cl CV47 . . . .**147** C4
Mill House Cl CV32 . . . .**109** C8
Mill House Ct CV32 . . . .**109** C8
Mill House Dr CV32 . . . .**109** C8
Mill House Terr CV32 . . . . . .**109** C8
Mill Ind Pk The B49 . . . .**143** B7
Milliners Way CV9 . . . .**18** D8
Millison Gr B90 . . . .**71** A7
Mill La
10 Kineton CV35 . . . .**132** B6
Alcester B49 . . . .**143** B2
Aston Cantlow B49,B95 . . .**119** F6
Atherstone CV9 . . . .**19** A6
Barford CV35 . . . .**122** A7
Bentley Heath B93 . . . .**71** F3

Mill La continued
Bramcote CV11 . . . . .40 F8
Broom B50. . . . . .148 B7
Bulkington CV12 . . . . .40 A3
Chipping Warden OX17 . . .134 F3
Cleeve Prior WR11 . . . . . . .128 A4
Clifton u D CV23 . . . . .83 E5
Coventry CV3. . . . . .62 F2
Cubbington CV32 . . . . .106 F5
Drayton OX15 . . . . .139 E4
Earlswood B94. . . . . .86 B8
Fazeley B78 . . . . .9 A8
Fenny Compton CV47. . . .133 D7
Fillongley CV7 . . . . .36 C5
Great Alne B49 . . . . .119 E6
Harbury CV33 . . . . .123 F7
Kingswood B94. . . . . .39 E2
Lowsonford,Finwood CV35 .113 E7
Lowsonford,Turner's Green
  CV35. . . . . .113 F8
Mickleton GL55 . . . . .135 B6
Newbold-on-S CV37. . . . . .136 F8
Shenington OX15. . . . . . . .138 F5
Shrewley CV35 . . . . .114 C6
Stratford-u-A CV37 . . . . . .145 A1
Tredington CV36 . . . . .136 F6
Welford-on-A CV37 . . . . . .129 A7
Witherley CV9 . . . . .19 A8
Wolvey LE10 . . . . .41 F5
Mill Pleck B80. . . . . .103 E3
Mill Pool La B93. . . . . .89 A8
Mill Race La CV6 . . . . .50 B3
Mill Race View CV9 . . . . . . .12 D2
Mill Rd
Napton on t H CV47. . . . . .125 C8
Royal Leamington Spa
  CV31. . . . . .110 A8
Rugby CV21 . . . . .83 C5
Southam CV47. . . . . .147 A5
Mill Row LE10 . . . . .41 F5
Mills La OX15. . . . . .139 D4
Mill St
Bedworth CV12 . . . . .39 B3
Harbury CV33 . . . . .123 E7
Kineton CV35. . . . . .132 B6
Nuneaton CV11 . . . . .29 C4
Royal Leamington Spa
  CV32. . . . . .110 A7
Shipston-on-S CV36. . . . . .149 D5
Warwick CV34 . . . . .108 F6
Mill Terr CV12 . . . . .39 B5
Millway Dr **1** CV33 . . . . . .122 F8
Mill Wlk CV11 . . . . .29 C4
Milner Cl CV32 . . . . .40 D2
Milner Cres CV2 . . . . .50 E1
Milner Dr B79 . . . . .8 E7
Milrose Way CV4 . . . . .75 F8
Milton Ave CV34 . . . . .108 C5
Milton Cl
Bedworth CV12 . . . . .39 D1
Bentley Heath B93. . . . . . . .71 F4
Redditch B97 . . . . .102 C8
Milton Rd
Bentley Heath B93. . . . . . . .71 F4
Stratford-u-A CV37 . . . . . .130 D8
Milton St CV2 . . . . .62 A4
Milverton Cres CV32 . . . . .105 E1
Milverton Cres W **3**
  CV32. . . . . .105 E1
Milverton Ct CV32 . . . . . . .109 E8
Milverton Hill CV32 . . . . . .109 E7
Milverton House Prep Sch
  CV32. . . . . .29 D3
Milverton Lodge **2**
  CV32. . . . . .105 E1
Milverton Prim Sch
  CV32. . . . . .105 E1
Milverton Rd
Coventry CV2 . . . . .50 D2
Knowle B93 . . . . .72 C5
Milverton Terr CV32 . . . . .109 E8
Miners Wlk B78 . . . . .4 F1
Minerva Mews B49 . . . . . .143 B4
Minions Cl CV9 . . . . .18 D8
Miniva Dr CV34 . . . . .13 A2
Minster Cl
Hampton Magna CV35. . . .114 F3
Knowle B93 . . . . .72 B8
Minster Rd CV1. . . . . .61 B3
Minton Rd CV2 . . . . .50 E1
Minworth Ind Pk B76. . . . . .22 B5
Minworth Jun & Inf Sch
  B76. . . . . .22 D5
Minworth Rd B46. . . . . .23 A3
Mira Dr CV10 . . . . .20 D3
Miranda Cl CV3. . . . . .78 D7
Miranda Dr CV34 . . . . .109 E2
Mistral Cl CV11 . . . . .31 F8
Mitchelldean Cl B98. . . . . .102 C8
Mitchell Ave CV4 . . . . .76 A7
Mitchell Cl CV23 . . . . .67 C2
Mitchell Ho
Coventry CV1. . . . . .76 A7
Warwick CV34 . . . . .108 E7
Mitchell Rd CV12 . . . . .39 C2
Mitchison Cl CV23 . . . . . . .117 E8
Mitford Villas GL56. . . . . . .140 A3
Mitre Ave CV3. . . . . .76 F5
Moat Cl
Bubbenhall CV8. . . . . .95 C6
Thurlaston CV23 . . . . .98 F2
Moat Croft
Birmingham B37 . . . . .33 A2
Sutton Coldfield B76 . . . . . .22 D7
Moat Dr B78 . . . . .8 E5
Moat Farm Cotts WR11. . .127 E5

Moat Farm Dr
Bedworth CV12 . . . . .49 C8
Rugby CV21 . . . . .101 A7
Moat Farm La B95. . . . . . . .112 E6
Moat Gn CV35 . . . . .108 A1
Moat House La
Coventry CV4. . . . . .76 C7
Shustoke B46. . . . . .25 B1
Moat House Prim Sch
  CV2 . . . . .50 D1
Moat La LE10 . . . . .41 F6
Mobbs La CV31 . . . . .142 D4
Mockley Wood Rd B93. . . . .72 B7
Modbury Cl CV3 . . . . .77 C2
Model Village The CV47 . . .115 D3
Molesworth Ave CV3. . . . . .62 A1
Mollington Gr CV35. . . . . .114 F6
Mollington La OX17. . . . . .133 D2
Mollington Rd
Claydon OX17 . . . . .134 B4
Shotteswell OX17 . . . . . . .139 E8
Whitnash CV31 . . . . .110 A3
Momus Bvd CV2 . . . . .62 C2
Moncrieff Dr CV31. . . . . . .110 C5
Monks Cl CV22 . . . . .99 A8
Monk's Croft The CV3. . . . .77 C7
Monks Dr B80 . . . . .103 C4
Monks Field Cl CV4 . . . . . . .60 A1
Monks Kirby La CV23 . . . . .53 F6
Monkspath Bsns Pk B90. . .70 F8
Monkspath Hall Rd B90,
  B91. . . . . .71 B7
Monkspath Jun & Inf Sch
  B90. . . . . .71 A6
Monks Rd
Binley Woods CV3 . . . . .79 C7
Coventry CV1 . . . . .61 F2
Monks Way CV34 . . . . .108 D6
Monkswood Cres CV22 . . . .62 D8
Monmouth Cl
Coventry CV5. . . . . .60 B3
Kenilworth CV8 . . . . .92 F6
Monmouth Gdns CV10 . . . . .28 E3
Monnington Ho CV6 . . . . . .93 B7
Montague Ho
13 Stratford-u-A CV37 . . .145 A3
Warwick CV34 . . . . .109 A8
Montague Rd
Coventry CV6. . . . . .99 D5
Warwick CV34 . . . . .109 A8
Montague's Cnr CV37 . . . .129 A6
Montalt Rd CV3. . . . . .77 E7
Montana Wlk CV10 . . . . . . .28 E3
Montfort Rd B46. . . . . .33 F5
Montgomery Ave CV35 . . .114 F3
Montgomery Cl
Coventry CV3. . . . . .78 C4
Stratford-u-A CV37 . . . . . .144 E1
Montgomery Dr CV22. . . . . .82 C1
Montgomery Rd CV31. . . .109 F4
Montilo La CV23 . . . . .66 D5
Montjoy Cl CV3 . . . . .78 D7
Montley B77. . . . . .10 C8
Montpelier Ho CV8. . . . . . .92 F5
Montpellier Cl CV3 . . . . . . .77 C6
Montrose Ave CV32. . . . . .106 B5
Montrose Dr
Birmingham B35 . . . . .22 A4
Nuneaton CV10 . . . . .28 F3
Montrose Rd CV22. . . . . . . .83 A1
Montsford Cl B93. . . . . .71 F6
Monument View B78 . . . . . .11 A8
Monument Cl B97. . . . . . . .102 B6
Monwode Lea La B46. . . . . .26 B4
Moorbrooke CV10. . . . . .28 A7
Moorcroft Cl
Nuneaton CV11 . . . . .30 B1
Redditch B97 . . . . .102 B6
Moorcroft Gdns B97. . . . . .102 B6
Moore Cl
Appleby Magna DE12. . . . . .3 F8
Coventry CV5. . . . . .50 A5
Warwick CV34 . . . . .104 E2
Moorend Ave B37. . . . . .33 B2
Moore Wlk CV34 . . . . .109 C7
Moor Farm Cl CV23 . . . . . . .96 F6
Moorfield Ave B93. . . . . . . .71 F6
Moorfield Rd B49. . . . . . . .143 B4
Moorfield The CV3. . . . . . . .78 B8
Moorhill Rd CV31. . . . . . . .110 A3
Moorhills Croft B90. . . . . . .70 B8
Moorings Bsns Pk The
  CV6 . . . . .50 A6
Moorings The CV31 . . . . . .109 D7
Moorlands Ave CV8. . . . . . .92 F3
Moorlands Lodge CV8. . . . .92 F3
Moor La
Tamworth B77 . . . . .4 A6
Willoughby CV23 . . . . .117 B6
Moorpark Cl CV11 . . . . .40 C8
Moor Rd CV10. . . . . .28 A8
Moors La CV23 . . . . .84 C1
Moor St CV5. . . . . .60 F1
Moor The B76. . . . . .22 A8
Moorwood Cres CV10 . . . . .28 A8
Moorwood La
Ansley Common CV10 . . . . .27 F8
Hartshill CV10 . . . . .28 A8
Morar Cl B35 . . . . .22 B4
Moray Cl LE10 . . . . .31 A8
Moreall Mdws CV4. . . . . . .146 E4
Morecroft Dr CV34. . . . . . .108 B4
Moreland Croft B76. . . . . . .22 B6
Moreton Cl CV37. . . . . .145 D2

Moreton-in-Marsh Hospl
  GL56. . . . . .140 A3
Moreton-in-Marsh Sta
  GL56. . . . . .140 A3
Moreton Morrell CE Prim
  Sch CV35 . . . . .122 F2
Moreton Morrell La
  CV35. . . . . .123 B2
Morfa Gdns CV6 . . . . .60 D5
Morgan Cl
4 Banbury OX16 . . . . . . .139 F4
New Arley CV7. . . . . .36 F8
Norton Lindsey CV35. . . . .114 C2
Studley B80 . . . . .103 F2
Morgan Gr B36. . . . . .22 F1
Morgans Rd CV5. . . . . .59 C4
Morgrove Ave B93. . . . . . . .71 F6
Morland Cl CV12. . . . . .40 D2
Morland Rd CV6 . . . . .49 C2
Morningside CV5 . . . . .77 B8
Mornington Ct B46 . . . . . . .34 A7
Morpeth B77 . . . . .9 C7
Morrell St CV32. . . . . .105 F1
Morris Ave CV2 . . . . .62 D4
Morris Cl CV21 . . . . .82 D8
Morris Croft B36. . . . . .22 F1
Morris Dr
10 Banbury OX16 . . . . . .139 F4
Nuneaton CV11 . . . . .29 D1
Whitnash CV31 . . . . .110 A2
Morris Hill B78. . . . . .11 A8
Morris Rd NN11 . . . . .117 F2
Morse Rd CV31. . . . . .110 B3
Morson Cres CV21. . . . . . . .83 E2
Morston B77 . . . . .9 C4
Mortimer Rd CV8 . . . . .92 F2
Morton Cl CV6 . . . . .49 A1
Morton Ct
1 Stratford-u-A CV37 . . .145 A3
Rugby CV21 . . . . .100 F8
Morton Gdns CV21 . . . . . . .83 C2
Morton Hall La B93. . . . . . .118 A6
Morton La B97 . . . . .102 B7
Morton St CV32. . . . . .105 F1
Morton Wood La WR7 . . . .127 B8
Morville Cl B93. . . . . .71 D3
Mosedale
Moreton-in-M GL56. . . . . .140 B3
Rugby CV21 . . . . .83 C7
Moseley Ave CV6 . . . . .61 A4
Moseley Prim Sch CV6. . . . .61 A4
Moseley Rd CV8 . . . . .93 B3
Moss Cl CV21. . . . . .82 E1
Mossdale Cl CV6. . . . . .61 B6
Mossdale Cres CV10 . . . . . .28 C8
Mossdale B77 . . . . .10 C8
Moss Gr CV8 . . . . .93 B7
Moss La
Newbold-on-S CV37. . . . . .130 E1
Redditch B98 . . . . .112 A8
Mossop Cl CV47 . . . . .144 E3
Mosspaul Cl CV21. . . . . . . .105 D2
Moss St **12** CV31. . . . . . . .110 A7
Mottisfone Cl CV3 . . . . .77 D6
Mott's Way B46. . . . . .34 A5
Moultrie Rd CV21,CV22. . . .83 B3
Mountbatten Ave CV37 . . .144 D1
Mountbatten Cl CV37 . . . .144 C3
Mount Dr CV12 . . . . .39 A3
Mount Field Ct CV11 . . . . .151 D4
Mountfield Gdns **4**
  CV47. . . . . .147 B4
Mountford Cl CV35. . . . . . .146 E3
Mountford Rise CV35. . . . .123 B2
Mount Gdns CV5. . . . . .77 B8
Mount Nod Prim Sch CV5 .60 A3
Mount Nod Way CV5. . . . . .60 B3
Mount Pleasant CV47 . . . .124 A4
Mount Pleasant Cl CV47 . .147 B4
Mount Pleasant Cotts
  CV2 . . . . .63 A7
Mount Pleasant La B95 . . .112 E6
Mount Pleasant Rd CV12 . .39 A3
Mount Pleasant
Stockton CV47. . . . . .147 F8
Stratford-u-A CV37 . . . . . .144 C3
Tamworth B77 . . . . .9 C8
Mount Pleasant Terr
  CV10 . . . . .28 F6
Mount Pleasant OX17 . . . .134 F1
Mount Rd
Henley-in-A B95. . . . . .113 B4
Hinckley LE10 . . . . .31 D8
Mount St
Coventry CV5. . . . . .60 F2
Nuneaton CV11 . . . . .29 B4
Mount Street Pas CV11 . . .29 B4
Mount The
Coventry CV3 . . . . .77 E8
Curdworth B76 . . . . .23 C6
Mowbray St CV2 . . . . .61 F3
Mowe Croft B37. . . . . .44 B7
Mows Hill Rd B94,B95. . . .113 A8
Moxhull Rd B37 . . . . .33 A5
Moyeady Ave CV22. . . . . . .100 E8
Moyle Cres CV5. . . . . .59 D4
Much Park St CV1 . . . . . . .151 C2
Muirfields Cl CV11 . . . . .40 C8
Muirfield B77 . . . . .4 C5
Mulberry Cl CV32. . . . . . . .106 C5
Mulberry Dr
19 Stratford-u-A CV37 . . .145 A3
Kenilworth CV8 . . . . .92 F4
Mulberry Rd
Coventry CV6. . . . . .62 A7
Rugby CV22 . . . . .82 B2

Mulberry St **20** CV37. . . . .145 A3
Mulberry Tree Ctr The
  CV37. . . . . .145 A3
Mulberry Way CV10 . . . . . .28 A8
Mullard Dr CV31. . . . . .110 B3
Mull Croft B36. . . . . .33 B7
Mullensgrove Rd B37. . . . . .33 A5
Mulliners Cl B37 . . . . .33 B2
Mulliner St CV6. . . . . .61 F5
Muntz Cres B91. . . . . .88 C6
Murcott Cl CV31 . . . . .110 A3
Murcott Rd E CV31. . . . . . .110 A3
Murcott Rd W CV31. . . . . .110 A3
Murrayfield Way CV3 . . . . . .78 C6
Murrayian Cl CV21. . . . . . . .83 B3
Murray Rd
Coventry CV6. . . . . .61 A7
Rugby CV21 . . . . .83 B4
Murton B77 . . . . .9 C4
Musborough Cl B36. . . . . . .22 C1
Museum of British Road
  Transport* CV1 . . . . .151 B3
Mus of British Road
  Transport* CV1 . . . . .151 B3
Mus of Country Bygones*
  CV23. . . . . .115 C7
Myatt Rd WR11 . . . . .127 D1
Myatt's Field WR11 . . . . . .127 D1
Myers Rd CV21 . . . . .101 C8
Mylgrove CV3 . . . . .77 D3
Mynors Cres B47 . . . . .69 A6
Myrtle Gr CV5. . . . . .60 F1
Mythe La CV9 . . . . .19 A8
Mythe View CV9 . . . . .12 E1
Myton Cres CV34. . . . . . . .109 A6
Myton Crofts CV31. . . . . . .109 D7
Myton Gdns CV34 . . . . . . .109 A6
Myton La CV34 . . . . .109 C6
Myton Rd CV31,CV34. . . . .109 B6
Myton Sch CV34 . . . . .109 B6
Mytton Rd B46. . . . . .22 F3

N

Nailcote Ave CV4 . . . . .75 C3
Nailcote La CV7 . . . . .75 A7
Nailsworth Rd B93. . . . . . . .71 D2
Nairn Cl CV10 . . . . .29 A2
Napier St CV1 . . . . .61 F3
Naples Rd CV35. . . . . .132 E5
Napton Cl CV22 . . . . .99 B6
Napton Dr CV32 . . . . .106 A2
Napton Ind Est CV47 . . . .125 B8
Napton Gn CV5 . . . . .60 A3
Napton Rise CV47. . . . . . .147 D4
Narberth Way CV2 . . . . . . .62 F8
Narborough Cl CV5 . . . . . .82 E1
Narrowboat Cl CV6. . . . . . .50 B6
Narrow Hall Mdw CV34 . .108 B4
Narrow La
Lowsonford B95,CV35. . . .113 F6
Stratford-u-A CV37 . . . . . .144 C3
Narrows The **1** LE10. . . . . .31 E8
Naseby Cl CV3. . . . . .78 F8
Naseby Rd CV22. . . . . .83 C1
Nash Croft B37 . . . . .44 B8
Nashes The CV37. . . . . . . .129 F7
Nash's La GL55 . . . . .135 E3
Nasmyth Rd NN11 . . . . . . .117 F3
Nathaniel Newton Inf Sch
  CV10 . . . . .28 B8
National Distribution Pk
  CV6 . . . . .50 B6
National Ex Ctr B40. . . . . . .44 E4
National Herb Ctr*
  OX17 . . . . .133 D1
National Motorcycle Mus
  The* CV7. . . . . .45 A2
Navigation Way CV6 . . . . . .49 B8
Nayler Cl CV21 . . . . .83 C6
Neale Ave CV4 . . . . .59 F4
Neale Cl CV12. . . . . .40 C1
Neale's Cl CV33. . . . . .123 F7
Nebsworth La CV36. . . . . .135 F5
Needhill Cl B93. . . . . .71 F6
Needle La CV7 . . . . .74 F2
Needlers End La CV7 . . . . .74 A7
Neilston St **18** CV31. . . . . .110 A7
Nelson Ave CV34. . . . . . . .109 A8
Nelson Cl CV37 . . . . .131 A4
Nelson La CV34 . . . . .109 A8
Nelson St **7** CV1 . . . . .61 E4
Nelson Way CV22 . . . . .82 C1
Nemesia B77 . . . . .4 B4
Nene Cl CV3 . . . . .78 D7
Nene Side Cl NN11 . . . . . .126 F6
Nene Wlk NN11 . . . . .117 F1
Nesfield Gr B92 . . . . .57 B7
Nesscliffe Rd CV47. . . . . . .132 F5
Nethercote Cl CV36. . . . . .136 B6
Nethercote Mdw CV36 . . .141 C4
Netherfield B98 . . . . .103 A4
Nethermill Rd **1** CV6. . . . . .61 A5
Nethersole CE Prim Sch The
  B78 . . . . .5 A2
Nethersole St B78 . . . . .5 A2
Netherwood Ind Est CV7 . .37 A2
Netherwood La B93. . . . . . .90 A7
Netting St OX15 . . . . .142 D4
Nevada Way B37. . . . . .33 C1
Nevill Cl CV31 . . . . .110 A6
Neville Cl **5** CV34 . . . . . . .108 E6
Neville Gr CV34. . . . . .104 F1

Neville Rd
Birmingham B36 . . . . .22 E1
Solihull B90 . . . . .69 F8
Nevill Wlk B35 . . . . .22 A2
Nevil Cl CV23 . . . . .83 E5
New Ash Dr CV5 . . . . .59 F5
New Barn OX15. . . . . .138 F5
New Bldgs CV1 . . . . .151 C3
Newbold Cl
Bentley Heath B93. . . . . . . .71 F5
Coventry CV3 . . . . .78 D8
Newbold Comyn Pk*
  CV32. . . . . .110 D8
Newbold Lawn CV32 . . . . .110 A8
Newbold Pl
Royal Leamington Spa
  CV32. . . . . .110 A8
Newbold Quarry Ctry Pk*
  CV21. . . . . .82 E6
Newbold Rd
Arnscote CV37 . . . . .136 E8
Rugby CV21 . . . . .83 A3
Rugby,Newbold on A CV21. .82 F6
Wellesbourne CV35 . . . . . .146 E4
Newbold Revel Coll CV23 .65 C6
Newbold Riverside Prim Sch
  CV21. . . . . .82 F4
Newbold St CV32. . . . . . . .110 A8
Newbold Terr E CV32. . . . .110 A8
Newbold Terr CV32. . . . . . .110 A8
Newbold & Tredington CE
  Prim Sch
  Newbold-on-S CV37. . . . .130 E1
  Tredington CV36. . . . . . .136 F1
Newborough Cl CV9 . . . . . . .3 A2
New Broad St CV37. . . . . .144 F1
New Brook St **3** CV32. . . .109 E8
Newburgh Cres CV34 . . . .108 E8
Newburgh Prim Sch
  CV34 . . . . .108 C4
Newbury Cl **4** CV31. . . . . .110 C6
Newby Gr B37 . . . . .33 B5
Newby Cl CV3 . . . . .77 E6
Newcastle Croft B35 . . . . . .22 C2
New Century Pk CV3. . . . . .62 C2
New Century Way CV11 . . .29 B4
New Cl CV35 . . . . .114 F3
New Combe Cl CV22 . . . . . .99 C3
Newcomen Cl CV12 . . . . . . .49 D8
Newcomen Rd CV12 . . . . . .38 D1
New Coppice Ct B97. . . . . .102 E6
New Cotts CV47 . . . . .144 E2
Newdegate Cl CV12 . . . . . . .39 A3
Newdegate Pl CV11 . . . . . . .29 C4
Newdegate Rd CV12 . . . . . .39 A3
Newdegate Prim Sch
  CV12 . . . . .38 C1
Newdigate Rd
Coventry CV6. . . . . .61 F6
Sutton Coldfield B75 . . . . . .13 A5
Newdigate CV31 . . . . .110 C5
New End Rd B46. . . . . .35 A4
Newent Cl B98 . . . . .112 A6
Newey Ave CV12 . . . . .49 D8
Newey Dr CV8. . . . . .93 A2
Newey Rd CV2 . . . . .62 D4
Newfield Ave CV8. . . . . .93 B3
Newfield Rd CV1. . . . . .61 C5
Newgale Wlk CV31. . . . . . .110 C7
New Gate Ct CV1 . . . . .151 C2
New Green Pk CV2 . . . . .62 D7
New Hall Inf Sch B75 . . . . .13 B5
New Hall Jun Sch B75 . . . .13 B5
Newhall Rd CV2 . . . . .62 D7
Newham Gn CV10 . . . . .28 C7
Newhaven Cl CV6. . . . . .60 E6
Newing Ct WR11. . . . . .127 D4
Newington Cl CV6 . . . . .60 E6
Newington Rd B37. . . . . . . .44 B8
New Inn La WR11. . . . . . . .127 D5
Newland Cl B98. . . . . .103 B7
Newland La CV7. . . . . .49 B7
Newland Rd
Coventry CV1. . . . . .61 D5
Royal Leamington Spa
  CV32. . . . . .106 C3
Newlands Cl CV3 . . . . .61 F2
Newlands La B37. . . . . .44 A6
Newlands Rd
Baddesley Ensor CV9. . . . . .11 C1
Bentley Heath B93. . . . . . . .71 F4
Newlands The B80 . . . . . . .103 D3
Newland St CV22 . . . . .82 C3
New Leasow B76 . . . . .22 B6
Newlyn Cl CV11. . . . . .29 F4
Newman Cl CV12 . . . . .39 B4
Newmarket Cl
Coventry CV6. . . . . .50 A4
Stratford-u-A CV37 . . . . . .129 F8
Newmarsh Rd B76. . . . . . . .22 A6
New Mill La B78 . . . . .9 A7
Newnham Ho B36. . . . . .33 B5
Newnham La B95. . . . . . . .120 C7
Newnham Rd
Coventry CV1. . . . . .61 F5
Royal Leamington Spa
  CV32. . . . . .106 B3
New Park Cotts OX15 . . . .137 F2
New Place & Nash's Ho
  (Mus)* CV37. . . . . .145 A2

New Pl OX17 . . . . 134 C1
Newport Cl B97 . . . . 102 B6
Newport Dr B49 . . . . 143 B3
Newport Rd CV6 . . . . 49 D1
Newquay Cl CV11 . . . . 29 F5
New Rd
 🔢 Moreton-in-M GL56 . . . . 140 A3
 Alderminster CV37 . . . . . . 130 D3
 Appleby Magna DE12 . . . . . . 3 E7
 Ash Green CV7 . . . . 49 B6
 Astwood Bank B96 . . . . . . 118 C8
 Corley CV12 . . . . 37 F2
 Coventry CV6 . . . . 48 F1
 Ebrington GL55 . . . . 135 E3
 Henley-in-A B95 . . . . 113 A4
 Hinckley LE10 . . . . 32 A6
 Hollywood B47 . . . . 69 A8
 Lowsonford CV35 . . . . 113 E6
 Norton Lindsey CV35 . . . . 114 C2
 Pebworth CV37 . . . . 128 F1
 Ratley OX15 . . . . 133 A2
 Shotteswell OX17 . . . . 139 E8
 Shuttington B79 . . . . 1 D2
 Studley B80 . . . . 103 E3
 Tamworth B77 . . . . 9 F7
 Temple Grafton B49 . . . . . 119 E1
 Temple Herdewyke CV47 . . 133 A6
 Water Orton B46 . . . . 23 B3
New Row
 Drayton Bassett B78 . . . . 8 E5
 Lower Quinton CV37 . . . . . 129 D2
Newscut La OX17 . . . . . . 134 C1
Newsholme Cl 🔢 CV34 . . 104 E1
New St
 Baddesley Ensor CV9 . . . . . 11 C1
 Bedworth CV12 . . . . 39 C2
 Birchmoor B78 . . . . 10 E7
 Bulkington CV12 . . . . 40 D2
 Cubbington CV32 . . . . 106 E5
 Dordon B78 . . . . 11 A5
Newstead Ave LE10 . . . . . 31 D4
Newstead Cl CV11 . . . . . . 29 F2
Newstead Dr CV47 . . . . . 147 A3
Newstead Way CV23 . . . . 63 B1
New St
 Fazeley B78 . . . . 9 B8
 Kenilworth CV8 . . . . 92 F6
 Napton on t H CV47 . . . . . 125 C7
 Royal Leamington Spa
 CV31 . . . . 110 A7
 Rugby CV22 . . . . 82 E3
 Shipston-on-S CV36 . . . . . 149 D5
 Stratford-u-A CV37 . . . . . 144 F1
 Tiddington CV37 . . . . 145 E4
 Warwick CV34 . . . . 108 E6
Newton Cl
 Coventry CV2 . . . . 62 F7
 Hartshill Green CV10 . . . . . 19 B2
 Redditch B98 . . . . 103 A6
Newton La
 Newton CV23 . . . . 68 A3
 Newton Regis CV9 . . . . 2 F2
 Seckington B79 . . . . 2 B3
Newton Manor La CV21,
 CV23 . . . . 83 E7
Newton Rd
 Clifton u D CV23 . . . . 84 A7
 Hinckley LE10 . . . . 30 E7
 Knowle B93 . . . . 72 B7
Newton Regis CE Prim Sch
 B79 . . . . 2 E3
Newtown Bldgs CV12 . . . . 39 B3
New Town CV36 . . . . 150 B8
Newtown Rd
 Bedworth CV12 . . . . 39 A2
 Nuneaton CV11 . . . . 29 C5
Newtown WR11 . . . . 127 E1
Nibbits La NN11 . . . . 117 E5
Nicholas Chamberlaine Tec
 Coll CV12 . . . . 39 D3
Nicholas Cl CV4 . . . . 39 C3
Nicholas Everton Cl CV8 . . 80 A5
Nicholls St CV2 . . . . 61 F4
Nicholson Cl CV34 . . . . . 104 F1
Nickson Rd CV4 . . . . 59 E1
Nightingale Ave B36 . . . . . 33 A8
Nightingale Cl
 Atherstone CV9 . . . . 12 E1
 Great Alne B49 . . . . 119 D6
Nightingale Ct CV31 . . . . 110 B8
Nightingale Gdns CV23 . . . 67 C1
Nightingale La
 Cleeve Prior WR11 . . . . . . 128 A4
 Coventry CV5 . . . . 76 E7
Nightingale Rd CV10 . . . . . 46 A6
Nimbus B77 . . . . 9 D4
Nineacres Dr B37 . . . . 33 A3
Nine Days La B98 . . . . . . 103 B6
Ninefoot La
 Tamworth,Belgrave B77 . . . . 9 E8
 Tamworth,Wilnecote B77 . . . 9 F7
Ninian Pk B77 . . . . 9 D6
Ninian Way B77 . . . . 9 E6
Niton Rd CV10 . . . . 29 C6
Niven Cl CV5 . . . . 60 A6
Noble Cl CV34 . . . . 108 D5
Noble Dr CV22 . . . . 99 A2
Node Hill Cl B80 . . . . 103 D3
Node Hill B80 . . . . 103 D3
Nod Rise CV5 . . . . 60 B3
Noel Ct
 Chipping Campden GL55 . . 135 B2
 Redditch B97 . . . . 102 C8
Nolan Cl CV6 . . . . 49 D4

No Man's Heath La CV9 . . . 3 A3
Nook The CV11 . . . . 29 E2
Norcombe Gr B90 . . . . 71 A5
Nordic Drift CV2 . . . . 63 A6
Norfolk Cl LE10 . . . . 31 D4
Norfolk Cres CV10 . . . . . . 28 E4
Norfolk St
 Coventry CV1 . . . . 61 B3
 Royal Leamington Spa
 CV32 . . . . 106 A1
Norluck Ct CV36 . . . . 149 D6
Norman Ashman Coppice
 CV3 . . . . 79 C7
Norman Ave
 Coventry CV2 . . . . 50 F1
 Nuneaton CV11 . . . . 29 B4
Normandy Mdws CV31 . . . 110 A2
Normandy Cl CV35 . . . . . 108 A7
Normandy Way LE10 . . . . . 21 F2
Norman Place Rd CV6 . . . . 60 F7
Norman Rd CV21 . . . . 82 F6
Norsefair The B95 . . . . . . 113 B4
Northampton La CV22 . . . . 99 D4
North Ave
 Bedworth CV12 . . . . 39 D2
 Birmingham B40 . . . . 44 F5
 Coventry CV2 . . . . 62 A3
Northbourne Dr CV11 . . . . 39 F7
North Brook Rd CV6 . . . . . 60 D8
North Circular Rd GL56 . . 140 C4
North Cl
 Braunston NN11 . . . . 117 E5
 Cubbington CV32 . . . . 106 E5
 Hinckley LE10 . . . . 31 E6
Northcote Rd CV21 . . . . . . 82 F3
Northcote St 🔢 CV31 . . . 110 B7
Northcote Wlk CV9 . . . . . . 12 D2
North Dr B95 . . . . 113 A5
Northend Rd CV47 . . . . . . 133 C7
Northey Rd CV6 . . . . 61 D8
Northfield Rd
 Coventry CV1 . . . . 61 F2
 Hinckley LE10 . . . . 31 C7
 Southam CV47 . . . . 147 A3
Northfolk Terr CV4 . . . . . . 76 B7
Northgate St CV34 . . . . . 108 E7
Northgate CV34 . . . . 108 E7
Northlands Prim Sch
 CV21 . . . . 83 B4
**North Leamington Com Sch
 & Arts Coll** CV32 . . . . . 105 F4
**North Leamington Com Sch
 & Arts Coll (Sixth Form)**
 CV32 . . . . 105 F2
Northolt Dr B35 . . . . 22 A4
North Rd CV23 . . . . 83 F6
Northside Cl B98 . . . . 102 E7
North St
 Atherstone CV9 . . . . 18 E8
 Coventry CV2 . . . . 62 B5
 Kilsby CV23 . . . . 101 F3
 Marton CV23 . . . . 115 C7
 Nuneaton CV10 . . . . 28 F3
 Rugby CV21 . . . . 83 A3
Northumberland Ave
 CV10 . . . . 28 F3
Northumberland Lodge
 CV32 . . . . 105 F1
Northumberland Mews
 CV32 . . . . 105 F1
Northumberland Pk
 CV32 . . . . 105 F1
Northumberland Rd
 Coventry CV1 . . . . 61 A3
 Royal Leamington Spa
 CV32 . . . . 105 E2
Northvale Cl CV8 . . . . 93 B6
North View CV7 . . . . 51 A1
North Villiers St CV32 . . . 106 A1
**North Warwickshire &
 Hinkley Coll (Atherstone
 Coll)** CV9 . . . . 18 E8
**North Warwickshire &
 Hinkley Coll**
 Hinckley LE10 . . . . 31 F8
 Nuneaton CV11 . . . . 29 E6
Northway
 🔢 Rugby CV21 . . . . 83 A3
 Birmingham B40 . . . . 44 F5
 Whitnash CV31 . . . . 110 A5
Norton Curlieu La CV35 . . 114 C3
Norton Dr
 Warwick CV34 . . . . 104 E2
 Wythall B47 . . . . 69 C4
Norton Gdns CV37 . . . . . 128 F1
Norton Grange CV5 . . . . . . 60 C6
Norton Green La B93 . . . . . 72 C2
Norton Hill Dr CV2 . . . . . . 62 E6
Norton La
 Austrey CV9 . . . . 3 D1
 Orton-on-H CV9 . . . . 6 D6
 Tidbury Green B47,B90,B94 . 69 E3
Norton Lea CV35 . . . . 114 C2
Norton Leys CV22 . . . . 99 F6
Norton Rd B46 . . . . 33 F8
Nortons Cl CV47 . . . . 133 B7
Norton's La CV35 . . . . . . 142 F8
Norton St CV1 . . . . 151 C3
Norton View GL55 . . . . . . 135 B6
Noral Cres WR11 . . . . . . 127 D1
Norwich Cl CV11 . . . . 30 A8
Norwich Dr CV3 . . . . 77 B5
Norwood Gr CV2 . . . . 50 E2
Norwood Ho 🔢 CV32 . . . 105 F2
Nova Croft CV5 . . . . 59 C4
Nova Lodge CV32 . . . . . . 105 E3
Nuffield Ho B36 . . . . 33 A8

Nuffield Rd
 Coventry CV6 . . . . 62 A7
 Hinckley LE10 . . . . 30 E7
Nugent Gr B90 . . . . 70 D3
**Nuneaton Borough Football
 Club** CV11 . . . . 29 A4
Nuneaton La CV13 . . . . . . 29 F2
Nuneaton Mus & Art Gal*
 CV11 . . . . 29 C3
Nuneaton Rd
 Ansley Common CV10 . . . . . 27 B6
 Atherstone CV9,CV10 . . . . . 19 B4
 Bedworth CV12 . . . . 39 B4
 Bulkington CV12 . . . . 40 B4
 Fillongley CV7 . . . . 36 F4
 Furnace End B46 . . . . 25 E2
 Furnace End,Monwode Lea
 B46 . . . . 26 C5
 Hartshill Green CV10 . . . . . 19 B2
Nuneaton Trent Valley Sta
 CV11 . . . . 29 C4
Nunhold Farm Bsns Ctr
 CV35 . . . . 114 D4
Nunts La CV6 . . . . 49 B3
Nunts Park Ave CV6 . . . . . 49 B4
Nunwood La CV23 . . . . 96 A2
Nursery Cl
 Mickleton GL55 . . . . 135 C2
 Moreton-in-M GL56 . . . . . 140 A4
Nursery Gdns B90 . . . . 69 E8
Nursery Hill Prim Sch
 CV10 . . . . 27 E8
Nursery La CV31 . . . . 110 A5
Nursery Rd
 Ansley Common CV10 . . . . . 27 B8
 Atherstone CV9 . . . . 18 F7
 Rugby CV22 . . . . 99 D6
Occupation Rd CV2 . . . . . . 62 C3
Oddfellows' Terr 🔢
 GL56 . . . . 140 A3
Oddicombe Croft CV3 . . . . 77 D5
Odingsel Dr CV47 . . . . . . 115 C4
Odstone Dr LE10 . . . . 30 F8
Offa Dr CV8 . . . . 93 A4
Offa Rd CV31 . . . . 110 B5
Offchurch La CV31 . . . . . 110 F6
Offchurch Rd CV32 . . . . . 106 E4
Offenham CE Fst Sch
 WR11 . . . . 127 D1
Ogley Dr B75 . . . . 13 A3
Okeford Way CV10 . . . . . . 29 A1
Okehampton Rd CV3 . . . . . 77 E5
Okement Gr CV23 . . . . 82 B5
Oken Ct CV34 . . . . 108 D7
Oken Rd CV34 . . . . 108 D8
Olaf Pl CV2 . . . . 63 A7
Oldany Way CV10 . . . . 28 F2
Oldberrow Cl 🔢 B90 . . . . 71 A6
Oldborough Dr CV35 . . . . 130 E8
Old Bowling Gn The
 CV36 . . . . 149 D5
Old Brewery Cl CV36 . . . . 149 E7
Old Budbrooke Rd CV35 . . 108 A8
Oldbury Rd CV10 . . . . 18 F1
Oldbury View CV10 . . . . . . 19 B1
Oldbutt Rd CV36 . . . . 149 C5
Old Chapel Wlk LE17 . . . . 43 E6
Old Church Rd
 Coventry CV6 . . . . 50 A1
 Water Orton B46 . . . . 23 B3
Old Council Hos The
 OX15 . . . . 139 D6
Old Courtyard The CV3 . . . 107 D7
Old Crown Mews CV2 . . . . 50 D5
Old Damson La B92 . . . . . . 44 A2
Old Dickens Heath Rd
 B90 . . . . 70 A5
Old Farm La B46 . . . . 25 A5
Old Farm Rd CV9 . . . . 18 F6
Oldfield Rd CV5 . . . . 60 E3
Old Ford Ave CV47 . . . . . . 147 A5
Old Forge Bsns Ctr B98 . . 103 C8
Old Forge Dr B98 . . . . 103 C8
Old Forge Rd
 Fenny Drayton CV13 . . . . . . 20 A6
 Great Rollright CV7 . . . . . . 142 A2
Old Forge The OX15 . . . . . 142 F8
Old Fosse Way CV36 . . . . . 136 F7
Old Gated Rd The CV33,
 CV35 . . . . 123 C4
Old Gram School Mews
 GL55 . . . . 135 B2
Old Green La CV8 . . . . 73 C1
Old Hall Ct B79 . . . . 2 C2
Oldham Ave CV2 . . . . 62 E4
Oldham Way CV23 . . . . 82 B4
Old Hedging La B77 . . . . . . 9 D5
Old Hinckley Rd CV10 . . . . 29 D5
Old Holly La CV9 . . . . 12 C3
Old House La CV7 . . . . 48 A7
Oldington Gr B91 . . . . 71 B8
Old Kingsbury Rd B76 . . . . 22 C5
Old Langley Hall B75 . . . . . 13 C4
Old La B48 . . . . 85 D4
Old Leicester Rd CV21 . . . . 83 A7
Old Manor Cl B78 . . . . 8 E5
Old Manor Gdns GL55 . . . 135 C6
Old Market Way 🔢 GL56 . 140 A3
Old Meeting Yd 🔢 CV12 . . 39 B3
Old Mill Ave CV4 . . . . 76 D5
Old Mill Rd B46 . . . . 23 B2
Old Milverton La CV32 . . . 105 E5
Old Milverton CV32 . . . . . 105 C3
Old Milverton Rd CV32 . . . 105 C4
Old Orchard The
 Birdingbury CV23 . . . . 115 F7
 Ebrington GL55 . . . . 135 E3
Old Penns La B46 . . . . 33 F7
Old Penn's Yd 🔢 CV12 . . . 39 A2

Oak St CV22 . . . . 83 A2
Oakthorpe Dr B37 . . . . 33 A5
Oak Tree Ave CV3 . . . . 77 A6
Oaktree Cl CV37 . . . . 120 D7
Oak Tree Cl B93 . . . . 71 E4
Oaktree Cl
 Kingsbury B78 . . . . 15 D6
 Moreton Morrell CV35 . . . . 122 E3
Oak Tree Cl CV32 . . . . . . 106 A2
Oak Tree Cl CV8 . . . . 106 A2
**Oaktree Farm Mobile Homes
 Pk** B94 . . . . 86 B7
Oak Tree La
 Cookhill B49 . . . . 118 D5
 Hollywood B47 . . . . 69 B6
 Sambourne B96 . . . . 103 B2
Oak Tree Rd
 Coventry CV3 . . . . 79 A7
 Harvington WR11 . . . . 127 C4
Oak Trees B47 . . . . 69 A7
Oak Way CV4 . . . . 59 D2
Oakwood Cl CV9 . . . . 11 C1
Oakwood Gr CV34 . . . . . . 105 A1
Oakwood Rd B47 . . . . 69 A6
Oakworth Cl CV2 . . . . 62 F8
Oaston Rd CV11 . . . . 29 D4
Oatlands Cl CV11 . . . . 49 C4
Oban Dr CV10 . . . . 29 A2
Oban Rd
 Coventry CV6 . . . . 49 F5
 Hinckley LE10 . . . . 31 A7
Oberon Cl
 Nuneaton CV11 . . . . 30 A1
 Royal Leamington Spa
 CV34 . . . . 109 E4
 Rugby CV22 . . . . 99 D6
Occupation Rd CV2 . . . . . . 62 C3

Old Pound Cotts CV36 . . . 137 A8
Old Pump Ho The WR11 . . 127 E2
Old Rd
 Bishops Itchington CV47 . . 124 B4
 Braunston NN11 . . . . 117 E4
 Meriden CV7 . . . . 46 E1
 Ratley OX15 . . . . 132 F2
 Shipston-on-S CV36 . . . . . 149 D5
 Southam CV47 . . . . 147 A3
Old Rectory Cl CV23 . . . . . 67 C6
Old Rectory Gdn B49 . . . . 143 B4
Old Rectory The CV37 . . . 130 A6
Old Red Lion Ct 🔢 CV37 . 145 A2
Old School Cl WR11 . . . . . 127 D1
Old School End OX15 . . . . 142 D4
Old School La
 Hampton Magna CV35 . . . . 114 F3
 Lighthorne CV35 . . . . 123 C2
 Wilmcote CV37 . . . . 120 C4
Old School Mews CV32 . . . 106 B3
Old School The CV36 . . . . 149 D6
Old School Yd The B77 . . . . 4 A5
Old Snitterfield Rd CV37 . . 121 B7
Old Sq The CV37 . . . . 144 D2
Old Sq CV34 . . . . 108 E6
Old Station Rd B92 . . . . . . 57 A8
Old Stone Yd CV32 . . . . . . 105 E1
Old Tollgate The CV37 . . . 145 D6
Old Town 🔢 GL56 . . . . . . 140 A3
Old Town Mews CV37 . . . . 144 F1
Old Town CV37 . . . . 145 A1
Old Tree Cotts CV36 . . . . . 136 C1
Old Tree La CV35 . . . . 138 B6
Old Vicarage Gdns B80 . . . 103 E4
Old Walled Gdn The
 CV35 . . . . 131 C3
Old Warwick Rd
 Kingswood B94,CV35 . . . . . 89 D3
 Rowington CV35 . . . . 114 A7
 Royal Leamington Spa
 CV31 . . . . 109 C7
Old Waste La CV7 . . . . 74 E6
Old Watling St CV9 . . . . . . 11 E3
Oldwich La E
 Balsall Common CV8 . . . . . 73 D1
 Honiley CV8 . . . . 90 E8
Oldwich La W B93 . . . . 90 C8
Old Winnings Rd CV7 . . . . 48 F6
Old Yd The CV2 . . . . 62 F7
Olive Ave CV2 . . . . 62 D5
Olivers Lock 🔢 CV37 . . . 145 A3
Oliver St
 Coventry CV6 . . . . 61 F6
 Rugby CV21 . . . . 82 F3
Olivier Way CV2 . . . . 63 B8
Olney Rd CV35 . . . . 132 D3
Olton Ave CV5 . . . . 59 E4
Olton Cl CV11 . . . . 41 A8
Olton Pl CV11 . . . . 28 F4
Olympus Ave CV34 . . . . . . 109 D5
Olympus Cl CV5 . . . . 59 B8
Omar Rd CV2 . . . . 62 D2
Ombersley Cl B98 . . . . . . 103 C7
Omega Pl CV21 . . . . 83 B4
Onley La CV22 . . . . 100 D6
Onley Pk CV23 . . . . 117 B8
Onley Terr CV4 . . . . 76 C7
Onslow Croft CV32 . . . . . 105 F2
Openfield Croft B46 . . . . . 23 C2
Ophelia Dr CV34 . . . . 109 E3
Oratory Dr CV3 . . . . 78 C6
Orchard Cl
 Austrey CV9 . . . . 3 A2
 Badby NN11 . . . . 126 F6
 Bidford-on-A B50 . . . . 148 D4
 Bishops Itchington CV47 . . 124 B4
 Coleshill B46 . . . . 33 F7
 Curdworth B76 . . . . 23 B7
 Hartshill B78 . . . . 28 B7
 Hinckley LE10 . . . . 32 A5
 Hurley CV9 . . . . 16 C4
 Lower Brailes OX15 . . . . . 137 F2
 Mickleton GL55 . . . . 135 C2
 Polesworth B78 . . . . 5 A3
 Shipston-on-S CV36 . . . . . 149 D5
 Welford-on-A CV37 . . . . . 129 B6
 Witherley CV9 . . . . 19 B8
 Wolvey LE10 . . . . 41 D4
Orchard Cnr B49 . . . . 119 E4
Orchard Cres CV3 . . . . 77 C8
Orchard Ct
 Atherstone CV9 . . . . 19 A4
 Coventry CV3 . . . . 63 A1
 Lower Quinton CV37 . . . . . 129 D2
Orchard Dr
 Alcester B49 . . . . 143 B3
 Coventry CV5 . . . . 59 D4
Orchard Gr
 Astwood Bank B96 . . . . . . 118 C8
 Stockton CV47 . . . . 147 F4
 Wood End B94 . . . . 93 C3
Orchard Meadow Wlk
 B35 . . . . 22 B3
Orchard Piece OX17 . . . . . 134 A2
Orchard Pl
 Clifford Chambers CV37 . . 129 F7
 Harvington WR11 . . . . 127 D4
 Redditch B80 . . . . 103 F8
Orchard Rd
 Hockley Heath B94 . . . . 88 C6
 Hook Norton OX15 . . . . . . 142 D4
Orchard Ret Pk CV3 . . . . . 78 D4
Orchard Rise
 Baddesley Ensor CV9 . . . . . 11 C1
 Binton CV37 . . . . 120 A1
Orchard St CV12 . . . . 39 A2

Orchards The
Astwood Bank B96 . . . . . . 102 D1
Cheswick Green B90 . . . . . . 70 D4
Hollywood B47 . . . . 69 A7
Newton CV23 . . . . 67 F1
Orchard St
Hinckley LE10 . . . . 31 E8
Nuneaton CV11 . . . . 29 C4
Orchard The
Baxterley CV9 . . . . 17 C7
Lower Quinton CV37 . . . . 129 D2
Marton CV23 . . . . 115 C7
Staverton NN11 . . . . 126 D8
Upper Boddington NN11 . . 134 E8
Whatcote CV36 . . . . 137 E7
Orchard View OX17 . . . . 134 C1
Orchard Way
Bubbenhall CV8 . . . . 95 D5
Hollywood B47 . . . . 69 A8
Long Itchington CV47 . . . 115 C4
Nuneaton CV10 . . . . 28 C6
Rugby CV22 . . . . 99 D8
Southam CV47 . . . . 147 B5
Stratford-u-A CV37 . . . . . 144 E2
Stretton-on-D CV23 . . . . . . 96 F6
Studley B80 . . . . 103 C2
Orchid Cl CV12 . . . . 38 E2
Orchid Way CV23 . . . . 83 D8
Ordnance Rd CV6 . . . . 61 E5
Orford Cl CV35 . . . . 146 E3
Orford Rise CV10 . . . . 27 E4
Oriel Cl GL56 . . . . 140 A2
Oriel Ho B37 . . . . 33 A3
Orion Cres CV2 . . . . 50 E2
Orkney Cl CV10 . . . . 28 C8
Orkney Croft B36 . . . . 33 B7
Orkney Dr B77 . . . . 9 F7
Orlando Cl CV22 . . . . 99 D6
Orlescote Rd CV4 . . . . 76 E6
Orpington Dr CV6 . . . . 49 D4
Orrian Cl CV37 . . . . 144 E5
Orsino Cl CV34 . . . . 109 E2
Orson Leys CV22 . . . . 99 F7
Orton Ave B76 . . . . 22 A2
Orton Hill CV9 . . . . 23 A3
Orton Hill CV9 . . . . 6 B8
Orton La
Austrey CV9 . . . . 6 B8
Orton-on-t-H CV9 . . . . 3 F2
Orton-on-t-H CV9 . . . . 6 D5
Orton-on-t-H CV9 . . . . 6 F2
Orton Rd
Coventry CV6 . . . . 49 D4
Warton B79,CV9 . . . . 5 E3
Orton Way B35 . . . . 22 A1
Orwell Cl
Clifton u D CV23 . . . . 84 A5
Nuneaton CV10 . . . . 28 A5
Orwell Ct CV1 . . . . 151 C4
Orwell Rd CV1 . . . . 61 F1
Osbaston Cl CV5 . . . . 59 E4
Osborne Ct CV31 . . . . 110 A4
Osborne Rd CV5 . . . . 77 A8
Osborne Croft B90 . . . . . . 70 D5
Osborne Ho CV1 . . . . 151 A2
Oslo Gdns CV2 . . . . 63 A7
Osney Cl OX15 . . . . 142 D4
Osprey Cl
Coventry CV2 . . . . 63 B6
Nuneaton CV11 . . . . 40 B8
Osprey Ho B80 . . . . 103 D4
Osprey B77 . . . . 10 A6
Ossetts Hole La CV35 . . . 113 E4
Oswald Rd CV32 . . . . 109 D8
Oswald Way CV22 . . . . 82 D3
Oswestry Cl B97 . . . . 102 C7
Oswin Gr CV2 . . . . 62 C4
Othello Ave CV34 . . . . . . 109 F3
Othello Cl CV22 . . . . 99 C5
Otter St CV6 . . . . 62 A8
Otterstone Rd CV7 . . . . . . 52 F5
Otters Rest CV31 . . . . . . 110 C5
Ottery B77 . . . . 10 B5
Our Lady of the Angels RC
Inf Sch CV11 . . . . 29 C3
Our Lady of the Assumption
RC Prim Sch CV4 . . . . 59 E1
Our Lady Of the Wayside RC
Prim Sch B90 . . . . 70 C8
Our Lady & St Teresa's RC
Prim Sch CV32 . . . . 106 D5
Our Lady's RC Prim Sch
Alcester B49 . . . . 143 B4
Princethorpe CV23 . . . . . . 96 D2
Ousterne La CV7 . . . . 36 D3
Outermarch Rd CV6 . . . . . 61 B6
Outlands Dr LE10 . . . . 21 F1
Outwood Cl B98 . . . . 102 E7
Outwoods Cl CV7 . . . . 18 C7
Outwoods The LE10 . . . . . 31 E8
Oval Rd CV22 . . . . 100 D8
Overbare Cl B94 . . . . 87 A1
Overberry Cl CV2 . . . . 50 D2
Overberry Orch CV23 . . . . 82 C1
Overdale B96 . . . . 102 E1
Overdale Rd CV5 . . . . 60 C3
Overell Gr CV32 . . . . 105 D2
Overslade Cres CV6 . . . . . 60 E8
Overslade La CV22 . . . . . . 99 E8
Overslade Manor Dr CV22 . 99 F8
Oversley Ho B49 . . . . 143 C4
Oversley Mill Pk B49 . . . . 143 B2
Oversley Rd B76 . . . . 13 A5
Over St CV6 . . . . 62 A8
Overstone Rd CV7 . . . . 52 F5
Overton Dr B46 . . . . 23 C3
Overtons Cl CV31 . . . . . . 110 F5
Overwoods Rd B77 . . . . . . 10 A4
Ownford Rd CV6 . . . . 61 C7

Owen Sq CV9 . . . . 18 D8
Owen St CV9 . . . . 18 D8
Owl End La NN11 . . . . . . 134 E7
Owl End Way NN11 . . . . . 134 E7
Owlets End B50 . . . . 148 F3
Ox Cl CV2 . . . . 62 A6
Oxendon Way CV3 . . . . . . 78 E8
Oxford Cl CV11 . . . . 29 F8
Oxford Pl 4 CV32 . . . . . 105 F1
Oxford Rd
Marton CV23 . . . . 115 D7
Princethorpe CV23 . . . . . . 96 D4
Oxford Row 16 CV32 . . . 105 F1
Oxford St
16 Moreton-in-M GL56 . . 140 A3
Coventry CV1 . . . . 61 E3
Royal Leamington Spa
CV32 . . . . 105 F1
Rugby CV21 . . . . 83 C3
Southam CV47 . . . . 147 B4
Oxford Way CV35 . . . . . . 146 B1
Oxhayes Cl CV7 . . . . 74 C6
Oxhey Hill OX17 . . . . 134 B2
Oxhill Bridle Rd CV35 . . 131 E3
Oxhill Rd CV35 . . . . 138 B6
Ox Leys Rd B75,B76 . . . . . 13 D3
Oxstall Cl B76 . . . . 22 D5
Oxstalls Cotts CV37 . . . . 145 D6
Oxway Cl CV36 . . . . 149 D6

P

Packhorse Rd CV37 . . . . 144 B4
Packington Ave CV5 . . . . . 60 B6
Packington La
Coleshill B46,CV7 . . . . 34 B2
Little Packington CV7 . . . . . 45 C6
Maxstoke B46 . . . . 35 B1
Packington Pl 6 CV31 . . 110 A7
Packmores B90 . . . . 70 A5
Packmore St CV34 . . . . . 108 F8
Packsaddle Hill CV37 . . . 145 E8
Packwood Ave CV21 . . . . 101 C8
Packwood Cl
Bentley Heath B93 . . . . 71 E4
Nuneaton CV11 . . . . 39 F8
Royal Leamington Spa
CV31 . . . . 110 C5
Packwood Cotts B93 . . . . . 71 F1
Packwood Gn CV5 . . . . 60 A3
Packwood Ho * B94 . . . . . 89 A5
Packwood Mews 5
CV34 . . . . 109 B8
Packwood Rd B94 . . . . 89 A7
Paddiford Pl CV10 . . . . 28 C3
Paddock Cl
Bidford-on-A B50 . . . . . . 148 C5
Napton on t H CV47 . . . . . 125 C8
Paddock Dr B93 . . . . 72 A2
Paddock La
Redditch B98 . . . . 102 E7
Stratford-u-A CV37 . . . . . 144 E1
Paddocks Cl
Polesworth B78 . . . . 4 F1
Wolston CV8 . . . . 80 A3
Paddocks The
Bulkington CV12 . . . . 40 B3
Kenilworth CV8 . . . . 93 B5
Mollington OX17 . . . . 133 F2
Norton WR11 . . . . 127 B2
Stretton-on-D CV23 . . . . . . 96 F5
Warwick CV34 . . . . 108 F7
Paddock The
Claybrooke Magna LE17 . . . 43 E6
Lower Boddington NN11 . . 134 E7
Newton CV23 . . . . 68 A1
Sutton Coldfield B76 . . . . . 13 A4
Paddock Way LE10 . . . . . . 30 E6
Paddox Cl CV22 . . . . 100 F8
Paddox Prim Sch
Rugby CV22 . . . . 100 D8
Rugby CV22 . . . . 100 D8
Padgate Cl B35 . . . . 22 B3
Padmore Ct CV31 . . . . . . 110 B6
Padstow Cl CV11 . . . . 29 F5
Padstow Rd CV4 . . . . 75 E8
Padua 3 CV37 . . . . 145 A3
Page Rd CV4 . . . . 75 E7
Pages La OX15 . . . . 139 B7
Paget Ct CV2 . . . . 50 B3
Paget Mews B76 . . . . 13 A2
Paget's La CV8 . . . . 95 D5
Pailton Cl CV2 . . . . 50 C2
Pailton Rd CV23 . . . . 66 B3
Painswick Cl B98 . . . . . . 102 E6
Pake's Croft 3 CV6 . . . . . 61 A5
Palefield Rd B90 . . . . 70 F6
Palermo Ave CV3 . . . . 77 E6
Pallett Dr CV11 . . . . 29 F7
Palmer La CV1 . . . . 151 B3
Palmer Rd CV31 . . . . 110 B6
Palmer's Cl CV21 . . . . . . 101 B8
Palmers Leys 5 CV35 . . 132 B6
Palmerston Ave B77 . . . . . . 9 E6
Palmerston Ct B77 . . . . . . 9 F6
Palmerston Rd CV5 . . . . . . 76 F8
Palm Tree Ave CV2 . . . . . . 50 C2
Pampas Cl CV37 . . . . 144 E5
Pancras Cl CV2 . . . . 50 E2
Pandora Rd CV2 . . . . 50 E1
Pangbourne Cl CV11 . . . . . 29 F8
Pangbourne Rd CV2 . . . . . 62 C8
Pangfield Pk CV5 . . . . 60 C4
Pantolf Pl CV21 . . . . 82 C7
Papenham Gn CV4 . . . . . . 76 A8

Parade CV32 . . . . 109 F8
Parade The
6 Hinckley LE10 . . . . 31 D8
Birmingham B37 . . . . 33 A5
Nuneaton CV11 . . . . 29 C4
Paradise Ho 4 CV6 . . . . . 61 F7
Paradise St
Coventry CV1 . . . . 151 C1
Warwick CV34 . . . . 108 F8
Paradise Way CV2 . . . . . . 51 B1
Paradise Works CV6 . . . . . 61 F7
Paragon Pk CV1 . . . . 61 D6
Paragon Way CV7 . . . . 50 B8
Parbrook Cl CV4 . . . . 75 E8
Parbury B77 . . . . 9 D5
Parish End CV31 . . . . 110 C4
Parkinstone Ho CV5 . . . . . 60 E2
Park Ave
Coleshill B46 . . . . 33 F6
Coventry CV6 . . . . 49 C3
Nuneaton CV11 . . . . 29 E3
Polesworth B78 . . . . 11 B8
Studley B80 . . . . 103 B3
Park Cl
Avon Dassett CV47 . . . . . 133 C4
Claverdon CV35 . . . . 113 F3
Hanwell OX17 . . . . 139 F6
Hook Norton OX15 . . . . . 142 D3
Kenilworth CV8 . . . . 93 B5
Wilmcote CV37 . . . . 120 C4
Park Cotts CV33 . . . . 115 B8
Park Croft B47 . . . . 69 A5
Park Ct
Allesley CV5 . . . . 60 A6
Stratford-u-A CV37 . . . . . 144 E4
Park Dr
Claverdon CV35 . . . . 113 F3
Royal Leamington Spa
CV31 . . . . 109 E7
Parkend CV21 . . . . 83 C7
Parke Row CV35 . . . . 138 B6
Parkers La GL56 . . . . 140 A3
Parkes Cl CV34 . . . . 108 D7
Parkes St CV34 . . . . 108 D7
Park Farm CV12 . . . . 22 B2
Park Farm Ind Est B98 . . 103 C7
Parkfield Cl B77 . . . . 9 C8
Parkfield Cres B77 . . . . . . 9 C8
Parkfield Ct 11 B46 . . . . . 23 F1
Parkfield B93 . . . . 72 A1
Parkfield Dr
Birmingham B36 . . . . 22 C1
Kenilworth CV8 . . . . 93 B5
Parkfield Rd
Coleshill B46 . . . . 33 F6
Keresley CV7 . . . . 49 A6
Rugby CV21 . . . . 82 E5
Parkfields CV47 . . . . 147 B4
Parkgate Prim Sch CV6 . . 49 B3
Parkgate Rd CV6 . . . . 49 C3
Park Gates CV33 . . . . 111 B8
Park Gr B46 . . . . 23 C2
Park Hall Cres B36 . . . . . . 22 E1
Park Hall Mews WR11 . . . 127 E6
Park Hall WR11 . . . . 127 E6
Parkhill Dr CV5 . . . . 60 A5
Park Hill OX15 . . . . 142 D4
Park Hill Jun Sch CV8 . . . 93 C5
Park Hill CV8 . . . . 93 B5
Park Hill La
Allesley CV5 . . . . 60 A6
Coventry CV5 . . . . 60 A6
Park Hill NN11 . . . . 116 F1
Park Hill Prim Sch CV5 . . . 60 A4
Parkinson Dr CV9 . . . . 12 E2
Park La
Astley CV10 . . . . 37 C5
Berkswell CV7 . . . . 58 B2
Birmingham,Castle Vale
B35 . . . . 22 C4
Galley Common CV10 . . . . 27 F3
Great Alne B49 . . . . 119 D6
Harbury CV33 . . . . 123 F7
Ilmington CV36 . . . . 135 F7
Lower Quinton CV37 . . . . 129 D2
Lower Shuckburgh NN11 . 116 F1
Parkland Cl CV6 . . . . 49 C3
Parklands Ave CV32 . . . . 106 C4
Park Lane Terr CV33 . . . . 123 F7
Park La
North Newington OX15 . . 139 E2
Snitterfield CV37 . . . . 121 C6
Southam CV47 . . . . 147 B4
Swalcliffe OX15 . . . . 142 F8
Park Paling The CV3 . . . . . 77 E7
Park Piece CV33 . . . . 123 F7
Park Rd
Baddesley Ensor CV9 . . . . . 11 B1
Bedworth CV12 . . . . 39 B2
Chipping Campden GL55 . 135 A1
Coleshill B46 . . . . 33 F6
Coventry CV1 . . . . 151 B1
Hinckley LE10 . . . . 31 C8
Hook Norton OX15 . . . . . 142 D4
Kenilworth CV8 . . . . 93 A4
Polesworth B78 . . . . 11 B8
Royal Leamington Spa
CV32 . . . . 106 A4
Rugby CV21 . . . . 83 A4
Stratford-u-A CV37 . . . . . 144 F4
Tamworth B77 . . . . 9 C5
Park Sq B37 . . . . 44 D8

Park St
Coventry CV6 . . . . 61 E7
Nuneaton CV11 . . . . 29 D3
Parkstone Rd CV6 . . . . 49 F2
Park St CV32 . . . . 105 F1
Park The
Lower Brailes OX15 . . . . . 137 F2
Stratford-u-A CV37 . . . . . 129 C8
Park View Ave 108 E4
Park View Cl CV7 . . . . 50 A8
Park View CV3 . . . . 62 A2
Parkview CV5 . . . . 151 A1
Park View B94 . . . . 88 C6
Park View La CV37 . . . . . 130 E1
Park View Cl CV6 . . . . 49 C3
Parkway CV2 . . . . 63 A8
Parkwood Ct CV8 . . . . 93 B5
Park Wood La CV4 . . . . 75 D7
Parmington Cl B97 . . . . . 102 B6
Parmiter Ho CV32 . . . . . . 105 F2
Parnell Cl CV21 . . . . 82 F3
Parolles Cl CV34 . . . . 109 E3
Parr Cl CV34 . . . . 109 D6
Parrotts Gr CV2 . . . . 50 D5
Parry Rd CV2 . . . . 62 F8
Parsonage Cl 13 CV33 . . 122 F8
Parsons Cl
Shipston-on-S CV36 . . . . 149 D5
Willey CV23 . . . . 54 F6
Parsons Hollow B77 . . . . . . 9 E7
Parson's La LE10 . . . . 31 F8
Parson's Nook CV2 . . . . . . 62 A5
Parsons Rd NN11 . . . . . . 117 F3
Parson St B77 . . . . 9 F7
Partridge Cl
Birmingham B37 . . . . 33 D3
Charwelton NN11 . . . . . . 126 D3
Partridge Croft CV6 . . . . . 50 A1
Partridge La B97 . . . . 102 A7
Partridge Rd CV37 . . . . . 144 C4
Passfield Rd B77 . . . . 9 C8
Pastures Way CV34 . . . . 108 B4
Patch La B98 . . . . 102 F6
Paterson Ct B93 . . . . 72 C6
Patience Gr CV34 . . . . . . 109 F3
Patricia Cl CV4 . . . . 59 C1
Pattens Rd CV34 . . . . . . 105 B1
Patterdale CV21 . . . . 83 D7
Patterton Dr B76 . . . . 22 A7
Pattison Coll CV3 . . . . 62 A2
Pauline Ave CV6 . . . . 50 A1
Paul Stacy Ho CV1 . . . . . 151 D4
Pavilions The B37 . . . . 44 E8
Pavilion The B37 . . . . 4 B3
Pavilion Way CV5 . . . . 60 F3
Paxmead Cl CV6 . . . . 49 A2
Paxton Rd CV6 . . . . 61 A4
Payne Cl CV32 . . . . 106 A2
Payne's La CV1 . . . . 61 F3
Paynes La CV21 . . . . 82 D3
Payton St CV37 . . . . 145 A3
Peace Wlk B37 . . . . 33 B1
Peacock Ave CV2 . . . . 50 F1
Peacock Ct CV35 . . . . . . 146 D3
Peacock La CV35 . . . . . . 138 C7
Peacocks The CV34 . . . . 108 B2
Peake Ave CV11 . . . . 29 E7
Pearl Hyde Com Prim Sch
CV2 . . . . 63 C8
Pearl Hyde Ho 4 CV1 . . 151 C4
Pearmans Croft B47 . . . . . 69 A6
Pears Cl CV8 . . . . 92 F5
Pearson Ave CV6 . . . . 50 B2
Pear Dr B80 . . . . 103 C4
Pear Tree Ave
4 Coventry CV2 . . . . 50 B2
Chipping Campden GL55 . 135 B1
Long Marston CV37 . . . . . 129 B3
Shuttington B79 . . . . 4 E7
Pear Tree Gdns B95 . . . . . 119 F7
Peartrees CV7 . . . . 133 B7
Pear Tree Way CV22 . . . . . 82 B1
Peat Cl CV22 . . . . 82 E1
Pebblebrook Way CV12 . . . 39 C1
Pebble Cl B77 . . . . 4 A3
Pebble Island Way CV31 . 110 C5
Peony Rd B94 . . . . 119 D5
Pebworth Cl CV5 . . . . 60 A4
Pebworth Ct CV5 . . . . 60 A4
Pebworth Dr CV35 . . . . . 114 F6
Pebworth Fst Sch CV37 . . 128 F1
Peckstone Cl CV1 . . . . . . 151 C1
Peddimore La B76 . . . . . . 22 C7
Peel Cl
Coventry CV6 . . . . 61 E6
Drayton Bassett B78 . . . . . . 8 E5
Hampton-in-A B92 . . . . 57 A7
Peel Cl
Fazeley B78 . . . . 9 B8
Tamworth B77 . . . . 9 F6
Peel Dr B77 . . . . 9 F6
Peel La CV6 . . . . 61 F5
Peel Rd CV34 . . . . 108 E8
Peel St CV6 . . . . 61 F5
Pegasus Prim Sch B35 . . . 22 B3
Pegmill Cl CV3 . . . . 77 F8
Pelham La B49 . . . . 119 D5
Pembridge Rd B93 . . . . . . 71 E3
Pembroke Cl
1 Warwick CV34 . . . . . . 108 F8
Bedworth CV12 . . . . 38 C1
Pembroke Ct 8 CV32 . . . 105 F2
Pembroke Gdns CV35 . . . 146 C1

Pembroke Way CV11 . . . . . 29 D3
Pembrook Rd CV6 . . . . 49 C2
Pembury Ave CV6 . . . . 50 A3
Penarth Gr CV3 . . . . 78 F7
Pencraig Cl CV8 . . . . 93 C5
Pendenis Cl CV6 . . . . 62 A8
Penderel Ct CV6 . . . . 49 C3
Pendicke Ct 8 CV47 . . . . 147 B4
Pendicke St CV47 . . . . . . 147 B4
Pendigo Way
Birmingham B40 . . . . 44 E3
Birmingham B40 . . . . 44 F4
Pendine Ct 4 CV32 . . . . 109 D8
Pendred Rd CV22 . . . . 82 C3
Pendrell Cl B37 . . . . 33 A3
Penelope Cl CV33 . . . . . . 123 F6
Penfold Cl 3 CV33 . . . . . 122 F8
Penmire Cl CV9 . . . . 11 C3
Pennant Rd LE10 . . . . 31 D5
Penn Ho CV4 . . . . 59 F1
Pennine Way
Nuneaton CV10 . . . . 28 B3
Tamworth B77 . . . . 10 C8
Pennington Mews CV21 . . 82 F3
Pennington St CV21 . . . . . 82 F3
Pennington Way CV6 . . . . . 61 B8
Penn La
Tanworth-In-A B94 . . . . . . 86 C4
Wibtoft LE17 . . . . 43 C2
Penns Cl CV32 . . . . 106 E5
Pennyford La B95 . . . . . . 113 B1
Penny Hapenny La CV37 . . 53 C8
Pennymoor Rd B77 . . . . . . 10 B7
Penny Park La CV6 . . . . . . 49 A3
Pennystone Cl CV31 . . . . 110 D6
Penrhyn Cl 14 OX16 . . . 139 F4
Penrith Cl
Coventry CV6 . . . . 49 C2
Royal Leamington Spa
CV32 . . . . 105 C2
Penrith Gr B37 . . . . 33 C2
Penrose Cl CV4 . . . . 76 A7
Penryhn Cl CV8 . . . . 93 C5
Penryn Cl CV11 . . . . 30 A4
Pensham Croft B90 . . . . . . 71 A6
Penshurst Way CV11 . . . . . 39 F8
Pensilva Way 2 CV1 . . . . . 61 E4
Pentire Cl CV11 . . . . 29 F5
Pentland Cl LE10 . . . . 31 A8
Pepper La CV1 . . . . 151 B2
Pepys Cnr CV4 . . . . 59 E3
Perch Ave B37 . . . . 33 A3
Perchfoot Cl CV1 . . . . . . 151 C1
Percival Dr CV33 . . . . . . 123 F6
Percival Rd CV22 . . . . . . 100 D8
Percy Cres CV8 . . . . 92 E2
Percy Rd
Kenilworth CV8 . . . . 92 E2
Warwick CV34 . . . . 108 E8
Percy St
Coventry CV1 . . . . 151 A3
Stratford-u-A CV37 . . . . . 145 A4
Percy Terr 5 CV32 . . . . . 105 D1
Peregrine Dr CV5 . . . . 60 A5
Pericles Cl CV34 . . . . 109 E3
Perimeter Rd
Birmingham B40 . . . . 44 D4
Birmingham B40 . . . . 44 E4
Periwinkle Cotts WR11 . . 127 F6
Perkins Cl
Hornton OX15 . . . . 139 B8
Salford Priors WR11 . . . . 127 F6
Perkins Gr CV21 . . . . 83 F1
Permian Cl CV21 . . . . 83 C6
Perryfields Cl B98 . . . . . . 102 F6
Perryford Dr B91 . . . . 71 C8
Perryman Dr B78 . . . . 15 F8
Perrymill La B96 . . . . 103 B1
Perry Mill La B95 . . . . . . 112 B6
Pershore Pl CV4 . . . . 76 B6
Perth Rise CV5 . . . . 60 A4
Petard Cl B77 . . . . 9 C8
Peterbrook Cl B98 . . . . . 102 F7
Peterbrook Rd B90 . . . . . . 69 E8
Peter Hall La CV2 . . . . 64 B6
Peterlee Wlk 6 CV2 . . . . . 63 A7
Peters Wlk CV6 . . . . 50 A4
Petitor Cres CV2 . . . . 50 C1
Peto Gr CV34 . . . . 109 F2
Pettiford La B95 . . . . 113 C3
Pettiphers Farm CV37 . . . 129 A3
Petton Cl B98 . . . . 103 C4
Pettyfields Cl B93 . . . . 72 A5
Petunia Cl CV10 . . . . 39 A8
Peveril Dr CV3 . . . . 77 B5
Peyto Cl CV6 . . . . 49 C2
Pheasant Cl
Bedworth CV12 . . . . 38 D1
Stratford-u-A CV37 . . . . . 144 C4
Pheasant Croft B36 . . . . . 33 A8
Pheasant La B98 . . . . 102 F7
Pheasant Oak CV4 . . . . . . 59 C2
Philip Ct
1 Royal Leamington Spa
CV31 . . . . 109 F6
Rugby CV21 . . . . 83 B4
Phillip Docker Ct CV12 . . . 40 B2
Phillippes Rd 6 CV34 . . . 104 F1
Phipps Ave CV21 . . . . 83 C1
Phoebe Cl CV34 . . . . 109 E3
Phoenix Bsns Pk LE10 . . . 30 E8
Phoenix Ct B35 . . . . 22 A3
Phoenix Pk Ind Est CV7 . . 50 B7
Phoenix Way CV6 . . . . 49 E3
Piccadilly Cl B37 . . . . 33 C1

Piccadilly Cres B78 . . . . 9 F1
Piccadilly B78 . . . . 9 F1
Pickard Cl CV21 . . . . .83 E7
Pickard St CV34 . . . . .109 A7
Pickford Cl CV11 . . . . .30 A1
Pickford Grange La CV5 . . .59 C7
Pickford Green La CV5 . . . .59 C7
Pickford Way CV5 . . . . .60 B6
Picton Croft **6** B37 . . . . . . .33 D2
Piers Cl CV34 . . . . .108 F8
Pike Cl CV10 . . . . .31 D5
Pike Dr B37 . . . . .33 C3
Pikehorne Croft B36 . . . . . .22 D2
Pikers La CV7 . . . . .48 A3
Pilgrims Gate LE10 . . . . .32 A6
Pilgrims La CV23 . . . . .67 F1
Pilgrims Wlk CV6,CV7 . . . . . .49 B6
Pilkington Rd CV5 . . . . .76 D8
Pillerton Rd CV35 . . . . .131 F4
Pilling Cl CV2 . . . . .62 F8
Pill La GL56 . . . . .140 F1
Pimlico La CV37 . . . . .121 D2
Pinbury Croft B37 . . . . .33 B1
Pinchester Cl GL56 . . . . . . .141 A1
Pinders Ct **3** CV21 . . . . . . .83 B3
Pinders La CV21 . . . . .83 B4
Pine Cl
  Stoke Golding CV13 . . . . . . .21 E7
  Stratford-u-A CV37 . . . . . .144 D1
Pine Ct
  Coventry CV5 . . . . .59 C4
  Royal Leamington Spa
  CV32 . . . . .106 B3
Pine Gr CV21 . . . . .84 A1
Pineham Ave CV33 . . . . . . .123 F6
Pinehurst CV32 . . . . .106 E6
Pine Sq B37 . . . . .33 B2
Pines The
  Bedworth CV12 . . . . .38 E2
  Cheswick Green B90 . . . . . .70 D5
  Coventry CV4 . . . . .75 D7
Pine Tree Ave CV4 . . . . .60 A2
Pine Tree Cres CV47 . . . . .147 C5
Pine Tree Ct CV12 . . . . .39 C4
Pine Tree Rd CV12 . . . . .39 D4
Pinewood Ave CV9 . . . . .10 C1
Pinewood Bsns Pk B37 . . .44 B8
Pinewood Dr CV5 . . . . .79 C7
Pinewood Gr CV5 . . . . .77 B8
Pinfold Cl LE10 . . . . .30 F7
Pinfold Gn NN11 . . . . .126 F6
Pinfold St CV21 . . . . .82 E3
Pingle Ct CV11 . . . . .29 D2
Pink Green La B98 . . . . .112 A8
Pinley Fields CV3 . . . . .78 B8
Pinnacle Ho B97 . . . . .102 E5
Pinner's Croft CV2 . . . . .62 A5
Pinnock Pl CV4 . . . . .59 F1
Pinwall La CV9 . . . . .12 E4
Pioneer Ho CV1 . . . . .151 D4
Pioneer Way B35 . . . . .22 B2
Pipe La CV9 . . . . .6 C4
Piper's Bath CV35 . . . . .123 A2
Piper's End LE10 . . . . .41 D4
Pipers La CV10 . . . . .27 C8
Piper's La CV8 . . . . .93 A5
Pipers Rd B98 . . . . .103 D7
Pipewell Cl CV22 . . . . .82 C1
Pipit Wlk CV23 . . . . .67 C1
Pipkin Ct CV1 . . . . .151 D1
Pippin Cl B50 . . . . .148 D5
Pirie Cl CV33 . . . . .123 F6
Pit Hill CV8 . . . . .95 C3
Pitmaston Ct **10** OX16 . . .139 F5
Pitt La B92 . . . . .44 D2
Pittoms La CV23 . . . . .101 C1
Pittway Ave CV36 . . . . .149 C6
Pixhall Wlk B35 . . . . .22 B3
Plain Rd The OX15 . . . . . . .139 A3
Plane Cl CV10 . . . . .28 E7
Plane Gr B37 . . . . .33 B1
Plank La B46 . . . . .23 A2
Plantagenet Dr CV22 . . . . . .99 E6
Plantagenet Pk CV34 . . . . .109 E3
Plantation The OX17 . . . . .134 C1
Planter Cl CV22 . . . . .99 A8
Plants Brook Rd B76 . . . . . .22 A6
Plants Hill Cres CV4 . . . . . . .59 E1
Plato Cl CV34 . . . . .109 F4
Pleasant Way CV32 . . . . . . .106 A2
Pleck Cl B50 . . . . .148 D4
Pleck The B50 . . . . .148 D4
Plexfield Rd CV22 . . . . .82 C1
Pleydell Cl CV3 . . . . .78 C5
Plomer Cl CV22 . . . . .99 C8
Plot Rd OX15 . . . . .139 A3
Plott La CV23 . . . . .96 E6
Plough Hill Rd CV10 . . . . . . .28 A6
Plough La CV47 . . . . .124 A4
Ploughmans Holt CV47 . . .147 B6
Plover Cl
  Alcester B49 . . . . .143 B5
  Stratford-u-A CV37 . . . . . .144 D5
Plowden Cl NN11 . . . . .134 F5
Plowman St CV21 . . . . .82 F3
Plymouth Cl CV2 . . . . .62 C7
Plymouth Pl CV31 . . . . .110 A7
Poins Cl CV34 . . . . .109 D5
Poitiers Rd CV3 . . . . .77 D6
Poland Ave CV37 . . . . .129 D2
Polesworth High Sch B78 .10 F7
Polesworth Sta B78 . . . . .5 A3
Polperro Dr CV5 . . . . .60 A5
Pomeroy Cl CV4 . . . . .75 D7

Pond Farm Mews CV5 . . . .59 E5
Pondthorpe CV3 . . . . .78 E6
Pontrilas Rd CV3 . . . . .132 D4
Pontypool Ave CV3 . . . . .78 F6
Pool Bank St CV11 . . . . .29 B4
Pool Close Cotts GL56 . . .140 F1
Pool Cl
  Rugby CV22 . . . . .99 D8
  Welford-on-A CV37 . . . . . .129 B6
Pool End Cl B93 . . . . .71 F6
Poole Rd CV6 . . . . .61 A6
Pooley Fields Heritage Ctr*
  B78 .5 A3
Pooley La B78 . . . . .4 F2
Pooley View B78 . . . . .5 A2
Poolgate CV35 . . . . .138 B6
Popes La B96 . . . . .102 B2
Pope St CV22 . . . . .82 E3
Poplar Ave
  Bedworth CV12 . . . . .39 D2
  Birmingham,Coleshill Heath
  B37 . . . . .44 C8
Poplar Cl
  Alcester B49 . . . . .143 D3
  Knightcote CV47 . . . . .124 B1
Poplar Dr B95 . . . . .113 B2
Poplar Gr
  Rugby CV21 . . . . .83 A4
  Ryton-on-D CV8 . . . . .79 B1
Poplar Ho CV12 . . . . .39 D2
Poplar N B95 . . . . .113 A2
Poplar Rd
  Bishops Itchington CV47 . .124 B4
  Coventry CV5 . . . . .60 F1
  Dorridge B93 . . . . .71 F3
  Napton on t h CV47 . . . . . .125 C8
Poplars Cl GL55 . . . . .135 A1
Poplars La B96 . . . . .102 A1
Poplars The
  Bidford-on-A B50 . . . . .148 E5
  Hartshill Green CV10 . . . . . .19 B2
  Napton on t h CV47 . . . . . .125 B8
  Nuneaton CV10 . . . . .28 D3
Poplars Trad Est B80 . . . . .103 D6
Poplar Terr CV37 . . . . .121 D3
Poplar Trees B47 . . . . .69 A6
Poplar Way CV11 . . . . .127 D4
Poppy Cl CV10 . . . . .39 A8
Poppy Ct CV3 . . . . .78 D6
Poppy Dr CV23 . . . . .83 E8
Poppyfield Ct CV4 . . . . .76 D3
Porchester Cl CV3 . . . . .63 A2
Porlock Cl CV3 . . . . .77 E5
Porter Cl CV4 . . . . .75 E8
Portia Cl CV11 . . . . .30 A1
Portia Way CV34 . . . . .109 E3
Portland Cl **9** CV32 . . . .109 F8
Portland Dr CV10 . . . . .28 C4
Portland Mews **8** CV32 .109 F8
Portland Pl E CV32 . . . . . . .109 F8
Portland Pl W **5** CV32 . .109 E8
Portland Pl CV21 . . . . .83 D2
Portland Rd CV21 . . . . .83 D2
Portland St CV32 . . . . .109 F8
Portleys La B79 . . . . .8 A5
Portmanteau Mews B94 . . .88 C6
Portreath Dr CV11 . . . . .30 A5
Portree Ave CV3 . . . . .62 F2
Portsea Cl CV3 . . . . .77 D6
Portway Cl
  Coventry CV4 . . . . .75 E8
  Royal Leamington Spa
  CV31 . . . . .110 D6
Portwrinkle Ave CV6 . . . . . .62 A6
Poseidon Way CV34 . . . . . .109 F4
Postbridge Rd CV3 . . . . . . .77 D5
Post House Gdns CV23 . . .66 A8
Postle Cl CV23 . . . . .101 F2
Post Office La
  Lighthorne CV35 . . . . .123 B2
  Stockton CV47 . . . . .147 F8
  Witherley CV9 . . . . .19 B7
Post Office Rd CV9 . . . . . . .11 C1
Post Office Row CV10 . . . . .37 E7
Post Office Wlk B96 . . . . . .102 C2
Post Office Yd CV23 . . . . . . .64 F4
Potters Cl CV23 . . . . .102 E3
Potters Green Prim Sch
  CV2 . . . . .50 E2
Potters Green Rd CV2 . . . . .50 E1
Potters La
  Darlingscott CV36 . . . . . . .136 D5
  Polesworth B78 . . . . .11 A8
Potters Rd CV12 . . . . .38 E1
Potton Cl CV3 . . . . .78 E6
Potts Cl CV8 . . . . .93 C4
Poultney Rd CV6 . . . . .61 A6
Pound Cl
  Berkswell CV7 . . . . .58 D3
  Lapworth B94 . . . . .89 B3
  Shipston-on-S CV36 . . . . .149 D6
Pound Field CV35 . . . . .113 B2
Pound House La
  Nuthurst B94 . . . . .88 A4
  Tanworth-in-A B94 . . . . . . .87 F4
Pound La
  Badby NN11 . . . . .126 F6
  Coleshill B46 . . . . .34 A4

Pound La continued
  Furnace End B46 . . . . .25 D4
  Mickleton GL55 . . . . .135 B6
  Royal Leamington Spa
  CV32 . . . . .106 A3
  Sibford Gower OX15 . . . . .138 D1
Pound The
  Harbury CV33 . . . . .123 F7
  North Newington OX15 . . .139 D2
Pound Way CV47 . . . . .147 C4
Poverty B96 . . . . .102 E2
Powell Cl **17** CV33 . . . . .122 F8
Powell Rd CV2 . . . . .62 A4
Powell Way CV11 . . . . .29 C4
Powers Ct **4** CV32 . . . . .105 F1
Powis Gr CV8 . . . . .93 C5
Powys Gr OX16 . . . . .139 F4
Poyser Rd CV10 . . . . .39 C8
Pratts La B80 . . . . .112 A4
Preachers Homes CV7 . . . .36 E4
Prebend The CV47 . . . . . . .133 B7
Precision Way B49 . . . . . . .143 C6
Prentice Cl CV23 . . . . .82 B5
Prescelly Cl CV10 . . . . .28 B3
Prescelly Ct **4** 92 F5
Prescott Ave OX16 . . . . . . .139 F3
President Kennedy Sch &
  Com Coll CV6 . . . . .49 B4
Prestbury Cl B98 . . . . .112 A6
Preston Cl CV4 . . . . .75 F4
Preston Fields La B95. . . . .113 D6
Preston La CV37 . . . . .130 A4
Prestwick Rd B35 . . . . .22 B4
Pretorian Way CV21 . . . . . . .83 A7
Prew Cotts OX7 . . . . .142 A2
Priam Cir CV34 . . . . .109 F3
Price Cl E CV34 . . . . .108 B4
Price Cl W CV34 . . . . .108 B4
Price Rd CV32 . . . . .106 E5
Pridmore Rd CV6 . . . . .61 D7
Priestfield Rd B97 . . . . .102 E5
Priesthills Rd LE10 . . . . .31 D8
Priest Meadow Cl B96 . . . .102 D1
Primary Wlk CV22 . . . . .99 B8
Primley Ave B77 . . . . .9 F5
Primrose Cl CV23 . . . . .83 E8
Primrose Ct
  Harborough Magna CV23 . .66 B3
  Moreton-in-M GL56 . . . . . .140 A3
Primrose Dr
  Bedworth CV12 . . . . .38 E1
  Hinckley LE10 . . . . .31 E5
Primrose Hill St CV1 . . . . .151 C4
Primrose Hill CV34 . . . . . . .104 E2
Primrose La
  Alcester B49 . . . . .143 C2
  Solihull B90 . . . . .70 A5
Primsland Cl B90 . . . . .71 C7
Prince Harry Rd B95 . . . . .113 B4
Prince Of Wales Rd CV5 . .60 E3
Prince Regent Ct **3**
  CV31 . . . . .109 F6
Prince Rupert Cl CV47 . . .133 A6
Prince's Ave CV11 . . . . .29 B3
Princes Cl CV3 . . . . .78 B8
Princes Ct CV21 . . . . .83 A4
Princes Dr
  Coventry CV6 . . . . .50 B1
  Kenilworth CV8 . . . . .93 B7
Prince's Dr CV31 . . . . .109 D7
Princes Rd CV9 . . . . .16 C5
Prince's Rd B78 . . . . .5 A2
Princess Rd
  Atherstone CV9 . . . . .18 E8
  Hinckley LE10 . . . . .31 E8
Princess St CV6 . . . . .61 F7
Prince's St
  Nuneaton CV11 . . . . .29 C3
  Royal Leamington Spa
  CV32 . . . . .106 B1
Princes St CV21 . . . . .83 A4
Princethorpe Coll CV23 . . .96 C3
Princethorpe Way CV3 . . . .78 E8
Prince William Cl CV6 . . . . .60 E8
Printers Pl CV37 . . . . .144 F3
Prior Deram Wlk CV4 . . . . .76 C7
Priors Cl CV7 . . . . .74 B6
Priors Ct CV47 . . . . .125 F4
Priors Field Prim Sch
  CV8 . . . . .92 D7
Priors Harnall CV1 . . . . . . .151 D4
Prior Deram Mkt NN11 . . .126 B5
Priors Mdw CV47 . . . . .147 C4
Priors Rd CV47 . . . . .125 F4
Priors The CV12 . . . . .39 C2
Priory Cl
  Coleshill B46 . . . . .34 A5
  Kingswood B94 . . . . .89 D5
Priory Croft CV8 . . . . .93 A4
Priory Ct
  Coventry CV5 . . . . .61 A1
  Nuneaton CV11 . . . . .29 A4
  Solihull B90 . . . . .71 B7
  Studley B80 . . . . .103 E5
Priory Ho CV8 . . . . .92 F4
Priory La CV35 . . . . .131 D2
Priory Mews CV34 . . . . . . .108 E7
Priory Pl CV1 . . . . .151 C3
Priory Rd
  Alcester B49 . . . . .143 B3
  Kenilworth CV8 . . . . .93 A4
  Warwick CV34 . . . . .108 E7

Priory Rd continued
  Wolston CV8 . . . . .80 B4
Priory Row CV1. . . . . .151 C3
Priory Sq B80 . . . . .103 E5
Priory St
  Coventry CV1 . . . . .151 C3
  Nuneaton CV10 . . . . .28 D3
  Royal Leamington Spa
  CV31 . . . . .109 F6
Priory Terr CV31 . . . . .110 A7
Priory Visitors Ctr* CV1. .151 C3
Priory Wlk
  10 Warwick CV34 . . . .108 F7
  Atherstone CV9 . . . . .18 F6
Privet Rd CV2 . . . . .50 B2
Proctor Way CV37 . . . . .144 A4
Proffitt Ave CV6 . . . . .50 A1
Progress Cl CV3 . . . . .79 A7
Progress Way CV3 . . . . .79 A8
Projects Dr CV21 . . . . .83 C6
Prologis Pk CV6 . . . . .49 B5
Prospect Rd CV31 . . . . .110 B5
Prospect Way
  Daventry NN11 . . . . .117 C2
  Rugby CV21 . . . . .83 D5
Prospero Dr CV34 . . . . .109 E3
Prossers Wlk B46 . . . . .33 F7
Providence St CV5 . . . . .76 F8
Provost Williams CE Prim
  Sch CV8 . . . . .79 A1
Ptarmigan Pl CV11. . . . . . . .29 F3
Puckering's La CV34 . . . . .108 E6
Pudding Bag La CV23 . . . . .98 F2
Pudlicott La GL55 . . . . .135 C1
Pughe's Cl LE10 . . . . .32 A6
Pullman Cl B77 . . . . .4 A2
Puma Way CV1 . . . . .151 C1
Pumphouse Cl CV6 . . . . . . .50 B6
Pump La CV7 . . . . .36 C3
Purbrook B77 . . . . .9 E8
Purcell Ave CV11 . . . . .40 A7
Purcell Cl CV32 . . . . .110 A8
Purcell Rd CV6 . . . . .62 B8
Purefoy Rd CV3 . . . . .77 D8
Purley Chase La CV9 . . . . . .18 D4
Purley View CV9 . . . . .18 F6
Purlieu La CV8 . . . . .92 D5
Purnells Way B93 . . . . .72 A5
Purser Dr CV34 . . . . .108 B4
Purton Cl B49 . . . . .143 C5
Purton Mews CV31 . . . . . . .110 C6
Putney Wlk B37 . . . . .33 B3
Pye Ct CV23 . . . . .117 B6
Pyeharps Rd LE10 . . . . .31 E5
Pyree Sq CV34 . . . . .108 B4
Pytchley Rd CV22 . . . . .83 C1
Pytman Dr B76 . . . . .22 A7
Pyt Pk CV5 . . . . .60 D4

Q

Quadrangle The B90 . . . . . .70 E8
Quadrant The
  Coventry CV1 . . . . .151 B2
  Nuneaton CV11 . . . . .29 E3
Quail Cl CV37 . . . . .144 C4
Quaker Cl CV13 . . . . .20 A6
Quantock Dr CV10 . . . . .28 B3
Quarry Berry La DE12 . . . . .2 E8
Quarry Cl
  Leek Wootton CV35 . . . . . .104 F7
  Rugby CV21 . . . . .82 F7
Quarryfield La CV1 . . . . . . .151 D1
Quarry Fields CV35 . . . . . .104 F7
Quarry La
  Cleeve Prior WR11 . . . . . .128 A4
  Nuneaton CV11 . . . . .29 F1
  Rowington Green CV35 . . . .90 C1
Quarry Rd
  Atherstone CV9 . . . . .18 E4
  Kenilworth CV8 . . . . .92 E6
Quarry St CV32 . . . . .109 C8
Quarrywood Gr CV2 . . . . . . .62 A4
Quarry Yd CV10 . . . . .28 C4
Queen Eleanors Dr B93 . . .72 B8
Queen Elizabeth Rd CV10 .28 F6
Queen Elizabeth Sch CV9 .18 F7
Queen Isabel's Ave CV3 . . .77 D7
Queen Margaret's Rd CV4 .76 C8
Queen Mary's Rd
  Bedworth CV12 . . . . .39 C5
  Coventry CV6 . . . . .61 E8
Queen Philippa St CV3 . . . .77 D6
Queens Ave CV11 . . . . .29 C4
Queen's Ave OX36 . . . . . . .149 C5
Queens CE Jun Sch CV11 .29 A4
Queen's Cl CV33 . . . . .123 F6
Queen's Cl CV8 . . . . .92 F3
Queen's Cl **5** CV37 . . . .144 F1
Queens Cl CV13 . . . . .29 A4
Queen's Cres OX15 . . . . . .139 E4
Queen's Ct **5** CV37 . . . .144 F1
Queens Ct CV11 . . . . .29 A4
Queen's Dr CV35 . . . . .132 B5
Queensferry Cl CV22 . . . . . .99 C8
Queensland Ave CV5 . . . . . .60 F2
Queensland Gdns **4** CV12 .38 F2
Queen's Own Hussars Mus
  The* CV34 . . . . .108 E6
Queen's Park Ct **3** LE10 .31 E8
Queen's Park Flats **2**
  LE10 . . . . .31 E8
Queen's Park Terr **4**
  LE10 . . . . .31 E8
Queen's Rd CV8 . . . . .18 E8
Queens Rd CV32 . . . . .80 E7
Queen's Rd
  Coventry CV1 . . . . .151 A2

Queen's Rd continued
  Hinckley LE10 . . . . .31 E8
  Kenilworth CV8 . . . . .92 F3
  Nuneaton CV11 . . . . .29 B4
Queens Rd CV36 . . . . .136 F6
Queen's Sq CV34 . . . . .108 D5
Queens St CV36 . . . . .136 F6
Queen St
  Astwood Bank B96 . . . . . .102 E1
  Bedworth CV12 . . . . .39 C2
  Coventry CV1 . . . . .151 C4
  Cubbington CV32 . . . . .106 E5
  Hook Norton OX15 . . . . . .142 D4
  Royal Leamington Spa
  CV32 . . . . .106 A1
  Rugby CV21 . . . . .83 A3
  Swalcliffe B50 . . . . .148 C5
Queens Way
  Dordon B78 . . . . .10 F6
  Hurley CV9 . . . . .16 C4
Queensway
  Nuneaton CV10 . . . . .29 E6
  Royal Leamington Spa
  CV31 . . . . .109 E6
Queensway Trad Est
  CV31 . . . . .109 E6
Queenswood Ct CV7 . . . . . .48 D4
Queen Victoria Rd
  Coventry CV1 . . . . .151 B2
  Coventry CV1 . . . . .151 B3
Queen Victoria St CV21. . .83 C3
Quillets Cl CV6 . . . . .50 A1
Quince B77 . . . . .4 B3
Quince Tree Sch B77 . . . . . .4 A3
Quiney's Leys CV37 . . . . . .129 A7
Quiney's Rd CV37 . . . . .144 D2
Quinn Cl CV3 . . . . .78 B7
Quinneys Cl B50 . . . . .148 E4
Quinneys La
  Bidford-on-A B50 . . . . .148 E5
  Redditch B98 . . . . .103 B6
Quinton Cl CV35 . . . . .114 E6
Quintondale **1** B90 . . . . .70 C8
Quinton Flats CV3 . . . . .77 D7
Quinton Grange CV37 . . . .129 E1
Quinton Par CV3 . . . . .77 D7
Quinton Pk CV3 . . . . .77 D7
Quinton Prim Sch CV37 . .129 D2
Quinton Rd CV1 . . . . .151 C1
Quorn Way CV3 . . . . .78 E7

R

Race Leys Inf Sch CV12 . . .39 B3
Race Leys Jun Sch CV12 . .39 B4
Racemeadow Prim Sch
  CV9 . . . . .12 E1
Racemeadow Rd CV9 . . . . .12 E1
Radbourne Cl CV47 . . . . . .147 C3
Radbourne La CV47 . . . . . .124 E5
Radbrook Way CV31 . . . . . .110 D6
Radburn Cl GL56 . . . . .140 B3
Radcliffe Gdns **6** CV31 .110 A6
Radcliffe Rd CV6 . . . . .76 F8
Radford Circ **5** CV6 . . . . .61 A4
Radford Cl CV9 . . . . .12 E2
Radford Hall CV31 . . . . .110 E6
Radford Ho CV6 . . . . .61 A7
Radford Prim Sch CV6 . . . .61 A5
Radford Rd
  Coventry CV1,CV6 . . . . .61 B5
  Royal Leamington Spa
  CV31 . . . . .110 C7
Radford Semele CE Prim Sch
  CV31 . . . . .110 E8
Radley Dr CV10 . . . . .29 C1
Radlow Cres B37 . . . . .44 B8
Radnor Dr CV10 . . . . .28 E2
Radnor Wlk CV2 . . . . .62 F8
Radway Ind Est B90 . . . . . .70 E7
Radway Rd B90 . . . . .70 E8
Raglan Cl CV11 . . . . .29 D4
Raglan Ct **7** CV1 . . . . . . .61 A2
Raglan Gr CV8 . . . . .93 B5
Raglan St CV1 . . . . .151 D3
Raglan Way B37 . . . . .33 D1
Ragley Cl B93 . . . . .72 B7
Ragley Hall* B96 . . . . .118 F2
Ragley Mill La B49 . . . . . . .143 B4
Ragley Rd WR11 . . . . .127 D4
Ragley Way CV11 . . . . .29 F2
Railway Cl B80 . . . . .103 D4
Railway Cres CV36 . . . . . . .149 D7
Railway Mews B47 . . . . . . .143 B4
Railway St CV23 . . . . .82 A4
Railway Terr
  Atherstone CV9 . . . . .18 D8
  Bedworth CV12 . . . . .39 C2
  Rugby CV21 . . . . .83 B3
Rainbow Fields CV36 . . . . .149 D6
Rainsbrook Ave CV22 . . . . .100 F8
Rainsbrook Cl CV47 . . . . . .147 D4
Rainsbrook Dr
  Nuneaton CV11 . . . . .30 A1
  Solihull B90 . . . . .71 B6
Rainsbrook Secure Training
  Ctr CV23 . . . . .100 C1
Rainsbrook Valley Rly*
  CV22 . . . . .100 C6
Rainscar B77 . . . . .10 B7
Rainsford Cl CV37 . . . . . . .129 F8
Raison Ave CV11 . . . . .29 F8
Raleigh Rd CV2 . . . . .62 C3
Ralph Cres B78 . . . . .15 C2
Ralph Rd CV6 . . . . .60 F6
Rambures Cl CV34 . . . . . . .109 F3
Ramp Rd B26 . . . . .44 C5

Ramsay Cres CV5........60 B7
Ramsay Gn CV35........146 D4
Ramsden Ave CV10.......28 D6
Ramsden Ct CV10........28 C7
Ramsden Rd CV9........19 A7
Ramsey Rd CV31........110 B7
Ramshill La B94,B95....112 E7
Ranby Rd CV7...........61 F4
Randall Rd CV8.........92 F3
Randle Ct CV10........28 D4
Randle St CV6..........61 B5
Randolph Cl 11 CV31...110 C6
Ranelagh St CV31......110 A6
Ranelagh Terr CV31...109 F6
Range Meadow Cl CV32.105 C3
Rangemoor CV3.........78 D6
Range Way B78.........15 D5
Rangeworthy Cl B97...102 C7
Rankine Cl CV21.......82 D7
Rannoch Cl LE10........31 B8
Rannoch Dr CV10.......28 C5
Rannock Cl CV3.........62 F2
Ransome Rd CV7........37 A8
Ransom Rd CV6.........61 E8
Ran-tan The B97......102 E5
Ranulf Croft CV3.......77 C7
Ranulf St CV3..........77 C7
Raphael Cl CV5........60 C3
Rashwood Cl B94........88 B6
Ratcliffe Ct CV10......28 C4
Ratcliffe La CV9.......12 F4
Ratcliffe Rd
  Atherstone CV9.......12 E1
  Hinckley LE10........31 F6
Ratcliffe St CV9......18 D8
Rathbone Cl
  Keresley CV7.........48 F6
  Keresley CV7.........49 A6
  Rugby CV21..........101 A8
Rathlin Croft B36......33 B6
Ratliffe Rd CV22.......99 F7
Rattlecombe Rd OX15..138 E5
Raveloe Dr CV11........29 D1
Raven Cragg Rd CV5....76 E8
Ravenglass CV21.......83 D7
Ravensdale Ave CV32..105 C2
Ravensdale Prim Sch CV2 62 D4
Ravensdale Rd CV2.....62 D3
Ravenshaw La B91......56 A4
Ravenshaw Way B91....56 A3
Ravensholt CV4........76 D6
Ravensthorpe CV3......78 E8
Ravenstone B77........10 B8
Ravenswood Hill B46...33 F7
Raven Way CV11........29 F2
Rawlins Croft B35......22 C3
Rawlinson Rd CV22.....106 B2
Rawnsley Dr CV8........93 C6
Rawn View CV9.........18 F6
Raygill B77...........10 B8
Raymond Cl CV6........49 F5
Raynor Cres CV12......38 D1
Raynsford Wlk CV34...104 D1
Raywoods The CV10....28 F3
Reading Ave CV11......29 F7
Reading Cl CV2.........50 B3
Readings The CV47....133 C4
Read St CV1............61 E3
Reardon Ct CV34......104 E1
Recreation Rd CV6....50 A3
Rectory Cl
  Allesley CV5.........60 C6
  Barby CV23..........101 C1
  Bedworth CV7.........39 A1
  Drayton Bassett B78...8 E5
  Harvington WR11.....127 D4
  Stockton CV47.......147 F8
  Warmington OX17.....133 D2
  Whitnash CV31.......110 B4
Rectory Dr CV7.........39 A1
Rectory Gdns OX15....139 E4
Rectory La
  Allesley CV5.........60 C6
  Barby CV23..........101 C1
  Lower Brailes OX15..137 F2
  Whatcote CV36.......137 D7
Rectory Rd
  Hook Norton OX15....142 D4
  Old Arley CV7.........26 E1
  Sutton Coldfield B75..13 A6
Redcap Croft CV6......49 F4
Redcar Cl CV32.......106 C4
Redcar Rd CV1.........61 E5
Red Deeps CV11........39 D8
Reddicap Heath Rd B75.13 A4
Reddings La B46........25 A5
Reddings The B47......69 A5
Redditch Rd B80.......103 D5
Redditch Wlk 4 CV2....63 A7
Redesdale Ave CV6.....60 F5
Redesdale Mews 10
  GL56................140 A3
Redesdale Pl GL56....140 A2
Redfern Ave CV8........93 A6
Redgrave Cl CV2........63 B8
Redhill Bank CV37....130 B3
Red Hill Cl B80.......103 E6
Redhill Cl CV35.......146 C1
Redhill Furrows CV31..110 C5
Red Hill Ho CV37.....129 F7
Red Hill CV35.........131 B8
Redhouse Cl B93.......71 E4
Red La
  Astley CV10..........37 E7
  Burton Green CV8......75 C2
  Coventry CV6.........61 F5
  Kenilworth CV8.......92 D8
Redlake B77............9 E8

Redland Cl CV2.........50 E2
Redland La CV8.........79 A2
Redland Rd CV31.......110 B5
Redlands Cres CV37...144 C3
Redlands Cvn Pk CV35.123 B3
Redlands Row GL56....141 A1
Redliff Ave B36........22 D1
Red Lion Cl CV47.....147 B5
Red Lion St OX17.....134 C1
Red Lodge Dr CV22.....99 E8
Redmoor Way B76......22 D6
Red Poll Cl OX16.....139 F4
Red Rd CV35..........132 B5
Redruth Cl
  Coventry CV6.........62 A8
  Nuneaton CV11........30 A4
Redthorne Gr CV8......93 B8
Redwing Cl CV37......144 C5
Redwing B77...........10 A6
Red Wing Wlk B36......33 A8
Redwood Croft CV10....29 A1
Redwood Dr B78........15 D7
Redwood Pk CV36.....149 D5
Reeds Pk CV33........111 F1
Rees Dr CV3...........77 D4
Reeve Dr CV8..........93 A4
Reeves Rd LE10........31 F6
Regal Cl B77...........9 C8
Regal Gr CV9..........18 E8
Regal Ho CV11.........29 D3
Regal Rd CV37........144 F4
Regal Road Trad Est
  CV37................144 F4
Regan Ct B75..........13 C5
Regency Arc 8 CV32..109 F8
Regency Cl CV10.......29 D6
Regency Ct
  Coventry CV6.........76 F8
  Hinckley LE10........32 A7
Regency Dr
  Alcester B49........143 A6
  Coventry CV3.........76 F5
  Kenilworth CV8.......92 F3
Regency Ho CV32......110 A8
Regency Mews CV32...110 A8
Regent Cl 5 LE10......31 D8
Regent Gr CV32.......109 F8
Regent Pl
  4 Royal Leamington Spa
  CV31................110 A7
  Rugby CV21...........83 A3
Regent St
  Bedworth CV12........39 C4
  Coventry CV1.........151 A2
  Hinckley LE10........31 D8
  Nuneaton CV11........29 D5
  Royal Leamington Spa
  CV32................109 F8
  Rugby CV21...........83 A3
Reg Hadden Ct CV10....29 D6
Regiment Ct CV6.......49 A1
Regina Cres CV2........63 A7
Regis Wlk CV2.........62 F7
Reignier Pl CV34.....109 F2
Reindeer Rd B78........8 F8
Relay Rd B77...........10 C7
Relton Mews CV6.......60 C3
Rembrandt Cl CV5......60 C3
Remburn Gdns CV34...108 E8
Remembrance Rd CV3...78 D6
Renfrew Sq B35........22 B4
Renfrew Wlk CV4.......76 A8
Renison Rd CV12.......38 E1
Renolds Cl CV4........60 C2
Renown Ave CV5........76 A3
Renshaw B91...........56 A3
Renshaw Ind Est B80.103 B4
Repington Ave CV9....12 D2
Repington Rd N B77....4 A5
Repington Rd S B77....4 A5
Repington Way B75....13 B5
Repton Dr CV6.........50 B2
Reservoir Dr B46......24 F2
Reservoir Rd CV21.....83 C6
Retreat St B96.......102 E1
Retreat The B95......113 B2
Reuben Ave CV10.......28 B6
Revel CE Prim Sch The
  CV23................53 F2
Rex Cl CV4............75 D8
Reynolds Cl CV21......84 B1
Reynolds Rd CV12......39 A8
Rhoose Croft B35......22 B3
Rhyl Rd CV11..........40 F6
Ribble Cl CV12........40 B2
Ribble Rd CV1.........61 F2
Ribblesdale B77.......10 B7
Ribbonbrook CV11......29 D3
Ribbonfields CV11.....29 D3
Richard Joy Cl CV6....49 A3
Richard Lee Prim Sch
  CV2.................62 E3
Richards Cl CV8.......92 F5
Richards Gr CV31.....110 A5
Richardson Cl CV34...104 F1
Richardson Way CV2....63 B8
Rich Cl CV34..........39 B2
Richman Gdns 3 OX16.139 F4
Richmond Cl B47......69 A6
Richmond Ct 6 CV31..110 B7
Richmond Ho 2 B37....33 C1
Richmond Rd
  Atherstone CV9.......18 C7
  Nuneaton CV11........29 A4
  Rugby CV21...........83 D2
Richmond St CV2.......61 F3
Richmond Way 2 B37..33 C3
Rickard Cl B78........71 E6

Rickyard Cl B78........5 A1
Rickyard The
  Easenhall CV23.......65 F4
  Shutford OX15.......139 A3
Ricoh Arena (Coventry City
  FC) CV6...........49 E3
Riddell Cl B49.......143 D4
Ridding Gdns B78.....11 A8
Riddings Hill CV7.....74 C8
Riddings La CV9.......11 C3
Riddings The
  Baddesley Ensor CV9..11 C2
  Coventry CV5.........76 E7
  Sutton Coldfield B76..22 B8
Riddon Dr LE10........31 B8
Rideswell Gr CV10....110 A1
Ridge Ct CV5..........60 A6
Ridge Dr CV21.........83 D4
Ridge La CV10.........26 D1
Ridgeley Cl CV34.....104 E2
Ridgethorpe CV3.......78 E6
Ridgeway Ave CV3......77 C6
Ridgeway Cl CV5.......60 A6
Ridgeway La CV13.....115 A5
Ridgeway Mid Sch B96.118 C8
Ridgeway Sch The CV34.105 A1
Ridgeway The
  Astwood Bank B96...118 D6
  Barby CV23..........117 F8
  Hinckley LE10........31 A6
  Warwick CV34.......105 A1
Ridgewood Cl CV32....105 C1
Ridgewood Rise B77....4 A5
Ridgley Rd CV4........75 E8
Ridgway The CV37.....120 C3
Ridley La B46..........25 A5
Ridsdale Cl WR11.....127 F6
Rigby Cl CV34.........109 D4
Rigdale Cl CV2........62 E2
Riley Cl
  Coventry NN11.......117 F2
  Kenilworth CV8.......93 D4
Riley Ct CV21.........83 C3
Riley Dr
  Banbury OX16........139 F4
  Birmingham B36.......23 A1
Riley Ho CV1.........151 B2
Riley Sq CV2..........50 B1
Rimell Cl CV37........29 B2
Ringway High Cross CV1.151 A3
Ringway Queens CV1...151 A2
Ringway Rudge CV1....151 A2
Ringway St Johns CV1.151 C2
Ringway St Nicholas
  CV1.................151 B3
Ringway St Patricks CV1 151 B1
Ringway Swanswell CV1 151 C3
Ringway Whitefriars
  CV1.................151 C3
Ringway Highway CV2..50 E2
Rinhill Gr CV31......110 D6
Riplingham 3 CV32...105 F2
Ripon Cl CV5..........60 B8
Risborough Cl CV6.....60 C3
Risdale Cl CV32......105 D2
Rise The B37..........44 A7
Rising La
  Chadwick End B93......90 B5
  Kingswood B94,B93....89 F5
Rising Rd B94.........89 C5
Riverbank Gdns CV37..145 B2
River Cl
  Bedworth CV12........38 F1
  Royal Leamington Spa
  CV32................109 D8
River Ct 3 CV1.......61 B3
River Dr CV9..........12 D2
Riverford Croft CV4...76 D4
Rivermead Cl B50.....148 D4
Rivermead Dr CV37...145 E4
Rivermead CV11........29 A4
Riverside 6 CV32....109 E8
Riverside CV11........29 A8
Riverside
  Alcester B49........143 D4
  Bubbenhall CV8.......95 B5
Riverside Cl CV3.......78 A7
Riverside Ct 11 B46....33 F7
Riverside Dr B95.....113 B2
Riverside Gdns B95...113 B4
Riverside Ind Est B46..9 B8
Riverside
  Royal Leamington Spa
  CV32................109 E8
  Studley B80.........103 F5
  Witherley CV9........19 B7
Riverslea Rd CV3......62 C1
Riversleigh Rd CV32..105 C1
Riversley Rd CV11.....29 C3
River Way CV36.......149 E2
River Wlk CV2.........50 C2
Rivington Glebe GL56.141 A1
Roach Cl B37..........33 C3
Roach B77.............9 D6
Roadway Cl CV12.......39 B2
Roanne Ringway CV11..29 B4
Robbins Ct 3 CV7.....39 A1
Robert Cl CV3.........78 C4
Robert Cramb Ave CV4.75 F8
Robert Hill Cl CV21...84 A1
Robert Rd CV7.........49 F8
Roberts Cl CV23.......96 F6
Roberts La WR11......127 F1
Roberts Rd CV23.......84 A5
Robey's La B78.........4 D3

Robin Cl
  Birmingham B36.......33 A8
  Tamworth B77..........9 C8
Robin Hood Rd CV3.....78 C6
Robinia Cl CV32......106 B2
Robinia B77............4 A4
Robins Cl OX7........142 A2
Robins Gr CV34.......108 C4
Robinson Rd CV12......49 D8
Robinson's Way B76....22 D5
Robinson Way LE10.....31 F4
Robins Way CV10.......28 A3
Robotham Cl CV21......82 F6
Rocheberie Way CV22...99 F8
Rochester Cl
  Nuneaton CV11........29 B3
  Redditch B97........102 C8
Rochester Rd CV5......76 E8
Rochford Cl B76.......22 A8
Rochford Ct
  Royal Leamington Spa
  CV31................109 E7
  Solihull B90.........71 A6
Rock Cl
  Coventry CV6.........50 B1
  Galley Common CV10...27 F4
Rocken End CV6........61 D8
Rockford Cl B98.......102 F5
Rockingham Cl B93.....79 F7
Rockingham Dr CV11....38 F7
Rock La CV7...........48 C7
Rock Mill La CV32....109 C8
Rock Mill Rd CV32....105 C1
Rocky La CV5..........93 D2
Rodborough Rd B93.....71 E3
Rodhouse Cl CV4.......59 D1
Rodney Cl CV22........82 C1
Rodway Dr CV5.........59 D4
Rodyard Way CV1......151 C1
Roebuck Pk B49......143 A5
Roe Cl CV34..........108 F8
Roe House La CV9,DE12..5 A2
Rofs Croft B78..........5 A2
Rogers La CV37.......131 A3
Rogers Way CV34......108 B4
Rokeby Ct CV22........99 E7
Rokeby Inf Sch CV22..100 A8
Rokeby Jun Sch CV22..100 A7
Rokeby St CV21........83 D3
Roland Ave CV6........49 C3
Roland Mount CV6.....49 C3
Rolan Dr B90..........69 E8
Rollason Cl CV6........61 B8
Rollason Rd CV6.......61 B8
Rollason's Yd CV6.....50 A4
Rolling Stones GL55..135 B2
Rollright Stones* OX7.141 D1
Rolph Ct GL56........140 A2
Roman Cl LE17........143 E6
Roman Ct B77..........9 E7
Romani Cl CV34.......108 D7
Roman Pk B46..........23 F1
Roman Rd CV2..........62 B3
Roman Row CV36......141 F5
Roman Way
  Alcester B49........143 A3
  Coleshill B46.........23 F2
  Coventry CV3.........77 D3
  Dordon B78..........11 A6
  Halford CV36........136 F6
  Rugby CV21...........83 A7
  Southam CV47........147 C4
Romeo Arbour CV34...109 E3
Romford Rd CV6........49 B2
Romilly Cl B76........13 A4
Romney Rd 23 OX16...139 F5
Romney B77............9 F8
Romsey Ave CV10.......28 C3
Romsley Rd CV6.......61 C6
Ronald Gr B36.........22 C7
Ro-Oak Rd CV6.........60 F5
Rookery Cl CV13.......20 A7
Rookery La
  Coventry CV6.........49 B4
  Ettington CV37......131 A3
  Newbold-on-S CV37...130 E1
  Preston Bagot B95...113 C5
Rookery The
  Birchley Heath CV10..17 F2
  Galley Common CV10...27 E5
Rooks Nest Cl CV37...144 F3
Rooks Nest CV23.......64 E3
Roosevelt Dr CV4......59 E2
Roper Cl CV21........101 A8
Ropewalk B49........143 A4
Rope Way OX15........142 D3
Rosaville Cres CV5....60 A6
Rose Ave
  Coventry CV6.........60 F5
  Henley-in-A B95.....113 B5
Rosebery Ave CV2.....50 C1
Rosebery Rd B77........9 D4
Rosebriars CV9........69 E7
Rose Cottage Flats CV5..59 D5
Rosecedadoc 9 CV35..132 B6
Rose Cres CV34.......129 C8
Rose Croft CV8........74 B8
Rosefield Pl 1 CV32..109 F8
Rosefield St CV32....110 A8
Rosefield Wlk 3 CV32.109 F8
Rosegreen Cl CV3......77 C6
Rosehall Cl B98......102 E6
Rose Hill CV9.........18 F7
Rosehip Dr CV2........62 B6
Rose La CV47.........125 C7
Roseland Rd CV8.......92 F3
Roselands Ave CV2.....62 D8

Rose La CV11..........29 C3
Rosemary Cl CV4.......59 E3
Rosemary Hill CV8.....92 F5
Rosemary Mews CV8....92 F5
Rosemary Way LE10.....31 B7
Rosemont Ho B93.......71 F3
Rosemount Cl CV2......62 E7
Rosemullion Cl CV7....50 B8
Roses La B46..........33 F8
Roseway CV13...........21 D7
Rosewood Ave CV22...100 A8
Rosewood Cl LE10......31 F6
Rosewood Cres CV32..106 B2
Rosewood CV11.........29 F1
Ross Cl CV5...........60 A5
Ross Ct CV21..........83 D3
Rossendale Way CV10..28 C2
Rosslyn Ave CV6......60 E6
Rosslyn Rd N CV6......22 A6
Ross Way CV11.........40 B7
Roston Dr LE10........31 A8
Rothay B77............9 F8
Rotherby Gr B37.......44 B7
Rotherfield Cl CV31..110 B7
Rotherham Rd CV6.....49 C2
Rotherhams Hill CV9..17 C8
Rotherhams Oak La B94..87 E7
Rother Rd 8 OX16...139 F5
Rother St CV37.......144 F2
Rotherwick Ct CV36..149 D6
Rothesay Ave CV4......60 B2
Rothesay Cl CV10......29 A2
Rothley Dr CV21.......83 E7
Rothwell Rd CV34....104 C1
Rotten Row Barns B93..72 C4
Rough Coppice Wlk B35 .22 A2
Rough Farm Ind Est
  CV37................130 C5
Rough Hill Dr B98....102 F6
Roughknowles Rd CV4..75 D6
Rouncil La B93.......104 C8
Round Ave CV23........82 A5
Round Close Rd OX15..142 D4
Round Cl B90..........70 A6
Roundhill Rd CV47....134 A2
Roundhouse Mews 8
  GL56................140 A3
Round House Rd CV3...78 B8
Round Moor Wlk B35....22 A3
Round Oak Sch The
  CV32................106 A3
Rounds Gdns CV21......82 F4
Rounds Hill CV8.......92 E2
Round St CV21.........82 F2
Rouse La CV35........137 F8
Rover Dr B36..........22 F1
Rover Rd CV1.........151 B2
Rowan Cl
  Binley Woods CV3.....79 D7
  Hollywood B47........69 B5
  Kingsbury B78........15 D6
  Stratford-u-A CV37..144 F5
Rowan Dr
  6 Warwick CV34.....108 F4
  Rugby CV22...........82 B2
Rowan Gdns B78.......11 B8
Rowan Gr CV2..........50 E2
Rowan Rd CV10.........28 C6
Rowans The
  Bedworth CV12........38 E2
  Harvington WR11.....127 D4
Rowan Way
  Birmingham,Chelmsley Wood
  B37.................33 C1
  Hartshill CV10.......28 A8
Rowborough Cl
  Astwood Bank B96...102 E2
  Hatton CV35.........114 F5
Rowbrook Cl B90.......69 E8
Rowcroft Rd CV2.......63 A6
Rowe Cl CV21.........101 C7
Rowington Cl CV6......60 D5
Rowington Gn CV35....89 F1
Rowland Ave
  Polesworth B78........5 A3
  Studley B80.........103 E3
Rowland Ct CV7........26 E1
Rowland St CV21.......82 F3
Rowlands Way CV36...137 E2
Rowland Way CV9......12 C2
Rowley Cres CV37....145 A4
Rowley Dr CV3.........78 B4
Rowley La CV3.........78 D3
Rowley Rd
  Coventry CV3,CV8.....78 B3
  Whitnash CV31.......110 A2
Rowley's Green La Ind Est
  CV6.................49 A4
Rowse Cl CV21.........83 C7
Row The
  Ansty CV7............51 D3
  Broadwell CV23......116 B4
  Mollington OX17.....133 F2
Rowthorn Dr B90.......71 A6
Roxburgh Croft CV32..105 B6
Roxburgh Rd CV11......29 E1
Royal Cres CV3........77 C6
Royal Ct LE10.........31 D7
Royal Leamington Spa
  Rehabilitation Hospl
  CV32................109 E4
Royal Meadow Dr CV9..12 E2
Royal Oak Ind Est NN11.117 F2

Royal Oak La CV7,CV12 . . . . . . .49 C7
Royal Oak Terr GL55 . . . . . 135 A1
Royal Oak Way N NN11. . .117 F2
Royal Oak Way S NN11. . .117 F2
Royal Oak Yd CV12 . . . . .39 B4
Royal Priors 18 CV32. . . . .105 F1
Royal Shakespeare Theatre*
CV37 . . . . 145 A2
Royston Cl CV3 . . . . .63 A3
Rubens Cl CV5 . . . . .60 C3
Rudgard Rd CV6 . . . . .50 A4
Rufford Cl
Alcester B49 . . . . 143 C5
Hinckley LE10 . . . . .31 D3
Rugby High Sch CV22 . . . .99 D6
Rugby La CV23 . . . . .97 B6
Rugby Rd
Barby CV23 . . . . 101 C1
Binley Woods CV3 . . . . .79 D8
Brandon CV8 . . . . .80 A5
Brinklow CV23 . . . . .64 F3
Bulkington CV12 . . . . .40 D2
Church Lawford CV23 . . . . . .81 C5
Clifton u D CV23 . . . . .83 F5
Cubbington CV32 . . . . 106 E6
Dunchurch CV22 . . . . .99 D4
Dunsmore CV23 . . . . .84 F6
Easenhall CV23 . . . . .65 F3
Harborough Magna CV23 . .84 A2
Hinckley LE10 . . . . .31 D5
Kilsby CV23 . . . . 101 E5
Long Lawford CV23 . . . . . . .82 B4
Pailton CV23 . . . . .66 A8
Princethorpe CV23 . . . . . . .96 F2
Royal Leamington Spa
CV32. . . . . 105 D1
Shawell LE17 . . . . .68 A8
Stockton CV47 . . . . 115 F3
Weston u W CV33 . . . . 107 D7
Wolston CV8 . . . . .80 C4
Rugby Sch CV22 . . . . .83 A2
Rugby Sta CV21 . . . . .83 C4
Ruislip Cl B35 . . . . .22 A4
Rumbush La
Earlswood B90,B94 . . . . . . .69 F3
Solihull B90 . . . . .70 A5
Rumer Cl CV37 . . . . 129 B4
Runcorn Cl
Birmingham B37 . . . . .33 C4
Redditch B98 . . . . 102 F8
Runcorn Wlk 10 CV2 . . . . . .63 A7
Runneymede Gdns CV10 . .28 F3
Runnymede Dr CV5 . . . . . . .74 C5
Rupert Brooke Rd CV22 . . .99 E7
Rupert Kettle Dr CV47 . . 124 B4
Rupert Rd CV6 . . . . .61 B8
Rushbrook La B94 . . . . .86 D3
Rushbrook Rd CV37 . . . . . 145 C1
Rushford Cl B90 . . . . .71 A7
Rush La B77,B78 . . . . .9 D4
Rushleigh Rd B90 . . . . .69 E8
Rushmoor Dr CV5 . . . . .60 F3
Rushmore St CV31 . . . . . . 110 B8
Rushmore Terr 8 CV31 . .110 B7
Rushock Cl B98 . . . . .103 C7
Rushton Cl CV7 . . . . .74 C7
Rushton Hall Sch CV7. . . . .49 D5
Rushwick Gr B90 . . . . .71 A6
Rusina Ct CV31 . . . . .109 F6
Ruskin Cl
Coventry CV6 . . . . .60 D6
Nuneaton CV10 . . . . .28 A5
Rugby CV22 . . . . .99 F6
Russell Ave CV22 . . . . .99 D4
Russell Cl
Long Ichington CV47 . . . . 115 D4
Tamworth B77 . . . . .9 E6
Russell Ct 7 CV31 . . . . . . .110 A7
Russell St N 2 CV1 . . . . . .151 C4
Russell St
Coventry CV1 . . . . 151 C4
Royal Leamington Spa
CV32. . . . . 105 F1
Russell Terr CV31 . . . . .110 A7
Russelsheim Way CV22. . . .83 A2
Russet Gr CV4 . . . . .76 D3
Rutherford Glen CV11 . . . .29 F1
Rutherford Way NN11 . . . .117 F2
Rutherglen Ave CV3 . . . . . .78 A6
Rutland Ave
Hinckley LE10 . . . . .31 C7
Nuneaton CV10 . . . . .28 F4
Rutland Croft 3 CV3 . . . . . .78 F8
Rydal Ave CV11 . . . . .30 A6
Rydal Cl
Allesley CV5. . . . . .60 B8
Hinckley LE10 . . . . .30 F7
Rugby CV21 . . . . .83 D6
Rydal B77 . . . . .10 A7
Ryde Ave CV10 . . . . .29 D7
Ryder Cl CV35 . . . . .114 F3
Ryder Row CV7 . . . . .37 A8
Ryders Hill Cres CV10 . . . . .28 C7
Rye Cl 9 OX16 . . . . .139 F5
Ryeclose Croft B37 . . . . .33 D3
Rye Croft CV37 . . . . .144 E5
Rye Croft B47 . . . . .69 A5
Ryefield La B76 . . . . .14 B2
Rye Fields 1 CV33. . . . . . 122 E8
Ryegrass La B97 . . . . .102 C6
Rye Grass Wlk B35 . . . . . . .22 B3
Rye Hill CV5. . . . . .60 A6
Rye Hill Office Pk CV5 . . . .60 A7
Ryelands The CV9. . . . . .98 D7
Rye Piece Ringway CV12 . .39 C3

Ryhope Cl CV12. . . . . .38 C1
Ryknild St B49. . . . . 143 A6
Ryland Cl CV31 . . . . .110 C6
Ryland Rd CV35. . . . . 122 B8
Ryland St CV37 . . . . .144 F1
Ryley St CV1. . . . . 151 A3
Rylston Ave CV6 . . . . .49 A1
Rylstone Way 4 CV34. . . .104 E1
Ryton Hill CV37 . . . . 145 E7
Ryton Cl CV4 . . . . .76 B8
Ryton Organic Gdns*
CV8. . . . . .79 E1
Ryton Pools Ctry Pk* CV8 .95 E5
Ryton Pools Visitor Ctr*
CV8. . . . . .95 E5
Ryton B77. . . . . .9 F8

S

Sabin Cl CV47. . . . . 115 C4
Sabin Dr CV33. . . . . 107 D7
Sackville Cl CV37 . . . . .144 C4
Sackville La CV37 . . . . .139 F6
Sackville Ho 1 CV1. . . . . .151 D4
Sacred Heart RC Prim Sch
CV2 . . . . .62 A3
Saddington Rd CV3 . . . . .78 E8
Saddlebow La CV35,CV37 .114 B2
Saddlers Cl LE10. . . . . .31 F6
Saddleton St CV35 . . . . . . 138 C7
Sadler Cl CV37 . . . . .144 F6
Sadler Gdns CV12. . . . . .39 C2
Sadler Rd CV6. . . . . .61 A8
Sadlers Ave CV36 . . . . .149 C5
Sadlers Cl CV36. . . . . .149 C6
Sadlers Mdw B46. . . . . .26 A2
Sadlerswell La B94 . . . . .88 B6
Saffron Cl CV23. . . . . .83 E8
Saffron Mdw CV37. . . . . . .144 F1
Saffron B77. . . . . .4 B4
Saffron Wlk 8 CV37 . . . . .144 F1
Sage Cl 2 OX16 . . . . .139 F5
St Agatha's Rd CV2 . . . . . . .62 A3
St Agnes Cl B80 . . . . .103 C4
St Agnes Way CV11. . . . . . . .29 F4
St Albans Cl CV32. . . . . . . .105 C2
St Andrews Benn CE Prim
Sch CV21. . . . . .83 D3
St Andrew's CE Inf Sch
CV5 .59 C5
St Andrews Cres CV2 . . . .100 A8
St Andrew's Cres CV37. . .144 F2
St Andrew's Ct CV21. . . . . .83 A4
St Andrews Dr CV11 . . . . . .30 B1
St Andrew's Rd
Coventry CV5. . . . . .76 F8
Royal Leamington Spa
CV32. . . . . 106 B5
St Andrews B77 . . . . .4 B4
St Annes Gr B93. . . . . .72 A6
St Anne's RC Prim Sch
Birmingham B37 . . . . .33 A2
Coventry CV3. . . . . .78 C6
Nuneaton CV10 . . . . .28 D7
St Anne's Rd CV22. . . . . .82 E1
St Ann's Cl CV31. . . . . .110 C7
St Ann's Rd CV2 . . . . .62 A3
St Anthony's RC Prim Sch
CV31. . . . . 110 C7
St Antony's RC Prim Sch
B37. .33 A5
St Asaphs Ave B80 . . . . . . 103 D4
St Athan Croft B35. . . . . . . .22 B3
St Augustine's RC High Sch
B97. 102 D5
St Augustine's RC Prim Sch
Coventry CV6. . . . . .61 A7
Kenilworth CV8 . . . . .92 E7
St Augustine's Wlk CV6 . . .61 A7
St Austell Cl CV11. . . . . .30 A5
St Austell Rd CV2 . . . . .62 E3
St Bartholemews Cl CV3 . .63 A3
St Bartholomew's CE Prim
Sch CV3 . . . . .78 E7
St Benedicts Cl B78 . . . . . . .18 D8
St Benedict's RC High Sch
B49. 143 C4
St Benedict's RC Prim Sch
CV9 . . . . .18 F7
St Bernard's Wlk CV3 . . . . . .78 D6
St Blaise Ave B46. . . . . .23 C2
St Bride's Cl CV31 . . . . . . .110 C6
St Buryan Cl CV11 . . . . .30 A5
Saintbury Cl CV37 . . . . . . .145 D1
Saintbury Dr B91 . . . . .71 C8
St Catharine's RC Prim Sch
GL55. . . . . 135 A2
St Catherine's Cl
Coventry CV3. . . . . .78 B8
Hinckley LE10 . . . . .31 F7
St Catherine's Cres CV34 109 F3
St Catherine's Lodge 7
CV6 .61 A4
St Chads Mews B94. . . . . . .89 D3
St Chads Rd
3 Bishops Tachbrook
CV33. . . . . 122 E8
Studley B80. . . . . .103 C4
St Christian's Croft CV3 . .77 E8
St Christian's Rd CV3 . . . . .77 E8
St Christopher Prim Sch
CV5 .60 D4
St Christopher's Cl CV34 108 D8
St Clements Ct CV2 . . . . . . .62 D8
St Columba's Cl CV1 . . . . .151 A4
St David's Cl CV31. . . . . . . .110 C7
St David's Ct GL56 . . . . . . .140 A3

St Davids Orch CV3 . . . . .78 F7
St David's Sch GL56 . . . . . .140 A3
St Davids Way CV10. . . . . . .39 A6
St Davids Wlk CV37 . . . . . .130 E1
St Denis View CV23 . . . . . . .66 A8
St Edithas Rd B78 . . . . .11 A8
St Edith's Cl CV23 . . . . .53 E3
St Edith's Cl 3 CV34 . . . . 109 B8
St Edith's Ho 2 CV34 . . . .109 B8
St Edmonds Rd CV6 . . . . . . .16 C5
St Edwards Ct GL56. . . . . . 140 A2
St Edward's RC Prim Sch
B46. .34 A3
St Egwin's Cl WR11 . . . . . .127 B2
St Elizabeth's Cl CV6. . . . . .61 E7
St Elizabeth's Rd CV6. . . . .61 E7
St Faith's Rd B49 . . . . .143 B5
St Francis RC Prim Sch
CV12 . . . . .39 C3
St Fremund Way CV31 . . 110 C5
St George & St Teresa RC
Prim Sch B93 . . . . .72 B7
St Georges Ave CV22. . . . . .99 F8
St George's Cl
24 Moreton-in-M GL56 . . . 140 A3
Stratford-u-A CV37 . . . . . 144 D4
St George's Rd
Atherstone CV9 . . . . .12 E1
Coventry CV1. . . . . .61 F2
Royal Leamington Spa
CV31. . . . . 109 F6
Solihull B90 . . . . .70 D8
St Georges Way CV10 . . . .39 B8
St Gerards RC Prim Sch
B35. .22 B4
St Giles Jun Sch CV7 . . . . . .49 F8
St Giles Rd
Coventry CV7. . . . . .49 D6
Gaydon CV35. . . . . 132 E8
St Govan's Cl 2 CV11. . . .110 C6
St Gregory's RC Prim Sch
Coventry CV2. . . . . .62 E3
Stratford-u-A CV37 . . . . . 145 A3
St Gregory's Rd CV37 . . . 145 A3
St Helena Rd B78 . . . . .11 A8
St Helen's Rd CV31 . . . . . .110 A5
St Helen's Way CV5. . . . . . . .60 B8
St Ives Rd CV2 . . . . .62 E3
St Ives Way CV11 . . . . .29 F5
St James' Ave CV35. . . . . .146 E4
St James CE Jun Sch
CV12 . . . . .40 C2
St James CE Prim Sch
CV47. . . . . 147 B5
St James Cl WR11 . . . . . . .127 D3
St James Cres CV47. . . . . .147 B5
St James Ct
Coventry CV3. . . . . .78 E6
Moreton-in-M GL56 . . . . . 140 A2
St James & Ebpton CE Jun &
Prim Sch GL55 . . . . .135 B4
St James Gdns CV12. . . . . .40 C2
St James' La CV3 . . . . .78 D6
St James Meadow Rd
CV32 . . . . 105 C2
St James Rd CV47 . . . . . . .147 B5
St James's Cl LE10. . . . . .31 D5
St John Fisher RC Prim Sch
CV2 . . . . .62 D5
St Johns Ave CV8 . . . . .93 A3
St Johns Ave CV22. . . . . . .100 E8
St John's CE Prim Sch
CV5 .60 C4
St John's Cl
Cherington CV36 . . . . 141 D7
Henley-in-A B95. . . . . .113 A4
St Johns Cl
Knowle B93. . . . . .72 B6
Stratford-u-A CV37 . . . . . 144 F1
St John's Ct
1 Stratford-u-A CV37 . . .144 F1
4 Warwick CV34 . . . . .108 F7
St John's Flats CV8 . . . . . . .93 A3
St John's House Mus*
CV34 . . . . 108 F7
St John's La CV23 . . . . .82 A5
St Johns Prim Sch CV8 . . .92 F2
St Johns Rd CV10. . . . . .27 E7
St John's Rd
Cherington CV36 . . . . 141 D7
Royal Leamington Spa
CV31. . . . . 110 A6
St John's St
Coventry CV1. . . . . 151 C2
Kenilworth CV8 . . . . .93 A3
St John's Terr 13 CV31 . .110 A6
St John St CV21 . . . . .83 A4
St Johns CV34 . . . . .108 F7
St Johns Way B93 . . . . .72 B6
St John the Baptist RC Prim
Sch B36 . . . . .33 B7
St John the Divine CE Prim
Sch CV3 . . . . .78 C5
St John Vianney RC Prim Sch
CV5 .60 B3
St Joseph B96. . . . . .118 D8
St Joseph's RC Jun Sch
CV11 . . . . .29 D3
St Joseph's RC Prim Sch
Banbury OX16 . . . . .139 F3
Whitnash CV31 . . . . .110 A3
St Judes Ave B80 . . . . .103 D4
St Jude's Cres CV3 . . . . .78 D7
St Laurence Ave CV34 . . .108 D5
St Laurence Cl CV35 . . . . .114 A8
St Laurence Way B50 . . . .148 D5

St Lawrence CE Prim Sch
CV47 . . . . 125 C7
St Lawrence Cl
Knowle B93. . . . . .72 B5
Napton on H CV47. . . . . . 125 C8
St Lawrence Rd CV10 . . . . .27 B4
St Lawrence's Rd CV6. . . . .49 F1
St Leonards Cl
Birmingham B37 . . . . .44 A7
Dordon B78. . . . . .11 A6
St Leonards View B78. . . . .10 F8
St Leonard's Wlk CV8. . . . .79 A1
St Luke's Rd CV6 . . . . .49 D3
St Lukes Way CV10. . . . . . . .28 C4
St Margaret Rd
Coventry CV1. . . . . .61 F2
Stoke Golding CV13 . . . . . .21 E7
St Margaret's Cl
CV31. . . . . 110 B3
St Margaret's CE Prim Sch
CV13 . . . . .21 D7
St Margaret's Rd CV31 . .110 B4
St Margaret's Rd CV31 . .110 B5
St Marie's RC Inf Sch
CV22 . . . . .83 A2
St Marie's RC Jun Sch
CV22 . . . . .82 F2
St Mark's Annexe (Coventry
& Warwickshire Hospl)
CV1 . . . . 151 C4
St Mark's Ave CV22 . . . . . .99 C7
St Mark's CV35. . . . . .132 E8
St Marks Cl CV10 . . . . .28 C4
St Mark's Cl CV35 . . . . . . .112 E6
St Mark's Mews CV32. . . .105 E1
St Mark's Rd CV32 . . . . . .105 D1
St Martins Ave B80 . . . . . .103 D4
St Martin's Cl CV37 . . . . . .144 E2
St Martin's LE10 . . . . .31 E6
St Martin's Rd CV3 . . . . .77 C2
St Martin's RC Sch CV13 . .21 E7
St Marys Acre CV37 . . . . .120 E7
St Mary & St Benedict RC
Prim Sch CV1 . . . . .61 E4
LE10. . . . . .31 D8
St Mary's Cl
Priors Hardwick CV47 . . . 125 D3
Southam CV47 . . . . .147 C5
Ullenhall B95. . . . . .112 E6
Warwick CV34 . . . . .108 D8
St Mary's Cres CV31 . . . . .110 B7
St Mary's Ct
Kenilworth CV8 . . . . .92 F2
Nuneaton CV11 . . . . .29 B5
St Marys Gr B79 . . . . .2 D3
St Mary's Immaculate RC
Prim Sch CV34 . . . . .108 E8
St Mary's La OX7 . . . . .142 F2
St Mary's RC Prim Sch
Aston le W NN11 . . . . .134 F5
Henley-in-A B95. . . . . .113 B4
Southam CV47 . . . . .147 C4
Studley B80. . . . . .103 E4
St Mary's Rd
Alcester B49 . . . . 143 D4
Atherstone CV9 . . . . .18 E8
Fillongley CV7 . . . . .36 E3
Hinckley LE10 . . . . .31 D8
Nuneaton CV11 . . . . .29 B5
Royal Leamington Spa
CV31. . . . . 110 B7
Stratford-u-A CV37 . . . . . 145 A4
St Mary St CV1 . . . . .151 C2
St Mary's Terr CV31 . . . . . .110 B7
St Matthew's Bloxam CE
Prim Sch CV22 . . . . .82 E2
St Matthews Cl
Nuneaton CV10 . . . . .28 C4
Salford Priors WR11 . . . . .127 E6
St Matthews St 2 CV21. . .83 A3
St Mawgan Cl B35. . . . . . . .22 C4
St Michael's CE Prim Sch
CV12 . . . . .39 D3
St Michaels Cl CV9 . . . . . . .12 F1
St Michael's Cl
Bishops Itchington CV47 . 124 A4
Claverdon CV35. . . . . .113 F3
New Arley CV7. . . . . .37 A8
South Littleton WR11. . . .127 F1
St Michaels Cl CV33 . . . . .111 F1
St Michael's Cl CV33. . . . .107 C2
St Michaels Ct CV3 . . . . . . .10 C1
St Michael's Cres CV47 . .147 F8
St Michael's Dr DE12 . . . . . .3 F8
St Michael's Hospl CV34 108 D8
St Michael's Rd
Claverdon CV35. . . . . .113 F3
Coventry CV2. . . . . .62 A3
Warwick CV34 . . . . .108 D8
St Michael's Way CV10. . . .28 C4
St Milburgh Cl WR11. . . . .127 D1
St Nicholas Ave CV8 . . . . . .92 F3
St Nicholas CE Com Prim
Sch CV8 . . . . .92 F5
St Nicholas CE Prim Sch
B49. 143 C4
St Nicholas Church St
CV34 . . . . 108 F6
St Nicholas Cl
Alcester B49 . . . . 143 C4
Austrey CV9. . . . . .3 A1
Coventry CV1. . . . . .61 C5
St Nicholas Ct
3 Coventry,Edgwick CV6 . .61 F7
Coventry,Radford CV6 . . . .61 B6
St Nicholas Est CV9. . . . . . .11 C1

St Nicholas Pk CV34 . . . . .108 F6
St Nicholas Rd
Henley-in-A B95. . . . . .113 B4
Radford Semele CV31. . . .110 F5
St Nicholas St CV1. . . . . . .151 B4
St Nicholas Terr CV31 . . . .110 E4
St Nicholas Wlk B76 . . . . . .23 B6
St Nicolas CE Prim Sch
CV11 . . . . .29 F6
St Nicolas Park Dr CV11 . .29 F7
St Nicolas Rd CV11 . . . . . . .29 D5
St Osburg's RC Prim Sch
CV1 . . . . 151 A3
St Osburg's Rd CV2 . . . . . . .62 A3
St Oswalds CE Prim Sch
CV22 . . . . .82 D3
St Patrick's CE Jun & Inf Sch
B94. .70 C2
St Patricks Dr
Birmingham B37 . . . . .33 C2
Coventry CV2. . . . . .50 D1
CV10 . . . . 109 F6
St Patrick's Rd CV1 . . . . . .151 B2
St Paul's CE Prim Sch
Nuneaton CV10 . . . . .28 C3
Royal Leamington Spa
CV32. . . . . 106 B1
St Paul's Cl CV34 . . . . .108 D6
St Paul's Cres 5 B46. . . . . .33 F7
St Pauls Cl GL56. . . . . .140 A2
St Paul's Ct B46. . . . . .9 C4
St Pauls Ct B46. . . . . .23 B3
St Paul's Rd
Coventry CV6. . . . . .61 C6
Nuneaton CV10 . . . . .28 D3
St Paul's Sq 4 CV32 . . . . .106 A1
St Paul's Terr CV34 . . . . . .108 D6
St Peter's Ave CV9 . . . . .19 B7
St Peter's Cl
Redditch B97 . . . . .102 E5
Water Orton B46. . . . . .23 B2
Witherley CV9 . . . . .19 A4
St Peters Cl 15 CV35. . . . .132 B6
St Peter's Ct CV1 . . . . .151 D4
St Peter's Ct GL56. . . . . . .140 A2
St Peter's Dr CV10 . . . . .27 F4
St Peters La B92. . . . . .44 D1
St Peter's Pl B78 . . . . .15 D5
St Peter's RC Prim Sch
CV32 . . . . 109 F8
St Peters Rd 12 CV35. . . .132 B6
St Peter's Rd CV32 . . . . . .109 F8
St Peters Rd
Atherstone CV9 . . . . .19 A7
Rugby CV21. . . . . .83 C3
St Peters Rd CV35. . . . . . .146 D4
St Peters Way CV37. . . . . .144 F6
St Philip's Ct B46. . . . . .34 A7
Saint's Peter & Paul RC Prim
Sch CV2 . . . . .62 F7
Saints Way CV10 . . . . .29 D5
St Swithin's Dr CV37 . . . .129 D2
St Thomas More RC Fst Sch
B98. 103 B7
St Thomas More RC Prim
Sch CV3 . . . . .77 D5
St Thomas Rd
St Thomas' Rd CV6. . . . . . .50 A3
St Thomas's Ct CV10 . . . . .28 C3
St Thomas's Cl CV10 . . . . .61 B2
St Thomas's Ho 17 CV1 . . .61 B2
St Wulstan Way CV47 . . . 147 C5
Salcombe Cl
Coventry CV3. . . . . .78 C6
Nuneaton CV11 . . . . .29 F5
Salemorton Ct CV22 . . . . . .99 B6
Salem Rd LE10 . . . . .31 F5
Salford Cl
Coventry CV2. . . . . .62 A3
Redditch B98 . . . . .103 B6
Salford Priors CE Prim Sch
WR11. . . . . 127 F6
Salford Rd B50 . . . . .148 C4
Salisbury Ave CV3 . . . . .77 C6
Salisbury Cl CV8 . . . . .79 F3
Salisbury Dr
Nuneaton CV10 . . . . .28 B7
Water Orton B46. . . . . .23 C3
Salisbury Rd LE10. . . . . .32 B7
Salters La B95 . . . . .120 C7
Salter St B94 . . . . .70 D2
Saltisford Canal Ctr*
CV34 . . . . 108 C8
Saltisford Gdns CV34. . . .108 C8
Saltisford CV34 . . . . .108 D7
Salt La CV1. . . . . .151 B2
Salts La B78. . . . . .8 E5
Salt Way B79,CV9 . . . . .8 B7
Salt Way B96 . . . . .118 B7
Salt Way La OX15 . . . . .137 F2
Sambourne La
Astwood Bank B96. . . . . .102 F1
Coughton B49,B96 . . . . . .118 E7
Sambourne Park La B96 . .103 A1
Sambourne Pk B96 . . . . . .118 D8
Sam Gault Cl CV3. . . . . .78 F7
Sammons Way CV4 . . . . . . .59 D2
Sampson Cl CV2. . . . . .62 C8
Samuel Hayward Ho 5
CV2 . . . . .50 B1
Samuel Vale Ho CV1. . . . .151 B4
Sanby Cl CV12 . . . . .39 D3
Sanctus Ct 2 CV37 . . . . . .144 F1
Sanctus Dr CV37 . . . . .144 F1
Sanctus Rd CV37 . . . . .144 F1
Sanctus St CV37 . . . . .144 F1

Sanda Croft B36 33 B6
Sandbarn Cl B90 70 F6
Sand Barn La CV37 121 D6
Sandel Cl CV37 144 E3
Sanders Cl
Atherstone CV9 12 E1
Braunston NN11 117 D5
Sanders Ct CV34 109 C8
Sanders Rd
Bedworth CV6 50 B6
Salford Priors WR11 127 F6
Sandfield Cl B90 70 B8
Sandfield Ct 12 CV37 144 F1
Sandfield La CV37 130 E1
Sandfield Rd CV37 144 F1
Sandfine Rd OX15 139 D1
Sandford Cl CV2 50 E3
Sandford Gn OX16 139 F4
Sandford Way CV22 99 C3
Sandgate Cres CV2 62 E2
Sandhills Cres B91 71 B8
Sandhurst Gr CV6 61 B5
Sandilands Cl CV2 62 E4
Sandon Rd CV11 29 B5
Sandown Ave CV6 49 F2
Sandown Cl
Royal Leamington Spa CV32 106 C4
Stratford-u-A CV37 144 D1
Sandown Rd CV21 83 C4
Sandpiper Cl
Rugby CV23 67 C1
Stratford-u-A CV37 144 D5
Sandpiper Rd CV2 50 B3
Sandpiper B77 10 A5
Sandpits Cl
Curdworth B76 23 C6
Upper Tysoe CV35 138 B6
Sandpits La CV6 48 F2
Sandpits Rd CV35 138 B7
Sandpits The CV12 40 C2
Sandringham Cl CV4 75 F5
Sandringham Ct CV10 28 F6
Sandstone Ct B77 10 A7
Sandwick Cl CV3 78 F8
Sandy La
Blackdown CV32 105 F6
Coventry CV1 61 C5
Fillongley CV7 37 A3
Furnace End B46 25 E3
Marton CV23 115 D7
Monks Kirby CV23 53 F4
Sandy Lane Bsns Pk CV1 61 C5
Sandy La
Newton Regis B79 2 D6
Royal Leamington Spa CV32 105 D4
Rugby CV21 82 E3
Sandythorpe CV3 78 E6
Sandy Way CV35 122 B7
Sandy Way La B78 11 C7
Sandy Way B77 4 B3
Sankey Gr GL56 140 A2
Santos Cl CV3 78 F8
Sapcote Gr CV2 50 B4
Sapcote Rd LE10 32 B7
Saplings The B76 22 A8
Sapphire Dr CV31 109 F5
Sapphire Gate CV2 62 C2
Saracen Dr
Balsall Common CV7 73 E6
Sutton Coldfield B75 13 A6
Sarawak Pl CV22 99 B8
Sargeaunt St CV31 109 F7
Sark Dr B36 33 B6
Satchwell Ct 15 CV32 109 F8
Satchwell Wlk 16 CV32 109 F8
Saumur Way CV34 109 C6
Saunders Ave CV12 39 B2
Saunders Ho 11 CV32 105 F2
Saunton Cl CV5 60 B8
Saunton Rd CV22 82 F1
Savages Cl CV33 122 F8
Savernake Rd CV35 132 C4
Saville Gr CV8 93 C5
Sawbridge Rd CV23 116 F5
Sawlcliffe Lea OX15 139 A1
Saxon Cl
4 Cawston CV22 99 A8
Binley Woods CV3 79 D7
Polesworth B78 4 F1
Stratford-u-A CV37 145 C2
Studley B80 103 E5
Tamworth B77 9 F6
Saxon Ct B50 148 D4
Saxonfields B50 148 D4
Saxon Mdws CV32 105 C2
Saxon Rd CV2 62 B4
Saxon Wood Rd B90 70 D5
Scafell Cl CV5 60 A4
Scafell CV21 83 D7
Scammerton B77 10 B7
Scar Bank CV34 104 E1
Scarborough Way CV4 75 F7
Scarman Rd CV4 76 B5
Schofield Rd B37 33 A5
Scholars Ct CV37 144 F3
Scholars Dr CV22 99 B8
Scholars La CV37 144 F2
Scholfield Rd CV7 49 A6
School Ave WR11 127 F6
School Bell Mews CV8 94 B6
School Cl
Birmingham,Castle Vale B35 22 B3
Birmingham,Kingshurst B37 33 A6
Braunston NN11 117 E5
Coventry CV3 61 F2
School Cl *continued*
Great Alne B49 119 D6
Hinckley LE10 32 A6
Long Compton CV36 141 C3
School Cotts CV35 90 F3
School Croft CV35 91 C2
School Dr B47 69 A3
Schoolfield Gr 1 CV21 83 A3
School Gdns CV21 84 A1
School Hill
Hartshill CV10 28 A8
Mollington OX17 133 F2
Napton on t H CV47 125 C8
Offchurch CV33 111 B8
Wootton Wawen B95 113 A3
School House La CV2 63 A6
School House Mews B95 113 B4
School La
Badby NN11 126 F6
Bearley CV37 120 E7
Bedworth CV7 49 F7
Galley Common CV10 27 E5
Kenilworth CV8 92 F5
Ladbroke CV47 124 D5
Lea Marston B76 24 A7
Little Packington CV7 45 D7
Lower Brailes OX15 137 F2
Middle Littleton WR11 127 F1
North Newington OX15 139 E2
Priors Marston CV47 125 E4
Radford Semele CV31 110 E5
Shuttington B79 4 F7
Stretton-on-D CV23 96 F6
Tamworth B77 9 D5
Tiddington CV37 145 E4
Warmington OX17 133 D2
Weston u W CV33 107 E5
Wolvey LE10 41 E4
Wroxall CV35 90 E4
School Rd
Alcester B49 143 B4
Bulkington CV12 40 C2
Great Alne B49 119 D6
Henley-in-A B95 113 B4
Hockley Heath B94 88 B7
Pebworth CV37 128 F1
Salford Priors WR11 127 F6
Snitterfield CV37 121 B6
Wellesbourne CV35 146 E3
School St
Church Lawford CV23 81 B5
Churchover CV23 67 C6
Dunchurch CV22 99 C3
Long Lawford CV23 82 A4
Rugby CV21 84 A1
Southam CV47 147 C4
Stockton CV47 147 F8
Wolston CV8 80 B4
School Wlk CV11 29 E2
Scotchill The CV6 49 A1
Scotland End OX15 142 D4
Scots Cl CV22 99 C7
Scots La CV6 60 F6
Scott Ave CV10 29 D8
Scott Cl
13 Stratford-u-A CV37 130 B8
Bidford-on-A B50 148 C5
Scott Rd
Kenilworth CV8 92 E2
Redditch B97 102 C8
Royal Leamington Spa CV31 110 B6
Scowcroft Dr CV47 124 A4
Seabroke Ave CV22 82 F3
Seafield La
Carpenter's Hill B98 86 A2
Portway B48,B98 85 E4
Seaford Cl CV6 50 B4
Seagrave Rd CV1 151 D1
Sealand Dr CV12 39 A3
Sear Hills Cl CV7 74 B6
Seathwaite CV21 83 C7
Seaton Cl
Hinckley LE10 32 B7
Nuneaton CV11 29 F5
Seaton B77 9 F8
Sebastian Cl CV3 78 B5
Seckington La B79 2 C3
Second Ave CV3 62 C1
Second Exhibition Ave B40 44 D4
Sedgemere Gr CV7 74 C5
Sedgemoor Rd CV3 78 B5
Sedlescombe Lodge CV22 99 E7
Sedlescombe Pk CV22 99 F8
Seed Field Croft CV3 77 E7
Seekings Dr CV8 93 B4
Seekings The CV31 110 B3
Seeney La B76 15 B2
Seeswood Cl CV10 28 C2
Sefton Rd
Coventry CV4 76 E6
Tamworth B77 9 D4
Seggs La B49 143 B3
Segrave Cl 14 CV35 132 B6
Selborne Rd CV22 99 D8
Selby Way CV10 28 B5
Selco Way B76 22 A5
Selina Dix Ho CV1 151 C4
Selsdon Cl B47 69 C5
Selsey Cl CV3 78 C4
Selside CV21 83 D7
Selworthy Rd CV6 49 E3
Selwyn Cl CV35 146 D4
Selwyn Ho B37 33 D3
Semele Cl CV31 110 E5
Seneschal Rd CV3 77 E7
Sennen Cl CV11 30 A5
Sentry Way B75 13 A6
Sephton Dr CV6 50 C6
Servite Ho
2 Coleshill B46 33 F7
Kenilworth CV8 92 F3
Sett The CV35 137 F8
Seven Acre Cl 4 CV33 122 E8
Seven Ho CV37 145 E4
Seven Meadows Rd CV37 144 F1
Seven Stars Ind Est CV3 78 A7
Severn Ave LE10 31 A8
Severn Cl CV32 106 C3
Severn Rd
Bulkington CV12 40 A3
Coventry CV1 61 F1
Sevilla Cl CV3 63 A2
Sevincott Cl CV37 144 C4
Sevington Cl B91 71 C8
Sewall Ct CV6 62 A8
Sewall Highway CV2 62 B6
Seymour Cl
Coventry CV3 78 C5
Hampton Magna CV35 114 F3
Seymour Gate GL55 135 B2
Seymour Gr CV34 109 D6
Seymour Ho CV3 77 C8
Seymour Homes B95 113 B2
Seymour Rd
Alcester B49 143 C5
Nuneaton CV11 29 D3
Rugby CV21 83 C6
Stratford-u-A CV37 144 D1
Shackelton Way LE17 55 D5
Shackleton Dr LE10 31 E4
Shadowbrook La B92 56 E7
Shadowbrook Rd CV6 61 A5
Shaftesbury Ave CV7 49 A7
Shaftesbury Rd CV5 76 F8
Shaft La CV7 47 A4
Shakels Cl B97 102 E4
Shakers La CV47 115 C5
Shakesfield Cl CV36 136 F6
Shakespeare Ave
Bedworth CV12 39 D2
Warwick CV34 108 C4
Shakespeare Ct 10 CV37 145 A3
Shakespeare Ctr Mus The★ CV37 145 A3
Shakespeare Dr CV11 30 A1
Shakespeare Gdns CV22 99 E7
Shakespeare La WR11 127 D3
Shakespeare Rd B90 70 D8
Shakespeares Birthplace Mus★ CV37 145 A3
Shakespeare's Grave★ CV37 145 A1
Shakespeare St
Coventry CV2 62 B4
Stratford-u-A CV37 145 A3
Shakleton Rd CV5 61 A2
Shanes Castle Rd CV35 132 D3
Shanklin Dr CV10 29 D6
Shanklin Rd CV3 78 B4
Shannon B77 9 F8
Shap Fell CV21 83 D7
Sharnford Rd LE10 32 F6
Sharp Cl CV6 49 C2
Sharpe Cl CV34 108 E8
Sharpe St B77 4 A5
Sharpless Rd LE10 31 F7
Sharpley Ct CV2 63 A8
Sharratt Rd CV12 39 A2
Sharries The GL56 136 C1
Sharry La CV37 129 C1
Shawberry Ave B35 22 B4
Shawbury Cotts B46 35 E7
Shawbury La
Fillongley CV7 36 A5
Shustoke B46 35 C7
Shawbury Village B46 35 E6
Shawe Ave CV10 29 C7
Shawell Rd
Shawell LE17 68 D8
Shawell LE17 68 F4
Shawfield B47 69 A5
Shawhurst Croft B47 69 A7
Shawhurst Gdns B47 69 B7
Shawhurst La B47 69 A6
Shaw's La CV35 114 C8
Shearings The OX15 142 D4
Shearwater Dr CV23 67 C1
Sheen Ho CV2 62 D8
Sheepclose Dr B37 33 A3
Sheepcote Cl CV32 106 A1
Sheep Dip La CV23 96 E2
Sheep St
Chipping Campden GL55 135 A1
Rugby CV21 83 A3
Shipston-on-S CV36 149 D6
Stratford-u-A CV37 145 A2
Sheepy La CV9 6 E3
Sheepy Rd
Atherstone CV9 12 D2
Atherstone,Pinwall CV9 12 E6
Shefford Rd CV35 132 D3
Shelbourne Rd CV37 144 B4
Shelby La CV37 121 C7
Sheldon Gr CV34 104 F2
Sheldon Rd B98 103 A8
Sheldons The CV36 149 D7
Sheldrake Cl CV3 63 A1
Shelfield Cl
Coventry CV5 60 B3
Hockley Heath B94 88 C6
Shelley Ave CV34 108 C4
Shelley Cl
Bedworth CV12 39 D1
Shelley Cl *continued*
Redditch B97 102 C8
Shelley Rd
Coventry CV2 62 C3
Stratford-u-A CV37 145 B1
Shellon Cl CV3 78 F8
Shelly Cres B90 71 B6
Shelly La B90 71 B6
Shelton Sq CV1 151 B2
Shelton St B77 9 F7
Shelwick Gr B93 71 F4
Shenington CE Prim Sch OX15 138 E5
Shenington Kart Club★ OX15 138 E5
Shenstone Ave CV22 83 E1
Shenstone Dr CV7 74 A6
Shenton Cl CV13 21 E7
Shepheards La CV7 46 A3
Shepherd Cl
Coventry CV4 59 F3
Long Itchington CV47 115 D3
Shepherd Pl CV35 132 B5
Shepherds Cl OX15 142 D8
Shepherds Hill CV47 147 D4
Shepherd St CV23 115 C7
Shepperton Bsns Pk CV11 29 C1
Shepperton Ct CV11 29 C1
Shepperton St CV11 29 C2
Sheppey Dr B36 33 B5
Sherard Croft B36 33 B6
Sherborne Cl B46 34 A4
Sherborne Rd LE10 32 B7
Sherbourne Arc CV1 151 B2
Sherbourne Ave CV10 28 B4
Sherbourne Cres CV5 60 E4
Sherbourne Ct CV1 151 B1
Sherbourne Fields Sch CV6 60 D5
Sherbourne St CV1 61 A2
Sherbrooke Ave B77 9 E6
Sherdmore Croft B90 70 F6
Sheridan Cl CV22 99 F7
Sheridan Dr CV10 27 F5
Sheridan Wlk B35 22 A3
Sheriff Ave CV4 76 B7
Sheriff Rd CV21 83 D3
Sheriffs Orch CV1 151 B2
Sheringham Cl CV11 29 F2
Sherington Ave CV5 60 C4
Sherlock Rd CV5 60 D3
Sherwell Dr B49 143 B4
Sherwood Cl CV9 10 C1
Sherwood Jones Cl CV6 61 B6
Sherwood Rd CV13 21 E7
Sherwood Wlk CV32 106 C4
Shetland Ave B77 9 F7
Shetland Cl CV5 60 A4
Shetland Dr CV10 29 A2
Shetland Wlk B36 33 B6
Shevlock Way CV6 62 A6
Shillingstone Cl CV2 63 A4
Shillingstone Dr CV10 29 A1
Shilton & Ansty CE Fst Sch CV7 51 E5
Shilton Cl B90 70 F6
Shilton Ind Est CV7 51 E7
Shilton La
Barnacle CV2,CV7 51 B4
Bulkington CV12 40 D1
Coventry CV2 50 F3
Shilton CV7,CV12 51 D8
Shinehill La WR11 128 A1
Shipston High Sch CV36 149 C6
Shipston Ind Est CV36 149 C7
Shipston Rd
Alderminster CV37 130 B5
Coventry CV2 62 C6
Long Compton CV36 141 C4
Upper Tysoe CV35 138 B6
Shipton-on-Stour Prim Sch CV36 149 D6
Shirebrook Cl CV2 50 D2
Shire Cl CV6 50 B1
Shires Gate Ret Pk CV31 109 E6
Shires Gate Trad Est CV31 109 E6
Shires Ret Pk CV34 109 D6
Shires The CV23 81 B6
Shirland Rd B37 33 A1
Shirlett Cl CV2 50 B4
Shirleydale 2 B90 70 C8
Shirley La CV7 59 A5
Shirley Rd CV2 63 A7
Shirrall Dr B78 7 E4
Shopping Ctr The CV31 110 B5
Shopping Prec The CV34 105 A1
Shorncliffe Rd CV6 60 E6
Shortacres CV35 132 C6
Shortfield Cl CV7 74 B7
Short La CV47 115 C4
Shortland Cl B93 72 A7
Shortlands CV7 49 D6
Shortley Rd CV3 77 F8
Short St
Coventry CV1 151 C2
Nuneaton CV10 28 D4
Solihull B90 70 A5
Shortwoods The B78 11 A6
Shottery Cl CV5 60 B3
Shottery Rd CV37 144 E2
Shottery St Andrew's CE Prim Sch CV37 144 D2
Shottery CV37 144 D2
Shotteswell Rd B90 70 B8
Shoulderway La CV36 149 D2
Showell La CV7 47 A1
Shreres Dyche CV34 108 C4
Shrewley Comm CV35 114 B6
Shrieve's Wlk 6 CV37 145 A2
Shrubberies The CV4 76 E4
Shrubland Street Com Prim Sch CV31 110 A6
Shrubland St CV31 110 A6
Shuckburgh Cres
Bourton on D CV23 97 E2
Rugby CV22 100 D8
Shuckburgh Gr 5 CV32 106 A2
Shuckburgh Rd
Napton on t H CV47 125 C8
Priors Marston CV47 125 E4
Shulman's Wlk CV2 62 D7
Shultern La CV4 76 D6
Shuna Croft CV2 63 B7
Shurnock Court Barns B96 118 A7
Shustoke CE Prim Sch B46 25 A2
Shustoke Resrs★ B46 24 F3
Shutford Rd
North Newington OX15 139 D2
Shutford OX15 139 B1
Shuttington Rd B77,B79 4 B6
Shutt La B94 70 B1
Shuttle St CV6 62 B8
Shuttleworth Rd CV23 83 F5
Shylock Gr CV34 109 E2
Sibford Gower Prim Sch OX15 142 D8
Sibford Rd
Hook Norton OX15 142 D4
Shutford OX15 138 F2
Sibford Sch OX15 142 D8
Sibree Rd CV3 78 B4
Sibton Cl CV2 50 C1
Sidbury Gr B93 71 E3
Sidbury Rd CV6 61 C6
Siddaway Ho CV21 83 C7
Siddeley Ave
Coventry CV3 62 B1
Kenilworth CV8 92 E3
Siddeley Way NN11 117 F2
Sidelands Rd CV37 144 C3
Sidenhill Cl B90 70 B8
Sidings Ind Est The CV23 115 D7
Sidings The
Rugby CV21 83 B4
Shipston-on-S CV36 149 D7
Sidmouth Cl
Coventry CV2 62 C7
Nuneaton CV11 29 F5
Sidney Rd CV22 100 D8
Sidney Stringer Com Tech Coll CV1 151 C3
Signal Hayes Rd B76 13 A2
Signal Rd CV36 149 D7
Signal Wlk B77 4 A2
Silica Rd B77 4 B2
Silken Ct CV11 29 B4
Silksby St CV3 77 D8
Silver Birch Ave CV12 38 E2
Silver Birch Cl CV3 79 D7
Silverbirch Cl CV10 28 A7
Silver Birch Dr B47 69 B6
Silver Birch Gr 5 CV31 109 F5
Silverdale Cl CV2 50 B4
Silver Link Rd B77 4 A2
Silver St
Coventry CV1 151 B3
Newton CV23 68 A1
Silverstone Dr CV6 49 E5
Silver St OX15 139 D4
Silverton Rd CV6 61 F7
Silver Trees Dr CV12 40 B4
Silver Wlk CV10 28 F3
Simmonds Way CV9 12 D2
Simmons Cl B78 8 B1
Simmons Ct CV35 146 D3
Simms La B47 69 A5
Simon Cl CV11 29 D2
Simon Ct CV7 50 A8
Simon Rd B47 69 A7
Simon Stone St CV6 61 F8
Simpkins Cl CV33 107 D7
Simpson Gr CV3 78 C6
Simpson Rd CV36 149 D5
Sinclair Ave 11 OX16 139 F4
Sinclair Dr CV6 50 C6
Singer Cl CV6 62 B8
Singer Croft B36 22 F1
Sir Frank Whittle Bsns Ctr CV21 83 D5
Sir Frank Whittle Prim Sch CV2 62 F8
Sir Henry Parkes Rd CV5 76 D7
Sir John Moore CE Prim Sch DE12 3 E7
Sir Thomas White's Rd CV5 60 F2
Sir Toby Belch Dr CV34 109 F3
Sir William Lyons Rd CV4 76 C6
Sir Winston Churchill Pl CV3 79 C7
Siskin Cl CV23 83 C8
Siskin Dr CV3 78 C4
Siskin Parkway E CV3 78 C1
Siskin Parkway W CV3 78 C2
Sitwell Ave CV47 115 D3
Sixteen Acres La B50 148 E1
Skelwith Rise CV11 30 A6
Sketchley Hall Gdns LE10 31 C5

Sketchley Hill Prim Sch
LE10 . . . . .31 E5
Sketchley La LE10 . . . . . . .31 C5
Sketchley La Ind Est LE10 .31 B5
Sketchley Manor La LE10. .31 D5
Sketchley Mdws LE10 . . . .31 C5
Sketchley Meadows Bsns Pk
LE10 . . . . .31 C4
Sketchley Old Village
LE10 . . . . .31 E5
Sketchley Rd LE10 . . . . . . .31 E5
Skey Dr CV10 . . . . .28 B6
Skiddaw CV21 . . . . .83 C7
Skidmore Ave B77 . . . . .9 C5
Skitts Sch B98 . . . . .112 B6
Skipton Gdns CV2 . . . . .62 B6
Skipton Lodge CV2 . . . . . . .62 B6
Skipwith Cl CV23 . . . . .64 D3
Skipworth Rd CV3 . . . . .63 A1
Sky Blue Way CV1 . . . . .61 E3
Skydome The CV1. . . . . . .151 A2
Skye Cl
Birmingham B36 . . . . .33 B6
Nuneaton CV10 . . . . .28 F2
Tamworth B77 . . . . .9 F7
Slack's Ave CV9 . . . . .18 D7
Slade Cl CV11 . . . . .40 C8
Slade Gr B93 . . . . .71 F6
Slade Hill CV35 . . . . .114 F4
Slade La
Sutton Coldfield B75 . . . . . . .7 A3
Tamworth B77 . . . . .9 C4
Slade Mdw CV31. . . . . . . .110 E5
Slade Rd
Rugby CV21,CV22 . . . . . . .83 C2
Sutton Coldfield B75 . . . . . .7 A4
Slade The OX17,CV47 . . .133 E6
Slateley Cres B90 . . . . .70 F6
Slater Rd B93 . . . . .71 F4
Sleath's Yd CV12. . . . . .39 B3
Sledmere Cl CV2 . . . . .50 B3
Sleets Yd CV12 . . . . .39 A2
Slimbridge Cl
[2] Solihull B90 . . . . .71 A6
Redditch B97 . . . . .102 E5
Slingates Rd CV37 . . . . . . .145 A4
Slingsby Cl CV11. . . . . .29 F2
Slingsby B77 . . . . .9 C7
Slingsby The B97,B80. . . .103 B4
Slowley Hill CV7 . . . . .36 A8
Smallbrook Bsns Ctr
B50 . . . . .148 E6
Smalley Pl CV8 . . . . .92 F4
Small Ho OX15 . . . . .142 D8
Small La B94 . . . . .86 E6
Smallman Rd CV10. . . . . . .28 A7
Smarts La CV35 . . . . .138 B6
Smarts Rd CV12 . . . . .38 F1
Smeaton La CV23 . . . . .64 E6
Smercote Cl CV12 . . . . . . .38 C1
Smite Cl CV23 . . . . .53 F3
Smithford Way CV1 . . . . . .151 B3
Smiths Cl B50. . . . . .148 E5
Smiths La B93 . . . . .71 E7
Smith's La CV37 . . . . .121 B6
Smiths Orch CV21 . . . . . . .83 C3
Smith St
[2] Royal Leamington Spa
CV31. . . . . .109 F7
Bedworth CV12 . . . . .38 E1
Coventry CV6. . . . . .61 F5
Warwick CV34 . . . . .108 F7
Wood End CV9. . . . . .10 C1
Smith's Way B49 . . . . .143 C5
Smiths Wood Sch B36 . . . .33 A6
Smithy La
Aston Flamville LE9 . . . . . .32 C8
Aston Flamville LE9 . . . . . .32 D8
Baxterley CV9 . . . . .17 D6
Church Lawford CV23 . . . . .81 B6
Tamworth B77 . . . . .9 F7
Smockington La LE10 . . . . .42 B7
Smorrall La
Bedworth CV12 . . . . .38 C2
Corley CV7,CV12 . . . . .37 E1
Smythe Gr CV34 . . . . .104 E1
Snape Rd CV2 . . . . .62 F5
Snarestone Rd DE12 . . . . . .3 F8
Snitterfield La
Norton Lindsey CV37. . . . .114 C1
Snitterfield CV37 . . . . .121 C7
Snitterfield Prim Sch
CV37. . . . . .121 B6
Snitterfield Rd CV37 . . . . .120 E7
Snitterfield St CV35. . . . . .121 F4
Snowdon Cl CV10. . . . . . . .28 B3
Snowdrop Cl CV12 . . . . . . .38 E1
Snowford Hill CV33,CV47. .115 A5
Snows Drive Hill B90 . . . . .70 D5
Snowshill Cl CV11 . . . . . . .39 F8
Snuff La OX17 . . . . .139 E8
Soar Way LE10 . . . . .31 A8
Soden Cl CV3. . . . . .78 D6
Soden's Ave CV8 . . . . .79 A1
Solent Dr CV2 . . . . .50 F1
**Solihull Coll (Chelmsley
Campus)** B37 . . . . .33 C4
Solihull Parkway B37 . . . .44 E8
Solihull Rd B92. . . . . .56 E6
Solihull Ret Pk B90 . . . . . .70 C8
Solway Cl CV31. . . . . .110 C6
Somerby Dr B91 . . . . .71 A8
Somerly Cl CV3. . . . . .78 F8
Somerset Dr CV10 . . . . . . .28 E4

Somerset Pl CV22 . . . . .82 B1
Somerset Rd CV1 . . . . .61 C5
Somers Pl [4] CV32. . . . . .109 E8
Somers Rd
Keresley CV7 . . . . .49 A6
Meriden CV7 . . . . .45 F1
Rugby CV22 . . . . .82 D3
Somerton Dr B37. . . . . .44 B7
Somerville Ho B37 . . . . . . .33 D3
Sommerville Rd CV2 . . . . . .62 C4
Soot La OX17. . . . . .133 D2
Sopwith Croft B35. . . . . . . .22 A2
Sorbus B77. . . . . .4 B4
Soredale Croft CV3 . . . . . . .63 A1
Sorrel Cl CV4. . . . . .75 E8
Sorrel Dr
Kingsbury B78 . . . . .15 D7
Rugby CV23 . . . . .83 D8
Sorrell Pl CV10 . . . . .39 D8
Sorrell Rd CV10. . . . . .39 D8
Sorrel B77 . . . . .4 B5
Southam Cl CV4 . . . . .75 E7
Southam Coll CV47 . . . . . .147 A5
Southam Cres CV33. . . . . .123 D2
Southam Dr CV47. . . . . . . .147 A2
Southam Prim Sch CV47 .147 B5
Southam Rd
Dunchurch CV22 . . . . .99 B2
Kineton CV35. . . . . .132 B6
Ladbroke CV47 . . . . .124 D6
Long Itchington CV47 . . . .115 D3
Mollington OX17 . . . . .134 A2
Priors Marston CV47. . . . .125 E4
Southam CV33,CV47 . . . .124 B8
Ufton,Radford Hall CV31,CV33,
CV47 . . . . .111 D3
Southam St CV35 . . . . . . .132 B6
South Ave CV2. . . . . .62 A2
Southbank Cl CV34 . . . . . . .92 F4
Southbank Ho [16] CV34. .109 D8
Southbank Rd
Coventry CV6. . . . . .60 E5
Kenilworth CV8 . . . . .92 F3
Southborough Terr [1]
CV31. . . . . .110 A6
Southbrook Rd CV22. . . . . .83 A1
South Car Park Rd B40 . . .44 E3
South Cl NN11. . . . . .117 E5
Southcott Way CV2 . . . . . . .50 F1
South Dr B46. . . . . .33 E6
South End OX7 . . . . .142 A4
Southern La CV37. . . . . . . .145 A2
Southey Cl B91 . . . . .71 B8
Southey Rd CV22 . . . . .99 E7
Southfield Cl CV10. . . . . . . .29 D5
Southfield Dr CV8 . . . . .93 A6
Southfield Rd
Hinckley LE10 . . . . .31 E7
Rugby CV22 . . . . .83 C1
Southam CV47 . . . . .147 A2
Southfields B46. . . . . .34 A4
Southfields Prim Sch CV1 .61 E3
Southfields Rd CV1. . . . . . .61 E3
South Green Dr CV37 . . . .144 C3
Southlands
[8] Royal Leamington Spa
CV31. . . . . .110 B7
Atherstone CV9 . . . . .18 E7
Southlea Ave CV31 . . . . . .109 E6
South Lea Cl CV13 . . . . . .109 E6
Southleigh Ave CV5 . . . . . .77 A4
South Lynn Gdns CV36. . .149 D5
Southmead Gdns B80 . . . .103 E3
South Par CV33. . . . . .123 F6
Southport Cl CV3 . . . . .78 B5
South Rd CV23 . . . . .84 A5
South Ridge CV5 . . . . .60 B4
Southrop Rd OX15 . . . . . .142 D3
South St
Atherstone CV9 . . . . .18 E8
Coventry CV1 . . . . .61 E3
Rugby CV21 . . . . .83 D3
South Terr CV31 . . . . .110 B3
South View
Hampton Magna CV35. . . .108 A6
Kingsbury B78 . . . . .15 D4
South View Rd
Long Lawford CV23 . . . . . . .81 A4
Royal Leamington Spa
CV32. . . . . .106 C5
South Way B40 . . . . .44 F3
Southway CV31 . . . . .110 A5
Sovereign Cl CV8 . . . . .92 F1
Sovereign Ct [9] CV47. . . .147 B4
Sovereign Rd CV5 . . . . .61 A2
Sovereign Row CV5 . . . . . .61 A2
Sowe Valley Prim Sch
CV3 . . . . .78 D7
Sparkbrook St CV1 . . . . . . .61 F3
Sparkbrook Workshops
CV1. . . . . .61 F3
Sparrow Cock La B93 . . . . .73 C1
Sparrowdale Sch CV9 . . . . .11 D4
Sparta Cl CV21 . . . . .83 A6
Spartan Cl CV34 . . . . .109 E4
Spa View CV31. . . . . .110 B4
Speedway La CV8. . . . . .79 F7
Speedwell Cl
[6] Bedworth CV12 . . . . . .38 D2
Rugby CV23 . . . . .83 E7
Speedwell Dr CV7 . . . . .74 A6
Speedwell La CV9 . . . . .11 B1
Spencer Ave CV5 . . . . .60 E4
Spencer Ct [10] CV47 . . . .144 F1
Spencer Rd CV5 . . . . .151 A1
Spencer's La CV7. . . . . .74 B4
Spencer St CV31 . . . . .109 F7
Spencer Yd CV31 . . . . .109 F7

Spernal Ash B80 . . . . .103 F1
Spernal La
Great Alne B80 . . . . .119 C7
Spernall B80 . . . . .112 A1
Spetchley Cl B97 . . . . .102 C6
Sphinx Dr CV3. . . . . .62 B1
Spicer Pl CV22. . . . . .82 D1
Spiers Cl B93 . . . . .72 A6
Spiers Ct B50. . . . . .148 D5
Spilsbury Cl CV32 . . . . . . .105 E2
Spilsbury Croft B91. . . . . . .71 A8
Spindle La B90 . . . . .70 A6
Spindle St CV1 . . . . .61 D6
Spindles The LE10 . . . . . . .31 F5
Spinners Bridge CV36. . . .149 D6
Spinney Cl
Binley Woods CV3 . . . . . . .79 E7
Lighthorne CV35 . . . . .123 B3
New Arley CV7. . . . . .36 E8
Polesworth B78. . . . . .10 F8
Spinney Dr B90. . . . . .70 D4
Spinney Hill
Braunston NN11 . . . . .117 E5
Warwick CV34 . . . . .105 A1
Spinney La CV10 . . . . .28 C4
Spinney Rd LE10. . . . . .31 C6
Spinney The
Atherstone CV9 . . . . .19 A7
Bishops Itchington CV47. .124 B4
Coventry CV4. . . . . .76 D3
Long Lawford CV23 . . . . . .82 A5
Royal Leamington Spa
CV32. . . . . .105 D1
Solihull B91 . . . . .71 C8
Spire Bank CV47 . . . . .147 B3
Spires The CV10 . . . . .28 C4
Spitfire Cl CV5. . . . . .60 C1
Spitfire Way B35. . . . . .22 A2
Spon End CV1,CV5 . . . . . . .61 A3
Spon Gate Ho CV1. . . . . . . .61 A2
Spon Gate Prim Sch CV1. .61 A3
Spon La
Bradley Green CV9 . . . . . . .11 E5
Grendon CV9 . . . . .11 D4
Spot St CV1 . . . . .151 A3
Spottiswood Cl CV22 . . . . . .99 A8
Springbrook Cl B36. . . . . . .22 D1
Springbrook La B94 . . . . . .87 A7
Spring Cl
[6] Coventry CV1 . . . . .61 E3
Ettington CV37. . . . . .131 A3
Spring Coppice Dr B93 . . . .72 A3
Spring Ct CV8 . . . . .95 C5
Springdale Ct CV11 . . . . . .29 D3
Springfield Bsns Pk B49 .143 B5
Springfield Cl CV36 . . . . . .149 C5
Springfield Cres
Bedworth CV12 . . . . .39 B2
Sutton Coldfield B76 . . . . . .13 A4
Springfield Ct CV5 . . . . . . .148 F3
Springfield Gr CV47 . . . . . .147 B5
Springfield Ho OX17 . . . . . .9 B4
Springfield House Com Specl
Sch B93 . . . . .73 A5
Springfield Pl CV1 . . . . . . .151 C4
Springfield Rd
Coventry CV1 . . . . .151 C4
Hinckley LE10 . . . . .31 D7
Nuneaton CV11 . . . . .29 B2
Shipston-on-S CV36. . . . .149 D4
Sutton Coldfield B75,B76. .13 A4
Tamworth B77 . . . . .9 B4
Springfields B46 . . . . .33 F5
Springfields Rd B49 . . . . .143 B5
Spring Hill
Bubbenhall CV8 . . . . .95 C5
Combrook CV35. . . . . .131 F7
Springhill CV10 . . . . .28 A4
Springhill Houses CV22 . .100 C8
Springhill Ind Pk CV7 . . . .36 F8
Spring Hill CV7 . . . . .36 F7
Spring Hill Rd CV10. . . . . . .28 C6
Spring La
Combrook CV35. . . . . .131 E6
Hockley Heath B94 . . . . . . .88 B5
Kenilworth CV8 . . . . .93 A5
Lapworth B94 . . . . .88 D3
Radford Semele CV31. . . .110 E5
Spring Pool CV34. . . . . . . .108 E7
Spring Rd
Barnacle CV7 . . . . .51 B6
Coventry CV6. . . . . .49 F1
Springs Cres CV47 . . . . . .147 B5
Springside B98. . . . . .103 C8
Spring St CV21 . . . . .83 B3
Springwell Rd CV31. . . . . .110 D6
Spruce Gr [4] CV31 . . . . . .109 F5
Spruce Rd
Coventry CV2 . . . . .50 B2
Nuneaton CV10 . . . . .28 E7
Spruce B77. . . . . .4 B4
Squadron Cl B35 . . . . .22 C4
Square La CV7 . . . . .37 B2
Square The
Clifford Chambers CV37 . .129 F7
Coventry CV2. . . . . .63 A7
Dunchurch CV22 . . . . .99 D3
Ettington CV37. . . . . .131 A3
Fazeley B78 . . . . .9 A4
Kenilworth CV8 . . . . .92 F4
Long Itchington CV47 . . . .115 D4
Middle Tysoe CV35. . . . . .138 B7
Nuneaton CV11 . . . . .29 C3
Stockton CV47 . . . . .147 F8
Swalcliffe OX15. . . . . .142 F8
Wolvey LE10 . . . . .41 D4

Square The continued
Wootton Wawen B95. . . . .113 A3
Squire Pl CV47 . . . . .133 D7
Squires Croft
Coventry CV2. . . . . .50 F1
Sutton Coldfield B76 . . . . . .13 A2
Squires Gate Wlk B35. . . .22 A3
Squires Gn LE10 . . . . .31 F6
Squires Rd CV23 . . . . .96 F6
Squires Way CV4 . . . . .76 D6
Squirhill Pl [1] CV31. . . . .110 B7
Squirrel Hollow B76 . . . . . .13 A2
Stableford Cl B97. . . . . . . .102 D7
Stables The
Berkswell CV7 . . . . .58 C4
Hinckley LE10 . . . . .31 D5
Longbridge CV35. . . . . . . .114 F1
Royal Leamington Spa
CV32. . . . . .105 C1
Stable Wlk CV11 . . . . .29 F2
Stable Yd The CV13 . . . . . .21 D7
Stacey Ct CV22 . . . . .99 C5
Stadium Cl CV6 . . . . .49 D2
Stafford Cl CV12. . . . . .40 C2
Stafford St CV9 . . . . .18 E8
Staines Cl CV11 . . . . .29 F7
Stainforth Cl CV11. . . . . . . .30 A2
Stainsby Croft B90 . . . . . . .71 A5
Staircase La CV5 . . . . .60 C7
Stamford Ave CV3 . . . . .77 C6
Stamford Gdns CV32 . . . . .105 E1
Stanbrook Rd B90 . . . . .71 A5
Standard Ave CV4. . . . . . . .60 B1
Standedge B77 . . . . .10 B7
Standish Cl CV2 . . . . .62 E2
Standlake Mews [14]
CV31. . . . . .110 C6
Stand St CV34 . . . . .108 D5
Stanford Cl B97 . . . . .102 B6
Stanier Ave CV1 . . . . .61 B4
Stanley Ct CV31. . . . . .110 C7
Stanley Rd
Atherstone CV9 . . . . .18 D7
Coventry CV5. . . . . .76 F8
Nuneaton CV11 . . . . .29 A5
Rugby CV21,CV22 . . . . . . .83 E1
Stannells Cl CV37 . . . . . . .129 E8
Stansfield Gr CV8 . . . . .93 D4
Stanton Bridge Prim Sch
CV6 . . . . .61 F6
Stanton Rd CV31 . . . . .110 C6
Stanton Wlk CV34 . . . . . . .104 D1
Stanway Rd CV5 . . . . .77 A8
Stanwilliams Ct CV6 . . . . . .50 A4
Stapenhall Rd B90 . . . . . . .71 A5
Stapledon Gn CV47 . . . . . .132 F7
Staple Hill Ho CV35 . . . . . .122 D2
Staples Cl CV12 . . . . .40 C3
Stapleton Cl
Studley B80 . . . . .103 D3
Sutton Coldfield B76 . . . . . .22 B6
Stapleton Dr B37 . . . . .33 A4
Stapleton La CV13 . . . . . . .21 F8
Stapleton Rd B80 . . . . .103 D4
Starbold Cres B93 . . . . .72 A6
Starbold Rd CV47 . . . . . . .124 A4
Star Cnr CV23 . . . . .101 C1
Starcross Cl CV2 . . . . .62 C7
Stare Gn CV4 . . . . .76 D5
Stareton Cl CV4 . . . . .76 F6
Star Ind Pk CV2 . . . . .62 F8
Starkey Croft B37 . . . . .33 D2
Star La CV35 . . . . .114 A4
Starley Ct CV3 . . . . .79 A7
Starley Rd CV1 . . . . .151 A2
Starley Way B37. . . . . .44 C6
Starmer Pl CV35 . . . . .114 D6
Startin Cl CV7 . . . . .49 F7
Station App
Dorridge B93. . . . . .71 F2
Royal Leamington Spa
CV31. . . . . .109 F7
Station Ave
Coventry CV4. . . . . .75 D8
Warwick CV34 . . . . .108 F8
Station Bldgs B46 . . . . .23 B3
Station Cotts
Chipping Campden GL55 . .135 D2
Long Itchington CV47 . . . .115 D3
Station Dr B94 . . . . .69 D1
Station La B94. . . . . .89 D3
Station Link Rd B26 . . . . . .44 D4
Station Rd
[12] Moreton-in-M GL56 . .140 A3
Alcester B49 . . . . .143 B4
Balsall Common CV7. . . . . .74 B7
Birmingham,Marston Green
B37 . . . . .44 A8
Bishops Itchington CV47. .124 A4
Chipping Campden GL55 . .135 C2
Claverdon CV35 . . . . .114 A3
Clifton u D CV23 . . . . .83 F5
Coleshill B46 . . . . .23 F1
Dorridge B93. . . . . .72 B4
Dunnsmore CV23 . . . . .84 F8
Fenny Compton CV47 . . . .133 E7
Hampton-in-A B92 . . . . . . .57 B7
Harvington WR11 . . . . . . .127 D3
Hatton CV35 . . . . .114 C5
Henley-in-A B95 . . . . .113 A5
Higham on t H CV13 . . . . . .20 F4
Hook Norton OX15. . . . . . .142 E4
Kenilworth CV8 . . . . .92 F4
Kingswood B94 . . . . .89 D4

Station Rd continued
Long Marston CV37. . . . . .129 C2
Old Arley CV7. . . . . .36 D8
Polesworth B79. . . . . .5 A2
Salford Priors WR11 . . . . .127 F6
Shipston-on-S CV36. . . . .149 D6
South Littleton WR11. . . .127 F1
Stockton CV47 . . . . .116 A3
Stoke Golding CV13. . . . . .21 C7
Stratford-u-A CV37 . . . . . .144 F3
Studley B80. . . . . .103 D4
Warwick CV34 . . . . .108 F7
Whitacre Heath B46 . . . . . .24 D4
Wilmcote CV37 . . . . .120 C5
Wythall B47. . . . . .69 B3
Station St E CV6 . . . . .61 E7
Station St W CV6 . . . . .61 E7
Station Sq CV1 . . . . .151 B1
Station St CV9. . . . . .18 D8
Station Street W Bsns Pk
CV6 . . . . .61 D7
Staunton Rd CV31 . . . . . . .110 A5
Staveley Way CV21. . . . . . .83 E6
Staverton CE Prim Sch
NN11 . . . . .126 E8
Staverton Cl CV5 . . . . .60 A3
Staverton Leys CV22 . . . .100 A2
Staverton Rd NN11 . . . . . .126 F8
Staverton Sports Ctr
NN11 . . . . .117 F1
Steeds Cl CV35 . . . . .122 A7
Steele St CV22. . . . . .82 E3
Steels La CV36. . . . . .141 D7
Steeping Rd CV23. . . . . . . .82 B5
Steeplefield Rd CV6 . . . . . .61 A5
Steeples The CV23 . . . . . . .116 F5
Stefen Way NN11 . . . . .126 F8
Stella Croft B37 . . . . .33 C2
Stennels Cl CV6 . . . . .60 F8
Stephanie Gr B77. . . . . .4 A6
Stephenson Cl
Daventry NN11 . . . . .117 F2
Royal Leamington Spa
CV32. . . . . .105 C2
Tamworth B77 . . . . .4 A2
Stephenson Dr CV23 . . . . .101 F2
Stephenson Dr B37 . . . . . . .33 B2
Stephenson Rd
Bedworth CV7 . . . . .50 C7
Hinckley LE10 . . . . .30 E7
Stephens Rd B76 . . . . .13 A4
Stephen St CV21 . . . . .82 F3
Stepney Rd CV2 . . . . .62 A4
Stepping Stones B50. . . . .148 C5
Stepping Stones Rd CV5 . .60 F4
Sterling Pk
Hinckley LE10 . . . . .30 D8
Tamworth B77 . . . . .9 F7
Sterling Way CV11 . . . . . . .39 E8
Stevenage Wlk [2] CV2 . . .63 A7
Stevens Ho CV1 . . . . .151 C4
Stevenson Rd CV6 . . . . . . .61 A8
Stewart Cl CV4 . . . . .60 D2
Stewart Ct CV7 . . . . .37 A8
Stewart St CV11 . . . . .29 C3
Stidfall Gr CV31 . . . . .110 D6
Stileman Cl CV37 . . . . .129 D2
Stiper's Hill B78. . . . . .5 B2
Stirling Ave CV32 . . . . . . .106 B6
Stirling Cl CV3. . . . . .78 F8
Stirling Ct [8] OX16 . . . . .139 F3
Stirling Pk B90 . . . . .70 E8
Stirling Rd B90 . . . . .70 E8
Stivichall Croft CV3 . . . . . .77 B6
Stivichall Prim Sch CV3 . . .77 A6
Stockingford Inf & Jun Schs
CV10 . . . . .28 B3
Stocking La OX15 . . . . . . .138 E5
Stocking La CV9 . . . . .18 A3
Stocking Mdw CV23. . . . . .53 B5
Stockley Rd CV6 . . . . .50 C6
Stocks Ct CV22 . . . . .99 B4
Stocks La CV23 . . . . .98 F3
Stockton Cl
Dorridge B93. . . . . .72 B4
Sutton Coldfield B76 . . . . . .22 C5
Stockton Prim Sch CV47 .147 F8
Stockton Rd
Coventry CV1. . . . . .151 D4
Long Itchington CV47 . . . .115 E3
Stockwell La NN11. . . . . . .126 B5
Stockwells GL56 . . . . .140 A3
Stoke Gn CV3 . . . . .62 A2
Stoke Green Cres CV3 . . . .62 B1
Stoke Heath Prim Sch
CV2 . . . . .62 A6
Stoke La
Higham on t H CV13 . . . . . .21 A4
Stoke Golding CV13. . . . . .21 C8
Stoke Park Mews CV2 . . . .62 B4
Stoke Park Sch & Com Tech
Coll CV2 . . . . .62 B4
Stoke Rd CV11. . . . . .62 A4
Stoke Row CV2 . . . . .62 A4
Stokesay Cl CV11. . . . . .30 A6
Stone Ave B75. . . . . .13 B4
Stonebow Ave B91. . . . . . . .71 B8
Stonebridge Highway
CV3 . . . . .77 C4
Stonebridge La CV47. . . . .115 B4
Stonebridge Rd
Birmingham B46. . . . . .45 A7
Coleshill B46. . . . . .23 F2
Lighthorne Heath CV33. . .123 C3
Stone Bridge GL56. . . . . . .140 D7

Stonebridge Trad Est CV3 78 B4
Stonebrook Way CV6 49 F3
Stonebury Ave CV5 59 E4
Stonechat Rd CV23 67 D1
Stone Cross B46 23 B3
Stone Ct OX7 142 A2
Stonefern Ct 21 GL56 140 A3
Stonefield Cl CV2 63 A8
Stonehall Rd CV22 99 A8
Stonehaven Dr CV3 77 C3
Stonehill Croft B90 70 F6
Stonehills CV21 83 C7
Stonehill Wlk 5 B77 9 F6
Stonehouse Cl CV32 106 D5
Stone House La CV7 47 F6
Stonehouse La
  Coventry CV3 78 C4
  New Arley CV7 36 E7
Stoneleigh Abbey* CV8 93 F3
Stoneleigh Ave
  Coventry CV5 76 F7
  Kenilworth CV8 93 A6
Stoneleigh Cl
  Hartshill Green CV10 19 B2
  Redditch B98 102 F6
  Stoneleigh CV8 94 B6
Stoneleigh Ct CV11 29 C3
Stoneleigh Deer Park Bsns Village CV8 94 D4
Stoneleigh Gdns CV11 29 C3
Stoneleigh Park National Ag Ctr* CV8 94 A4
Stoneleigh Rd
  Baginton CV8 77 F1
  Blackdown CV32 106 A7
  Coventry CV4 76 E2
  Kenilworth CV8 93 A6
  Stoneleigh CV8 94 B3
Stoneley Rd CV13 21 D6
Stone Mdw CV7 49 A6
Stonepits La B97 102 D4
Stone Pits Mdw CV37 120 C5
Stoneton Cl CV47 147 C3
Stoneton Cres CV7 74 A6
Stoneway NN11 126 F5
Stoneway Gr CV31 110 D6
Stonewell Cres CV11 40 B8
Stoney Ct CV3 79 A7
Stoneydelph Prim Sch B77 4 A1
Stoney La CV35 114 C6
Stoneymoor Dr B36 22 D1
Stoney Rd
  Coventry CV1,CV3 151 B1
  Nuneaton CV10,CV11 29 B6
Stoney Stanton Rd CV1, CV6 61 E5
Stoneywood Rd CV2 62 F8
Stonydelph La B77 10 A7
Stoop The CV3 63 B1
Stornoway Rd B35 22 B4
Storrage La B48 85 A3
Stour Ct CV36 149 D5
Stour B77 10 A5
Stourton Cl B93 72 B7
Stour View CV36 137 A8
Stowe Dr CV47 147 B3
Stowe Pl CV4 59 C1
Stow Rd GL56 140 A2
Strachey Ave CV32 105 E2
Stradey Cl CV3 63 B1
Straight Mile CV23 98 A4
Stratford Ave CV9 18 C7
Stratford Bsns & Tech Pk CV37 130 C8
Stratford Butterfly Farm* CV37 145 B2
Stratford Coll CV37 144 E3
Stratford Prep Sch CV37 144 F2
Stratford Rd
  Alcester B49 143 D3
  Banbury OX15,OX16 139 E4
  Bidford-on-A B50 128 D7
  Dorridge B94 71 B3
  Hampton Lucy CV35,CV37 121 E4
  Harvington WR11 127 D3
  Henley-in-A B95 113 A3
  Ilmington CV36 136 B8
  Lighthorne Heath CV33 123 D2
  Longbridge CV34 108 C3
  Loxley CV35 130 F8
  Mickleton GL55 135 B7
  Newbold-on-S CV37 130 E1
  Nuthurst B94 88 C5
  Shenington OX15 138 F7
  Shipston-on-S CV36 149 D7
  Solihull B90 70 D7
  Temple Grafton B49 119 E3
  Wellesbourne CV35 146 B3
  Wroxton OX15 139 B5
Stratford St
  Coventry CV2 62 A4
  Nuneaton CV11 29 C4
Stratford-upon-Avon Gram Sch For Girls CV37 144 D2
Stratford-upon-Avon High Sch CV37 144 E3
Stratford-upon-Avon Hospl CV37 144 F3
Stratford-upon-Avon Prim Sch CV37 144 F2
Stratford-upon-Avon Shire Horse Ctr* CV37 129 F7
Stratford-upon-Avon Sta CV37 144 F3
Strath Cl CV21 101 A7
Strathearn Rd CV32 105 E1
Strathmore Ave CV1 61 E1
Strathmore Rd LE10 31 A7
Stratton St CV9 18 E7
Strawberry Fields CV7 46 B1
Strawberry Wlk CV2 50 D2
Streamside Cl CV5 60 A8
Stretton Ave CV3 78 C6
Stretton Cl LE10 31 D6
Stretton Cres CV31 110 B5
Stretton Ct
  Hinckley LE10 31 D3
  Rugby CV21 83 D7
Stretton Rd
  Nuneaton CV10 29 A3
  Solihull B90 70 B8
  Wolston CV8 80 A2
Stroma Way CV10 28 F2
Strutt Rd LE10 32 A5
Stuart Cl CV34 108 D5
Stuart Ct
  7 Royal Leamington Spa CV32 105 E1
  Coventry CV6 62 A8
Stuart Gdns CV47 132 F7
Stubbs Cl CV12 39 A4
Stubbs Gr CV2 62 B5
Stud Farm Cl OX17 134 F1
Studland Ave CV21 83 F1
Studland Gn CV2 63 A4
Studley High Sch B80 103 E3
Studley Inf Sch B80 103 E4
Studley Rd B98 103 B8
Studley St Mary's CE Jun Sch B80 103 E3
Sturley Cl CV8 93 B6
Sturminster Cl CV2 63 A4
Styles Cl
  Hampton Magna CV35 114 F4
  Royal Leamington Spa CV31 110 A7
Styvechale Ave CV5 77 A8
Sudbury Cl CV32 106 C3
Sudeley Cl B36 22 B1
Sudeley Rd CV10 39 C8
Sudeley B77 9 C8
Suffolk Cl
  Bedworth CV12 39 A3
  Coventry CV5 60 B3
  Nuneaton CV10 28 E3
Suffolk St CV32 106 A1
Sugarswell La OX15 138 D7
Sugarwell Cotts OX15 138 E8
Sulgrave Cl CV2 62 E7
Sullivan Ct CV6 62 B7
Sullivan Rd CV6 62 B7
Sumburgh Croft B35 22 A3
Summerhouse Cl B97 102 A6
Summer La B76 22 D6
Summerton Rd CV31 110 A3
Sumner Cl CV35 114 F3
Sumner Rd B46 34 A6
Sunart Way CV10 28 C5
Sunbeam Cl
  Birmingham B36 22 F1
  Rugby CV21 83 C3
Sunbridge Terr CV21 83 C3
Sunbury Rd CV3 78 C5
Suncliffe Dr CV8 93 A2
Sunderland Pl CV35 146 C1
Sundew St CV2 50 D2
Sundorne Cl CV5 60 A4
Sunfields Cl B78 11 B8
Sunningdale Ave
  Coventry CV6 49 D2
  Kenilworth CV8 93 B4
Sunningdale Cl CV11 30 A1
Sunningdale B77 4 C5
Sunnybank Ave CV3 78 B5
Sunny Bank
  Coventry CV1 151 A3
  Great Rollright OX7 142 A2
Sunnydale Cres LE10 31 A7
Sunnydale Rd LE10 30 F7
Sunnyhill LE10 31 F7
Sunnyhill S LE10 31 F6
Sunnyside B95 119 F7
Sunnyside Cl
  Balsall Common CV7 74 C7
  Coventry CV5 60 F3
Sunnyside Ct CV10 28 F3
Sunnyside La CV7 74 C7
Sun Rising Hill OX15 132 D1
Sunset Cl B78 11 A8
Sunset Dr CV37 129 C8
Sunshine Cl CV8 93 A2
Sun St CV21 83 C3
Sunway Gr CV3 77 B6
Surrey Cl
  Hinckley LE10 31 E4
  Nuneaton CV10 28 E3
Surrey Ct CV34 108 E8
Sussex Cl CV10 28 E3
Sussex Ct CV34 108 E8
Sussex Dr 21 OX16 139 F5
Sussex Rd CV5 60 F4
Sutcliffe Ave CV37 130 D3
Sutcliffe Dr CV33 123 E6
Sutherland Ave CV5 60 A4
Sutherland Cl CV34 104 E1
Sutherland Dr CV12 39 A4
Sutton Ave CV5 59 D4
Sutton Cl NN11 134 F6
Sutton Ct CV6 50 C6
Sutton Ho CV22 82 C1
Sutton La OX15 137 E1
Sutton Pk CV10 28 B7
Sutton Rd B78 8 A8
Sutton Sq B76 22 E6
Sutton Stop CV6 50 B5
Swadling St CV31 109 F6
Swain Crofts CV31 110 B6
Swains Gn LE10 31 F6
Swalcliffe Barn Mus* OX15 142 F8
Swalcliffe Park Sch Trust OX15 142 F8
Swaledale CV4 76 D6
Swale Rd B76 13 A1
Swallow Ave B36 33 A8
Swallow Cl CV37 145 A5
Swallow Ct
  Bedworth CV12 49 C8
  Hinckley LE10 30 F6
Swallowdean Rd CV6 60 E8
Swallowgate Bsns Pk CV6 49 D1
Swallow Rd CV6 49 C1
Swallows Ind Est The B90 70 D8
Swallows' Mdw B90 70 D8
Swanage Gn CV2 63 A4
Swan Cl GL56 140 A3
Swan Croft B95 113 A5
Swancroft Rd CV2 62 A5
Swan Ct
  Alcester B49 143 B3
  Stratford-u-A CV37 145 B2
Swanfold CV37 120 C5
Swan La CV2 61 F4
Swans Cl CV37 120 C5
Swan's Nest CV37 145 B2
Swan St
  Alcester B49 143 B3
  Royal Leamington Spa CV32 106 A1
  Warwick CV34 108 E6
Swanswell St CV1 151 C4
Swanswood Gr 3 B37 33 C3
Swedish Houses CV23 116 B6
Sweet Knowle Farm Cotts CV37 130 A2
Swerford Rd OX15,OX7 142 D3
Swift Cl
  Birmingham B36 33 A8
  Kenilworth CV8 93 A2
Swift Pk CV21 83 A7
Swift Point CV21 66 F1
Swift Rd CV37 145 A5
Swift's Cnr CV3 77 E8
Swift Valley Ind Est CV21 82 F8
Swillington Rd CV6 61 B5
Swinburne Ave CV2 62 D2
Swinburne Cl CV10 28 A5
Swinburne Rd B97 102 C7
Swindale Croft CV3 78 F8
Swindale B77 10 B7
Swinford Gr B93 71 E3
Swinford Rd LE17 68 F8
Swiss Lodge Dr B78 8 F8
Sycamore Ave B78 11 A8
Sycamore Cl
  Hinckley LE10 31 E5
  Sibford Gower OX15 142 D8
  Stockton CV47 147 E8
  Stratford-u-A CV37 144 F5
  Wellesbourne CV35 146 E3
Sycamore Cres
  Birmingham,Marston Green B37 44 A8
  New Arley CV7 37 B8
Sycamore Ct
  Allesley CV5 59 F7
  Kineton CV35 132 B5
Sycamore Dr B47 69 B6
Sycamore Gr
  Rugby CV21 83 A4
  Southam CV47 147 B6
  Warwick CV34 105 A1
Sycamore Ho B98 102 F8
Sycamore Rd
  Coventry CV2 50 B2
  Kingsbury B78 15 D7
  Nuneaton CV10 28 D6
Sycamores The CV12 38 E2
Sycamore B77 9 E7
Sydenham Dr CV31 110 B6
Sydenham Ind Est CV31 110 B6
Sydenham Prim Sch CV31 110 C6
Sydnall Fields CV6 49 F4
Sydnall Rd CV6 49 F4
Sydney Ct 1 CV12 38 F2
Sykes Cotts CV37 129 B6
Sykesmoor B77 10 B7
Sylvan Dr CV3 76 F6
Synkere Cl CV7 49 A6
Sywell Leys CV22 99 F6

T

Table Oak La CV8 74 B1
Tachbrook Cl CV2 50 C2
Tachbrook Link CV34 109 E4
Tachbrook Park Dr CV34 109 E5
Tachbrook Rd CV31 109 F4
Tachbrook St CV31 110 A6
Tackford Cl B36 22 D1
Tackford Rd CV6 62 A8
Tackley Cl B90 70 B8
Tailor's La CV37 129 D1
Tainters Hill CV8 93 A6
Talbot Cl 6 OX16 139 F4
Talbot Ct
  Royal Leamington Spa CV32 106 A1
  Wellesbourne CV35 146 E3
Talbot Rd CV37 145 A4
Talisman Cl CV8 92 F3
Talisman Sq CV8 92 F4
Talland Ave CV6 62 A6
Tallants Cl CV6 62 A8
Tallants Rd CV6 62 A8
Talton Cl B90 71 A5
Tamar Cl CV23 82 B5
Tamar Dr B76 22 B7
Tamar Rd
  Bulkington CV12 40 B2
  Tamworth B77 10 A5
Tame Bank B78 15 C6
Tame Ct B78 9 B8
Tameside Dr B35 22 A1
Tame Valley Bsns Pk B77 9 E6
Tame Valley Ind Est B77 9 E6
Tame Way LE10 31 A8
Tamora Cl CV34 109 D3
Tamworth Bsns Ctr B77 4 B3
Tamworth Bsns Pk B77 4 B3
Tamworth Rd (Amington) B77 4 A5
Tamworth Rd B78 9 C2
Tamworth Rd (Dosthill) B77 9 C6
Tamworth Rd
  Fillongley,Corley Ash CV7 37 A1
  Fillongley CV7 36 C6
  Keresley CV6,CV7 48 D5
  Kingsbury B78 15 C7
  Polesworth B78 4 E1
  Sutton Coldfield B75 7 A2
  Tamworth,Two Gates B77 9 D8
  Wood End CV9 10 C1
Tancred Cl CV31 109 F5
Tangmere Dr B35 22 A3
Tanhill B77 10 B7
Tankards Hill GL56,GL55 136 B1
Tanners Ctyd CV34 108 D5
Tanners Gr CV6 49 D4
Tanners Green La B47,B94 69 B2
Tanners' La CV4,CV7 59 B1
Tannery Cl CV9 18 E8
Tannery Ct CV8 92 F4
Tannery The CV36 149 C6
Tanser Ct CV22 99 C3
Tansley Cl B93 71 F4
Tanwood Cl
  Redditch B97 102 A6
  Solihull B91 71 B8
Tanworth-in-Arden CE Prim Sch B94 87 A2
Tanworth La
  Henley-in-A B95 113 A7
  Redditch B98 112 B8
  Solihull B90 70 C5
Tanyard Cl CV4 59 D1
Tanyard The B95 113 B5
Tapcon Way CV2 62 F5
Tappinger Gr CV8 93 C5
Tapster La B94 88 F2
Tara Ct CV2 62 B4
Tarlington Rd CV6 60 E6
Tarn Cl CV12 39 A2
Tarquin Cl CV3 78 D7
Tarragon Cl CV2 50 D1
Tarrant B77 9 F8
Tarrant Wlk CV2 63 A5
Taskers Way 3 CV37 145 A2
Tatchbrook Ct 5 CV31 109 F6
Tatnall Gr CV34 108 E8
Tattle Bank CV47 147 B3
Taunton Way CV6 49 A2
Taverners La CV9 18 D7
Tavern La CV37 144 D2
Tavistock St CV32 105 F1
Tavistock Way CV11 29 E5
Tavistock Wlk CV2 62 C7
Tay Croft B37 33 C4
Taylor Ave CV32 106 B2
Taylor Cl CV8 93 B6
Taylor Ct CV34 108 D7
Tay Rd CV6 61 B6
Teachers Cl CV6 61 A5
Tea Gdn The CV12 49 E8
Teal Bsns Ctr LE10 30 D7
Teal Cl CV37 144 C5
Teal Dr LE10 31 A6
Teal Rd B80 103 F4
Teasel Cl CV23 83 D8
Teddy Bear Mus The* CV37 144 F3
Ted Pitts La CV5 48 B2
Teign B77 10 A5
Telegraph St CV36 149 D6
Telephone Rd CV3 62 C2
Telfer Rd CV6 61 B7
Telford Ave CV32 106 B5
Telford Inf & Jun Schs CV32 106 C5
Telford Rd CV7 50 C8
Templar Ave CV4 60 A1
Templar Ct CV11 29 C3
Templars' Fields CV4 76 B7
Templars Prim Sch CV4 60 A1
Templars The CV34 108 F5
Temple Ave CV7 73 F6
Temple Ct
  Coleshill B46 23 F1
  Rugby CV22 83 C2
Temple End CV33 123 E6
Temple Grafton CE Prim Sch B49 119 E1
Temple Gr CV34 108 D5
Temple Herdewyke Prim Sch CV47 133 A7
Temple Hill Rd OX15 142 D8
Temple Hill LE10 41 E5
Temple La B93 73 A4
Temple Rd B93 72 A3
Temple St CV21,CV22 83 C2
Templeton Cl B93 72 A3
Temple Way B46 23 F1
Ten Acres B49 143 D4
Tenby Cl CV12 38 C1
Tenby Ct CV32 109 E8
Teneriffe Rd CV6 49 F1
Tenlons Rd CV10 28 F2
Tennant Cl CV21 83 E1
Tennant St CV11 29 E3
Tennyson Ave
  Rugby CV22 99 E7
  Warwick CV34 108 C4
Tennyson Cl CV8 93 C4
Tennyson Rd
  Coventry CV2 62 C3
  Redditch B97 102 C8
  Stratford-u-A CV37 130 A8
Ten Shilling Dr CV4 75 E6
Tenter St CV9 18 D8
Terrace Rd CV9 18 D8
Terrace The
  Moreton Morrell CV35 122 F2
  Snitterfield CV37 121 B6
  Welford-on-A CV37 129 B6
Terrett Ct 2 CV37 145 A2
Terry Ave CV32 105 C1
Terry Rd CV1 61 F1
Tewkesbury Dr CV12 39 C3
Thackeray Cl
  Lower Quinton CV37 129 D2
  Nuneaton CV10 28 A4
  Rugby CV22 99 F7
Thackhall St CV2 61 F4
Thames Cl CV12 40 A3
Thames Rd NN11 117 F1
Thamley Rd CV6 61 A4
Thane Cl B80 103 F4
Thatchers Cl OX15 138 D3
Thatchings The CV22 99 D3
The Archbishop Grimshaw RC Sch B37 33 A3
Theatre Ct CV34 108 D6
Theatre St CV34 108 D7
Thebes Cl CV5 59 B8
Theddingworth Cl CV3 78 E8
Thickthorn Cl CV8 93 B2
Thickthorn Mews CV8 93 B2
Thickthorn Orchs CV8 93 B2
Thimble End Rd B76 13 A2
Thimbler Rd CV4 76 C7
Third Exhibition Ave B40 44 D4
Thirlestane Cl CV8 93 C6
Thirlmere Ave CV11 29 F6
Thirlmere Cl CV4 59 E3
Thirlmere Rd
  Bedworth CV12 39 A2
  Hinckley LE10 31 A7
Thirlmere CV21 83 C7
Thirsk Rd CV3 77 C5
Thistle Way CV23 83 D8
Thistlewood Gr B93 90 B6
Thistley Field E CV6 61 A7
Thistley Field N CV6 61 A7
Thistley Field S CV6 60 F6
Thistley Field W CV6 60 F7
Thomas Jolyffe Prim Sch CV37 145 A5
Thomas King Ho 6 CV1 61 E4
Thomas Landsdail St CV3 77 D8
Thomas Lane St CV6 50 A1
Thomas Naul Croft CV4 59 F3
Thomas Sharp St CV4 76 A7
Thomas St
  Bedworth CV12 39 A2
  Royal Leamington Spa CV32 106 A1
Thomas Way CV23 82 A5
Thomas Wlk B35 22 B3
Thompson's La CV7 48 E6
Thompson's Rd CV7 48 F6
Thomson Cl CV21 83 B6
Thornbury Ho CV8 93 A3
Thornbury Rise OX16 139 F3
Thornby Ave
  Kenilworth CV8 93 B3
  Tamworth B77 9 E8
Thorncliffe Cl B97 102 A6
Thorncliffe Way CV10 27 F8
Thorn Cl CV21 83 C6
Thorney Rd CV2 62 B6
Thornfield Ave CV13 21 E7
Thornfield Way LE10 31 E8
Thorngrove Ave 7 B91 71 C8
Thornhill Dr CV11 40 C8
Thornhill Rd CV1 61 D5
Thornley Cl CV31 110 F5
Thornley Gr B76 22 C6
Thorns Com Inf Sch CV8 93 B4
Thorn Stile Cl CV32 106 E6
Thornton Cl
  Coventry CV5 59 C4
  Warwick CV34 104 F1
Thornton Rd B90 70 F6
Thorntons La CV47 125 C7
Thorntons Way CV10 28 A3
Thornton Way B77 9 C8
Thorn Way CV47 115 D4
Thornycroft Rd LE10 31 E8
Thorpe Rd OX17 134 F1
Threadneedle St CV1 61 D6
Three Acres La B90 69 F6
Three Cocks La WR11 127 D1
Three Corner Cl B90 69 E8

Three Cornered Cl CV32 .106 E6
Three Oaks Rd B47 ....69 B8
Three Pots Rd CV11 ....31 E4
Three Spires Ave CV6 ....61 A6
Three Spires Ind Est CV6 ..50 A5
Three Spires Jct CV6 .....49 E1
Three Spires Sch CV6 ....60 D6
Throckmorton Cl CV35 ..114 C8
Throckmorton Rd
  Alcester B49 ....143 D4
  Redditch B98 ....103 A8
Thrupponce Cl CV4 ......75 E6
Thurlaston Dr CV22 ....99 B6
Thurlestone Rd CV6 ......60 F8
Thurlow Cl CV9 ....12 D2
Thurne B77 ....9 F8
Thurnmill Rd CV23 ....82 C4
Thursfield Rd CV32 ......106 B3
Tibberton Cl B91 ....71 A8
Tibbets Cl B49 ....143 C4
Tibbits Ct [4] CV34 .....108 E6
Tibblestone B90 ....70 A5
Tiber Cl CV5 ....59 F4
Tiberius Cl B46 ....23 F1
Tiber Way CV21 ....82 F7
Tidbury Cl B97 ....102 C6
Tidbury Green Sch B90 ...69 E4
Tiddington Cl B36 ....22 B1
Tiddington Ct CV37 .....145 E4
Tiddington Rd CV37 .....145 C3
Tideswell Cl CV3 ....63 A1
Tidmarsh Cl CV7 ....74 A6
Tidmarsh Rd CV23 ....105 A7
Tidmington Cl CV35 .....114 F5
Tile Gr B37 ....33 A5
Tile Hill La
  Coventry,Allesley CV4,
  CV5 ....60 D2
  Coventry,Tile Hill CV4 ..60 B1
Tile Hill Sta CV4 ....75 C8
Tile Hill Wood Sch &
  Language Coll CV4 ......59 D2
Tilehouse Green La B93 ..71 F6
Tilehouse La B90 ....69 E6
Tilehurst Dr CV4 ....75 A8
Tilemans La CV36 ....149 D7
Tilesford Cl B90 ....71 A6
Tilewood Ave CV5 ....59 F4
Tilia Rd B77 ....4 B5
Tilton Rd LE10 ....31 E6
Timber Ct CV22 ....83 C2
Timberlake Cl B90 ....71 B6
Timon View CV34 ....109 E3
Timothy Gr CV4 ....60 B1
Timothy's Bridge Rd
  CV37 ....144 D4
Timsa Rd CV35 ....132 E5
Tink-A-Tank CV34 ....108 E6
Tinker's Cl [28] GL56 ...140 A3
Tinkers Green Rd B77 ....9 F6
Tinkers La
  Earlswood B94 ....87 E7
  Lapworth B94 ....88 E1
  Mollington OX17 ....133 F2
Tintagel Cl CV8 ....78 D5
Tintagel Gr CV8 ....93 B4
Tintagel Way CV11 ....30 A5
Tintern Way CV12 ....39 C3
Tipper's Hill La CV7 .....36 E6
Tippett Cl CV11 ....40 A7
Tipping's Hill B97 ......102 C5
Tisdale Rise CV8 ....93 B6
Titan Bsns Ctr CV34 ....109 F4
Tite La OX15 ....142 D4
Tithe Barn Cl CV35 .....114 F4
Tithe Barn La B94 ....87 C6
Tithe Cl CV13 ....21 D6
Tithe Ct WR11 ....127 F2
Titheway WR11 ....127 F2
Tithings The OX15 ......142 F8
Tiverton Dr CV11 ....29 F5
Tiverton Gr CV2 ....62 D5
Tiverton Rd CV2 ....62 D5
Tiverton Sch CV6 ....60 D5
Tiveycourt Rd CV6 ....50 A3
Tocil Croft CV4 ....76 D4
Todenham Way CV35 ....114 F6
Toft Hill CV23 ....99 B1
Tokchong Rd CV35 ......132 E5
Toledo Cl CV5 ....60 C1
Toler Rd CV11 ....29 B5
Tollard Cl CV2 ....62 F5
Toll Gate Cl CV37 ......144 B3
Toll Gate Rd CV47 ......147 B5
Tolson Ave B78 ....9 B8
Tolson Cl B77 ....9 D5
Tom Brown St CV21 ....83 C3
Tom Ellis Ct CV7 ....50 A8
Tom Henderson Cl CV3 ..78 F7
Tom Hill B94 ....87 E4
Tomkinson Rd CV10 ......28 F4
Tomlinson Rd B36 ....22 D1
Tommy's Turn La OX15 ..133 F7
Tompson Cl NN11 ....117 E5
Tomson Ave CV6 ....61 B4
Toms Town La B80 ......103 E3
Tom Ward Cl CV3 ....78 E7
Tomwell Cl CV47 ....147 B5
Tom Williams Way B77 ....9 C8
Tonbridge Rd CV3 ....78 A6
Tongue Ave B78 ....9 A8
Tookeys Dr B96 ....118 C8
Topcliffe Prim Sch B35 ..22 A3
Topp's Dr CV12 ....38 D1
Topp's Heath CV12 ....38 E1

Top Rd CV7,CV12 ....51 B7
Top St
  Appleby Magna DE12 .....3 F7
  Northend CV47 ....133 B2
Torbay Rd CV5 ....60 C4
Torcastle Cl CV6 ....61 F7
Torcross Ave CV2 ....62 C6
Torpoint Cl CV2 ....62 C7
Torrance Rd CV21 ....82 F3
Torres Cl CV34 ....108 B4
Torridge B77 ....10 A5
Torrington Ave CV4 ......75 E8
Torside B77 ....10 B7
Torwood Cl CV4 ....75 F6
Totnes Cl CV2 ....62 C7
Touchstone Rd CV34 ....109 F2
Tove Ct CV23 ....82 B5
Towbury Cl B98 ....102 F5
Tower Cl
  Bidford-on-A B50 ......148 E5
  Stratford-u-A CV37 ...145 A5
Tower Croft
  Bidford-on-A B50 ......148 E5
  Birmingham B37 ....33 B4
Tower Hill B50 ....148 E5
Tower Rd
  Bedworth CV12 ....39 B2
  Rugby CV21 ....83 C1
Towers Cl CV8 ....92 F2
Tower St
  [6] Royal Leamington Spa
  CV31 ....110 A7
  Coventry CV1 ....151 B3
Tower View Cres CV10 ...28 B3
Townesend Cl CV34 .....104 F1
Town Feilds Cl CV5 ....60 B7
Town Ground CV35 ......131 F5
Townhill OX15 ....133 A2
Townsend Cl
  Binton CV37 ....120 A1
  Newton Regis B79 ....2 D4
Townsend Croft CV3 .....77 C7
Townsend Dr CV11 ....29 F3
Townsend La
  Long Lawford CV23 ......82 B4
  Upper Boddington NN11 ..134 E8
Townsend Rd
  Coventry CV3 ....77 C8
  Rugby CV21 ....83 D3
  Tiddington CV37 ......145 E3
Townsends Cl CV11 ......31 A1
Town Sq CV37 ....145 A2
Towpath Cl CV6 ....50 B6
Trafalgar Ct B50 ....148 D4
Trafalgar Ho [3] CV1 ....61 B2
Trafford Cl CV9 ....12 D2
Trafford Dr CV10 ....28 C6
Trafford Lodge [4] CV3 .110 B7
Traitor's Ford La OX15,CV36,
  OX7 ....141 A8
Trajan Hill CV8 ....23 F1
Tramway Ct CV37 ....145 B2
Travellers Way B37 ......33 D3
Tredington Cl B98 ......103 B7
Tredington Rd CV5 ....59 F4
Treedale Cl CV4 ....75 D8
Trefoil B77 ....4 B5
Treforest Rd CV3 ....78 C8
Tregaron [4] CV37 .....145 A4
Tregorrick Rd CV7 ......50 A8
Tregullan Rd CV7 ....50 B8
Trehern Cl B93 ....72 A5
Treherne Rd CV6 ....61 B8
Trelawney Rd CV7 ....50 A7
Tremelling Way CV7 .....36 F8
Trenance Rd CV7 ....50 A8
Trench La B49 ....143 F3
Treneere Rd CV7 ....50 B8
Trensale Ave CV6 ....60 F4
Trentham Cl CV11 ....39 F8
Trentham Gdns CV8 ......93 C5
Trentham Rd
  Coventry CV1 ....61 F4
  Hartshill Green CV10 ...19 B2
Trent Rd
  Bulkington CV12 ....40 A2
  Hinckley LE10 ....31 A8
  Nuneaton CV11 ....29 D5
Trent Wlk NN11 ....117 F1
Tresillian Rd CV7 ....50 B8
Tressel Croft CV34 .....109 E2
Trevelyan Cl
  Claverdon CV35 ....113 F3
  Stratford-u-A CV37 ...144 C4
Trevelyan Cres CV37 ...144 C4
Trevelyan Ho [1] B37 ...33 C1
Treviscoe Cl CV7 ....50 A7
Trevor Cl CV4 ....75 D8
Trevor White Dr CV22 ...83 B1
Trevose Ave CV7 ....50 B8
Trewint Cl CV7 ....50 A8
Triangle The CV5 ....60 B4
Tribune Trad Est CV37 ..83 A6
Trident Bsns Pk CV11 ...29 D3
Trident Bvd B35 ....22 B2
Trident Cl B37 ....44 E8
Trident Rd B26 ....44 C4
Trimpley Cl B93 ....71 E3
Trimpley Dr CV6 ....61 C6
Trinculo Gr CV34 ....109 F2
Trinity Churchyard CV1 .151 B3
Trinity Cl
  Banbury OX16 ....139 F4
  Stratford-u-A CV37 ...145 A1
  Warton B79 ....5 B2
Trinity Coll [2] CV37 ..144 F2

Trinity Ct
  Hinckley LE10 ....31 C8
  Rugby CV21 ....83 B3
Trinity La
  Coventry CV1 ....151 B3
  Hinckley LE10 ....31 C8
Trinity Pk B40 ....44 D3
Trinity RC Sch CV32 ...105 D2
Trinity RC Sch The CV34 .109 C6
Trinity Rd
  Freasley B78,CV9 ....10 B3
  Kingsbury B78 ....15 E7
Trinity St
  Coventry CV1 ....151 B3
  Royal Leamington Spa
  CV32 ....105 F1
  Stratford-u-A CV37 ...145 A1
Trinity Vicarage Rd LE10 .31 C8
Trinity Way CV37 ....130 B8
Trinity Wlk CV11 ....29 E3
Triton Pk CV21 ....82 F8
Triumph Cl CV2 ....62 E3
Triumph Ho CV1 ....151 B2
Triumph Wlk B36 ....23 A1
Troilus Ct CV34 ....109 F3
Troon B77 ....4 C4
Troon Way LE10 ....31 D4
Trossachs Rd CV5 ....59 F3
Troubridge Wlk CV22 ....82 C2
Troughton Cres CV6 .....61 A5
Troutbeck Ave CV32 ....105 C2
Troutbeck Rd CV5 ....59 B3
Troyes Cl CV3 ....77 E7
Troy Ind Est B96 ....103 A3
Trueman Cl CV34 ....108 E8
Truemans Heath La B47,
  B90. ....69 C7
Truggist La CV7 ....74 E8
Trundalls La B90 ....70 A5
Truro Cl CV11 ....29 F5
Truro Wlk B37 ....33 B1
Trussell Way CV22 ....99 A8
Trust Cotts B49 ....118 D8
Trusteel Hos CV23 ......67 C5
Tryan Rd CV10 ....28 E4
Tuckwell Cl CV47 ......147 E8
Tudman Cl B76 ....22 A7
Tudor Ave CV5 ....59 F4
Tudor Cl CV7 ....74 A6
Tudor Cres CV9 ....12 D1
Tudor Ct
  Bedworth CV7 ....49 E7
  Coventry CV7 ....77 C8
  Warwick CV34 ....108 D5
Tudor La CV47 ....147 B3
Tudor Rd CV10 ....28 C6
Tuer The WR11 ....127 A6
Tulip Tree Ave CV8 ......93 B5
Tulip Tree Ct CV8 ....93 B5
Tunnel Rd CV10 ....27 D4
Tulip Wlk B37 ....44 C8
Tulliver Cl CV12 ....39 B3
Tulliver Rd CV10 ....29 C1
Tulliver St CV6 ....61 B5
Tunnel Rd CV10 ....27 D4
Turchil Dr B76 ....22 B8
Turchil Rd CV22 ....99 A8
Turchil Wlk CV22 ....99 A8
Turlands Cl CV2 ....63 A7
Turnberry Dr CV11 ......40 C8
Turnberry B77 ....4 C5
Turner Cl
  Bedworth CV12 ....39 A4
  Rugby CV21 ....101 B8
  Warwick CV34 ....108 B4
Turner Rd CV5 ....60 D3
Turnhouse Rd B35 ....22 B4
Turnpike Cl
  [18] Moreton-in-M GL56 ..140 A3
  Balsall Common CV7 ....74 B7
Turnpike Dr
  Lower Quinton CV37 ...129 D2
  Water Orton B46 ....23 C2
Turnstone Cl CV23 ......83 C8
Turpin Ct CV31 ....109 F6
Turpin Ho CV22 ....99 A2
Turton Way CV8 ....93 C4
Turville Cl LE10 ....31 F5
Turvins Mdw CV47 ....125 E4
Tutbury Ave CV4 ....76 E6
Tutbury B77 ....9 C7
Tutehill B77 ....10 B7
Tuthill Furlong CV23 ....67 D1
Tutnall Dr B94 ....88 B6
Tuttle Hill CV10 ....28 E8
Tweed Cl NN11 ....126 F8
Twenty One Oaks CV9 ...17 E6
Twickenham Way CV3 ....63 B1
Two Gates Com Prim Sch
  B77 ....9 C8
Two Gates Ind Est B77 ...9 D7
Twycross La CV9 ....6 F6
Twycross Rd LE10 ....31 E6
Twycross Wlk CV34 ....104 D1
Twycross Zoo* CV9 ......3 F1
Tybalt Cl
  Coventry CV3 ....78 C5
  Royal Leamington Spa
  CV34 ....109 D4
Tylers Gr B90 ....70 F6
Tyler St [18] CV37 ....145 A3
Tylney Cl CV3 ....63 B2
Tyne Cl B37 ....33 C4
Tynemouth Cl CV2 ......50 D5
Tyne Rd NN11 ....126 F8
Tynward Cl CV3 ....77 B5
Tysoe CE Prim Sch CV35 .138 C7
Tysoe Cl B94 ....88 C6

Tysoe Croft CV3 ....78 F8
Tysoe Rd
  Kineton CV35 ....132 B4
  Oxhill CV35 ....137 F8
  Radway CV35 ....132 E3
Tyte End OX7 ....142 A2
Tythe Barn Cotts WR11 .127 B2
Tythe Barn La B90 ....70 A6
Tything Rd B49 ....143 C6

U

Ufton Croft CV5 ....60 A3
Ufton Fields CV33 .....123 F8
Ufton Hill CV33 ....111 F1
Ullapool Cl B97 ....102 D5
Ullenhall La B95 ....112 D6
Ullenhall Rd
  Dorridge B93 ....72 A6
  Ullenhall B95 ....112 E5
Ullenhall St B95 ....112 E6
Ullswater Ave
  Nuneaton CV11 ....29 F6
  Royal Leamington Spa
  CV32 ....105 C2
Ullswater Rd
  Bedworth CV12 ....39 A2
  Coventry CV3 ....62 E1
Ullswater B77 ....10 B7
Ulverscroft Rd CV3 ......77 D7
Ulverston CV21 ....83 D7
Umberslade Children's
  Farm* B94 ....87 C2
Umberslade Rd
  Earlswood B94 ....87 C7
  Tanworth-In-A B94 ......87 E3
Underhill Cl
  Coventry CV3 ....77 D3
  Redditch B98 ....102 F6
Underpass The B40 ....44 E4
Underwood Cl B97 .....102 A7
Unicorn Ave CV5 ....59 F4
Unicorn La CV5 ....59 F4
Union Bldgs CV1 ....151 B2
Union Pl CV6 ....49 F4
Union Rd CV32 ....105 E1
Union St
  Rugby CV22 ....83 A2
  Stratford-u-A CV37 ...145 A3
Unity Ho CV1 ....151 C4
University Farm [15] GL56 140 A3
University Hospl-Walsgrave
  CV2 ....63 A5
University Rd CV4 ....76 C5
Univ of Birmingham (The
  Shakespeare Inst)
  CV37 ....144 F2
Univ of Warwick CV4 ....76 C4
Univ of Warwick (Gibbet Hill)
  CV4 ....76 C5
Univ of Warwick Science Pk
  CV4 ....76 C5
Univ of Warwick (Westwood)
  CV4 ....76 B6
Upavon Cl B35 ....22 A4
Uplands CV2 ....62 A5
Upleadon Cl B97 ....102 A6
Upper Abbey St CV1 .....29 B5
Upper Cape CV34 ....108 D8
Upper Crossgate Rd B98 103 C8
Upper Eastern Green La
  CV5 ....59 E5
Upper Farm Mdw CV35 .123 E1
Upperfield Way CV3 .....63 A1
Upper Grove St [6] CV32 105 E1
Upper Hill St
  Coventry CV1 ....151 A3
  Royal Leamington Spa
  CV32 ....106 A1
Upper Holly Wlk CV32 ..106 A1
Upper Ladyes Hills CV8 ..93 A6
Upper Pk CV3 ....78 D6
Upper Prec CV1 ....151 B3
Upper Ride CV3 ....78 D5
Upper Rosemary Hill CV8 ..92 F5
Upper Spon St CV1 ......61 A3
Upper Spring La CV8 ....92 F7
Upper Well St CV1 .....151 B3
Upper York St CV1 ......61 B2
Upton Dr CV11 ....39 F8
Upton Rd CV22 ....82 D3
Upton La CV13 ....21 B7
Uplands B94 ....88 E5
Usher Dr [11] OX16 ....139 F5
Utrillo Cl CV5 ....60 C3
Uxbridge Ave CV3 ....62 C2

V

Valanders La CV36 .....136 B6
Vale Cl CV21 ....101 A8
Valencia Croft B35 ......22 B4
Valencia Rd CV3 ....62 E3
Valentine Cl CV37 .....129 F8
Vale The CV3 ....78 C8
Vale View CV10 ....28 E4
Valiant Cl LE10 ....31 F6
Vallet Ave B49 ....143 B5
Valletta Way CV35 ......28 E4
Valley Dr CV21 ....83 A8
Valley La
  Kingswood B94 ....89 E7
  Tamworth B77 ....9 E7
Valley Rd
  Coventry CV2 ....62 A6

Valley Rd continued
  Earlswood B94. ....70 A1
  Galley Common CV10 ....27 F4
  Radford Semele CV31 ..110 E4
  Royal Leamington Spa
  CV32. ....106 C3
Valley The CV31 ....110 E4
Van Dyke Cl CV5 ....60 C3
Vanguard Ave CV5 ....60 C1
Vanguard Ctr CV4 ....76 C6
Vanguard Rd B26 ....44 C4
Vanguard B77 ....9 D6
Vardon Dr CV3 ....77 D4
Vauxhall Cl [4] CV1 .....61 E3
Vauxhall Cres B36 ....22 F1
Vauxhall La B49 ....119 D1
Vauxhall St CV1 ....61 E3
Vaynor B97 ....102 D8
Vaynor Fst Sch The B97 .102 C7
Veasey Cl CV11 ....29 E3
Vecqueray St CV1 ....61 E2
Ventnor Cl CV2 ....62 E3
Ventnor St CV10 ....29 D6
Venture Ct LE10 ....30 E8
Verbena Cl CV2 ....50 B1
Verden Ave CV34 ....108 B4
Verdon Pl CV35 ....122 B8
Verdun Cl CV31 ....110 B2
Vere Rd CV21 ....83 F1
Vermont Gr CV31 ......110 D6
Verney Cl
  Butlers Marston CV35 ..131 F4
  Lighthorne CV35 ......123 B2
Verney Dr CV37 ....144 F5
Verney Gdns CV37 .....144 F5
Verney Rd
  Lighthorne Heath CV33 ..123 D2
  Temple Herdewyke CV47 ..133 A6
Vernon Ave CV22 ......100 E8
Vernon Cl
  [5] Coventry CV1 ....61 E3
  Royal Leamington Spa
  CV32. ....105 C3
Vernon St [9] CV1 ......61 E4
Vernons Cl CV10 ....28 E4
Vernons La CV10,CV11 ..28 F4
Vernons Mews CV11 .....28 F4
Verona [6] CV37 ....145 A3
Verona Cl CV11 ....30 A1
Vesey Cl B46 ....23 B2
Viaduct Cl CV21 ....83 D4
Vicarage Cl
  Atherstone CV9 ....18 E7
  Dordon B78 ....10 F5
Vicarage Cotts GL55 ...135 B2
Vicarage Field CV34 ...109 B8
Vicarage Flats OX17 ...134 C1
Vicarage Gdns OX17 ...134 C1
Vicarage Hill
  Badby NN11 ....126 F5
  Clifton u D CV23 ....83 E5
  Middleton B78 ....8 B3
  Tanworth-In-A B94 ......86 F3
Vicarage La
  Coventry CV7 ....49 D7
  Dunchurch CV22 ....99 D3
  Harbury CV33 ....123 F6
  Longbridge CV35 ......108 A1
  Long Compton CV36 ...141 C3
  Priors Marston CV47 ..125 F4
  Water Orton B46 ....23 B2
Vicarage Rd
  Cheswick Green B90,B94 ..70 D3
  Flecknoe CV23 ....117 B2
  Hockley Heath B94 ......88 F7
  Napton on t H CV47 ...125 C8
  Royal Leamington Spa
  CV32. ....106 B3
  Rugby CV22 ....82 F3
  Stoneleigh CV8 ....94 F5
Vicarage Rise [8] CV33 .122 F8
Vicarage St CV11 ....29 C4
Victor Hodges Ho [2]
  CV47 ....147 B4
Victoria Ave CV21 ....82 F4
Victoria Bsns Ctr [1]
  CV31 ....109 F7
Victoria Cl [2] CV37 ...145 A3
Victoria Ct CV5 ....60 D4
Victoria Dr B78 ....9 A8
Victoria Mews
  Coventry CV5 ....62 E2
  Warwick CV34 ....108 D7
Victoria Rd
  Atherstone CV9 ....18 F6
  Bidford-on-A B50. .....148 C6
  Hartshill CV10 ....28 B8
  Hinckley LE10 ....31 F5
  Royal Leamington Spa
  CV31. ....109 E8
Victoria St
  Coventry CV1 ....151 A4
  Nuneaton CV11 ....29 C4
  Royal Leamington Spa
  CV31. ....109 E8
  Rugby CV21 ....82 E3
  Warwick CV34 ....108 D7
Victoria Terr
  Royal Leamington Spa
  CV31. ....109 F7
  Stockton CV47 ....147 F8
Victoria Way B50 ......148 C5
Victory Rd CV6 ....49 E1
Victory Terr B78 ....9 A4
Vienna Ho CV5 ....60 E2
Viking B77 ....9 D7

Vil Ci LE10 . . . . .31 F4
Villa Cl CV12 . . . . .40 C2
Villa Cres CV12 . . . . . . .40 C1
Village Hall Yd CV47 . . . 115 D4
Village Mews CV22 . . . . .99 C2
Village Rd OX17 . . . . . . 133 D2
Village St
 Harvington WR11 . . . . . 127 D4
 Offchurch CV33 . . . . . . 111 B8
Villa Rd CV6 . . . . .61 B6
Villebon Way CV31 . . . . 110 A2
Villiers Rd CV8 . . . . .93 B5
Villiers St
 Coventry CV2 . . . . .62 A3
 Nuneaton CV11 . . . . . . .29 B3
 Royal Leamington Spa
  CV32 . . . . 106 A1
Vincent Ave CV37 . . . . . 145 A4
Vincent Cl 2 CV37 . . . . . 145 A4
Vincent St
 Coventry CV1 . . . . .61 B2
 Royal Leamington Spa
  CV32 . . . . 106 A1
Vincent Wyles Ho CV2 . . .62 E3
Vinecote Rd CV6 . . . . . . .49 F4
Vine Cottage Est CV35 . . 121 F4
Vine Ct CV34 . . . . 108 F8
Vine La CV34 . . . . 108 F8
Vinery Ct CV37 . . . . 144 F2
Vine St CV1 . . . . 151 C3
Vineyard The LE17 . . . . . .43 E6
Violet Cl
 Bedworth CV12 . . . . . . .38 E2
 Coventry CV2 . . . . .50 C3
 Rugby CV23 . . . . .83 E8
Virginia Pl CV10 . . . . . . .28 E3
Virginia Rd CV1 . . . . . . .61 E3
Viscount Cl
 Birmingham B35 . . . . . .22 A2
 Royal Leamington Spa
  CV31 . . . . 109 F6
Viscount Dr B35 . . . . . . .22 B2
Vittle Dr CV34 . . . . 108 D7
Vodena Cl 5 CV32 . . . . . 105 C1
Vogue Cl CV1 . . . . 151 D3
Vulcan Way LE17 . . . . . . .55 C7

W

Wackrill Dr CV32 . . . . . . 106 C3
Wadbarn B90 . . . . .70 A5
Wade Ave CV3 . . . . .77 B5
Wadebridge Dr CV11 . . . .29 F5
Wade Gr CV34 . . . . 104 E2
Wade La CV33 . . . . 123 D2
Wadham Ho B37 . . . . . . .33 D3
Wadleys Cl B50 . . . . 148 D5
Waggestaff Dr CV10 . . . . .28 A7
Waggoners Cl CV8 . . . . .95 C5
Waggoner's La B78 . . . . . .7 E8
Wagstaffe Cl CV33 . . . . 123 E6
Wagstaff Way B37 . . . . . .44 A8
Wainbody Ave N CV3 . . . .77 A6
Wainbody Ave S CV3 . . . .76 F5
Wainbody Wood Sch CV4 .76 D2
Wain Cl B49 . . . . 143 D5
Wainrigg B77 . . . . .10 B7
Wakefield Cl
 Coventry CV3 . . . . .78 F7
 Hurley CV9 . . . . .16 B4
Wakefield Gr B46 . . . . . .23 B3
Wakeford Cl CV10 . . . . . .18 A3
Wake Gr CV34 . . . . 108 B5
Wakehurst Cl CV11 . . . . . .39 F8
Wakelin Rd B90 . . . . .70 B7
Walcote Cl LE10 . . . . . . .30 F8
Walcot Gn B93 . . . . .72 A2
Waller Cl CV35 . . . . 104 F7
Waller St CV32 . . . . 106 A2
Wall Hill Rd CV5,CV7 . . . . .48 B3
Wallingford Ave CV11 . . . .29 F7
Wallsgrove Cl CV32 . . . . 106 B3
Wallwin Ct CV34 . . . . . . 108 D6
Walmer Way B37 . . . . . . .33 C3
Walmley Ash La B76 . . . . .22 C6
Walmley Ash Rd B76 . . . . .22 A7
Walmley Jun & Inf Schs
 B76 . . . . .22 A7
Walnut Cl
 Birmingham B37 . . . . . .33 B1
 Braunston NN11 . . . . . . 117 E5
 Hartshill CV10 . . . . .28 A8
 Harvington WR11 . . . . . 127 D3
 Nuneaton,Camp Hill CV10 . .28 E6
 Warton CV9 . . . . .17 C8
Walnut Dr
 Atherstone CV9 . . . . . . .18 F7
 Royal Leamington Spa
  CV32 . . . . 106 B3

Walnut Gdns OX17 . . . . . 134 B5
Walnut St CV2 . . . . .50 B2
Walnut Tree Cl CV8 . . . . .93 A3
Walnut Way CV22 . . . . . .82 B1
Walsal End La B92 . . . . . .56 F3
Walsall St CV4 . . . . .76 B7
Walsgrave CE Prim Sch
 CV2 . . . . .63 A6
Walsgrave Gdns 5 CV2 . . .63 A7
Walsgrave Rd CV2 . . . . . .62 B3
Walsgrave Ret Pk CV2 . . . .63 B7
Walsh La CV7 . . . . .46 E2
Walsingham Dr CV10 . . . .39 A7
Walter Scott Rd CV12 . . . .39 C1
Waltham Cres CV10 . . . . .28 B5
Walton Cl
 Coventry CV3 . . . . .78 E7
 Nuneaton CV11 . . . . . . .40 A7
Walton Cotts CV35 . . . . 132 C6
Walton Fields CV35 . . . . 132 C5
Walton Rd CV35 . . . . . . 146 E2
Walton W ay CV35 . . . . . 146 C1
Walton Way CV35 . . . . . 146 D2
Wandsbeck B77 . . . . .9 E8
Wanley Rd CV3 . . . . .77 D6
Wansfell Cl CV4 . . . . .75 F7
Wantage Rd B46 . . . . . . .23 E1
Wappenbury Cl CV2 . . . . .50 C2
Wappenbury Rd CV2 . . . . .50 D2
Wapping La B98 . . . . 112 A7
Warden Rd CV6 . . . . .61 B6
Wardens Ave The CV5 . . . .60 B6
Wardens The CV8 . . . . . .93 C5
Ward Gr CV34 . . . . 109 C7
Wardour Dr B37 . . . . . . .33 C2
Wareham Gn CV2 . . . . . . .63 A5
Ware Orch CV23 . . . . . . 101 C2
Ware Rd CV23 . . . . 101 C2
Warings Green Rd B94 . . . .70 D1
Waring Way CV22 . . . . . .99 D4
Warkworth Cl OX16 . . . . 139 F4
Warmington Cl CV3 . . . . . .78 E8
Warmington Gr CV34 . . . 108 B8
Warmington Rd B47 . . . . .69 A6
Warmwell Cl CV2 . . . . . . .62 F4
Warneford Mews 9
 CV31 . . . . 110 A2
Warneford Pl 2 GL56 . . . 140 A3
Warner Cl CV34 . . . . . . 104 D1
Warner Row 2 CV6 . . . . . .61 F7
Warren Cl
 Earlswood B94 . . . . .87 A8
 Royal Leamington Spa
  CV32 . . . . 106 A3
 Ryton-on-D CV8 . . . . . . .79 A1
Warren Dr B93 . . . . .72 A3
Warren Field CV8 . . . . . . .79 A1
Warren Gn CV4 . . . . .75 F7
Warren Rd CV22 . . . . . . .83 D1
Warrington Cl B76 . . . . . .13 A1
Warton Cl CV8 . . . . .93 C4
Warton La
 Austrey CV9 . . . . .3 A1
 Orton-on-t-H CV9 . . . . . . .6 C4
 Warton B79 . . . . .5 F8
Warwick Ave CV5 . . . . . .77 A8
Warwick By-Pass
 Hampton Magna CV34,
  CV35 . . . . 108 A5
 Warwick CV34 . . . . 109 A1
Warwick Castle* CV34 . . 108 E6
Warwick Cl B80 . . . . 103 D3
Warwick Cres CV37 . . . . 145 B3
Warwick Ct
 5 Birmingham,Chelmsley
  Wood B37 . . . . .33 D2
 Coventry CV3 . . . . 151 B1
 Stratford-u-A CV37 . . . . 145 A3
Warwick Dr CV9 . . . . .12 C2
Warwick Gdns CV10 . . . . .28 E4
Warwick Gn CV12 . . . . . .40 C1
Warwick Highway
 Mappleborough Green
  B80 . . . . 112 A5
 Redditch B98 . . . . 102 F8
Warwick Hospl CV34 . . . 108 E8
Warwick House Ind Pk
 CV47 . . . . 147 B2
Warwick La CV1 . . . . 151 B2
Warwick Mews CV37 . . . 145 B3
Warwick New Rd CV32 . . 109 C8
Warwick Parkway CV35 . . 108 A7
Warwick Pl
 Royal Leamington Spa
  CV32 . . . . 105 C1
 Shipston-on-S CV36 . . . 149 C6
 Southam CV47 . . . . 147 B4
Warwick Race Course
 CV34 . . . . 108 C6
Warwick Rd
 Chadwick End B93 . . . . . .90 A7
 Coventry CV3 . . . . 151 B1
 Ettington CV37 . . . . 131 A4
 Hanwell OX16,OX17 . . . . 139 F5
 Henley-in-A B95 . . . . . . 113 C4
 Kineton CV35 . . . . 132 B6
 Knowle B93 . . . . .72 D3
 Leek Wootton CV35 . . . . 104 F7
 Norton Lindsey CV35 . . . 114 C2
 Shrewley CV35 . . . . 121 E7
 Snitterfield CV37 . . . . . . 121 C5
 Southam CV47 . . . . 147 A3
 Stratford-u-A CV37 . . . . 145 C5
 Tiddington CV37 . . . . . . 145 E2
 Upper Boddington NN11 . . 134 E8

Warwick Rd continued
 Wellesbourne CV35 . . . . 146 D4
 Wolston CV8 . . . . .80 A3
Warwick Row CV1 . . . . . 151 B2
Warwick Sch CV34 . . . . . 109 A6
Warwickshire Coll (Moreton
 Morrell Ctr) CV35 . . . . 122 C2
Warwickshire Coll
 Royal Leamington Spa
  CV32 . . . . 109 D8
 Rugby CV21 . . . . .83 D2
Warwickshire Ex Ctr
 CV31 . . . . 111 C4
Warwickshire Mus* CV34 . 108 E6
Warwickshire Nuffield Hospl
 The CV32 . . . . 105 B2
Warwick Sta CV34 . . . . . 108 F7
Warwick St CV5 . . . . .60 F1
Warwicks The CV35 . . . . 114 F3
Warwick St
 Royal Leamington Spa
  CV32 . . . . 105 F1
 Rugby CV21 . . . . .83 A2
 Southam CV47 . . . . 147 B4
Warwick Tech Pk CV34 . . 109 B5
Warwick Terr CV32 . . . . . 105 E1
Wasdale Cl CV32 . . . . . . 105 C2
Washbourne Rd CV31 . . . 110 A2
Washbrook La CV5 . . . . . .48 A1
Washbrook Pl CV36 . . . . 136 B6
Washford Dr B98 . . . . . . 103 D7
Washford Ind Est B98 . . . 103 E8
Washford La B98 . . . . . . 103 D8
Wasperton Cl 6 CV35 . . . .78 F8
Wasperton La CV35 . . . . 122 C7
Waste La
 Baddesley Ensor CV9 . . . . 11 E1
 Balsall Common CV7 . . . .74 F5
 Coventry CV6 . . . . .48 F1
Watchbury Cl B36 . . . . . .22 C1
Watch Cl CV1 . . . . 151 A3
Watchmaker Ct CV1 . . . . 151 A2
Watcombe Rd CV2 . . . . . .62 E8
Watercall Ave CV3 . . . . . .77 C6
Waterdale B90 . . . . .70 D5
Waterfall Cl CV7 . . . . .46 C1
Waterfield Gdns CV31 . . . 110 C7
Waterfield Way LE10 . . . . .31 C5
Waterford Way CV3 . . . . . .62 C1
Water Lily Way CV10 . . . . .39 A8
Waterloo Ave B37 . . . . . .33 B4
Waterloo Cl CV35 . . . . . 146 C2
Waterloo Cres B50 . . . . . 148 B5
Waterloo Dr CV37 . . . . . 145 D1
Waterloo Ind Est
 Bidford-on-A B50 . . . . . 148 E6
 Birmingham B37 . . . . . . .33 B5
Waterloo Pk B50 . . . . . . 148 E6
Waterloo Pl 5 CV32 . . . . 105 F1
Waterloo Rd
 Bidford-on-A B50 . . . . . 148 E6
 Hinckley LE10 . . . . .31 D8
Waterloo Rise 1 CV37 . . 130 B8
Waterloo St
 1 Coventry CV1 . . . . . . .61 E4
 Royal Leamington Spa
  CV31 . . . . 110 B7
Waterman Rd CV6 . . . . . .61 F6
Water Orton La B46,B76 . . .22 E4
Water Orton Prim Sch
 B46 . . . . .23 B2
Water Orton Rd B36 . . . . .22 E1
Water Orton Sta B46 . . . . .23 A3
Watersbridge Gdns CV10 . .29 C1
Waterside CV6 . . . . .50 C6
Waterside Ct
 Hinckley LE10 . . . . .30 F7
 Royal Leamington Spa
  CV37 . . . . 145 A5
Waterside Dr CV21 . . . . . .83 C5
Waterside
 Polesworth B78 . . . . .5 A1
 Stratford-u-A CV37 . . . . 145 A2
Watermeet Gr CV2 . . . . . .62 B6
Watermeet Ho B78 . . . . . .9 B8
Watermeet Rd CV2 . . . . . .62 B6
Waterson Croft B37 . . . . .33 D3
Watery La
 Baddesley Ensor CV9 . . . . 11 B2
 Cheswick Green B90 . . . .70 D4
 Corley Moor CV7 . . . . . . .47 D5
 Coventry CV6 . . . . .49 A4
 Hook Norton OX15 . . . . 142 D4
 Keresley CV7 . . . . .48 F4
 Kineton CV35 . . . . 132 C7
 Knowle B93 . . . . .72 E4
 Longbridge CV35 . . . . . 114 B1
 Pillerton Hersey CV35 . . 131 E3
 Portway B47,B48 . . . . . . .85 D7
 Shipston-on-S CV36 . . . 149 D6
 Shustoke B46 . . . . .24 D2
 Ullenhall B95 . . . . 112 A6
Wathen Rd
 Royal Leamington Spa
  CV32 . . . . 106 A2
 Warwick CV34 . . . . 108 E8
Watling Cl LE10 . . . . .31 C4
Watling Cres CV23 . . . . . .68 C1
Watling Ct CV11 . . . . .29 F3
Watling Dr LE10 . . . . .31 C4
Watling La CV9 . . . . 11 B2

Watling Rd CV8 . . . . .93 B6
Watling St
 Dordon B77,B78 . . . . . . .10 D6
 Grendon B78,CV9 . . . . . .11 C4
 Hinckley CV11,LE10 . . . . .30 C8
 Tamworth,Wilncote B77 . . .9 E7
Watson Cl 3 CV34 . . . . . 104 E1
Watson Rd CV5 . . . . .60 D2
Watson Way CV7 . . . . . . .74 C8
Wattisham Sq B35 . . . . . .22 A4
Watton Gn B35 . . . . .22 A2
Watton La B46 . . . . .23 D2
Watton's La CV47 . . . . . 147 B4
Watton's Lodge CV47 . . . 147 B4
Watts La CV21 . . . . 101 B8
Watts Rd B80 . . . . 103 E2
Waugh Cl B37 . . . . .33 B2
Wavebeck Ct CV23 . . . . . .82 B5
Waveley Rd CV1 . . . . .61 A3
Wavendon Cl CV2 . . . . . .50 F1
Waveney Cl LE10 . . . . . . .31 A8
Waveney B77 . . . . .9 E8
Wavere Ct CV21 . . . . .83 D7
Waverley Ave CV11 . . . . . .29 F1
Waverley Edge CV8 . . . . .95 B3
Waverley Rd
 Kenilworth CV8 . . . . . . .93 A4
 Royal Leamington Spa
  CV31 . . . . 110 B6
 Rugby CV21 . . . . .84 A1
Waverley Sq CV11 . . . . . .29 F1
Wavers Marston B37 . . . . .44 A8
Waverton Ave B79 . . . . . . .5 E4
Waverton Mews 15 CV31 . 110 C6
Waytrec Cl CV34 . . . . . . 108 D7
Wawensmere Rd B95 . . . 113 A2
Wayside B37 . . . . .44 A8
Weale Gr CV34 . . . . 104 F2
Weatheroak Rd B49 . . . . 143 D4
Weaver Ave B76 . . . . .13 A1
Weaver Dr CV23 . . . . .82 C4
Weavers Cl
 Bedworth CV12 . . . . . . 102 D4
 Shipston-on-S CV36 . . . 149 D6
Weavers Cotts CV3 . . . . 141 C3
Weavers Hill B97 . . . . . . 102 A4
Weavers Row OX15 . . . . 139 A3
Weavers Wlk CV6 . . . . . . .62 B8
Webb Dr CV23 . . . . .83 D8
Webb Ellis Bsns Pk CV21 . .83 B4
Webb Ellis Rd CV22 . . . . .82 E2
Webb St CV10 . . . . .28 D3
Webster Ave CV8 . . . . . . .93 B5
Webster St CV6 . . . . .61 E7
Webster Way B76 . . . . . . .22 A8
Weddington Country Wlk*
 CV10 . . . . .20 C1
Weddington Ctry Wlk*
 CV10 . . . . .20 B3
Weddington La CV10 . . . . .20 A3
Weddington Prim Sch
 CV10 . . . . .29 C7
Weddington Rd CV10 . . . .29 C7
Weddington Terr CV10 . . . .29 D5
Wedgewood Cl CV2 . . . . .62 E8
Wedgewood Ho B37 . . . . .33 B4
Wedge-Woods CV5 . . . . . .76 F8
Wednock Cl CV34 . . . . . 104 C8
Wednock Ind Est CV34 . . 108 C8
Wedon Cl CV4 . . . . .75 E7
Weigh Bridge Ct GL55 . . 135 B2
Weilerswist Dr CV31 . . . . 109 F4
Weland Cl B46 . . . . .23 B2
Weland Ct B46 . . . . .23 A2
Welbeck Ave LE10 . . . . . .31 D4
Welby Gate CV7 . . . . . . .74 B5
Welcham Pl CV35 . . . . . 138 C6
Welcombe Ct 1 CV37 . . . 145 A4
Welcombe Hills Ctry Pk (Nat
 Res)* CV37 . . . . 145 B7
Welcombe Hills Sch
 CV37 . . . . 145 A5
Welcombe Rd CV37 . . . . 145 B4
Welcome St CV9 . . . . . . .18 E8
Welford Cl B98 . . . . 102 F5
Welford Gr CV35 . . . . . . 114 E6
Welford-on-Avon Prim Sch
 CV37 . . . . 129 A6
Welford Pl CV6 . . . . .61 D7
Welford Rd
 Bidford-on-A B50,CV37 . . 128 D6
 Long Marston CV37 . . . . 129 B4
 Rugby CV21 . . . . .83 C4
 Tamworth B77 . . . . .9 C5
Welgarth Ave CV6 . . . . . .60 F6
Welham Croft B90 . . . . . .71 A6
Welland Cl
 Long Lawford CV23 . . . . .82 C5
 Staverton NN11 . . . . . . 126 F8
Welland Rd CV1 . . . . .61 F1
Welland Way B76 . . . . . . .22 A7
Well Bank OX15 . . . . . . 142 D4
Well Cl B97 . . . . 102 C5
Wellesbourne CE Prim Sch
 CV35 . . . . 146 B3
Wellesbourne Farm
 CV35 . . . . 146 E3
Wellesbourne Gr CV37 . . 144 F2
Wellesbourne Ho CV35 . . 146 D2
Wellesbourne Rd
 Alveston CV37 . . . . 121 D3
 Barford CV35 . . . . 122 B7
 Coventry CV5 . . . . .60 A6
 Lighthorne CV35 . . . . . . 123 B2
 Loxley CV35 . . . . 130 F8
Wellesbourne Sch (Annexe)
 CV35 . . . . 146 E4

Wellesbourne Water Mill*
 CV35 . . . . 146 E1
Wellfield Cl CV7 . . . . .74 D5
Wellington Aviation Mus
 The* GL56 . . . . 140 A3
Wellington Cl
 Hinckley LE10 . . . . .31 E4
 Wellesbourne CV35 . . . . 146 C1
Wellington Dr CV37 . . . . 145 D1
Wellington Gdns 1 CV1 . . .61 B2
Wellington Parkway LE17 . .55 D6
Wellington Rd
 Moreton-in-M GL56 . . . . 140 B3
 Royal Leamington Spa
  CV32 . . . . 106 C2
Wellington St CV1 . . . . . 151 D4
Wellington Terr GL56 . . . 140 B3
Wellington Way B35 . . . . .22 B2
Well La
 Shenington OX15 . . . . . 138 F5
 Staverton NN11 . . . . . . 126 D8
 Tanworth-In-A B94 . . . . . .87 A1
Wellmeadow Gr B92 . . . . .57 A7
Wells Cl CV10 . . . . .28 A8
Wells Ct CV3 . . . . .77 F7
Well Spring Cl CV9 . . . . . .18 F8
Wells La B95 . . . . .83 B3
Well St CV1 . . . . 151 B3
Wells Wlk B37 . . . . .33 A1
Welsh Cl CV34 . . . . 104 E2
Welsh Rd
 Aston le W NN11 . . . . . . 134 F6
 Bascote CV47 . . . . 115 B2
 Coventry CV2 . . . . .62 B4
 Cubbington CV32,CV23 . . 106 F2
Welsh Rd E CV47 . . . . . . 147 D2
Welsh Rd W
 Lower Boddington NN11 . . 134 F7
 Napton on t H CV47 . . . . 125 C5
 Offchurch CV33 . . . . . . 111 C6
Welsh Rd W CV47 . . . . . 147 A5
Welton Cl B76 . . . . .13 A2
Welton Rd CV22 . . . . . . 100 D8
Welton Rd
 Braunston NN11 . . . . . . 117 E5
 Warwick CV34 . . . . 104 D1
Wembrook Cl CV11 . . . . . .29 D2
Wembrook Ho CV11 . . . . .29 C2
Wembrook Prim Sch
 CV11 . . . . .29 C2
Wendiburgh St CV4 . . . . . .76 B7
Wendover Dr LE10 . . . . . .31 F5
Wenlock Way CV10 . . . . . .28 B3
Wensum Cl LE10 . . . . . . .31 B8
Wentworth Ave CV47 . . . 133 A6
Wentworth Dr
 Coventry CV6 . . . . .49 B4
 Nuneaton CV11 . . . . . . .30 A1
Wentworth Rd
 Royal Leamington Spa
  CV31 . . . . 110 D6
 Rugby CV22 . . . . .82 F1
Wesley Rd CV21 . . . . . . 101 A8
Wessenden B77 . . . . .10 B7
Wessex Cl CV12 . . . . .39 A4
Wessex Ct B79 . . . . .4 F7
Wessons Rd B50 . . . . . . 148 E5
West Ave
 Bedworth CV12 . . . . .39 D2
 Coventry CV6,CV7 . . . . . .49 A5
 Coventry,Middle Stoke CV2 . .62 A2
Westbourne Gr CV22 . . . . .82 F1
Westbrook Ct CV5 . . . . . .60 A4
Westbury Ct
 Coventry CV2 . . . . .62 A3
 Warwick CV34 . . . . 109 A7
Westbury Rd
 Coventry CV5 . . . . .60 D5
 Nuneaton CV10 . . . . . . .28 D3
West Cl LE10 . . . . .31 D7
Westcliff Dr CV34 . . . . . 104 E2
Westcliff Dr CV3 . . . . .77 B5
Westcotes CV4 . . . . .60 B1
Westcroft Gr CV35 . . . . . 114 E6
West Dr B95 . . . . 113 B2
West End CV35 . . . . 138 F5
West End Cres CV37 . . . . 144 F1
West End Ct CV34 . . . . . 108 D6
West End
 Hornton OX15 . . . . 139 B7
 Radway CV35 . . . . 132 E2
Westend Terr GL55 . . . . 135 A2
Westham Gr CV31 . . . . . 110 B5
Western Dr LE17 . . . . . . .43 E5
Western Hill Cl B96 . . . . 102 E1
Western Rd CV37 . . . . . . 144 F3
West End
 CV37 . . . . 144 F3
Western Road Ind Est
 CV37 . . . . 144 F3
Westfield Barns CV47 . . . 125 E4
Westfield Cl
 Dorridge B93 . . . . .71 F2
 Nuneaton CV10 . . . . . . .29 D5
 Stratford-u-A CV37 . . . . 144 F5
Westfield Cres CV35 . . . . 146 D3
Westfield Ct LE10 . . . . . . .31 C7
Westfield Ho B36 . . . . . . .33 A7
Westfield Inf Sch LE10 . . . .31 B7
Westfield Jun Sch LE10 . . .31 B7
Westfield Rd
 Hinckley LE10 . . . . .31 B7
 Rugby CV22 . . . . .82 F2
 Southam CV47 . . . . 147 A3
Westfields B78 . . . . .10 D8
Westgate Cl CV34 . . . . . 108 D6
Westgate Ho 10 CV34 . . . 108 E6

Westgate Prim Sch CV34 108 D6
Westgate Rd CV21 83 E1
West Green Dr CV37 144 B3
Westgrove Ave 6 B90 71 A6
Westgrove Terr 1 CV32 109 D8
Westham Ho
Barford CV35 122 A7
Birmingham B37 33 B4
Westham La CV35 122 A7
Westhill Rd
Blackdown CV32 106 A6
Coventry CV6 60 F6
Westholme Ct B50 148 D4
Westholme Rd B50 148 D5
West Hyde LE10 30 F7
Westlea Rd CV31 109 E6
Westleigh Ave CV5 76 F7
West Leyes CV21 83 A3
Westmead Ave B80 103 E4
Westmede Ctr CV5 60 C4
Westminster Dr
Hinckley LE10 31 F4
Nuneaton CV10 28 B7
Westminster Rd CV1 151 A1
Westmoreland Ave CV10 28 E4
Westmorland Rd CV2 62 F4
West of St Laurence CV35 114 A8
Westonbirt Cl CV8 93 C6
Weston Cl
5 Royal Leamington Spa CV31 110 C6
Dorridge B93 72 A2
Dunchurch CV22 99 C4
Warwick CV34 108 F7
Weston Ct
Long Compton CV36 141 D3
Rugby CV21 83 C4
Weston Hall Stables CV12 40 A3
Weston La
Bubbenhall CV8,CV33 95 B3
Bulkington CV12 40 A3
Weston St CV1 151 C4
West Orchards Sh Ctr CV1 151 B3
West Park Cl CV37 144 B3
West Ridge CV5 60 A5
West Rock CV34 108 D7
West Side Bsns Ctr CV4 75 F8
West Side WR11 128 A2
West St
17 Royal Leamington Spa CV31 110 A7
Coventry CV1 61 E3
Long Lawford CV23 82 A4
Shipston-on-S CV36 149 D6
Shutford OX15 139 A3
Stratford-u-A CV37 144 F1
Warwick CV34 108 D5
West View CV10 27 E8
West View Rd
Royal Leamington Spa CV32 106 C5
Rugby CV22 82 E2
Westway CV21 83 A3
Westwood Bsns Pk CV4 75 F6
Westwood Cl CV10 28 E3
Westwood Cres CV9 18 D7
Westwood Heath Rd CV4 75 E6
Westwood Rd
Atherstone CV9 18 D7
Coventry CV5 61 A1
Rugby CV22 100 F7
Westwood Way CV4 76 A6
Wetherby Way CV37 144 E1
Wetherell Way CV21 83 C7
Wexford Rd CV2 50 D1
Weymouth Cl CV3 78 D5
Whaley's Croft CV6 61 B8
Wharf Ind Est The CV23 65 A7
Wharf La B94 88 D4
Wharf Lodge CV31 109 D7
Wharf Rd
Coventry CV6 61 F5
Stratford-u-A CV37 144 F4
Wharf St CV34 109 A8
Wharf The
Shipston-on-S CV36 149 D7
Wilmcote CV37 120 C5
Wharf Yd LE10 31 A7
Wharrage Rd B49 143 D4
Wharrington Cl B98 103 A8
Wharrington Hill B98 103 A8
Whatcote Rd CV35 137 F8
Whateley Ct CV11 29 B4
Whateley Hall Cl B93 72 C7
Whateley Hall Rd B93 72 B7
Whateley La B77,B78 9 F4
Whateley's Dr CV8 93 A5
Whateley Villas CV9 10 A2
Wheatcroft Dr B37 33 C1
Wheate Croft CV4 59 F2
Wheaten Cl B37 33 D3
Wheatfield Cl B36 33 A7
Wheatfield Ct GL55 135 B6
Wheatfield Rd CV22 82 D1
Wheathill Cl CV32 105 E2
Wheatley Grange B46 33 F6
Wheatmoor Rd B75 13 A6
Wheatsheaf La B94 113 C8
Wheat St CV11 29 D4
Wheelbarrow La CV35 114 A3
Wheeler Cl B93 90 B7
Wheeley Moor Rd B37 33 A5
Wheelwright Ct 6 CV37 144 F3
Wheelwright La CV6,CV7 49 C4
Wheelwright Lane Prim Sch CV7 49 D5
Wheler Rd CV3 78 A7
Whernside CV21 83 C7
Whetstone Dr CV21 83 E7
Whichcote Ave CV7 46 C1
Whiley Cl CV23 83 F5
Whimbrel Cl CV23 83 C8
Whitacre Rd 3 CV32 106 A2
Whitacre Rd Ind Est CV11 29 E4
Whitacre Rd
Knowle B93 72 B7
Nuneaton CV11 29 E4
Whitaker Rd CV5 60 C3
Whitburn Rd CV12 38 C1
Whitchurch Cl B98 102 F6
Whitchurch Way CV4 75 F8
Whitebeam Cl CV4 59 D1
White Beam Rd B37 44 D8
Whitebeam Way CV10 28 D7
Whitefield Cl CV4 75 D6
Whitefriars Dr CV22 82 A1
White Friars La CV1 151 C2
White Friars St CV1 151 C2
Whitehall Cl CV10 19 A2
Whitehall Rd CV21 83 B2
White Hart La CV33 111 F1
Whitehead Dr
Kenilworth CV8 93 C7
Minworth B76 22 D6
Wellesbourne CV35 146 E4
Whitehead Gr CV7 74 B7
Whiteheads Ct 17 CV32 105 F1
Whitehorse Cl CV6 50 B6
White Horse Hill CV37 121 B6
White Ho The B95 113 B4
Whitehouse Cres CV10 28 D3
White House Hill B95 120 B7
Whitehouse Rd B78 11 A7
Whitelaw Cres CV5 60 C6
Whitemoor Dr B90 71 A7
Whitemoor La B96 118 D8
Whitemoor Rd CV8 93 B5
Whitemoors Cl CV13 21 E7
Whitemoors Rd CV13 21 E7
Whitepits La B48 85 F4
Whitepump La B95 112 E7
White Rose Ho 4 CV32 105 F2
Whiteside Cl CV3 78 F8
Whiteslade Cl B93 72 A7
Whites Row CV8 93 A3
White St CV1 151 C3
Whitestitch La CV7 46 C3
Whitestone Inf Sch CV11 40 A8
Whitestone Rd CV11 40 B7
Whitethorn Dr CV32 106 B2
Whiteway OX17 133 F2
Whitfield Cl CV37 145 E4
Whitford Dr B90 71 C7
Whiting B77 9 D7
Whitley Abbey Com Sch CV3 77 F6
Whitley Abbey Prim Sch CV3 78 A6
Whitley Ct CV3 77 F7
Whitley Rd B95 113 B4
Whitley Village CV3 77 F7
Whitlocks End Halt B90 69 E7
Whitmore Park Prim Sch CV6 49 A1
Whitmore Park Rd CV6 49 D3
Whitmore Rd CV31 110 A3
Whitnash Cl CV7 74 A6
Whitnash Gr CV2 62 D5
Whitnash Prim Sch CV31 110 A4
Whitnash Rd CV31 110 B4
Whittington Cl 4 CV34 109 B8
Whittington La CV9 12 B2
Whittle Cl
Coventry CV3 78 F8
Daventry NN11 117 F3
Rugby CV22 99 D7
Whittle Ct 9 CV32 106 A1
Whittleford Gr B36 22 C1
Whittleford Rd CV10 28 C4
Whittle Rd LE10 30 E7
Whittons Cl OX15 142 D4
Whitwell Cl B90 71 A6
Whitworth Ave
Coventry CV3 62 B1
Hinckley LE10 30 F7
Whitworth Cl CV35 146 C2
Whoberley Ave CV5 60 D2
Whoberley Hall Prim Sch CV5 60 C3
Wickham Cl CV6 48 F2
Wickham Ct CV32 106 B3
Wickham Rd B80 103 F4
Wickmans Dr CV4 59 C2
Wiclif Way CV10 28 B3
Widdecombe Cl CV2 62 D7
Widdrington Rd CV1 61 C5
Widney Cl B93 71 F5
Widney La B91 71 B8
Widney Manor Rd B91, B93 71 D7
Widney Manor Sta B91 71 C8
Widney Rd B93 71 F5
Wigford Rd B77 9 C5
Wiggins Cl CV21 101 B8
Wiggins Hill Rd B76 22 F7
Wight Croft B36 33 B6
Wigston Hill CV9 17 D5
Wigston Rd
Coventry CV2 50 F1
Wigston Rd *continued*
Rugby CV21 101 A8
Wike La B96 118 E8
Wilcox Cl CV47 124 A4
Wilcox Leys CV35 122 F2
Wildcroft Rd CV5 60 C3
Wilderness B95 113 B2
Wildey Rd 1 CV12 38 D2
Wild Goose La B98 103 D8
Wildmoor Cl CV2 50 B4
Wilford Gr B76 22 B6
Wilhelmina Cl CV32 109 E8
Wilkes Way B50 148 D5
Wilkins Cl CV35 122 A7
Wilkinson Way B46 25 A2
Willday Dr CV9 12 D2
Willenhall La CV3 78 F7
Willenhall Wood Prim Sch CV3 78 D6
Willes Ct 2 CV31 110 B7
Willes Rd CV31,CV32 110 A8
Willes Terr CV31 110 B8
Willett Gdns CV35 146 D4
Willett Ho CV35 146 D4
William Arnold Cl CV2 62 A4
William Batchelor Ho CV1 151 B4
William Beesley Cres CV11 40 E6
William Bree Rd CV5 59 C5
William Bristow Rd CV3 77 E7
William Cl 12 OX16 139 F4
William Cree Cl CV8 79 F3
William Groubb Cl CV3 78 D7
William Iliffe St LE10 31 B7
William Kirby Cl CV4 60 A1
William McCool Cl CV3 78 F7
William McKee Cl CV3 78 E7
William Malcolm Ho CV2 62 E3
William Morris Sch OX16 139 F4
William Sheriden Ho CV2 62 E3
Williams Rd CV31 110 E4
William St
Bedworth CV12 39 D2
Nuneaton CV11 29 E3
Royal Leamington Spa CV32 110 A8
Rugby CV21 83 B3
William Tarver Cl CV34 109 A7
William Thomas Ho 7 CV32 106 A1
William Thomson Ho 2 CV1 151 D4
William Tolson's Ind Est B78 9 A8
Willington St CV11 29 B5
Willis Croft B79 5 E4
Willis Gr CV12 39 C3
Willis Ho CV11 29 E1
Willoughby Ave CV8 92 E3
Willoughby Cl
Alcester B49 143 A6
Coventry CV3 78 E8
Willoughby Pl CV22 100 D7
Willowbank Rd LE10 31 C7
Willow Bank Rd B93 71 F6
Willow Bank CV37 129 A7
Willow Brook Rd CV8 80 A4
Willowbud Ho B98 102 F8
Willow Cl
Alcester B49 143 B2
Bedworth CV12 39 A5
Hinckley LE10 31 E5
Kingsbury B78 15 D7
Nuneaton CV10 28 A7
Whitnash CV31 110 B2
Willow Ctyd CV2 62 D7
Willowdale LE10 31 A7
Willowdene Cvn Site CV37 120 B5
Willow Dr
Cheswick Green B90 70 D4
Wellesbourne CV35 146 E3
Willow End GL56 141 A1
Willowfields Rd CV11 30 A1
Willow Gdns CV47 147 B4
Willow Gr
Coventry CV4 60 B2
Long Itchington CV47 115 D4
Willowherb Cl 5 CV3 78 F8
Willowherb Way B90 70 A5
Willow Ho 11 CV34 109 D8
Willow La
Fillongley CV7 36 C5
Rugby CV22 83 C2
Willow Meer CV8 93 B5
Willow Park Ind Est CV13 21 C7
Willow Rd CV10 28 F5
Willows CE Prim Sch The CV37 144 E2
Willows Dr N CV37 144 E3
Willow Sheets Mdw CV32 106 E6
Willows The
Atherstone CV9 12 E2
Bedworth CV12 38 E2
Hollywood B47 69 A6
Portway B47 85 F7
Stratford-u-A CV37 144 E2
Willow Tree Gdns CV21 101 B8
Willow Way
Birmingham B37 33 B1
Studley B80 103 E2
Willow Wlk CV7 26 E1
Wilmcote CE Prim Sch CV37 120 C4
Wilmcote Gn CV5 60 A3
Wilmcote La B95 120 A5
Wilmcote Sta CV37 120 C5
Wilmhurst Rd CV34 108 C8
Wilmot Ave B46 33 F6
Wilmot Cl CV7 74 B8
Wilnecote Gr CV31 110 B5
Wilnecote High Sch B77 9 F6
Wilnecote Jun Sch B77 9 F7
Wilnecote La B77 9 E8
Wilnecote Sta B77 9 D7
Wilson Cl CV22 82 C2
Wilson Dr B75 13 A5
Wilson Gn CV3 62 F1
Wilson Gr CV8 93 C4
Wilson Rd CV37 144 E3
Wilsons La CV7 50 A6
Wilson's La CV6 49 F6
Wilsons Rd B93 72 C6
Wilton Rd CV7 74 B5
Wiltshire Cl
Bedworth CV12 39 A3
Coventry CV5 60 B3
Wimborne Dr CV2 63 A4
Wimbourne Cl CV10 28 B5
Wimbourne Rd B76 13 A4
Wimpstone La CV37 130 B4
Winceby Pl CV4 59 D1
Winchat Cl CV3 62 F1
Winchcombe Rd B49 143 D4
Winchelsea Cl 3 OX16 139 F5
Winchester Ave CV10 29 C7
Winchester Ct CV22 99 C3
Winchester Dr
Birmingham B37 33 A2
Hinckley LE10 32 B7
Winchester St CV1 61 E3
Wincott Cl CV37 145 C1
Windermere Ave
Coventry,Binley CV3 62 E1
Coventry,Upper Eastern Green CV5 59 E4
Nuneaton CV11 29 F6
Windermere Cl CV21 83 C7
Windermere Dr CV32 105 D2
Windermere B77 10 A7
Winderton Ave CV35 114 E5
Winding House La CV6, CV7 49 C4
Windmill Ave 4 B46 33 F7
Windmill Cl
Ilmington CV36 136 B6
Kenilworth CV8 93 A6
Warton B79 5 E3
Windmill Croft CV32 106 D5
Windmill Ct CV6 50 A3
Windmill Dr B97 102 C6
Windmill Gdns
Redditch B97 102 B6
Staverton NN11 126 E8
Windmill Hill
Bidford-on-A B50 128 E8
Cubbington CV32 106 D5
Windmill Hill La CV33, CV35 123 C5
Windmill Hill The CV5 60 A7
Windmill Ind Est CV5 59 F7
Windmill La
Astley CV10 37 E6
Austrey CV9 3 C3
Balsall Common CV7 74 D4
Baxterley CV9 17 D6
Corley Moor CV7 47 D6
Dorridge B93 71 F1
Dunchurch CV22 99 A4
Ladbroke CV47 124 D6
Ladbroke CV47 124 E5
Staverton NN11 126 E8
Tanworth-in-A B94 89 A8
Windmill Rd
Atherstone CV9 12 D1
Bedworth CV7 50 A8
Coventry CV6 50 A3
Nuneaton CV10 28 D7
Whitnash CV31 109 F5
Windmill Way
Southam CV47 147 A5
Upper Tysoe CV35 138 B6
Windridge Cl CV3 78 C6
Windrush Cl B97 102 D6
Windrush Dr LE10 31 A8
Windrush Rd B47 69 B7
Windrush Way CV23 82 B5
Windsor Ct
12 Royal Leamington Spa CV32 109 F8
9 Stratford-u-A CV37 144 F3
Coventry CV4 60 B2
Hinckley LE10 32 A5
Nuneaton CV10 28 E6
Windsor Gdns CV10 28 E4
Windsor Pl 10 CV32 105 F1
Windsor Rd B78 5 A3
Windsor St
Coventry CV1 61 B2
Hinckley LE10 32 A5
Nuneaton CV11 29 B4
Royal Leamington Spa CV32 109 F8
Rugby CV21 83 C3
Stratford-u-A CV37 144 F3
Windward Way B36 33 B6
Windy Arbor Prim Sch B37 33 D2
Windy Arbour CV8 93 B4
Windyridge Rd B76 22 A6
Winfield Rd CV11 29 B5
Winfield St CV21 83 D3
Wingfield Rd B46 33 F5
Wingfield Way CV6 49 A2
Wingrave Cl CV5 60 A6
Winifred Ave CV5 61 A1
Winnallthorpe CV3 78 E6
Winsford Ave CV5 60 B4
Winsford Cl CV7 74 A6
Winsford Ct CV5 60 C4
Winsham Wlk CV3 77 C3
Winslow Cl
Coventry CV5 60 B3
Royal Leamington Spa CV32 105 C1
Winslow Ho 11 CV1 61 B2
Winspear Cl CV7 46 B1
Winster Ave B93 71 E4
Winster Cl CV7 49 A7
Winston Ave CV2 62 D8
Winston Cl
Coventry CV2 62 D8
Stratford-u-A CV37 144 D1
Winston Dr 15 OX17 139 F5
Winterborne Gdns CV10 29 A2
Winterdene CV7 74 B7
Winter Gardens Way 1 OX16 139 F5
Winterton Rd CV12 40 C2
Winthorpe Dr B91 71 C8
Winton Gr B76 22 A6
Winwick Pl CV22 99 C8
Winyates Rd CV33 123 D2
Wise Gr
Rugby CV21 83 F2
Warwick CV34 104 E2
Wise St CV31 109 F7
Wise Terr CV31 109 F7
Wishaw Cl B98 103 A8
Wishaw La
Curdworth B76 23 A7
Middleton B76,B78 14 C6
Minworth B76 22 E7
Wisley Gr CV8 93 C5
Wistaria Cl 2 CV2 50 B2
Witham Cl B76 13 A1
Witham The NN11 117 F1
Witherley CE Prim Sch CV9 19 B7
Witherley Rd
Atherstone CV9 18 F7
Witherley CV9 19 B6
Withington Gr B93 71 E4
Withybrook Cl CV2 50 D2
Withybrook La CV7 51 F5
Withybrook Rd
Bulkington CV12 40 D2
Solihull B90 70 B8
Withycombe Dr OX16 139 F3
Withy Hill Rd B75 13 B8
Witnell Rd CV6 61 C6
Wixford Lodge B50 148 D8
Wixford Rd B49,B50 119 B1
Woburn Cl CV31 110 C6
Woburn Dr CV10 29 A2
Wolds End Cl GL55 135 B2
Wolds La LE10 41 E4
Wolfe Rd CV4 75 F8
Wolford Rd GL56 140 D6
Wolseley Cl B36 23 A1
Wolsey Rd CV22 99 D6
Wolston La CV8 79 E2
Wolston St Margaret's CE Prim Sch CV8 80 A4
Wolston Way CV3 78 C6
Wolverton Prim Sch CV35 114 B2
Wolverton Rd
Birmingham,Marston Green B37 44 B7
Coventry CV5 60 A3
Norton Lindsey CV35 114 C2
Snitterfield CV37 121 B7
Wolvey CE Prim Sch LE10 41 D4
Wolvey Rd
Bulkington CV12 40 E2
Hinckley LE10 31 E4
Woodbank LE10 32 A7
Woodberrow La B97 102 D6
Woodberry Dr B76 13 A2
Woodbine Cotts
2 Royal Leamington Spa CV32 109 E8
Kingswood CV35 89 D3
Woodbine St 1 CV32 109 E8
Woodbine Wlk B37 33 D2
Woodbridge Ct CV21 83 A3
Woodbridge Pk CV9 16 C4
Woodbrook Ho 9 B37 33 B2
Woodburn Cl CV5 60 B4
Woodbury Cl B97 102 A6
Woodby La LE17 55 E8
Woodchester Rd B93 71 E2
Wood Cl B46 33 F7
Woodclose Ave CV6 60 F6
Woodclose Rd B37 33 A3
Woodcock Cl B94 86 E3
Woodcote Ave
Kenilworth CV8 92 D6
Nuneaton CV11 29 F8
Woodcote Dr
Dorridge B93 72 B2
Leek Wootton CV35 104 F7
Woodcote La CV8,CV35 104 F7
Woodcote Rd
Royal Leamington Spa CV32 105 F3
Warwick CV34 108 F8
Woodcot Park Dr CV37 120 B5
Woodcot Park Homes Est CV37 120 B5

Woodcraft Cl CV4..........60 A2
Wood Croft B47...........69 B6
Wood Ct CV2..............62 D7
Woodend Croft CV4.......75 E8
Wood End La
 Fillongley CV7..........37 A3
 Tanworth-In-A B94......86 F5
Wood End Prim Sch CV9...10 C1
Wood End Sta B94........86 F4
Woodfield Rd
 Coventry CV5............76 E8
 Hinckley LE10...........31 C6
Woodford Cl
 Coventry CV7............49 D5
 Nuneaton CV10..........28 D4
Woodford La CV10.........19 C4
Woodgate Rd LE10........32 A8
Woodgreen Cl B97.......102 B7
Woodhall Cl CV11.........30 A2
Woodhams Rd CV3........78 C3
Wood Hill Rise CV6........49 D2
Woodhouse Cl CV3........78 E8
Woodhouse La B77.........4 A5
Woodhouse St CV34.....108 D6
Woodington Rd B75.......13 B5
Wood La
 Aston Cantlow B49,B95...119 F5
 Birmingham,Marston Green
 B37....................44 A8
 Cherington CV36.......141 D7
 Cookhill B96...........118 C6
 Earlswood B94..........69 E1
 Eastcote B92...........56 F2
 Hartshill CV10..........28 A8
 Higham on t H CV13.....20 E3
Woodland Ave
 Claybrooke Magna LE17...43 E6
 Coventry CV5............76 F7
 Hinckley LE10...........32 A7
Woodland Rd
 Kenilworth CV8..........93 B7
 Tamworth B77............4 A4
Woodlands Ave B46.......23 B2
Woodlands Cl B78........11 A5
Woodlands Ct
 Binley Woods CV3........79 D7
 Coventry CV5............77 A8
Woodlands Farm Rd B24..22 A4
Woodlands Inf Sch B90...70 B8
Woodlands La
 Bedworth CV12..........38 E4
 Solihull B90............70 B8
Woodlands Rd
 Bedworth CV12..........38 F3
 Binley Woods CV3........79 D7
 Stratford-u-A CV37.....144 F5
Woodlands Sch The CV5...59 D3
Woodlands Terr B78......11 A5
Woodlands The
 Hartshill CV10..........19 A1
 Staverton NN11........126 D8
 Sutton Coldfield B75....13 A6
 Wood End CV9...........10 C1
Woodlands Way B37......33 D3

Woodland Way B78.......10 F8
Wood La
 Old Arley CV7...........26 D2
 Shilton CV7.............51 D5
Woodleigh Rd CV4........75 F5
Woodloes Ave N CV34...104 F2
Woodloes Ave S CV34...104 F1
Woodloes Inf Sch CV34..104 E1
Woodloes Jun Sch CV34..104 E1
Woodloes La CV34,CV35..104 F2
Woodloes Rd B90.........70 B7
Woodman Ct CV37.......144 F4
Woodmill Mdw CV8.......93 B6
Woodpecker Gr B36......33 A7
Woodridge Ave CV5.......60 A6
Woodroffe Wlk CV6.......50 A4
Woodrow Cres B93.......72 A5
Woodrow Ctr B98........103 B8
Woodrow Dr B98.........103 B6
Woodrow Fst Sch B98...103 B7
Woodrow N B98..........103 A7
Woodrow S B98..........103 B7
Woodrow Wlk B98.......103 A7
Woodrush Com High Sch The
 B47....................69 A6
Woodrush Dr B47.........69 A5
Woodshires Rd CV6.......49 F5
Woodsia Cl CV23.........83 C8
Woodside Ave N CV3......76 F6
Woodside Ave S CV3......76 F5
Woodside CV9.............11 D1
Woodside Bsns Pk CV21...83 A4
Woodside CE Prim Sch
 CV9....................96 B6
Woodside Cl CV9..........11 D1
Woodside Cl CV9..........10 C1
Woodside Cotts CV9......18 A5
Woodside Cres B93.......72 B4
Woodside CV7............26 D1
Woodside Park Cvn Pk
 CV8....................96 B6
Woodside Pk Mobile Homes
 Pk B94.................86 B7
Woodside Pk CV21........83 B5
Woods Piece CV7.........48 F6
Wood St
 Bedworth CV12..........39 B5
 Nuneaton CV10..........28 F4
Woodstock Cl LE10.......32 A5
Woodstock Cres B93......71 F3
Woodstock Rd
 Coventry CV3...........77 D7
 Nuneaton CV11..........29 E1
Wootton Gr B91..........71 C8
Wood St
 Royal Leamington Spa
 CV32..................110 A8
 Rugby CV21.............83 B4
 Southam CV47..........147 B4
 Stratford-u-A CV37.....145 A2
Wood Terr B96..........118 D8
Woodview Rd CV9........18 E7
Woodville Ct CV34......108 F7
Woodville Rd CV34......108 E8

Woodward Cl CV31......110 A2
Woodward Ct CV37......121 B6
Woodway Ave CV35......114 F3
Woodway Cl CV2..........62 F8
Woodway CV35..........114 F3
Woodway La
 Claybrooke Parva LE17...43 D4
 Coventry CV2............50 F1
Woodway Park Sch & Com
 Coll CV2................50 F1
Woodway Rd 0X15......142 D8
Woodway Wlk CV2........62 E8
Woolaston Rd B98.......103 C8
Woolaway Bglws GL56...140 A6
Woolgrove St CV6.........50 A3
Wooll St 6 CV21.........83 A3
Woolpack The 8 CV34...108 E6
Woolpack Way CV9.......18 D8
Woolscott Rd CV23.....117 B6
Woolwich Rd CV11........40 F6
Wootton Cl CV37........145 D2
Wootton Ct
 6 Royal Leamington Spa
 CV32.................105 F2
 Coventry CV2............62 D7
Wootton Green La CV7....74 A8
Wootton Hall B95.......113 B2
Wootton La CV7..........57 E1
Wootton St CV12.........39 D3
Wootton Wawen CE Prim
 Sch B95...............113 A2
Wootton Wawen Sta
 B95...................113 A2
Worcester Cl CV5........60 B7
Worcester Ct CV6........50 B4
Worcester Ho B36........33 A8
Worcester Pl CV36.....149 C6
Worcester Rd CV8........93 B3
Worcester St CV21.......83 A4
Worcester Wlk B37.......33 A1
Wordsworth Ave
 Redditch B97...........102 C8
 Stratford-u-A CV37....130 B8
 Warwick CV34..........108 D5
Wordsworth Dr CV8.......93 C4
Wordsworth Rd
 Bedworth CV12..........39 D1
 Coventry CV2............62 C8
 Rugby CV22.............99 E6
Workhouse La LE10.......32 A4
Works Rd B26............44 A3
World of Shakespeare
 (Mus) * CV37..........145 A2
Worsdell Cl CV1..........61 B4
Worsfold Cl CV5..........60 A7
Worths Way CV37.......144 D6
Worthy Down Wlk B35....22 B3
Wortley Cl
 Cawston CV6............99 A8
 Cawston CV22...........99 A8
Wrenbury Dr CV6.........50 A4
Wren Cl DE12..............3 E8
Wren's Nest Cl B90......70 A5
Wren St CV2.............61 F3

Wright Cl B78............15 D5
Wrighton Gr B78..........9 A8
Wright St CV1...........61 E4
Wrigsham St CV3........77 D8
Wroxall Dr CV3..........78 D5
Wroxton CE Prim Sch
 0X15..................139 D4
Wroxton Coll 0X15......139 D4
Wroxton Ct 0X15........139 D4
Wroxton Ho 0X15.......139 D4
Wr Twr La CV8...........92 F6
Wulfstan Dr CV47.......115 D4
Wyatt Ho CV2............62 D7
Wyatt Rd B75............13 B5
Wyatts Ct CV12..........39 B3
Wychbold Cl B97........102 A6
Wychbury Rd CV13.......13 A1
Wych-Elm Cl CV22........82 B1
Wych Elm Dr 6 CV31...109 F5
Wychwood Ave
 Coventry CV3............77 C3
 Knowle B93..............72 B8
Wychwood Cl CV33.....122 F8
Wychwood Dr B97.......102 D6
Wycliffe Gr CV2..........62 B5
Wycliffe Rd W CV2.......62 C5
Wye Cl
 Bulkington CV12........40 B2
 Hinckley LE10...........31 A8
Royal Leamington Spa
 CV32.................106 C3
 Sutton Coldfield B76....22 B7
Wyegate Cl B36..........33 A8
Wykeham Ho CV21........83 C7
Wykeley Rd CV2..........62 C4
Wyken Ave CV2...........62 D5
Wyken Cl B93............71 E2
Wyken Croft CV2..........62 D6
Wyken Croft Nature Pk*
 CV2...................62 D6
Wyken Croft Prim Sch
 CV2...................62 E5
Wyken Grange Rd CV2....62 C5
Wyken Way CV2..........62 B5
Wyke Rd CV2............62 C4
Wykham La 0X15,0X16...139 F1
Wykin La CV13,LE10......21 E5
Wykin Rd LE10...........21 F3
Wyld Ct CV5.............60 B5
Wyley Rd CV6............61 B5
Wynbrook Gr B90.........71 A4
Wyncote Cl CV8..........93 A4
Wyndshiels B46..........34 A6
Wynter Rd CV22.........82 D3
Wyre La CV37..........129 B3
Wythall Sta B47.........69 C4
Wythburn Way CV21......83 D7
Wythwood Gr B47........69 C6
Wythwood Rd B47........69 C6
Wyver Cres CV2..........62 C3
Wyvern Cl
 Hinckley LE10...........31 E4
 Wellesbourne CV35....146 C2

Y

Yardley Chase Rd CV35...132 D4
Yardley Cl CV34........104 F2
Yardley St CV1...........61 E4
Yard The CV37..........120 E7
Yarmouth Gn CV4........75 E8
Yarn Cl B47.............69 A5
Yarningale Cl B98......102 F6
Yarningale La CV35.....113 E5
Yarningale Rd CV3.......78 D5
Yarningdale 7 B90.......70 C8
Yarn La B90.............70 A6
Yarranton Cl CV37.....144 E5
Yarrow Cl CV23..........83 D8
Yates Ave CV21.........82 F6
Yatesbury Ave B35.......22 A3
Yeats Rd 6 CV37.......130 B8
Yelverton Rd CV6........61 D8
Yeomanry Cl
 12 Warwick CV34......108 F7
 Sutton Coldfield B75....13 A6
Yew Cl CV3..............62 C1
Yewdale Cres CV2........50 E1
Yewdale Cl CV2..........50 F1
Yews The CV12...........38 E2
Yew Tree Cl B94.........89 D3
Yew Tree Ct
 1 Royal Leamington Spa
 CV31.................109 F5
 Austrey CV9.............3 A2
Yew Tree Farm Craft Ctr*
 B95...................113 B2
Yew Tree Gdns B95.....113 A4
Yew Tree Hill CV23......64 E3
Yew Tree La B94........113 D8
Yew Trees The B95.....113 B4
Yew Wlk B37............33 B2
York Ave
 Atherstone CV9.........12 E1
 Bedworth CV12.........39 D2
York Cl
 Coventry CV3...........78 C5
 Studley B80............103 C4
Yorkminster Dr B37......33 D3
York Rd CV31...........109 F8
Yorksand Rd B78.........8 F8
York St
 Coventry CV1...........61 B2
 Nuneaton CV11..........29 A4
 Rugby CV21.............82 F4
Young Cl CV34..........108 B5
Yule Rd CV2.............62 D5
Yvonne Rd B97.........102 D7

Z

Zorrina Cl CV10..........28 B5

Name and Address	Telephone	Page	Grid reference

Addresses

Name and Address	Telephone	Page	Grid reference

NG	NH	NJ	NK
NM	NN	NO	NP
NR	NS	NT	NU
NX	NY	NZ	
SC	SD	SE	TA
SH	SJ	SK	TF	TG
SM	SN	SO	SP	TL	TM
SR	SS	ST	SU	TQ	TR
SW	SX	SY	SZ	TV

Any feature in this atlas can be given a unique reference to help you find the same feature on other Ordnance Survey maps of the area, or to help someone else locate you if they do not have a Street Atlas.

The grid squares in this atlas match the Ordnance Survey National Grid and are at 500 metre intervals. The small figures at the bottom and sides of every other grid line are the National Grid kilometre values (**00** to **99** km) and are repeated across the country every 100 km (see left).

To give a unique National Grid reference you need to locate where in the country you are. The country is divided into 100 km squares with each square given a unique two-letter reference. Use the administrative map to determine in which 100 km square a particular page of this atlas falls.

The bold letters and numbers between each grid line (**A** to **F**, **1** to **8**) are for use within a specific Street Atlas only, and when used with the page number, are a convenient way of referencing these grid squares.

Example The railway bridge over DARLEY GREEN RD in grid square B1

Step 1: Identify the two-letter reference, in this example the page is in **SP**

Step 2: Identify the 1 km square in which the railway bridge falls. Use the figures in the southwest corner of this square: Eastings **17**, Northings **74**. This gives a unique reference: **SP 17 74**, accurate to 1 km.

Step 3: To give a more precise reference accurate to 100 m you need to estimate how many tenths along and how many tenths up this 1 km square the feature is (to help with this the 1 km square is divided into four 500 m squares). This makes the bridge about **8** tenths along and about **1** tenth up from the southwest corner.

This gives a unique reference: **SP 178 741**, accurate to 100 m.

Eastings (read from left to right along the bottom) come before Northings (read from bottom to top). If you have trouble remembering say to yourself "Along the hall, THEN up the stairs"!

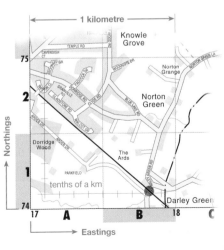